THE BLUE HOUSE

THE WORLD OF FRIDA

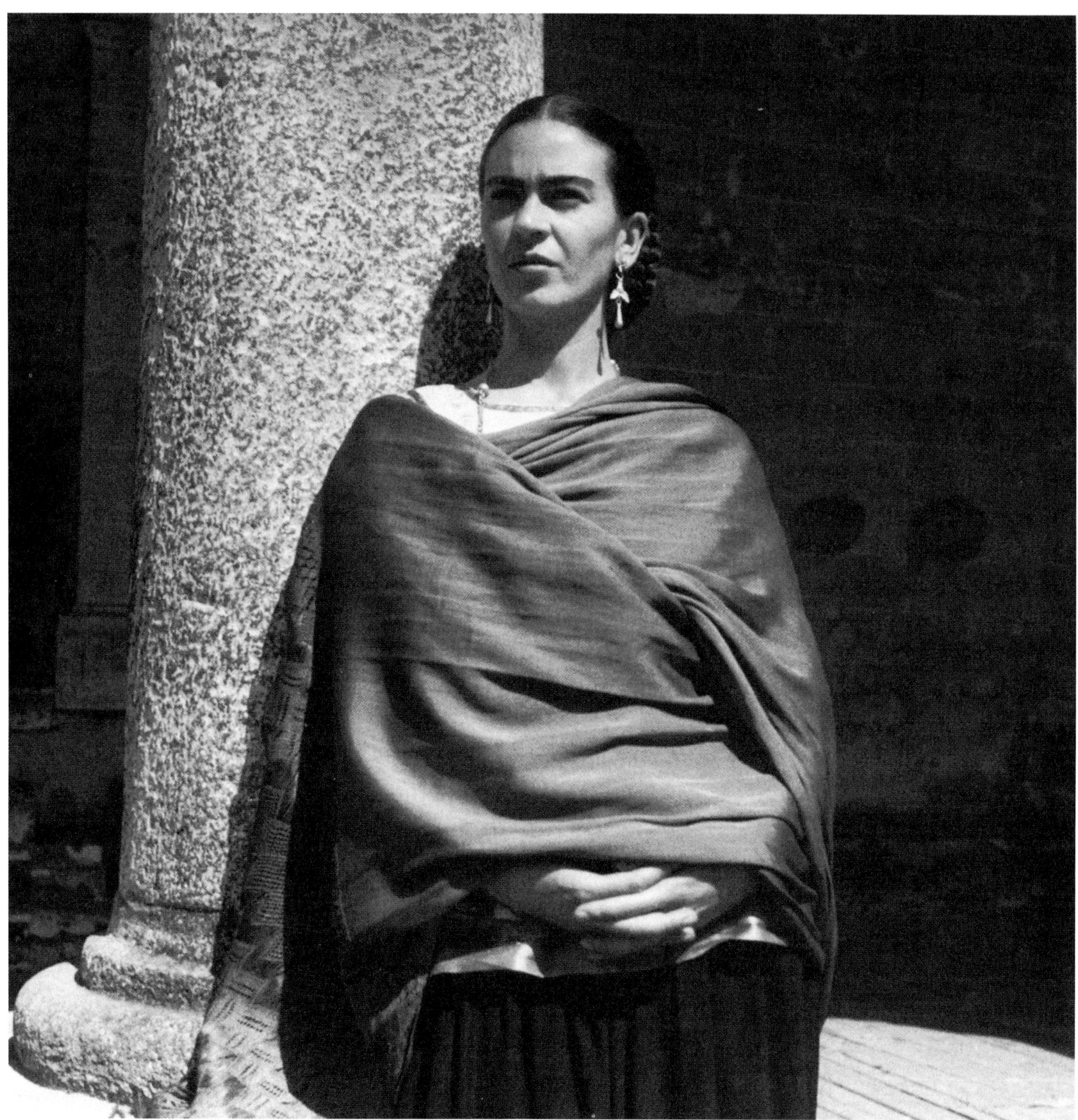

Fritz Henle, Frida Kahlo at the church of Coyoacán, 1936.

THE BLUE HOUSE

THE WORLD OF FRIDA KAHLO

EDITED BY ERIKA BILLETER

UNIVERSITY OF WASHINGTON PRESS

IN ASSOCIATION WITH

MUSEUM OF FINE ARTS, HOUSTON

The World of Frida Kahlo is published in conjunction with the exhibition organized by the Schirn Kunsthalle Frankfurt and held at:

Schirn Kunsthalle Frankfurt
March 6 – May 23, 1993

Museum of Fine Arts, Houston
June 6 – August 29, 1993

The World of Frida Kahlo is sponsored by PHILIP MORRIS COMPANIES INC.

International transportation from Frankfurt to Houston is provided by Continental Airlines.

In Houston, additional support has been provided by Anchorage Foundation, Inc., Anchorage Foundation of Texas, Celina and Alfredo Brener, and an anonymous donor.

Originally published as *Die Welt der Frida Kahlo*,

Printed in Switzerland.

Translation: Kathleen Jameson-Cemper (pp. 10–22, 48–49, 192–193) Edith M. Pross (pp. 23–32, 67–72, 187–191, 227–229, 238–243), and Arturo Sanchez (pp. 244–263).

Editor: Cynthia Newman Bohn

Curator in Houston: Janet Landay

ISBN 0-295-97328-5

For the SCHIRN KUNSTHALLE FRANKFURT

Director: Christoph Vitali
Curator and Catalogue Editor: Erika Billeter
Coordination and Consultation in Mexico: Armando Colina, Víctor Acuña, Patricia Feria
Organization: Margarete Heck and Elke Walter
Office Staff: Gerlinde Gumpinger and Antje Longhi
Exhibition Design: Holger Wallat
Restoration Management: Stefanie Gundermann
Technical Direction: Ronni Kammer
Photography: Jesús Sánchez Uribe, Gerardo Suter, Javier Orozco, Bob Schalkwijk
Translation: Bela Wohl, Maria Dettmers-Schreieck
Publishers: Benteli-Werd Verlags AG, Berne
Layout: Benteliteam Berne
Typesetting and Printing: Benteli Druck AG, Wabern-Berne

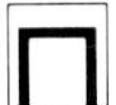 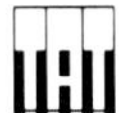 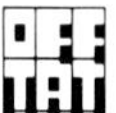 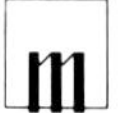

Kulturgesellschaft Frankfurt mbH

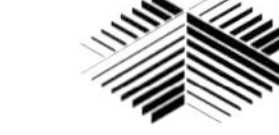

EUROPALIA 93
MEXICO

For EUROPALIA 93 MEXICO

Organizing Committee Mexico:

Rafael Tovar y de Teresa
President of the National Council for Culture and the Arts

Dolores Olmedo Patiño
Executive President of the Museo Dolores Olmedo Patiño

Committee Europalia Mexico:

Alfredo del Mazo G.
General Commissioner

Victor E. Bravo Ahuja R.
Adjunct Cultural Commissioner

Juan Morales Doria
Adjunct Economic Commissioner

Daniel Leyva Santiago
Coordinator of the Cultural Program

Armando Colina
Commissioner of the Exhibition

Front cover: Frida Kahlo, *Self-Portrait with Loose Hair*, 1947 (cat. 65)
Back cover: Fritz Henle, *Frida in her Studio*, photograph, 1943

CONTENTS

FOREWORD

"Is that the exhibition of Frida Kahlo?" That was the question asked by many female and, of course, male visitors when they bought entrance tickets for our exhibition *Images of Mexico* in the winter of 1987/88. Their attention was concentrated on the small group of works by Frida Kahlo, which was part of the large panorama of modern Mexican art being displayed. For them her name stood as an archetype for Mexico and its art and, in that, they were not entirely wrong. For hardly another artist-personality has been so strongly shaped by all the facets of the unique Mexican cultural mixture – Indian/pre-Columbian elements and the influences of folk art as well as, at the same time, the atmosphere of idealistic-universal openness that encouraged artists to explore and comprehend the cultural developments of the old world, Cubism and Surrealism. Frida Kahlo's singular, charismatic aura has no less power today than it did four years ago. On the contrary, her community of admirers grows with every year. Works of hers that appear on the market for the first time are traded at enormous prices, and her personality is made use of for social-political aims and other matters about which, were she confronted with them today, she would be speechless and uncomprehending.

The cultural-political phenomenon of this unique admiration, almost religious devotion, for the person Frida Kahlo could not have endured if beyond the ability of her person to fascinate there were not also magnificent works of art, rich and versatile despite their limitation to a few themes and small size. The high aim of this project is to collect these in an exhibition and so make it possible to examine and compare. The difficulties of realizing this goal seemed, in part, almost insurmountable. The majority of the works are still in the possession of private collectors. Their owners have lived for decades with the little pictures in their living rooms or bedrooms, in constant dialogue, and now, in many cases being advanced in years, they do not want to part with them, not even for the short period of an exhibition. A great deal of friendly persuasion was needed to get the collectors to send their treasures on a long journey, and some could ultimately not agree to that. Still, a selection which one can term representative was collected in Frankfurt. Among more than seventy works by Frida, all genres and media are represented: Portraits and, of course, self-portraits, taken from all ages of the artist, in whose features the battle with life and pain dug deeper and deeper; compositions of a magically super-elevated realism, for instance, *The Little Deer* or *Roots*, the work that caused André Breton to think so highly of her, and in which he wished to see once again the Surrealism he proclaimed; the pictures of pain such as *The Broken Column* or *Henry Ford Hospital*, in which her own existence becomes a cipher for the pain of all creatures; the encyclopedic compositions such as *Moses*, in which Frida displays an entire artistic cosmos, reducing it from the monumental dimensions of the murals by her partner through life, Diego Rivera, to such a small size that it almost bursts the frame; and finally, the drawings, which in their groping awkwardness and directness are particularly touching.

The World of Frida Kahlo is presented in this exhibition in all its facets. Apart from her own artistic works, there are those of her friends and contemporaries. At the top of the list is Diego Rivera, to whom she was tied in love and hate for a lifetime. Frida alone and Frida and Diego are the subjects of a very extensive documentation in contemporary photographs, some published for the first time. And finally, works and objects of folk art, votive paintings, traditional Indian dress, and pre-Columbian ceramics, show the source of Frida's stimulation and the ambience in which she lived her life.

A large number of people have contributed to the success of this exhibition, who must now be given due recognition. First of all, I reiterate my deep gratitude to the lenders, who have generously agreed to let us show their pictures, first and foremost among them Dolores Olmedo Patiño, whose collection forms the heart of the exhibition. Erika Billeter, a good friend for many years, and comrade-in-arms already for the exhibition *Images of Mexico,* has poured her profound knowledge, her sensitivity, and her great love for Mexico and its art into this project. We owe our thanks to her both for the concept of the exhibition and for the empathetic catalogue that departs from the beaten path of some of the earlier publications about Frida Kahlo and sheds light on entirely new aspects in the life and work of the artist. During the organization of the exhibition we experience once again the selfless help of Armando Colina and his partner, Victor Acuña, of the Galería Arvil, who coordinated all the Mexican loans. Finally, a word of thanks to the Mexican government, represented by Rafael Tovar y de Teresa, president of the National Council for Culture and the Arts in Mexico, and his deputy, José Luis Martinez, ambassador Jorge Alberto Lozoya, head of the cultural department in the foreign ministry, and Gerardo Estrada, director of the Instituto Nacional de Belles Artes. The committee appointed by the government for Europalia 1993 Mexico in Brussels is headed by Alfredo del Mazo. To him and to Baron Jacques Groothaert, director of the festival Europalia itself, as well as to the head of the exhibition, Anne Mommens, for their cooperation during the entire period of preparation. Before travelling to Brussels in September, however, the exhibition is now being presented in Houston thanks to the unwavering enthusiasm of Peter Marzio. He and his curator, Janet Landay, have brought about this unique encounter with Frida Kahlo for the American public efficiently, dedicatedly and at very short notice indeed. The Museum of Fine Arts, Houston has every reason to be proud of this magnificent performance, which the audiences will be sure to adequately appreciate. In the autumn our exhibition will be one of the main themes of the Europalia program in Brussels, which this year will be dedicated to Mexico. I wish the exhibition a good reception.

Christoph Vitali

LENDERS

Grateful acknowledgement is made to the Museo Dolores Olmedo Patiño, Mexico City, for the generous loan of its Frida Kahlo collection.

Mexico:
Victor Acuña
Manuel Arango
Banco Naçional de México, S.A.
Armando Colina
Gerardo Contreras Gómez
Juan Coronel Rivera
Agustín y Angel Cristóbal
Ruth y León Davidoff
María Estela Elizondo de Santos
Victor Fosado
Galería Arvil
Galería de Arte Mexicano
Galería Juan Martin
Enrique García Formentí
Margarita Garza Sada de Fernández
Gunther Gerzso
Jesús González Vaquero
Instituto Tlaxcalteca de Cultura, Tlaxcala
Gustavo Lailson
Adrian Lajous
Ruth D. Lechuga
Alberto Misrachi
Sylvia Misrachi de Assael
Museo de Arte Moderno, INBA, Mexico D.F.
Museo Dolores Olmedo Patiño
Museo Regional de Guanajuato,
Alhóndiga de Granaditas, Gto. INAH
Francisco Osio Morales
Patrimonio de la Pinacoteca
de la Universidad de Colima
Mariana Pérez Amor
Elva C. Podesta
Teresa Salazar de Gómez Arias †
Claudia Thompson Balaguer
Alejandra R. de Yturbe
Joaquin Zendejas Pérez and family

United States of America:
Art Collection, Harry Ransom Humanities Research Center, The University of Texas at Austin
Gretchen and John Berggruen Collection, San Francisco, California
Collection IBM Corporation, Armonk, New York
Michele and Howard Lazar, New York
María Reyero Collection, New York
B.Lewin Galleries, Palm Springs, California
The National Museum of Women in the Arts, Washington D.C.
as well as the public and private lenders not listed here.

For their advice and support we thank the following:
Fred and Steve Banks, San Francisco, California
Richard Berglund, New York
Malú Block
Concepción Casas Ahuja
CDS Gallery, Clara D. Sujo, New York
Flavio Díaz
Marisol Espina
Patricia Fería
Jorge García Murillo
Rogelio García Espinoza
Lucio García Noriega
Fritz Henle
Gabriel Loera
Mary-Anne Martin/Fine Art, New York
María del Carmen Mazarazzo
Fernando Moreno Peña
Fernando Ondarza and Carlos Santos
Lisa Palmer, Christie, Manson & Woods, New York
Alicia Pinal
Graciela de Reyes Retana
Juan Diego Suárez Dávila
Ignacio A. Tapia Echavarri
Graciela Toledo
Eugenio Zubiría Maqueo

To produce the exhibition in Houston, we thank the following:
Cynthia Newman Bohn
Dianne Cauble
Thomas Chingos
Jack Eby
Alison Eckman
Janet Landay
Diane Lovejoy
Ellen Osborne
Mariana Servitje
Margaret Skidmore
Sandy Zavaleta

PREFACE

The exhibition *The World of Frida Kahlo* is presented at the Museum of Fine Arts, Houston thanks to the valuable cooperation and resolute support of its Director, Peter C. Marzio, and exhibition curator, Janet Landay. The exhibition presents one of the most appealing figures in Mexican culture, Frida Kahlo.

Conceptualized by Christoph Vitali and Erika Billeter from the Schirn Kunsthalle in Frankfurt, *The World of Frida Kahlo* has been possible thanks to the significant participation of the Museo Dolores Olmedo Patiño. The museum's president and founder, Mrs. Olmedo herself, has dedicated her life to preserve and diffuse the work of this great Mexican artist. A unique effort has been made by many institutions and individuals to organize this successful exhibition, including numerous museums and private collectors in Mexico and the United States, the National Council for Culture and the Arts of the Mexican government, and the directors of Galeria Arvil, Victor Acuña and Armando Colina.

To all of them, in the name of the Committee Europalia Mexicano, our gratitude.

Alfredo del Mazo
General Commissioner

STATEMENT BY THE SPONSOR

The opportunity to sponsor an exhibition of such importance as *The World of Frida Kahlo* does not occur very often. When the Museum of Fine Arts, Houston approached us with the idea, we were captivated. This would be the most important exhibition of Kahlo's work that had been organized to date. The people of the United States should have the chance to see this remarkable collection, which was originally scheduled to tour only in Europe.

The exhibition offers rare and significant insight into the understanding of Frida Kahlo's art and life. An impassioned and brilliant artist, Kahlo overcame considerable struggles and created a powerful and inspirational body of work. She overturned established expectations of women in art and searched to address universal issues through her own distinctive and personal voice.

Philip Morris' 35th anniversary in support of the arts takes place in 1993, and it seems fitting to celebrate with an exhibition of works by one of the most influential artists of the 20th century. We applaud and thank the Museum of Fine Arts, Houston for its leadership role in bringing this vital exhibition to us, and to the United States.

Stephanie French
Vice President
Corporate Contributions and Cultural Affairs
Philip Morris Companies Inc.

ERIKA BILLETER

WORLD OF TRUTH – WORLD OF UTOPIA FRIDA KAHLO

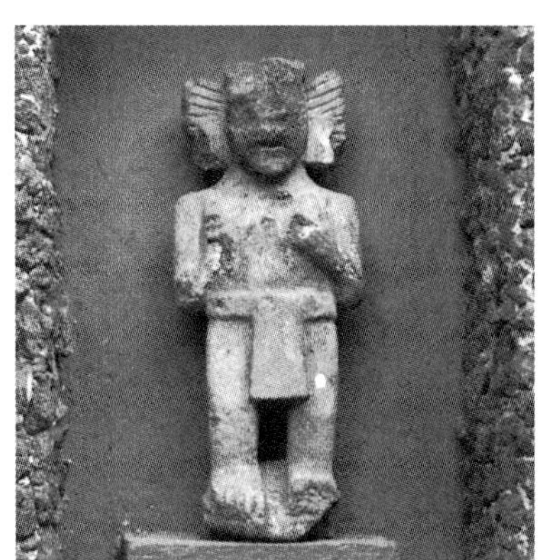

"I have to leave everything hanging in the air or let distance come dangerously, mysteriously close."

"Tree of hope – keep firm."

Today Frida Kahlo's works are among those that draw the keenest attention of the public. One publication replaces another, one exhibition follows another. For how much longer? Her works are small in number; there are not many more than 100 pictures in oil and a few dozen drawings, which, one of these days, will not be able to travel anymore, because they have become as fragile as their creator. What is the secret of Frida Kahlo's fascination? Why is her name associated with what is mysterious and yet present? Why do we, when contemplating her pictures, recall our own fate, why do we recall love, suffering, death? Why do these pictures, usually small in size, disturb us more than the large monumental wall paintings by her husband, Diego Rivera, and his contemporaries?

Perhaps Frida Kahlo is particularly liked by women, because, through her person and her work, they can identify themselves, for the first time, as women. Frida Kahlo is the first artist in history to have departed from the male principle of art. She escaped and created her own iconography. Ever since art has been a topic, it has been dominated by men. Men have painted, made music, written. Until the twentieth century, the few women who managed to accomplish something, did not change art history. They worked within the pattern of the world, the principle of which was arranged by men. The beginning of the twentieth century brings change. Female artists begin to reflect on their situation and become more active in the public eye. Names like Paula Modersohn-Becker, Marianne von Werefkin, Gabriele Münter, Sonia Delaunay, Georgia O'Keeffe, Sophie Tauber make a deep impression. But, at least at the beginning of their work, they are all at the side of an important man who shares in the shaping of their work. They have no part in the decisive achievements of art history. But all these women continued to develop, achieving glory late in life, sometimes only after their death. On June 6, 1902 Paula Modersohn wrote in her diary that people looked upon her artistic activity with pity and tact as one would upon a droll little eccentricity that one has to accept in a person. Yet her friend, none other than the poet Rainer Maria Rilke, recommended her to Rodin as a "very distinguished woman painter."

With Frida Kahlo it was entirely different. Of course she, too, had at her side a man who, even today, is considered one of Mexico's most eminent painters: Diego Rivera. But Frida Kahlo went her own way, far from contemporary history and contemporary trends, and placed herself on the most dangerous path, that of the loner. She followed this path unconditionally, free from the desire for approval from others. She painted for herself and still captured the interest of the art world. Artists thought highly of her, and, no sooner were her pictures finished than collectors tried to pull them off the easel. Among the admirers of her work, Rivera was one of the first and one of the most convinced. "Frida began with a series of masterpieces which had no model whatsoever in art history – they were paintings which acknowledge the special capacity of the woman to look truth in the face and, even, with an eye on cruel reality, to endure suffering. Never before has a woman so poetically transformed her deeply felt agony and placed it on canvas, as Frida did in Detroit at that time."[2] He is referring to the first picture Frida painted after her miscarriage and which gave iconography a new theme: abortion. That was by far not the first time that Rivera expressed his admiration for Frida's art. We also know from Rivera that, when Kandinsky and Picasso saw Frida's exhibition in Paris in 1939, they spoke enthusiastically about her work. Kandinsky was so touched that he had tears in his eyes, and Picasso prostrated himself before her. The Louvre bought a portrait that is now to be found in the collection of the Centre Georges Pompidou.[3] André Breton saw her as the embodiment of the woman invented by the Surrealists as the beginning and end of the female as such. "There is no art more exclusively feminine, in the sense that, in order to be as seductive as possible, it is only to willing to play alternately at being absolutely pure and absolutly pernicious." The art of Frida Kahlo is a ribbon around a bomb.[4] Indeed, her personality seems to unite all the characteristics which set the wishful fantasies of the Surrealists in motion: *la beauté du diable,* the way André Breton imagined it. "In Frida, a genuine *'monstre sacré'* the *'amour fou'* is embodied in her terrible and painful love for Diego Rivera," writes Lourdes Andrade, while "the *'beauté convulsive'* is expressed in the dramatic beauty of her wounded body." For Breton, there is another reason why Frida Kahlo is the epitome of the female Surrealist: her *"personalité féerique"* and, in the realization of her work, her dedication to the inner model (*"modèle intérieur"*). Sensuality becomes almost morbid; humor and cruelty form the structure of the work, in which the ordinary is clothed in the dreams and obsessions of the artist. It was the fire of erotic ambiguity in such art that caused Breton to term it "the purest and most dangerous."[5]

But admiration for Frida went way beyond Surrealism. In 1940 the art critic Meyer Schapiro recommended her for a Guggenheim scholarship with the following words: "She is an excellent painter with true originality, one of the most interesting figures I know of on the Mexican art scene. Her works compare well with the best pictures by Orozco and Rivera. In a certain sense she is more Mexican than they. She might not have their heroic and tragic dimension, but she is closer to Mexican tradition and its decorative form.

The times were few and far between when female artists of that time could enjoy such words of praise. Of course, Meret Oppenheim managed to sell her famous *Déjeuner en fourrure* to the Museum of Modern Art in New York in 1936, but her real success came late, only in the last years of her life.

Frida Kahlo differs from the other female artists of her time in that she did not originally intend to pursue an artistic career. As a young girl she did like to draw and often accompanied her father, the photographer Guillermo Kahlo, on his Sunday watercoloring excursions. She had decided on medicine and wanted to become a doctor. She started painting when, after an accident in 1925, she was bedridden for months. To kill time, she occupied herself with brush and paints. But as early as 1926 she drew her accident (she never painted it). The painting over of an *ex-voto* in which she portrayed her accident also seems to spring from that time. These are the first expressions of her suffering, which sometimes retreated, only to appear again all the more strongly, but which, until her death, never disappeared from her life. "She lived while dying," the poet Andrés Henestrosa once said of her.[6]

Already with the first portraits Frida Kahlo painted (*Self-Portrait,* 1926, *Portrait of Alicia Galant,* 1927, *Portrait of Christina, My Sister,* 1928), her talent was evident and, despite the influences of the Italian Renaissance and of contemporary Art Deco, that can be seen in these portraits, something appears that is characteristic of Frida's portraits: the tendency to aesthetically isolate the person portrayed. Only after her experience at Henry Ford Hospital in Detroit in 1932, will she find the mode of expression that typifies her thematic pictures. There she lost a baby for the second time and it started to become clear to her that, although she can conceive a child, she cannot bear one to the full term. It is as if this realization and the suffering she experienced opened her eyes to a new picture of the world, as if it moved something within her that led her to her own vision of pictorial representation. Her suffering created her iconography, and it is tied to her for all time. It is neither transposable nor imitable. Her iconography is independent of the pictorial systems known to art history. In Mexico it is said that her accident was, in the broader sense, no accident, that Frida Kahlo had to create this stirring experience, which altered her life entirely, in order to find her true vocation. It helped her walk the road, not of life, but of art. It gave her a pictorial imagination without her having to avail herself of the wealth of art already in existence.

In this way an existential art was created, which belongs to the fears, loves, sufferings of a woman. She visualizes feelings, emotions, not in competition with the man, but in a solidary dialogue with herself. Painful, fearful circumstances are described which are far removed from the male conception of the world. She does not set herself against the man (in today's feminist sense) but remains conscious of her uniqueness. Frida Kahlo does not ask for pity. Through her sorrow new images are created, mythical images that make visible a spiritual experience.

Despite its extreme vividness, her work is completely closed, in a mysterious way that belongs only to her. Perhaps that is why so many collectors today want to possess her paintings, because they want to live in a world that someone else has lived in and suffered through for them. This completely closed realm does not belong to Surrealism, as André Breton would have liked so much, but to a distant place of female thinking and feeling. I can recall something similar only in literature: Virginia Woolf, whose writing emerged from the experience of much suffering, who knew the solitude of female thought and belonged to a world "outside." There is a story which, in a literally magic way, leads us to Frida's world, right into the Blue House: "A Room of One's Own" written in 1929, which describes the necessity of having one's own room, of claiming a room for one's own fantasies.

Frida Kahlo was born in 1907 in the Blue House and died there in 1954. It was her parents' house, which they had built in 1904. In 1936 she included it in her painting *My Grandparents, My Parents, and I,* and one can see that it was always blue. This blue is like a sign. Frida spend most of her lifetime in that blue house. It was her refuge, the place in which most of her pictures were created. It was her *"lieu sacré,"* her home, her recourse. It was her birthplace and her grave. (Today her ashes are kept there in a pre-Columbian urn.) At the same time it is – like the room of Virginia Woolf – a symbol of her independence, of her breaking away from conventions. It is a signal of liberation. "The exile of an uncensored experience."[7] Within the walls of the Blue House Frida's suffering was transformed into a creativity that liberated her from all traditions. Suffering is a great theme in art history. We have been acquainted with it ever since the story of the sufferings of Christ and the saints became a pictorial theme. To make suffering in the profane world worthy of art is a process that begins first in modern times, and even then appears relatively late.

We owe one of the first stirring cycles about human suffering to Ferdinand Hodler, who tried to capture the suffering and death of his life-companion, Valentine Godé-Darel, in pictures and drawings. Edvard Munch drew the sick Nietzsche and, in his last self-portrait, from 1940–44, he himself is shown in the process of dissolution. His chest resembles an X-ray picture. Munch's constant feeling that his existence was threatened is very close to Frida Kahlo's sense of her life when he writes "My way has led me along an abyss, a bottomless deep. Now and again I have left the path, have plunged myself into the human throng of life. But ever and ever again I have had to return to the road along the abyss. That is the road I have to follow until I fall into the deep. Fear of life has been my companion as far back as I can remember."[8] The beginning of the twentieth century introduced pictures of suffering such as these which finally led to the Viennese movement known as *Aktionismus* with its staged tortures.

Frida Kahlo made suffering the leitmotiv of her artistic conception. She portrayed herself in situations that do not obviously reveal illness, but for the observer this state becomes more and more evident. The self-portrait was the instrument she chose for the artistic realization of her innermost being.

As she herself said, she painted herself, over and over again, because she was so often alone and had to paint while lying in bed, or in a wheelchair, because she could not leave the house. In this way, she created the story of her life in pictures.

There are two types of self-portraits in Kahlo's oeuvre: those that presuppose a look in the mirror, and which I would like to describe as her "official" portraits, but which – as we shall see – are at the same time utopian portraits, and those narrative portraits in which she describes certain events in a form similar to that of *ex-votos*. In none of the self-portraits is there a single indication that she is a painter. She never painted herself

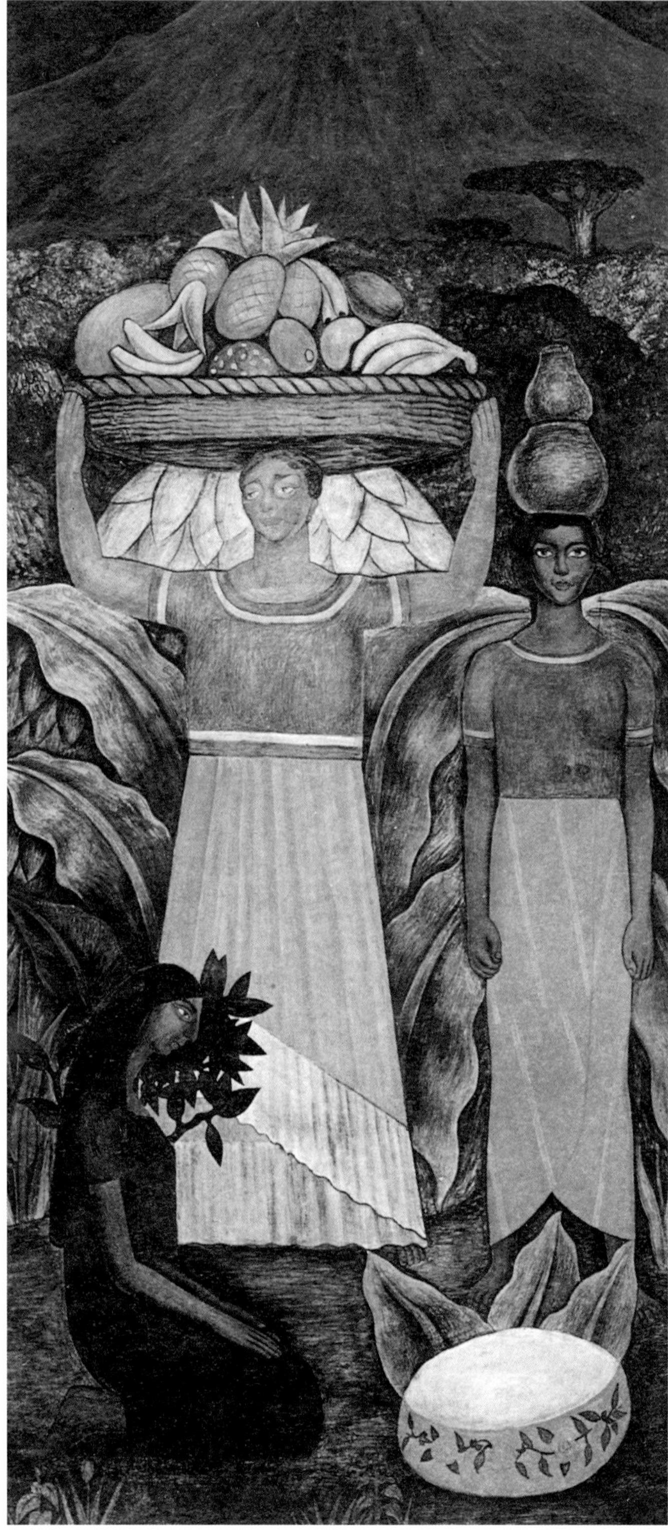

Diego Rivera, *Women of Tehuana*, fresco, Secretaría de Educación Pública, Mexico City, 1923–1928.
The dress of the women of Tehuana is the most beautiful of all Mexican folk costumes. Frida Kahlo wore such a costume as her second skin until her death.

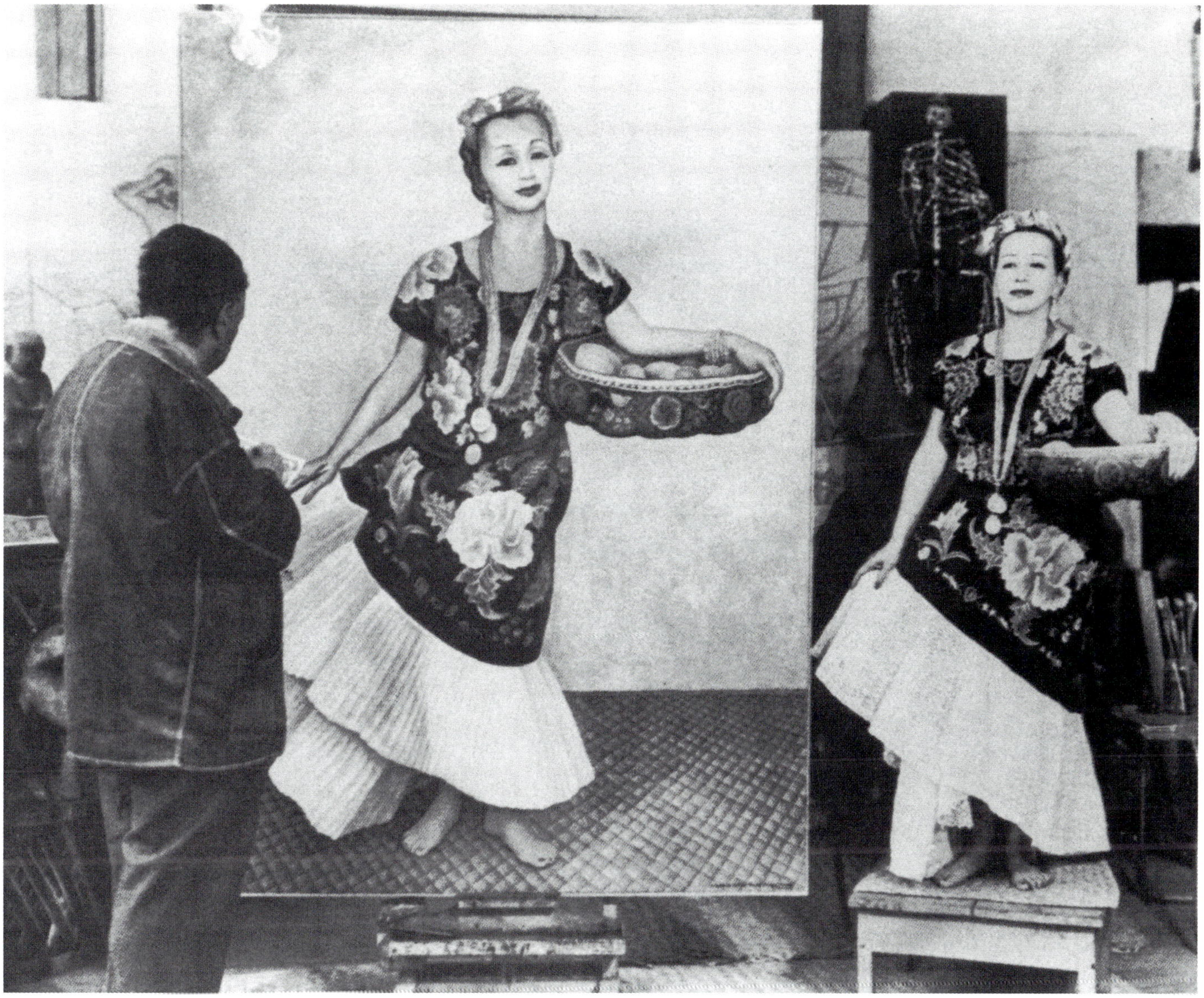

Diego Rivera painting Dolores Olmedo in the dress of a Tehuana, photograph.

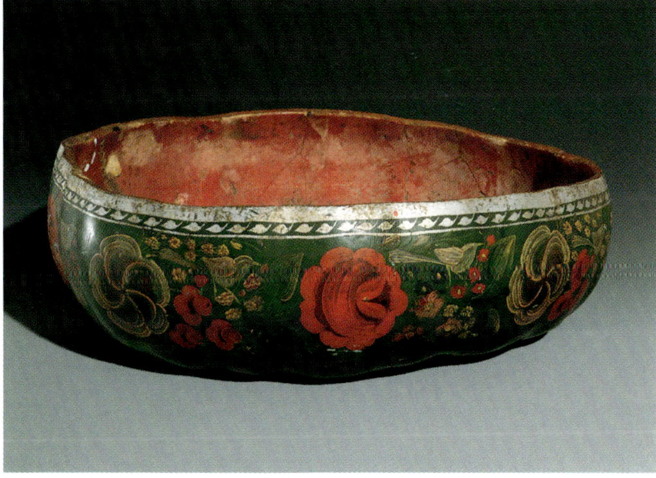

Xicalpextli, lacquerwork (cat. no. 149). This is the same bowl that Dolores Olmedo holds in her arm in Rivera's portrait.

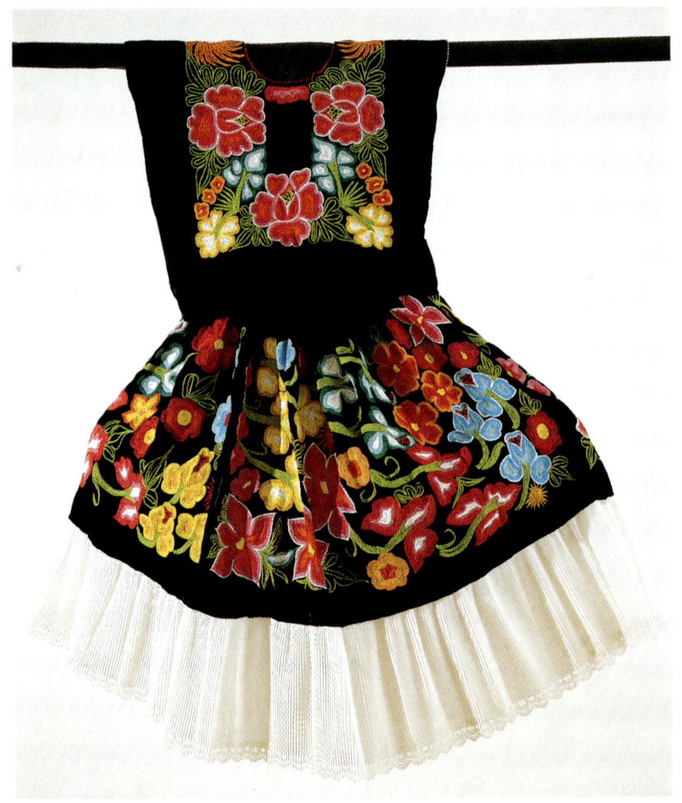
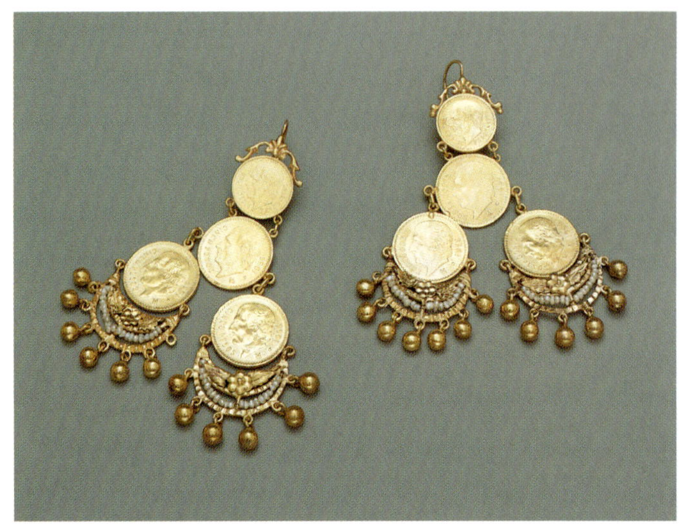
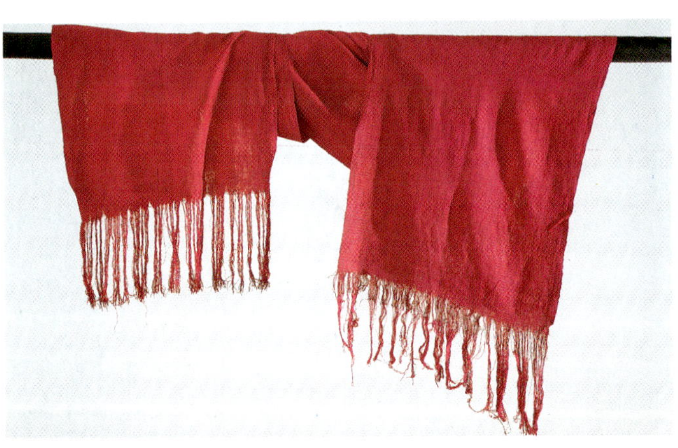
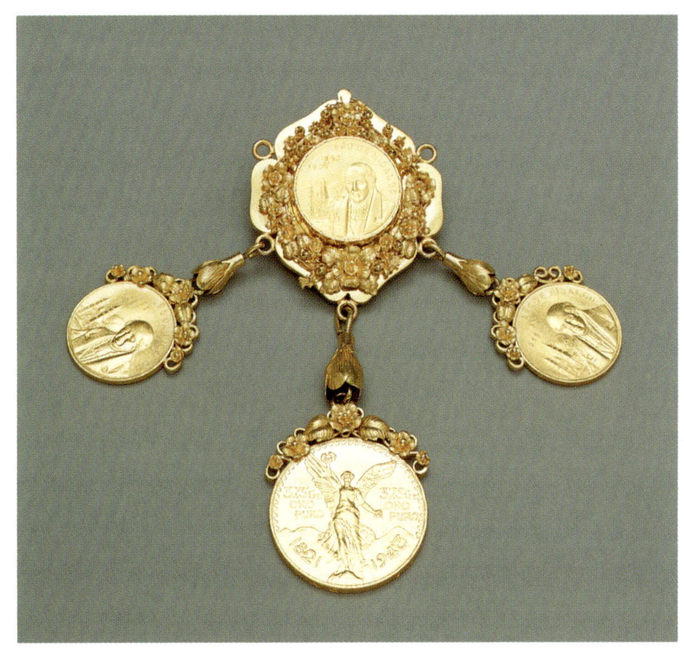
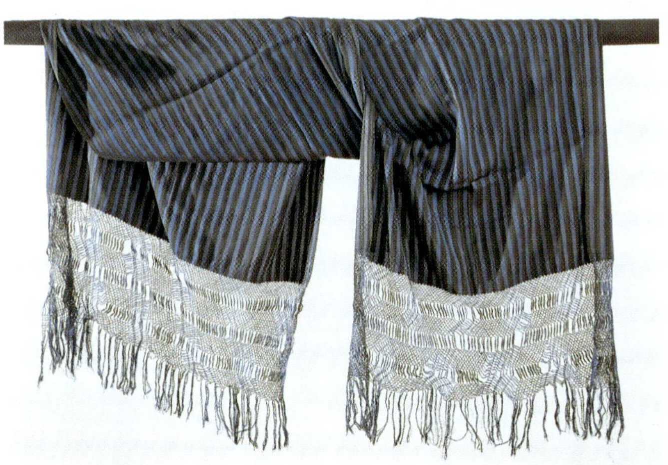
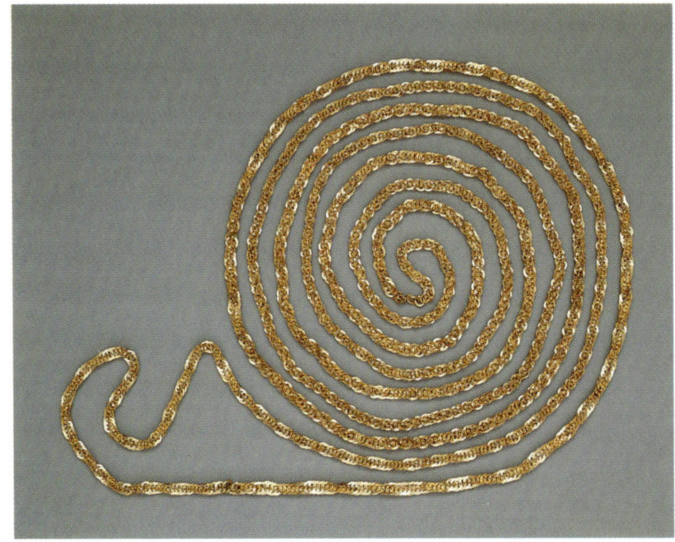

Tehuana dress, *rebozos* (cotton shawls), and jewelry like those Frida Kahlo loved to wear (cat. nos. 144–148).

with brush and palette – the insignia of her profession. That was left to Rivera who, in 1940, portrayed her with a palette in his fresco Pan-American Unity in San Francisco (now in the library of the City College) to symbolize Latin American culture. In her self-portrait with Dr. Farill, Frida converted her palette into an open heart and her brushes into arrows. Could she have said anymore clearly that for her painting did not emerge from the craft but from the fact of her suffering? The person in the mirror always looks back at Frida Kahlo with an almost masklike, expressionless countenance. It is the decor and the atmosphere that give each portrait its own mood; one could almost exchange the faces. In the case of other painters who made a diarylike series of portraits – for instance Vincent van Gogh, Ferdinand Hodler, Lovis Corinth, Kathe Kollowitz – their perception of their own expression fluctuated. Their portraits provide evidence of momentary moods. In Frida Kahlo's portraits, we must observe things other than her face: her clothes, her hair decoration, the things surrounding her, the background. In every portrait she is dressed up for an occasion. The clothes, the jewelry, were part of her life. A daily ritual took place when she selected the various parts of the traditional Tehuana dress and put the jewelry together. She changed her hairstyle from one day to the next. This was perhaps the clearest expression of her moods. With this festive outward appearance she tried to please Rivera, who liked the traditional dress of this region above all others. But at the same time she used it to hide her suffering. The dress became a second skin, a magic armour that protected her from the world. She once wrote that the traditional Tehuana dress made "the absent portrait of only one person," her "absent self," Hayden Herrera adds.[9] Even when she was very ill in the last year before her death and practically entirely confined to her bed, she was dressed up as if for a fiesta.

During Frida's visit to Paris in 1940, the traditional dress of the Tehuanas fascinated even the haute couture. In Mexico itself the Tehuanas had been a popular subject in art ever since Rivera first included Tehuana women in his wall paintings for the Secretaría de Educación Pública (1923–28). In the thirties, Mexican art without the Tehuana was unthinkable. "The Tehuanas are festivity per se. In the magnificence of their dress they express their pride and their grace. To glitter, gold is not enough; it is the entire cultural inheritance that gives the Tehuana their mythos."[10]

Even Dolores Olmedo had Rivera portray her in the traditional dress of the Tehuana. Even today the women of the isthmus are admired as the most beautiful and the strongest in Mexico. At the same time, however, the Tehuana embodies female power. Today Juchitán is still governed by women, and for centuries the matriarchy has been an essential part of the society. This aspect

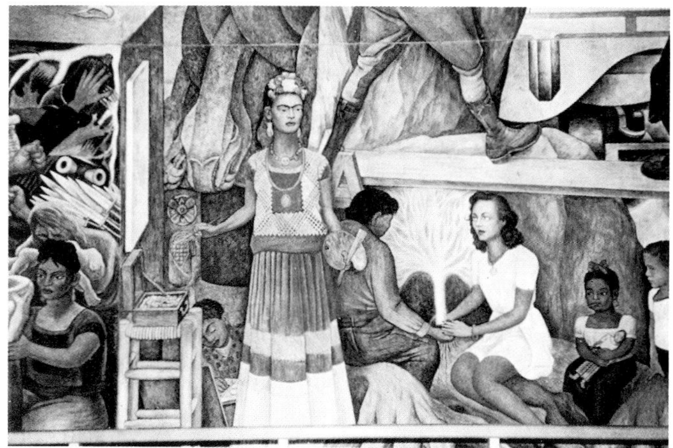

Portrait of Frida Kahlo in a Tehuana costume in Diego Rivera's fresco *Allegory of California* in San Francisco, 1939/40.

must have attracted Frida Kahlo when she decided to live in the clothing of the Tehuana. There was, however, a deeper, entirely personal reason. As we have already said, the long festive robes hid the outward marks of her suffering and her inner pain at the same time. Every self-portrait was for her a victory over pain. The festive robe pushes it out of the picture. The things that surround her as well as the atmosphere in the picture contribute greatly to making us feel that Frida is a happy, normal woman. Usually the background is filled right to the edge with lush, green foliage. Only in later years do her backgrounds become more neutral spaces, like the lavastones in one of her most moving self-portraits *Self-Portrait with loose Hair,* 1947, in which the facial mask reveals a hint of suffering for the first time. Otherwise, however, she veils her physical and inner suffering with the things she loves, things that make her happy and distract her from her pain: her parrots, the monkeys she kept as pets, and the dogs which inhabited the garden of the Blue House. How important they were for her mood and her art is expressed in a letter to Alejandro Gómez Arias in 1934: "Alex, the light ended and I am not painting little monkeys.".. In that year she once again had a miscarriage, her right foot was operated on, and Diego begin an affair with her sister Cristina. And indeed, in that year, she produced not a single picture.

Objects of pre-Columbian and Mexican folk art can also be seen in the portraits. The Rivera's house was a treasury of such objects. It was a Mexican house through and through – the incarnation of what the Revolution had achieved: the recollection of the Mexican people's own roots and cultural values. Frida and Diego lived that *Mexicanidad* and pulled everyone else under its spell. From the Blue House it shone out unto the town, and there were hardly any artists who did not integrate *Mexicanidad* in their own homes.

It is interesting to compare examples of how Frida was

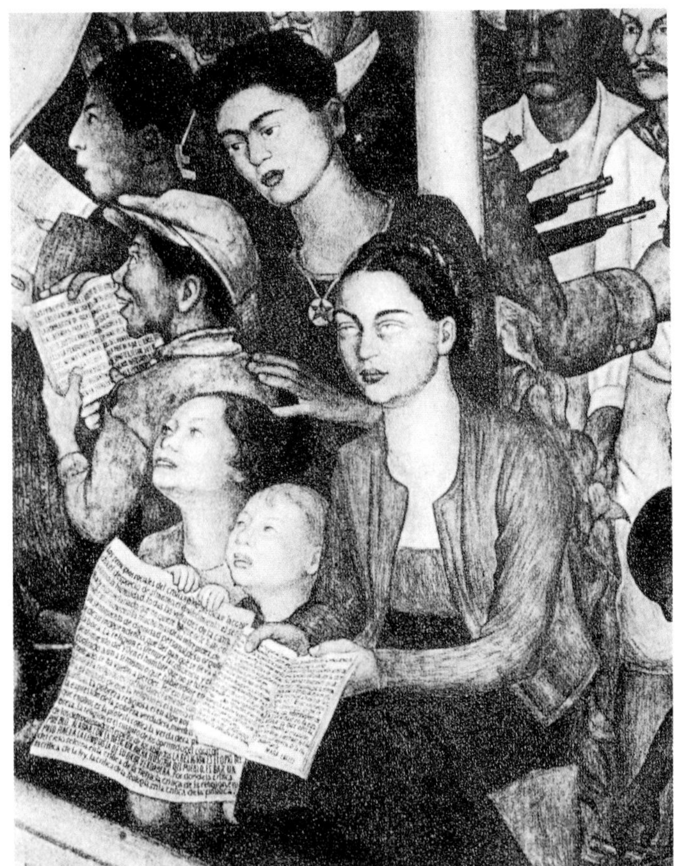

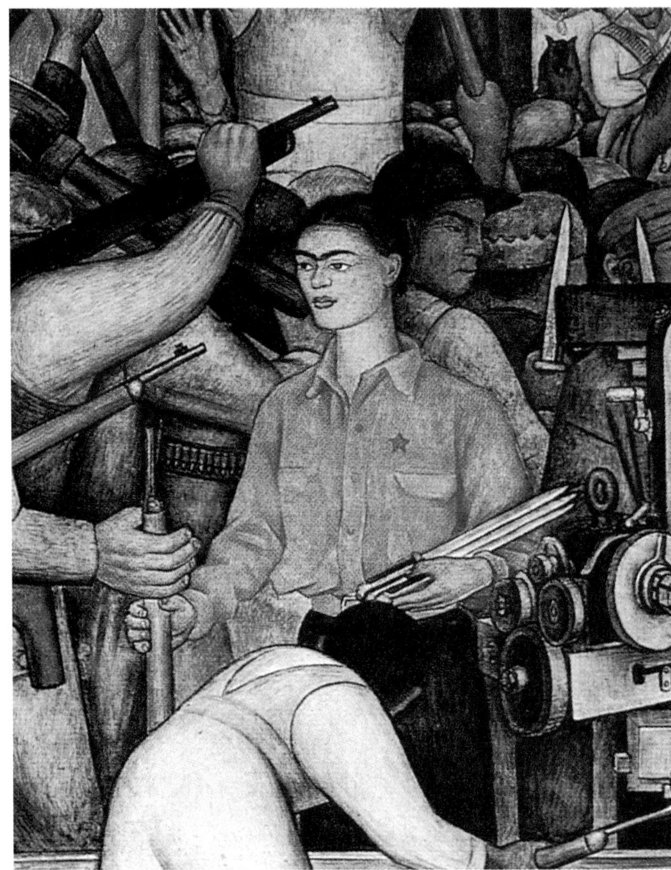

Diego Rivera, portraits of Frida in his frescoes: Palacio Nacional, Mexico City, 1934; Secretaría de Educación Pública, 1928.

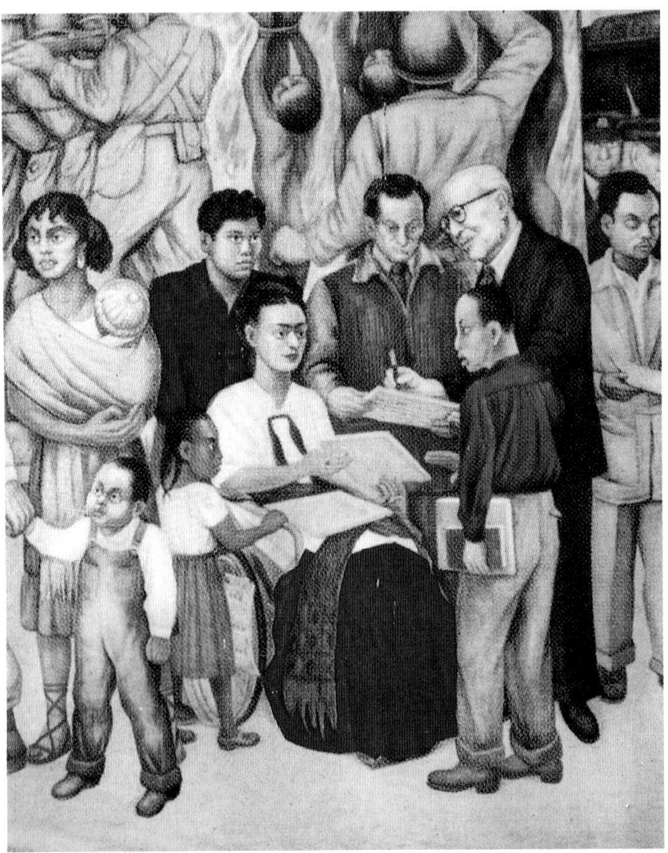

The Nightmare of War and the Dream of Peace, 1952 (Beijing?).

seen by other painters. The woman who, becaue of her exotic beauty, was so often portrayed by famous photographers, seems seldom to have inspired a desire to paint her. Rivera never painted a real portrait of her. A lithograph of 1930 shows her as a nude without any particularly recognizable characteristics. But for his frescoes he used her as a model on several occasions for figures embodying the symbolic content of his historical-mythical panoramas, where she is included among many others as a narrative element in the story being told.

Apparently only Roberto Montenegro painted her several times. Compared with her own festive self-portraits, her image in the eyes of another artist seems reserved, almost plain. The traditional Tehuana dress is not so magnificent, the atmosphere is restrained. Which is the real Frida: the one in the self-portraits or the one portrayed by her friend Montenegro? Montenegro must be nearer the truth, Frida's "official" self-portraits are utopian portraits – wisful pictures of a woman who was denied the most natural thing in the world: to bear children and to be healthy.

Even in that portrait which shows scars, she is nearer Utopia than reality. *The Broken Column*, produced in 1944, is not a picture of sorrow, although the beautiful body is pierced through with nails like that of Saint Sebastian. This is not the posture of a suffering person

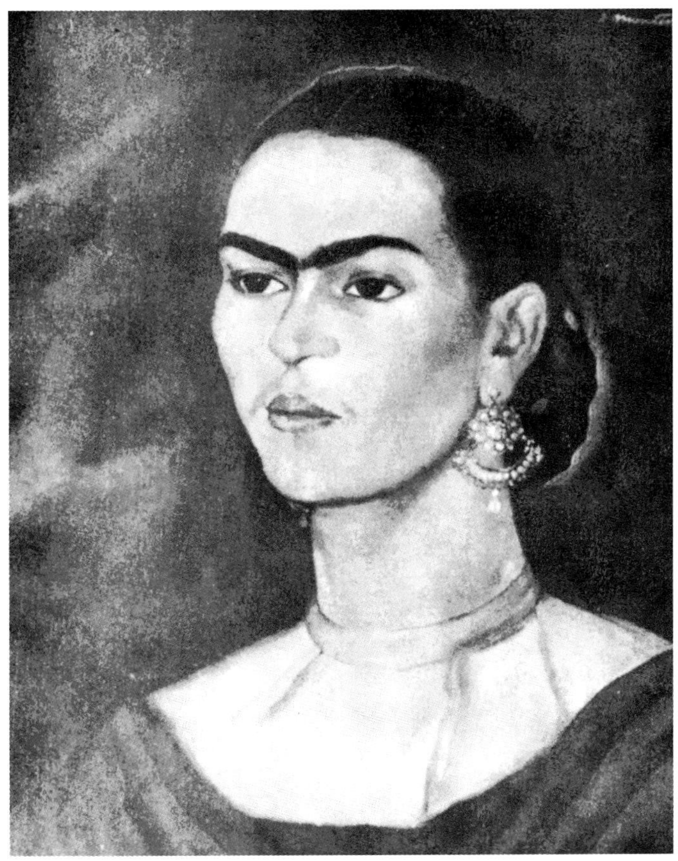

Roberto Montenegro, *Portrait of Frida Kahlo* (location unknown).

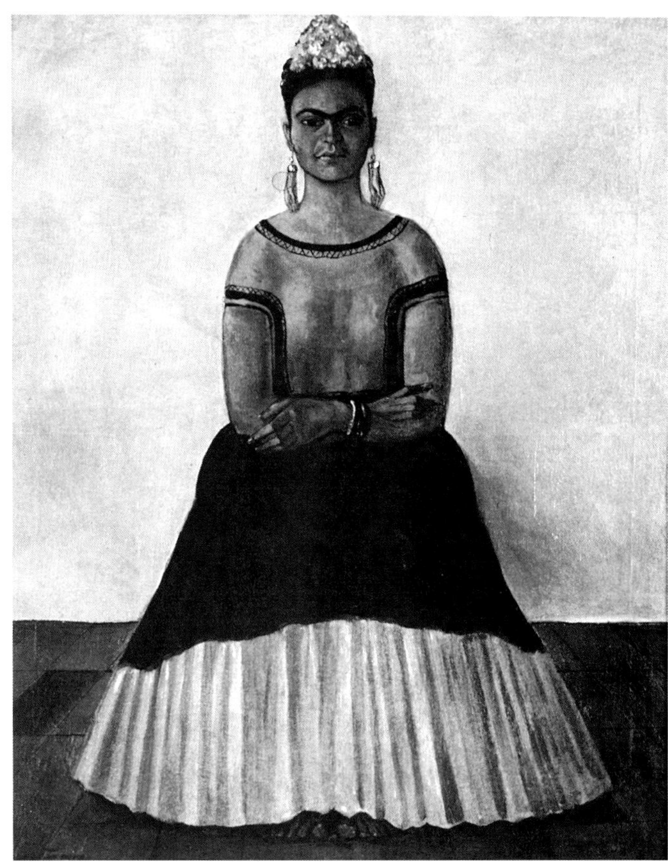

Roberto Montenegro, *Portrait of Frida Kahlo* (cat. no. 97).

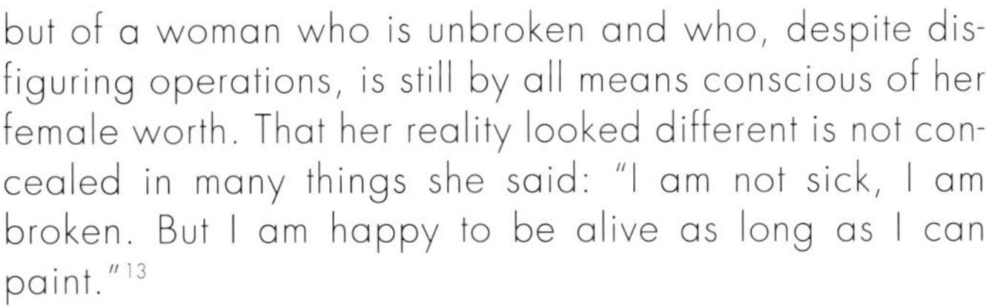

but of a woman who is unbroken and who, despite disfiguring operations, is still by all means conscious of her female worth. That her reality looked different is not concealed in many things she said: "I am not sick, I am broken. But I am happy to be alive as long as I can paint."[13]

The self-portraits in the form of narrative representations are certainly nearer the truth, although it is often obscured by symbolic metaphors and made less personal through humor. For these pictures Frida usually chose the folk-art style of *ex-votos* and *retablos,* which have a long tradition in Mexico. Frida was one of the first artists to let herself be inspired by them. In these portrayals, a new iconography unfolds. To liberate herself from her unhappy experiences, she transformed them into pictures: the miscarriage in *Henry Ford Hospital, The Birth* (her own), *A Few Small Nips,* which was a response to the fact that Diego had started an affair with her sister. At that time, Frida considered her works "all small and unimportant, with the same personal portrayals which are only of importance for myself and no one else."[14]

But sometimes she also painted these painful portrayals for friends, as for instance, *The Litle Deer* of 1946, a picture that only measures 22×30 cm but which is one of her most endearing in its portayal of belief in life over-

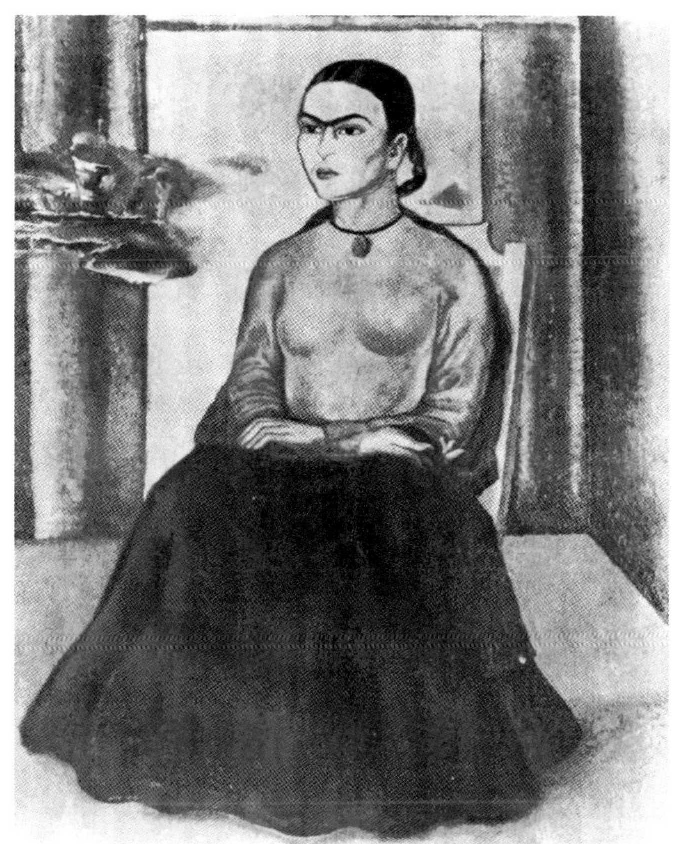

Roberto Montenegro, *Portrait of Frida Kahlo* (location unknown).

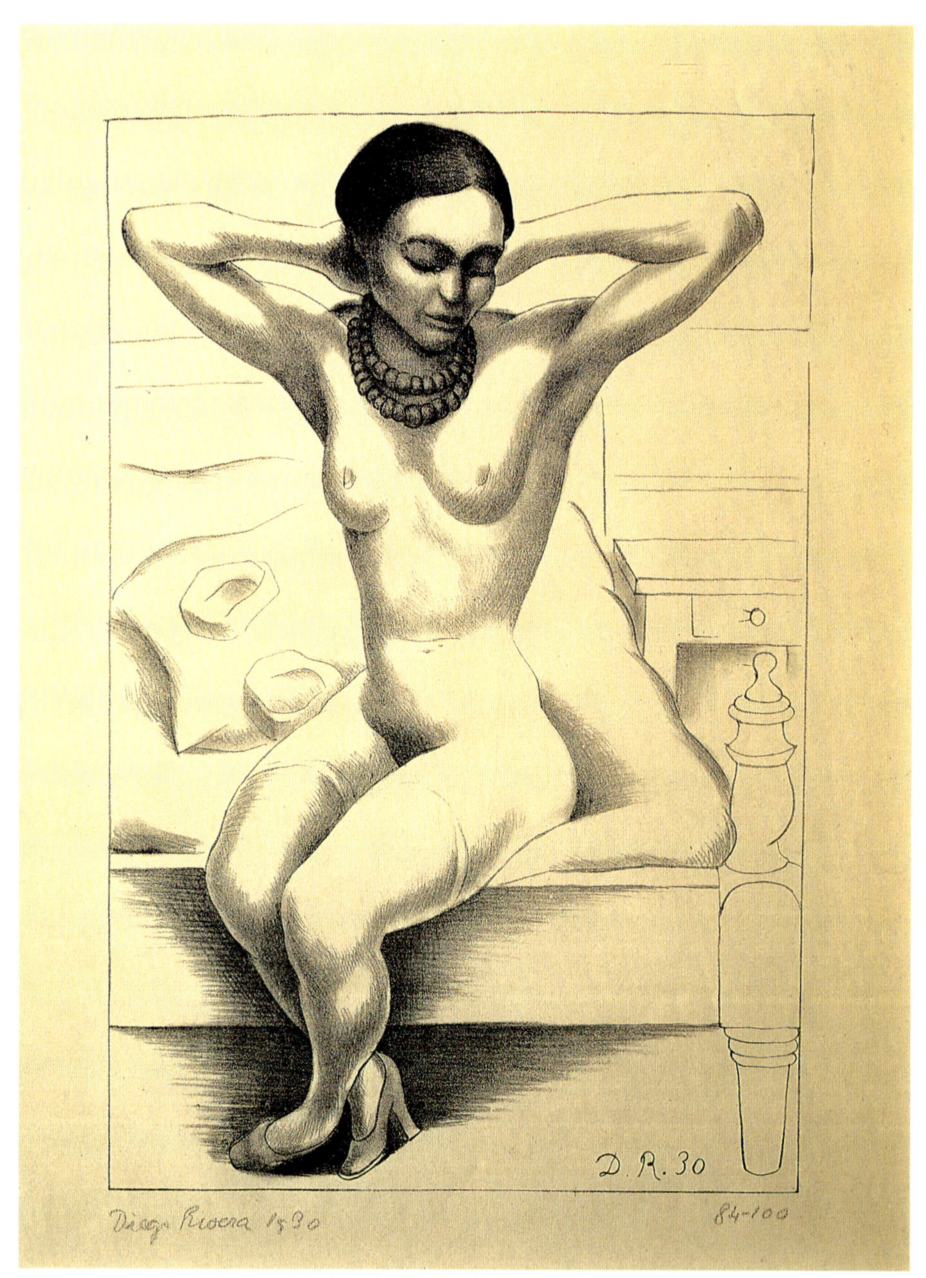

Diego Rivera, *Nude Study of Frida Kahlo*, 1930, lithograph (cat. no. 110).

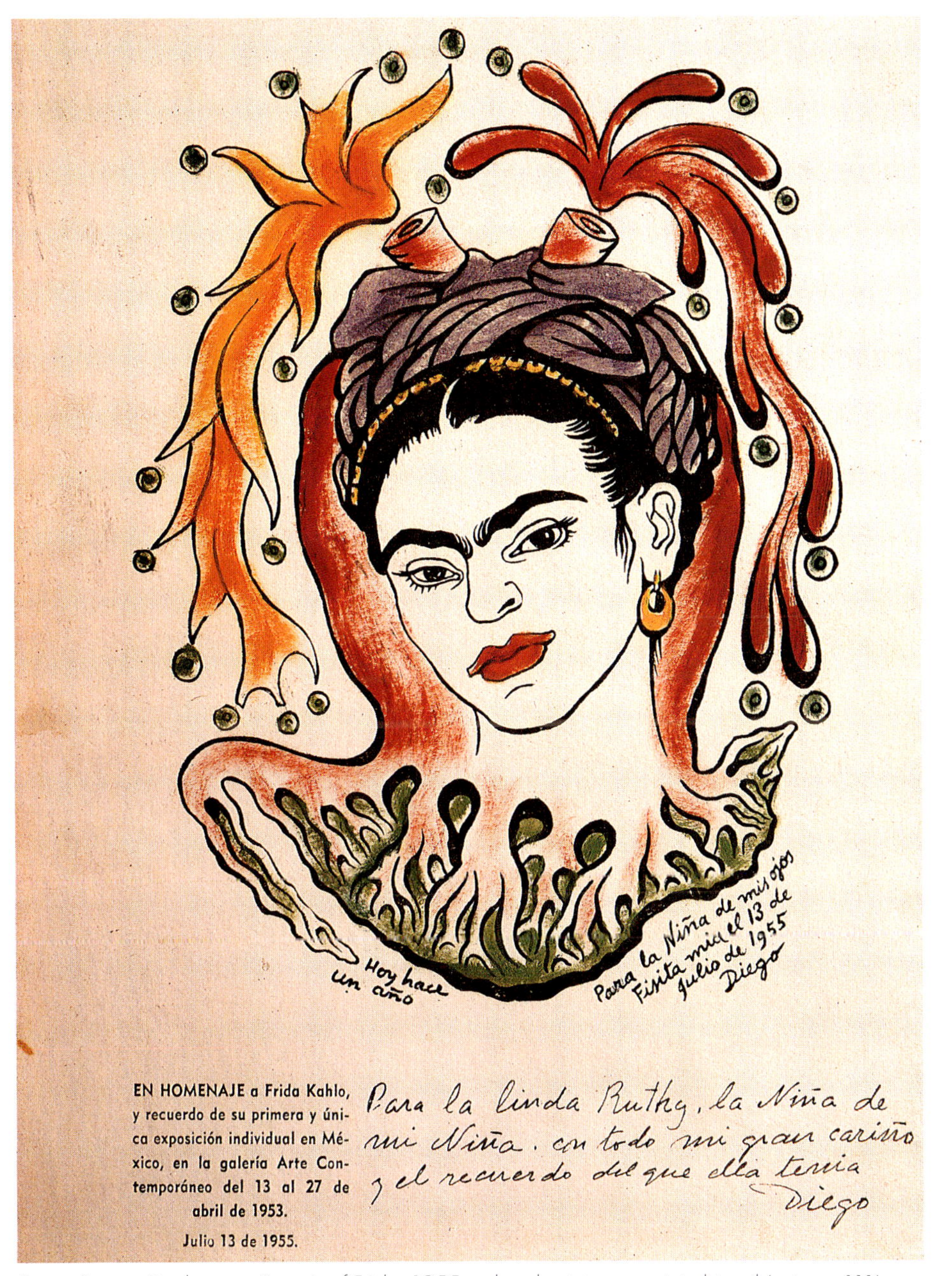

Diego Rivera, *Posthumous Portrait of Frida*, 1955, colored print, overpainted in oil (cat. no. 111).

coming pain. Despite her pain she neither weeps nor complains. Although only the stumps of the forest can be seen, she still springs through. Elena Poniatowska, whose favorite picture this is, recalls that Frida Kahlo once wrote on a drawing: "Feet – what do I need them for – after all, I have wings to fly."[15] She had just been told that her right leg would have to be amputated. Her readiness to believe in life, which was crystallized primarily in her dedication to art, remained hers, like a valuable gift, until the end of her life. In her last years she painted many still lifes full of sumptuous fruits, and even if in one work a coconut sheds tears, still the watermelons and exotic fruits are surely a song to the life and nature of Mexico. A little Mexican flag appears again and again as a kind of symbol. "Viva la Vida," she wrote on her last still life, painted in 1954. Eight days before her death she wrote this inscription on an open watermelon (a *sandia,* also a great theme in Mexican art).[16]

While the self-portrait was Frida Kahlo's primary focus, sometimes she also portrayed friends. These pictures were usually gifts. Now and again they were commissions, for example, the portraits of the Morillo Safa family, which the engineer Eduardo Morillo Safa ordered in 1944. In this series of portraits, one is particularly endearing: that of Doña Rosita Morillo, the mother of the client, and the only one that is still in the collection of Dolores Olmedo, who once owned the entire series of family portraits. It was one of Frida's favorite pictures. Indeed, it is quite different from all the portraits she painted of other people. These portraits were usually produced on a neutral or not very conspicuous background, but here the figure sits in front of a blossoming cactus of luxuriant red that parts and spreads itself over the red foliage. The blossoming background emphasizes Doña Rosita's imposing appearance. This is the only portrait in which Frida lets the hands play an expressive part in the composition. Emerging from the dark, they are active – knitting – and form a counterpoint to the head. Never before nor afterward did Frida, who was in the final analysis really only inierested in self-portraits, pay so much attention to another personality. There is gripping realism here, but the work is still full of symbolic content. The dark dress, the dark red are not the colors of life but call to mind death. Doña Rosita's thoughts seem to be already in another world as the thread of life approaches its end. Frida could identify with Doña Rosita. There is another portrait that has a special place in Frida Kahlo's work, that of the Californian horticulturalist Luther Burbank. It is, in the true sense of the word, the most "fantastic" of her portraits and, indeed, embraces the two fundamental laws of life: life and death in unity, the way the Mexicans understand it in their deep philosophy of life.

The posthumous portrait (Luther Burbank died in 1926) was painted when Frida first visited San Francisco in 1931. Both Frida and Rivera admired Burbank's work. Rivera gave him a place in his fresco *Allegory of California* in San Francisco. Frida painted a portrait of him that shows Mexican Surrealism as no other picture of hers does. The Surrealism is based on the reality that life always leads to death: Luther Burbank grows out of a tree, the roots of which spring from a skeleton. He is part of the earth: his body inhabits the ground while his head reaches into the heavens. The Mexican principle of life and death could not be illustrated more convincingly. The portrait also makes it clear that Frida Kahlo – as she herself always declared – had nothing whatsoever in common with Breton's Surrealistic theories.

Everything in her work that seems Surrealistic to us has a profound bases in Mexican thought. The "reality" of Mexican history, which is her cradle, is reflected in the subjects of many of her paintings, for example, *Birth.*[17] Hayden Herrera and Irene Herner (elsewhere in this catalogue) point out the pre-Columbian iconographic roots of this portrayal, which from the Middle Ages until now has been unthinkable in European art. One has to go back to the beginning to find the most elemental experiences of mankind presented in art. The Aztecs represented the goddess, Tlazolteotl, in the ceremonial act of birth. But I first became aware of how deeply Frida Kahlo had tapped into the subconscious of the primitive creators of this image when I visited the Museum of Archaeology in Ankara. There, the famous statuette of the mother goddess of Catalhöyük from the sixth millennium before Christ is portrayed as a women giving birth. It was excavated ten years after Frida Kahlo's death.

Mexican history is always present in Frida Kahlo's pictures beginning with the wood engravings of José Guadalupe Posada and ending with pre-Columbian art. Posada, the first Mexican artist to portray the everyday life of Mexicans, has played no small part in the development of Mexican art in the twentieth century. His numerous satirical illustrations, with their humour and their constant exaggeration of events, which finally takes away the horror even from violence, inspired not only the Mexican muralists. In the little *ex-voto* à la Frida (e.g., *A Few Small Nips*) one can comprehend this satiric mind.

Motifs from Mexican folk art are recurring themes in her art. The mask appears many times, most stirringly, to be sure, in *My Nurse and I* (1937). The wet nurse holding Frida, who has the body of a child and the face of an adult, is an Indian woman and she is wearing a precolumbian mask with preatures reminiscent of Frida's own. Frida carries within her both distant history and the present.

Frida painted portraits of children only occasionally at the beginning of her career as a painter. But in 1937 she

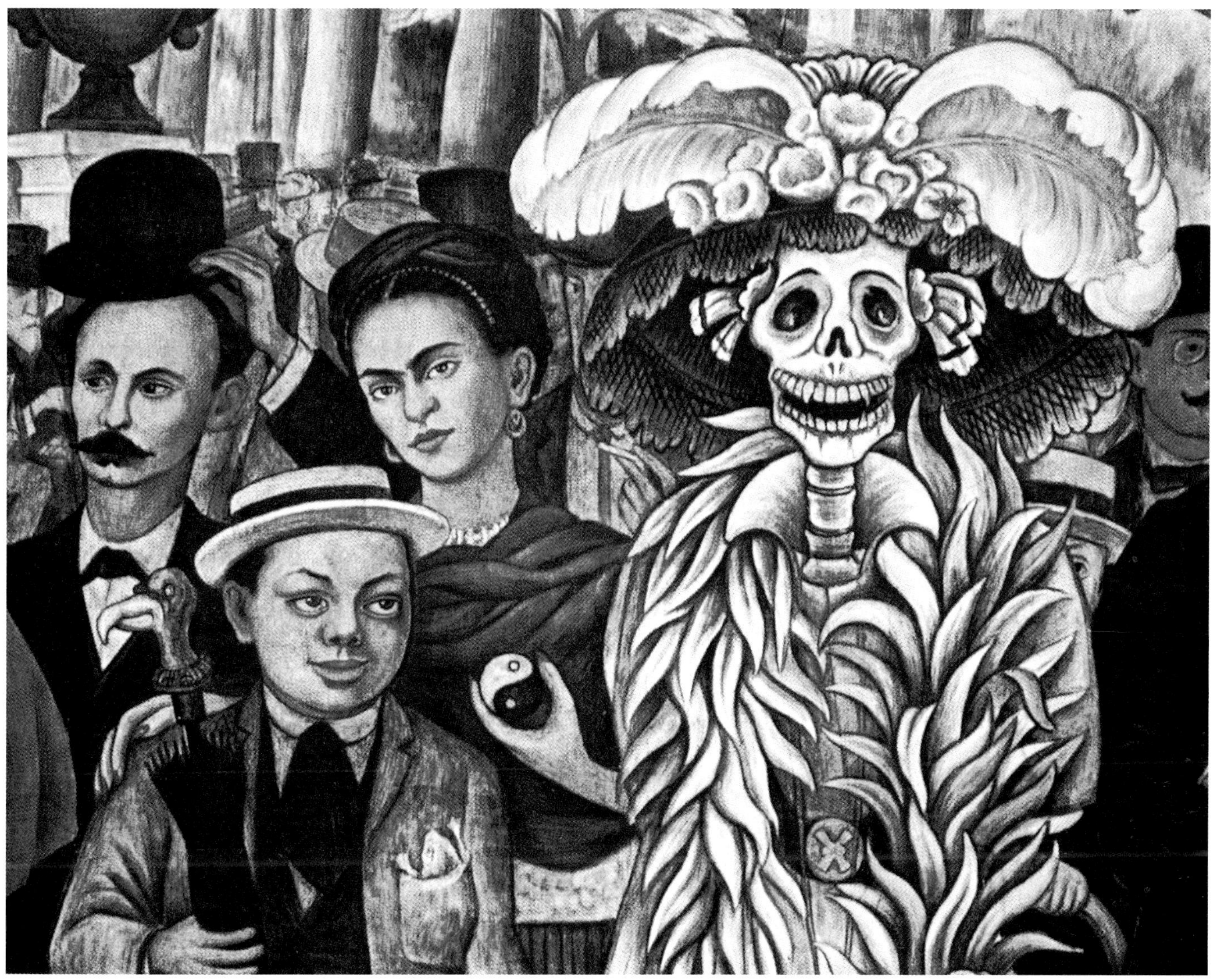

Portrait of Frida Kahlo (with self-portrait of Diego Rivera as a boy) by Diego Rivera, fresco, *Dream of a Sunday afternoon in the Alameda*, 1947.

painted one that is of profound significance: *The Deceased Dimas*. In Mexico it is the tradition to memorialize a dead child through a painted picture (today this task has been taken over by photography). In these pictures, the child appears to sleep peacefully, reconciling its parents to death since the child now no longer has to undergo the sufferings of the world. In the Blue House Frida had such a painted portrait of the dead over her bed. In art the theme constantly appears in the nineteenth and early twentieth centuries. Thus, it is not surprising that Frida painted the child of Delfina, an Indian woman who often sat for Diego, when he died at the age of three. On the inscription she tenderly calls him "Difuntito," the little dead one. The little dead one is dressed as a king. What he could not be when alive Frida gives him on his way to eternal life. As a sign of the pains he suffered she puts the picture of the suffering Christ on his pillow. At the time, the picture was bought by an American collector, but when she realized it was the portrayal not of a sleeping child but of a dead one, she gave the picture back.[17] Death is often present in Frida's art. He was her companion in life, and in her art as well. He appears as a skeleton, as a *calavera*. He once took root in her thoughts, and she painted him on her forehead, where the wise men of Asia believed the third eye to be. Diego, also, could occupy the place that usually belongs to the eye of wisdom. Here, too, one has to go very far back into Mexican history to encounter this theme. An artist has hammered it in stone as the eternal metaphor on a classic Maya head, the *cabeza con personaje en el tocado*. Frida portrays quite directly what she is thinking: in her head there is Diego, there is death. This thought stands out on her forehead. But, at the same time, it has been contained in Mexican art for centuries. As Diego Rivera said in his article "Frida Kahlo and Mexican Art" in 1943. "Frida was the greatest proof of the renaissance of art in Mexico."[18]

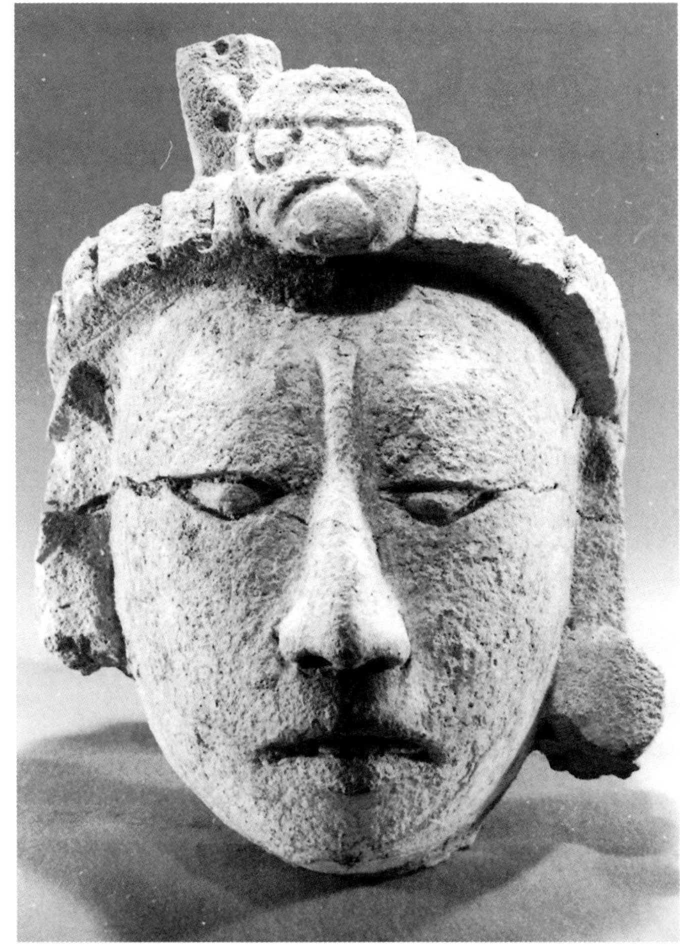

Mayan figure with the sculpture of a head as hair decoration.

---

1 *Paula Modersohn-Becker*. (Kunstverein Hamburg, 1976), 12.
2 Martha Zamora, *Frida Kahlo: The Brush of Anguish* (San Francisco: Chronicle Books, 1990), 100.
3 Hayden Herrera, *Frida: A Biography of Frida Kahlo* (New York: Harper & Row, 1983), 251.
4 Hayden Herrera, *Frida*, 214.
5 Lourdes Andrade, "La femme et le surréalisme au Mexique," in *La femme et le surréalisme*, ed. Erika Billeter (Bern: Benteli Verlag, 1988).
6 Quoted in Hayden Herrera, *Frida*, 62.
7 Gisela von Wysocki, "Die Fröste der Freiheit: Aufbruchsphantasien," *Syndikat* (1980/81), 35.
8 Uwe Schneede, "Selbstprüfung in Schwierigen Jahren: Munchs Selbstporträts," in *Edward Munch: Höhepunkt des malerischen Werks im 20. Jahrhundert*, (Kunstverein Hamburg, 1984/85), 72.
9 Heyden Herrera, *Frida*, 112.
10 G. Estrada in *Del Istmo y sus mujere-Tehuanas en el Arte Mexicano* (Museo Nacional de Arte Mexico, 1992).
11 Raquel Tibol, *Frida Kahlo: Una vida abierta* (Mexico: Editorial Oasis, 1983), 56–57.
12 Diego Rivera painted Frida's portrait in five of his frescoes: *In the Arsenal* in the series, The Ballad of the Proletarian Revolution, Patio de las Fiestas, Secretaría de Educación Pública, 1928; "The Exploitation of the Mexican People" section of *Mexico Today and Tomorrow*, Palacio Nacional (with her sister Cristina), 1934; *Pan-American Unity* (originally painted for the Palace of Fine and Decorative Arts at the Golden Gate International Exposition, San Francisco, 1939/40; now in the library of City College, San Francisco); *Dream of a Sunday Afternoon in the Alameda* (orginally for the Hotel Prado, 1947/48, Mexico City; now in its own museum, Jardin de la Solidaridad), and *The Nightmare of War and the Dream of Peace*, 1952 (this mural is said to be in Beijing, China).
13 Hayden Herrera, *Frida*, 410.
14 *Frida Kahlo: Das Gesamtwerk*, eds. Helga Prignitz-Poda, Andrea Kettenmann, and Salomon Grimberg (Frankfurt: Verlag Neue Kritik, 1988), 79.
15 Ibid., 158.
16 Ibid., 263.
17 Ibid., 240–241.
18 Hayden Herrera, *Frida*, 162.

ELENA PONIATOWSKA

FRIDA KAHLO'S BLUE HOUSE

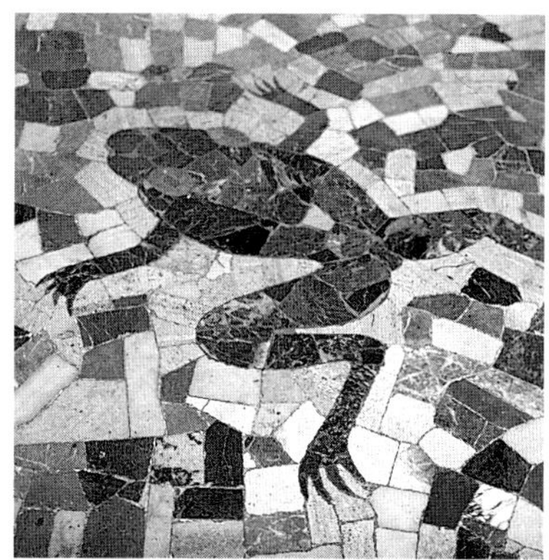

There are several signs in the neighborhood of Coyoacán that read: *Museo Frida Kahlo,* but there are absolutely none for the Trotsky Museum just a few blocks down the street. The *Casa Azul,* at the corner of Berlin and Allende streets, has become a fortress; the tall windows overlooking the street, long since walled up, are blind eyes. How would Frida Kahlo be able to escape it? By blowing through her fist to make a narrow tunnel through the vapor on the glass as she did as a child? Her house no longer sings, it is tightly sealed. Behind the door the tall papier-mâché Judas figures[1] wait without hope.

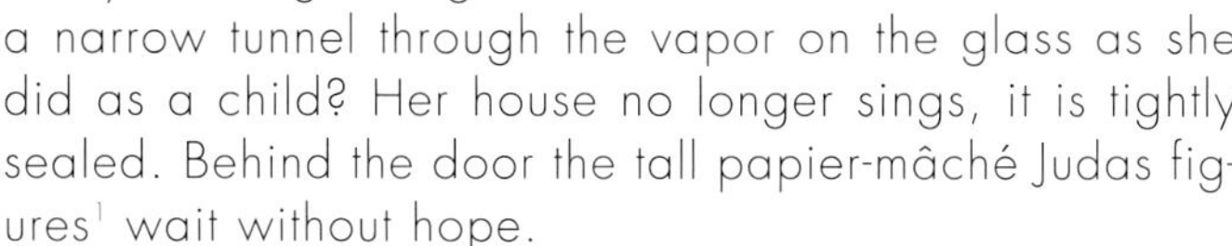

The color of the house is indigo, a deep unyielding blue. The house is more forbidding than the Trotsky Museum even though the latter has at its corners the lookout towers which were built to stop unwanted guests and to shoot from if necessary. Although Trotsky's house was intentionally constructed to resemble a bunker, today it looks more vulnerable than the unassailable fortress that was Frida Kahlo's home.

Yet, when the poet Carlos Pellicer first turned it into a museum, it was an inviting house, open to both birds and people. The curious would come by the dozens to sit in the sun after the obligatory visit to the various rooms. Frida and Diego would have liked that, to watch them there, in the garden, enjoying the sun and chatting. Pellicer wanted the museum to be a house that would sing, one in which each room would have its treble clef and staff, but now the museum, closed off, looks more like a black piano, a locked Steinway whose key has been lost.

The entrance is flanked, on the inside, by two black-and-white Judas figures made of wire and papier-mâché. They were commissioned by Diego from Carmen Caballero, his favorite folk artist. The inner patio of this typically Mexican home then opens into what must have been an austere sitting room or receiving room, now turned into an exhibit hall where there is very little to see. Many downstairs doors open onto the the garden, and the kitchen, which also overlooks the garden, draws enraptured exclamations, with its typical country kitchen look, its avalanche of clay pottery hanging from the ceiling, its sink and stove of clay and tiles, its palm-leaf fans, its huge earthenware pots marked with the names *Frida and Diego,* its tall, colorful water pitchers, its cans and jars for beans and rice, its straw brooms, and its small, hard chairs made of woven palm leaves. Nothing is missing in this Mexican kitchen, which resembles those of Puebla with its Talavera tiles that resonate like silver. The stone for grinding maize, the hanging garlic strands, the chile peppers laid out to dry, the spice mortar with its curved stone, the *comal* for cooking and turning over tortillas without burning one's fingertips, the wooden rod for stirring foamy chocolate, the ladles, and the woven baskets in which tortillas, wrapped in a napkin, are kept warm. One can still hear in the air the clap of hands molding dough. A sauce bowl is inscribed "I belong to my mistress, Niña Frida."

Downstairs it is the kitchen that reigns supreme; upstairs it is Frida's bedroom with its bright study where large windows invite King Sun in; he follows her to Diego's room, where she sometimes slept and then to the other rooms, the successive rooms of her agony and death. The ones with hard beds, orthopedic beds, hospital beds that can be cranked up or down, the beds of her loneliness and her amputated leg, of her broken spine and her crown of flowers, of her corset with the painted hammer and sickle. And those canopied beds, one with a big mirror so she could see herself, the bed of her infinite self-portraits, the other in the room of mystery and self-affirmation, of love and desire between women, its painted banner, clearly announcing: "The room of María Felix, Diego Rivera, Frida Kahlo, Elenita and Teresita."

What a wonderful statement in Palmer script and blood-red ink at the top of the four walls! Frida was afraid María Felix would take Diego Rivera away from her. Earlier in his marriage to Frida, Diego had always been unfaithful. Women had passed through the painter's life like whirlwinds; they were affairs, adventures, and the ladies did not come to stay. But with María Felix, Frida was fearful. So she won María over to her cause, turning her into an ally, an accomplice, like her other accomplices: the Cuban Teresita Proenza and Elenita Vásques Gómez, a strong and very beautiful woman. The niece of Francisco Vásquez Gómez, who was

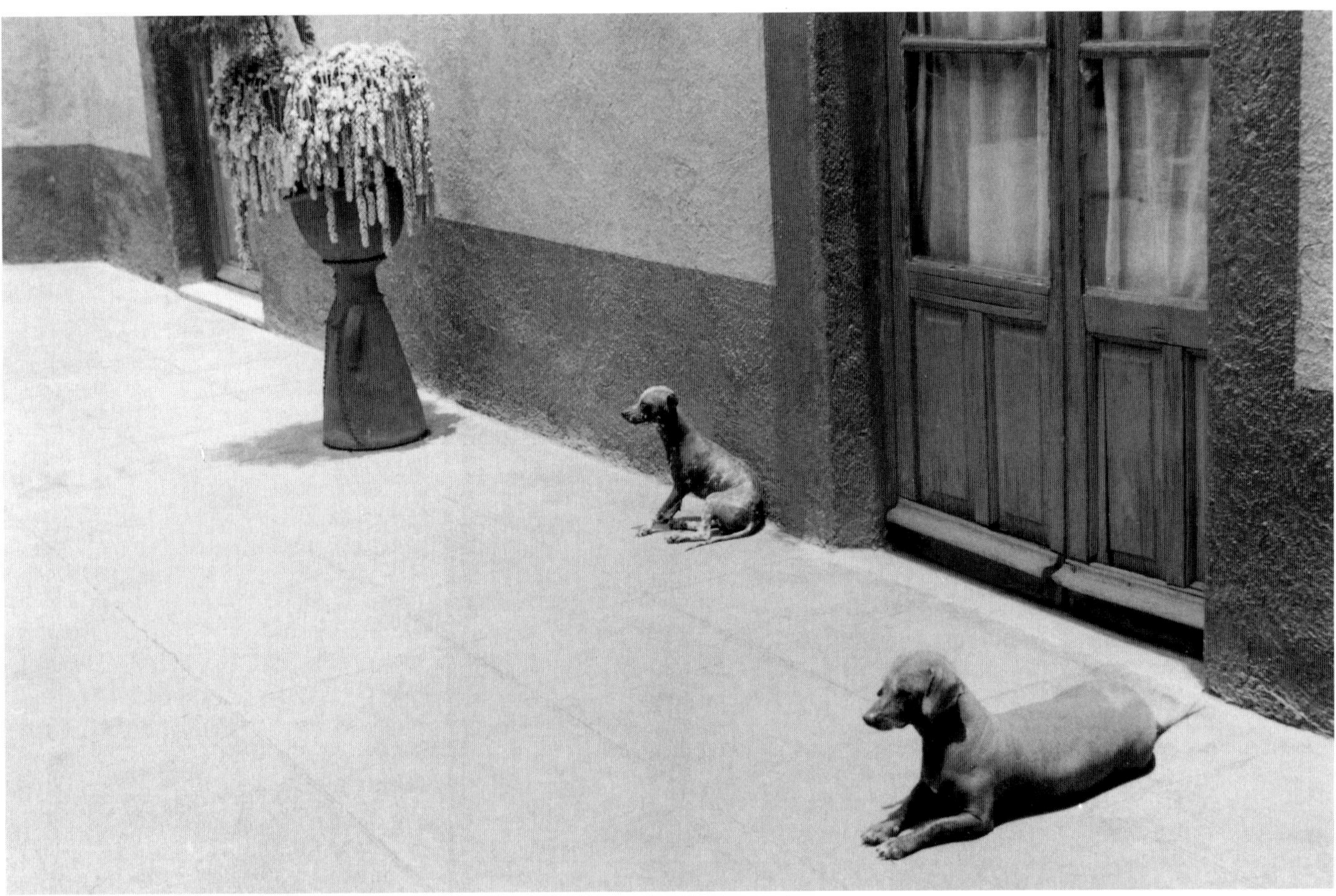

Frida Kahlo's dogs (Mexican Itzcuintli) in the courtyard of the Blue House, 1944. Photograph by Lola Alvarez Bravo.

briefly president of the republic, Elena was Lazaro Cardena's secretary and courageously accepted her homosexuality. Teresita Proenza died in Fidel Castro's Cuba. Both were part of the household: Teresita, Diego's secretary, archivist, friend; Elenita, a woman who always stood out among Mexican intellectuals for her strong personality. All of them consecrated by history as committed Communists and fighters. Well, not all of them. María Felix was never a Communist, but she had other virtues. Or other defects.

In the same room, in another corner, there is a handwritten inscription: "The house of Machila Armida." In a few places "Pita," the nickname of the poet Guadalupe Amor, appear's clumsily scrawled in red. Machila, the niece of Mother Conchita Armida, a saintly nun who invented sins so she could confess them, turned out to be more fun that her aunt, more open, a better cook. She would prepare octopus in its own ink, plunging her guests into the lustful abyss of the darkest hell. Diego painted her as if she were just another huge and round fruit, like those spread out on her lap. Had one not known Frida, one could at least look at Machila, her hair braided with flowers and fruit the way Frida used to wear it. What a beautiful woman!

The Frida Kahlo Museum is not so much intimate as it is impudent, or at least that is what it was like until they started to empty it and then closed it down. When I visited it almost thirty years ago, two girls sat chatting on the couch where Frida and Diego once chatted; with a timid hand a lady smoothed down the handmade lace cover on Frida's bed; another fluffed the embroidered pillows, one of which bore the message "Sleep peacefully, my love," held in the beaks of two pigeons, while another announced in cross-stitch "Yours for love." No museum is as revealing as Frida Kahlo's, nothing is private here: soon we will hear the toilet flush; in the kitchen the rice will start to boil in the pan, the oil will sizzle and the cutting of onions will make us cry; on the flat roof we will hear the steps of one of Frida Kahlo's favorite spider monkeys, *Guayabito,* or those of *Xolotl,* her black hairless Mexican Itzcuintli dog which has roamed the world; meanwhile, in the hallway, the parrot repeats incessantly: "Perico perro, perico perro, the little parrot plays the trumpet, tu turu tu tu tu tu."

Everything in the house is laid bare, very little is left to the imagination. I see Frida smoking like the workers at the Mercado de San Juan, her *Delicado* held between her thumb and index finger; the smoke puffs out of her lungs, those two crushed wings at the sides of her broken spine, as if from a steam locomotive. I see Diego lean-

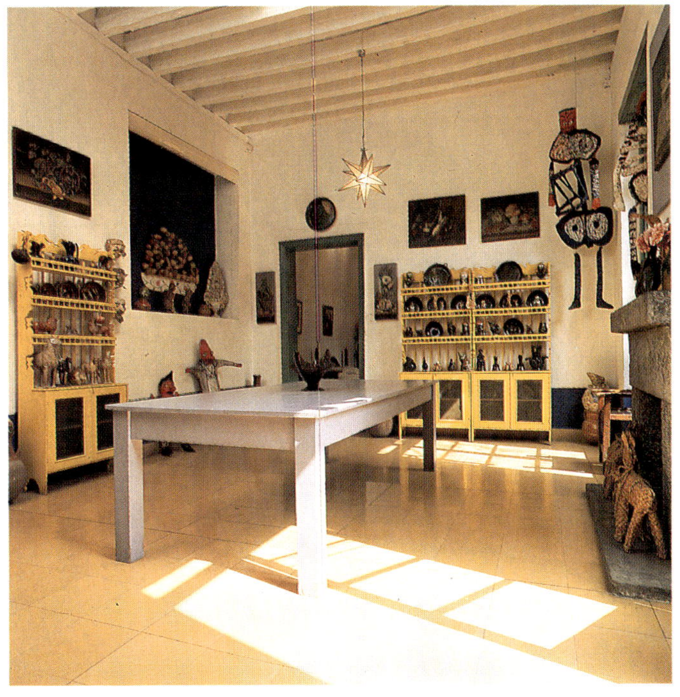

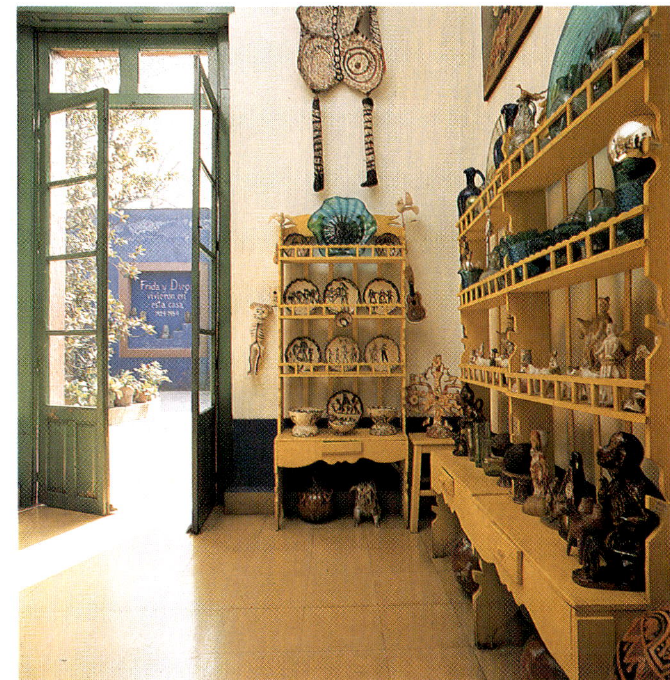

ing over to kiss her, I see the little pet deer trying to flee, I see the servants calling Frida by her name, Frida who cries because the pain is too much to bear, I see the nurse brandishing the syringe as she injects her a dose of morphine.

Frida loved Diego, painted, chatted, sang, and laughed whith her *cuates*, her comrades[2], told rough jokes and talked nonsense with a glass in her hand, met with her students, "Los Fridos," attended political rallies and railed against the government. Frida especialy loved Mexican food: tequila with salt and lime, sangrita, tacos, black *mole* (meat seasoned with black pepper), *capirotada* (a mixture of eggs, herbs, garlic, and other ingredients), and coconut candies. She delighted in the smell of chile peppers roasting in the kitchen, of beans with *epazote* (Mexican herbs) starting to boil, of squeezed oranges spreading their aroma throughout the house. She loved to arrange paper flowers from the Mercado de La Merced in different transparent flower vases to see if they would bloom, to wear dresses with long, lacy petticoats to hide her leg atrophied by polio; these were her other pastimes. She wore long skirts not only to hide her defect but also because the Tehuana petticoats[3] that swept the floor made her feel like a queen and lent her a majesty that other women lacked.

Back then, during the fifties, one could see Frida's diary, kept under glass, and read some of the messages Diego had scribbled in haste before leaving for his studio and museum on Avenida Altavista. All their letters lay open. Diego called his wife "My little Fisita," and she addressed him as "My number one toad frog." There also lay the simple flying eyes made from a page torn

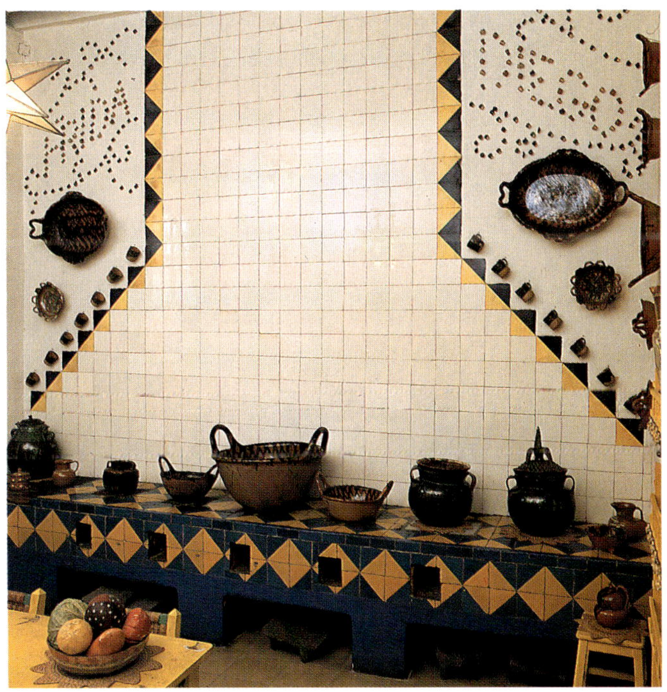

Dining room, kitchen of the Blue House. Photographs by Laura Cohen.

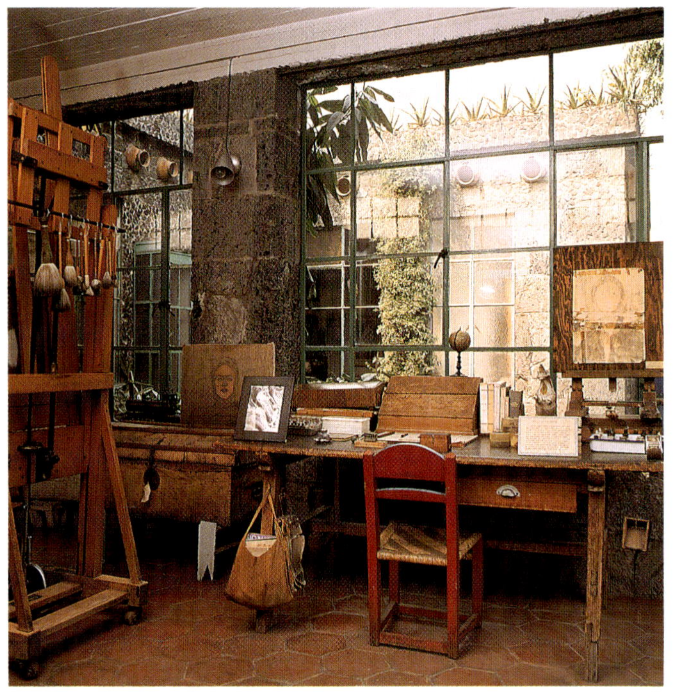

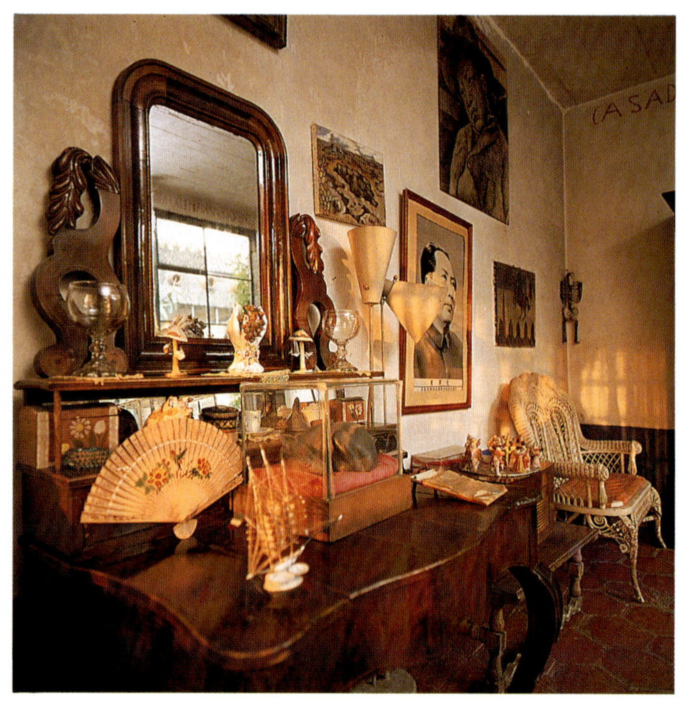

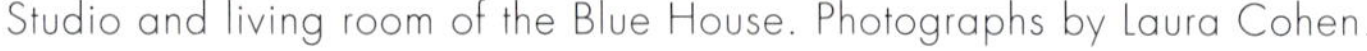

Studio and living room of the Blue House. Photographs by Laura Cohen.

out of a notebook: "I left without seeing you because you were still asleep." Also preserved were the newspapers with the statements that each of them made to the press about the other. They lived in a showcase, and that is what they wanted, to be seen, to be heard; they were always on display. My mother would have said that they had no manners, because the press does not write about decent people. But their rules of decency were different; for them it was indecent not to keep their doors open, shouting out to the passersby "Come on in, come on in, come and make yourselves comfortable, because here learning is made easy." The most moving thing in Frida Kahlo's diary, among pages covered with writing and drawings, may be the illustrated scream: "Diego, I am lonely," and later, "Diego, I am no longer lonely!"

Visitors linger especially in the study with her palette and brushes, her unfinished paintings, one of Stalin, barely outlined, the studies by the masterful José María Velasco whom Frida admired, the easel and wheelchair in which she almost always sat while painting. From the study one can see the bedroom of her last days and the smaller room in which she died. There, displayed on the bed by the headboard, the impressive plaster death mask of her face, wrapped in a *rebozo* (a Mexican shawl), makes a deep impression.

"Look, those were her corsets." One bears the hammer and sickle and looks ugly to me, the other, bright, yellow, joyful, painted orange, is more attractive.

"How's that for an assembly of Russians?" Facing the bed there is a series of gray portraits: Engels, Marx, Lenin, Stalin, and Mao Tse Tung.

In another room there is a huge photograph of Mao, head of the Chinese Communist Party, and one of Diego Rivera. Diego's is by Edward Weston, I believe.

Both of Frida's beds have a canopy, to one is affixed a large mirror, to the other a framed butterfly collection. In those beds Frida suffered, sweated, tossed about, burned up with fever, got morphine shots, cried, cursed, anathematized. The curious inspect the Frida Kahlo Museum in silence, not because it is a sad museum, quite the contrary, it is joyful and even grotesquely festive, but the display of intimacy and of someone's everyday life always inspires a feeling of embarrassment. They hesitate, not knowing whether to ask for more or say: "*Basta*" (That's enough). Frida's combs, her Spanish combs, perhaps still holding some trapped strand of hair; the colorful wool yarn she used to braid flowers and leaves into her hairdo, the only luxury that her illness granted her at the end; her brushes, still encrusted with paint; her china and cloth dolls in a glass cabinet; a few small pieces of inexpensive jewelry (it is said that her valuable jewelry was stolen before her cremation and that Diego flew into a hell-raising rage); all of that is here displayed and the light of publicity is merciless. But not more so than the life that Frida led on this earth, a strangled life, slit open like a carcass, with ribs laid bare, her spine pulverized, her pelvis shattered, her whole body hacked to pieces by the crash between a bus and a streetcar. From that moment on Frida Kahlo lived by picking up the pieces and holding them together by the sheer power of her lust for life. "Why should I want feet if I have wings to fly."

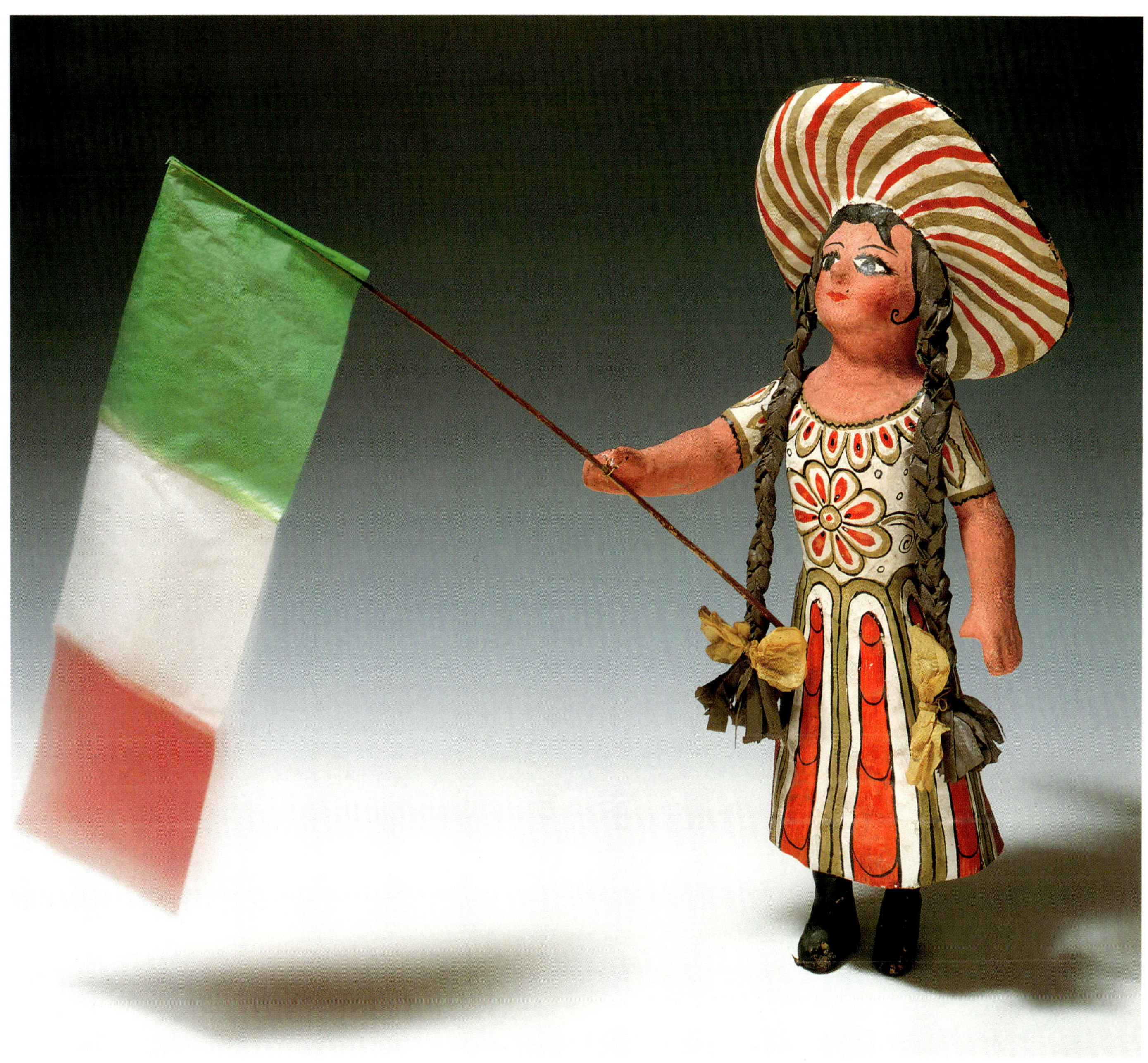

Adelita (campfollower of the Revolution), figure by Carmen Caballero made out of papier-mâché, a popular subject in folk art (cat. no. 141).

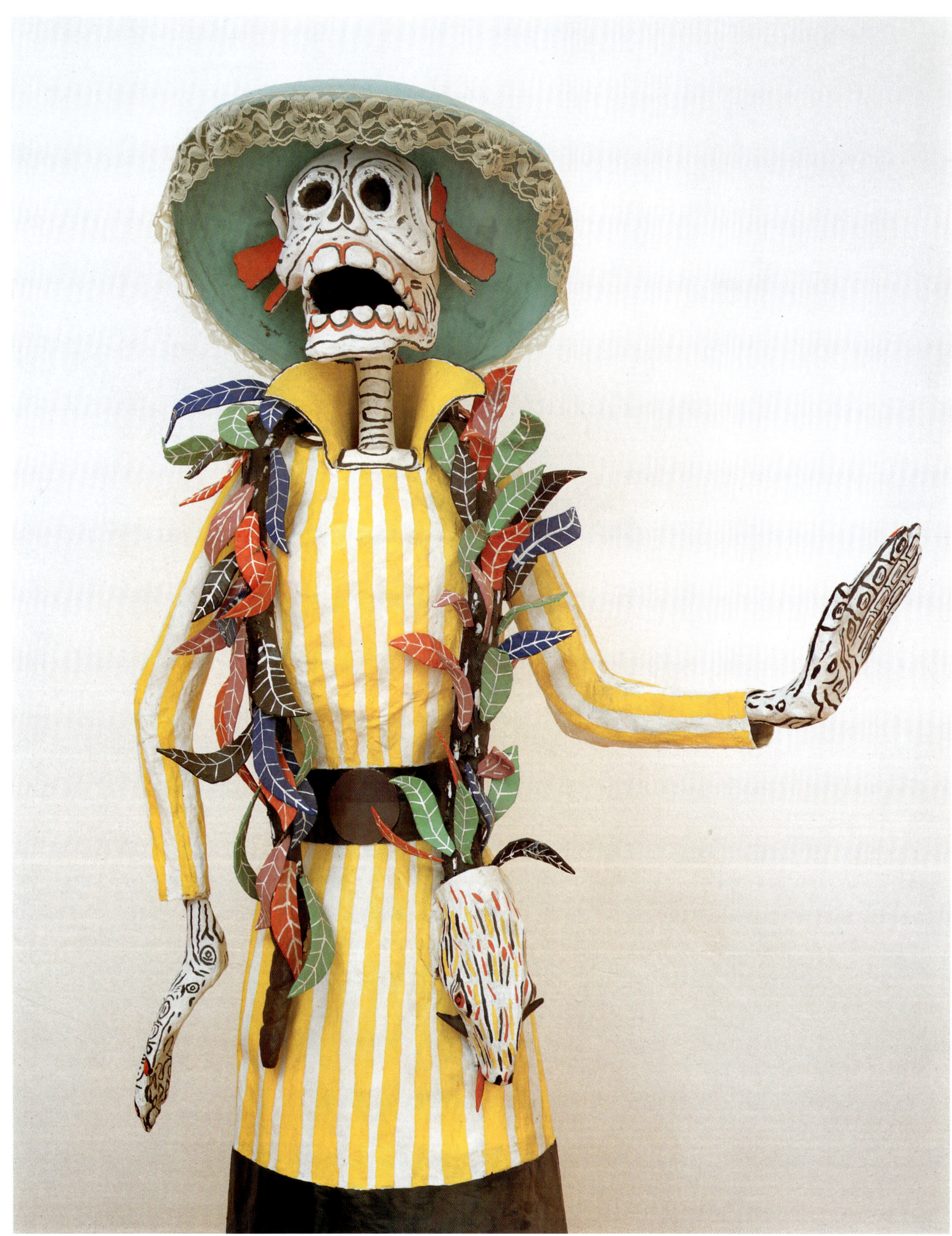

Papier-mâché Judas figures by Carmen Caballero (cat. nos. 138–139). Frida Kahlo and Diego Rivera collected such figures.

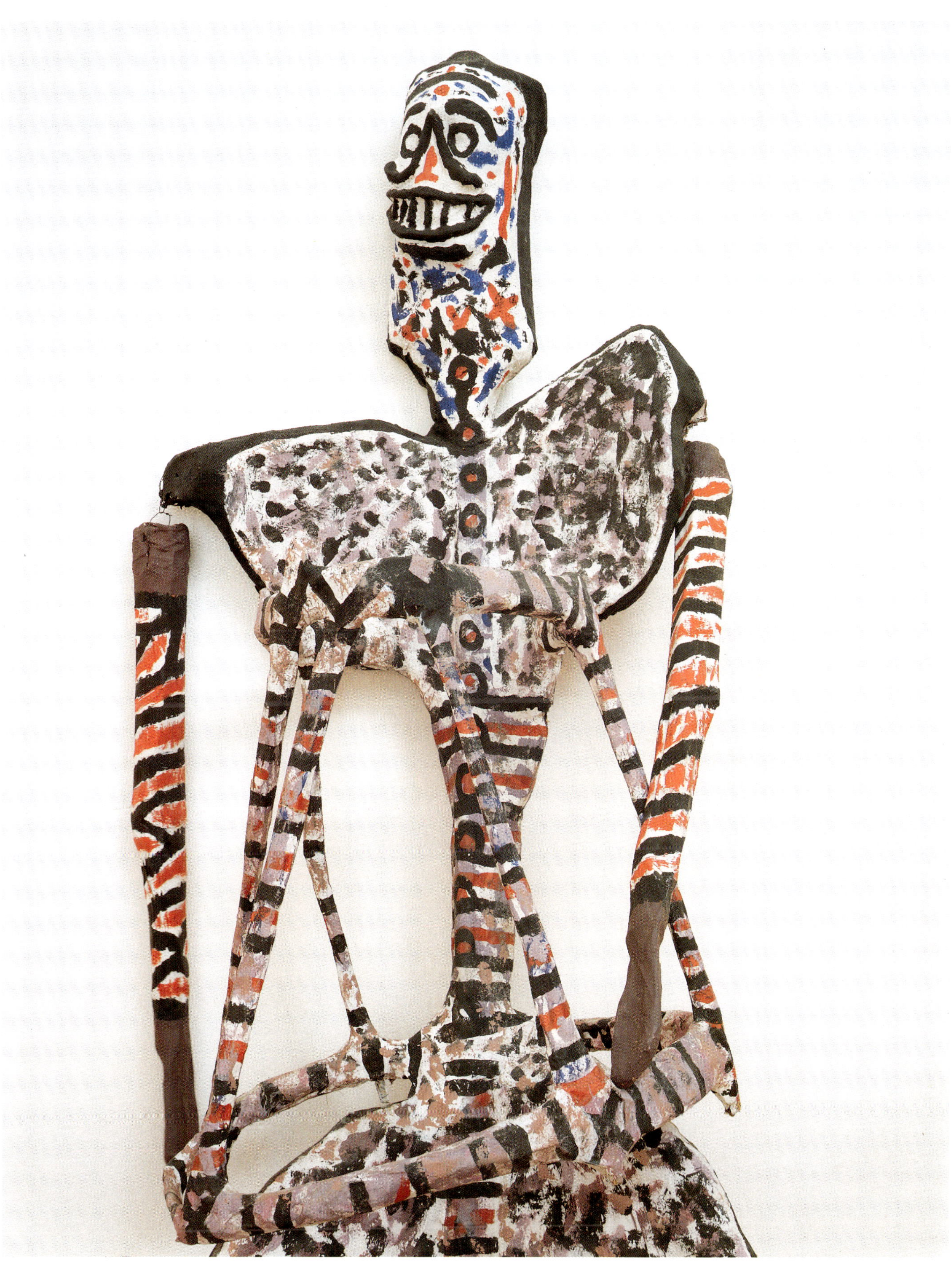

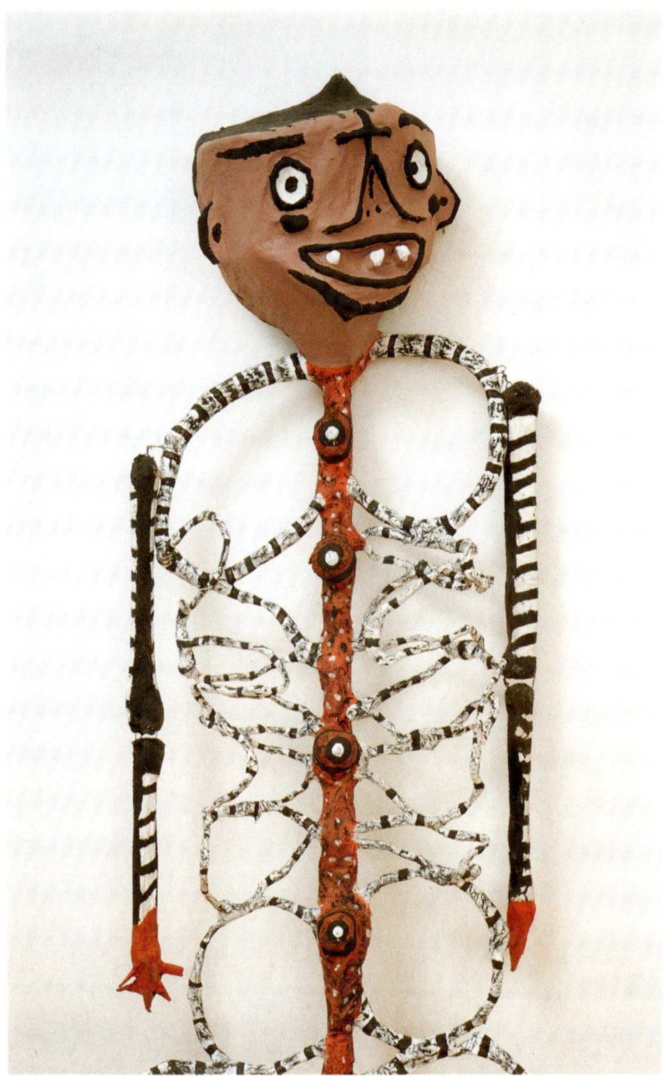

Judas figure by Carmen Caballero (cat. no. 140).

During the fifties, after leaving the Blue House in Coyoacán, Frida's fans could go see her paintings at the *pulquería* "La Rosita" at the corner of Londres street, almost across from her house. These funny and naive murals were done by "Los Fridos" under her guidance and in her company. There, one could admire María Felix in high heels seated on a cloud watching all the men plunge headlong into hell because of her. On another wall, Diego and Pita Amor, both with the same tired pink eyes, look at the sky. But soon the colors faded, the *pulquería* very quickly gave way to an apartment building, and Frida's murals were lost. Another mural painted at a school in collaboration with Ignacio Aguirre was also destroyed.

Frida Kahlo was born on July 6, 1907 in this house, in a room overlooking the corner of Londres and Allende streets, and she died there on July 13, 1954 in an upstairs room. It is said that to be born and to die in the same house is a blessing. The unconventional Frida always felt welcome and sheltered in the Blue House of Coyoacán. An expansive, open house, free and unprejudiced, willful and creative, it resembled her. She died at forty-seven, her body marked by suffering like that of Christ. Twenty-eight of those forty-seven years were years of pain and agony, during which she underwent thirty-nine operations and months of hospitalization that left her bedridden for many months afterward. Added to these were the miscarriages that further endangered her life. The originator of Frida's house-museum, Carlos Pellicer, Tabascan poet and museologist, wrote three sonnets for her, among them the one reproduced below:

You, who held flowers in your hands
and embraced a whole people
offering them your heart, I love you.
(I could not be your good Samaritan)

None of our pain has been in vain;
let me have the paint brushes: the first
dipped in blood will sing like a finch
about her tears roaming the plain.

You are nailed with little nails,
the blood set on fire by the brushes
A blood-drenched child rises to heaven.

I set up camp in an abyss of tenderness,
parched with thirst. Your heart, in flight,
has let fall a piece from on high.

---

[1] These figures, made out of papier-mâché, are hung with firecrackers as part of the mass celebrations on the Saturday before Easter. They commemorate not only Judas's betrayal of Christ but over time have come to symbolize the oppressors of the people, those on whom they wish to take revenge. For that reason, these figures take the form of policemen, soldiers, politicians, landowners – anyone who has earned the hatred of the masses.

[2] Literally: twins. This, among others, is the term Frida used for her friends Ella and Bertram Wolfe and her students at the Escuela de Pintura y Escultura "La Esmeralda."

[3] The dresses Frida loved best were based on the traditional clothing of the woman of Tehuantepec. No doubt the belief that the women of this region were especially statuesque, pretty, strong, sensuous, intelligent, and brave contributed to this preference.

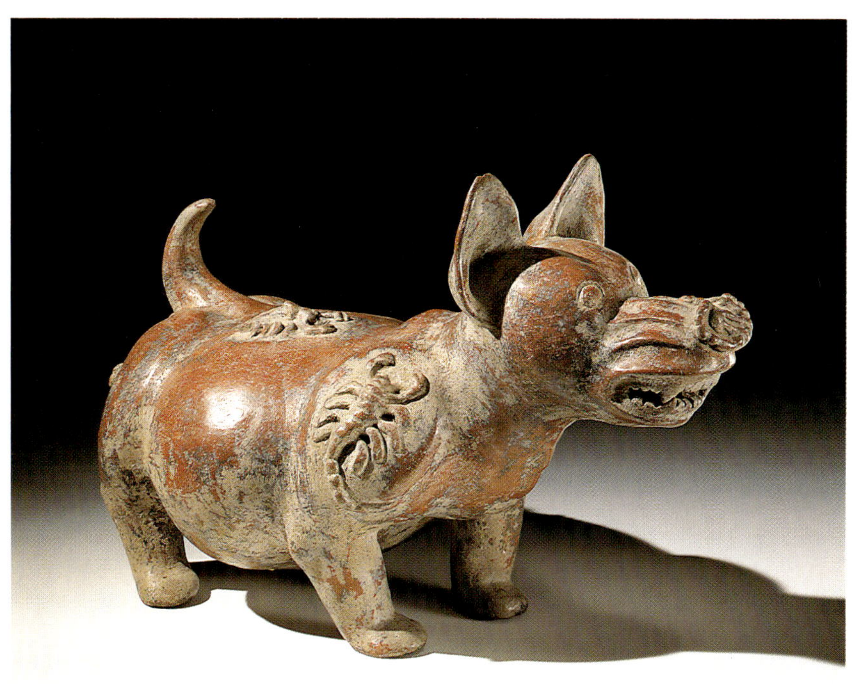

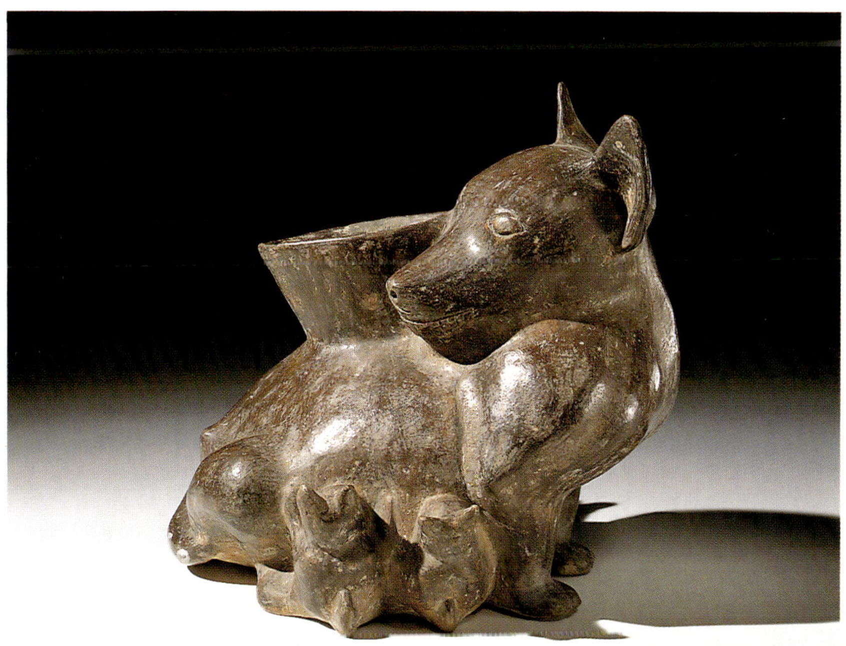

Frida Kahlo and Diego Rivera were passionate collectors of Mexican folk art and pre-Columbian artifacts, among others these unique clay vessels in the form of Itzcuintli dogs (cat. nos. 150, 155).

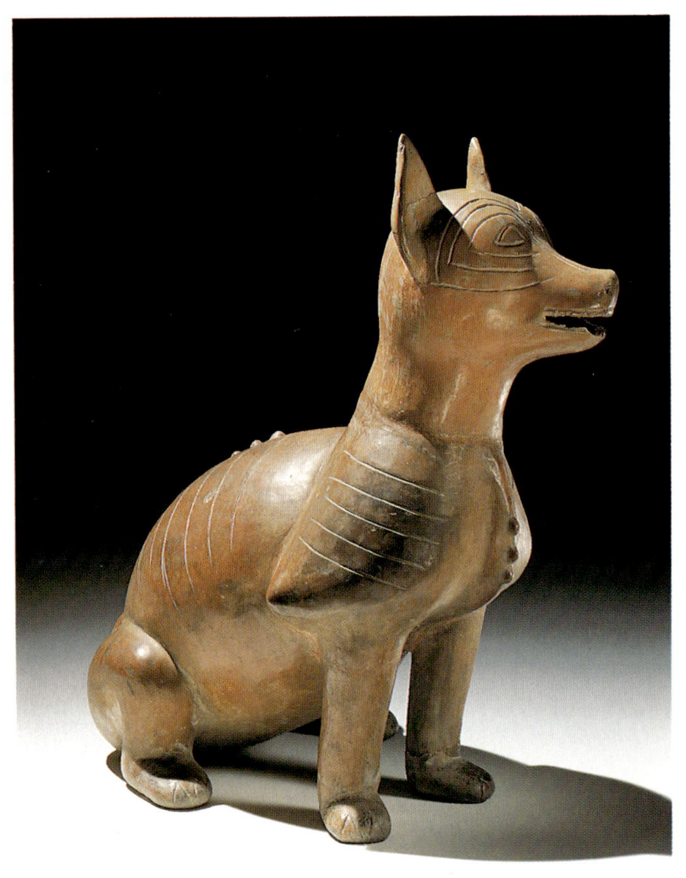

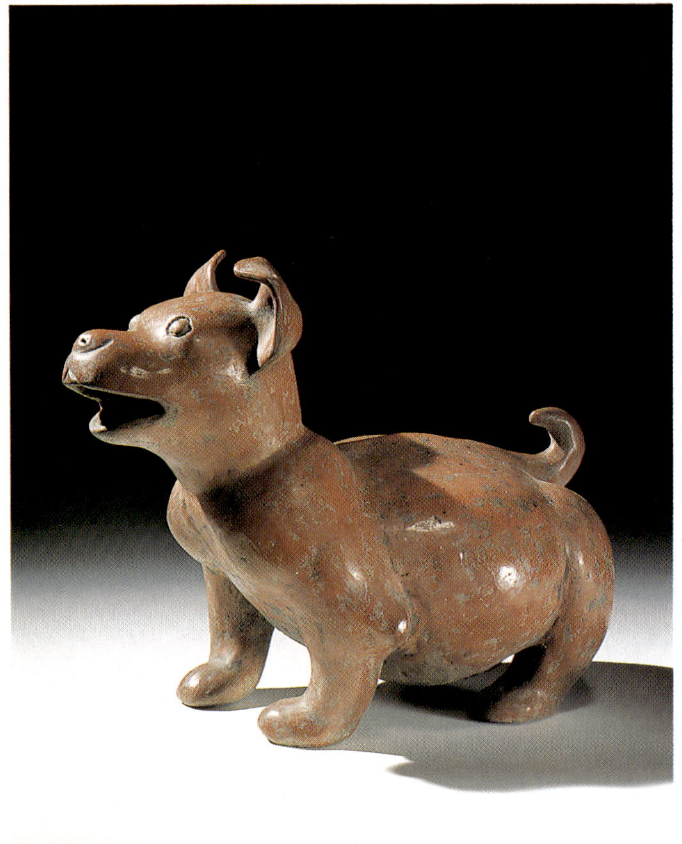

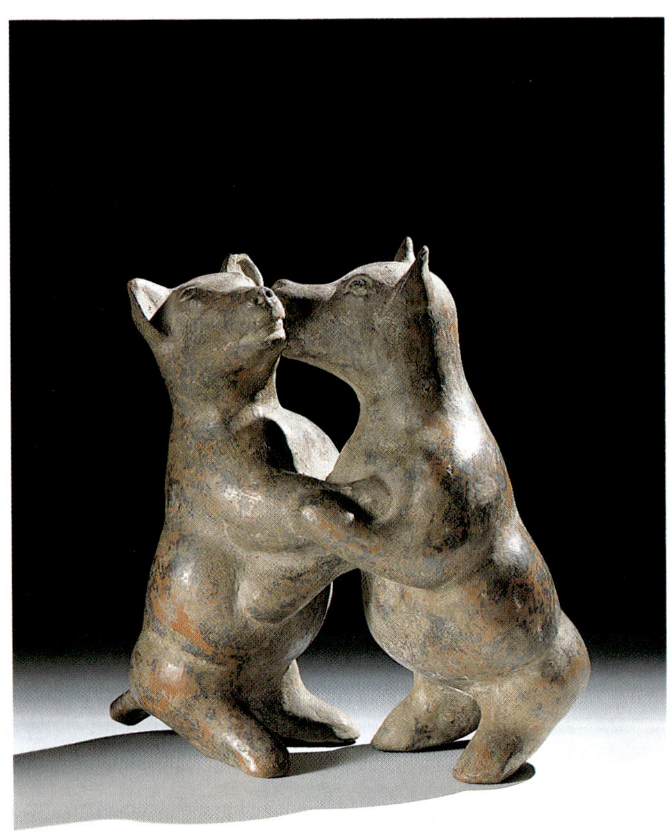

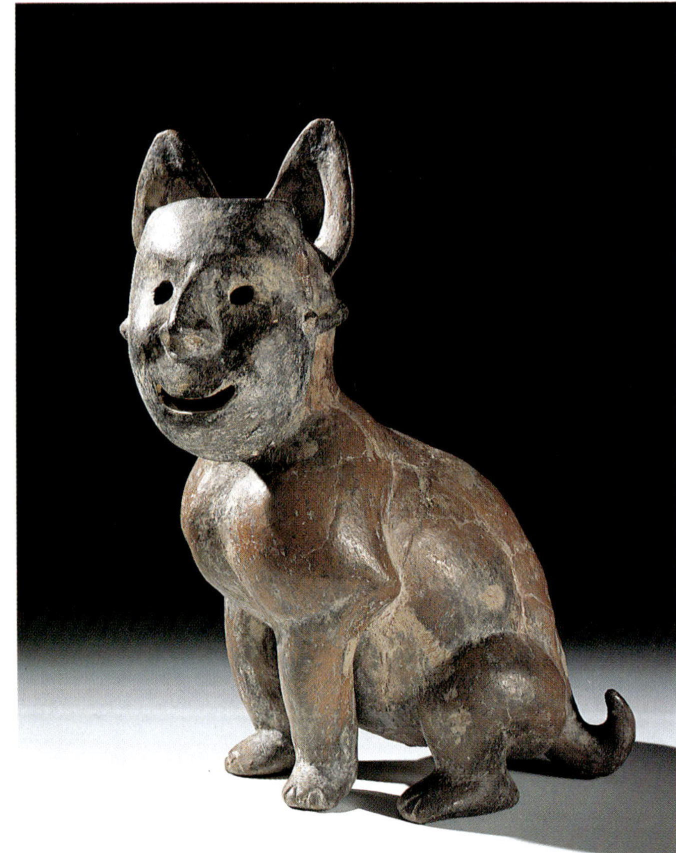

Clay dogs from the graves at Colima, 200–600 A.D. (cat. nos. 151–52, 154, 156).

THE BLUE HOUSE

PHOTOGRAPHED BY
MARIANA YAMPOLSKY

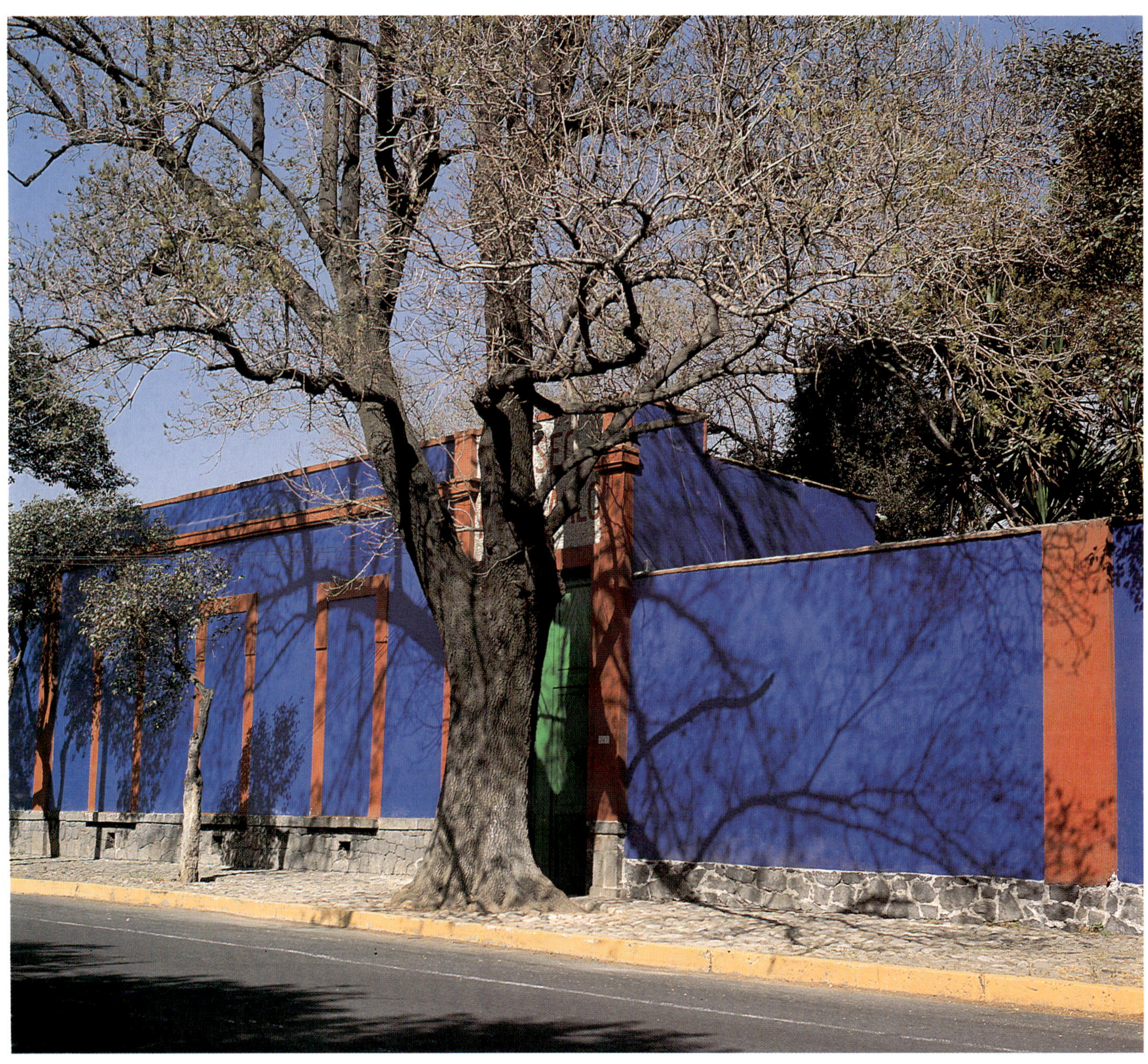

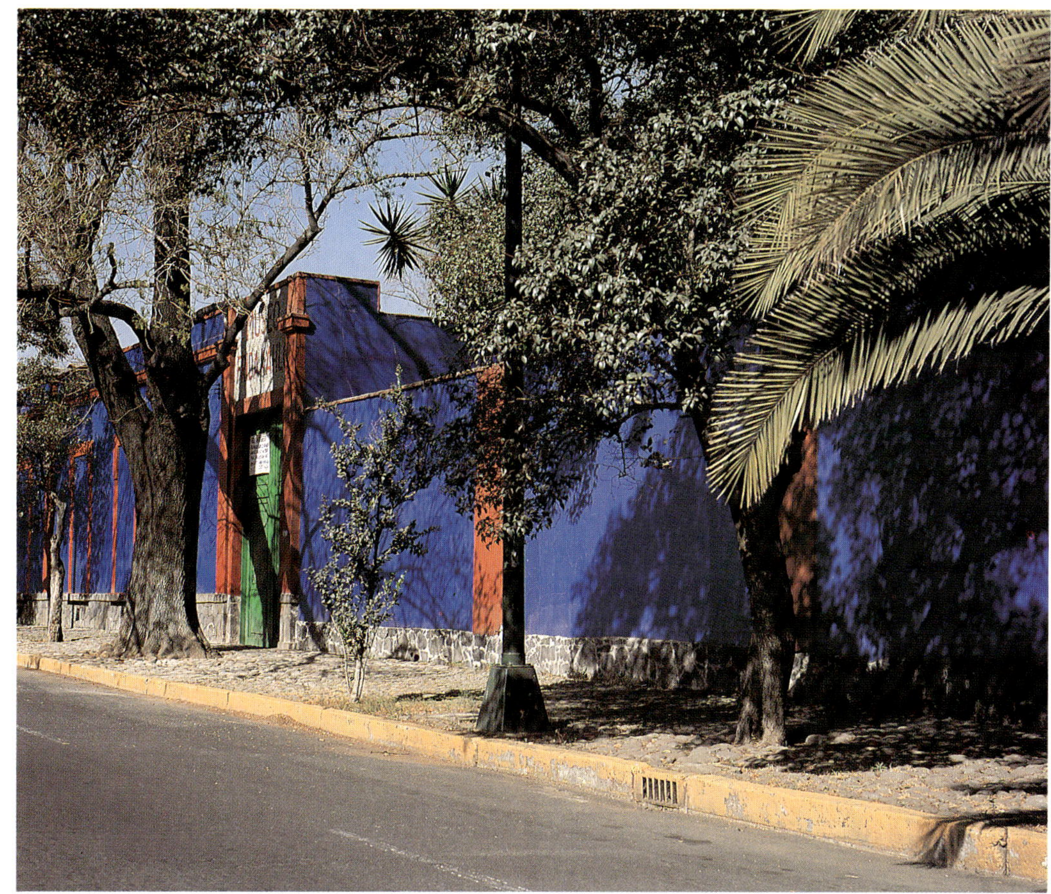

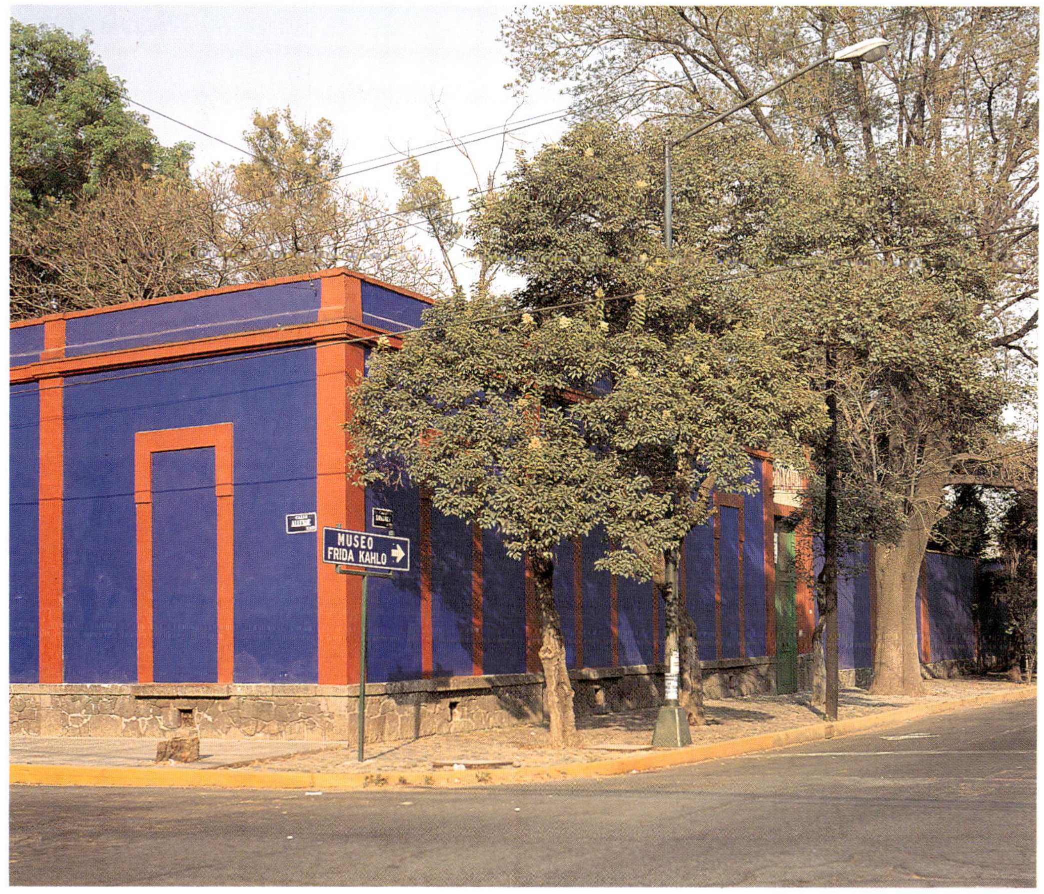
MUSEO
FRIDA KAHLO

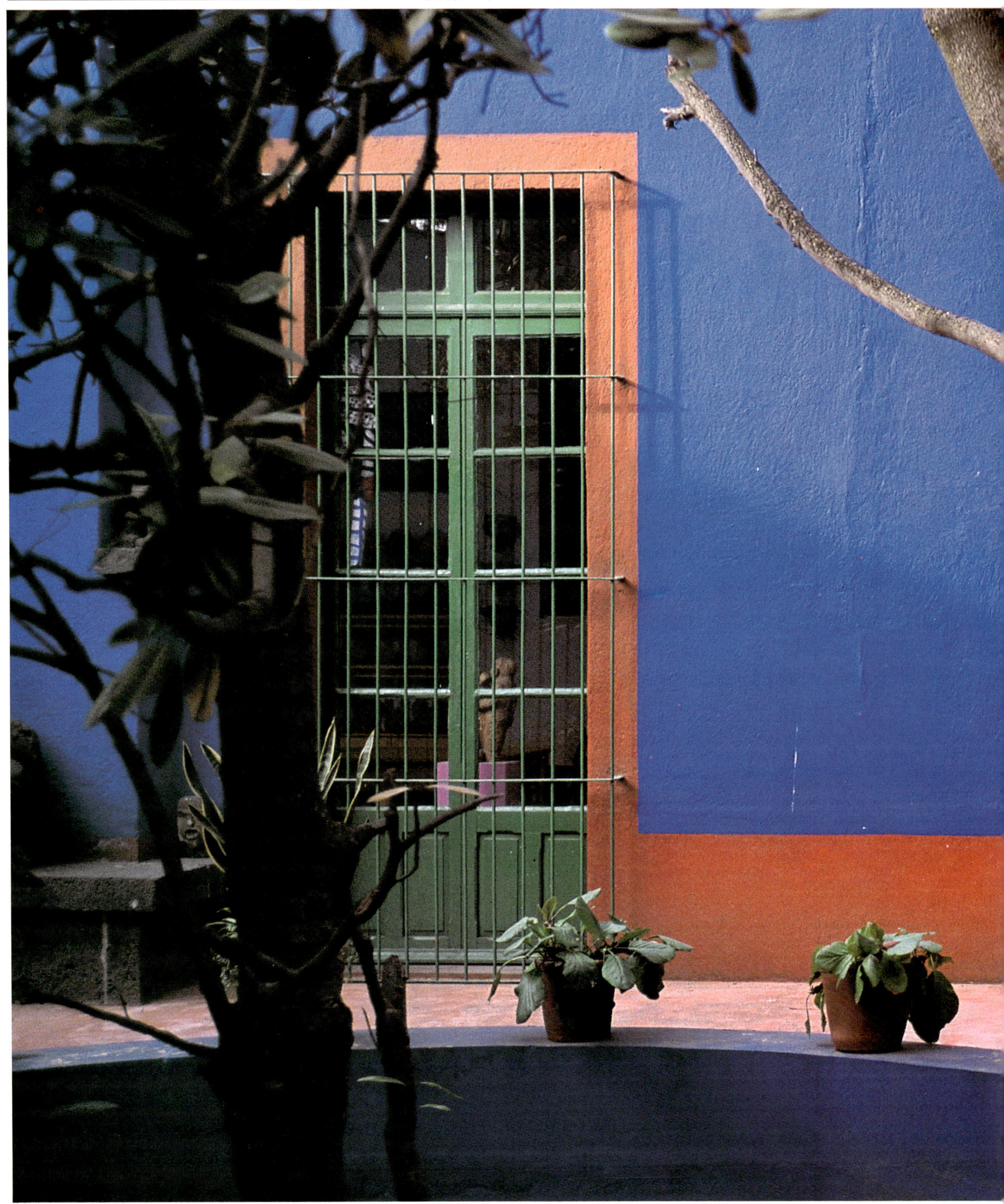

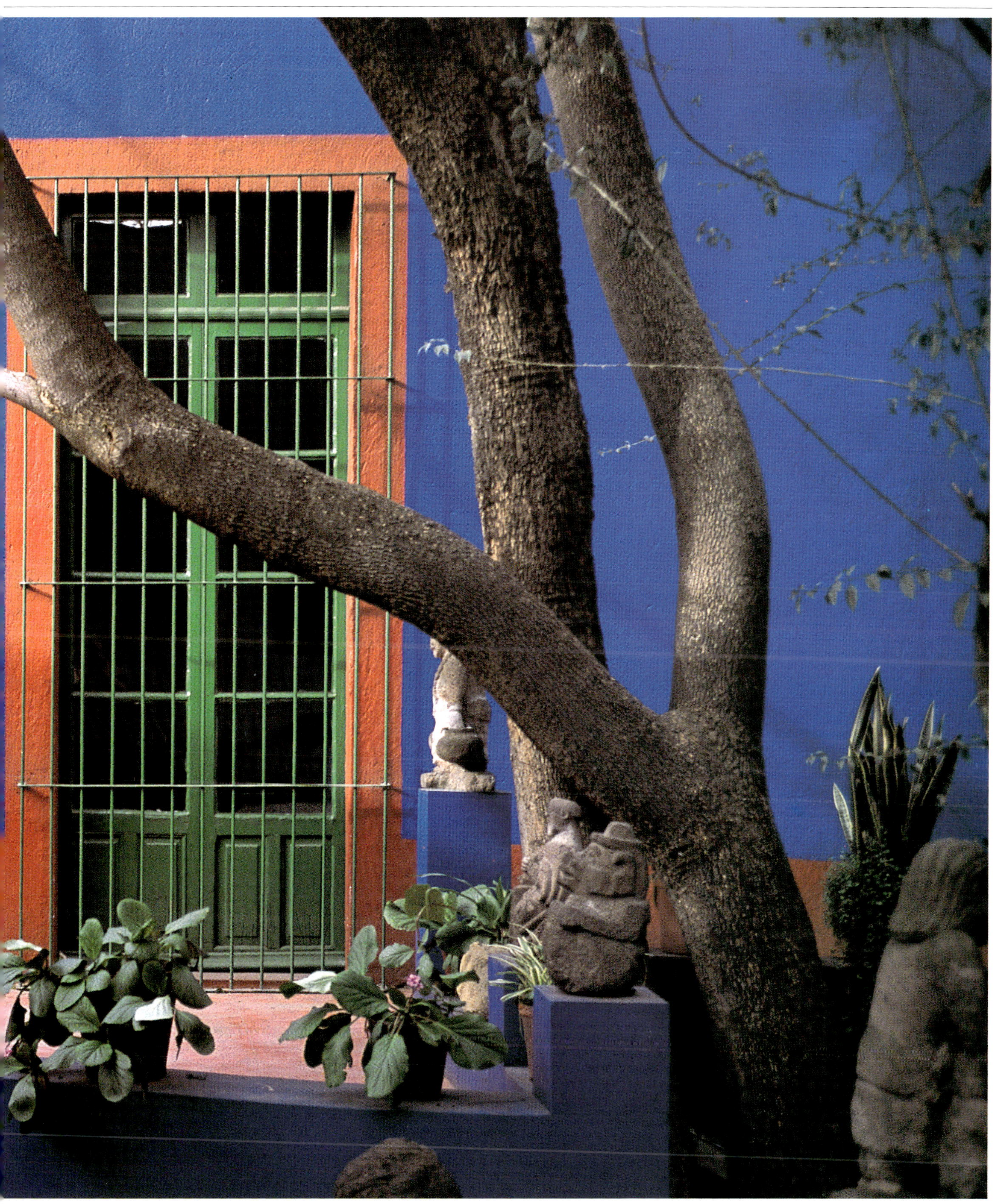

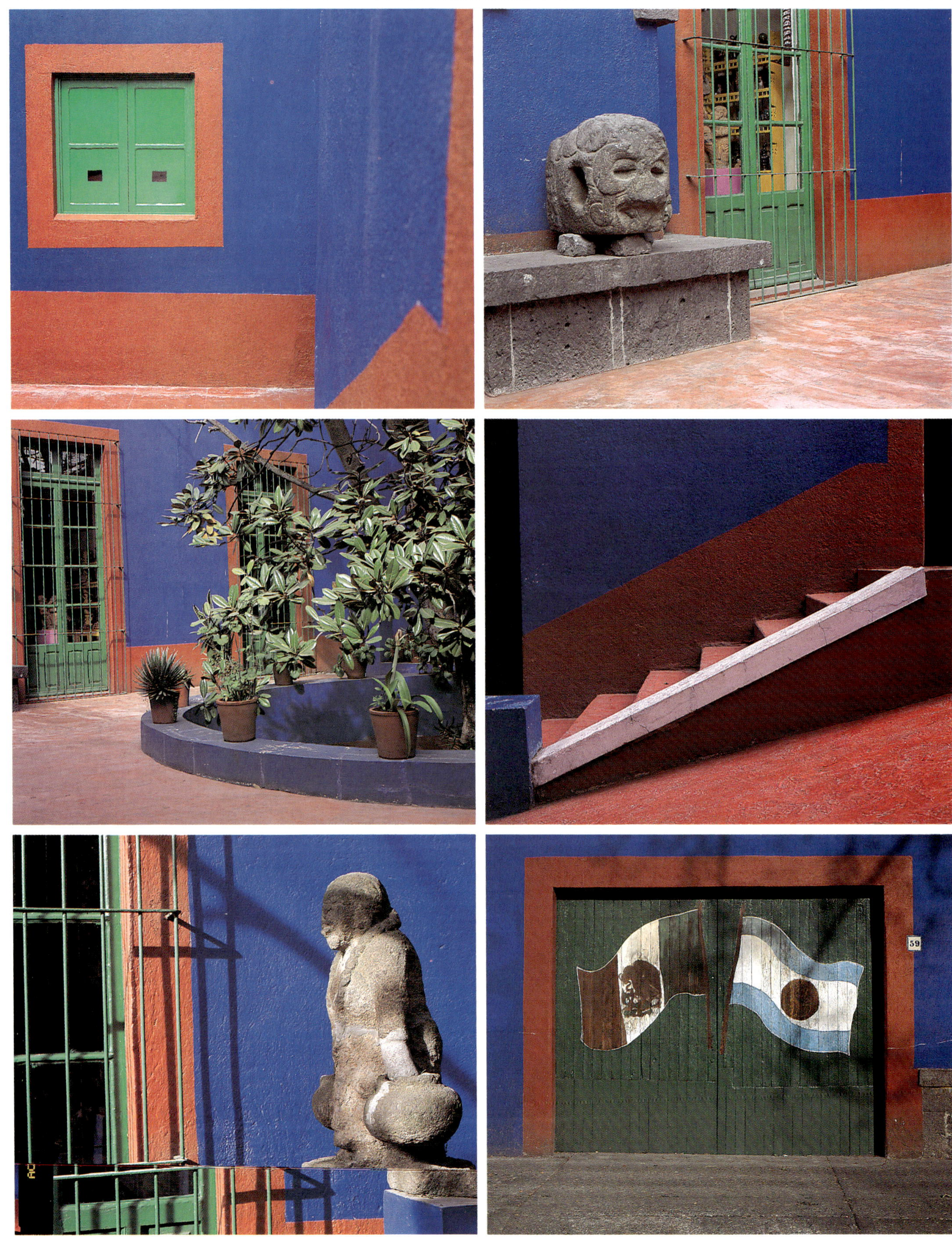
59

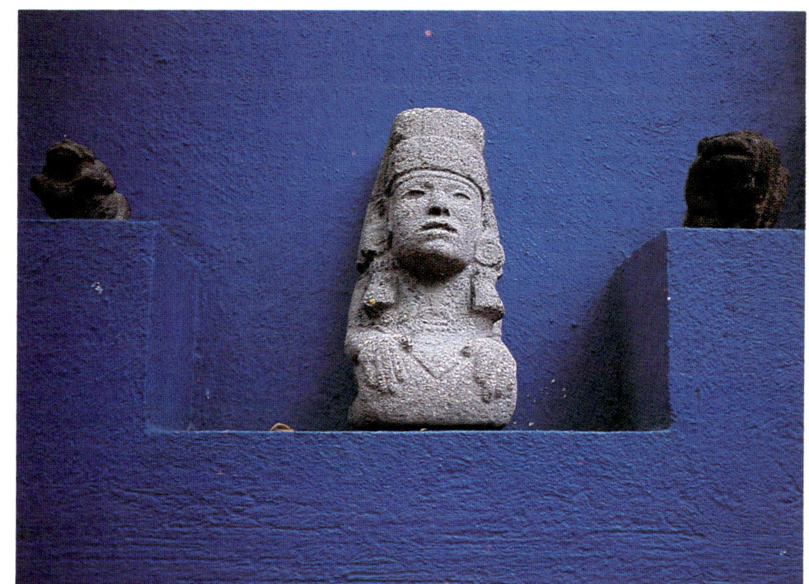

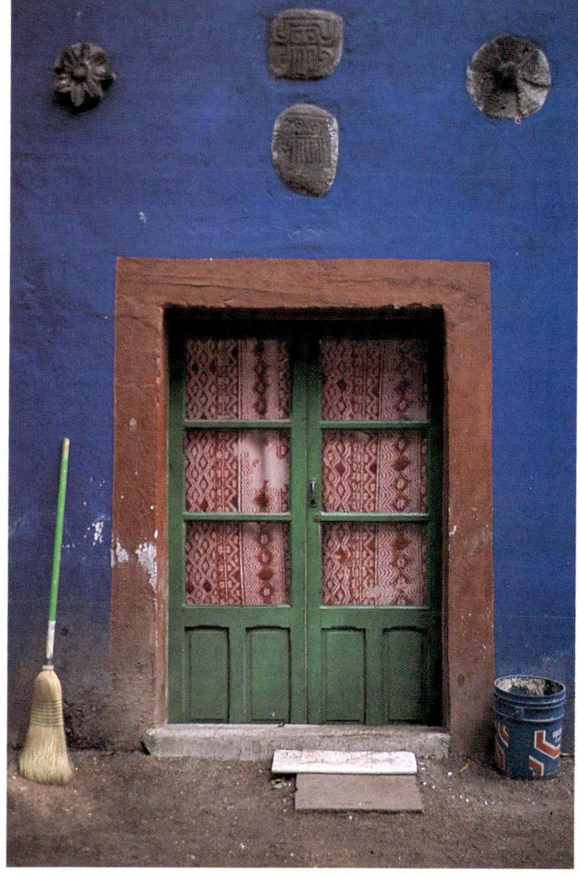

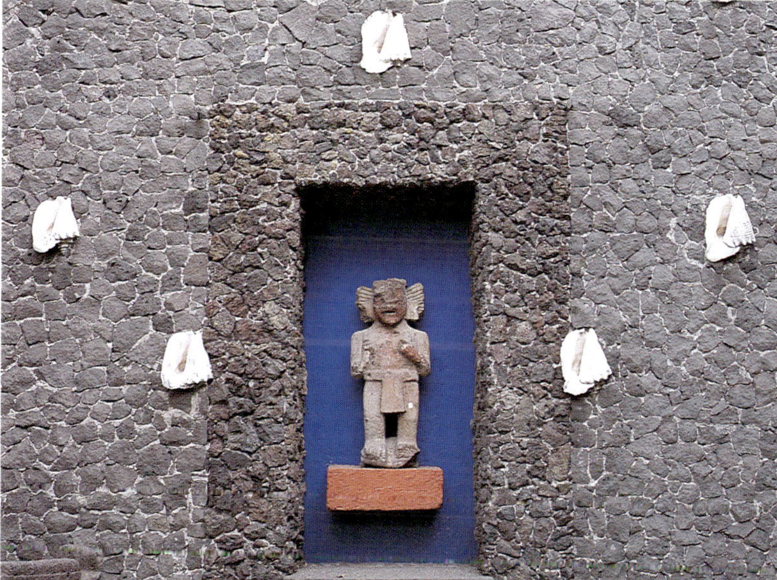

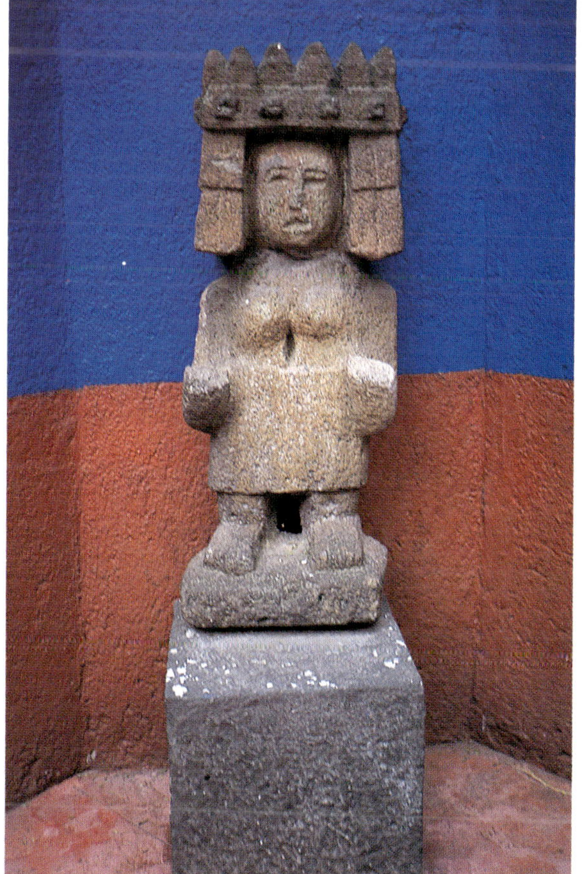

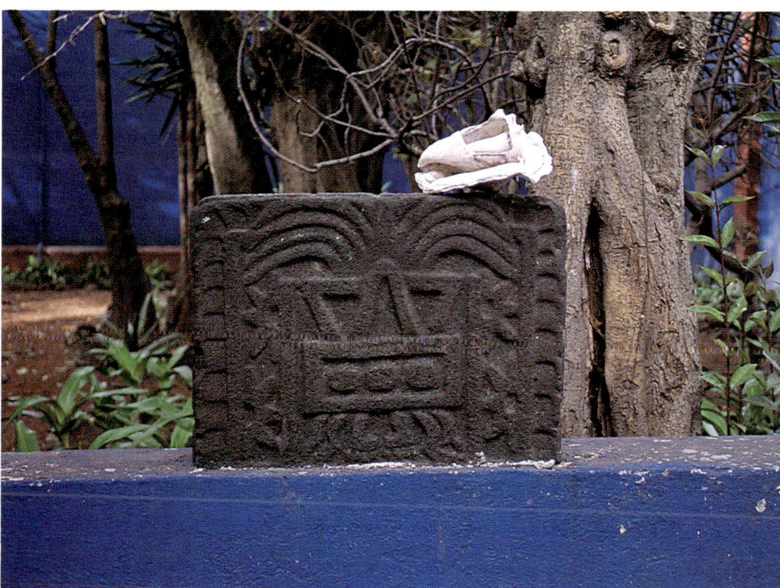

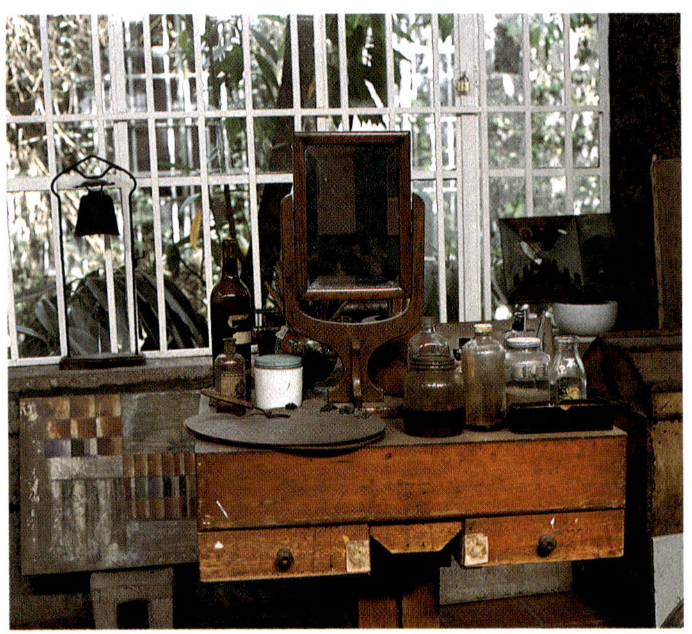

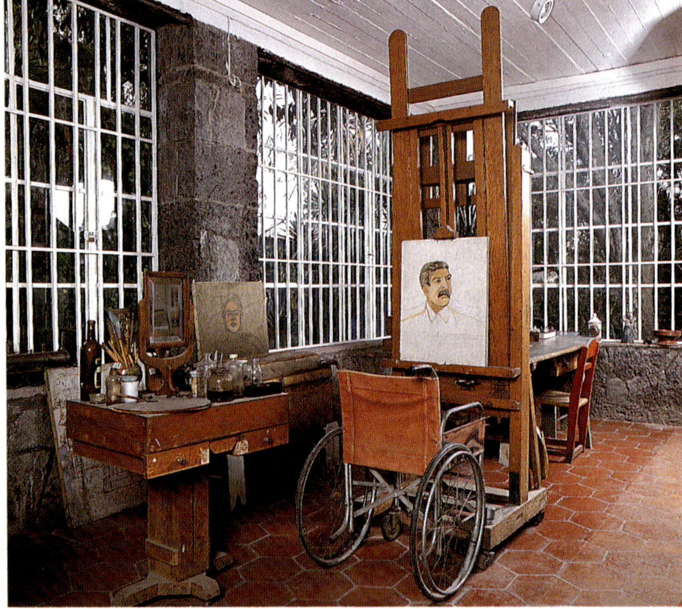

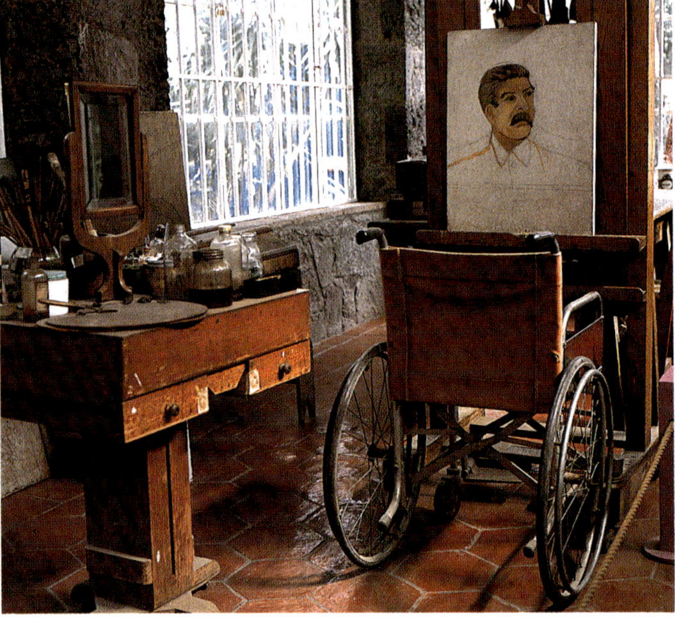

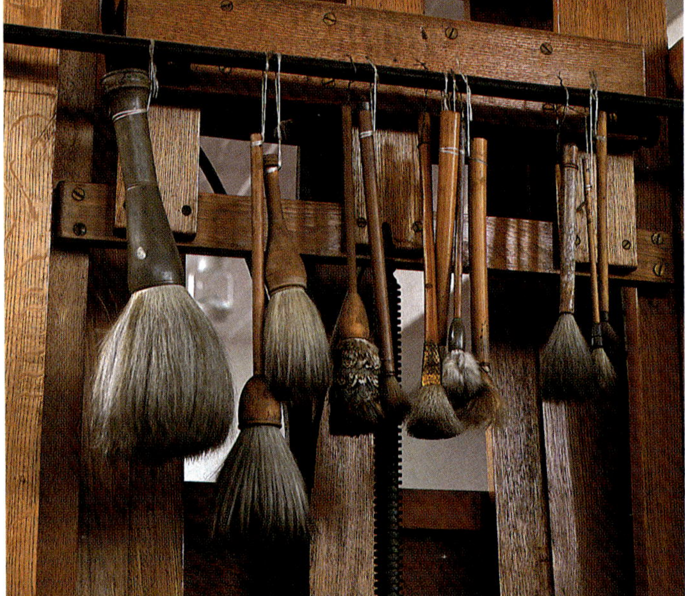

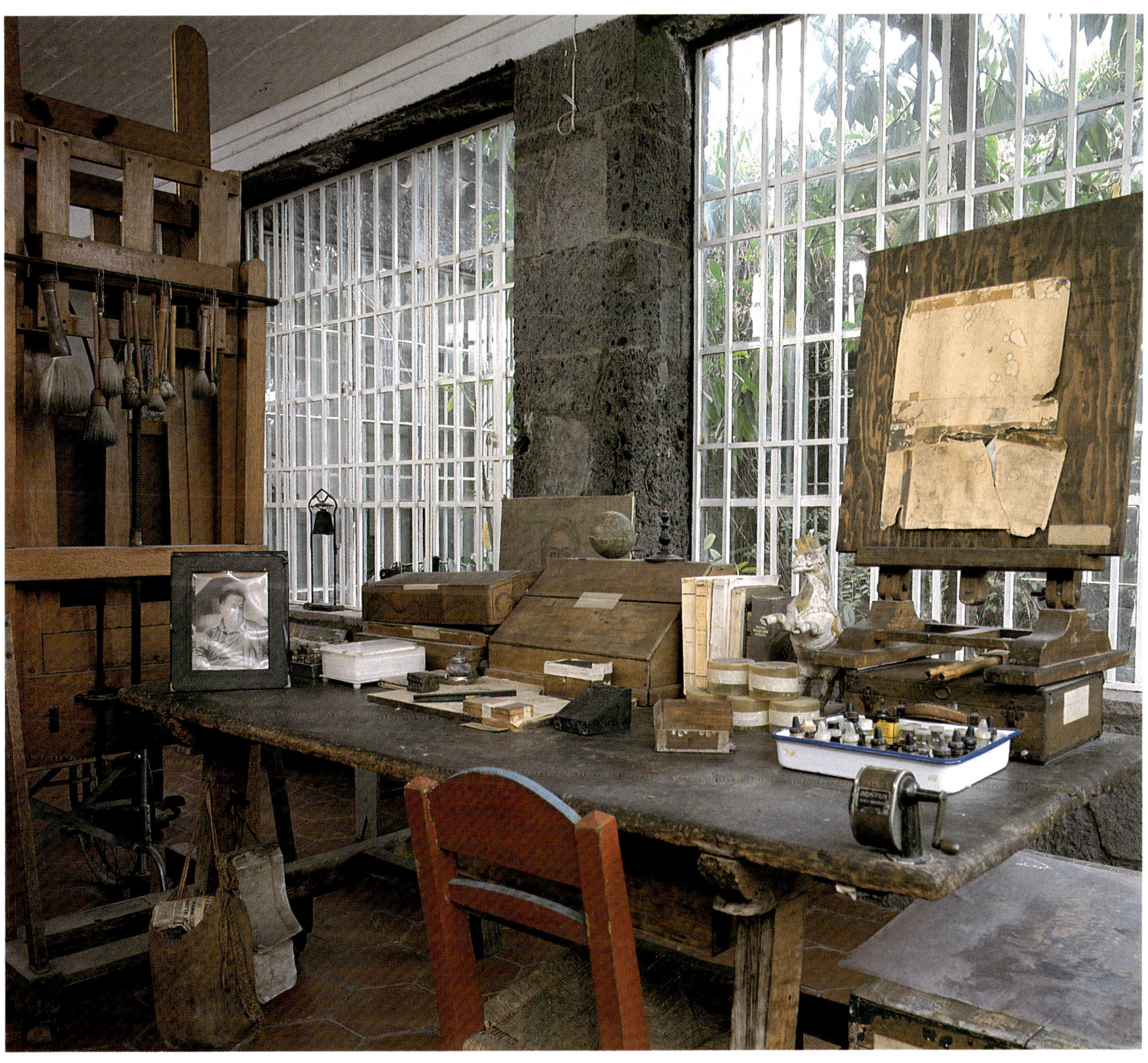

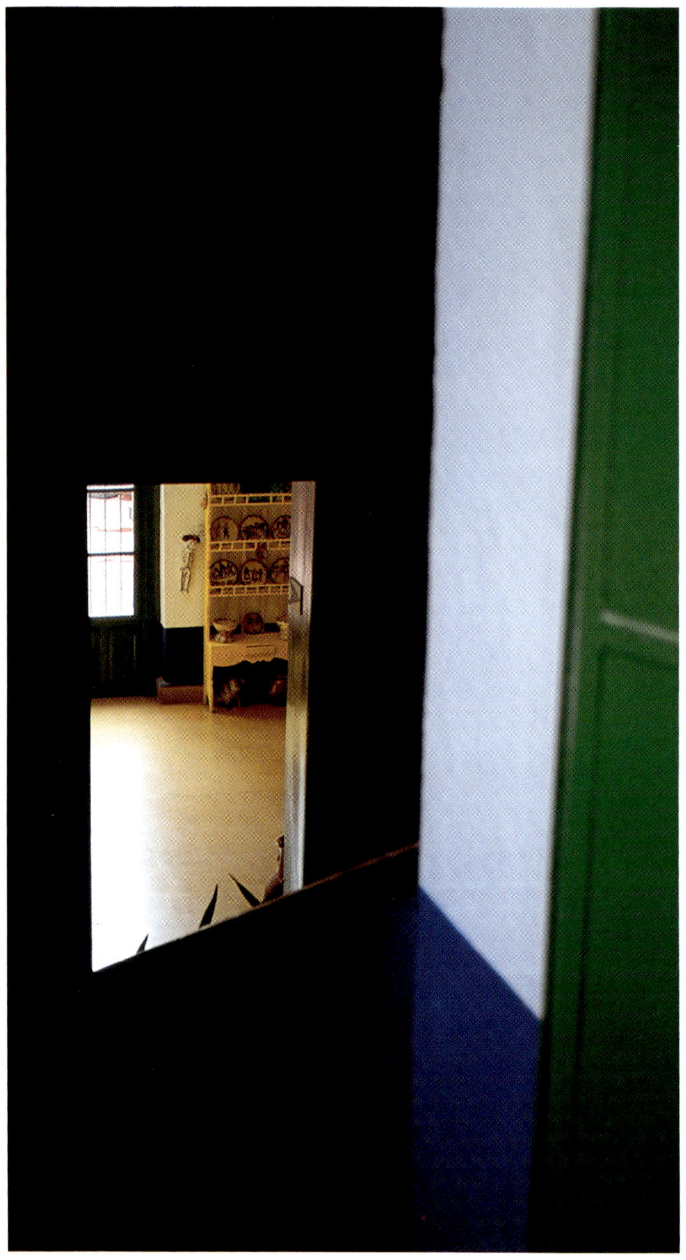

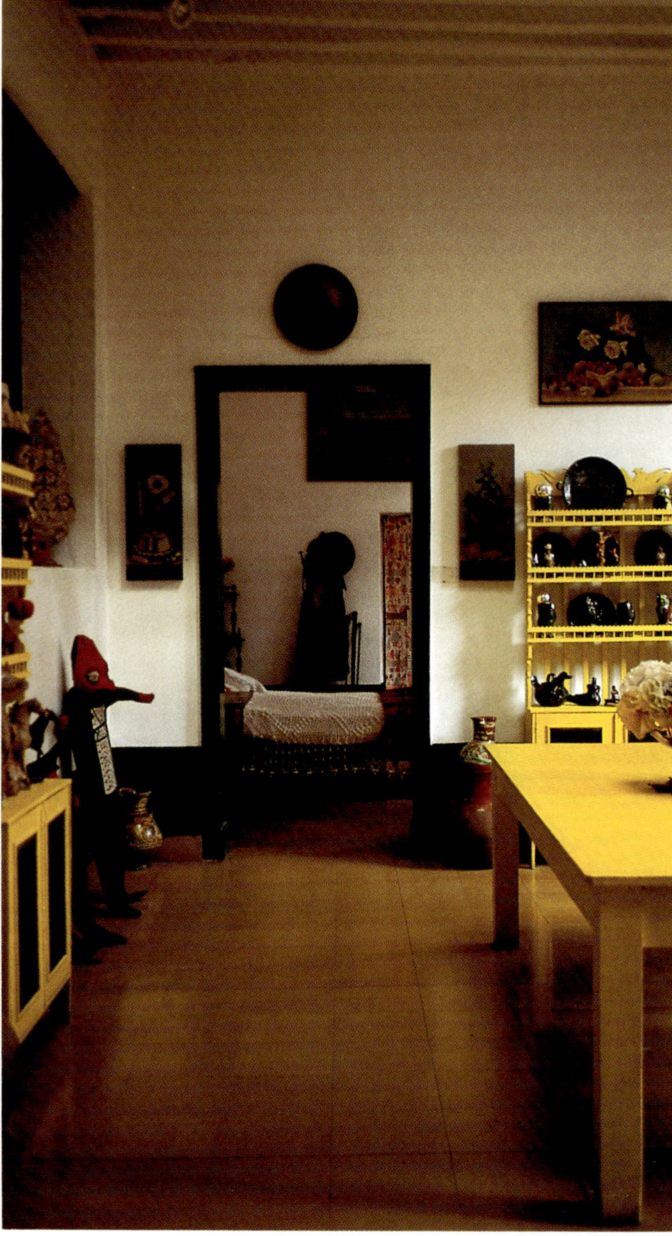

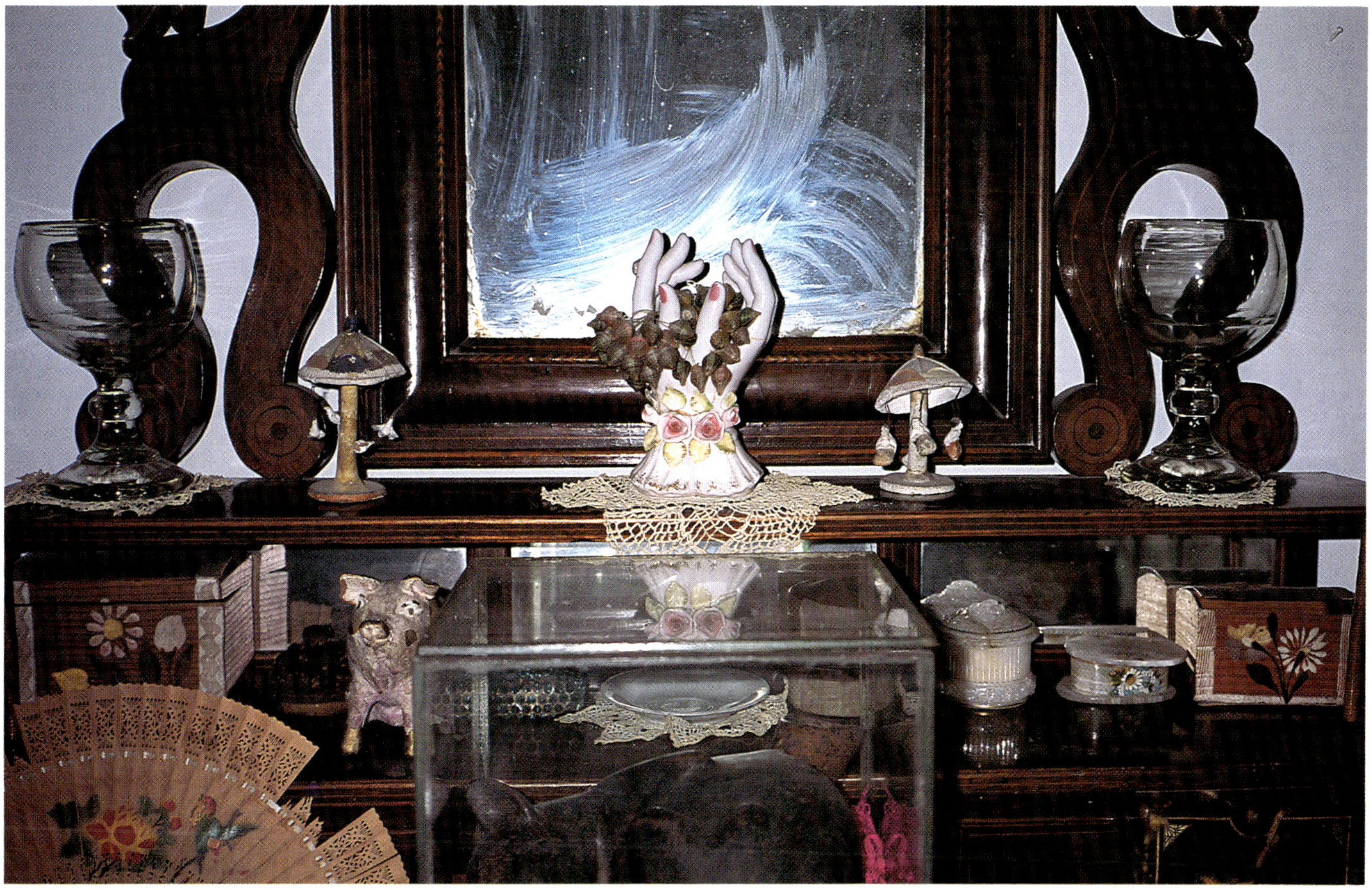

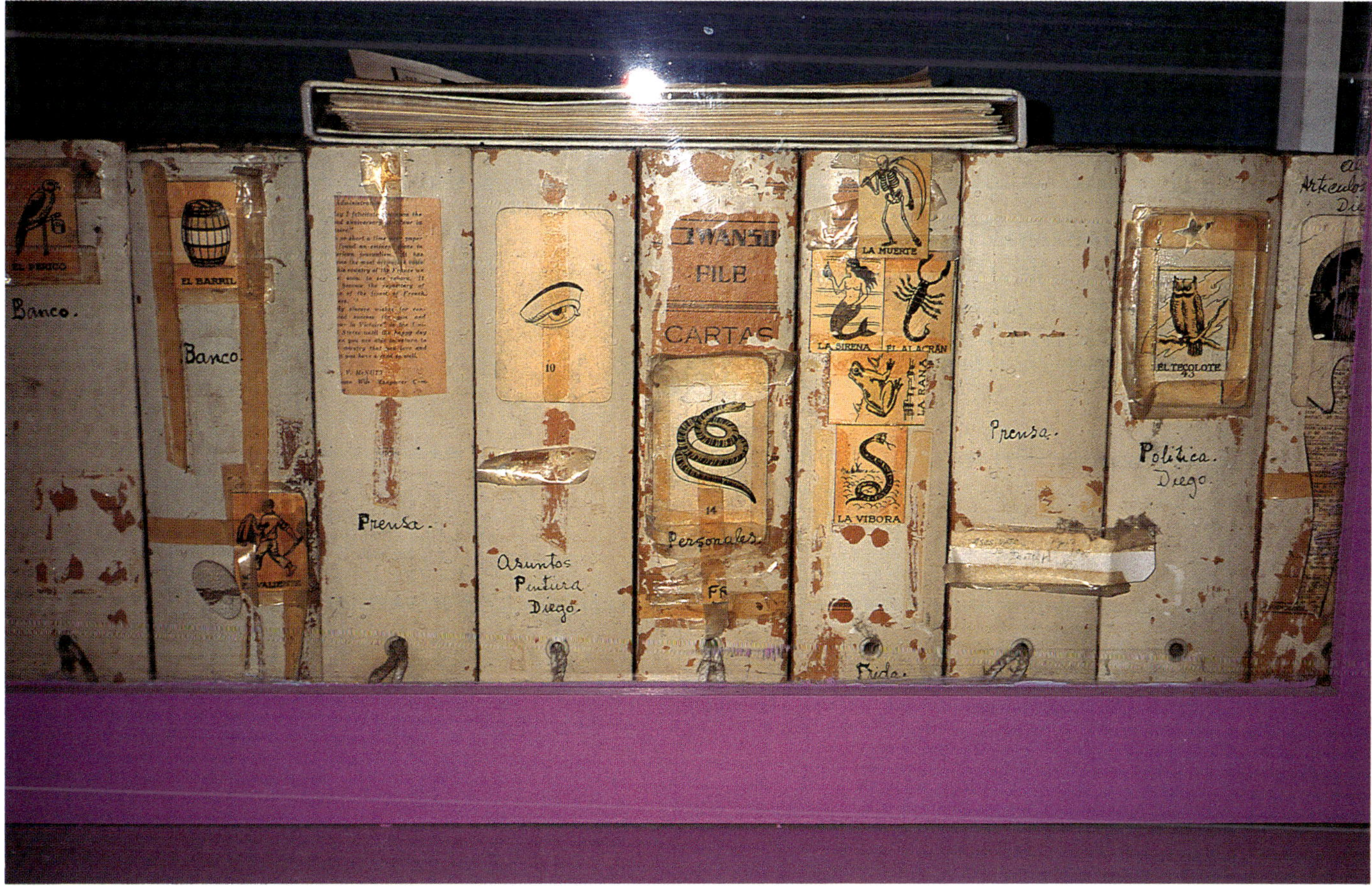
Banco.
EL BARRIL
Banco
Prensa.
Asuntos
Pintura
Diego.
FILE
CARTAS
Personales.
LA MUERTE
LA SIRENA
EL ALACRAN
LA VIBORA
Prensa.
EL TECOLOTE
Politica.
Diego.

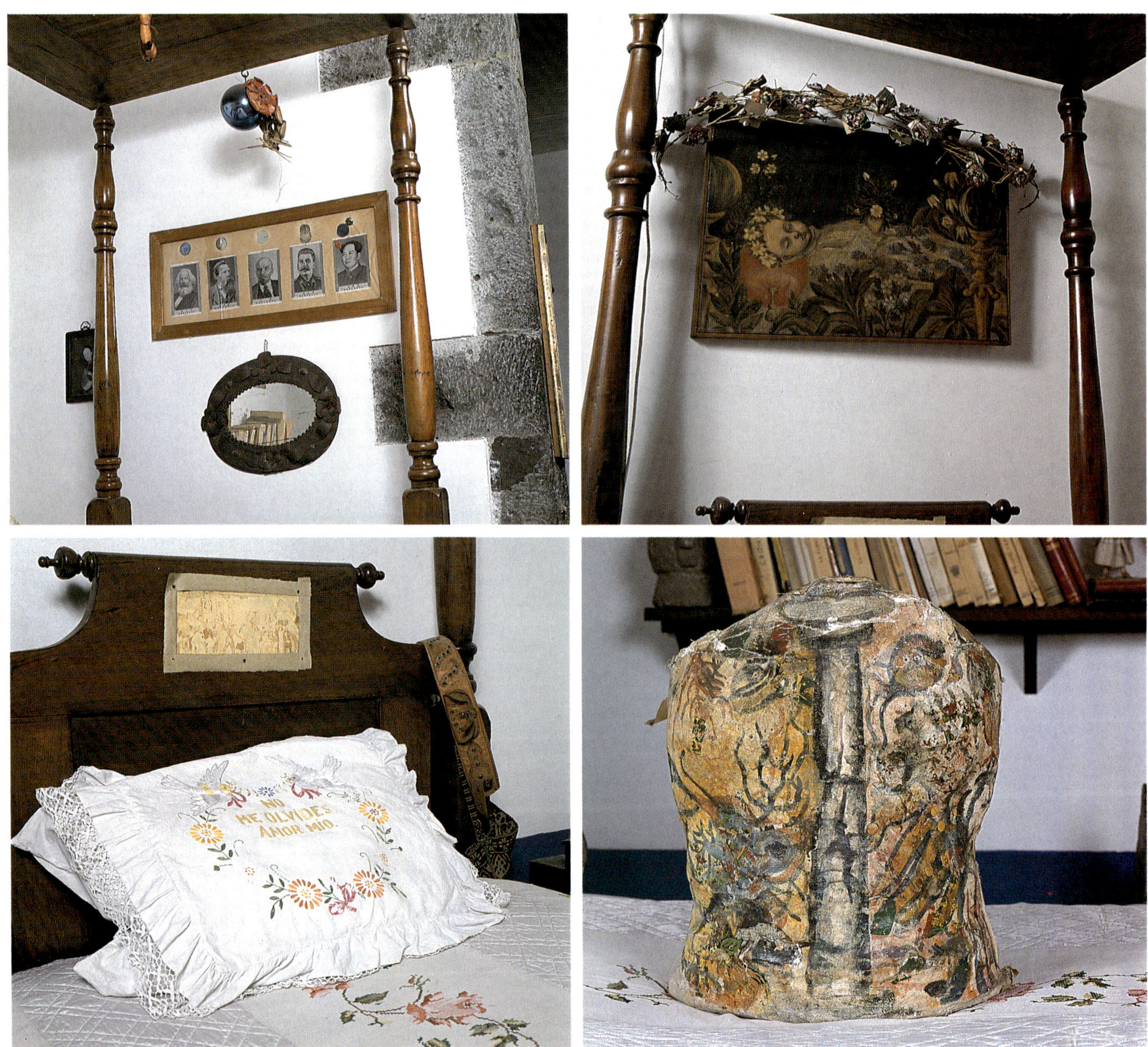
NO
ME OLVIDES
AMOR MIO

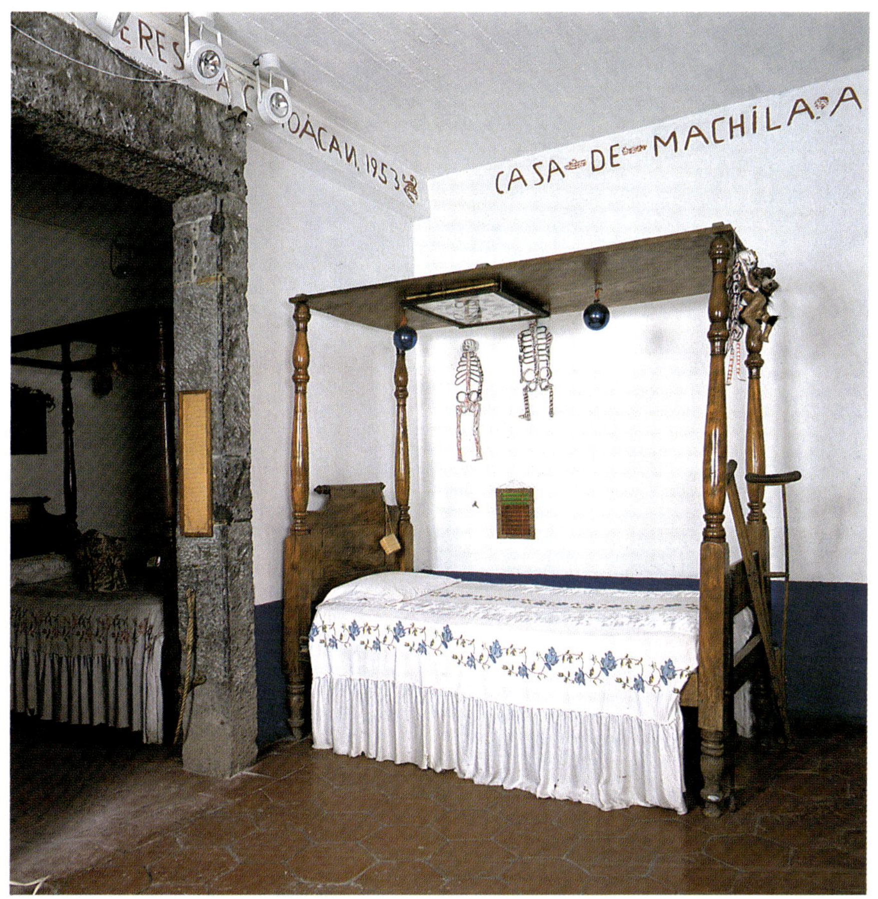
CASA DE MACHILA A
1953

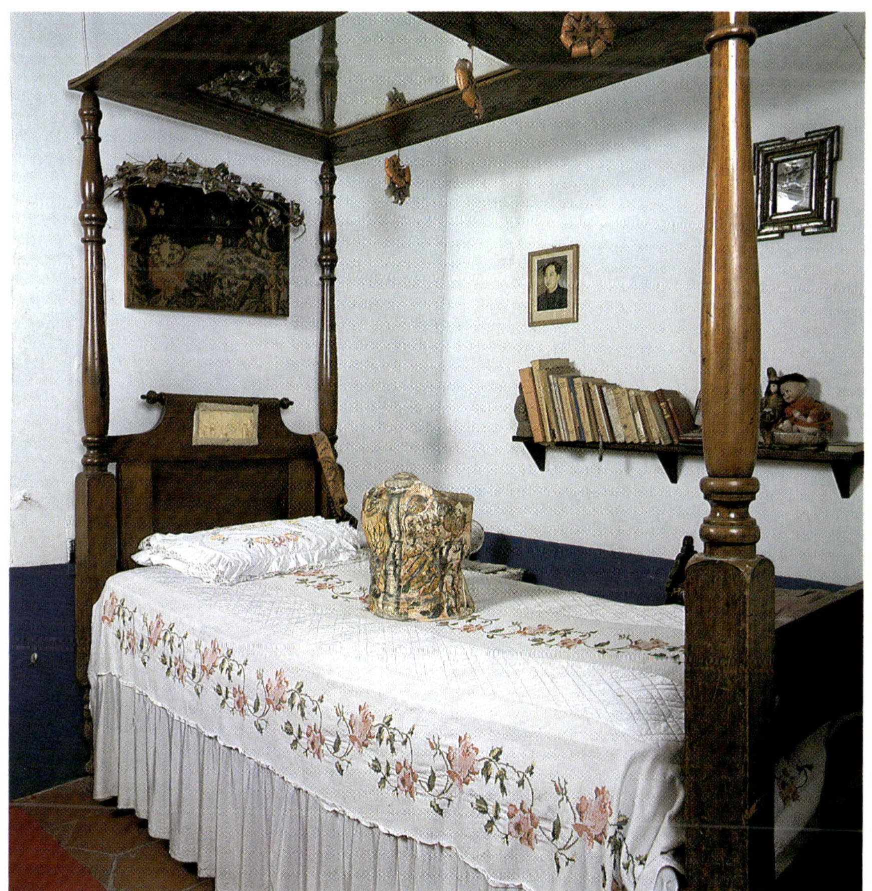

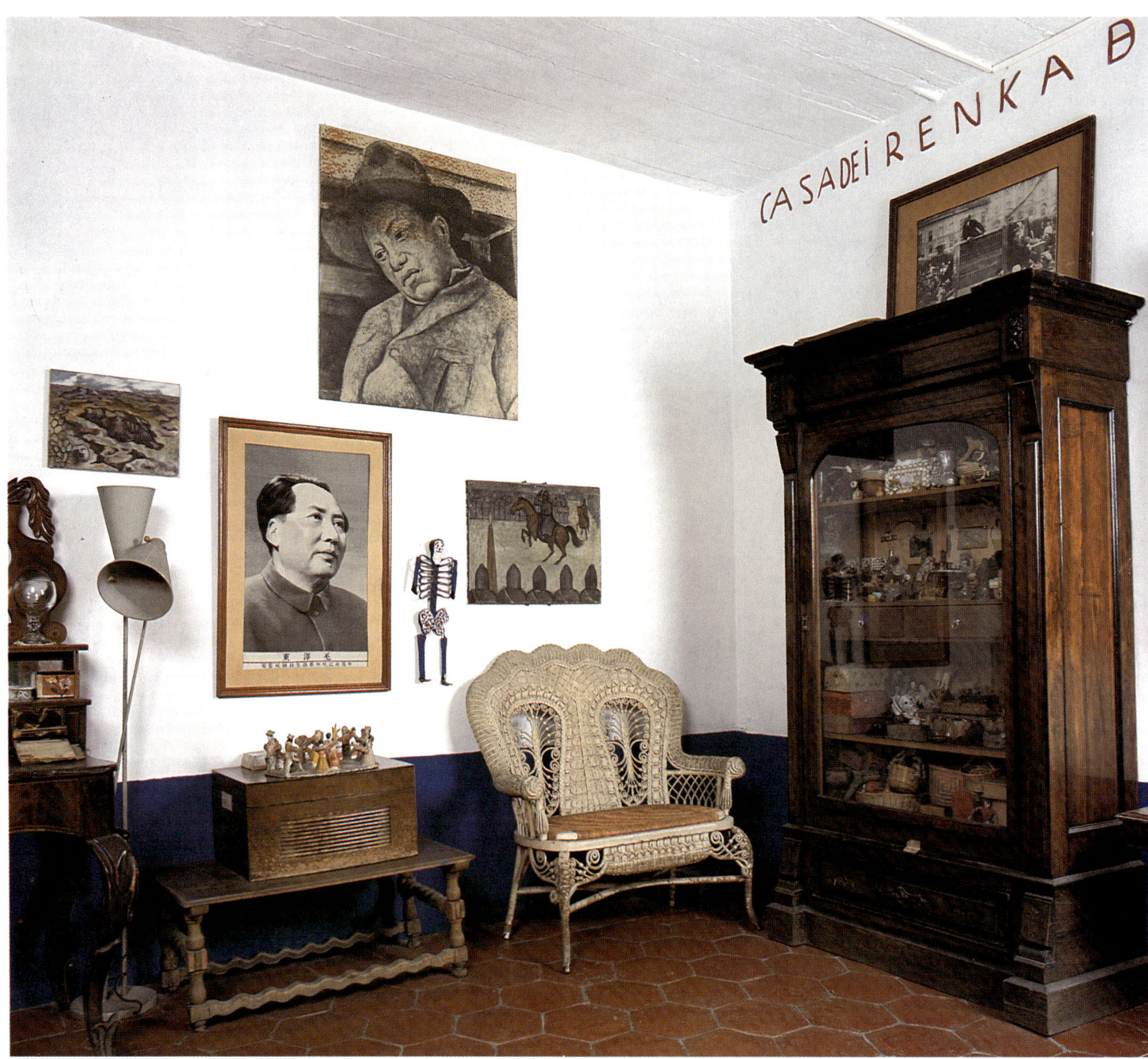
CASADEI RENKA

ERIKA BILLETER

FRITZ HENLE PHOTOGRAPHS FRIDA KAHLO AND DIEGO RIVERA

In remembrance of Fritz Henle, who died during the preparations for this exhibition.

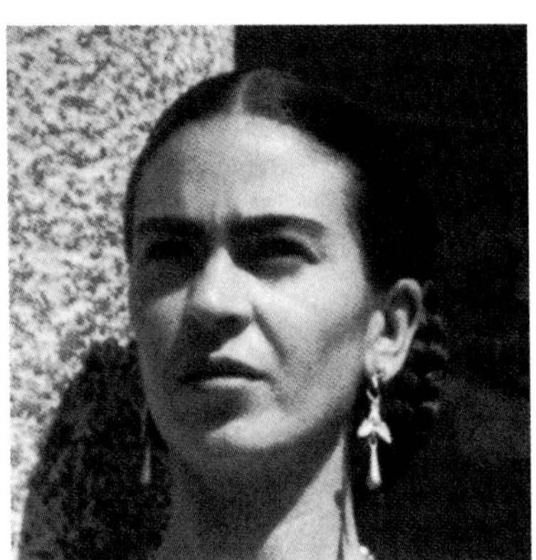

Fritz Henle, who was born in 1909 in Dortmund, Germany, and who died in 1993 in a hospital in Puerto Rico, belonged to a great generation of photography. His contemporaries were Cartier-Bresson, Werner Bischof, Gisèle Freund, Margaret Bourke-White, Robert Capa, and Bill Brandt. Like them, he photographed situations as quickly as lightning, but was always aware of the scope of the reality he was fixing in his pictures. "I do not want to prove anything, I do not want to demonstrate anything. Things and beings speak enough." That credo by Cartier-Bresson applies to the entire generation.

In 1936 Henle emigrated to America, where he began a brilliant career as photographer for the most important American magazines. *Life, Harper's Bazaar,* and *Vogue* were his clients. But meanwhile he continued his personal work. Today tens of thousands of his negatives are in the collection of the University of Texas in Austin. A lot of these Henle never developed. Some of his photos of Frida and Diego, which he took during trips to Mexico in 1936 and 1943/44, are being published here for the first time. In the forties Henle published a volume about Mexico which is forgotten today. The photographs in this book are primarily landscapes and pictures of *campesinos* – the picturesque subjects that inspire all photographers who come to Mexico. In this he followed his great predecessor, Hugo Brehme, who came to Mexico about the time Henle was born and never left again. Brehme's book *Malerisches Mexico,* published in Berlin in 1923 by the Wachsmuth Verlag, is considered one of the first photo volumes about a country: To judge by photographic portraits of him, Henle must have been a good-looking young man. I first became acquainted with him in 1992, when he was eighty-three years old, and he was still a charming man, obsessed by his only passion, photography. I can imagine that he charmed Frida, and that it was easy for him to convince her to let him take photos of her. Frida liked being photographed. For her, posing was almost a natural way of behaving. The most famous photographers of her time portrayed her. Henle achieved more. He accompanied her on walks in Coyoacán. He went with her to the floating gardens of Xochimilco, which Frida liked to visit on Sundays when the boats on the channels were full of flowers and life. She also let him direct his camera at her, while she examined the goods in the market of Toluca, where she liked to buy ribbons for her hair from the Indian women.

Frida must have known the market of Toluca quite well. We recall that she mentioned it in a letter to Nickolas Muray after her return from Paris, saying he would have preferred to "sell in the market of Toluca than have anything to do with the rotten artists of Paris." Henle photographed Frida in the garden of the Blue House with her favorite monkey Fulang-Chang, which she so often included in her self-portraits, on her arm. And he made the unique photograph of her in her studio, in which she sits pensively before her easel. In the background one can see the painting *The Two Fridas* of 1939, which she always kept hanging in her studio until pecuniary problems caused her to sell it to the Museo de Arte Moderno in Mexico City. There it hangs today well-protected against any sale. Her other pictures in private collections have, for the most part, made a long migration through various private collections in Mexico and the United States.

Until the end of his days Henle valued his memories of the atmosphere in the Blue House. "One got an impression of compressed creativity. It was she who dominated the house." Frida had come to trust him, so he managed to make completely natural photographs of her. Apart from Henle, only Frida's best friend, the photographer Lola Alvarez Bravo, was able to do that. But even in these pictures Frida remains strangely still. No smile moves her face. "She was strikingly beautiful," said Henle, "and there was no bitterness in her." Henle succeeded in making what is surely the most beautiful picture ever made of Diego Rivera, Frida's "Froggy," as she lovingly called him. Henle photographed him in the garden of the Blue House, resting in the midst of luxuriant plants. There also exist a few portraits that Rivera agreed to "pose" for.

The photographs taken in Frida's studio show the host of

pre-Columbian idols and objects of folk art that she collected and which she needed not only for her mental stimulation but also perhaps for the daily establishment of *Mexicanidad*. Even a life-size Judas figure made of papier-mâché leans against the wall. Both Frida and Diego loved the Judas figures. And in these creations of anonymous folk artists they saw creativity personified. Frida's Blue House and Diego's studio in San Angel were crowded with Judas figures. They were the real other occupants.

But in all the photographs by Henle one thing becomes clear, and it is something that all her contemporaries have always emphasized about Frida: her love for traditional Mexican dress that lent her something special and went very well with her *mestiza* beauty. The photographs of 1939 are practically studies of how one can wear a *rebozo* with elegance. As if, symbolically speaking, nothing but the traditional Tehuana dress belonged to that expressive head, she presents herself in complete harmony within and without and reflects what Rivera also said about her art: that she painted within and without at the same time. She painted the inside and outside of herself and of the world at the same time.

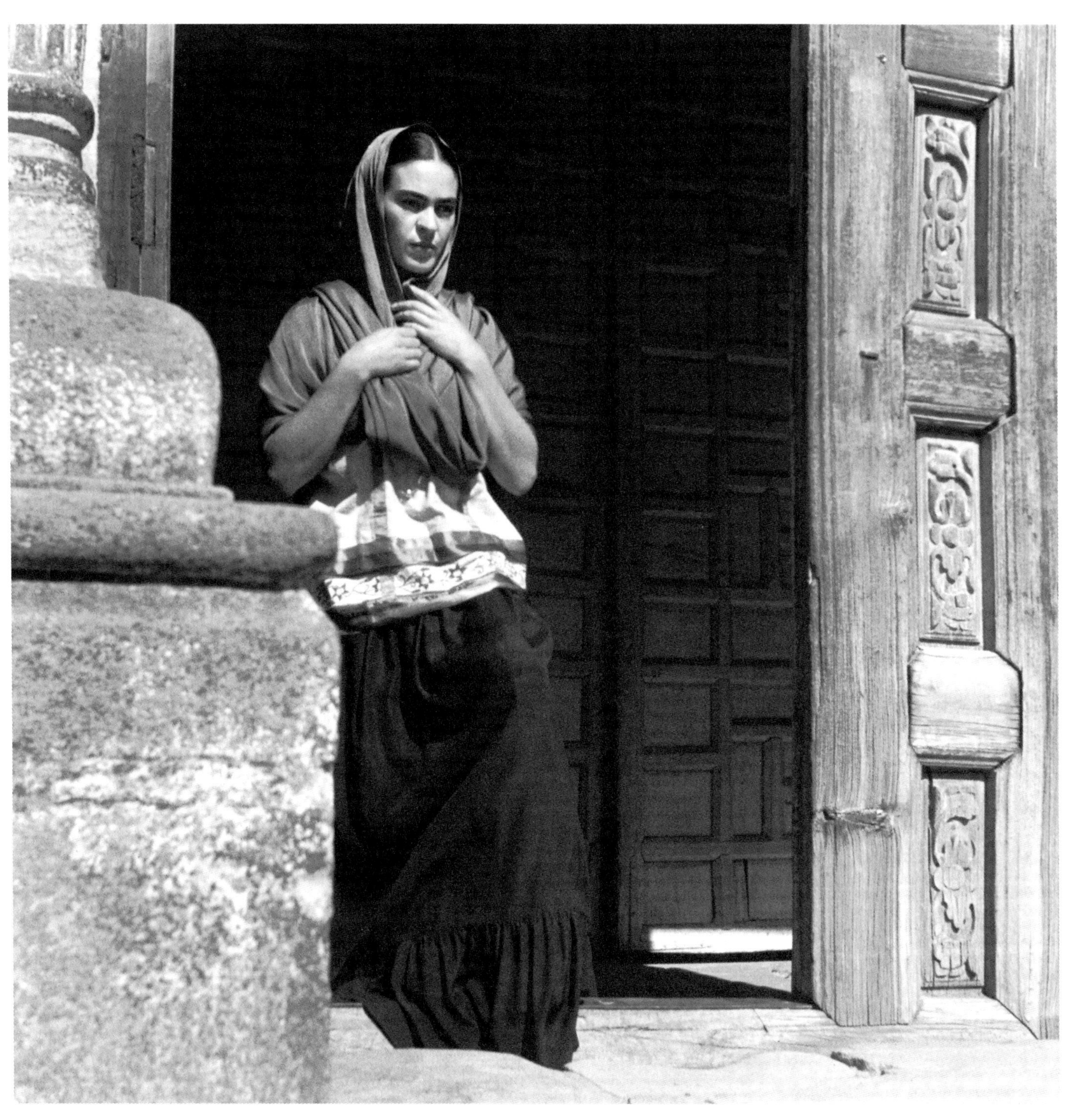

FRITZ HENLE, FRIDA KAHLO AT THE CHURCH OF COYOACÁN, 1936

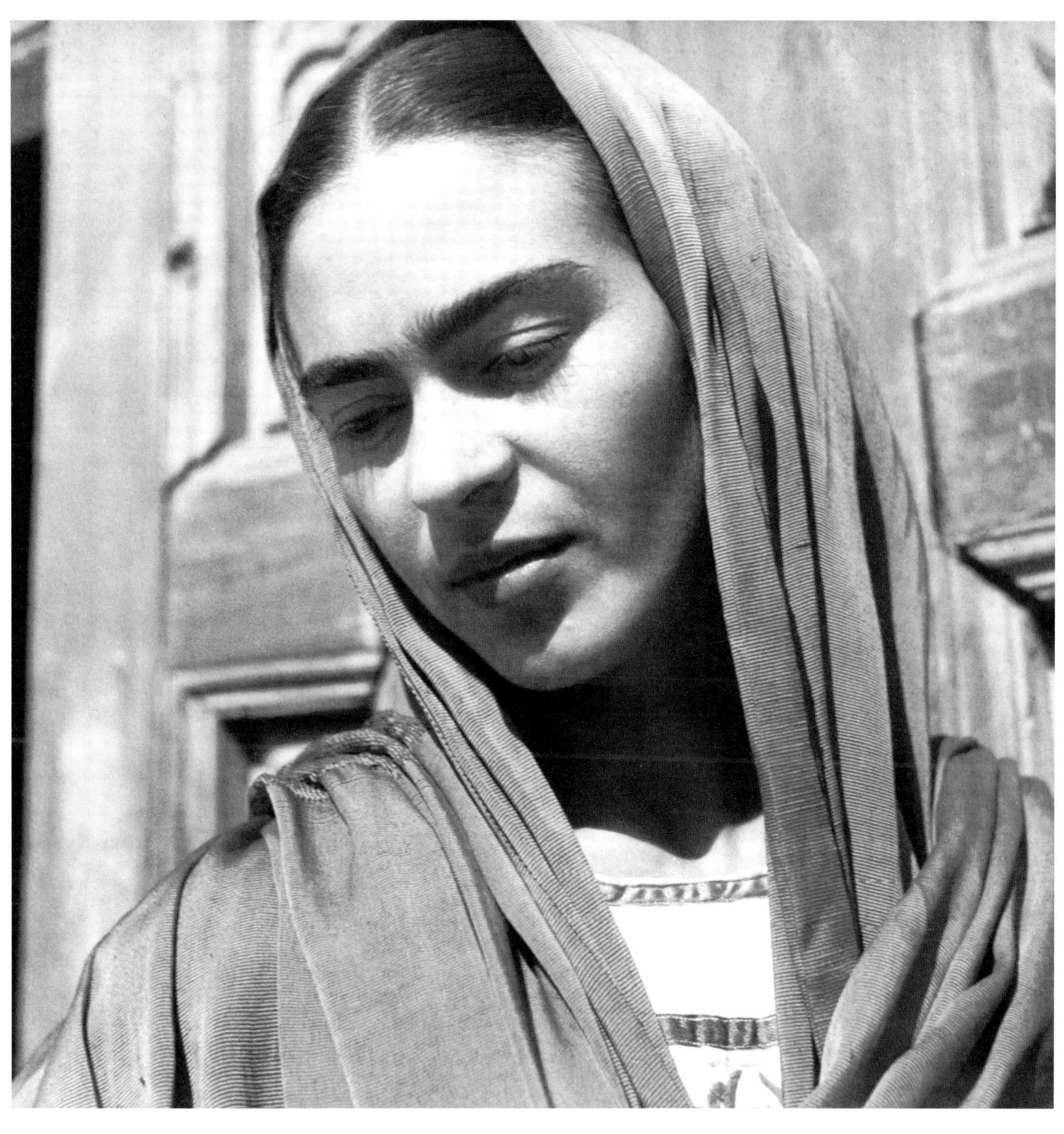

FRITZ HENLE, FRIDA KAHLO WEARING A REBOZO, 1936

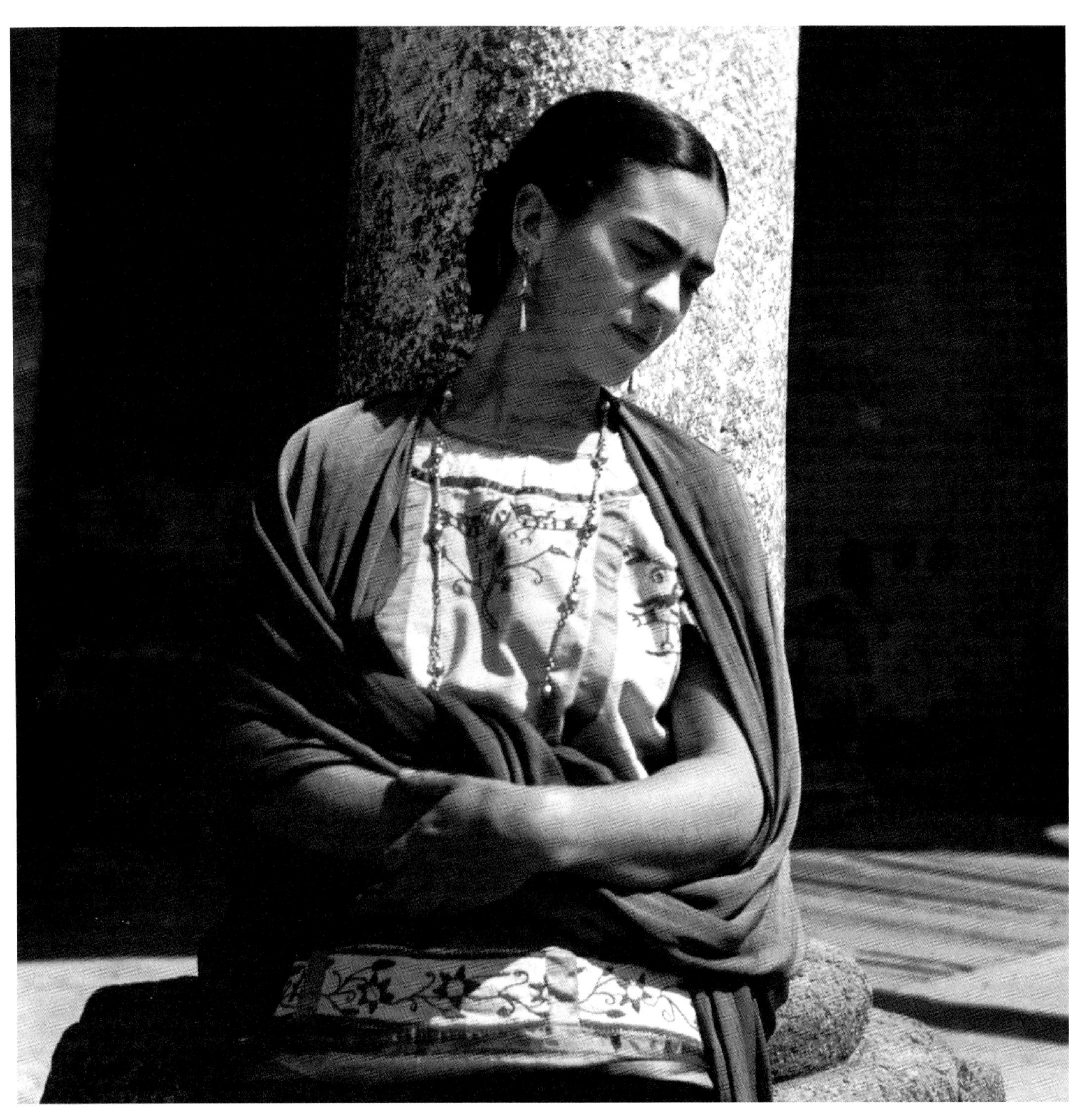

FRITZ HENLE, FRIDA KAHLO IN COYOACÁN, 1936

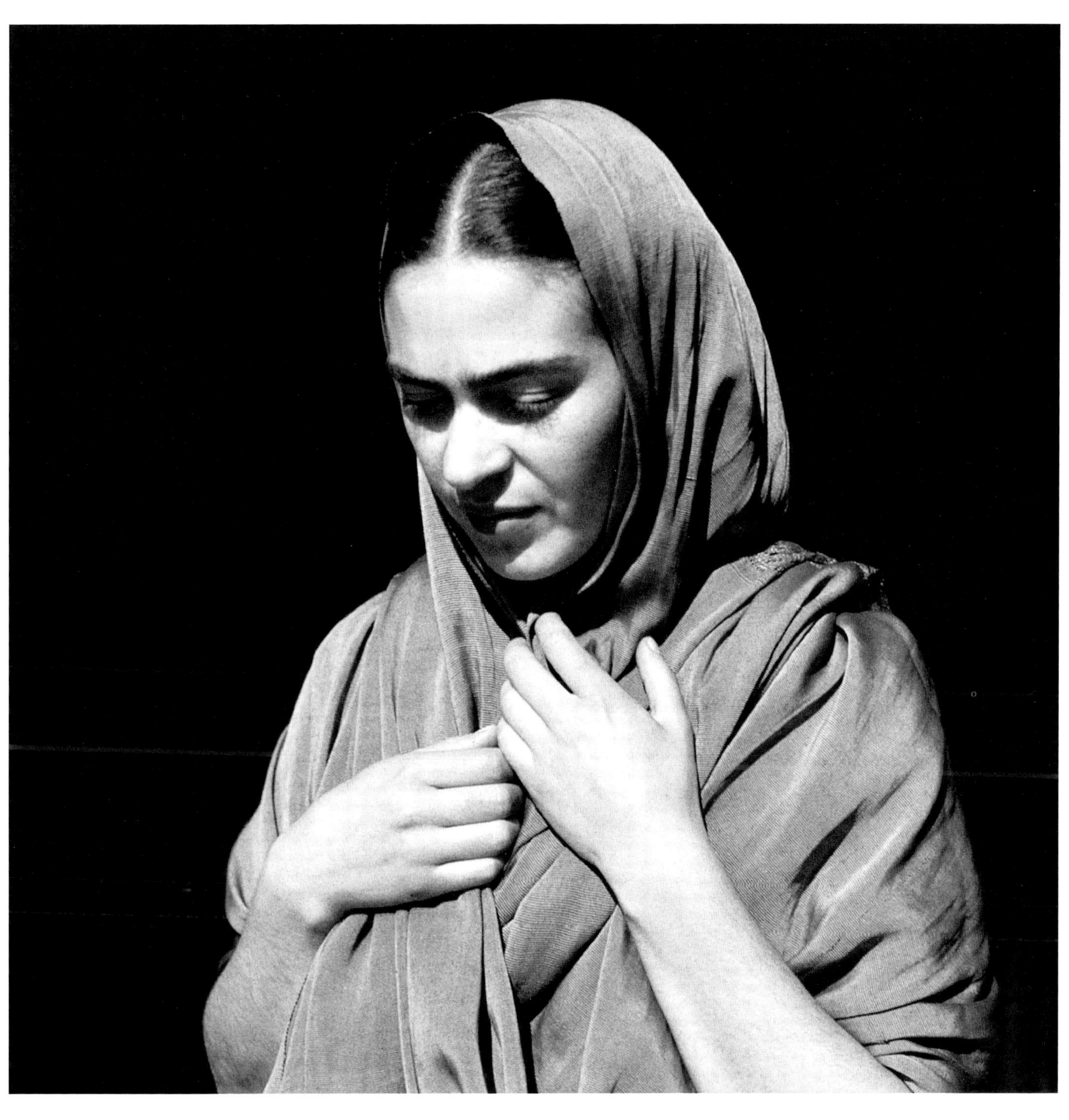

FRITZ HENLE, FRIDA KAHLO IN COYOACÁN, 1936

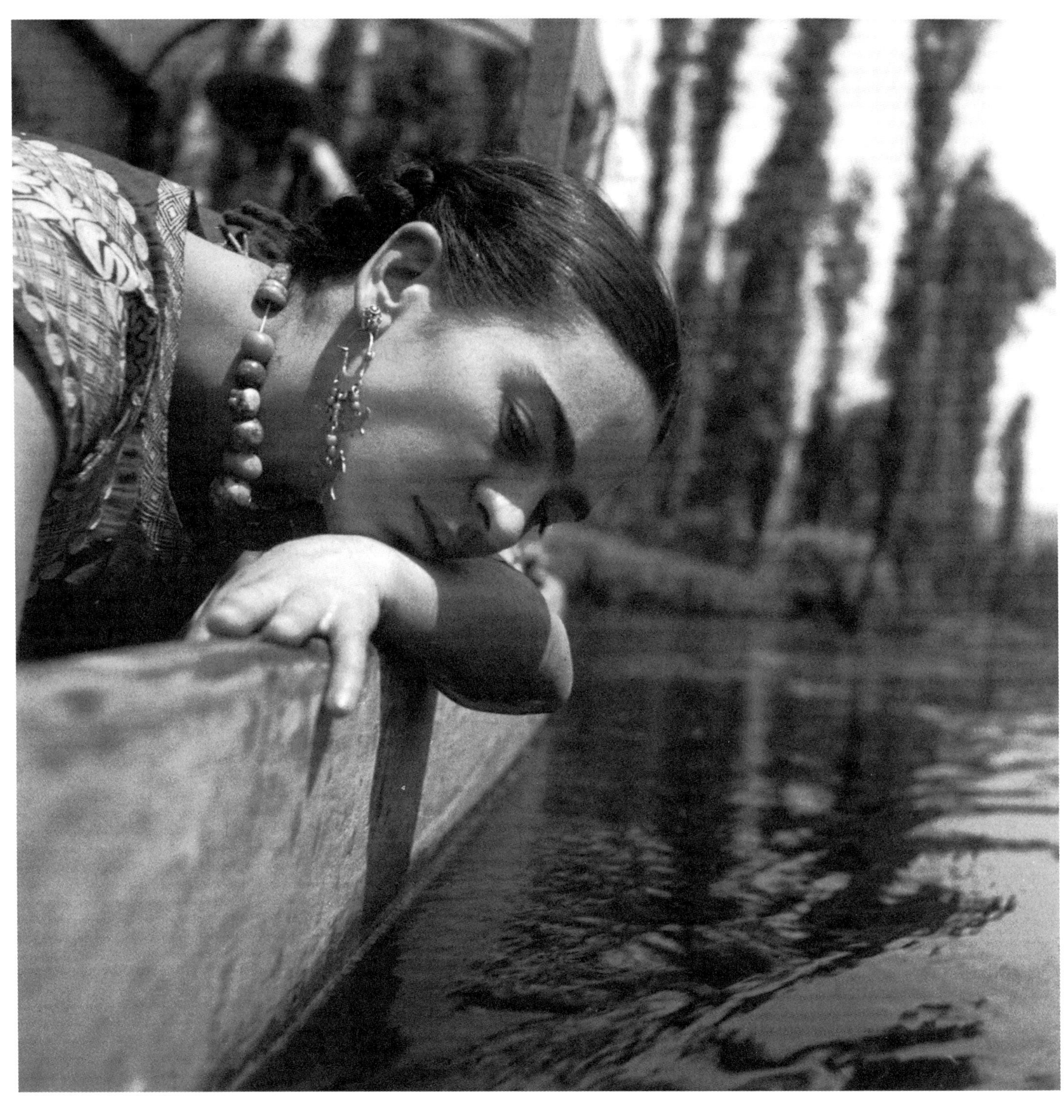

FRITZ HENLE, FRIDA KAHLO IN XOCHIMILCO, 1936

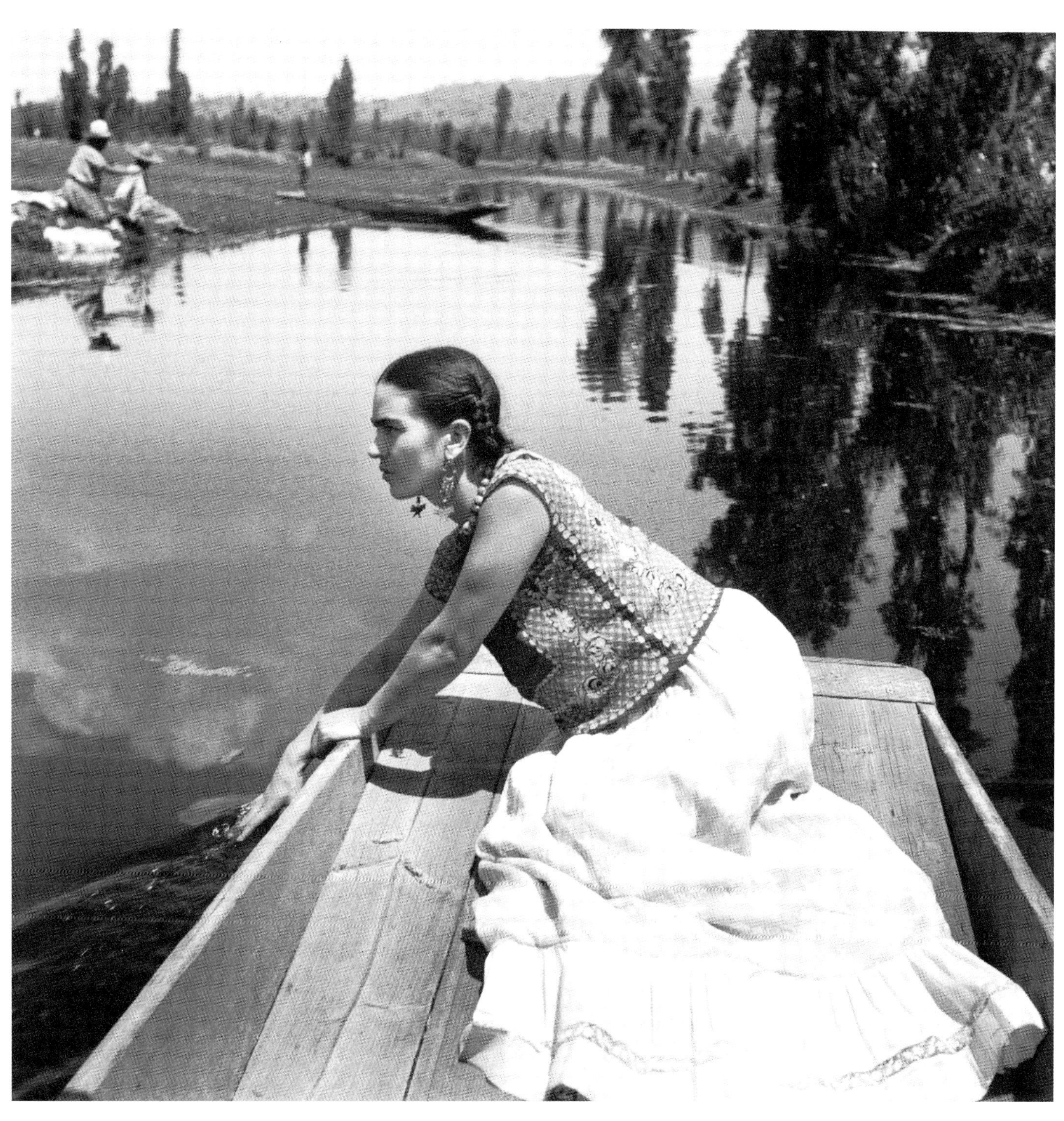

FRITZ HENLE, FRIDA KAHLO ON A BOAT RIDE IN XOCHIMILCO, 1936

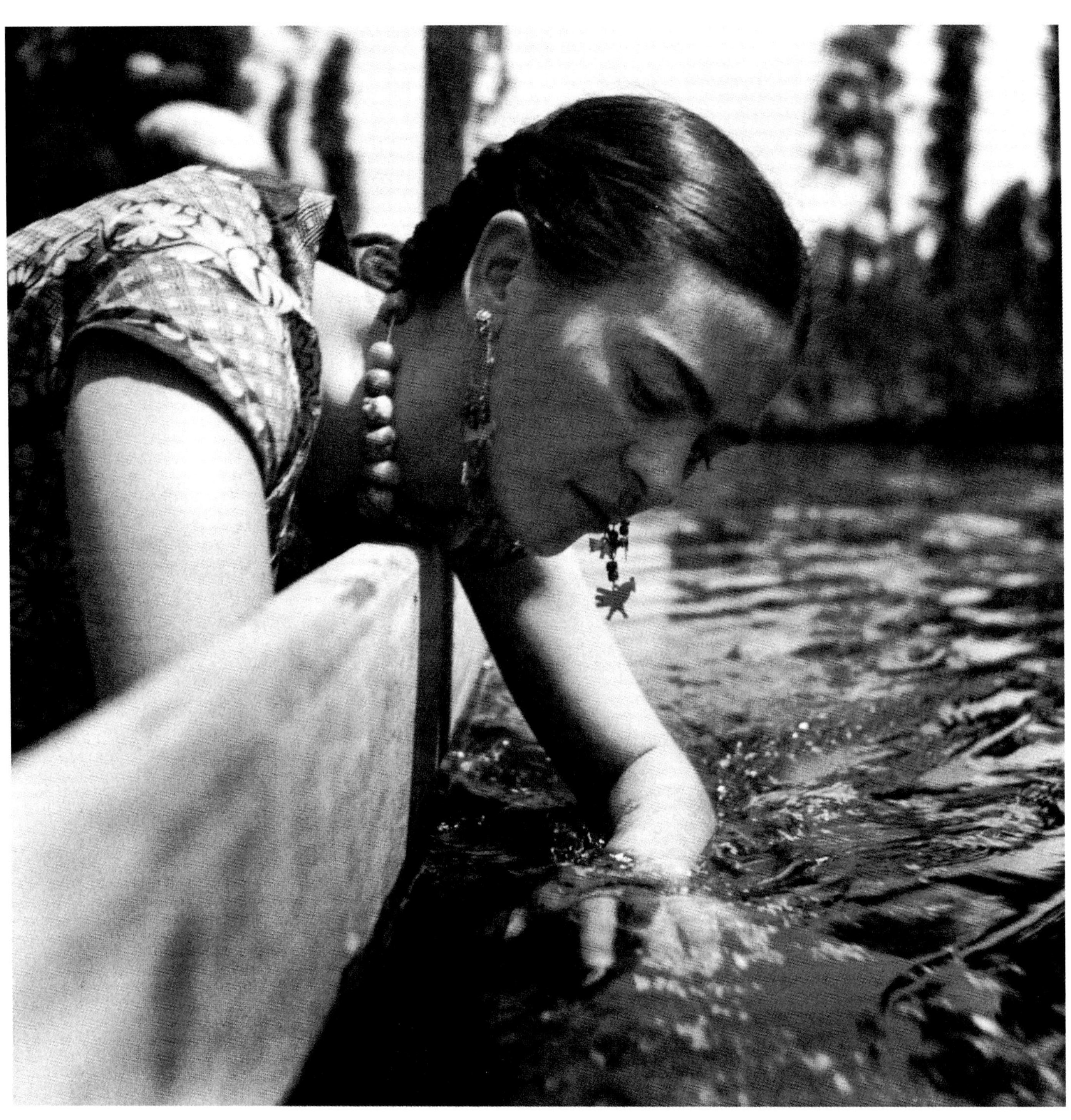

FRITZ HENLE, FRIDA KAHLO IN XOCHIMILCO, 1936

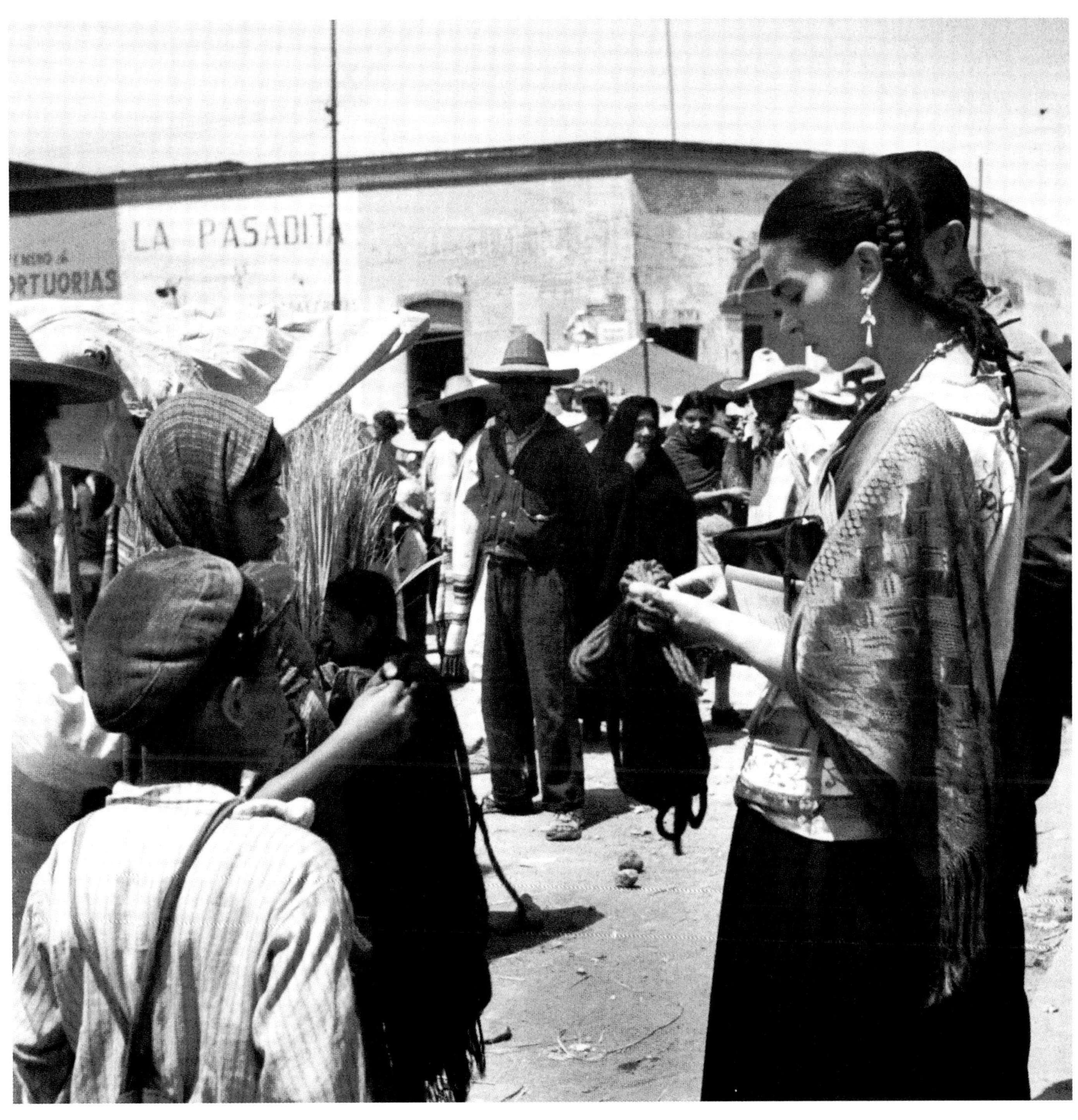

FRITZ HENLE, FRIDA KAHLO AT THE TOLUCA MARKET, 1943

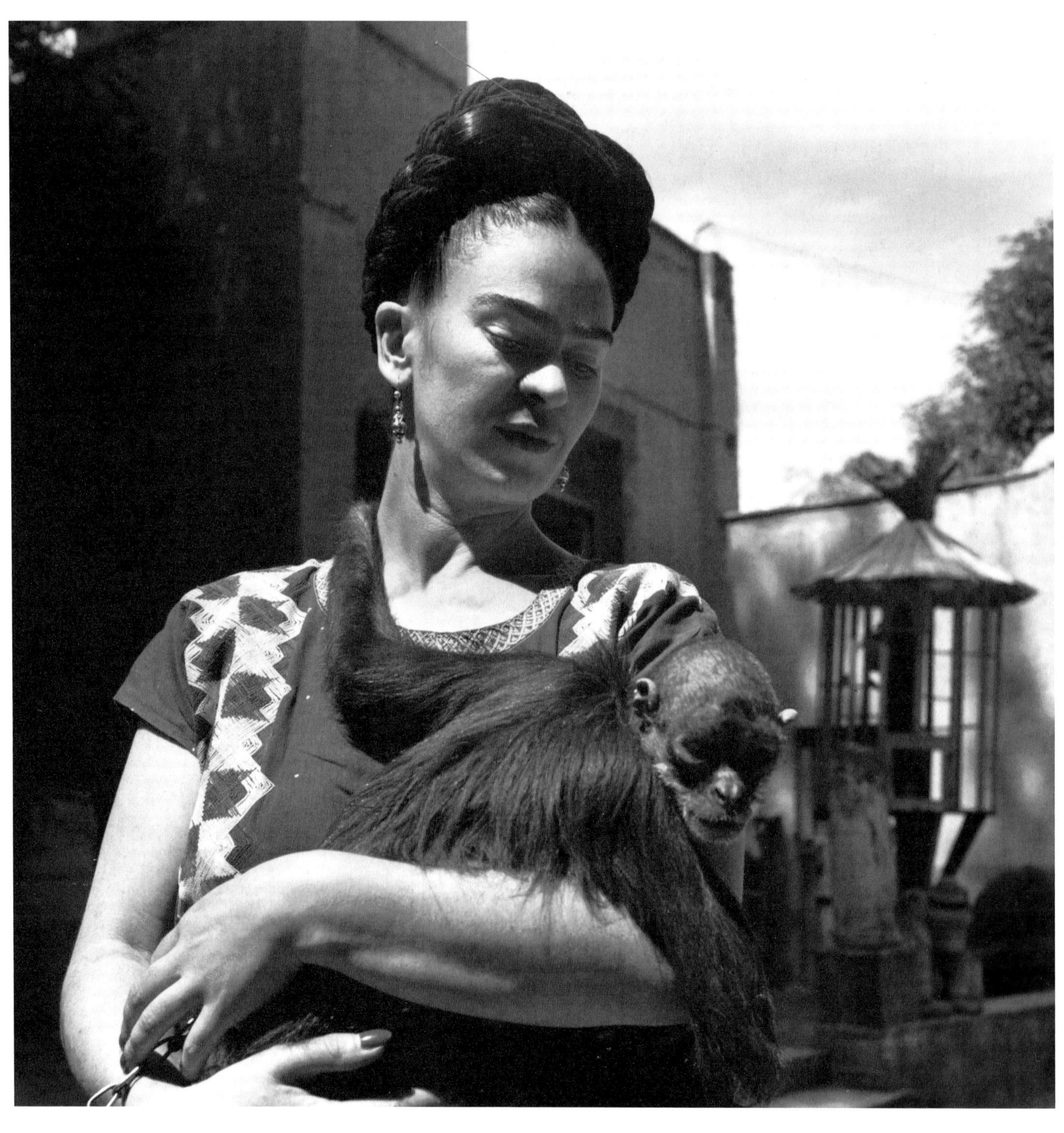

FRITZ HENLE, FRIDA KAHLO WITH HER PET MONKEY FULANG-CHANG
IN THE GARDEN OF THE BLUE HOUSE, 1943

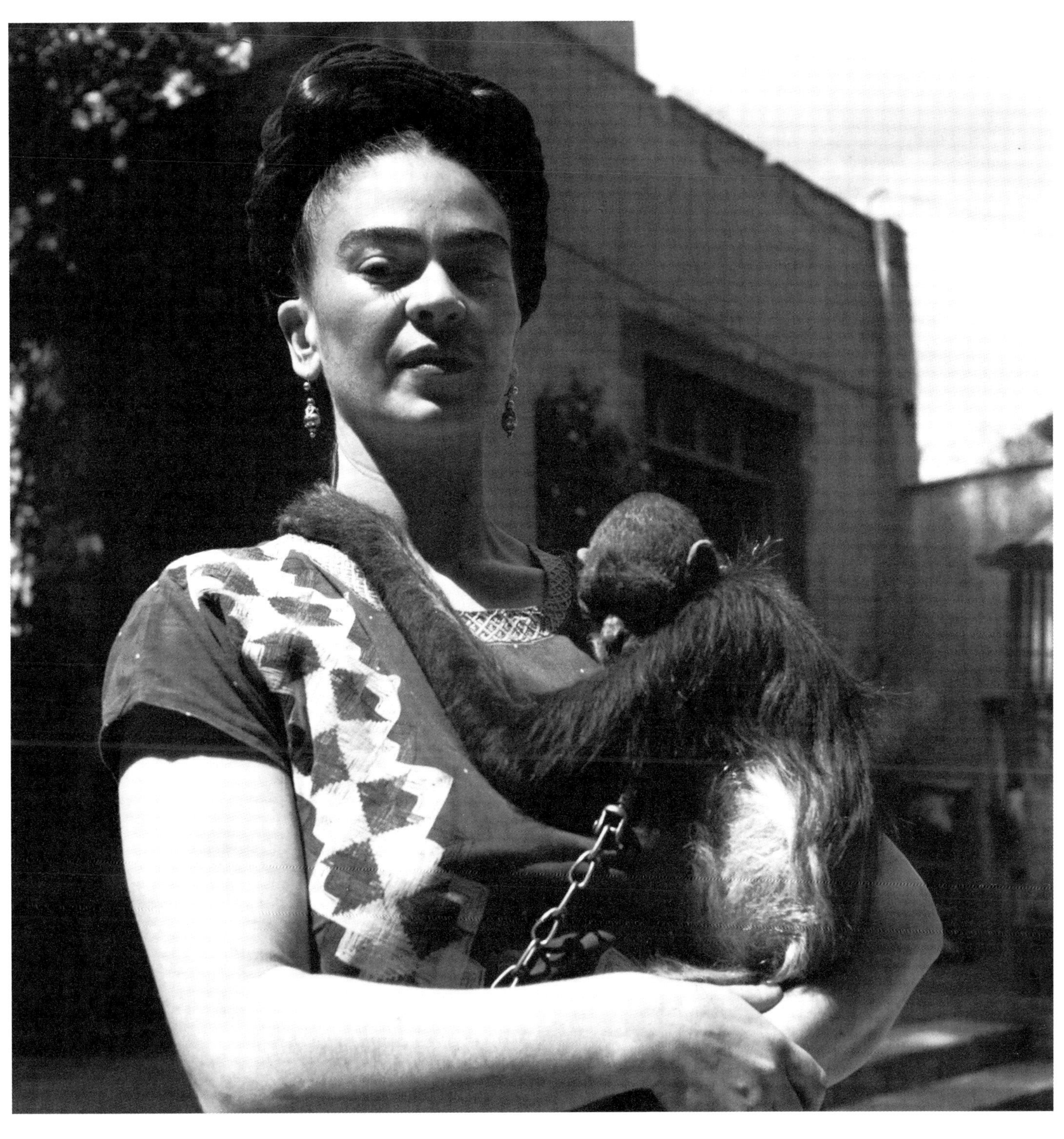

FRITZ HENLE, FRIDA KAHLO WITH HER PET MONKEY FULANG-CHANG
IN THE GARDEN OF THE BLUE HOUSE, 1943

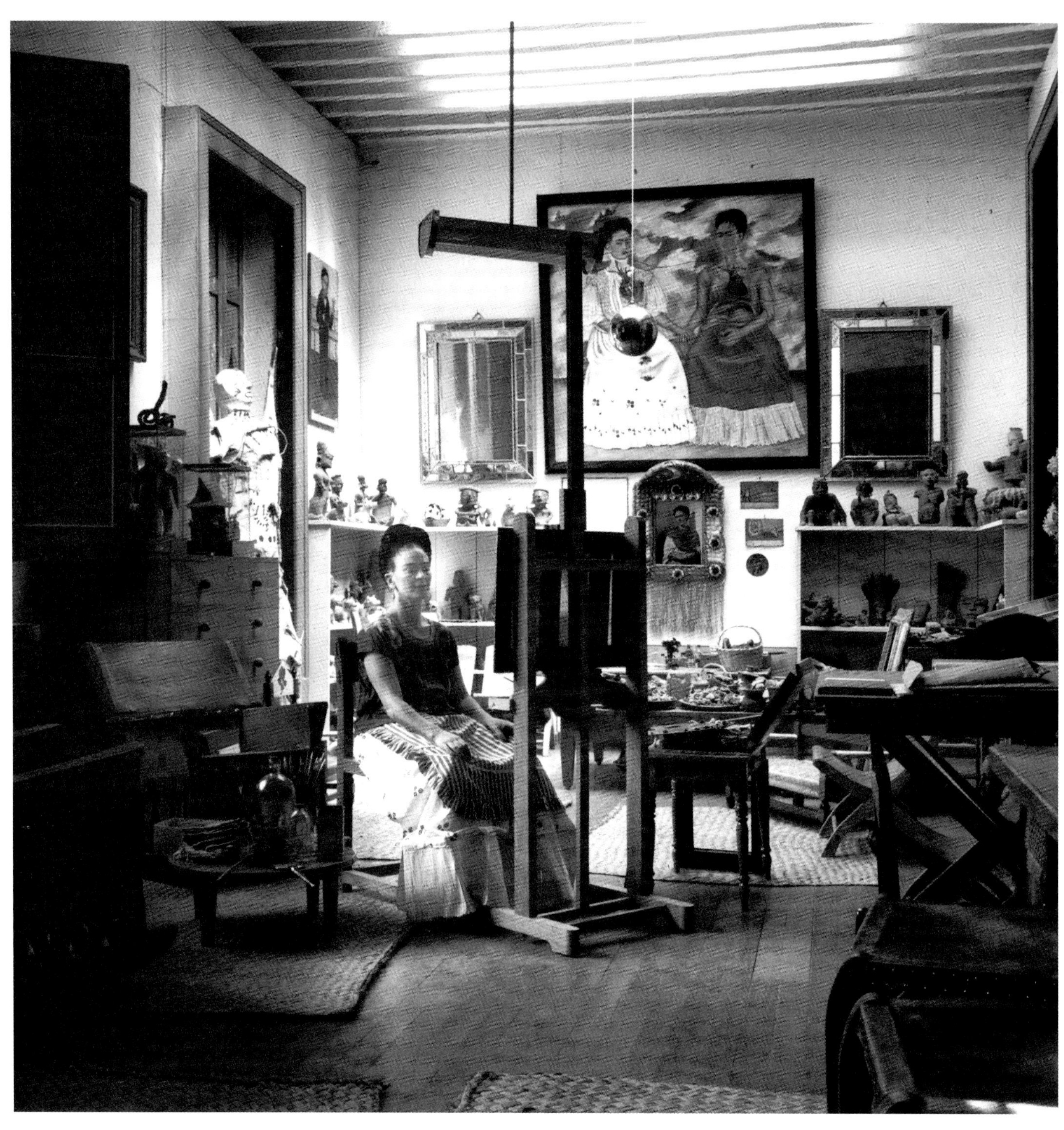

FRITZ HENLE, FRIDA KAHLO IN HER STUDIO IN THE BLUE HOUSE, 1943

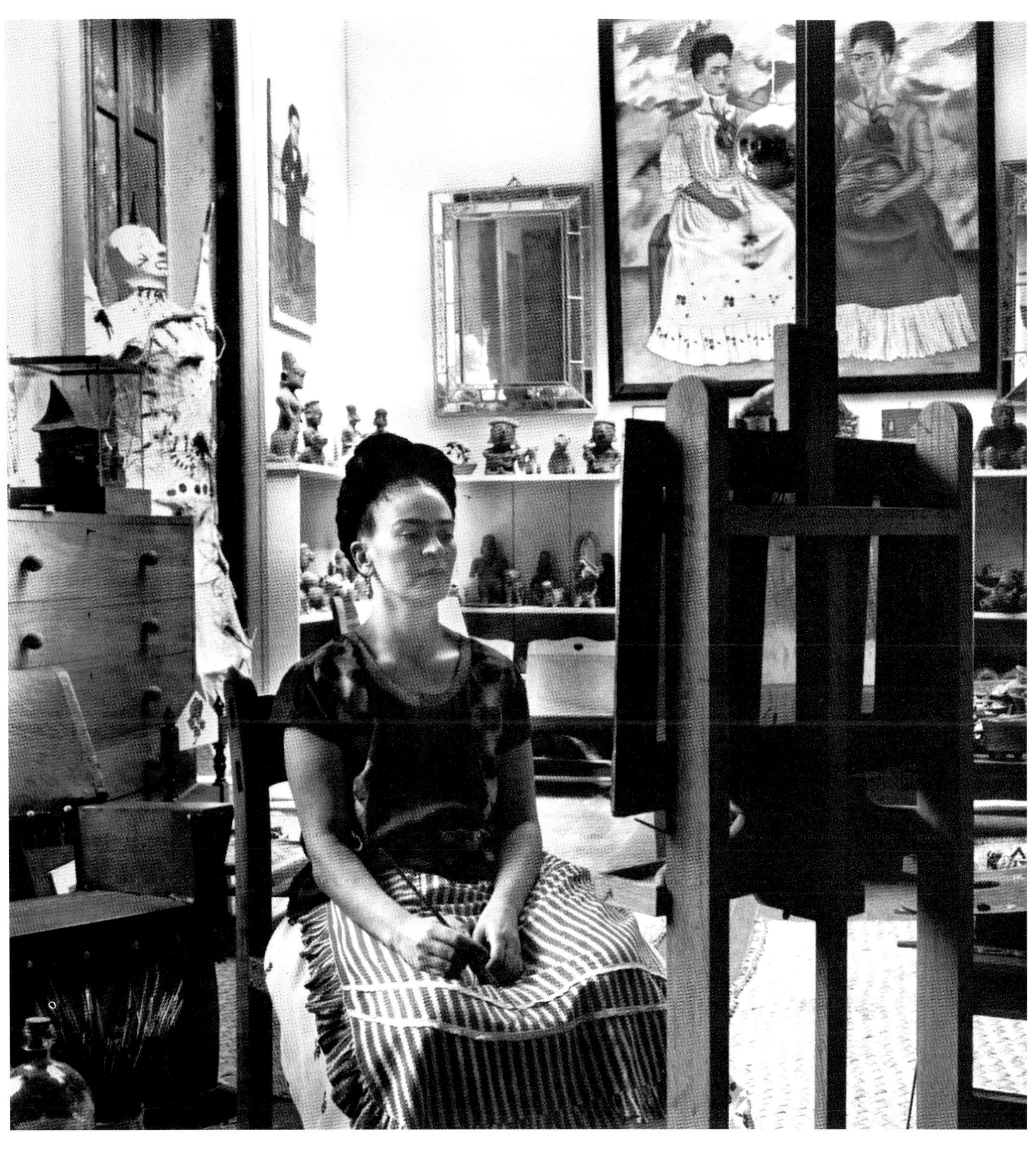

FRITZ HENLE, FRIDA KAHLO IN HER STUDIO IN THE BLUE HOUSE, 1943

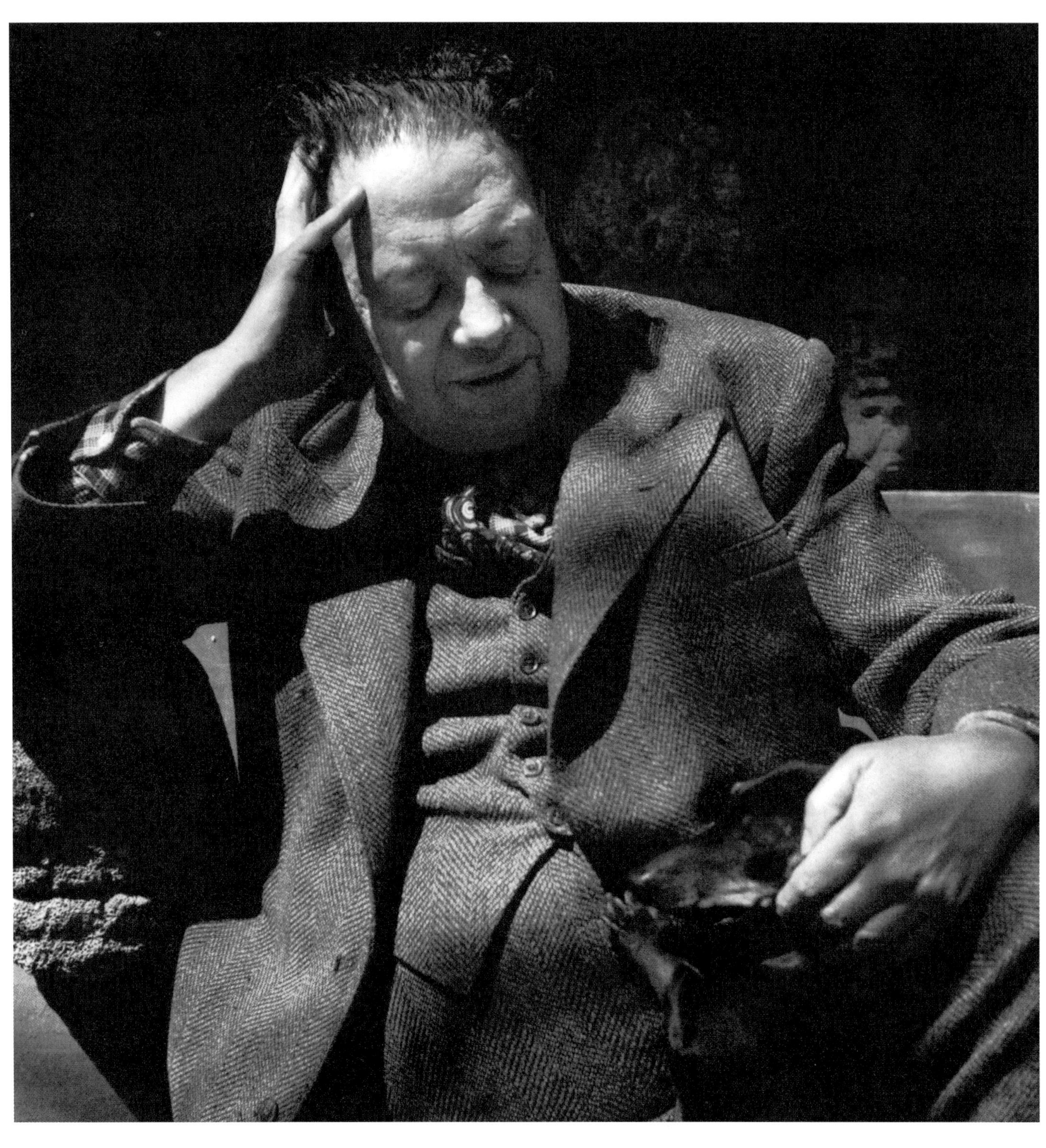

FRITZ HENLE, DIEGO RIVERA WITH ONE OF HIS DOGS IN THE BLUE HOUSE, 1943

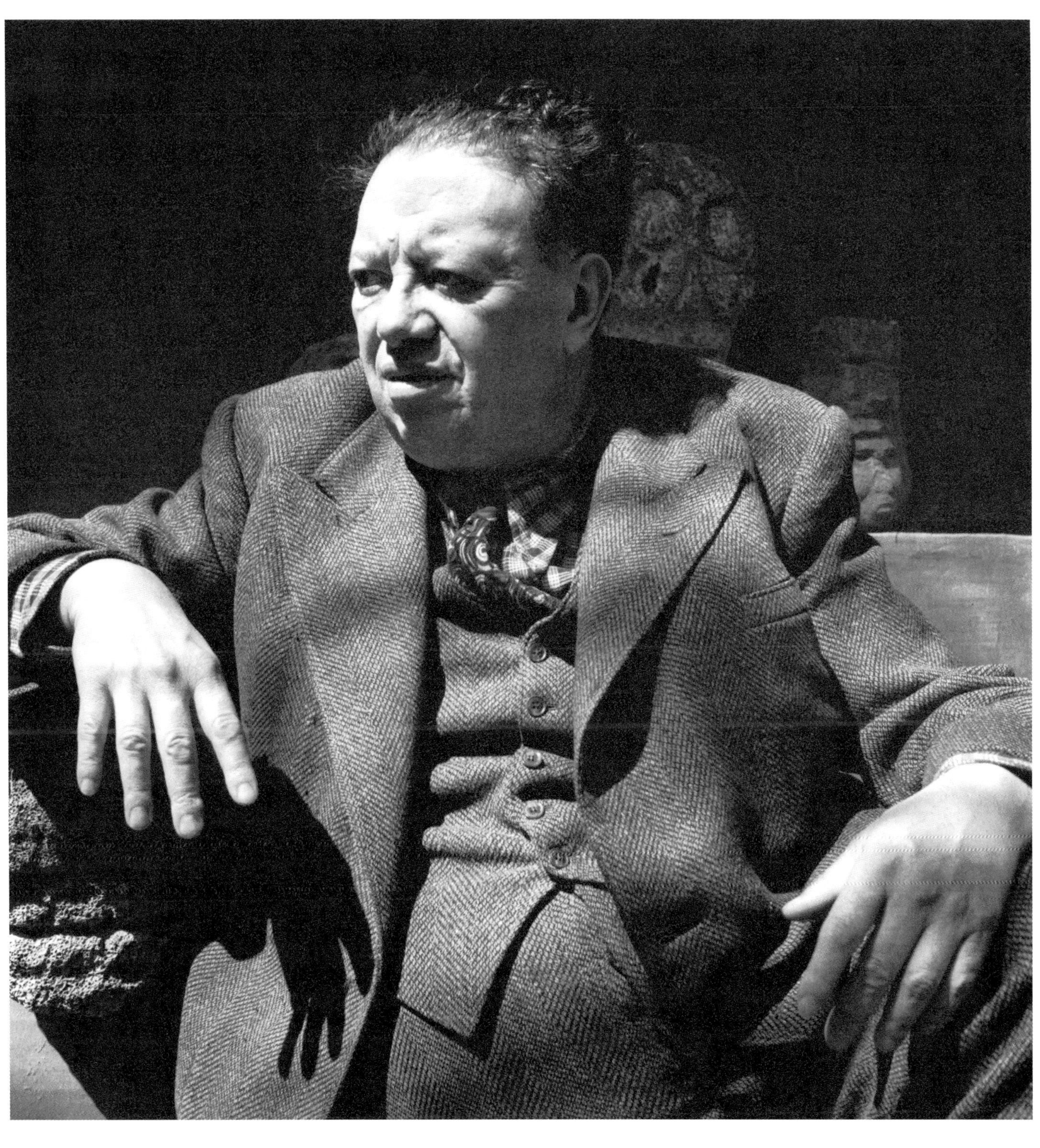

FRITZ HENLE, DIEGO RIVERA IN THE BLUE HOUSE, 1943

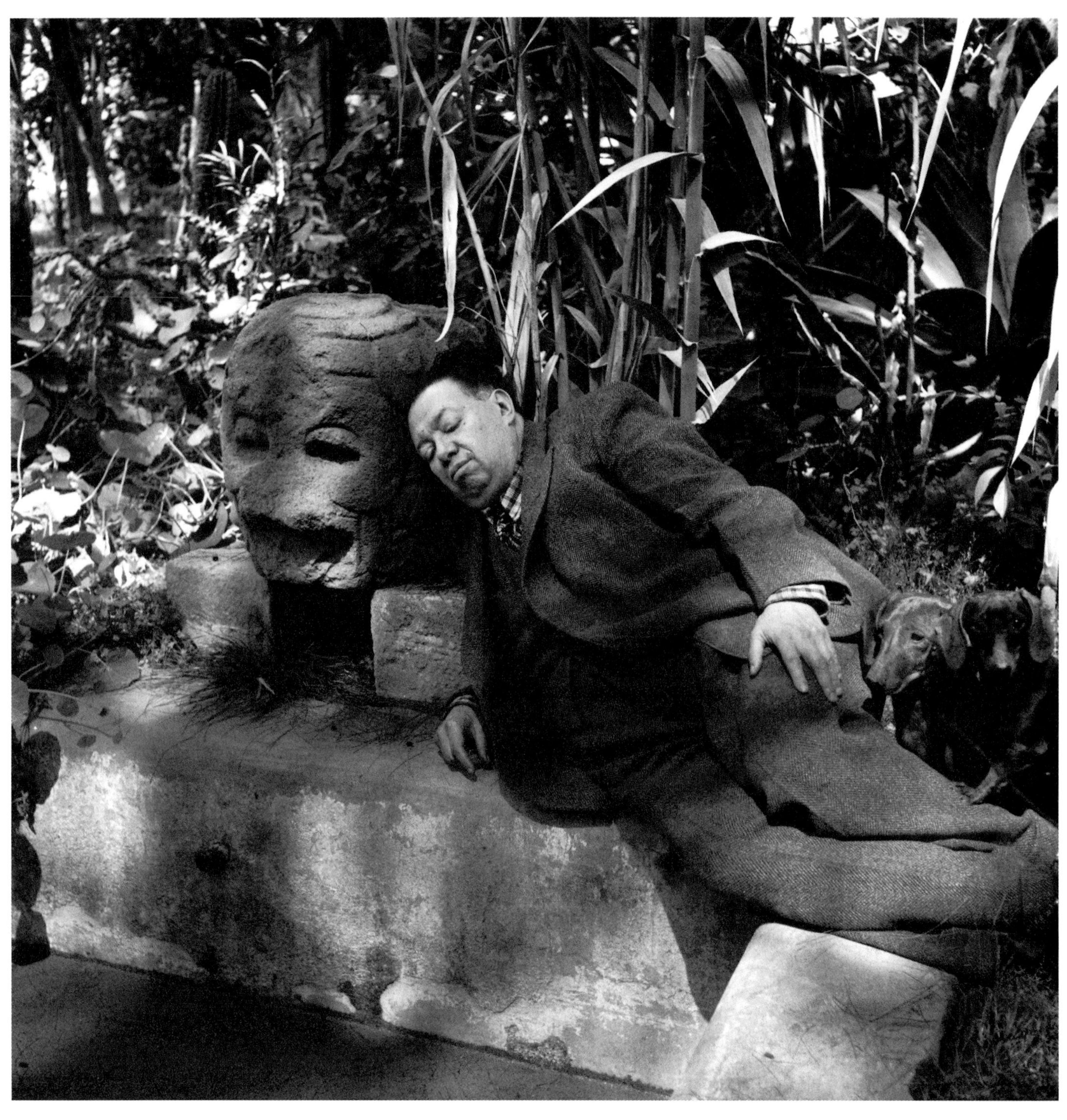

FRITZ HENLE, DIEGO RIVERA SLEEPING IN THE GARDEN OF THE BLUE HOUSE, 1943

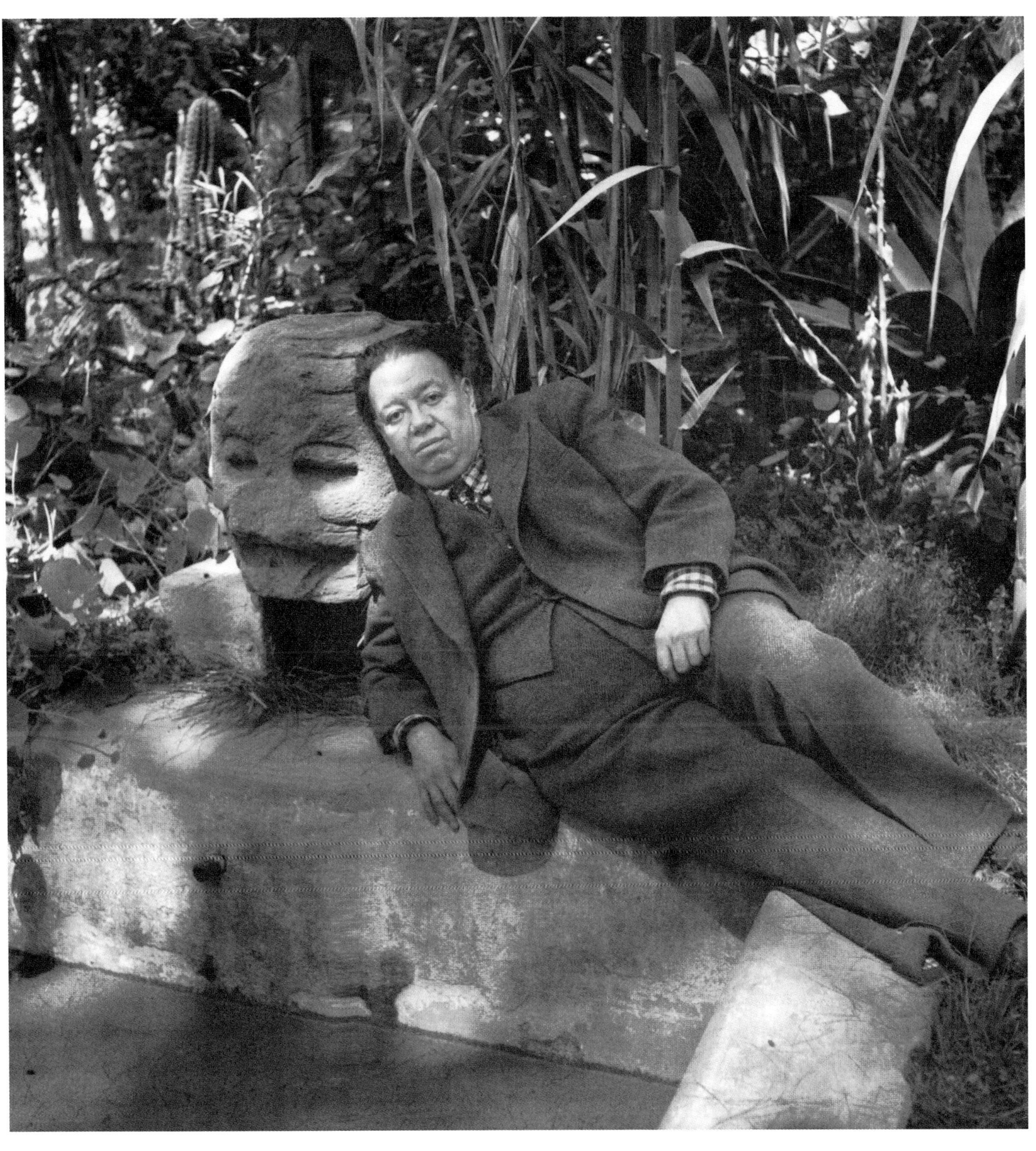

FRITZ HENLE, DIEGO RIVERA IN THE GARDEN OF THE BLUE HOUSE, 1943

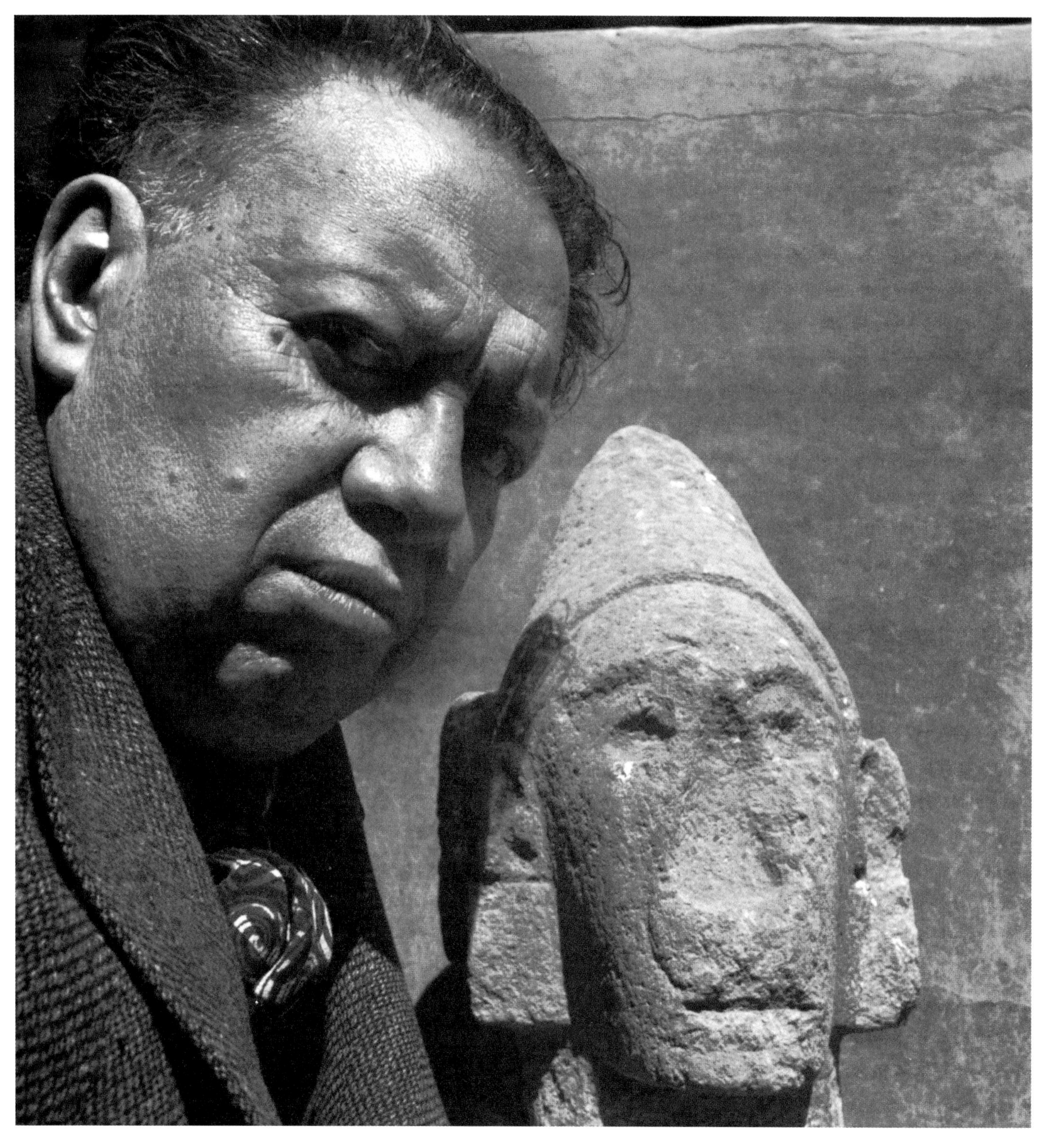

FRITZ HENLE, DIEGO RIVERA WITH A PRE-COLUMBIAN FIGURE
IN THE GARDEN OF THE BLUE HOUSE, 1943

IRENE HERNER DE LARREA

FRIDA KAHLO: MY BIRTH

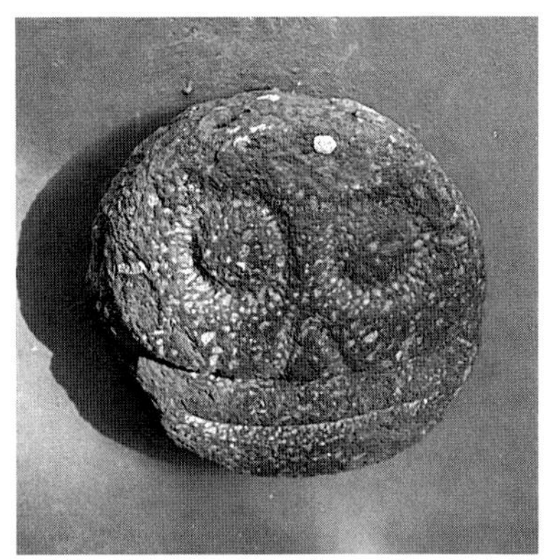

Dedicated to Erika Billeter

My Birth, a 1932 painting by Frida Kahlo, deals with a subject not treated until then in Western painting. It portrays birth and sexuality. It is a truthful representation of the body at the very moment of giving birth, a view of what it means to be a woman that borders on the unbearable. An image that would have been banned during the Christian era, it was a pioneering achievement vis-à-vis the visual exploration of the female body during the seventies and eighties. What is revolutionary and lends import to this painting, however, is that it finds its direct inspiration in pre-Columbian sculpture, in one of the most important motifs in Mexican culture: Tlazolteotl. *"Diosa de la impureza, Diosa de la tierra, de la luna, del amor carnal, de la confesion"* (Goddess of impurity, Goddess of the earth, of the moon, of carnal love, of confession)[1]. Tlazolteotl is an Aztec stone sculpture from the beginning of the sixteenth century that represents the deity at the moment of giving birth to an adult male warrior. It is reminiscent of the figure of Coatlicue, a portrayal of duality, of the law of origins, of the mother of the Aztec pantheon, protected at the hour of delivery by her oedipal son Huitzilopochtli through the bloody sacrifice of her daughters, the moon and the stars, in order to ensure the continuity of the universe, in its succession of days and nights.

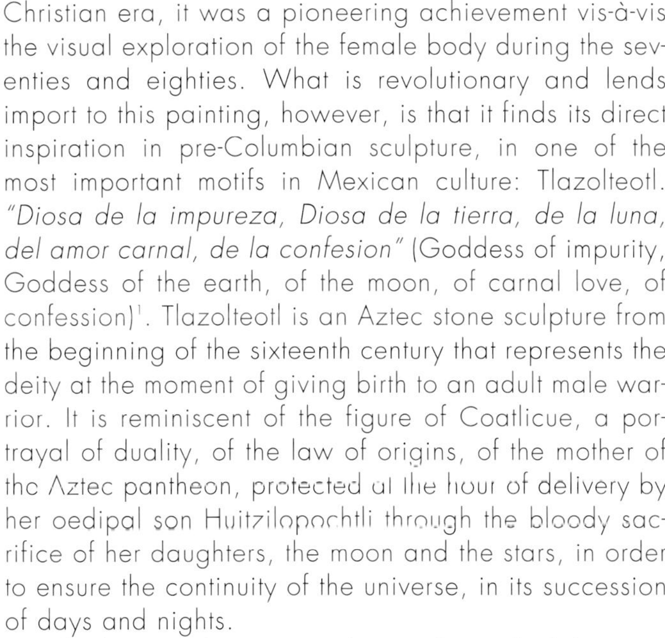

Freud's hysterical patients who, at the end of the nineteenth and beginning of the twentieth century, preferred to faint and get sick rather than honor their desires, the broomstick-riding witches who were burnt at the stake by the Inquisition, the "easy" ladies, the dissatisfied, the adulterers and the seductresses, all of them ushered in, after the First World War, the femmes fatales who, like Marlene Dietrich, disguised as sirens or peacocks, thought and acted unter the pretense of being more independent than men. The feminine image that had traditionally been dictated by men gave way to the explorations and fantasies about femininity undertaken by twentieth-century women. Frida Kahlo is a pioneer in the pictorial exploration of women's sexuality. The theme, forbidden by religion, good manners, and Queen Victoria, moves to the foreground in the artist's work and is courageously dissected, without giving up its mystery a pictorial exploration of the dark void and the fear of blood. Frida, the Tehuana who wrapped her infirmity in finery, did not hesitate to portray its naked reality.

As opposed to many of Frida's paintings, which are full of joyful detail, this work is especially radical and gloomy. It shows an impersonal room, in spite of the bright yellow wooden floor that resembles those of her Blue House. On crisp white sheets and an embroidered lace-trimmed pillow lies a brown nude body, face and chest covered with a shroud like a corpse, at the moment of giving birth to a tiny Frida Kahlo. The mother is a ghost, a hidden presence, depersonalized. "My head is covered, Frida said, because my mother died at the time I was working on this painting." A painting or colored print of the grieving Virgin hangs above the headboard. Rivera described her as "the *mater dolorosa* with her seven daggers of pain which make possible the opening from which the child Frida emerges, the only human force since the marvelous Aztec master... who has given plasticity to the actual phenomenon of birth."[2]

The scene portrays a body with no face and no breasts, delivering a newborn – whether dead or alive we cannot tell – watched over by the picture of a weeping woman, the Mater Dolorosa. In Frida's chronology of suffering, this painting is also visual evidence of the painter's recent miscarriage in Detroit, and thus is a pendant to her painting *Henry Ford Hospital*. In the latter the miscarriage happens in an open space, against the desolate background of industrial Detroit as opposed to *My Birth* which takes place in the secluded intimacy of a room, with a mother who is simultaneously a golem, earth, and death. This painting differs from *Henry Ford Hospital* in that it does not utilize symbols as the artistic medium, instead, it represents a change, a symbolic act. Noteworthy in *My Birth* is the blank space the painter left at the bottom, which recalls the space where the text of a votive painting (*retablo*) would be inscribed.

This small oil painting on metal, 12 by 15 inches in size, is a confirmation of the idea that art allows us to transcend horror and to marvel at it. Painting transforms dreams, fantasies, fears, and yearnings into public

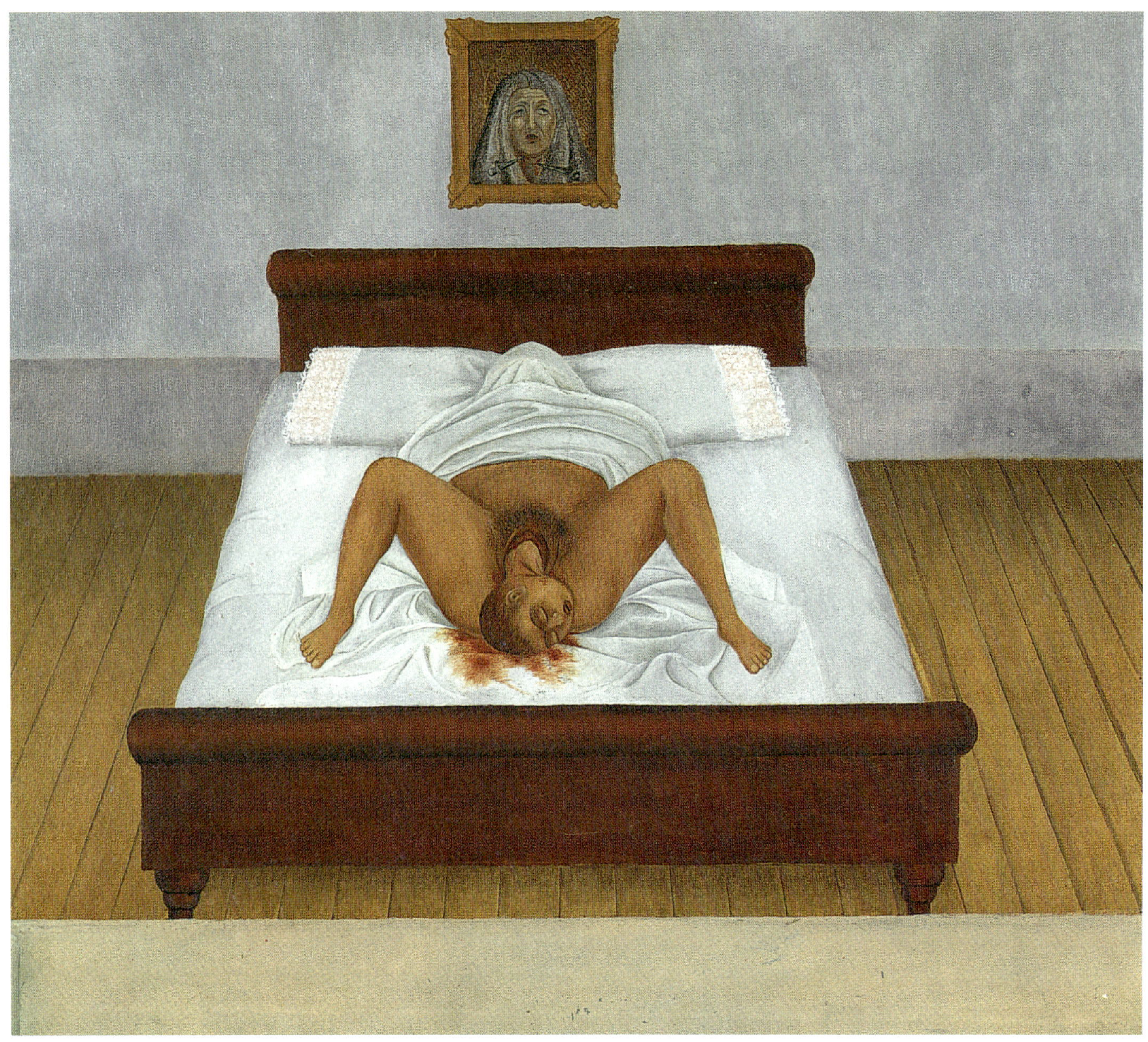

Frida Kahlo, *My Birth,* 1932, oil on metal, 12×13 ¾ inches (30.5×35 cm), private collection, United States (not in the exhibition).

images. One can witness one's own birth, show surprising metaphors like this painting, in which the obvious meaning evokes its opposite, overwhelming the signifier: the enfolding legs are arms, the newborn is the genitalia, the missing face is one's own or that of the Mater Dolorosa. The mixing of races in which the witness, the painting of the Virgin within the painting, is reminiscent of the paintings of those virgins/mothers in Western art, who never gave birth, while at the same time the woman in labor in this painting embodies all mothers, the archetypal mother, mother earth, the unique mother of the newborn Frida Kahlo. "Beauty is convulsive," André Breton insisted.

My Birth is not an isolated work; its meaning unfolds throughout the course of the painter's life. It appears in the flowers and fruits that she painted, especially in *Xochitl, The Flower of Life* (1938) and in *Roots* (1943), in which Frida's body is rooted to the earth, penetrated by roots and branches. In *Moises (Moses),* painted in 1945, she deals with an epic subject infrequent in her work: the birth of the Judeo/Christian era and its historical role in the mixing of races. In her treatment it becomes an autobiographical statement that harks back to the universal myth of the origin of the world. But undoubtedly the 1946 *El abrazo de amor de El universo, la tierra (Mexico) yo, Diego y el senor Xolotl (The Love-*

Embrace of the Universe, The Earth (Mexico), Diego, Me and Señor Xolotl), is the conclusion of this journey of exploration: an image of the paradisaical fulfillment of the *mestizo*.

Frida Kahlo's art is autobiographical because she is her main referent. She herself as mask, as disguise, tied to the *Tehuana* image, to the myth of Eve. The disguise as symbol wrapped around a void, and a question: What does it mean to be a woman?

Self-portraits, reconstructions within a boundary, concrete figures of others, Frida, her features. And yet, next to her many portraits of herself in the guise of a *Tehuana,* there are others in which she painted herself wearing men's clothes or nude. Nudity almost always appears in relation to images of maternity – failed maternity – or infirmity (*Remembrance of an Open Wound*). A search for a formal identity, a longing for the lost indigenous ancestry. The most powerful contrast: barrenness/fertility.

My Birth revisits a type of religious art in which birth is the ultimate myth, the myth of origin, as seen through the amazed eyes of a foreigner who claims as her own the Mexican heritage.

Birth, the coming together of beginning and end, the fleeting moment when life and death meet. Source of the original sin of Christian mythology, and of its redemption. Locus of the sacred and of lust. Earth, creation, and woman who, at the moment of giving birth, conquers the phallus.

The center of the earth is the place of birth. The center of sight is the reflection in the mirror, the place of mastery of oneself.

Frida Kahlo's contribution to Surrealism was her unique way of bringing to light the hidden secrets of a woman's soul by combining popular and pre-Columbian art forms with her knowledge of Western art.

The mixing of races as a visual artist's option. A paradise of tropical plants. The fruits in *Viva la Vida (Long Live Life),* the watermelons, the symbol of the Mexican esthetic, the sensuality of warm places and the colors of Oaxaca. Beyond that, the recapturing of a cosmogony, a *Weltanschauung,* founded on duality. For Frida it implied the exploration of Mexico beyond the eyes of her Jewish/Hungarian father, who took pictures of Mexican architecture; it meant to further her knowledge of what was Mexican, to take root – she always painted roots – to make the ancient culture and the popular customs her own, and to create an image of herself tied to her mother's soil.

Frida Kahlo is the incarnation of the mythos of the mixing of races that came out of wars and migrations during the twentieth century. Jewish, Hungarian, Spanish and Indian, she stood at the crossroads, cosmopolitan and nationalistic, so powerful and explosive that today, almost forty years after her death, she is more valued than ever, an international celebrity. Not by chance does Madonna own *My Birth,* which she bought a few years ago at the Gagosian Gallery in New York.[3]

Frida Kahlo has become a cultural icon, and her works the fetishes of mass culture. But her paintings retain their standing as works of art.

Frida Kahlo's world, a private pictorial reality out of which she constructed a unique and yet universal self, is sourrounded by a universe of acts, gestures, and objects. Transfigurations of popular visions; of markets and styles of dress; of her fascination with the culture of hand embroidery, of looms which Indians operate by attaching them to their waist; of long hair in rich black braids, with flowers, ribbons, nets, and woolen strands woven into them like the precious stones of fairy tales or like roots from the bowels of the earth. Frida made herself into a *Tehuana,* with a bird's face, a man's eyes, the mouth of the Mediterranean sea. The Blue House was a magical place.

The artist shared her foreigner's eyes not only with her father but also very uniquely with Diego Rivera who, during the twenties, upon returning from Europe, created with other artists a national aesthetic that mixed elements

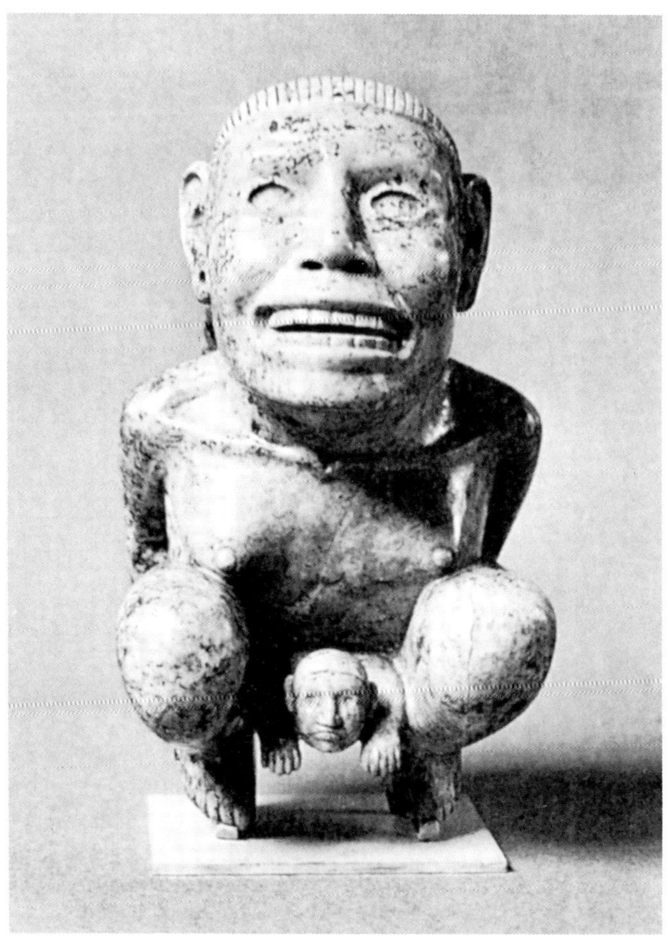

The goddess Tlazolteotl giving birth. Aztec, early 16th century.

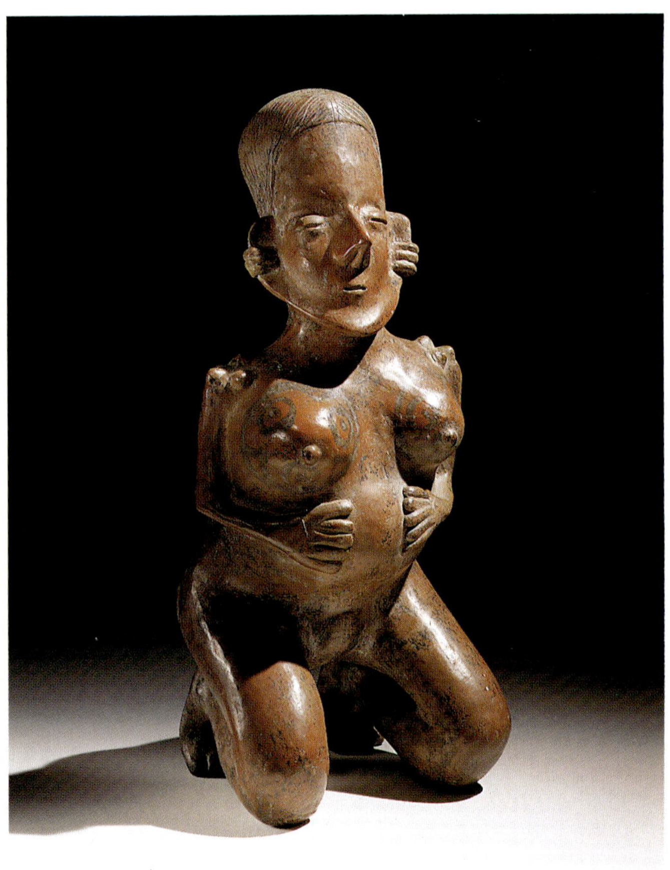

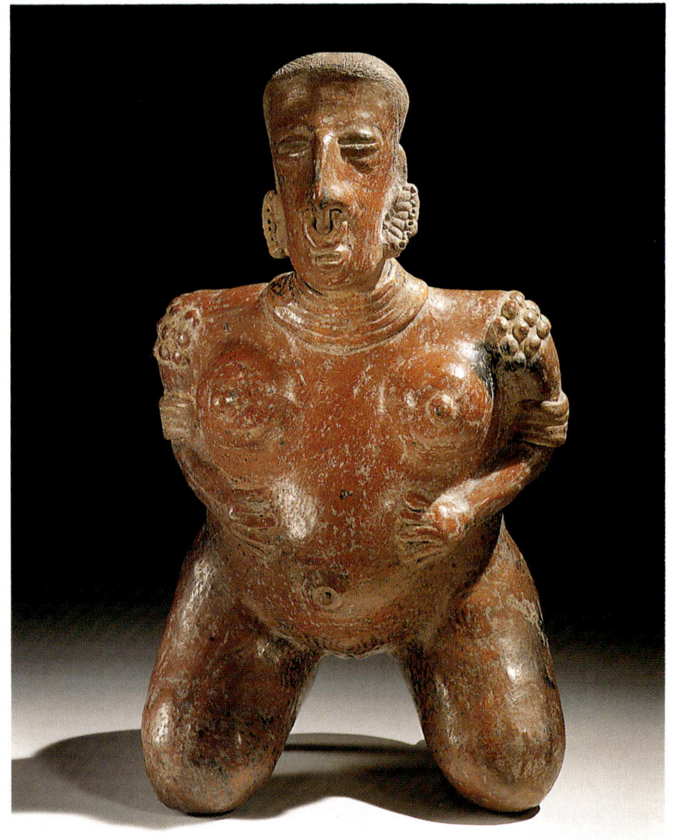

Women Giving Birth, pre-Columbian clay vessels (cat. nos. 157–158).

reminiscent of the modernists with the colors, textures, and shapes of their Mexican surroundings. Frida loved what Diego loved.

The naiveté of popular votive paintings achieves in *My Birth* an impressive intellectual sophistication. The sincerity of the artist's subconscious and her pictorial craft combine to recapture the mystic power of the act of birth. The work endows this act with transcendent artistic themes, the telluric force, the nature of woman.

We believe that before "I" there is you, "The Other," an ideal. And the "I" of Frida the artist was an "I" of paintings. Paintings that portray a self that is broken, wounded like Saint Sebastian and like *Pobre Venadito (Poor Little Deer),* an "I" reconstructed with brushstrokes, with an artificial spine that is broken and clumsily held together with nails, an artist who in *Giver of Life* painted herself as a duality: the mother of flowers or the woman who despairs of her barrenness.

"I am not sick, " Frida said, "I am broken. But I am happy to be alive as long as I can paint."[4] The vision of a shattered body is a nightmare for any human being. Frida painted what she felt in the core of her being. She compelled her body to be reborn and recomposed through her painting. Daily ritualistic acts of survival.

Frida created herself in front of the mirror, thus her "I" is composed as a reflection of "The Other." The impossibility of giving birth makes her the witness of her own birth. *My Birth* could very well be the first page of a book. Frida Kahlo is an inexhaustible exploration.

[1] Jacques Soustelle, *El Universo de los Aztecas* (Mexico City: Fondo de Cultura Economica, 1962), 54.

[2] Hayden Herrera, *Frida: A Biography of Frida Kahlo* (New York: Harper & Row, 1983), 158.

[3] The painting was originally purchased from the artist in 1941 by Edgar J. Kaufmann, Jr.

[4] Martha Zamora, *Frida Kahlo: The Brush of Anguish* (San Francisco: Chronicle Books, 1990), 126.

JORGE ALBERTO LOZOYA

KAHLO AND AMBIGUITY

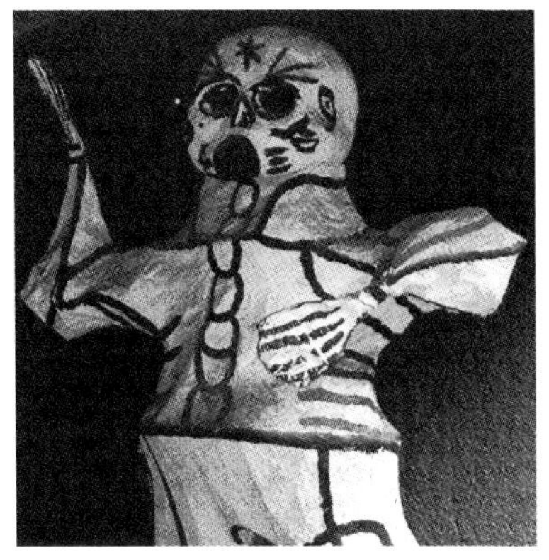

It is difficult to approach Frida Kahlo without getting caught by the virus of fetishism. In this hopeless era, the tendency is to adore idols in an equivocal manner. Of course, as things go, this is not the worst of vices.

The Blue House could be approached as a ritual, a prelude to an announced canonization. Possibly the Blue House was a desert shared by two souls, Frida and Diego de Rivera, who frequently distanced themselves from society – the basis of the myth that pretends to proclaim the artist the creator and not the victim of his work.

Frida Kahlo died when I was eleven years old. I never met her. However, my father, a well-known surgeon, was a friend of Rivera, and because of that I have clear memories of the era and the environment in which the painters lived. Later, Juan Somolinos, a great physician of my generation, and a great friend from the years of our youth, used to tell me moving stories of the serene intimacy he experienced with Frida when he was a child. An afternoon in 1956, when I was thirteen years old comes to mind. I had accompanied my parents to a dinner at the home of movie director Emilio Fernández. We went with Vicente Lombardo Toledano, a dear friend of my father, and the main ideologist of the Mexican Revolution, to whom deserved recognition had been denied. The small group of guests included Diego Rivera. Frida had been dead for over a year, and the painter referred to her more as an imaginary ghost than as his wife of flesh and blood.

Rivera frequently talked as if narrating a Mexican version of a tale by the Brothers Grimm, and the Fernández's home, set in a park full of trees in the beautiful Coyoacán district, was a dramatic castle, cold and gloomy. Perhaps the strange place and the strong rain of a summer afternoon in Mexico City contributed to stamp in my memory the huge Diego, talking about a Frida more invented than real.

My father was a passionate admirer of Rivera but never did understand Frida, I don't think he even tried to make an effort to understand her. The themes of Frida's paintings seemed to my father painful and tormented. On the other hand he was fascinated by the presence surrounding Rivera of cinematographic luminaries such as Dolores del Rio and María Felix. Obviously Frida, in that context, came to be anti-climatic and even hostile. The way Frida dressed was considered extravagant in that era. In Mexico the years of the 40s and 50s were very westernized. The Second World War, and later on, the economic "boom" with its subsequent closeness to the United States, surely had an influence. Frida's dresses displeased women, and did not attract men either. This paraxodically, accented the foreign condition of the painter, in what seems to be a failed intent of "Mexicanization" at all cost.

The "otherness" of Frida, her insistence on being different, is one of the characteristic traits of her identity. By boasting about her extravagant ways she sought a refuge, almost always inadequate, from the oppressive sensation of knowing herself to be an outsider. And she was, like so many others, an outsider in the front of the unaissailable fortress of bourgeois morality and the social graces, wielded without pity by those who, being sure of their normalcy, made of it a dagger, a gallow, a fire.

When not dominated by terror, the outsider answers this constant aggression by wrapping herself with the only costume that can partially hide her: ambiguity.

Ambiguity, product of genius and adornment of the spirit, is a fragile defense with which to oppose the hostility of those who domineer, corrupt, and condemn, but it is also a blind alley at whose end waits a mirror without a reflection. Simone de Beauvoir, distressed, searched the mirror for the story of her own existence. Standing before the murky glass, she agonized: "Never can I get hold of myself as an entire object. I feel in myself the emptiness that is my being, and I have the feeling that I do not exist."[1]

Thus paralized, de Beauvoir pleads for an Ethic of Ambiguity, a cause that Frida would embrace in the long hours of Diego's absences, in the nights of pain, in the heartless statements of an ideological orthodoxy marked by treason.

The sense of being alien always ends up expressing itself as an interior tension, which, if overcome, makes one resistant to pain and provides a means for penetrating the darkness. With discipline one can get to the core of that darkness, a journey that culminates in the recognition of horror. Ambiguity sometimes creates the presupposition that the pain is itself an antidote to experience. William James, the scientist that coined the term "threshold of pain", described his encounter with the dreadful informer of the futility of life: "Being in a state of philosophical pessimism, and of a general spiritual depression, facing my future, one night I entered a dark room... Suddenly and without any warning, coming from the darkness a horrible terror of my own life assaulted me. Simultaneously, an epileptic patient, that I have seen in the hospital, came to my mind; a young man, with black hair and greenish skin, a complete idiot, who used to spend the entire day seated, moving only his dark eyes and appearing to be absolutely non-human. That image and my horror were combined. Potentially, I felt *that form was me*. It came to me that nothing I own, could defend me from that fate, as my hour arrived. I was so afraid of him and had such a clear perception that only a mere moment makes me different from him. It was as if something in my breast, up to this moment solid, fell down, converting me into a mass of trembling fear. From then on, the Universe changed completely for me. Every morning I wake up, with a dreadful fear in my stomach and with a sensation of insecurity with life that I had never felt before.[2]

In the sudden sensation of irrelevancy is one faced with the enigma of freedom, and, as in the case of the outsider, this can end in absolute negation, in inescapable slavery to fortuitous events, transformed into the essence of evil.

Van Gogh, Hesse, or Camus – great outsiders – took refuge in the practical uselessness of consciousness, astonished by the ordinary individual, who not only is not free but does not even known it. The torment is that without renouncing consciousness, one aspires to quit being. But while it is not pleasing being left out, neither does the average, adaptable individual please us. Where can one go and who can one be?

Without mask we can then face and see the enigma of life. Initiation explained up to the last consequences by Leonid Andreyev in which Frida, always alone, found vocation and death.

---

[1] Simone de Beauvoir, *Pyrrhus and Cineas*, cited by Colin Wilson in *Mysteries* (London: Grafton Books, 1979), 44.

[2] William James, *The Varities of Religious Experiences* (1903). Quoted by Colin Wilson, *The Outsider*, Boston, Houghton Miffin, 1956, 110–111.

PAINTINGS AND DRAWINGS BY FRIDA KAHLO

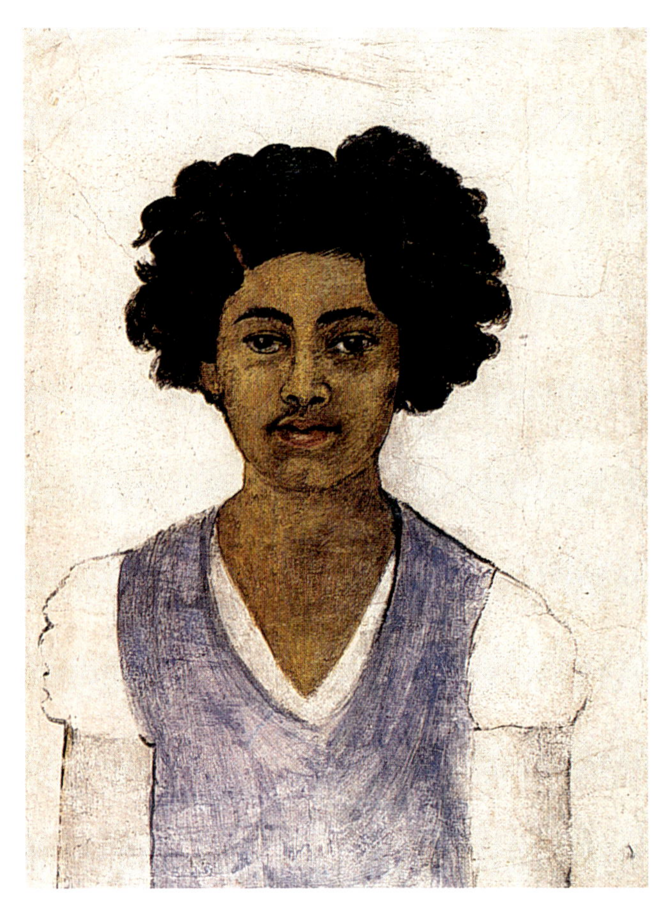

1 SELF-PORTRAIT, 1923–1933

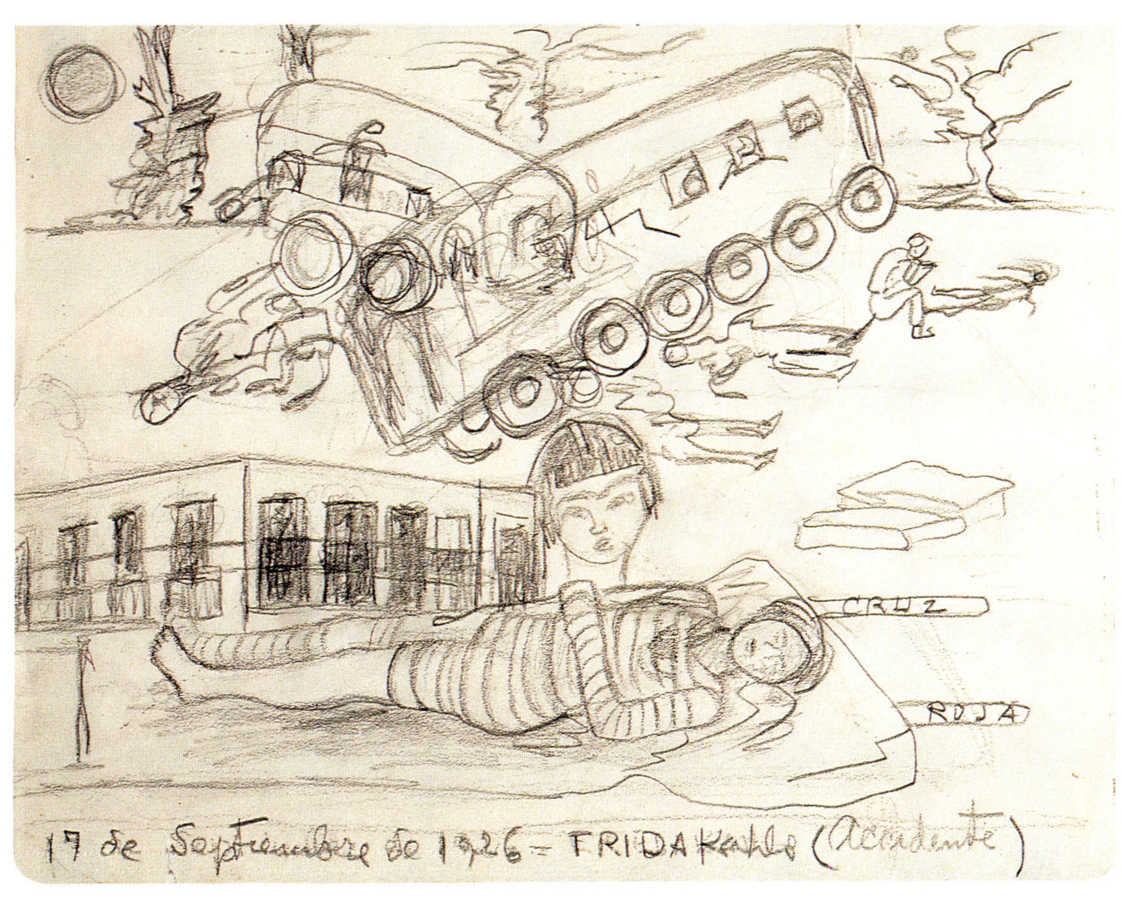

4 THE ACCIDENT, 17 SEPTEMBER 1926

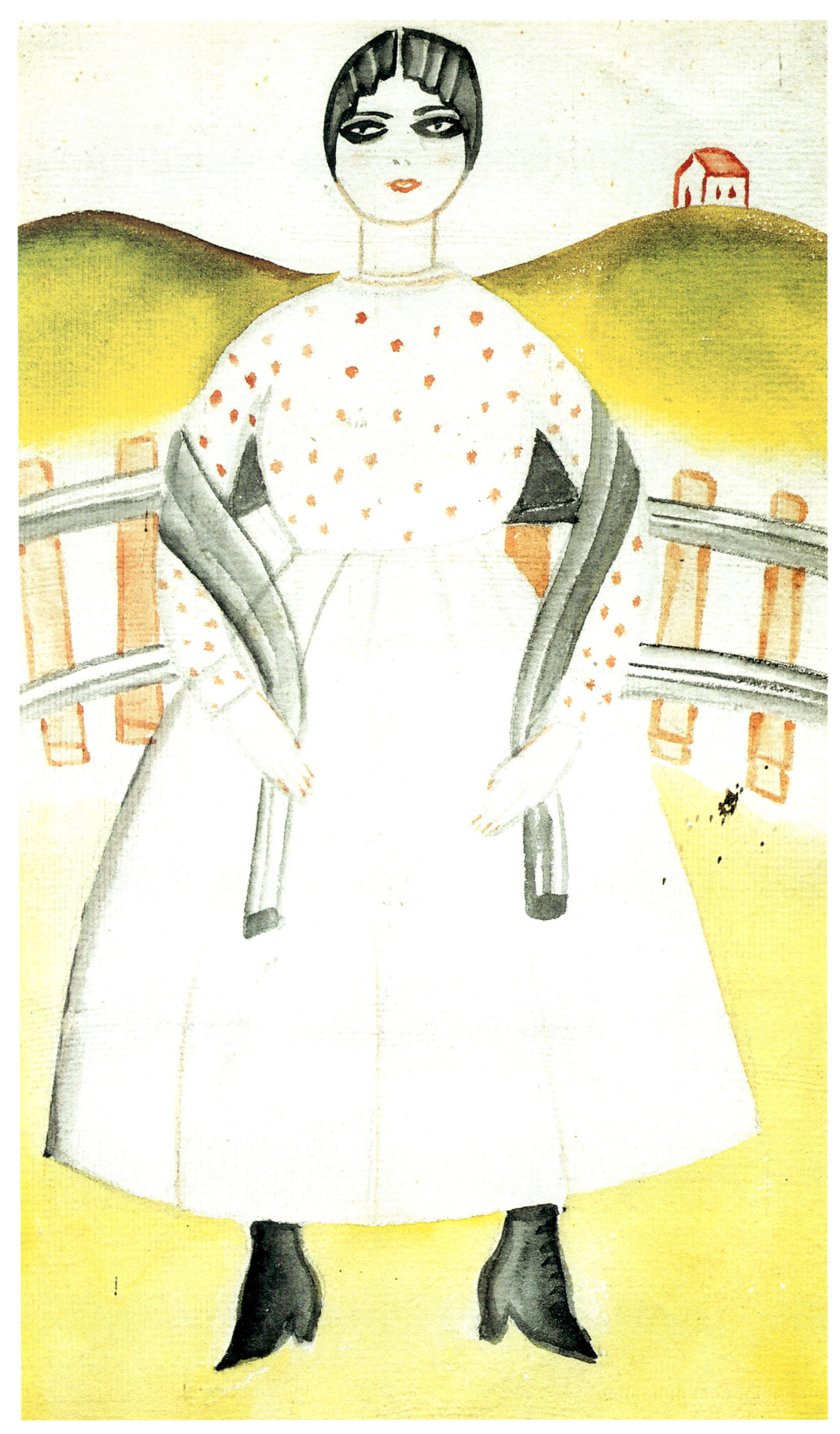

2 VILLAGE GIRL, before 1925

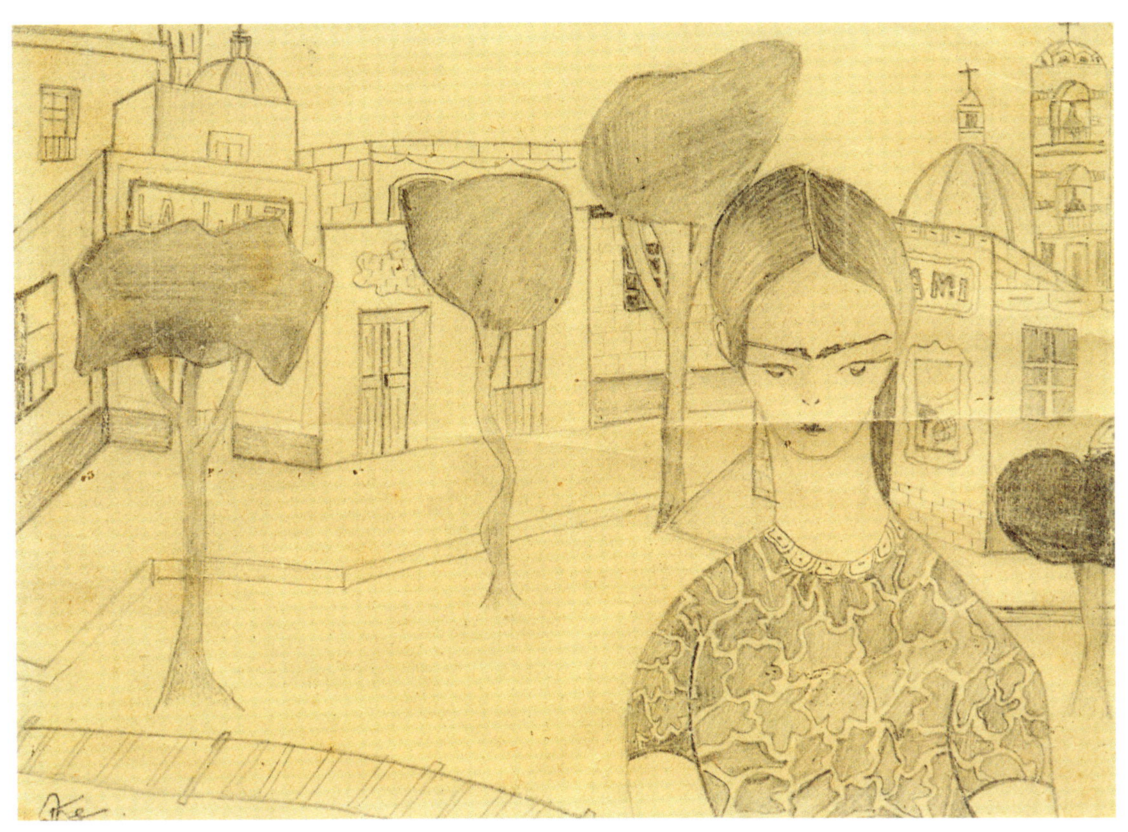

8 FRIDA IN COYOACÁN, circa 1927

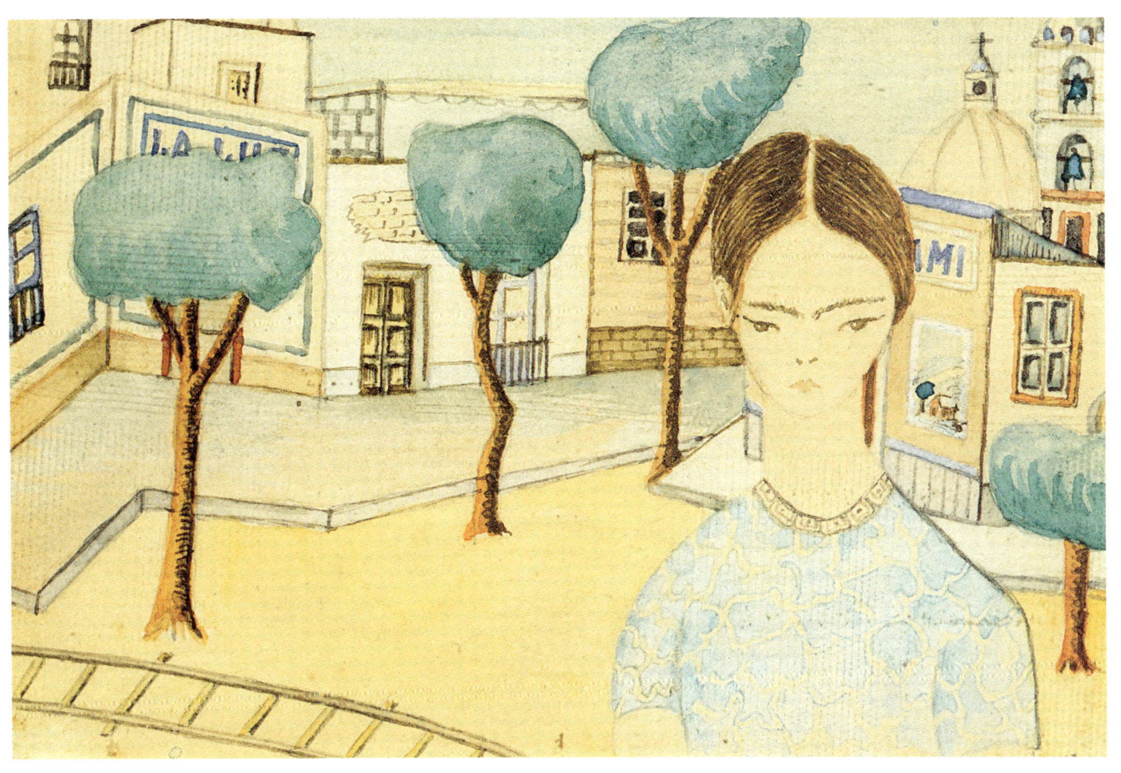

9 FRIDA IN COYOACÁN, circa 1927

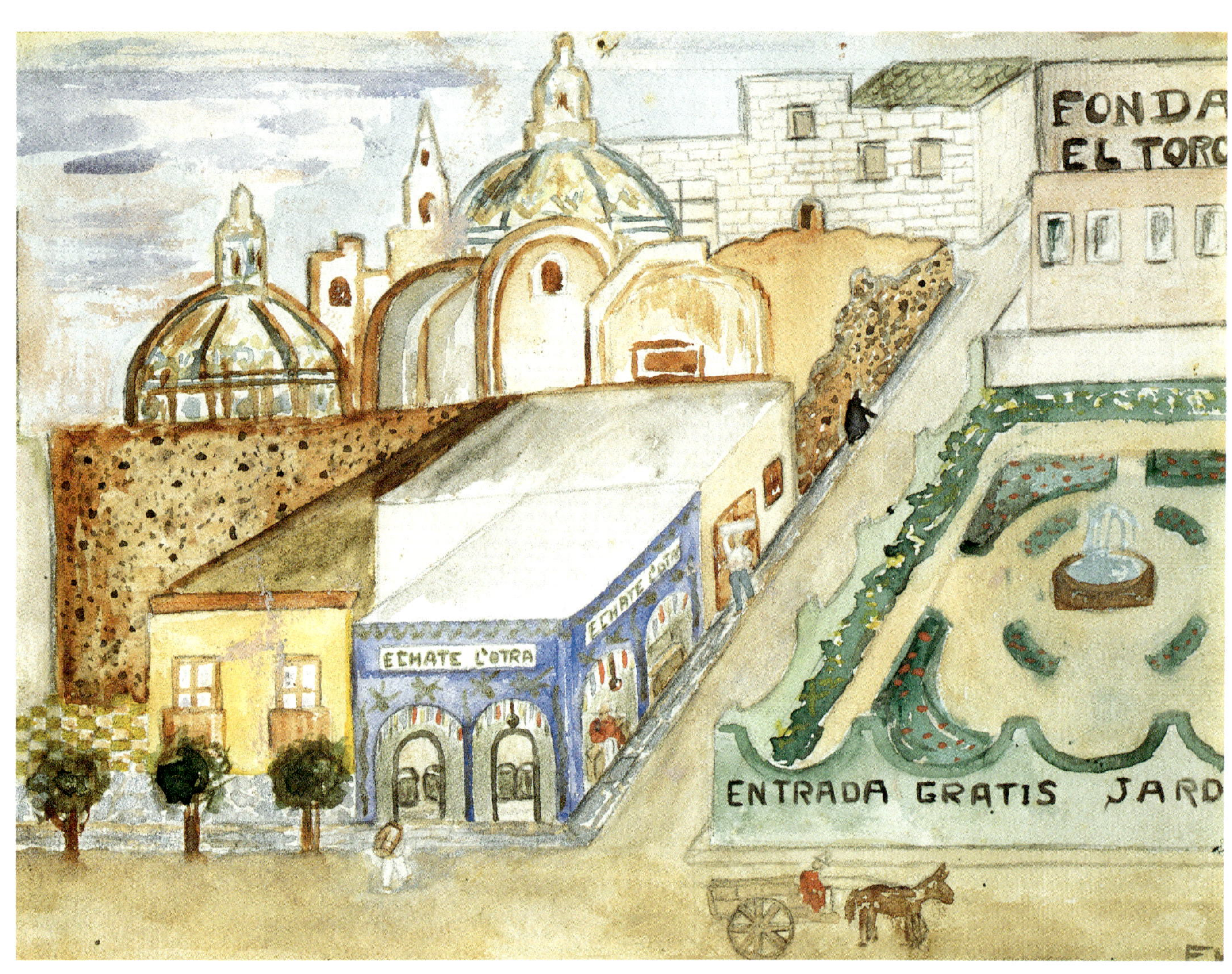

3 HAVE ANOTHER DRINK, before 1925

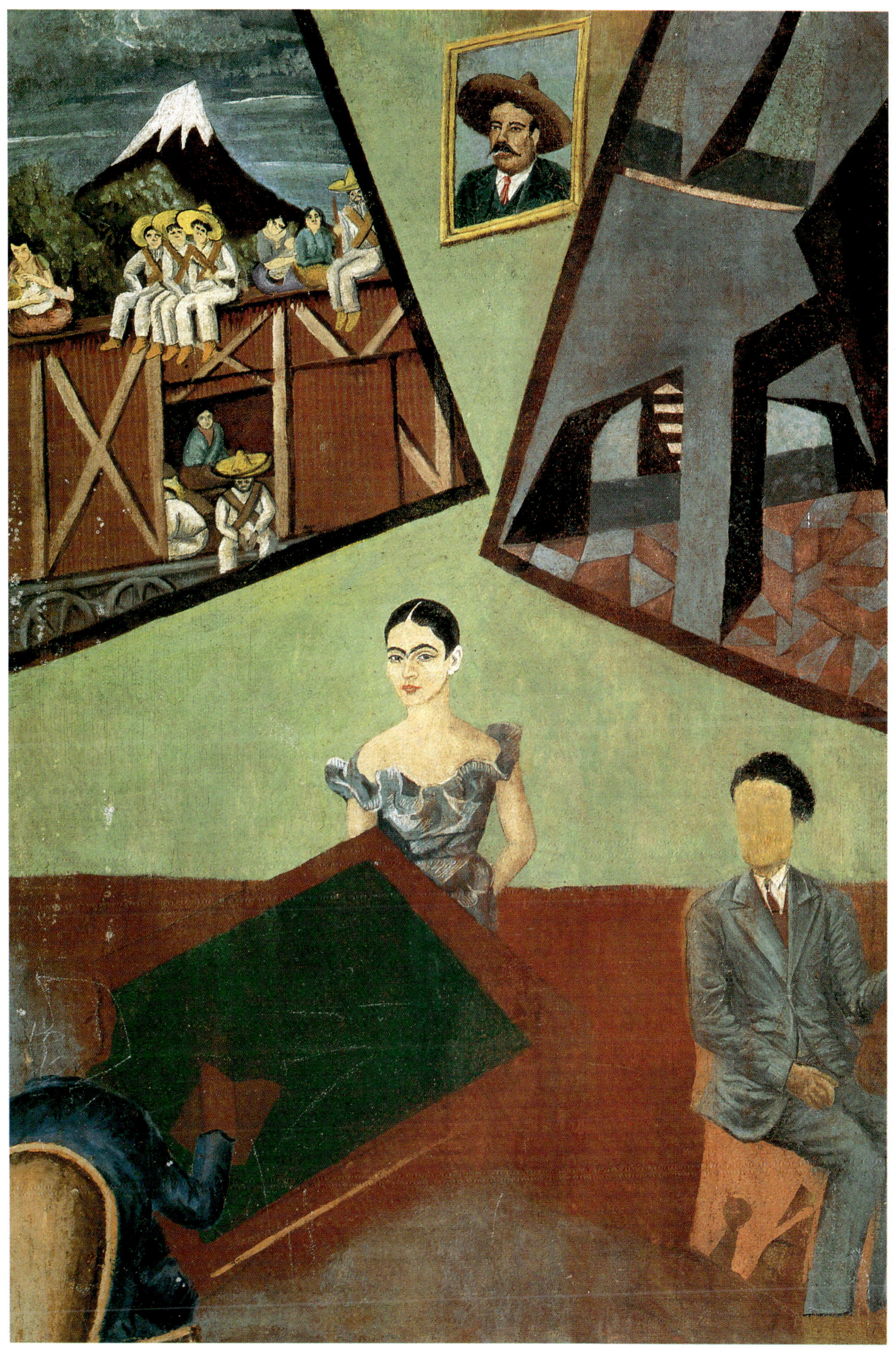

5 PANCHO VILLA AND ADELITA, before 1927

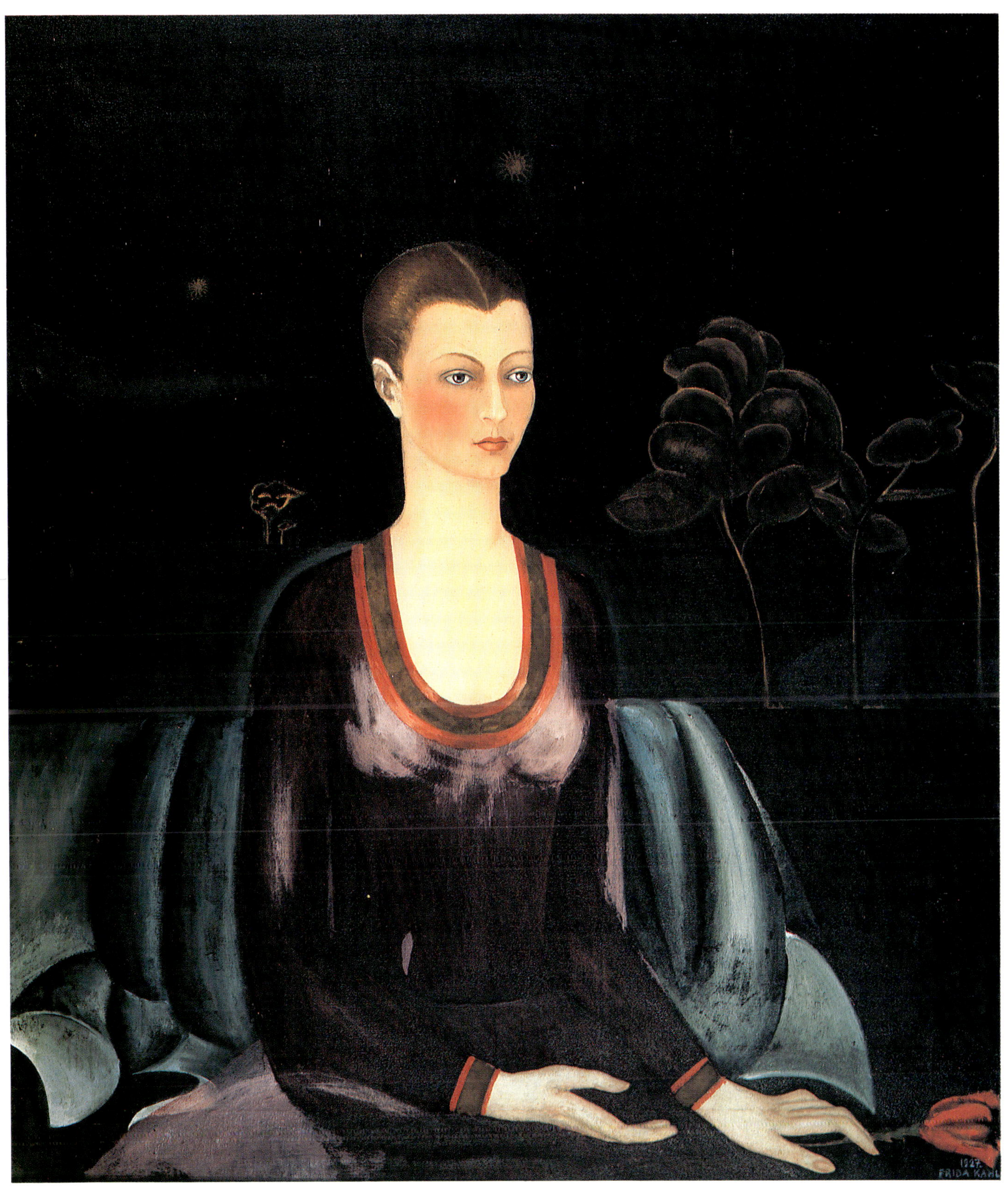

7 PORTRAIT OF ALICIA GALANT, 1927

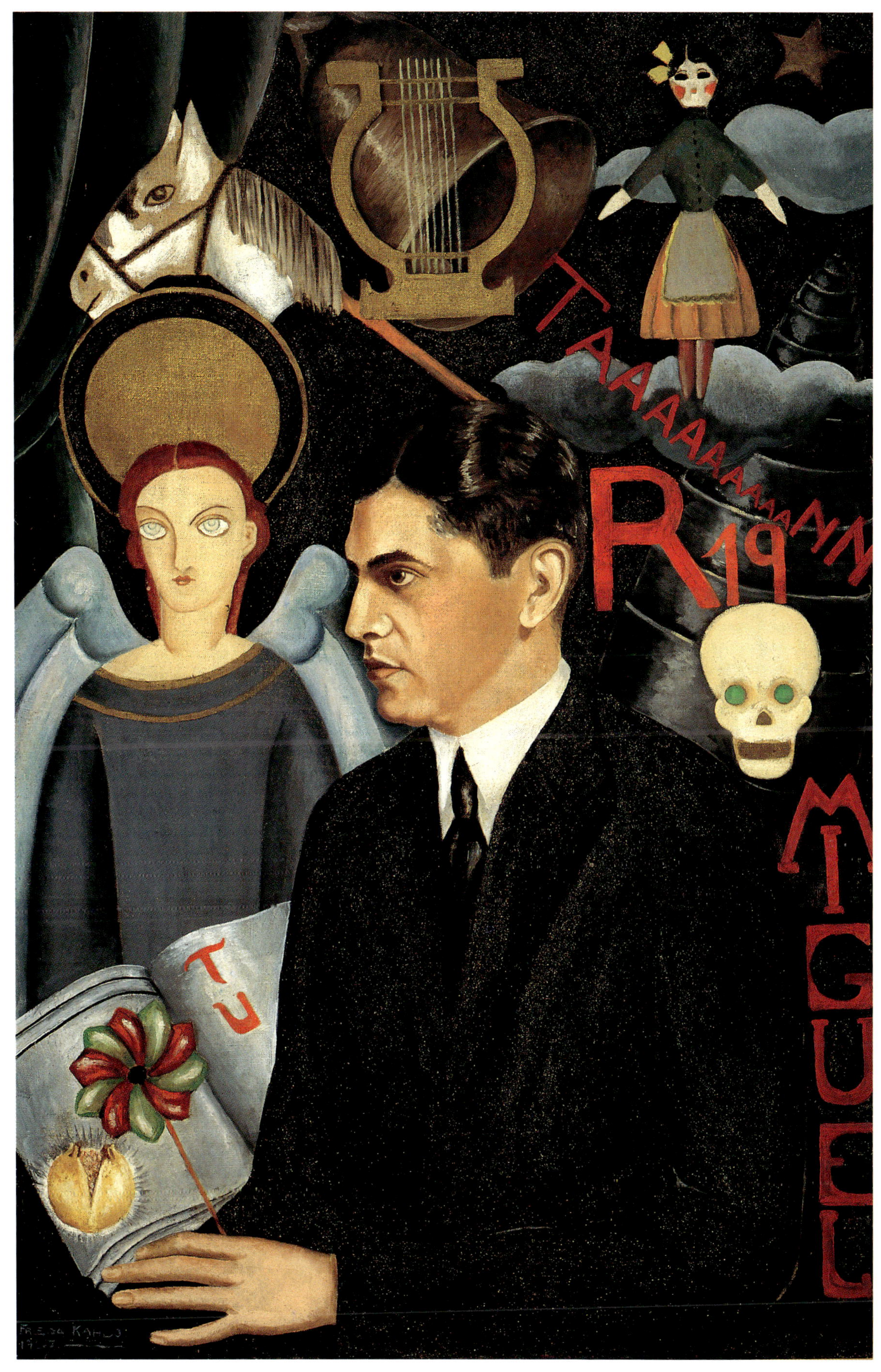

6 PORTRAIT OF MIGUEL N. LIRA, 1927

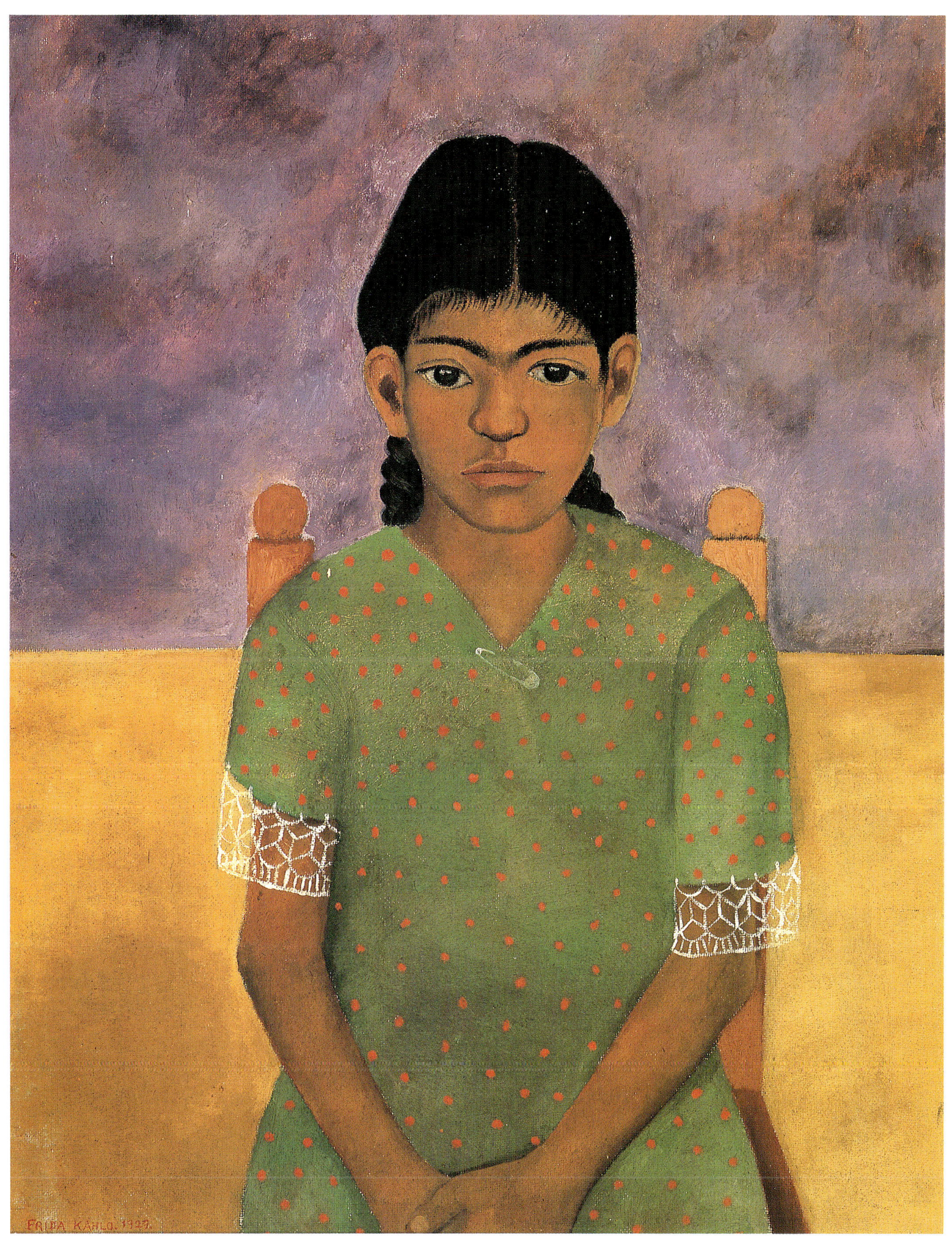

12 PORTRAIT OF VIRGINIA (NIÑA), 1929

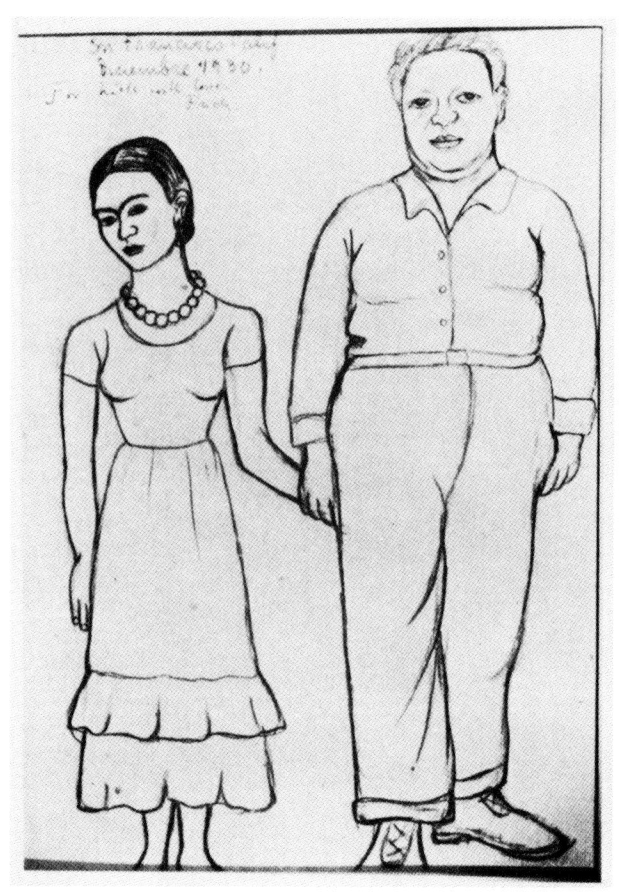

14 FRIDA KAHLO AND DIEGO RIVERA, 1930

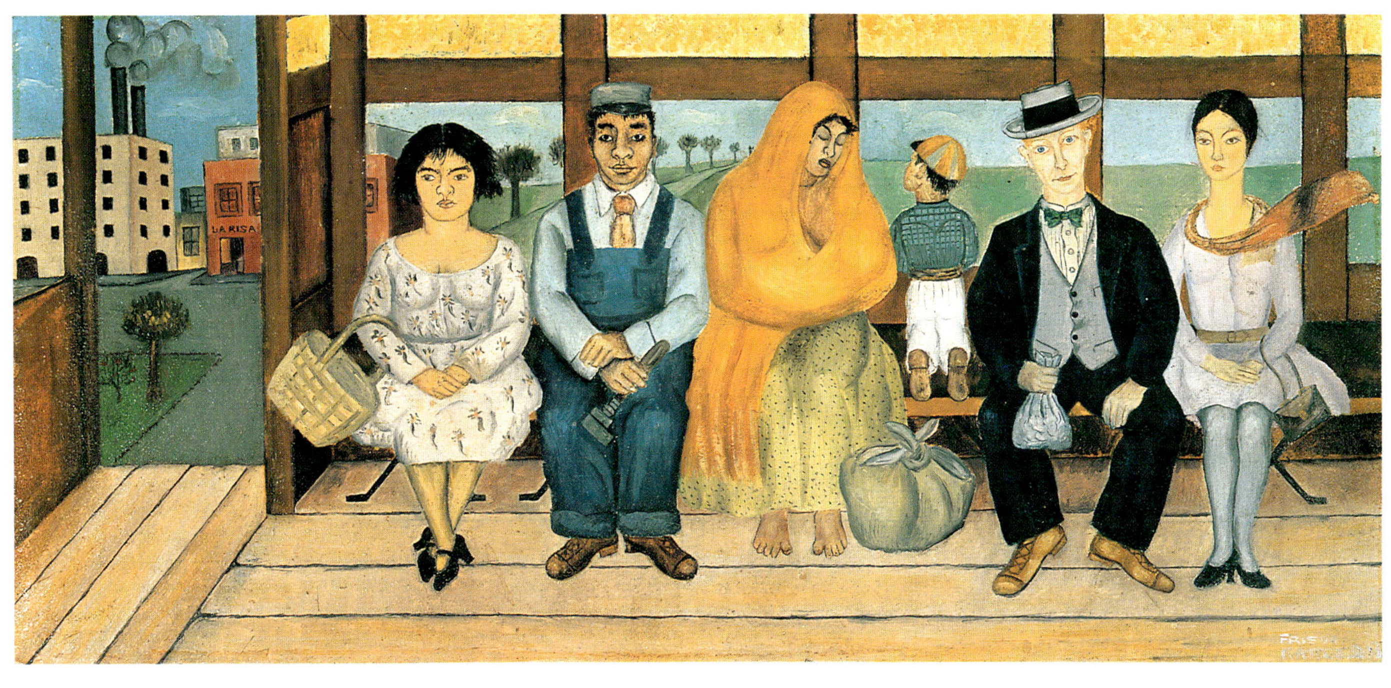

13 THE BUS, 1929

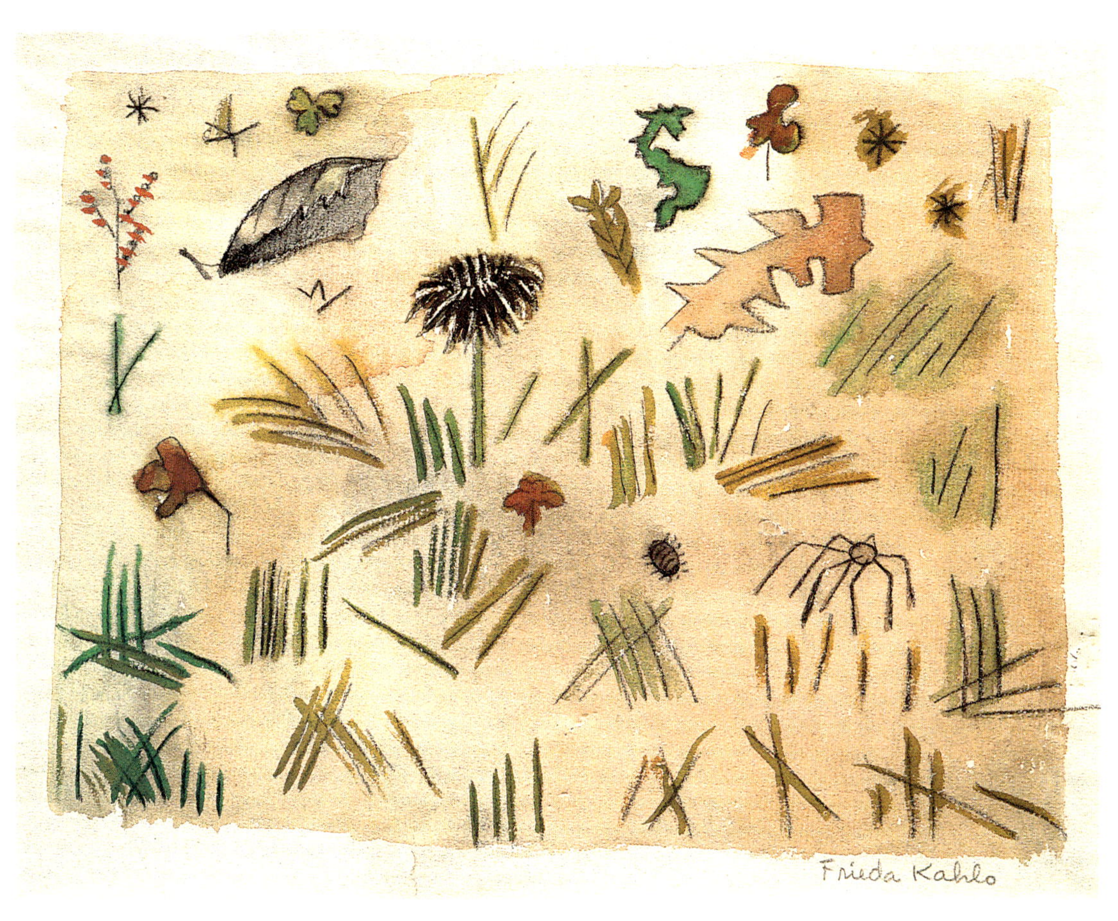

10 UNTITLED – LITTLE LIFE (II), circa 1928

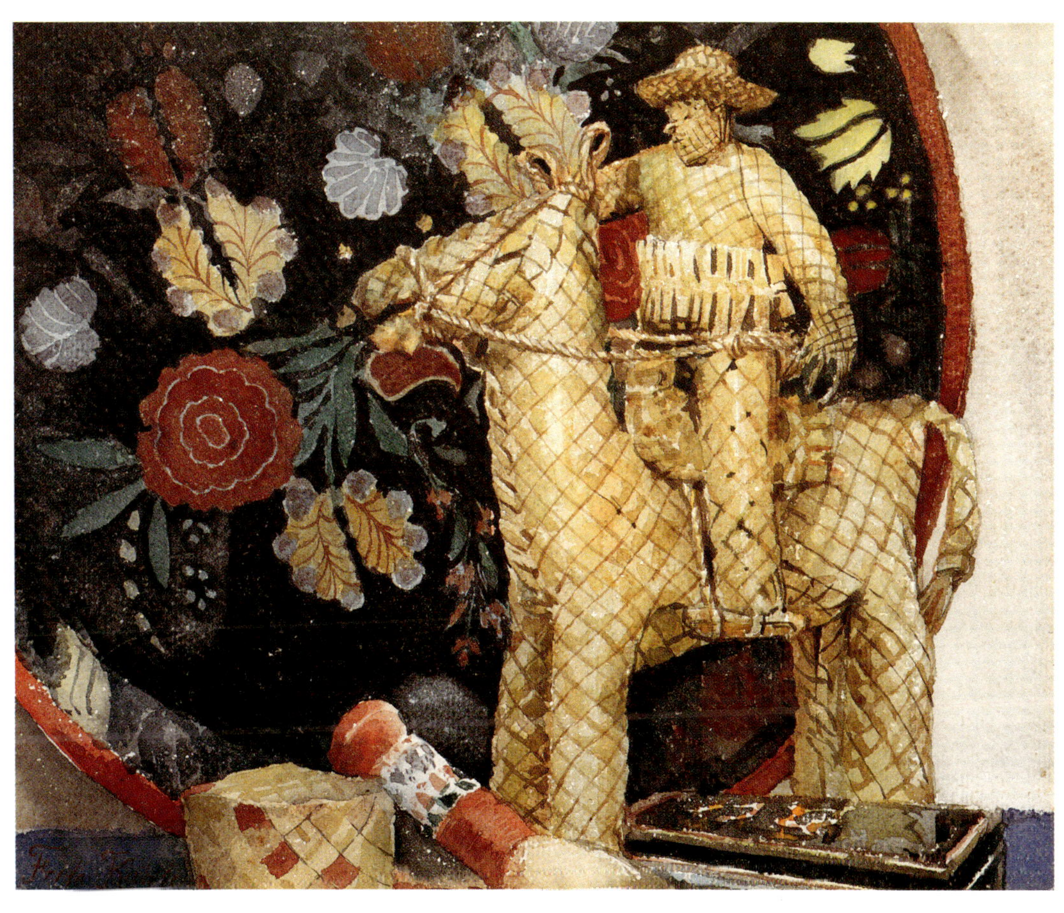

11 TINY CABALLERO, 1928

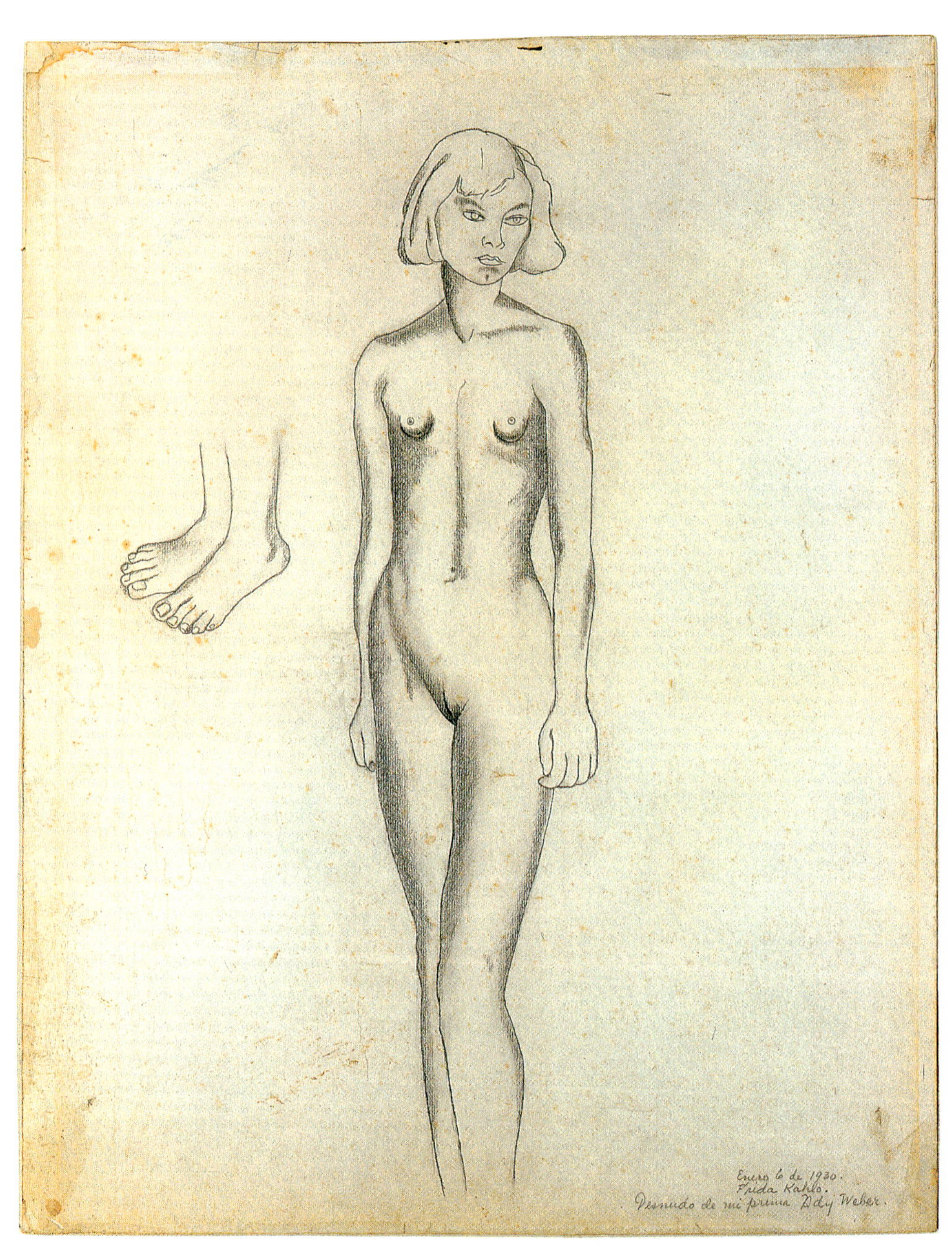

15 NUDE STUDY OF MY COUSIN ADY WEBER, 1930

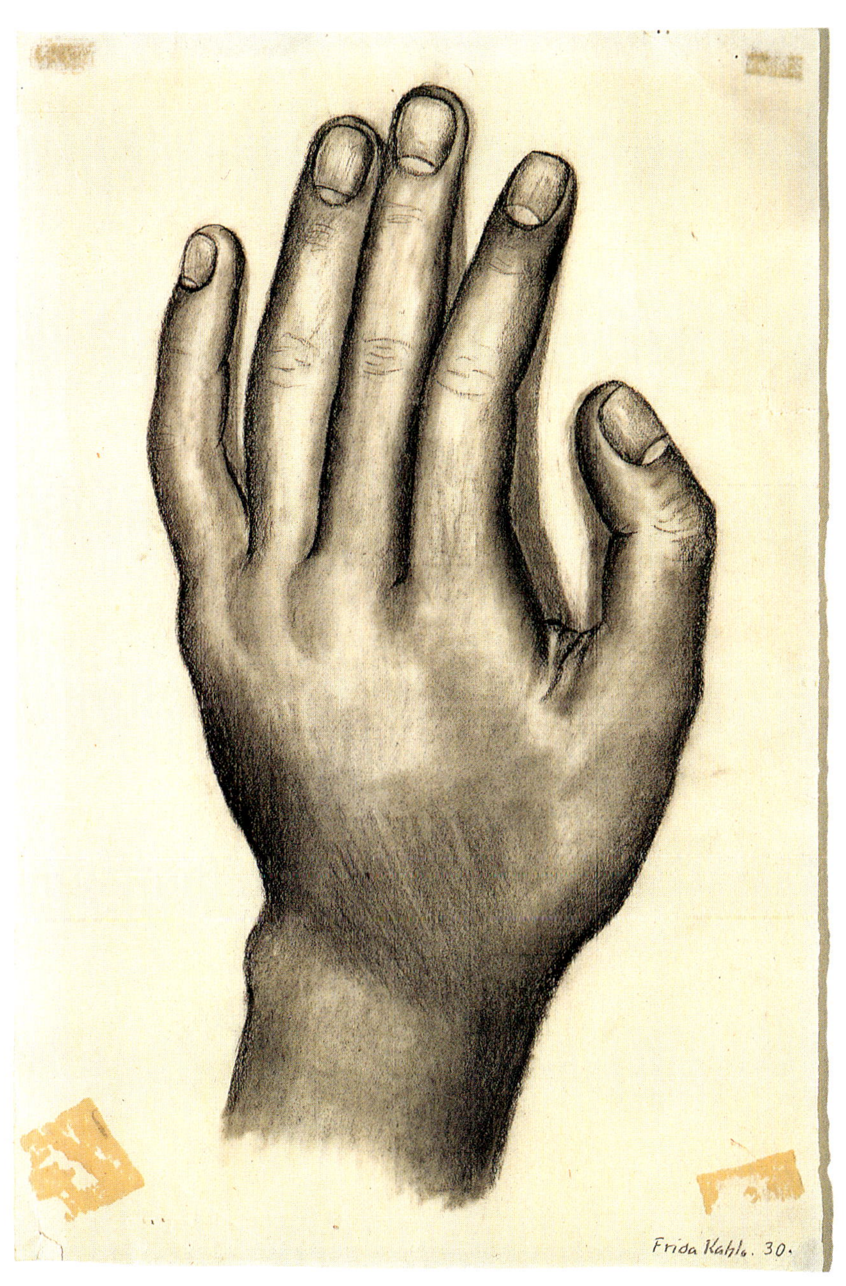

16 THE HAND, 1930

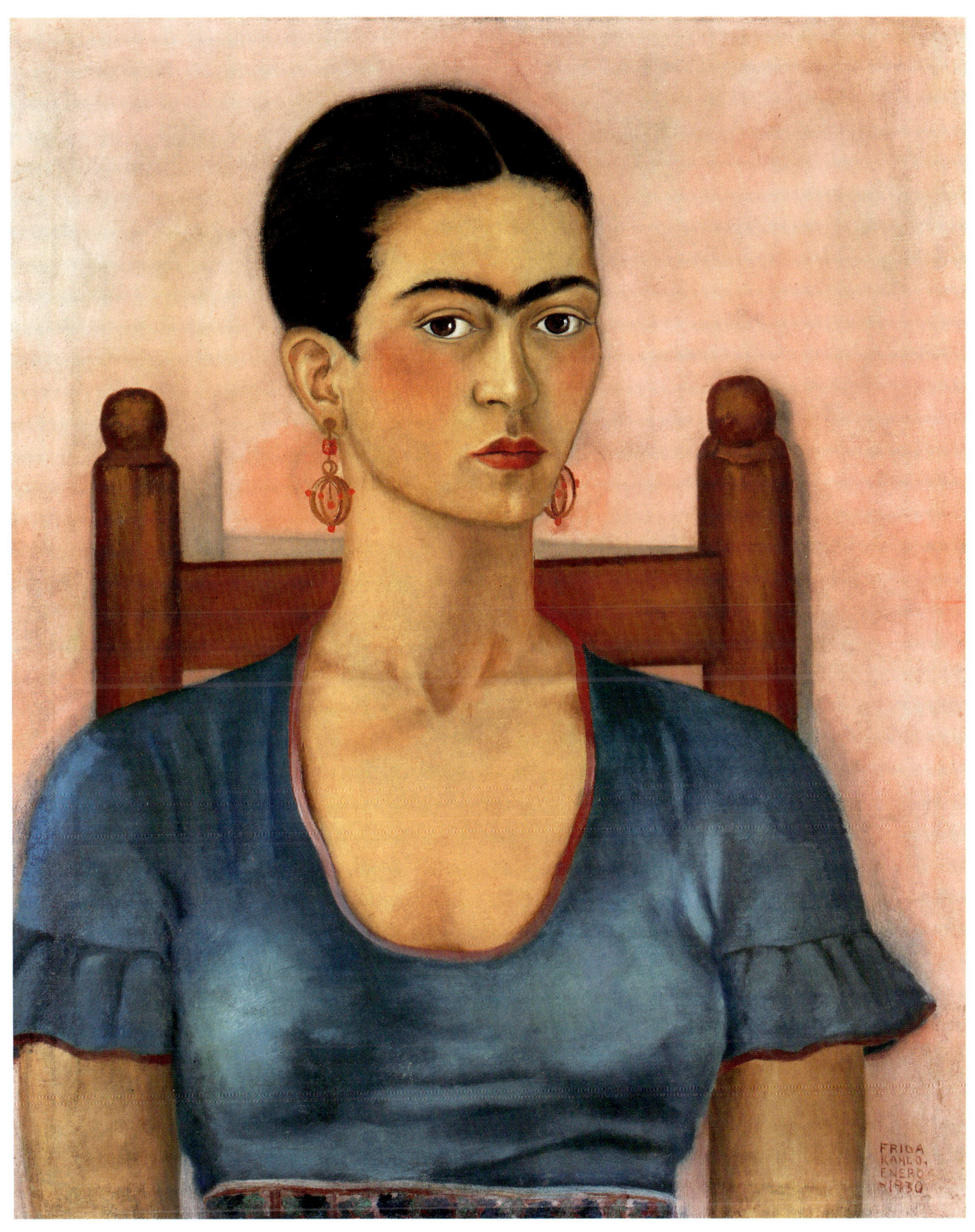

17 SELF-PORTRAIT, 1930

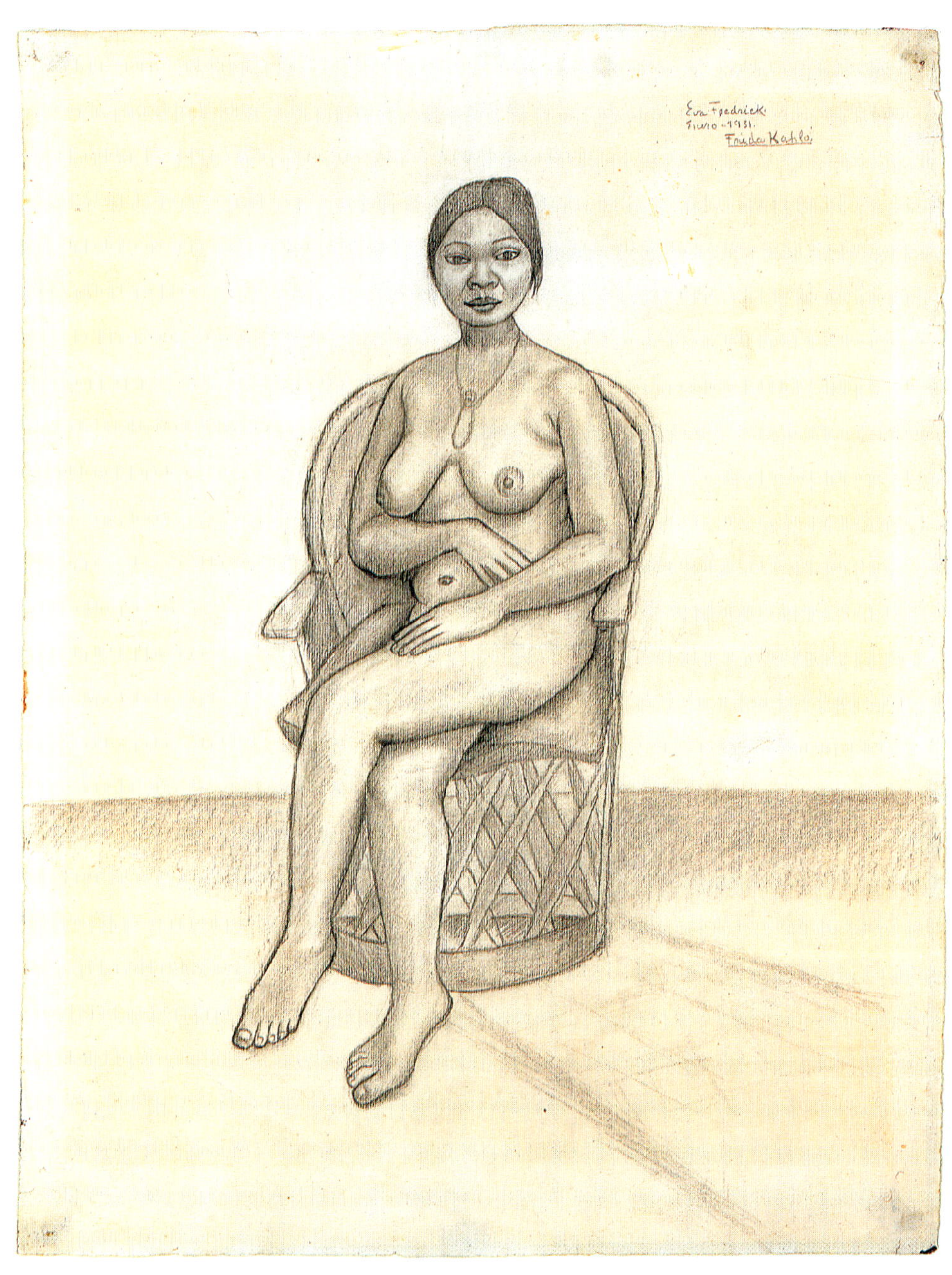

18 NUDE STUDY OF EVA FREDERICK, 1931

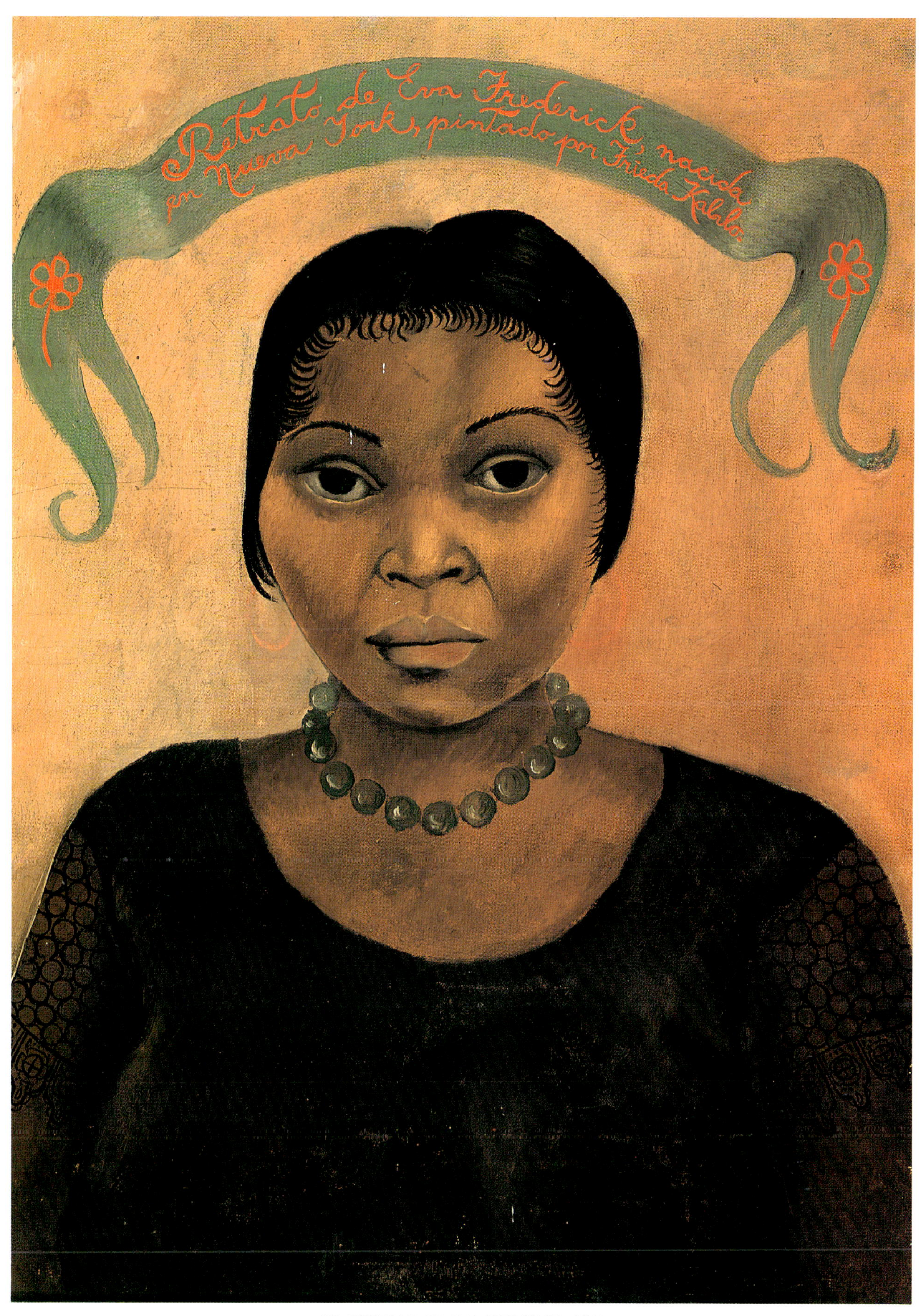

19 PORTRAIT OF EVA FREDERICK, 1931

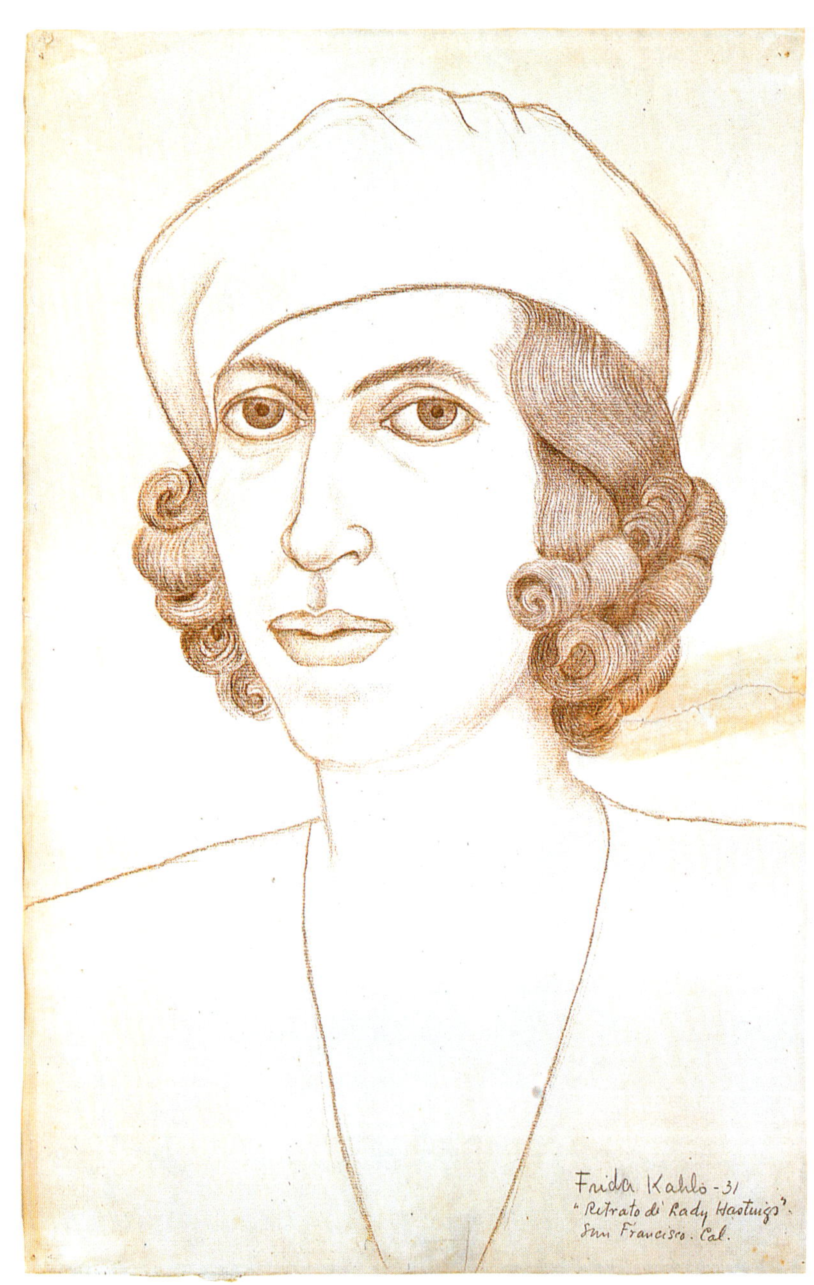

20 PORTRAIT OF LADY CRISTINA HASTINGS, 1931

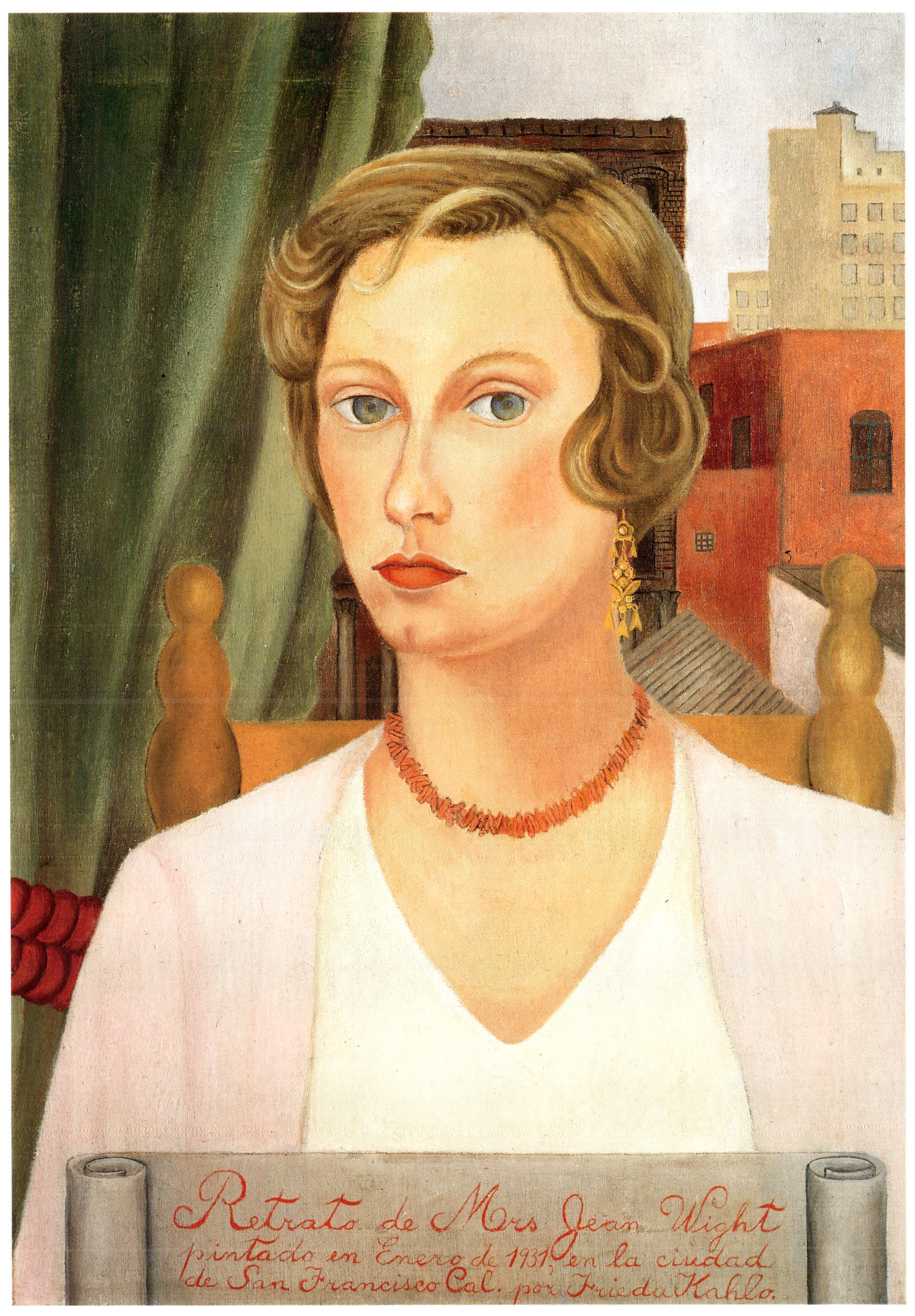

21 PORTRAIT OF MRS. JEAN WIGHT, 1931

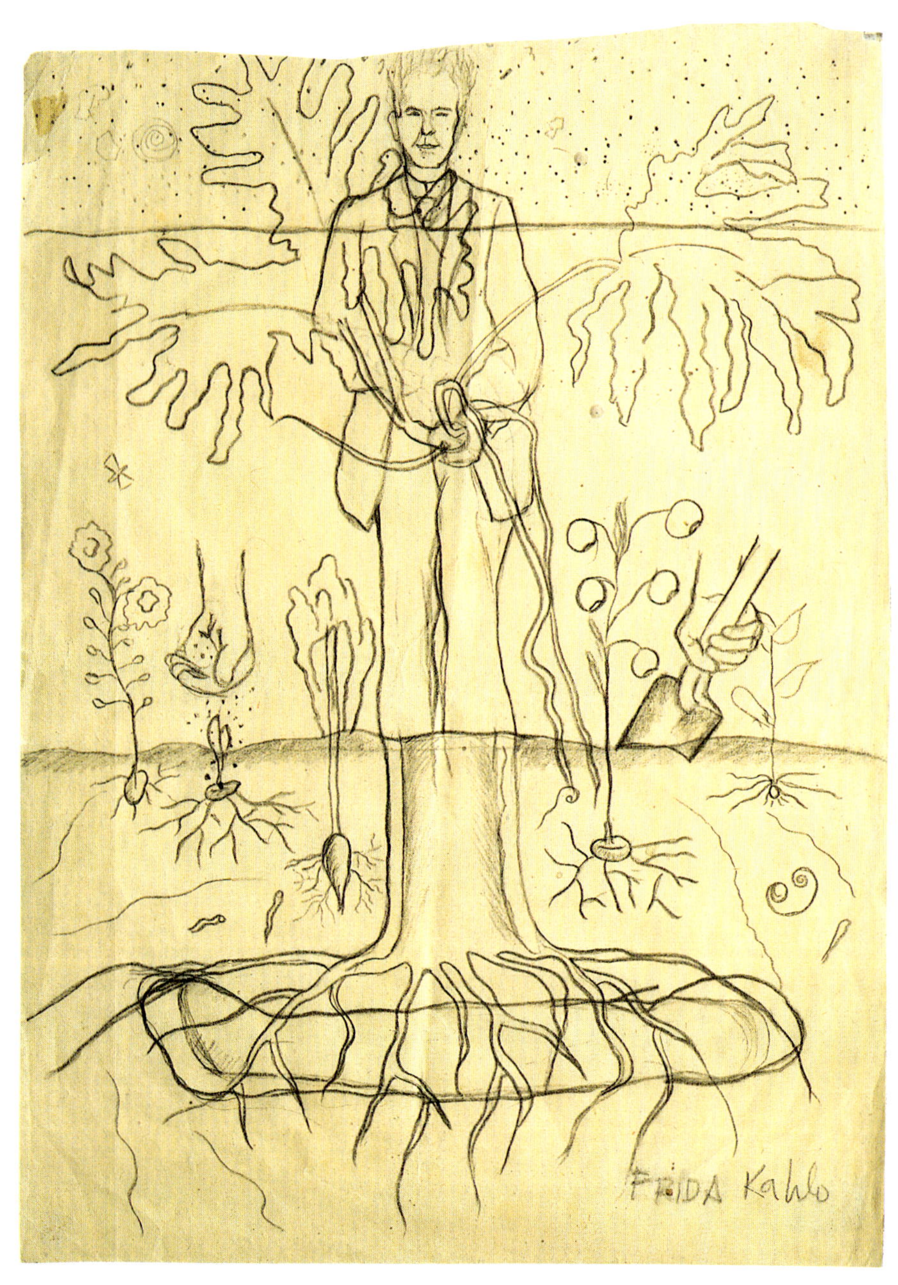

22 PORTRAIT OF LUTHER BURBANK, 1931

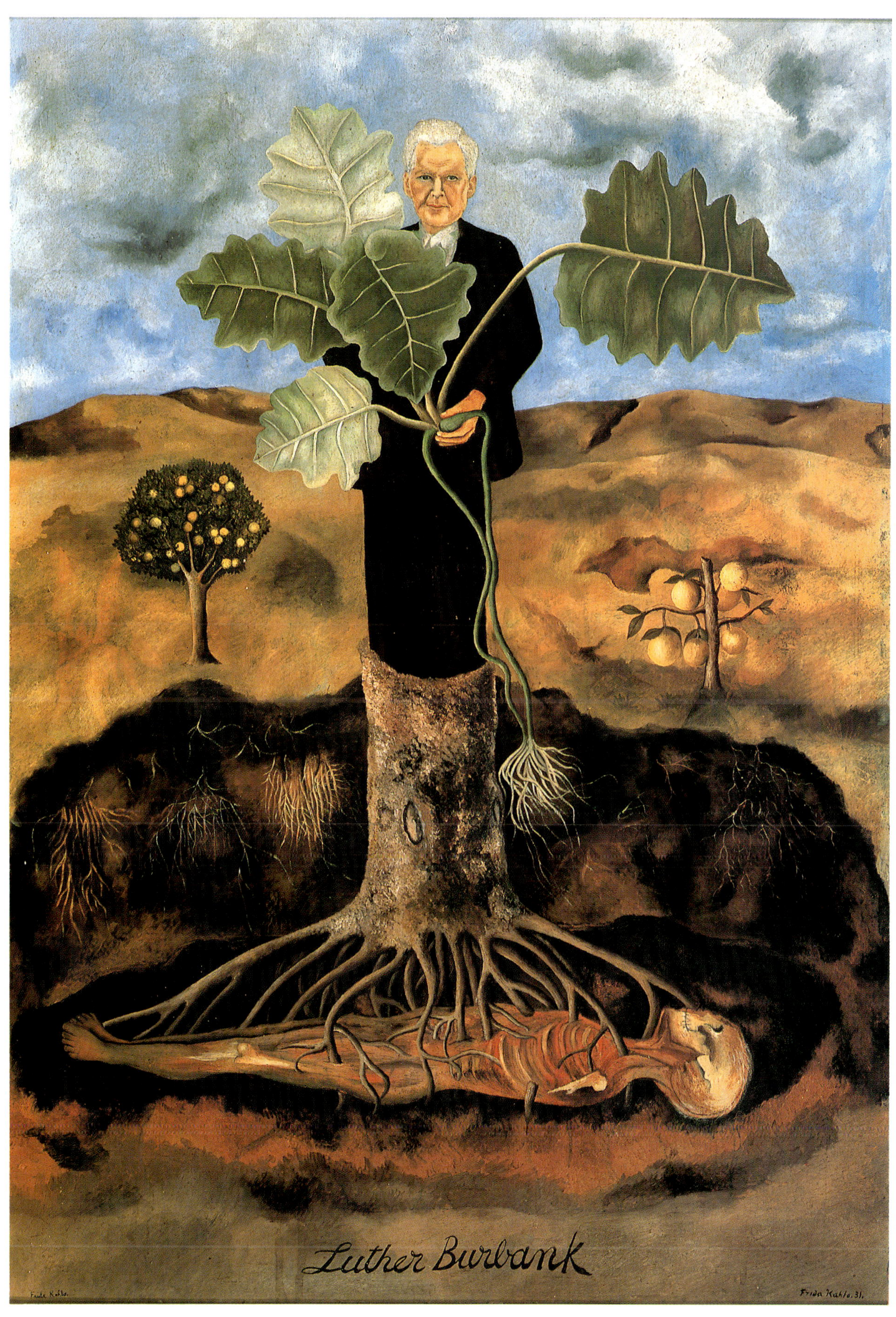

23 PORTRAIT OF LUTHER BURBANK, 1931

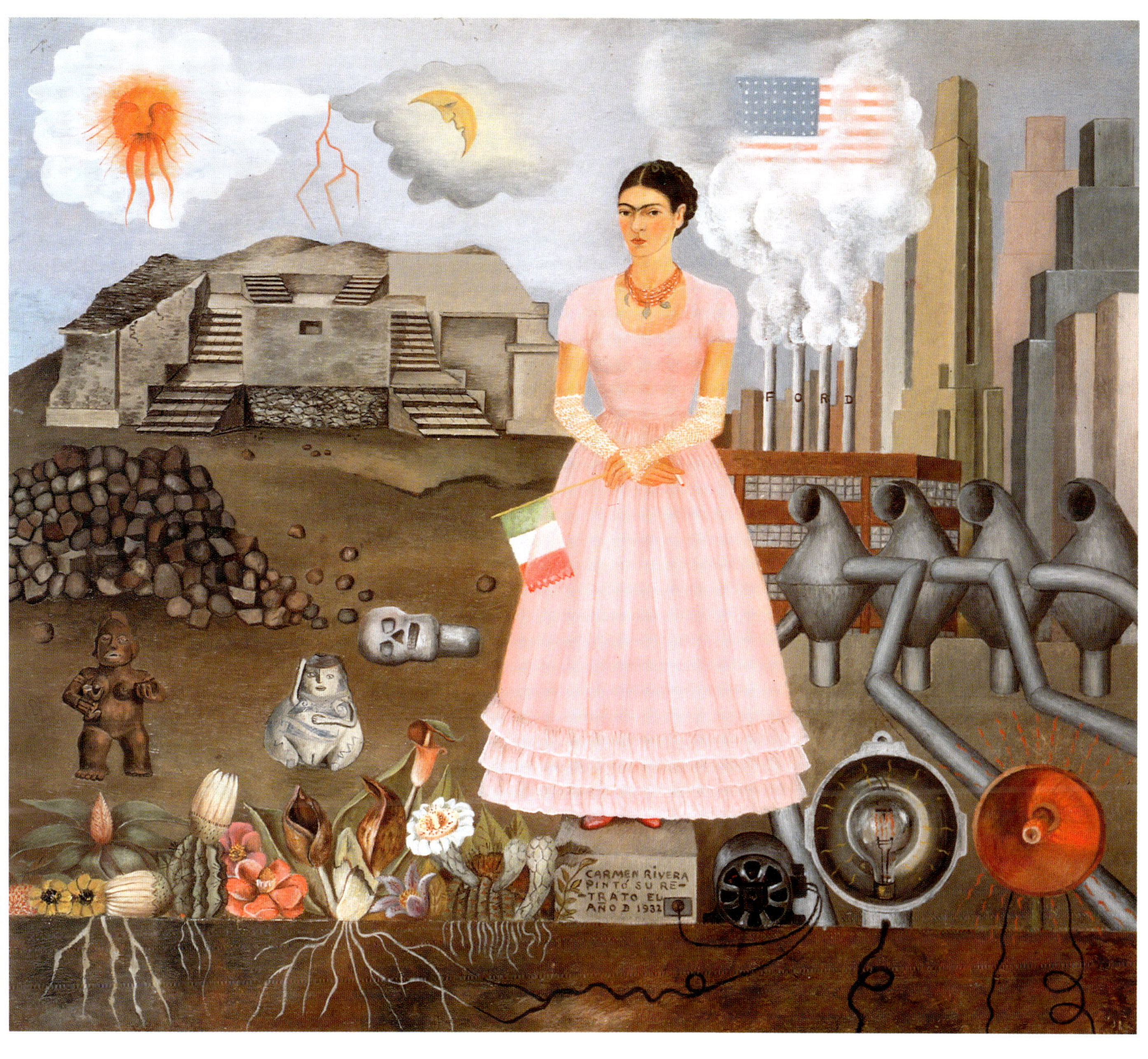

25 SELF-PORTRAIT ON THE BORDER BETWEEN MEXICO AND THE UNITED STATES, 1932

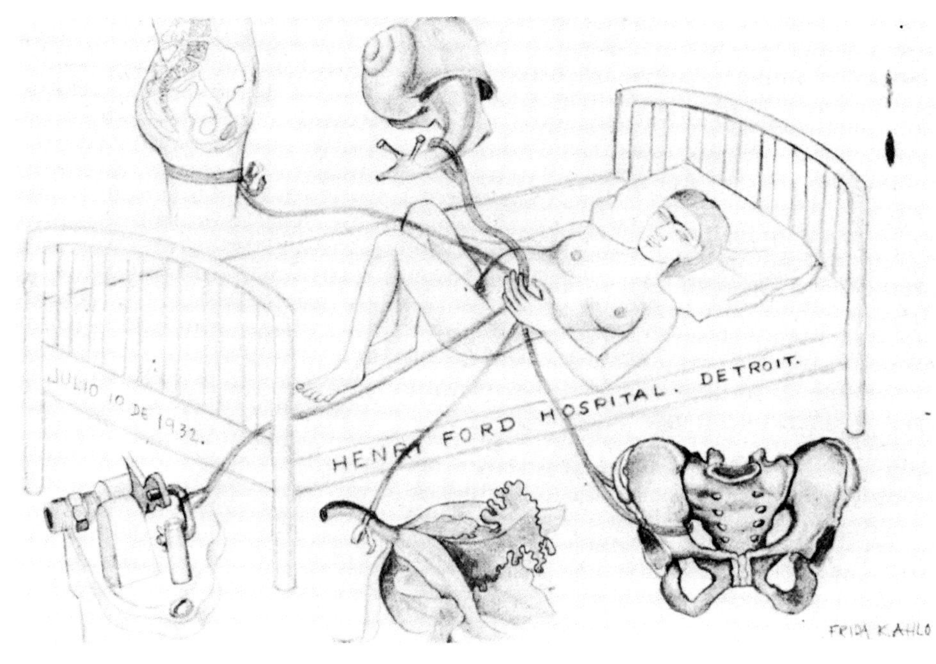

26 STUDY FOR "HENRY FORD HOSPITAL," 1932

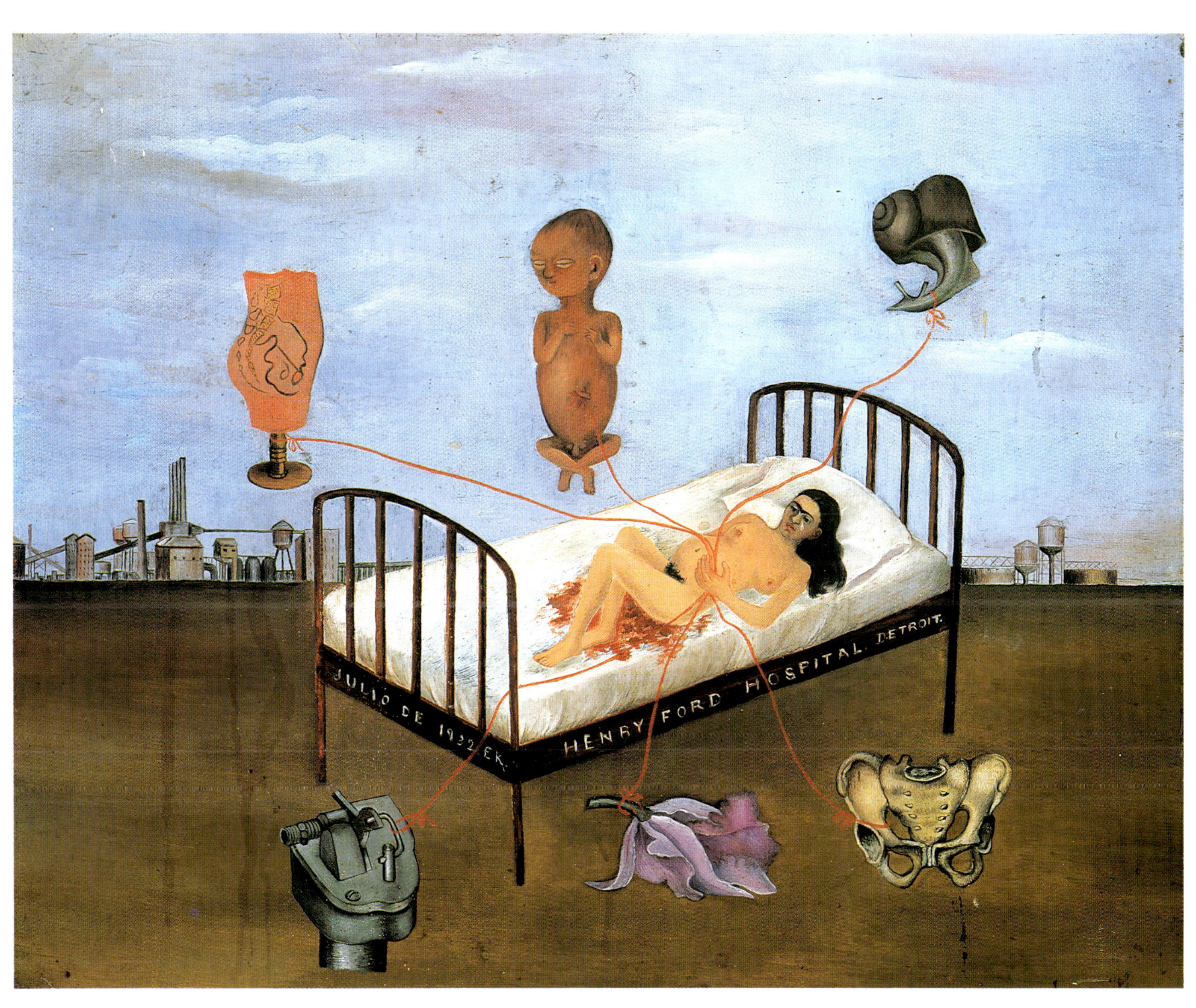

27 HENRY FORD HOSPITAL, 1932

Shortly after her stay at Henry Ford Hospital, Frida Kahlo set out to learn lithography and used this technique in her work *The Miscarriage* (1932), which portrays the kind of anguish she must have felt at the hospital. She probably used as a model the illustrations in a book on histology or embryology, because the final result resembles a page of one of those textbooks, an accurate illustration of the evolution of pregnancy.

On the left is an enlarged male fetus attached to Frida, who is standing in the center, by a vein that winds in a spiral around her healthy leg. Inside her uterus there is a smaller physiologically accurate fetus. Above the male fetus, images of the first phases of cellular development are accompanied by small lateral arrows that separate them. On the right side of the lithograph Frida's body is shaded, perhaps hinting that this is the side that causes her suffering. Big tears streak her face and drops of blood stream down to form a puddle that gives life to several large plants. The foliage of these plants resembles human organs, very similar to those of the male fetus. The shaded and unshaded halves of Frida's body represent the dualities of pain and joy, life and death. On the right side of the print there is a weeping moon, a third arm holding a heart-shaped palette, sperm lined up on a precise, straight line, and many small droplets. This is the first of Frida's works in which the lower limb affected by polio is clearly visible. The atrophied leg and the stiff foot with its cramped toes, both on the shaded side of the lithograph, are typical of the disease. There is no clear proof that repercussions from her accident had any effect on Frida's fertility, since only one of her labia majora was injured, and she became normally pregnant after marrying Rivera. It therefore appears that her sterility was secondary, namely, that it resulted from her miscarriages.

Rafael Vázquez Bayod

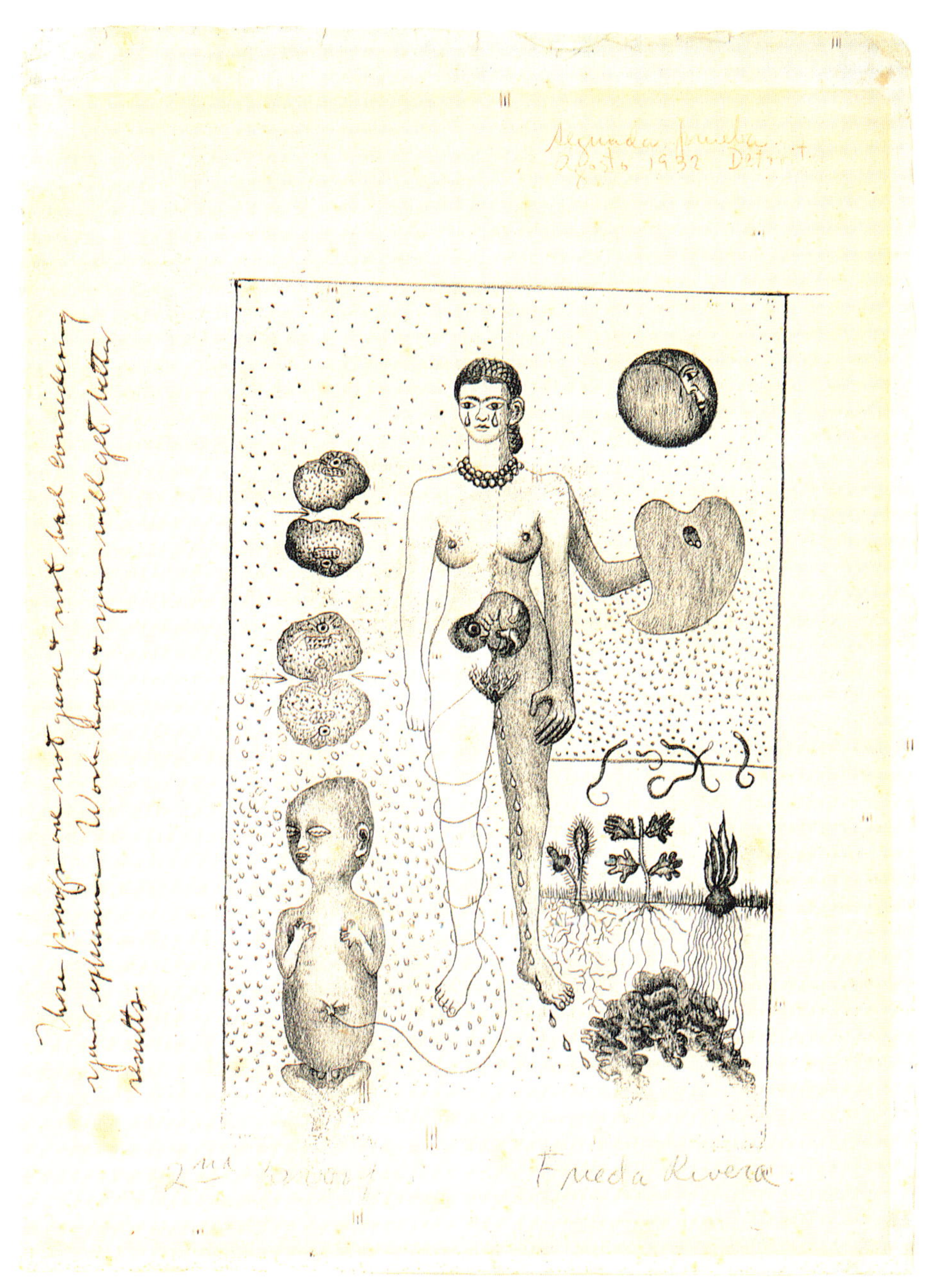

28 THE MISCARRIAGE, 1932

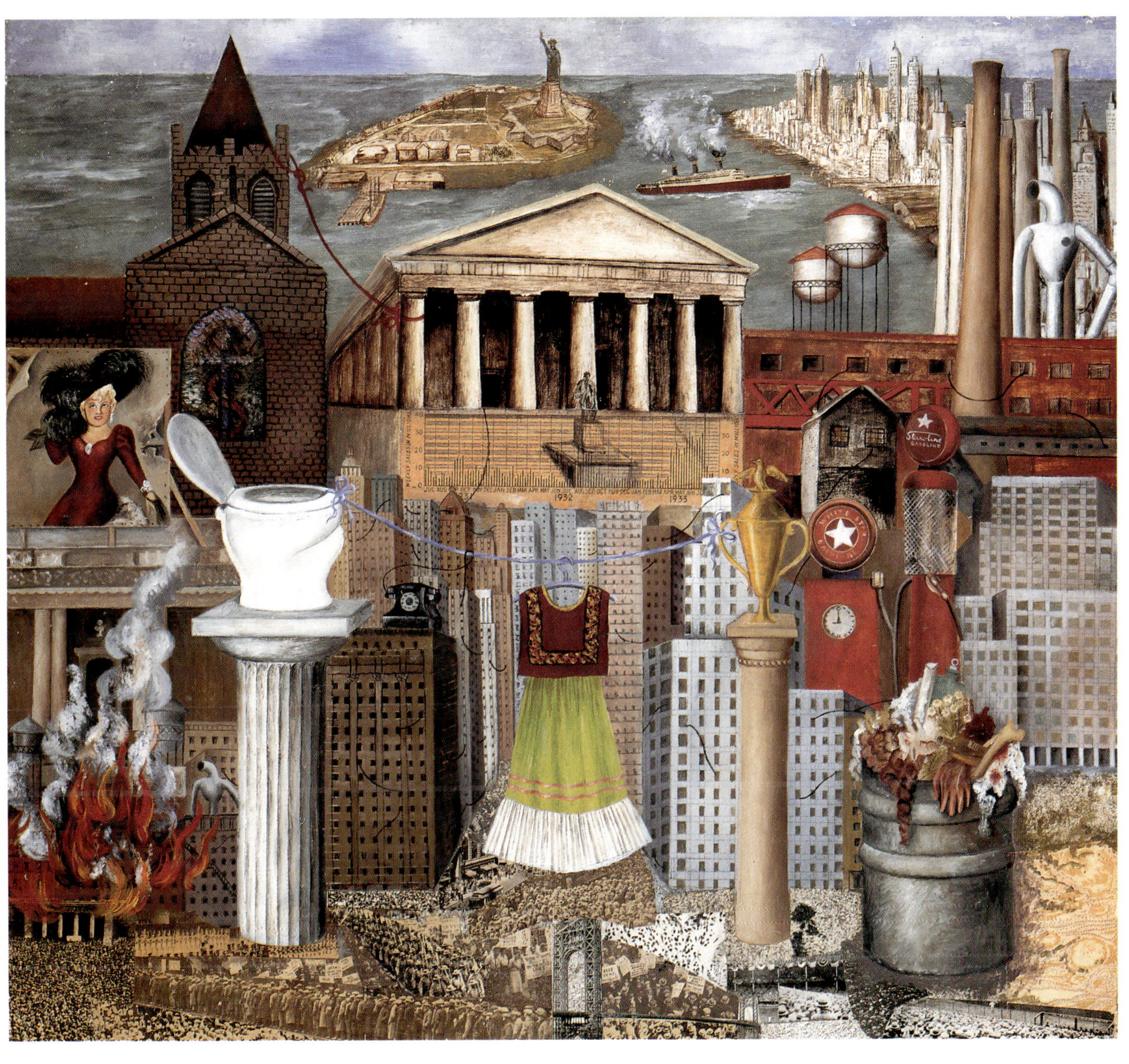

32 MY DRESS HANGS THERE, 1933

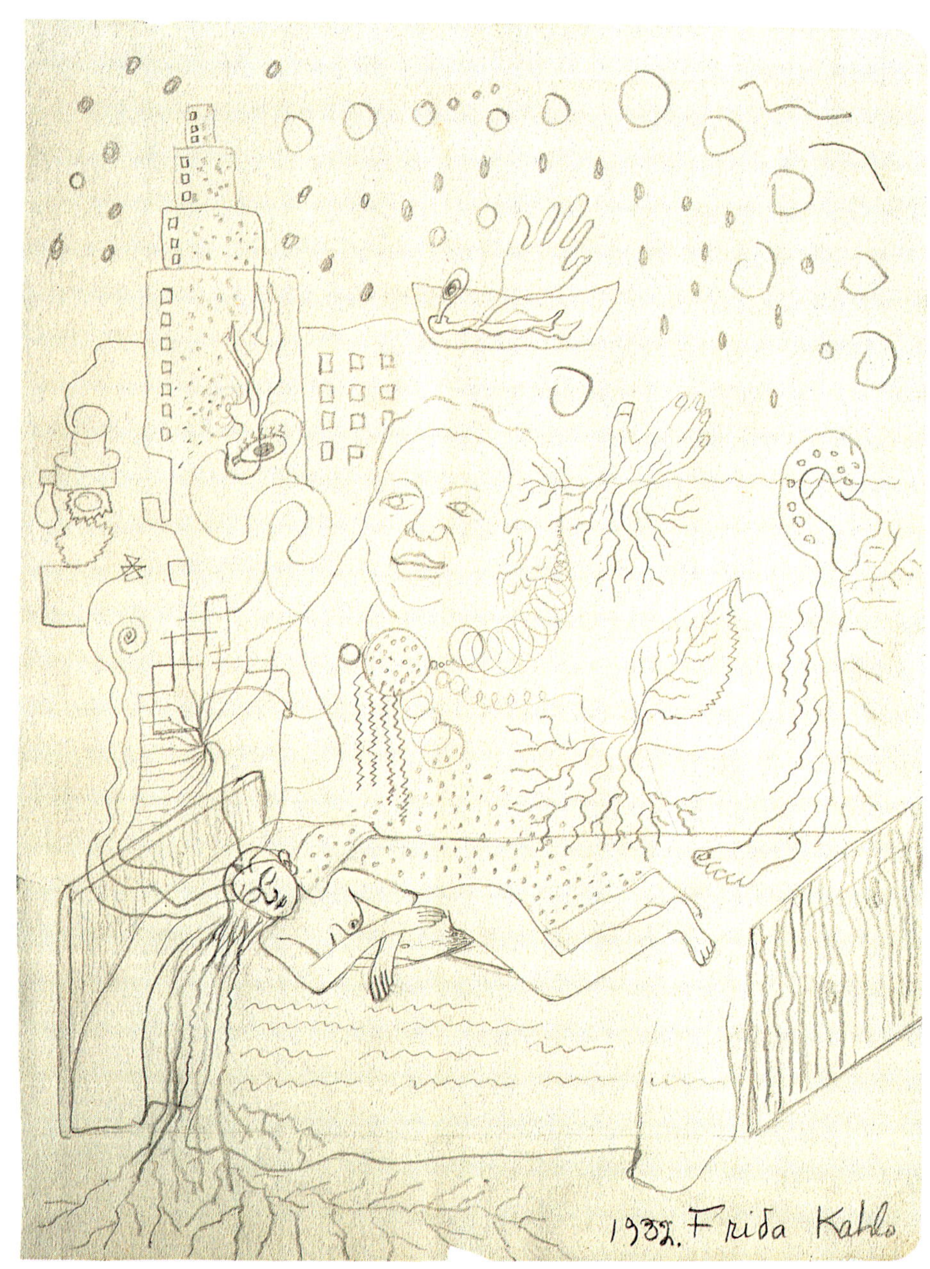

24 SELF-PORTRAIT DREAMING (I), before 1932

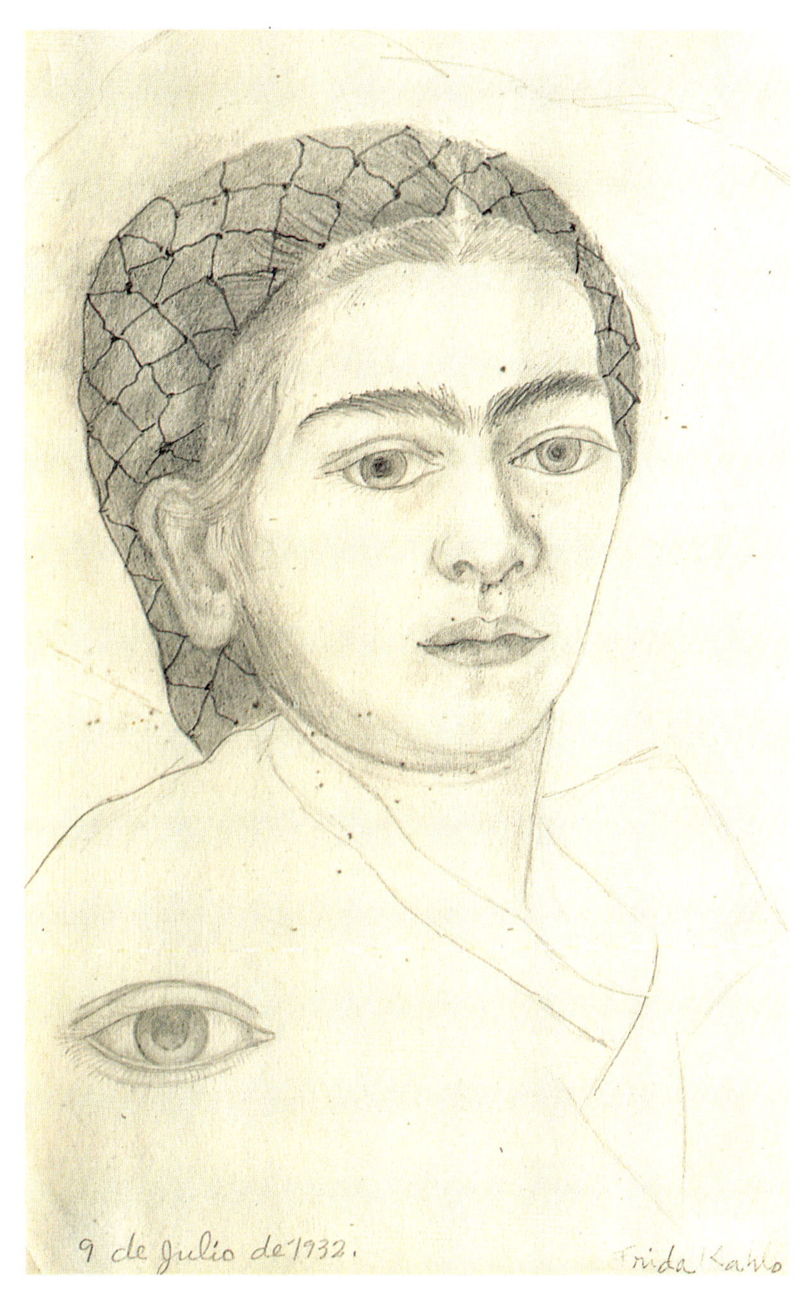

29 SELF-PORTRAIT, «9 JULY, 1932»

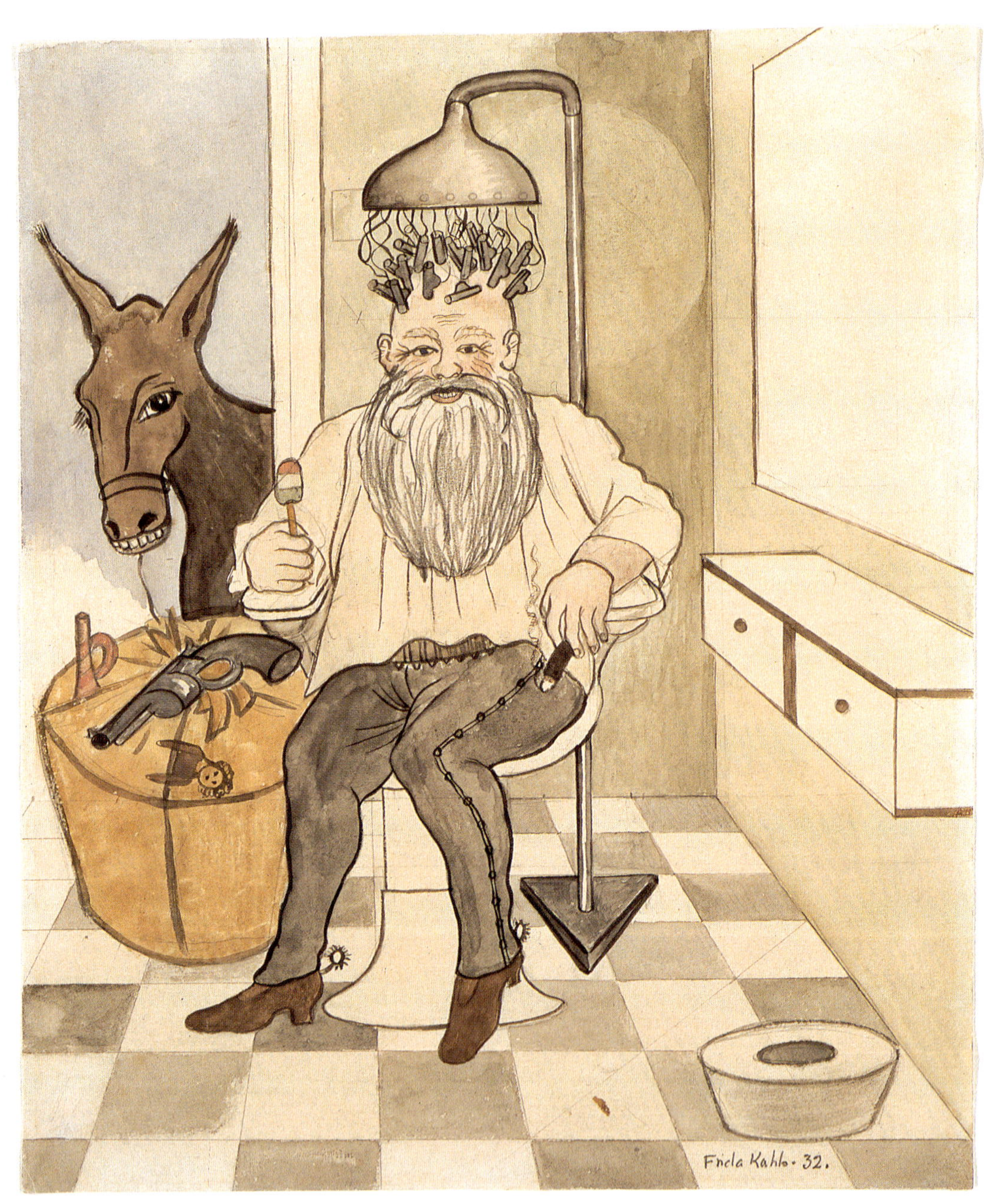

30 BEAUTY PARLOR, 1932

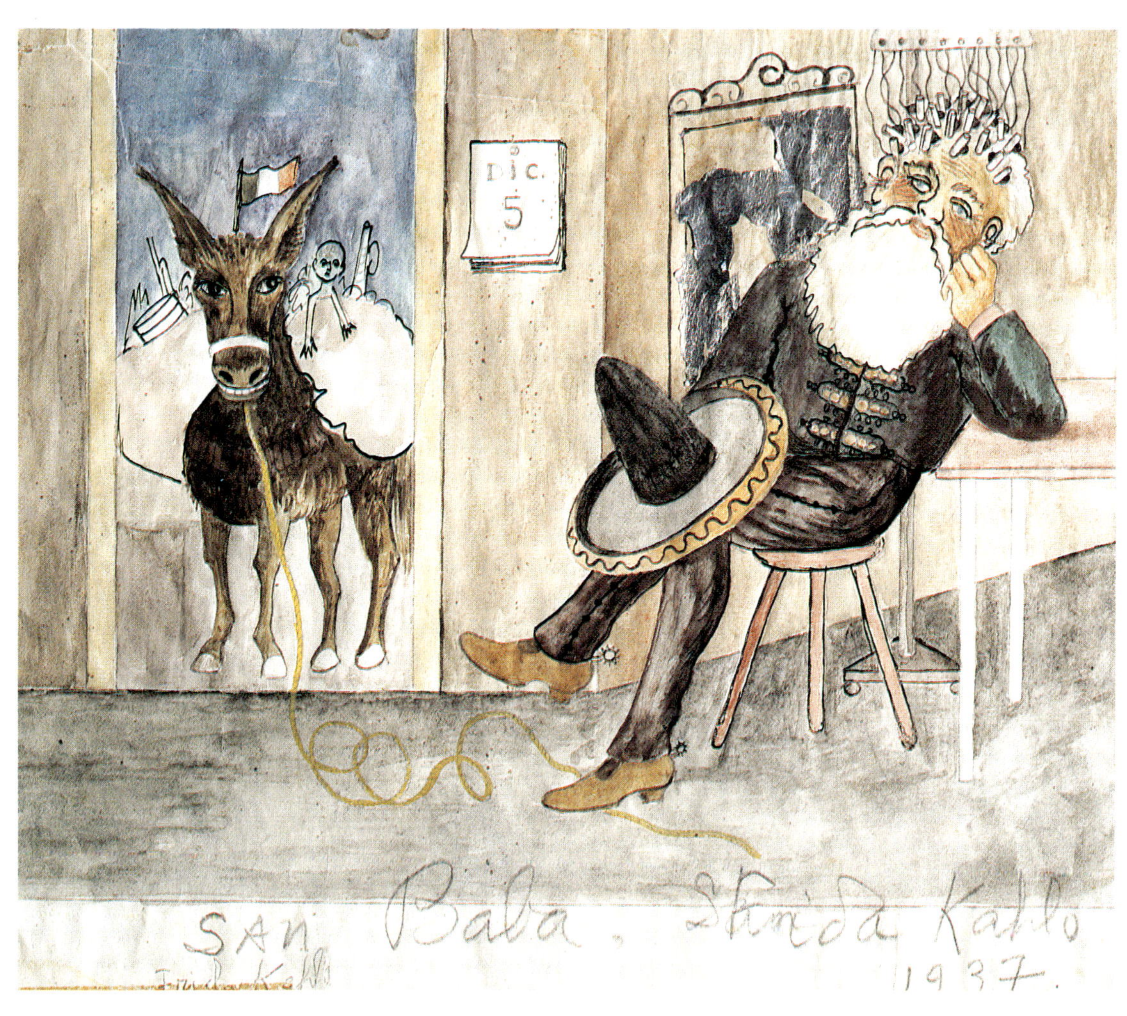

37 SANTA CLAUS, circa 1932, dated 1937

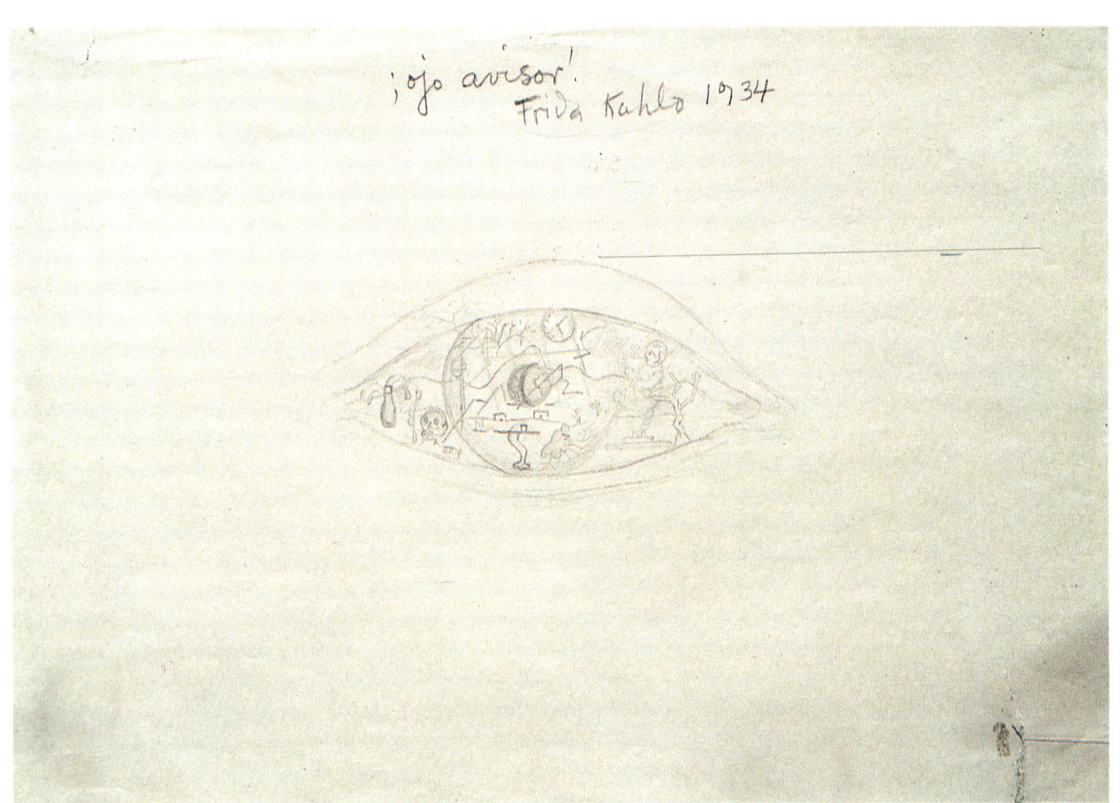

34 ALL-SEEING EYE, 1934

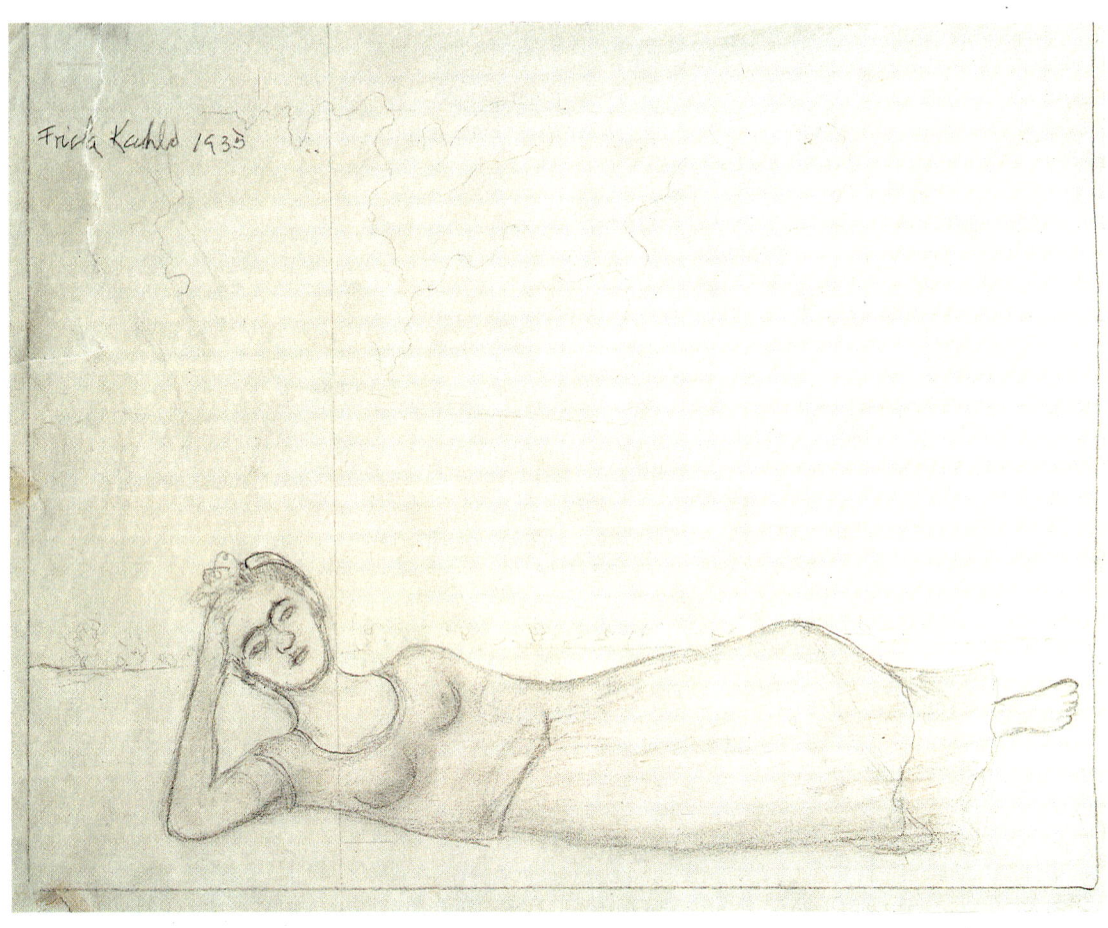

35 RECLINING SELF-PORTRAIT, 1935

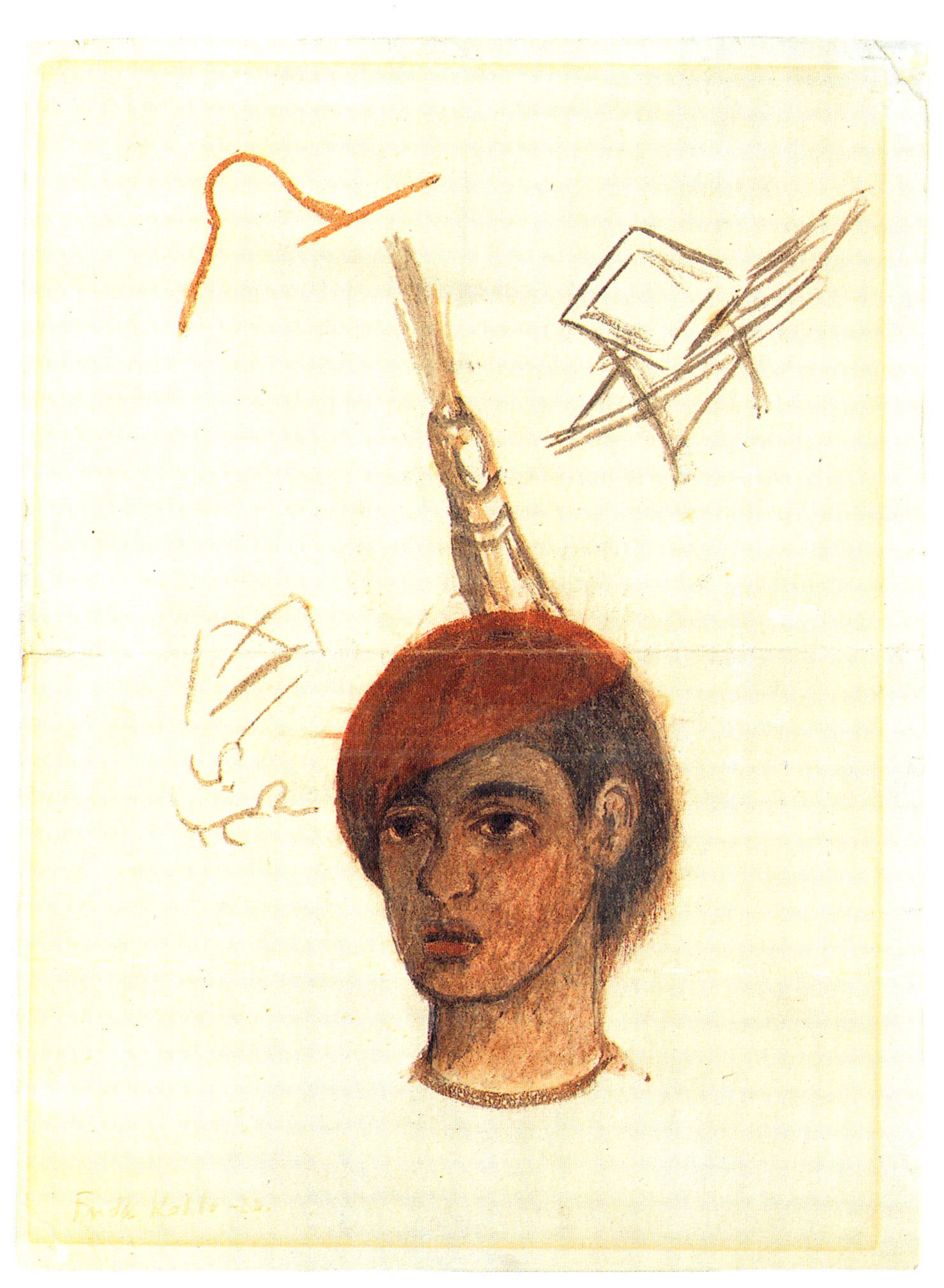

31 HEAD, 1932

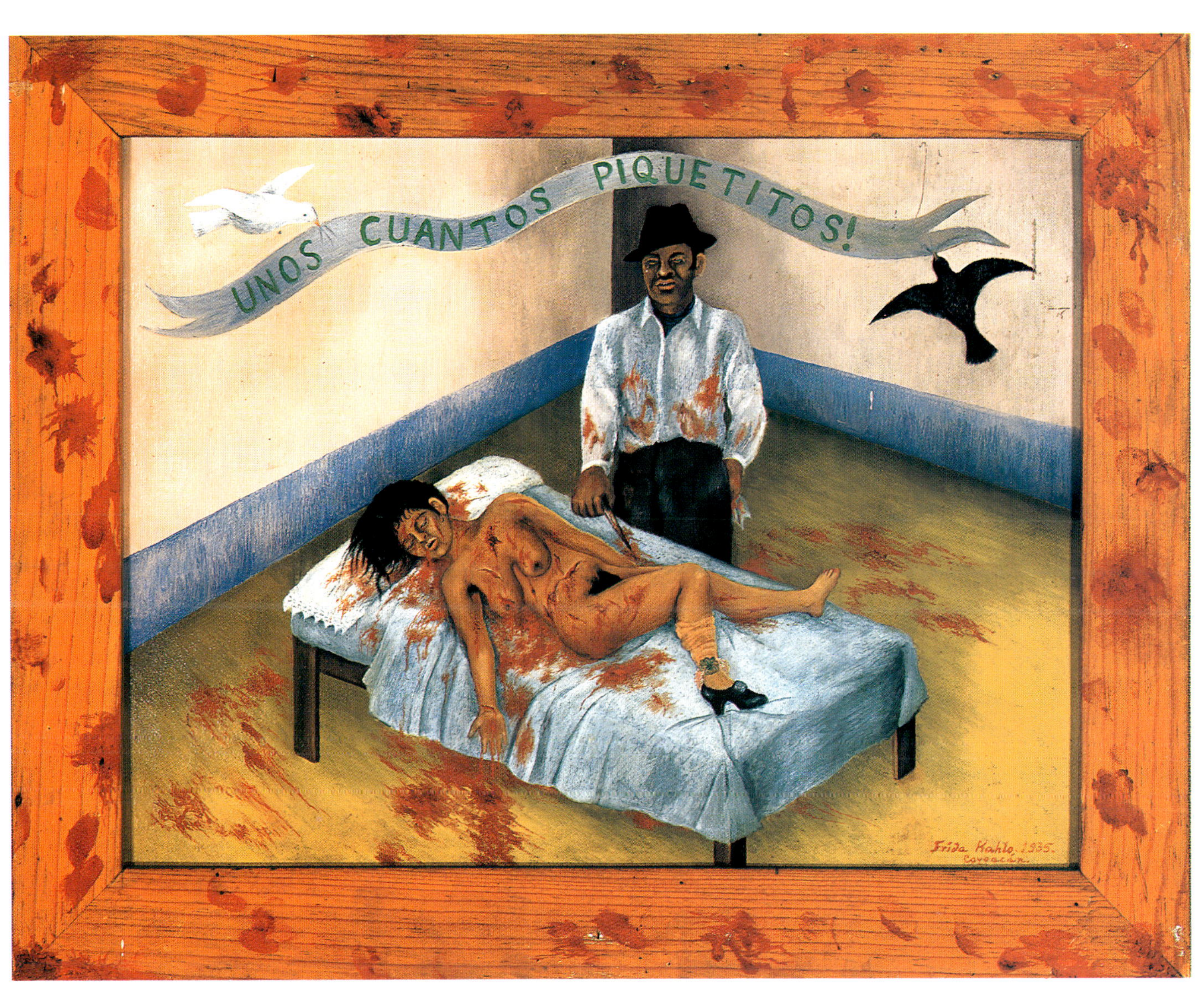

36 A FEW SMALL NIPS, 1935

Frida is the only example in the history of art of someone who ripped open her insides and her heart to tell the biological truth of her feelings. She painted her mother and her wet nurse although she knew that, in reality, she did not know their faces. The picture of the wet nurse is only an Indian mask of hard stone and her milk glands are grapes from which milk drops, like the rain that fertilizes the earth and the tears that fertilize joy; and the one of the mother, a mother in pain with the seven daggers of grief who made the rupture out of which Frida comes possible. She is the first person since the expressive Aztec master who made a sculpture of black basalt, to portray the real process of birth. A birth which brought forth the only woman who, with unparalleled physical dedication, portrayed in her works of art the feelings, tasks, and creative possibilities of the woman. A birth that brought into the world the most important female painter, who is the best proof of the existence of a renaissance in Mexican art.

Diego Rivera

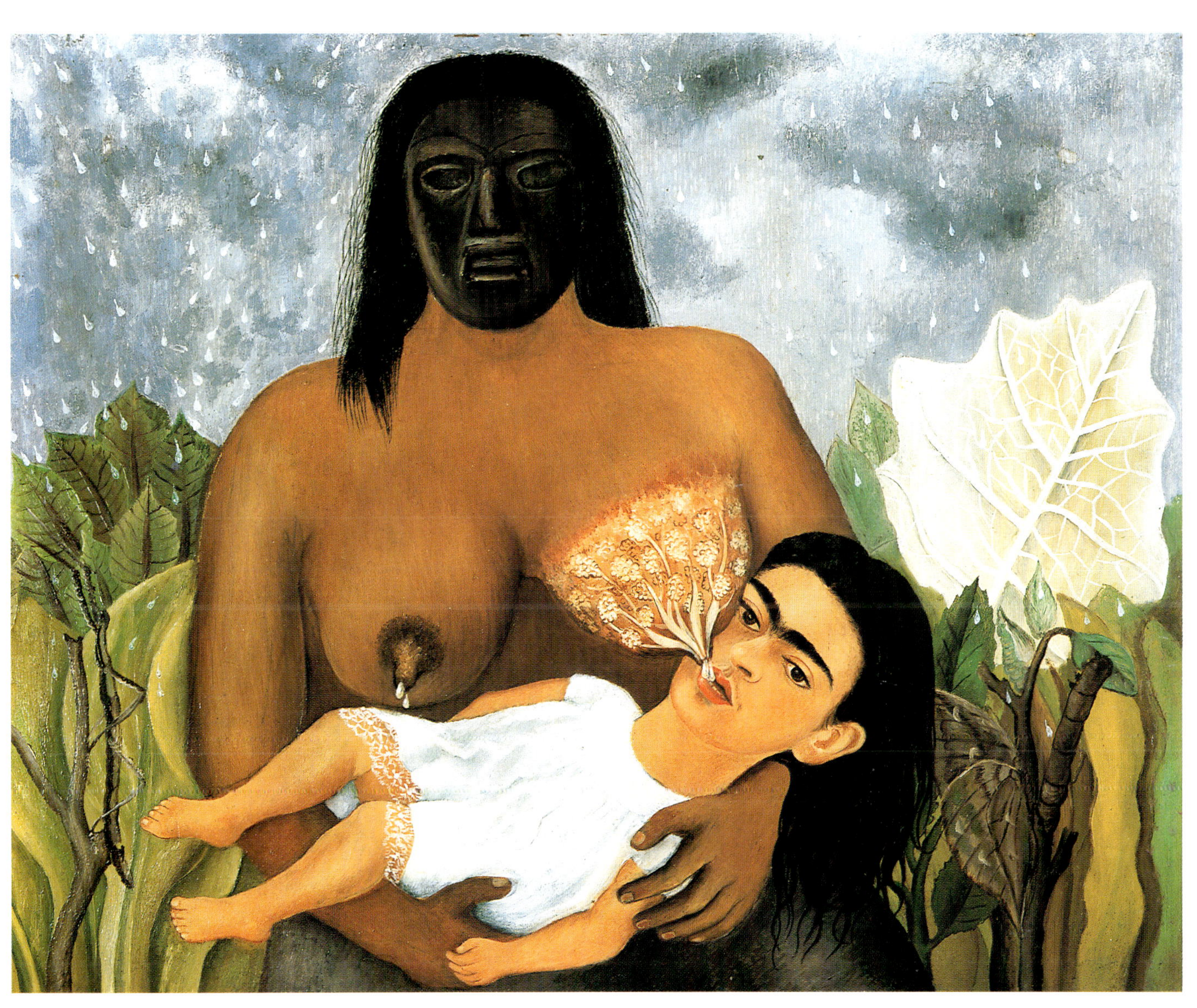

39 MY NURSE AND I, 1937

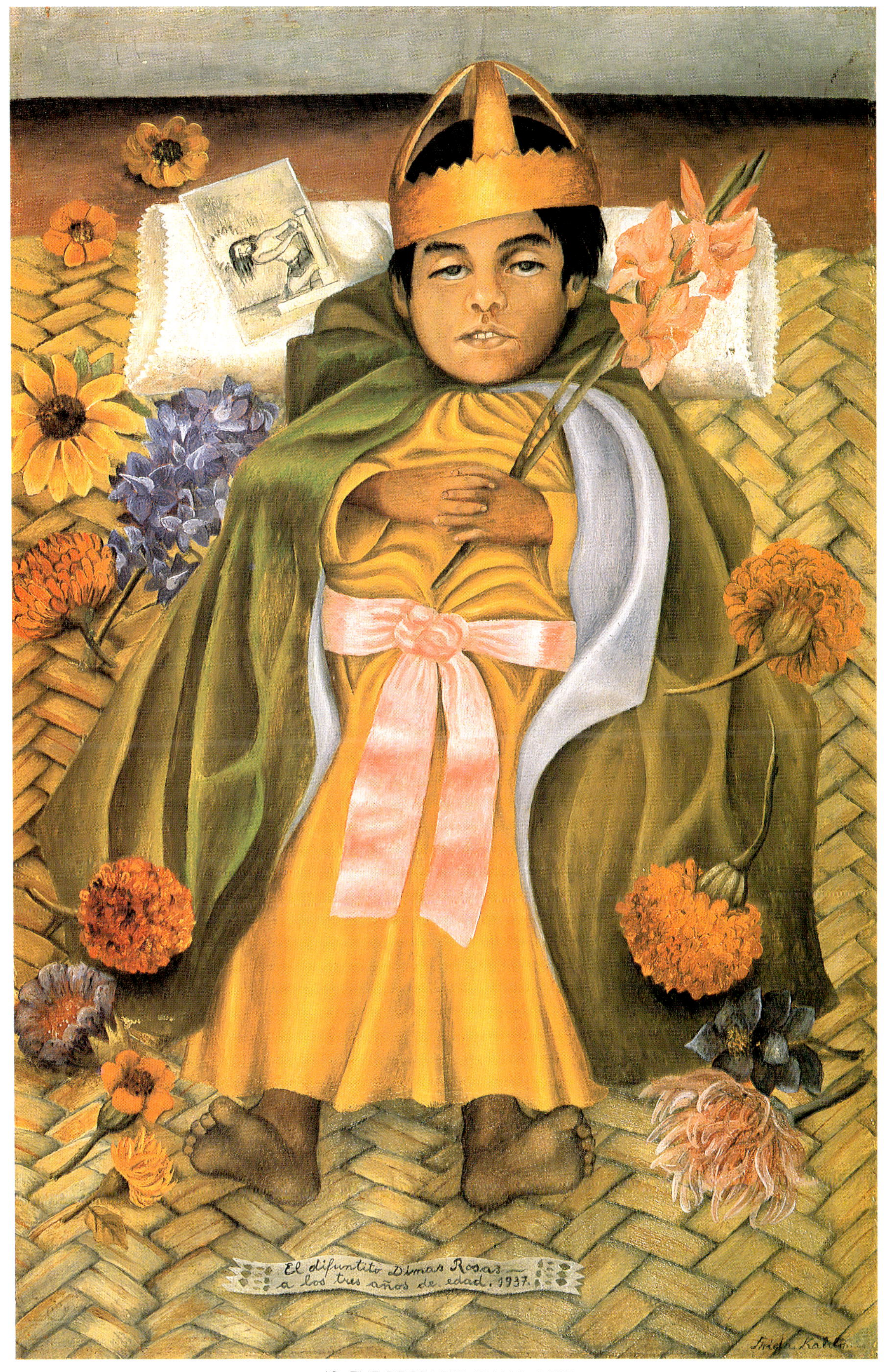

40 THE DECEASED DIMAS, 1937

For a long time I have admired the self-portrait by Frida Kahlo de Rivera that hangs on a wall in Trotsky's study. She has portrayed herself in a dress that looks like folded wings and is studded with golden butterflies. And just in this dress she succeeds in removing the mental veil from our familiar perceptions. We are allowed to be present as observers when a young woman, equipped with every possible art of enticement – exactly in the sense of the glorious days of German Romanticism – enters the society of men of genius.

André Breton

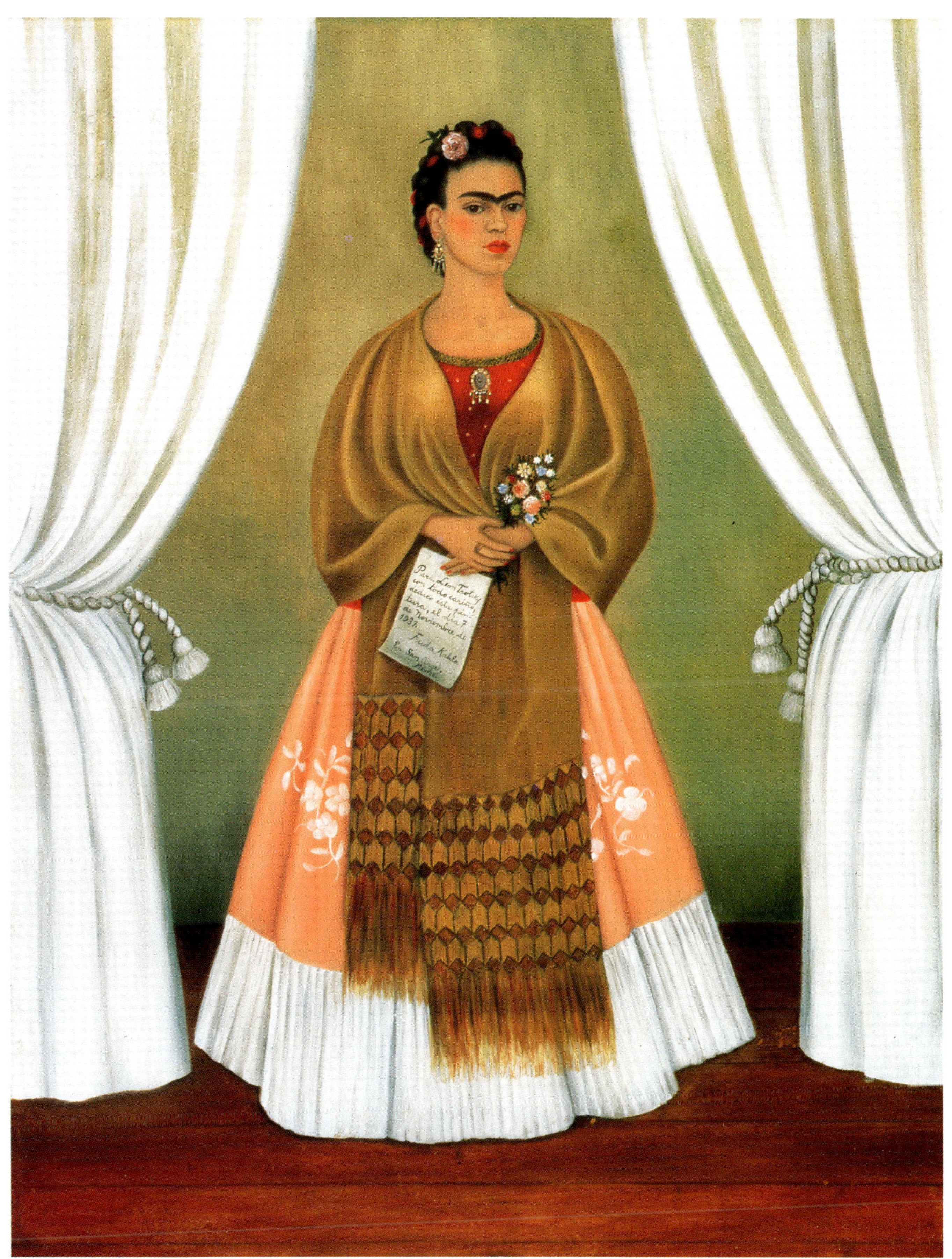

41 SELF-PORTRAIT DEDICATED TO LEON TROTSKY, 1937

I never suspected that the world of fruits could bring forth something as wonderful as the *pitahaya,* the pulp of which has the color and appearance of rolled-up rose leaves – the *pitahaya* with its juicy flesh and its taste like a kiss of love and desire; I had never held in my hand a lump of that red earth that the statuettes of Colima – half woman, half cricket – and made up like goddesses, emerged from; and finally I had never set eyes on those things that, in their posture and jewelry, are so much like a fairy princess with magic powers in her fingertips, in the ray of light of the bird Quetzal which, when he flies away, scatters opal on the edges of the rock: Frida Kahlo de Rivera.

André Breton

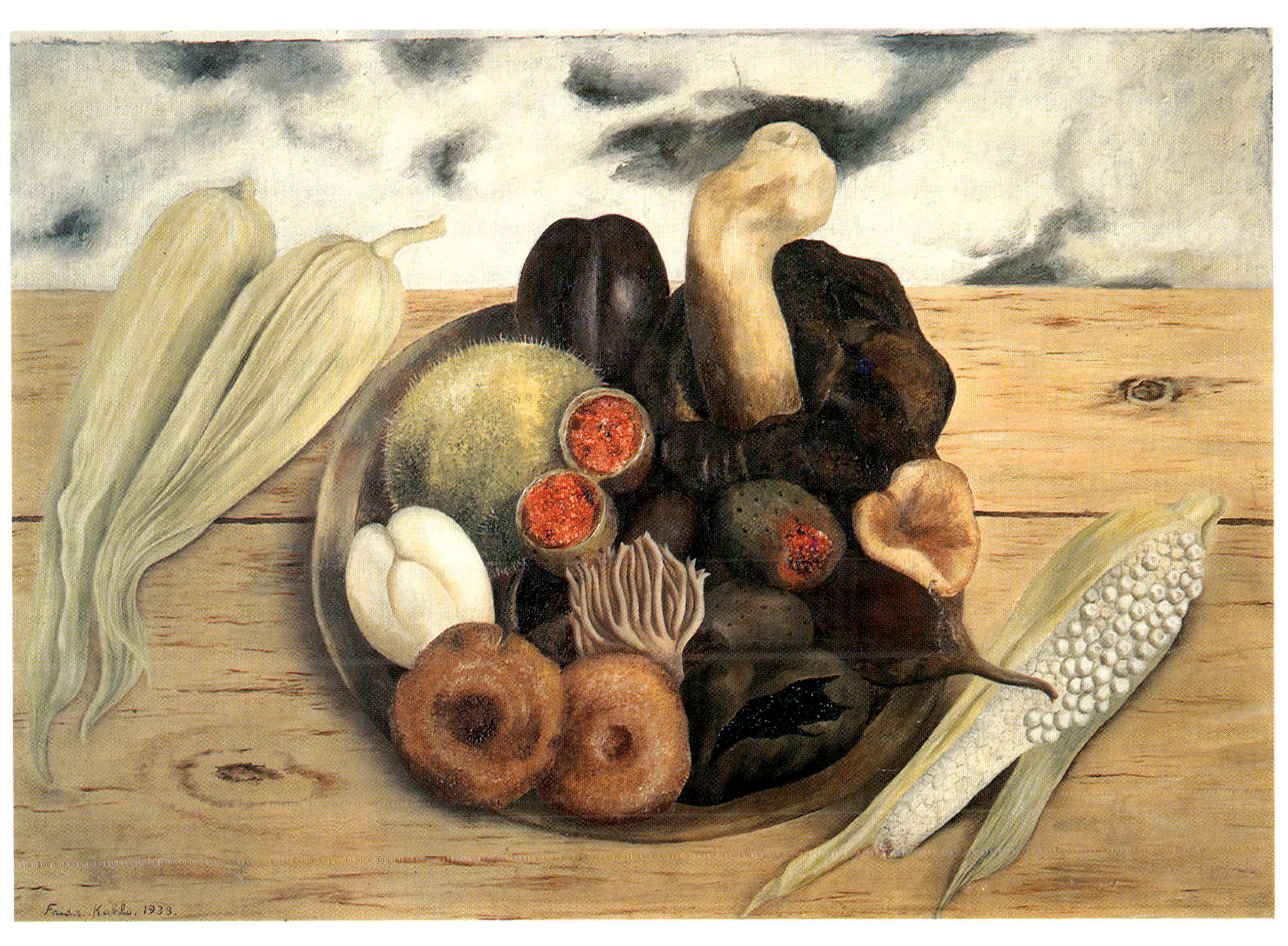

42 FRUITS OF THE EARTH, 1938

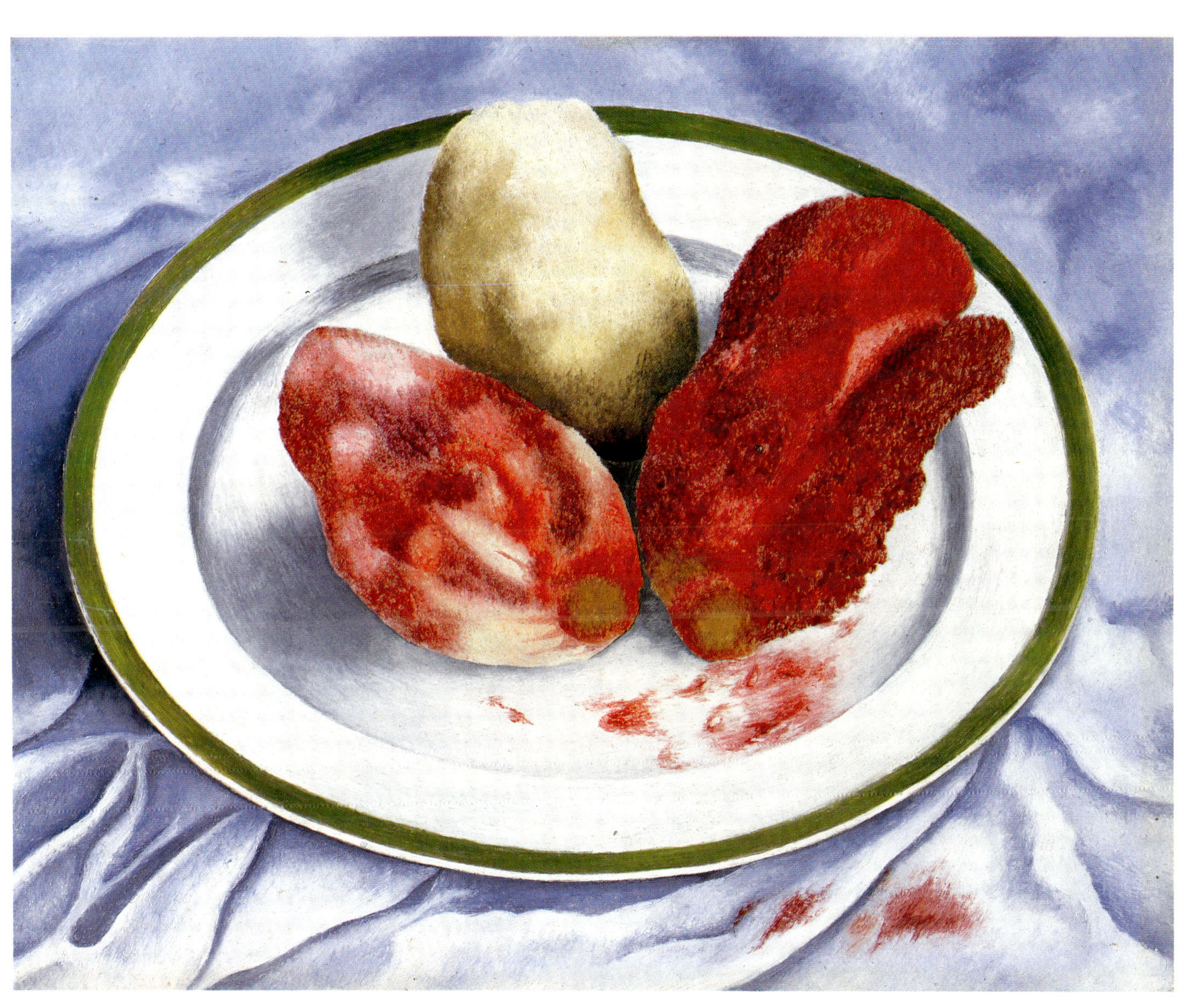

43 TUNAS (STILL LIFE WITH PRICKLY PEAR FRUIT), 1938

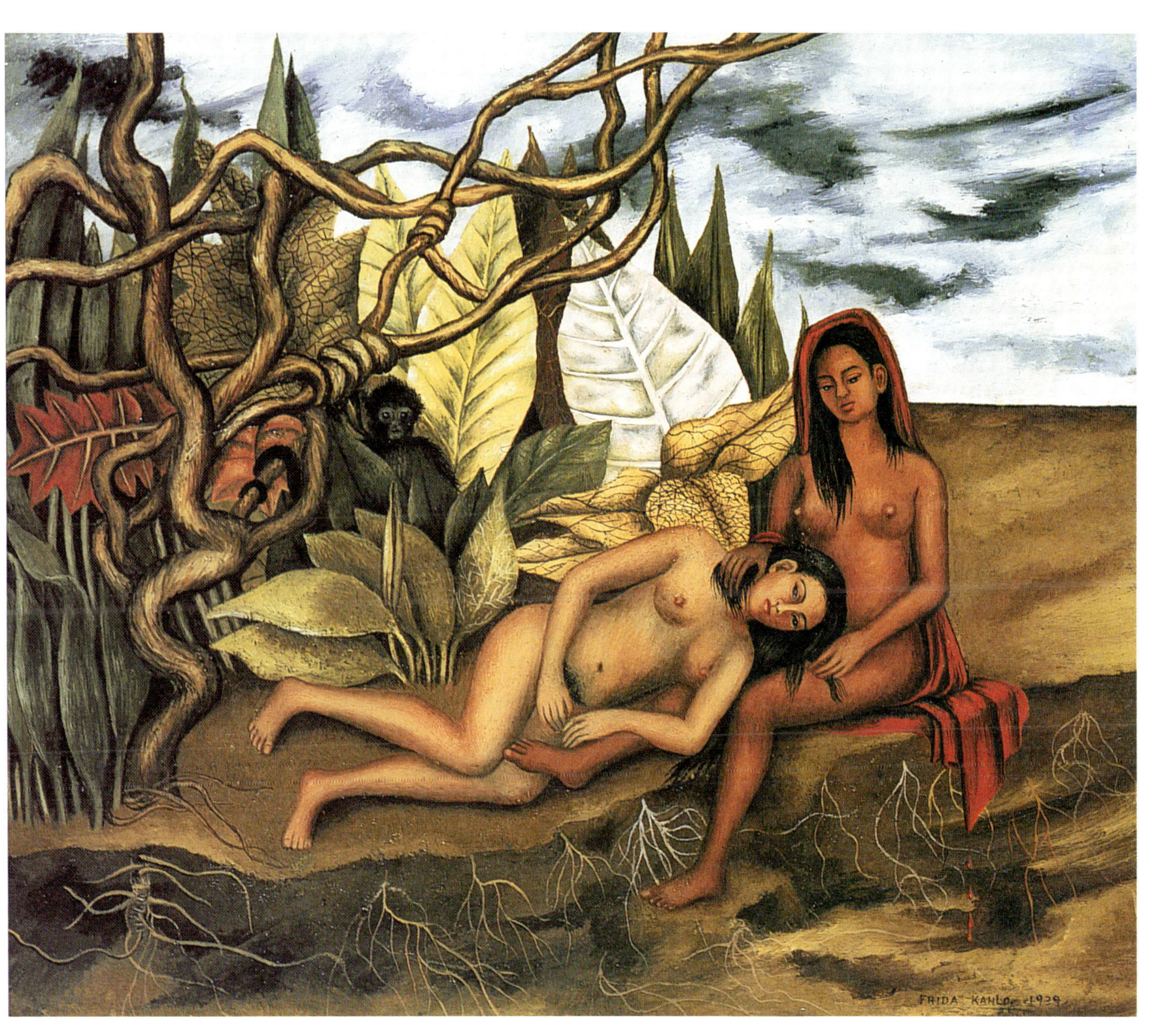

44 TWO NUDES IN THE FOREST, 1939

In spite of the power that characterizes all of her work, *The Two Fridas* (1939) is perhaps one of her best-known paintings. It consists of two life-size self-portraits that the artist completed almost at the same time as her divorce from Rivera, an event that partially explains the painting. The Frida dressed as a Tehuana is the one that Rivera loved; the other, in Victorian dress, is the one he no longer loves. Both are seated on a bench, holding hands, while their other hands rest close to their genitalia. The loved Frida holds a picture of Rivera as a child. From it a vein winds up to her vena cava and continues behind the other Frida's back to connect with her. The vein then bifurcates in her body; one of its branches enters the vena cava and the heart, while the other reaches her hand where, stopped by pincers, it gushes blood that stains the whiteness of the dress. Although Frida said to Rivera about this painting: "My Blood is the miracle that flows through the veins of the air, from my heart to yours," a detailed analysis leads to a radically different interpretation, since the blood stream, the vital liquid, starts from Rivera pictured as a child, and nourishes both Fridas. Joined by the same vein, the unloved Frida lets the blood flow; the loved Frida, instead, by the placement of Rivera's portrait and the open stance of her legs, noticeable under her skirt, provocatively evokes the attitude of the sexual act.

The artist's remarkable knowledge of anatomy and physiology deserves mention. In both portraits her painting of the hearts is so perfect that they seem to come directly from a medical textbook. The very idea for the painting seems to have been inspired by the process of a blood transfusion. From the medical point of view, it could well be an illustration of the cardiovascular hemodynamics of a person-to-person transfusion, a quite common procedure at the time. The surgical pincers themselves are impressive; they are exactly like those used in such cases.

Rafael Vázquez Bayod

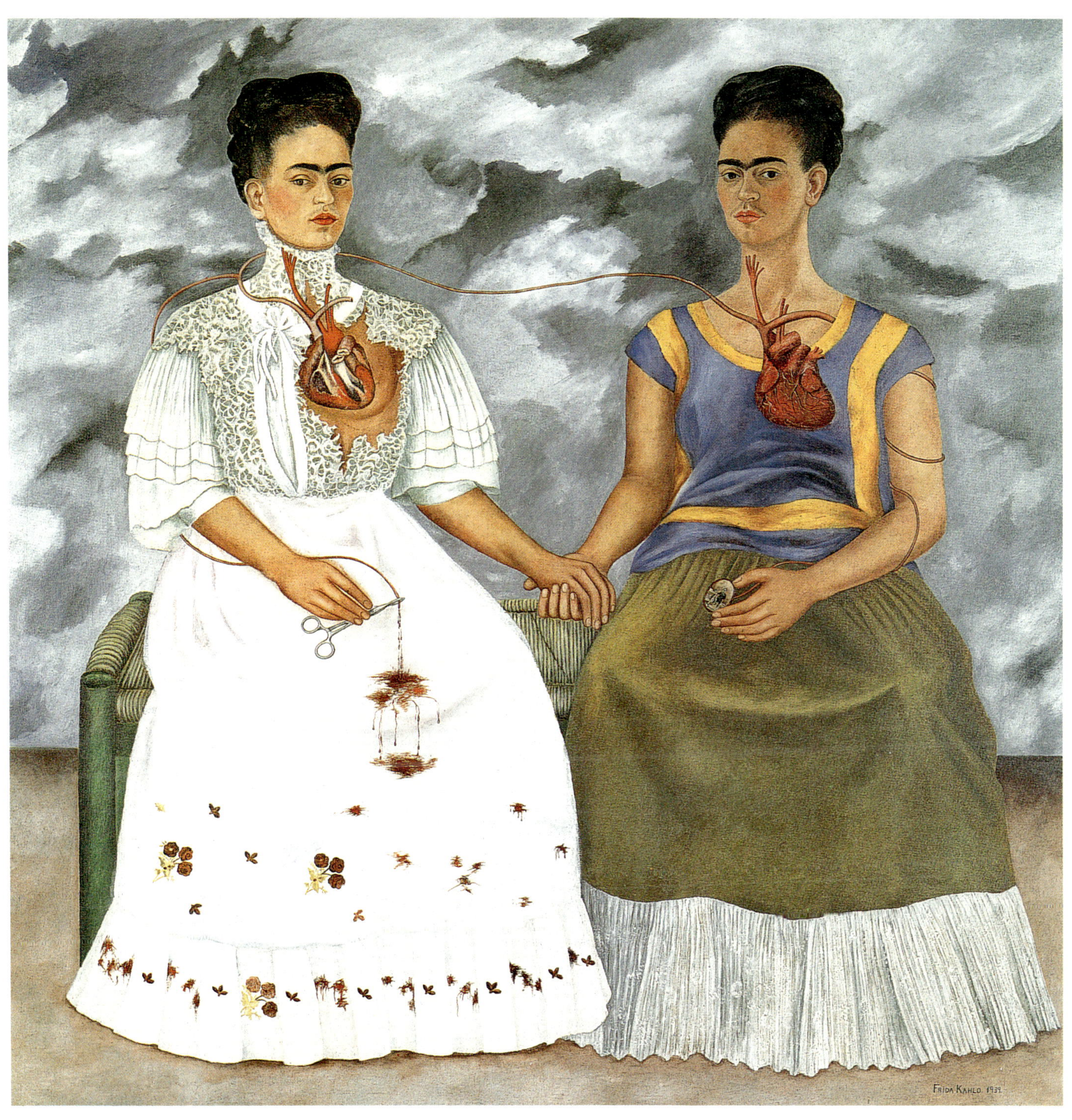

45 THE TWO FRIDAS, 1939

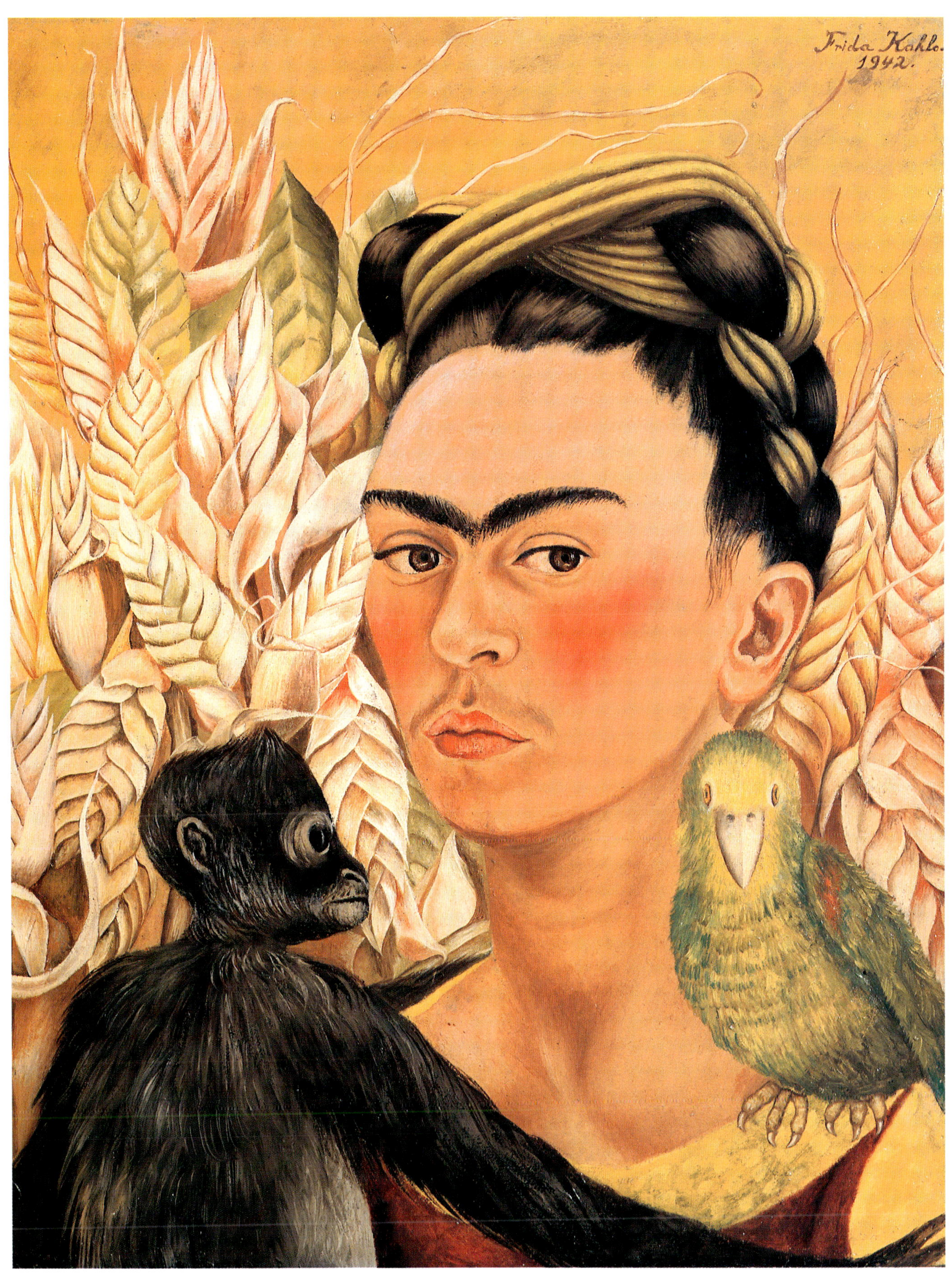

46 SELF-PORTRAIT WITH MONKEY AND PARROT, 1942

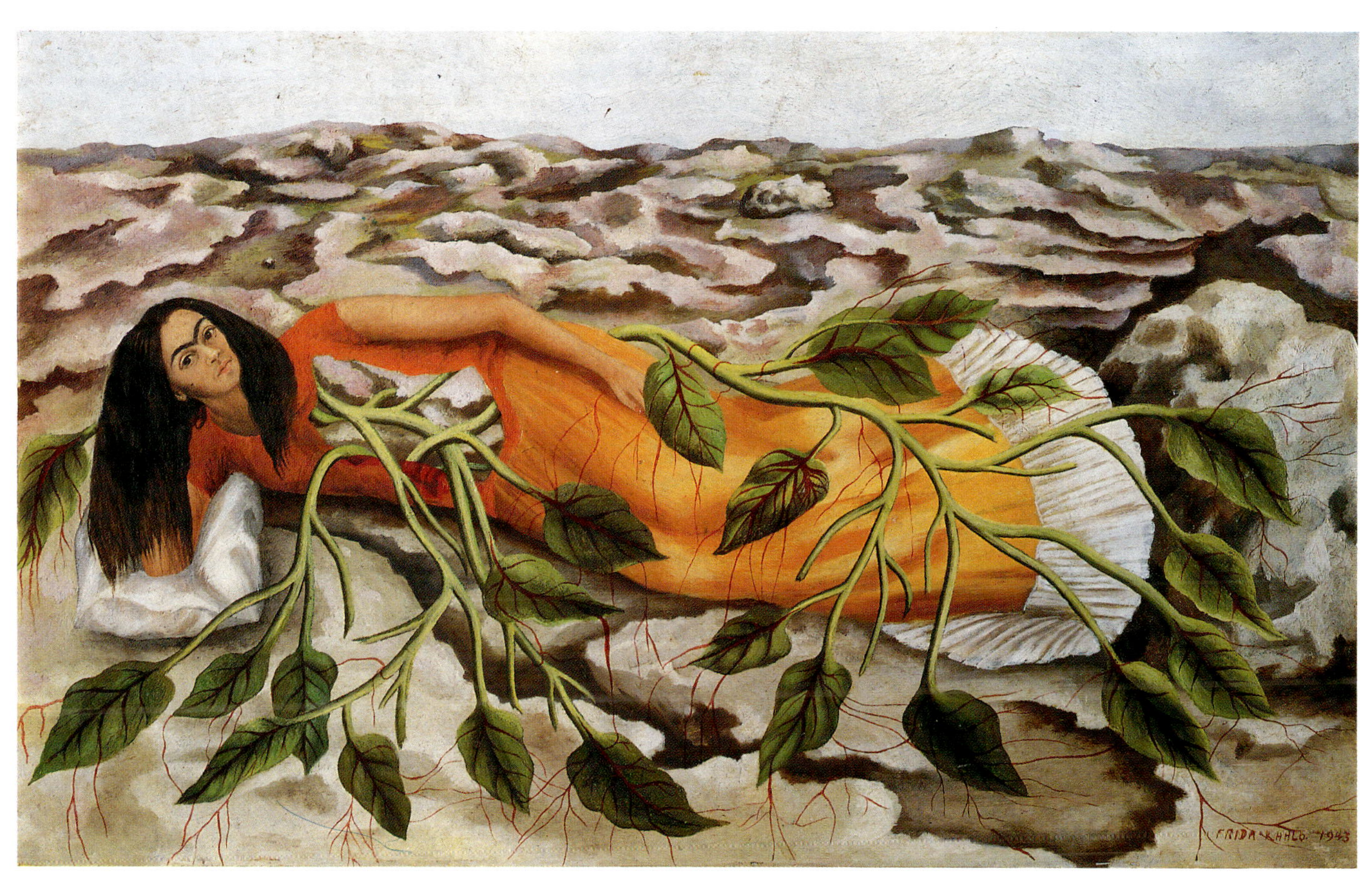

47 ROOTS, 1943

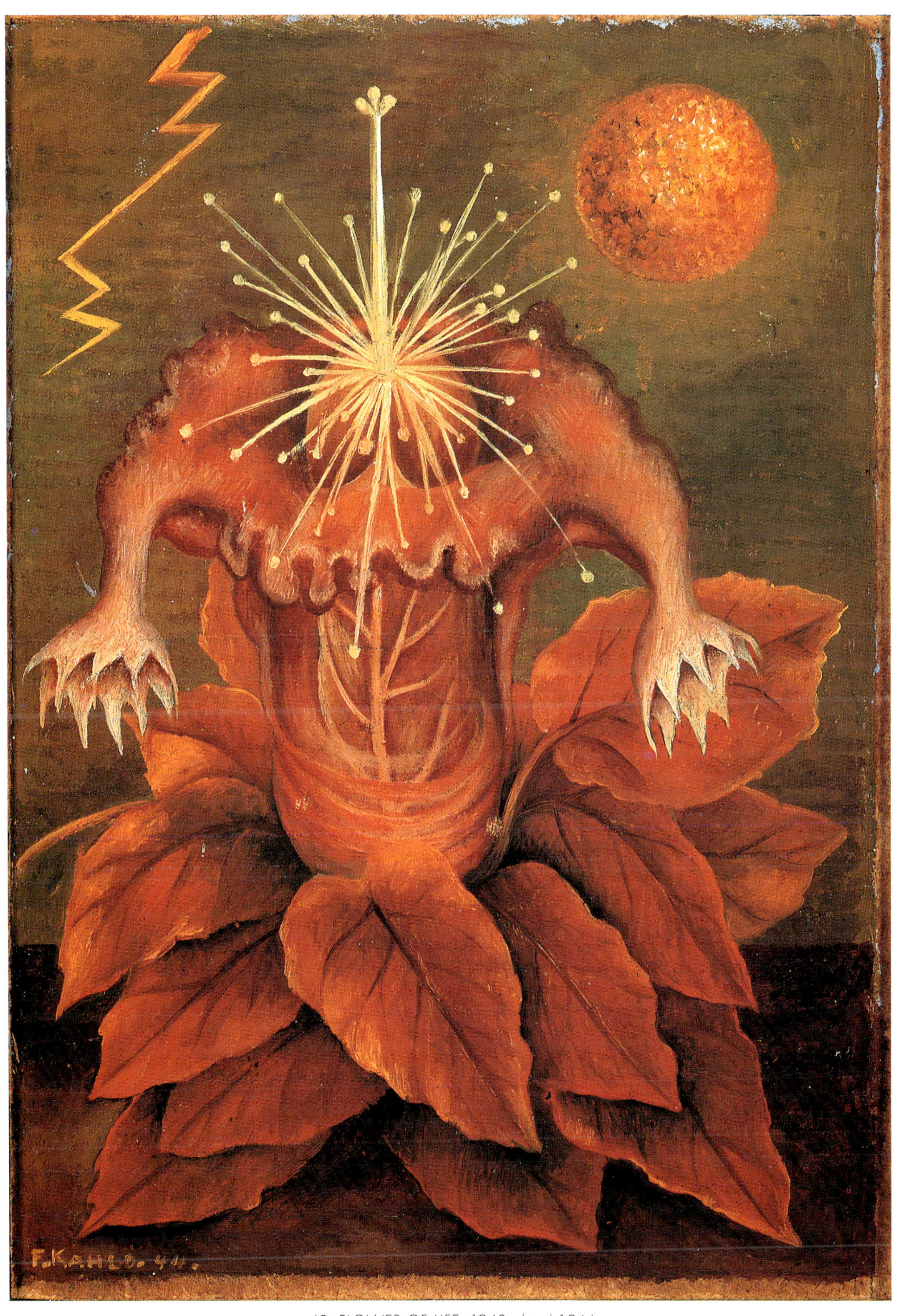

48 FLOWER OF LIFE, 1943, dated 1944

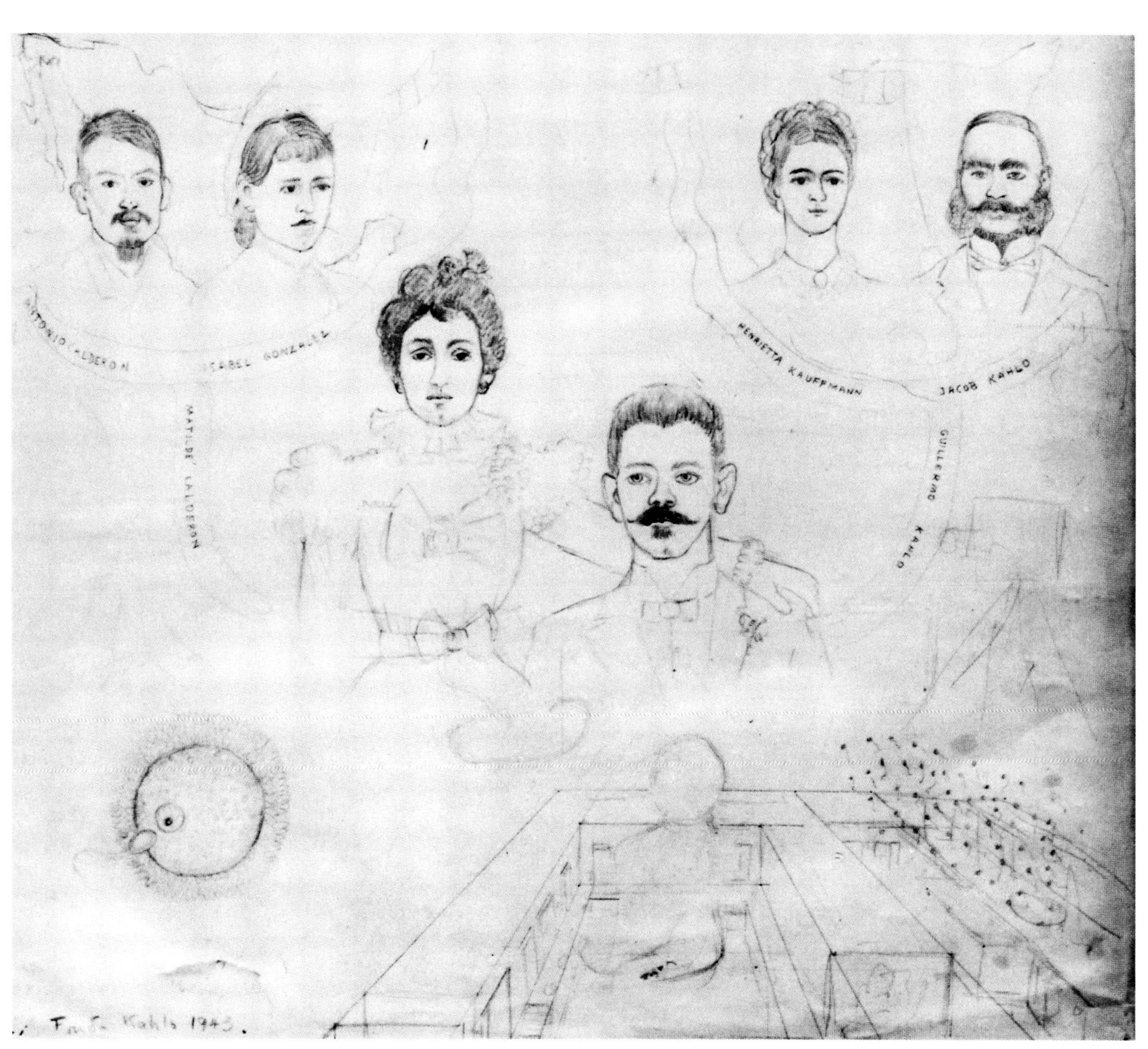

49 STUDY FOR "MY GRANDPARENTS, MY PARENTS, AND I", 1943

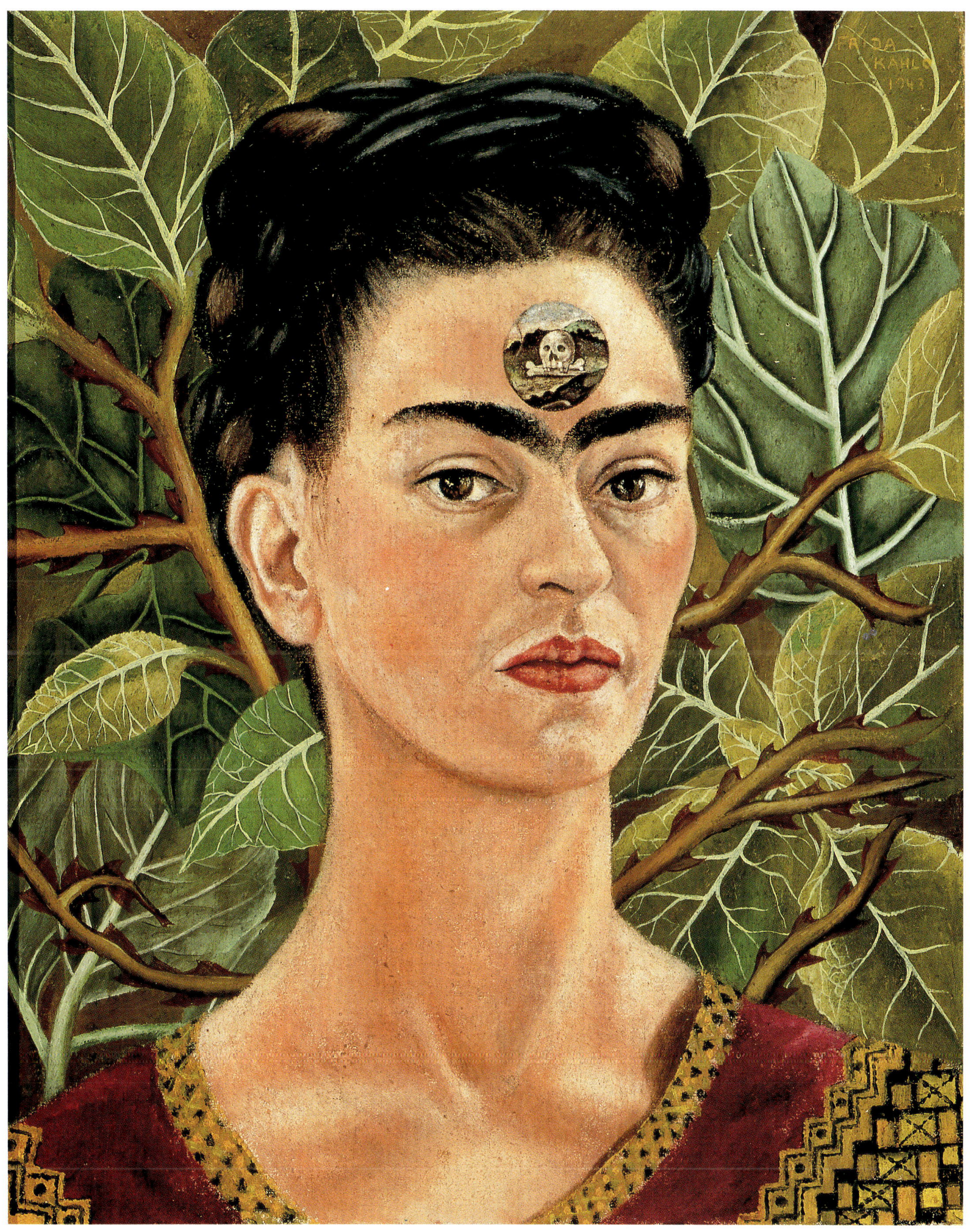

50 THINKING ABOUT DEATH, 1943

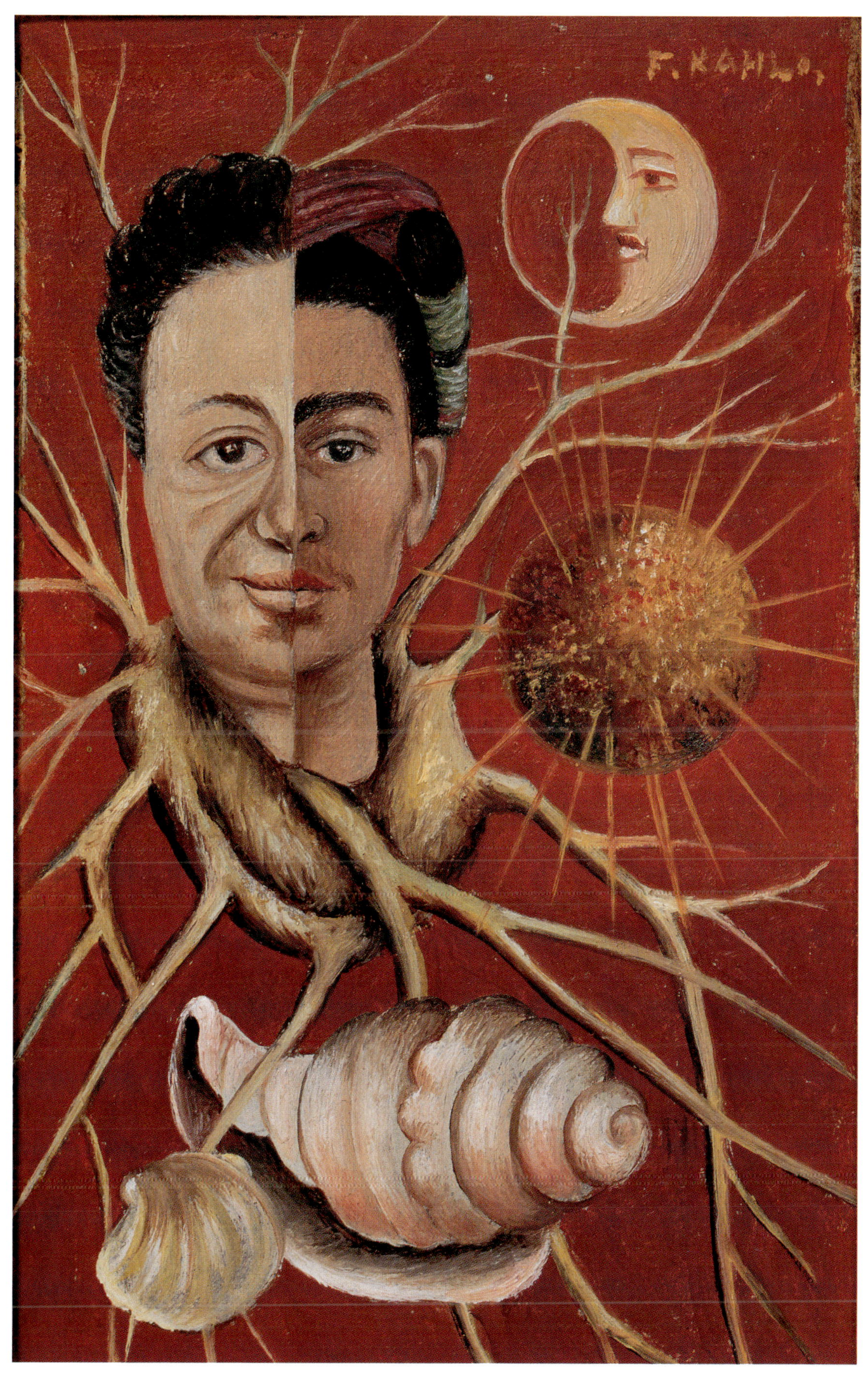

51 DIEGO AND FRIDA 1929–1944 (II), 1944

The Broken Column is a kind of homage to all those who suffer from spinal injuries. Although most critics believe that it expresses the artist's suffering after her first spinal operation, this work precedes that intervention and bespeaks the terrible agony that results from such injuries. In this self-portrait Frida is nude and standing upright, her torso split in two by a wide gap inside of which is a broken Ionic column. The architectural element is the artist's way of glorifying her infirmity, conferring on her fractures a certain art and beauty. An orthopedic corset like the ones she often had to wear wraps around the fragmented torso; it has the leather straps and metal buckles common to such contraptions. The beauty of the breasts, which Frida painted with utmost perfection, contrasts with the rest of the composition. The tears and nails that mar her face and body lend great drama to the work, as does the cold and challenging gaze in her eyes, which look straight ahead, with great determination. The cloth wrapped around her hips recalls religious images, while the background is once again a barren landscape.

Rafael Vázquez Bayod

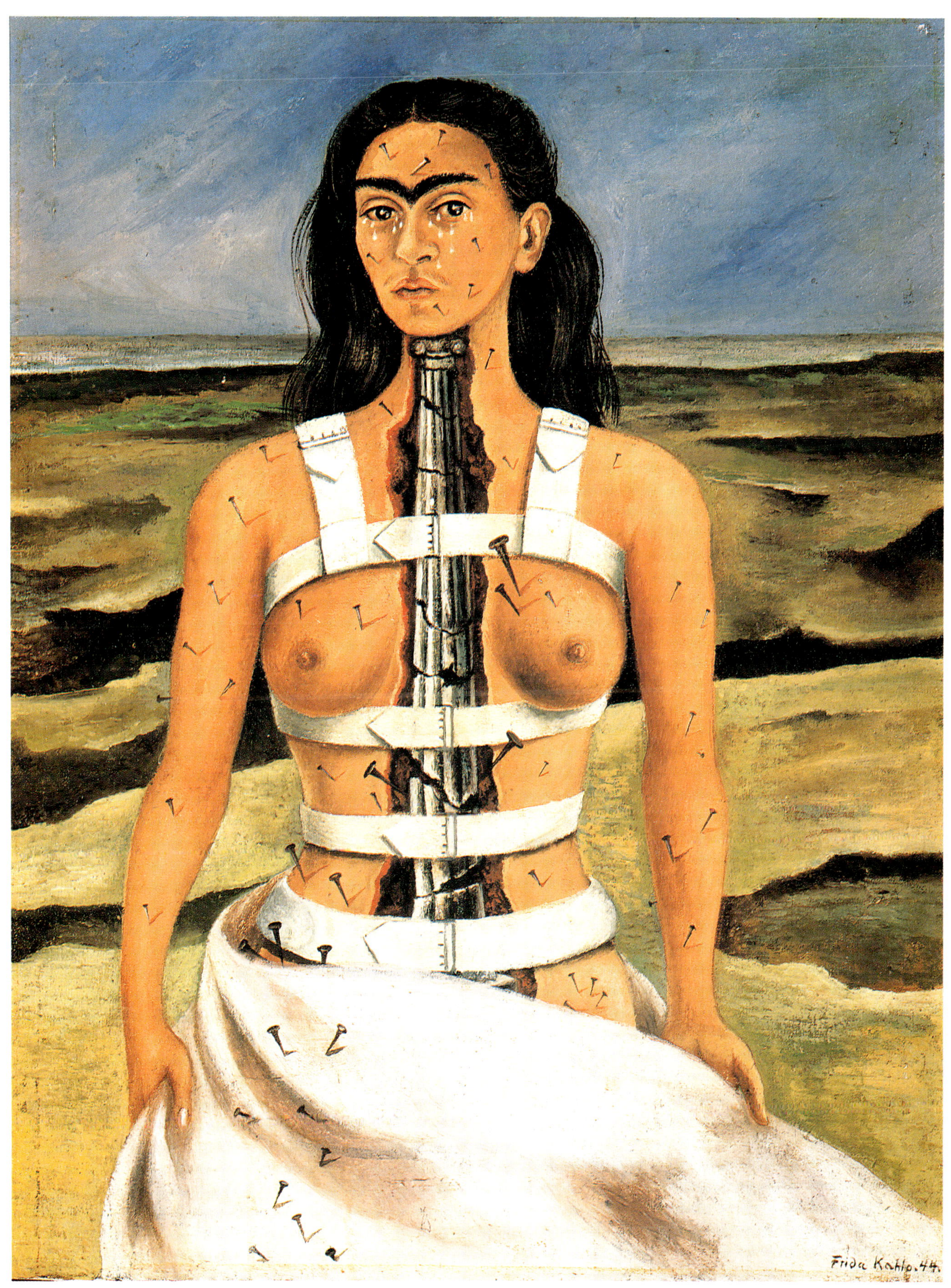

52 THE BROKEN COLUMN, 1944

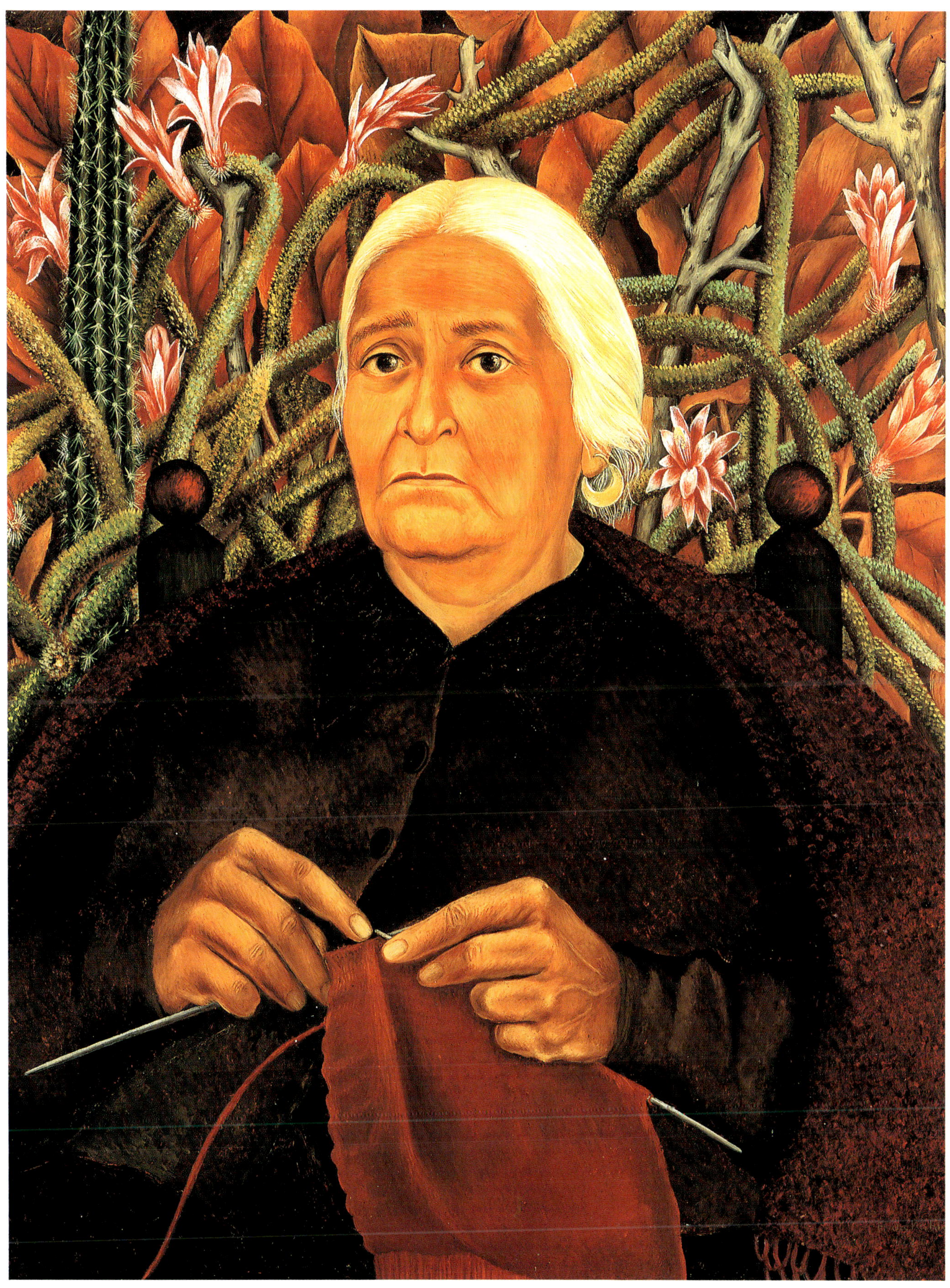

53 PORTRAIT OF DOÑA ROSITA MORILLO, 1944

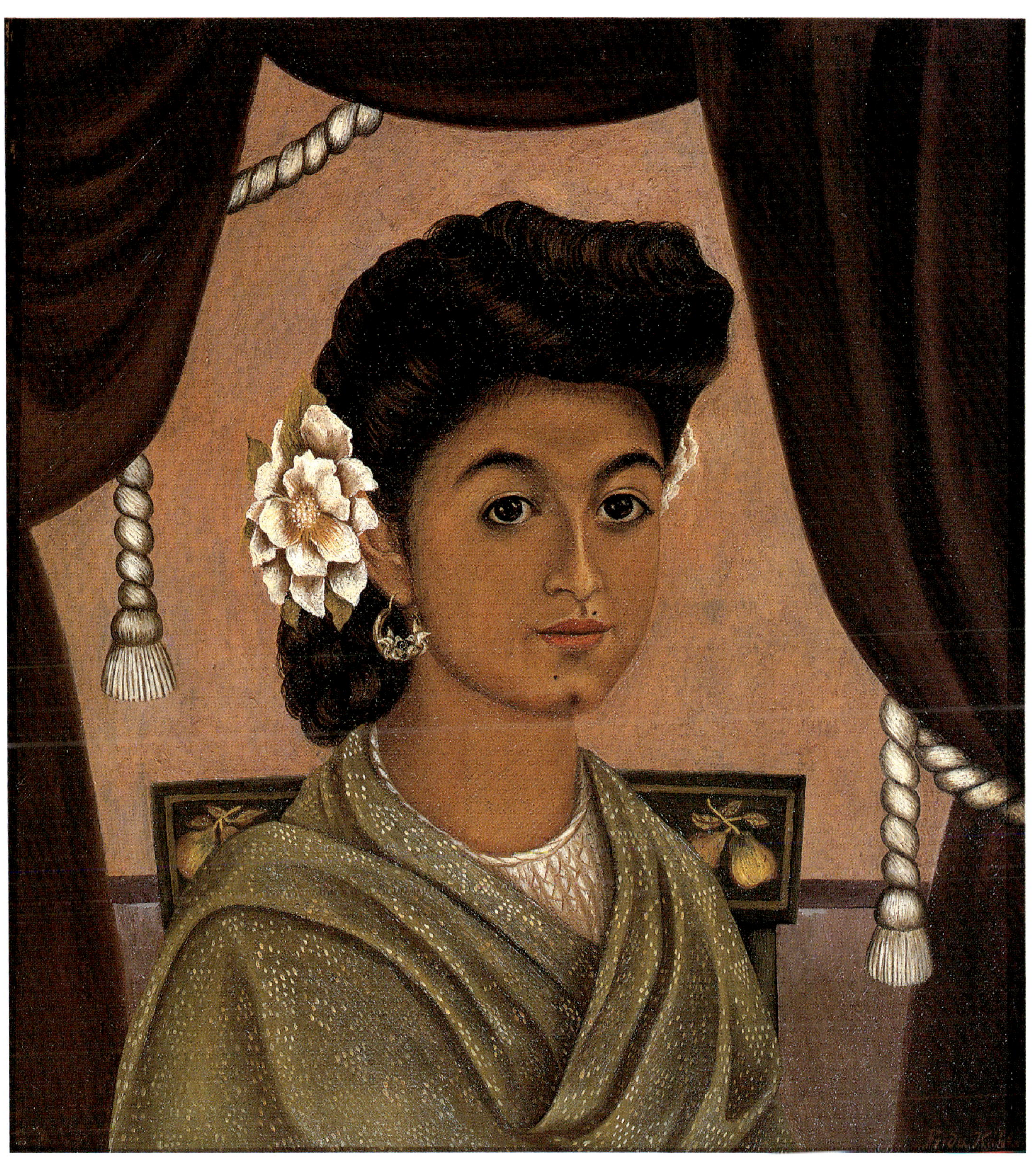

54 PORTRAIT OF LUPITA MORILLO SAFA, 1944

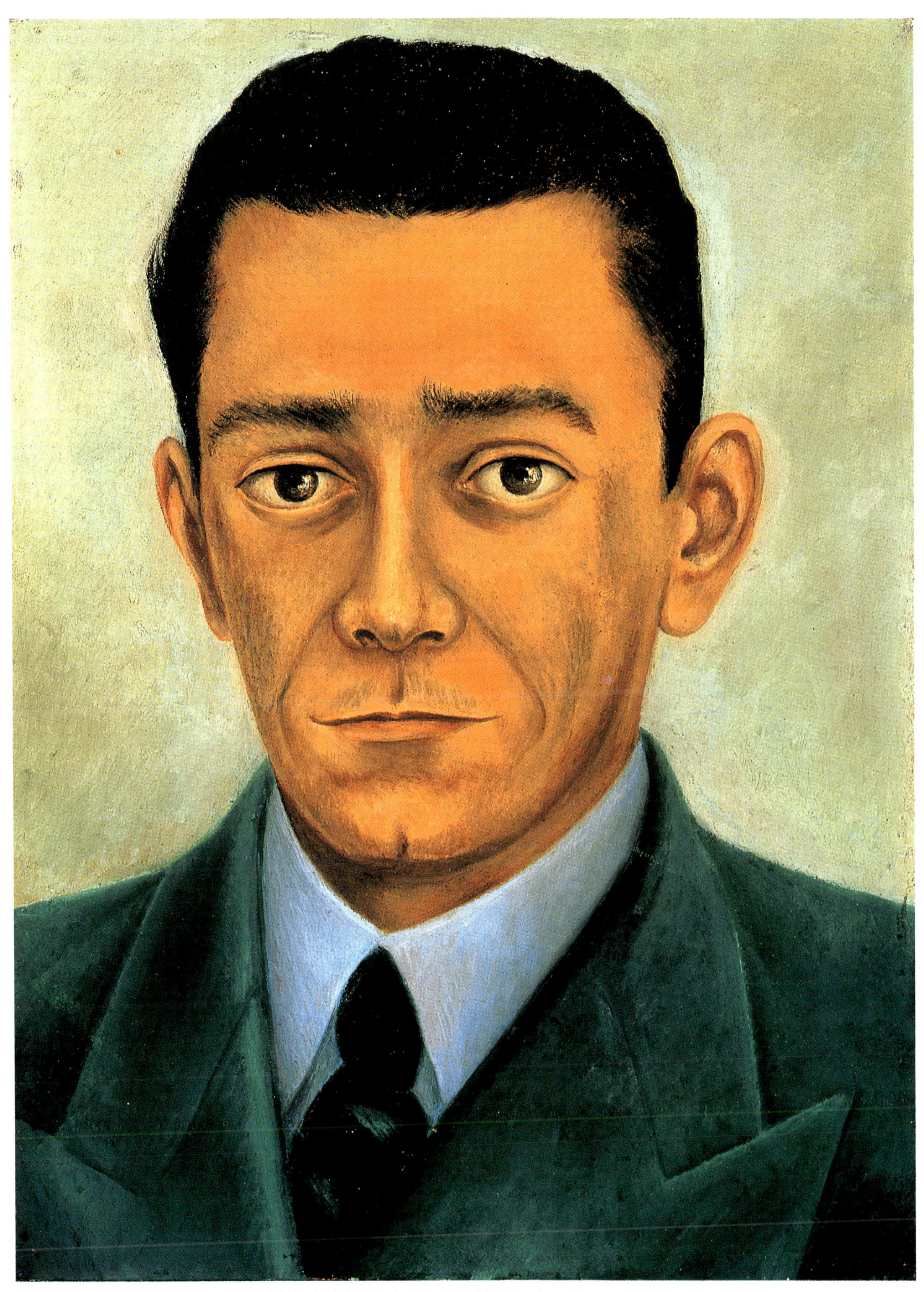

55 PORTRAIT OF THE ENGINEER EDUARDO MORILLO SAFA, 1944

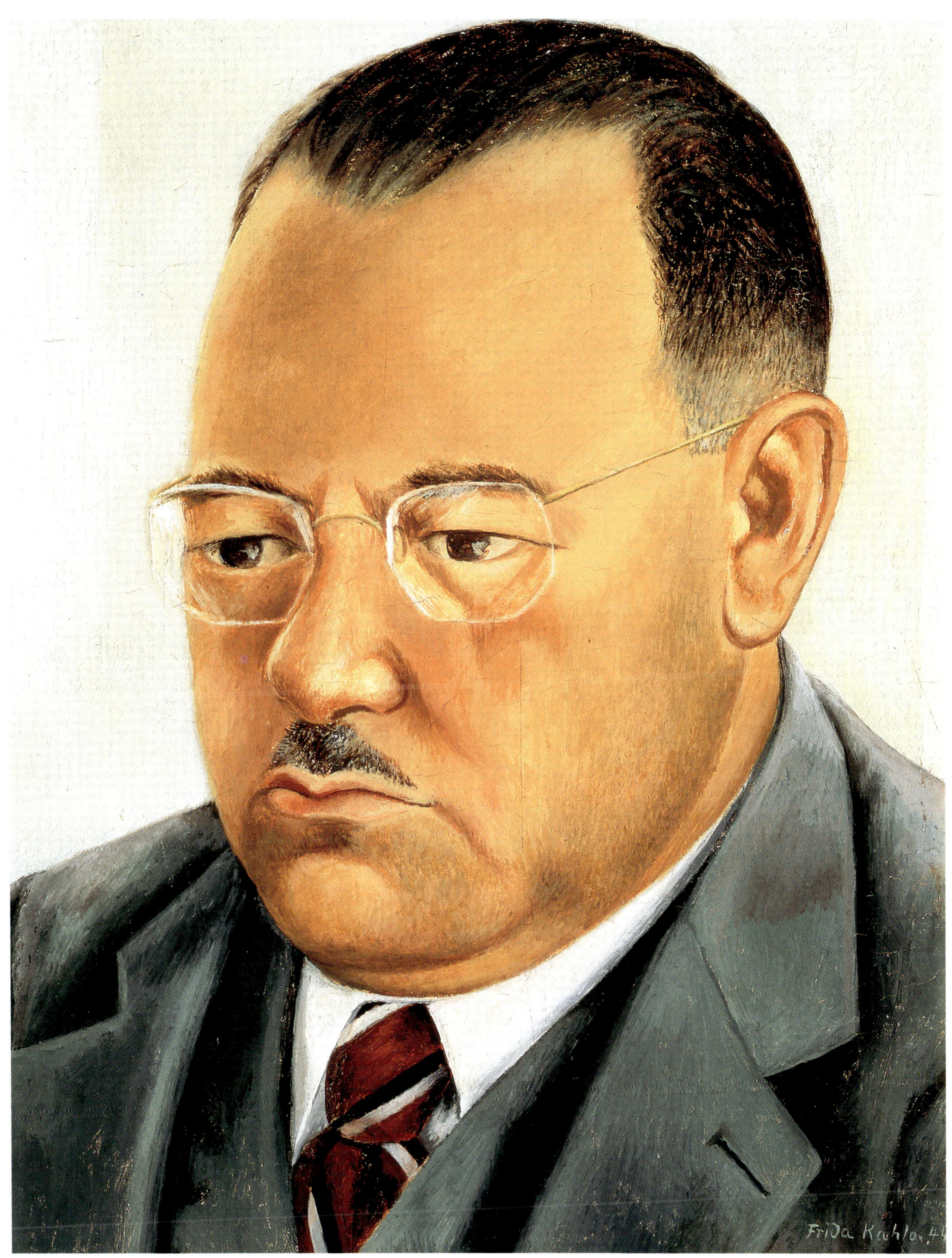

56 PORTRAIT OF THE ENGINEER MARTE R. GÓMEZ, 1944

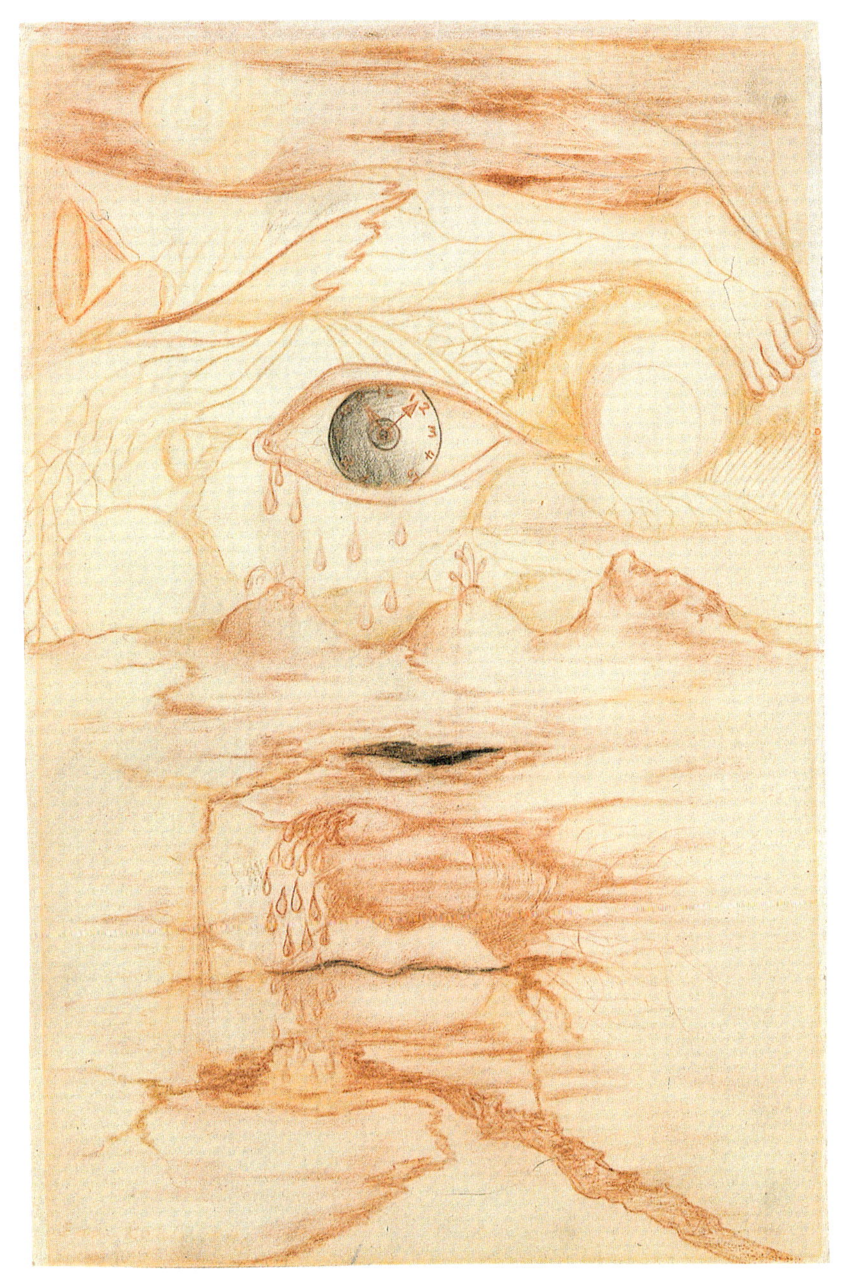

57 FANTASY (I), 1944

About a year ago José Domingo Lavin said that it would be good if I read Freud's *Moses* and painted my interpretation of the book. This picture is the result of that conversation.
I read the book only a single time and at once began to paint under the influence of that first impression. Yesterday I read it anew and must admit, that now the picture seems very inadequate and very far away from a good interpretation of the excellent analysis of Moses by Freud. But now, of course, I cannot alter or add anything, and so I have to stand by the picture as it is and the way you can see it.
The actual theme is, of course, Moses, or to put it better, the birth of the hero. But in my own (very weird) way I have generalized the facts and pictures of the book, which left a special impression on me while I was reading it. But of course, you can tell me whether I was mistaken or not. What I wanted to bring out particularly clearly and distinctly is that pure fear that pushes people to invent and imagine heroes and gods. Fear of life and fear of death.
I began by painting the figure of the boy Moses (in Hebrew Moses means "the one who was pulled out of the water" but in Egyptian it means "Child.") I painted him the way he is described in many legends, that is, floating in a basket left on the river. I tried to form the basket which is covered with an animal skin in the picture so that it resembles a womb as far as possible, because, according to Freud, the basket depicts the womb, and the water signifies the motherly sources during birth. To include that, I painted the human fetus in its last stage in the placenta. The oviducts resemble hands and are stretched out towards the world. At the sides of the begotten child I portrayed the elements of its creation: the fertilized egg and cell division.
As far as I can understand, Freud analyzes very clearly and, at the same time in a very complicated way, the significant fact that Moses was not a Jew but an Egyptian; now, for my picture I painted only a little boy who was to embody quite generally both Moses as well as all the others that the legends say have such an origin and who later become important personalities, leaders of their people and heroes (more frequently than others and that is why I gave him the third eye). That applies to Sargon, Kyros, Romulus, Paris and so on. Freud's other extremely interesting conclusion is that Moses, although not a Jew, gave the chosen people a religion as a guide and a salvation that was likewise not Jewish, but Egyptian. Amenophis IV, revived the sun cult, the very old religion of Heliopolis. That is why I painted the sun as the center of all religions, as the first god, as the creator and preserver of life. This is the relationship of the three main figures in the front of the picture.
There have been many "visionary" changers of religions and of human history like Moses, and they will come over and over again. One can describe them as a sort of mediator between humans and the gods they invented. Some of these gods are in the picture. Of course, not all of them fit in, and so right and left of the sun I painted those which, whether they like it or not, have a direct relationship to the sun. On the right are those of the west and on the left those of the east. The winged bull of Assyria, Amon, Zeus, Osiria, Horus, Jehova, Apollo, the Moon, the Virgin Mary, Heavenly Providence, the Holy Trinity, Venus, and ... the Devil. On the left side; Lightning, the flash of light and the consequences of lightning, that is, the hurricane, Kukulkan and Gukamatz; Tlaloc, the mother of all gods, the magnificent Coatlique, Quetzalcoatl, Tezcatlipoca, Centeotl, the Chinese dragon god and

the Hindu Brahma. An African god was missing. But I could not find any. I cannot tell you about the origin and meaning of each and every one of them, because I do not know all that.
After I had painted the gods in their respective heavens I wanted to separate the heavenly world of poetry and imagination from the earthly world of fear and death, and I painted human and animal skeletons. The earth spreads its protecting arms over them. Between the dead and the group of heroes there is no separation whatsoever because these must also die and the earth will make no difference between them and accept them generously. To make a difference from the masses I painted on the same earth, somewhat bigger, the heads of some of the heroes (but only the very few chosen ones), the changers of religion, the inventors or creators of religions, the conquerors, the rebels, that is, the really important people. On the right one can see the hero of the eighteenth dynasty, Amenophis, who was later also called Akhenaton (I had to stress this figure much more strongly than all the others), who imposed on his subjects a strictly monotheistic religion, which had its origins in the old On-cult (Heliopolis), the religion of Aton and the sun, and which moved away from the traditional practice of polytheism. They were far more advanced than modern scientific knowledge about the sun's energy as expressed in its powerful rays and honored the sun, not only as a material being but also as the creator of all living creatures inside and outside Egypt. Later, according to Freud in his analysis, Moses gave his people the same religion as Akhenaton in a slightly altered version that fit the interests and circumstances of his time. This is the conclusion Freud comes to after a minute examination of the close relationships between these two monotheistic schools of thought, the Aton-religion and the Mosaic belief. (I did not know how I could convey this extremely important chapter in my picture).
Then come Christ, Zarathustra, Alexander the Great, Caesar, Mohammed, Luther, Napoleon, and the prodigal son: Hitler, on the left side, the wonderful Nofretete, the wife of Akhenaton. I imagined that she was not only exceptionally beautiful but also a secret genius, an extremely intelligent assistant to her husband. Buddha, Marx, Freud, Paracelsus, Epicurus, Genghis Khan, Gandhi, Lenin, and Stalin. The order is very poor, but I painted them as well as my historical knowledge allowed, and that is also very poor. Between them and the other masses of people in a huge conglomeration of all kinds; the warriors, the peaceful, the scientists and the uneducated, those who make history, the rebels, the standard-bearers, the medal-wearers, the great speakers, the intelligent, the happy and the sad, the healthy and the sick, the poets and the simpletons, and who knows how many other types that exist on this immense globe. The only thing is that those in the forefront can be seen a bit more distinctly than the others ... those in the shade cannot be seen.
On the left side man, the constructor, stands in the forefront. His four colors portray the four races. On the right side, the mother, the creator, holds her child in her arms. Behind her is a monkey. The two trees form a triumphal arch.New life continuously takes root in their old trunks. In the bottom center there is what is most important for Freud and many others: love, portrayed by a shell and a snail, the two sexes embraced by constantly new and living roots.
That is all I can say about this picture.

Frida Kahlo, Mexico City
August 1945

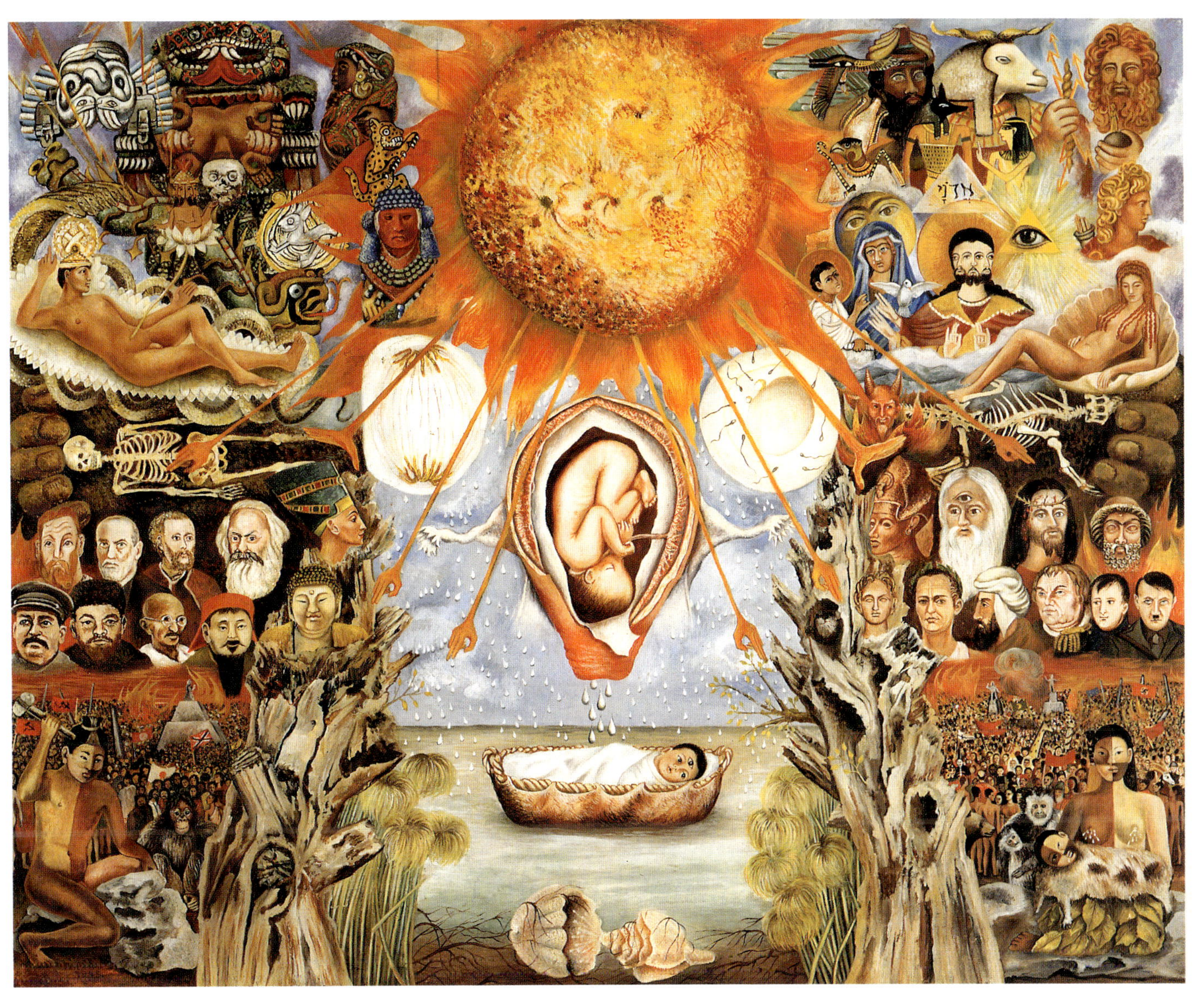

58 MOSES, 1945

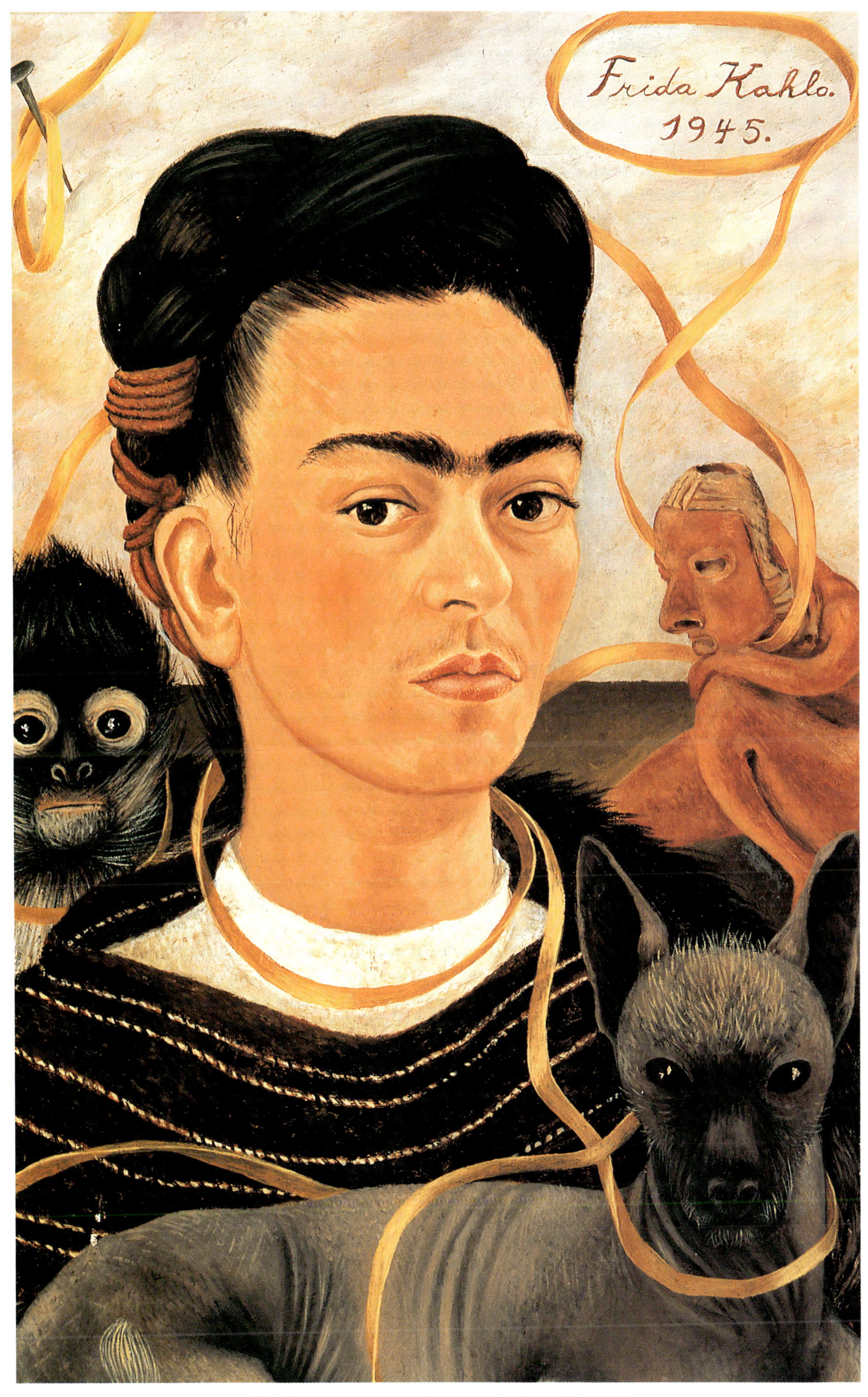

59 SELF-PORTRAIT WITH SMALL MONKEY, 1945

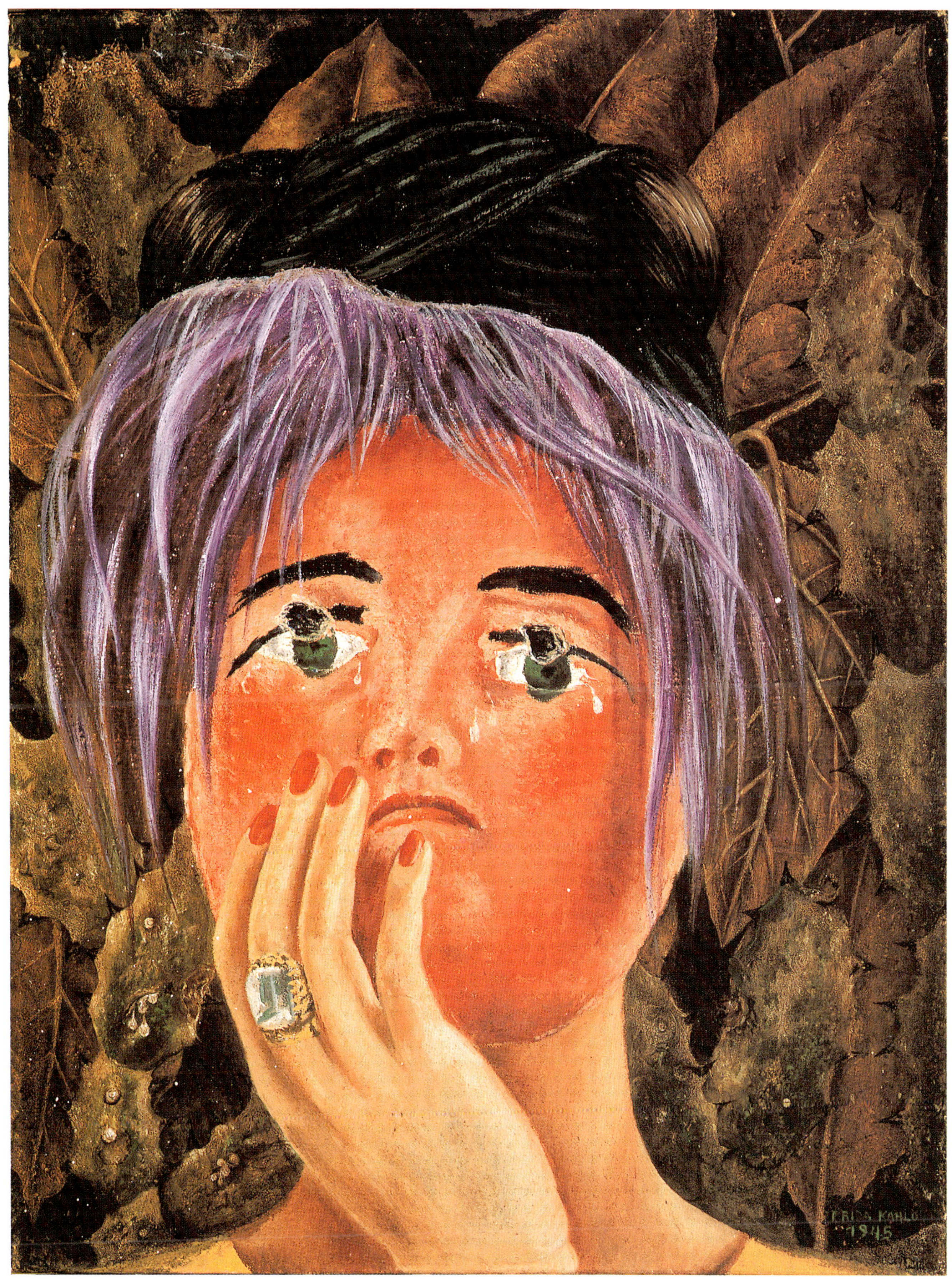

60 THE MASK, 1945

I have no hope left ...
everything moves in time with what the belly contains.
Frida Kahlo

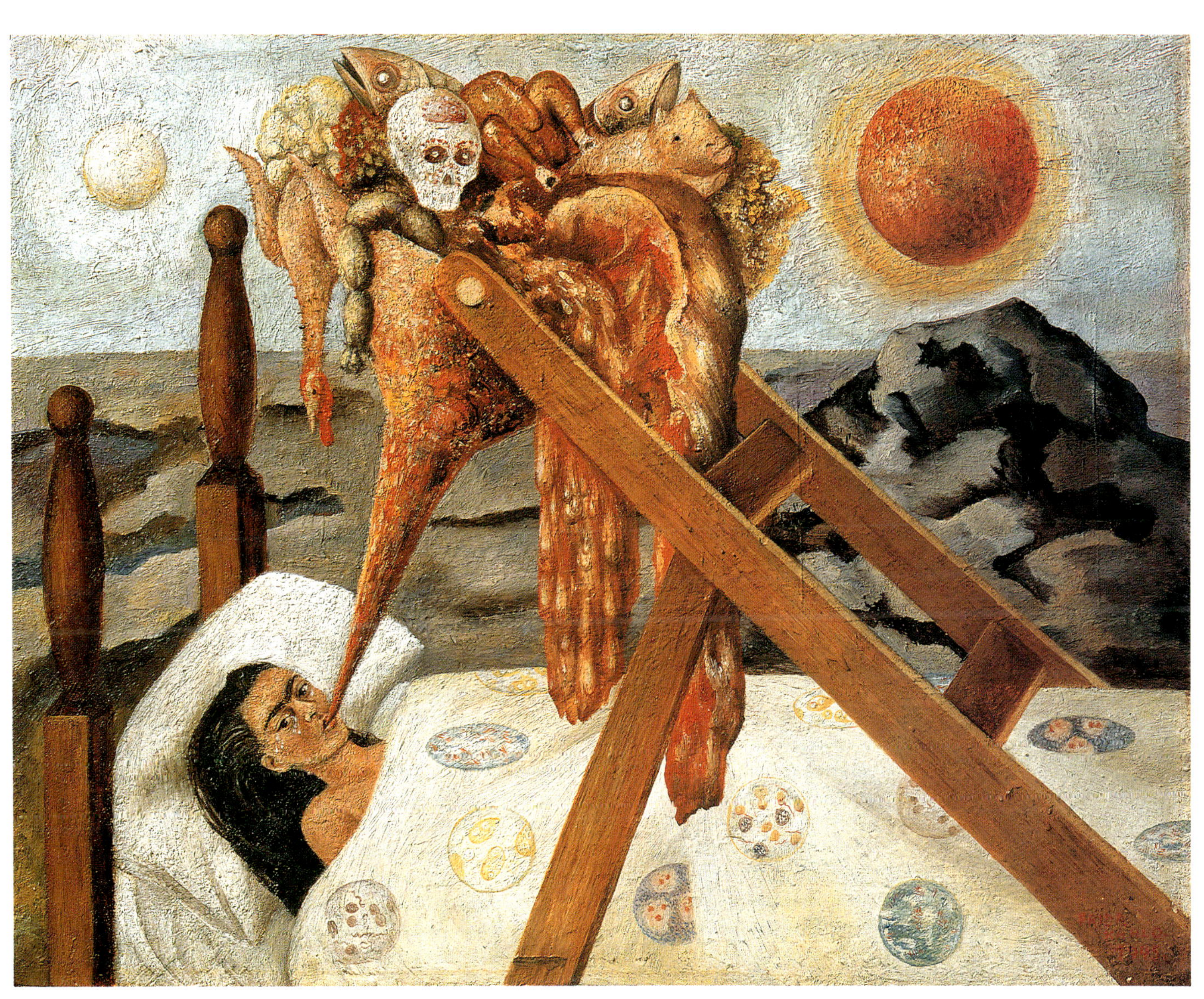

61 WITHOUT HOPE, 1945

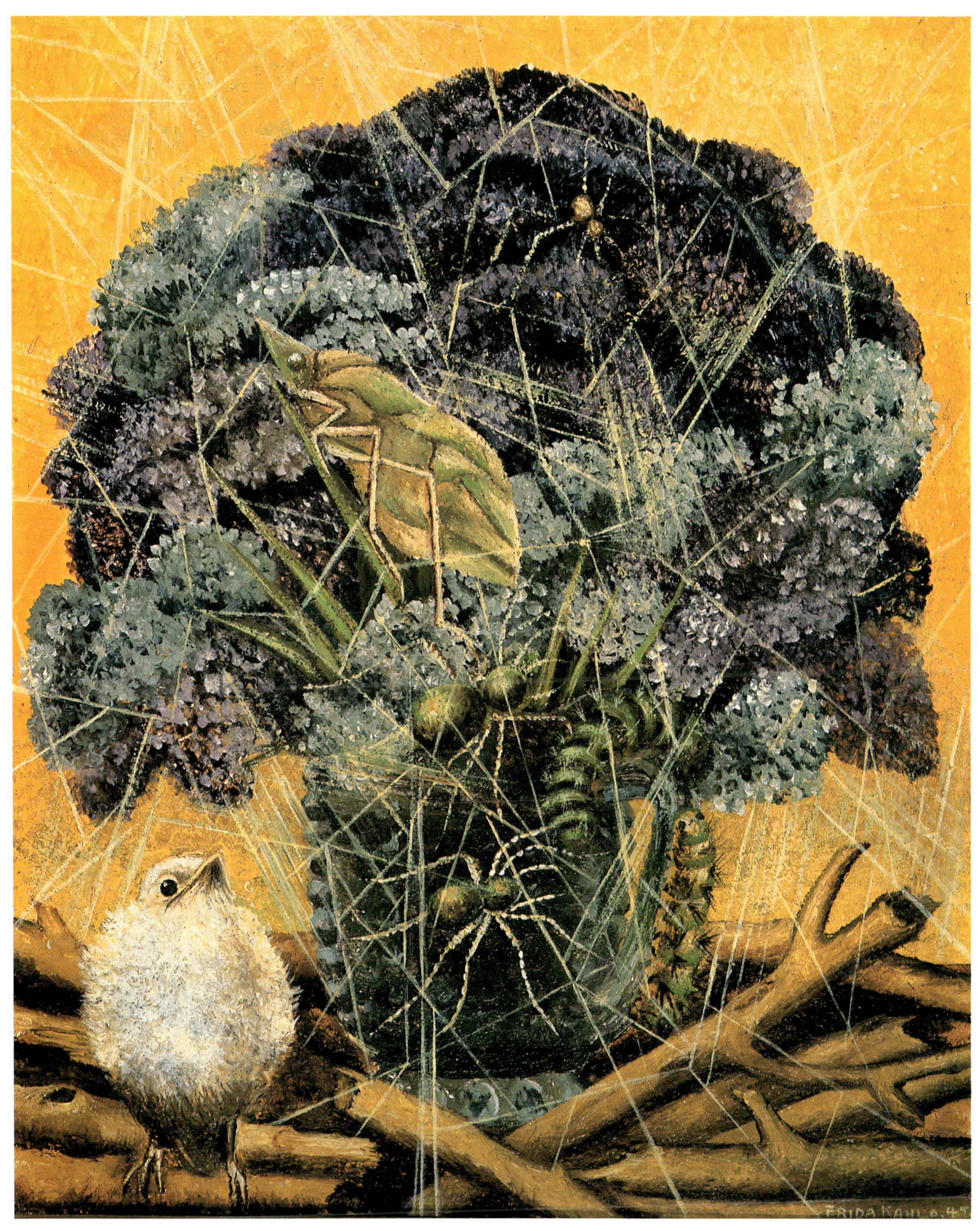

62 THE CHICK, 1945

Alone the deer roams about
very sad and full of wounds,
until he finds warmth and a nest
near Arcady and Lina.

When the deer returns once again,
strengthened, happy and recuperated,
the wounds of today
will have long been forgotten.

Thank you, children of my life,
thank you for all the comfort.
In the deer's forest
the sky is already clearing up.

Here I leave you my portrait
so that you do not forget me,
all the nights and days
I am away from you.

There is sorrow
in all my pictures,
my life was simply like that,
complaining will not help.

But deep down in my heart
I preserve the joyful fact
that Arcady and Lina
love me as I am.

Accept this little picture
which I painted full of love
as a gift for your care
and your endless gentleness.

Frida Kahlo

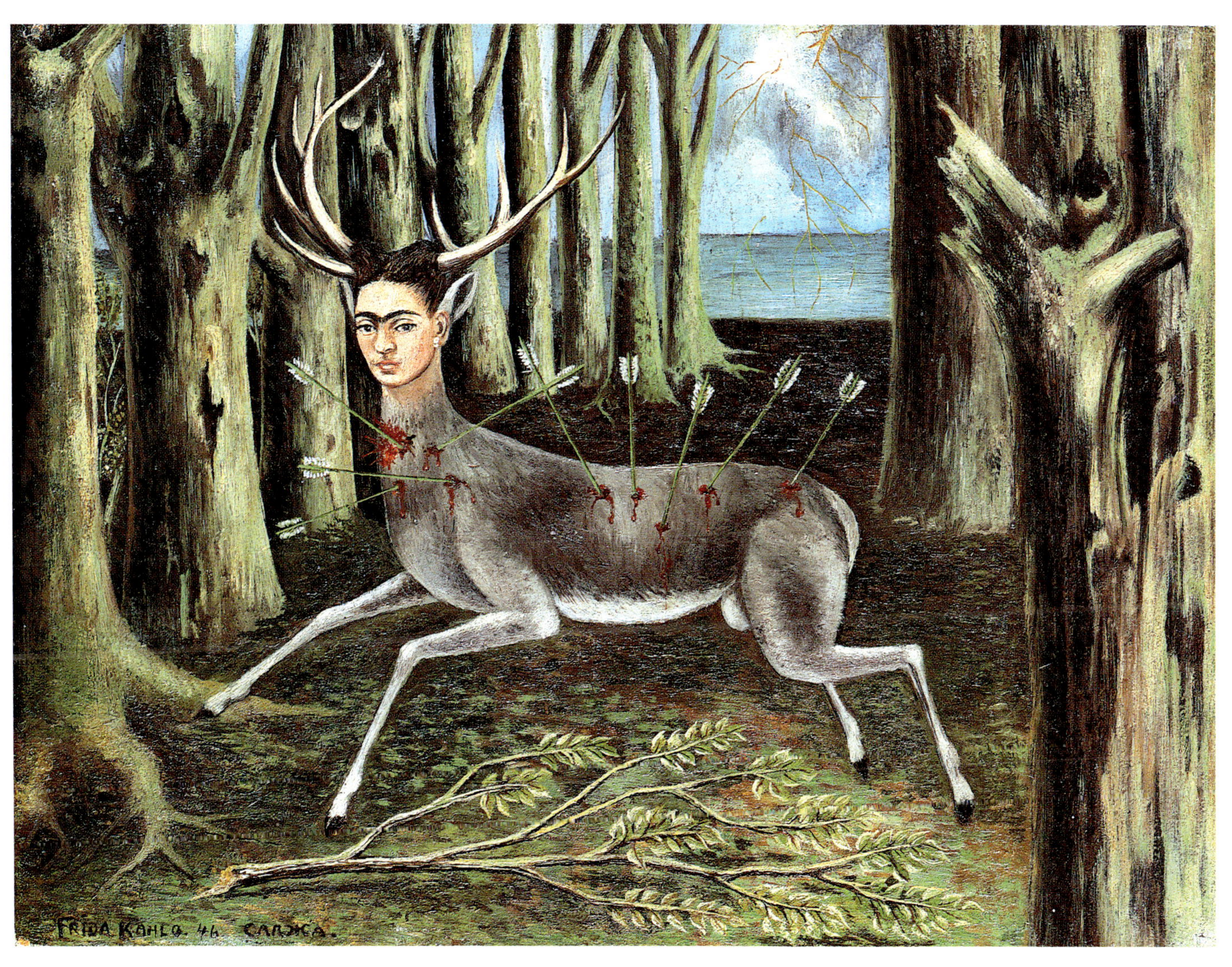

63 THE LITTLE DEER, 1946

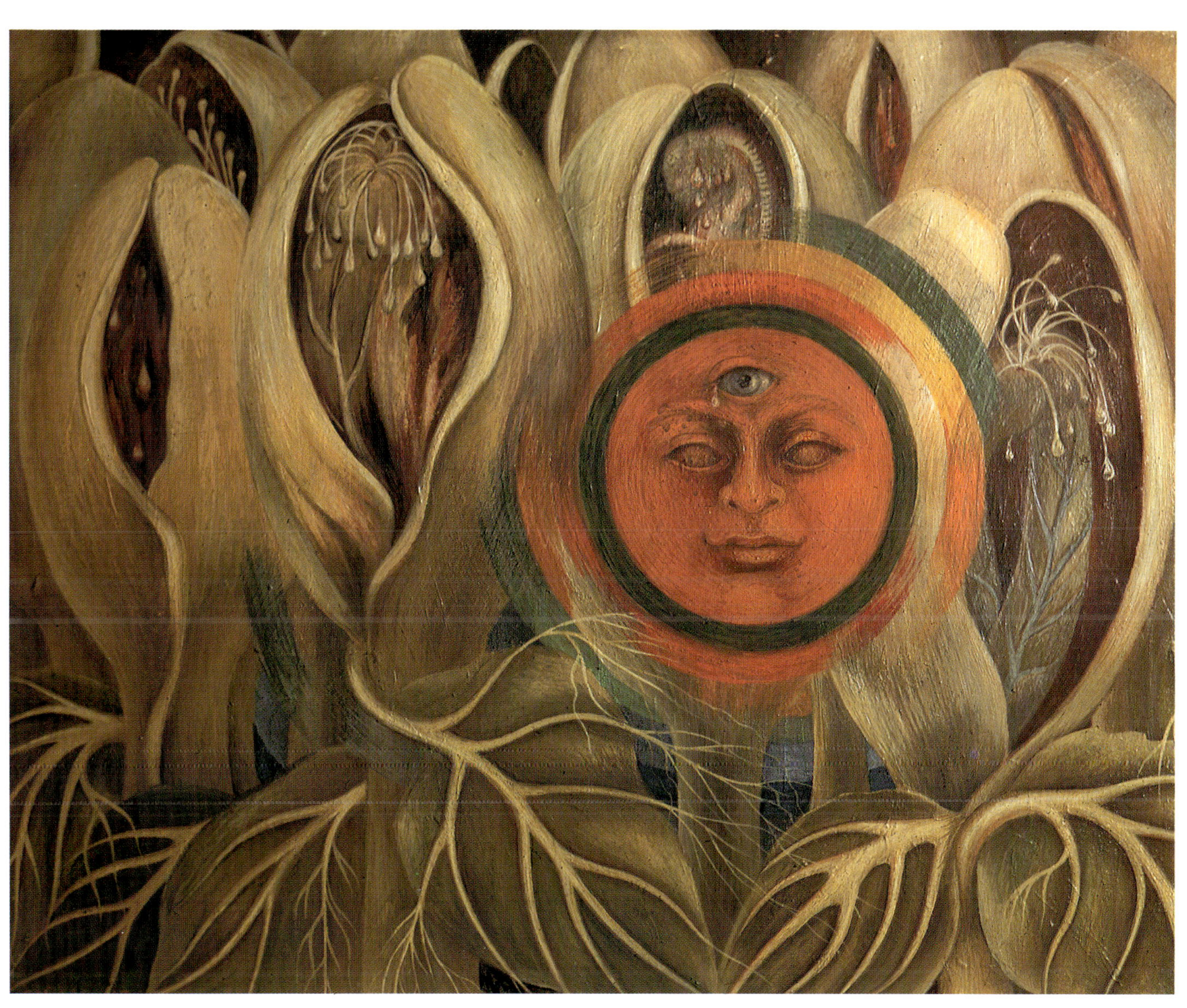

64 SUN AND LIFE, 1947

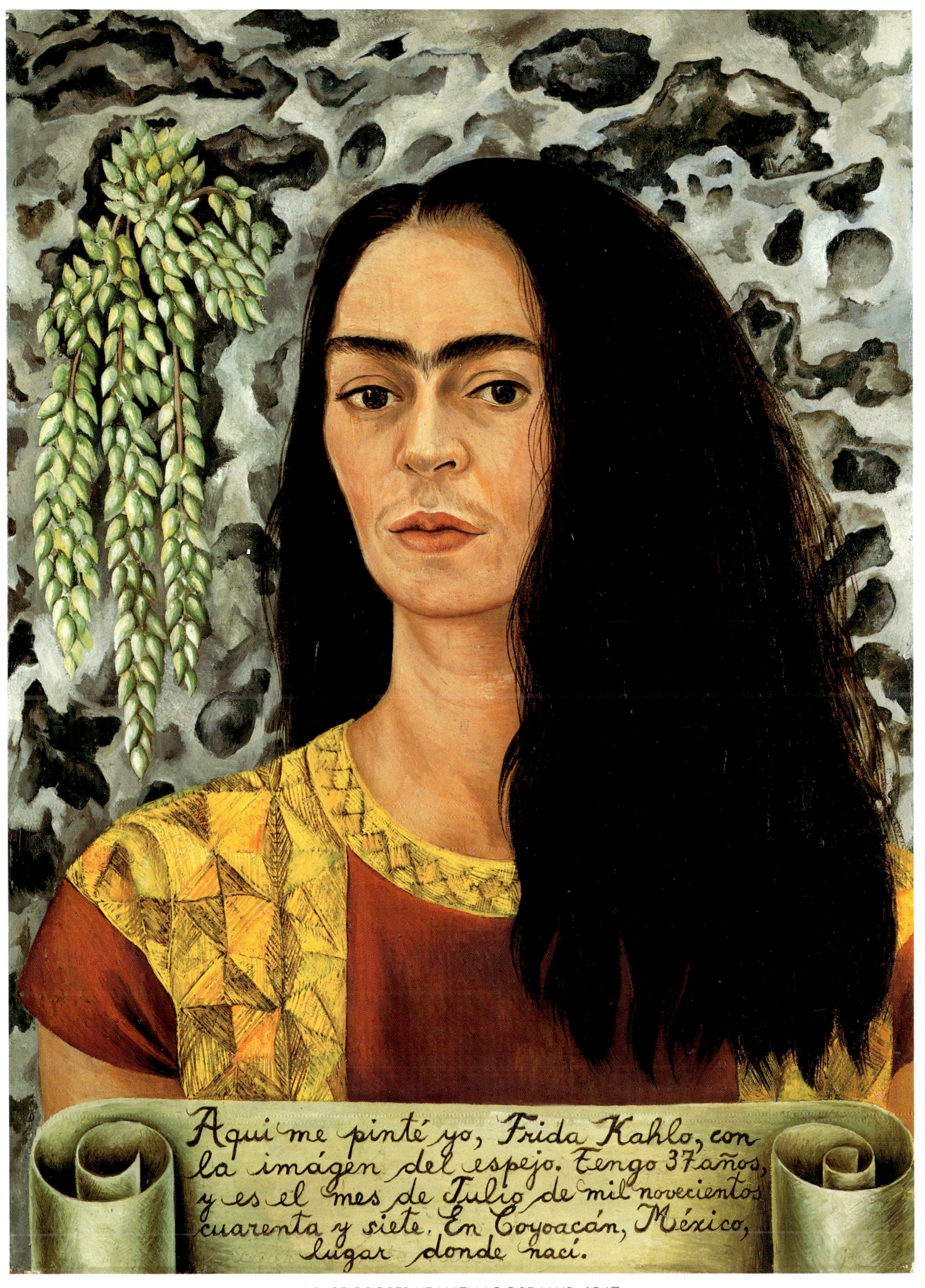

65 SELF-PORTRAIT WITH LOOSE HAIR, 1947

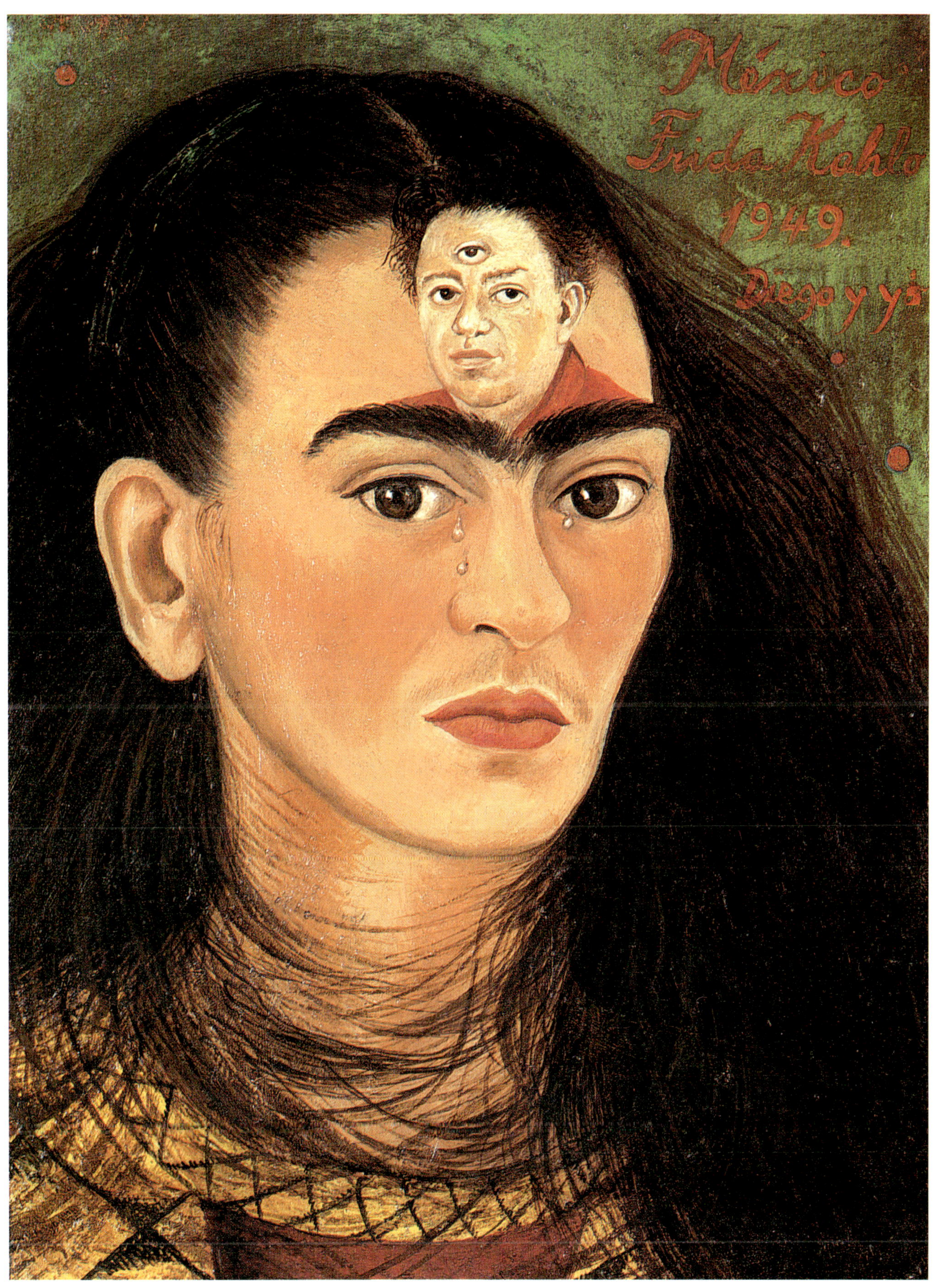

66 DIEGO AND I, 1949

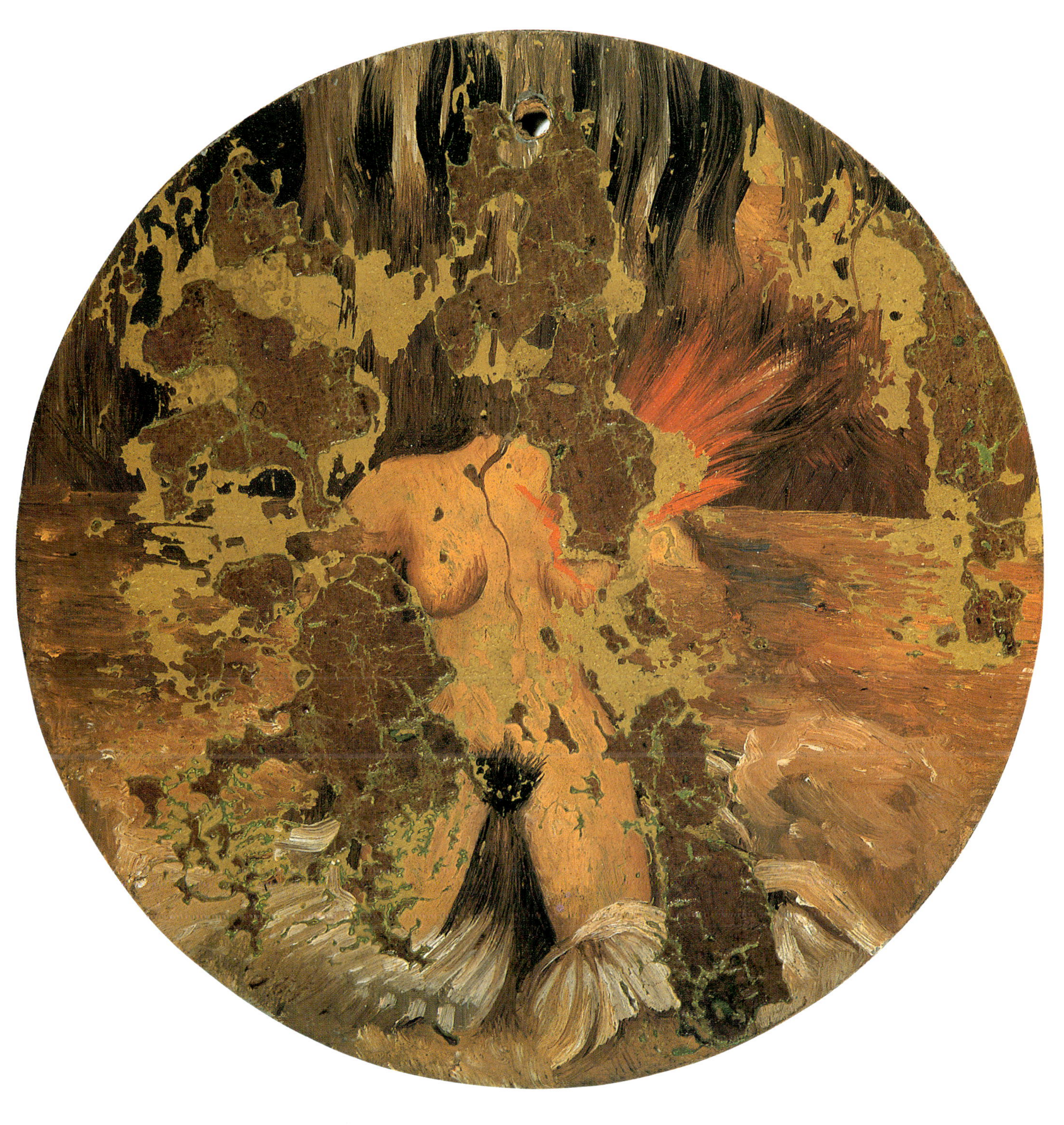

67 THE CIRCLE, circa 1950

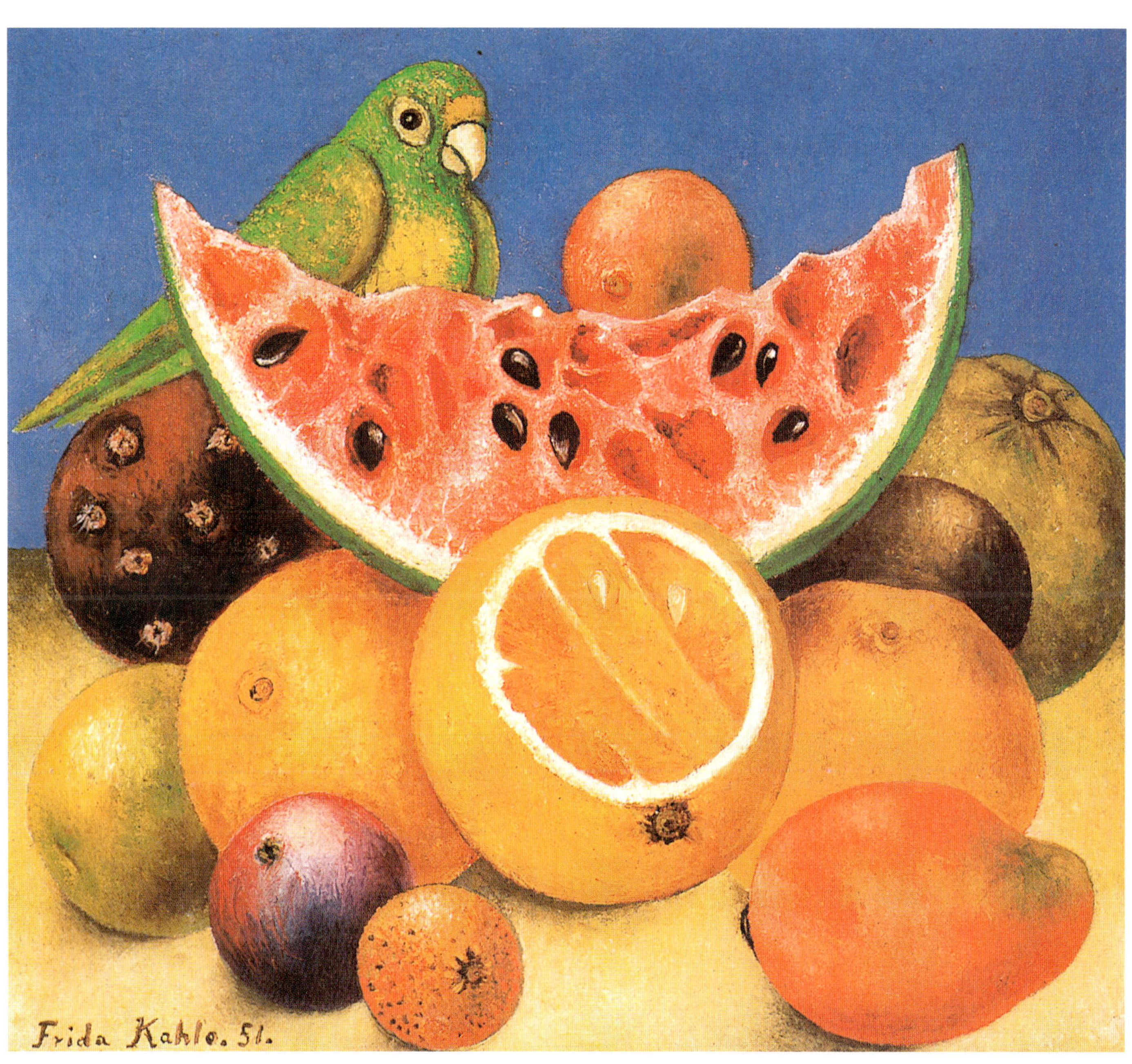

68 STILL LIFE WITH PARROT, 1951

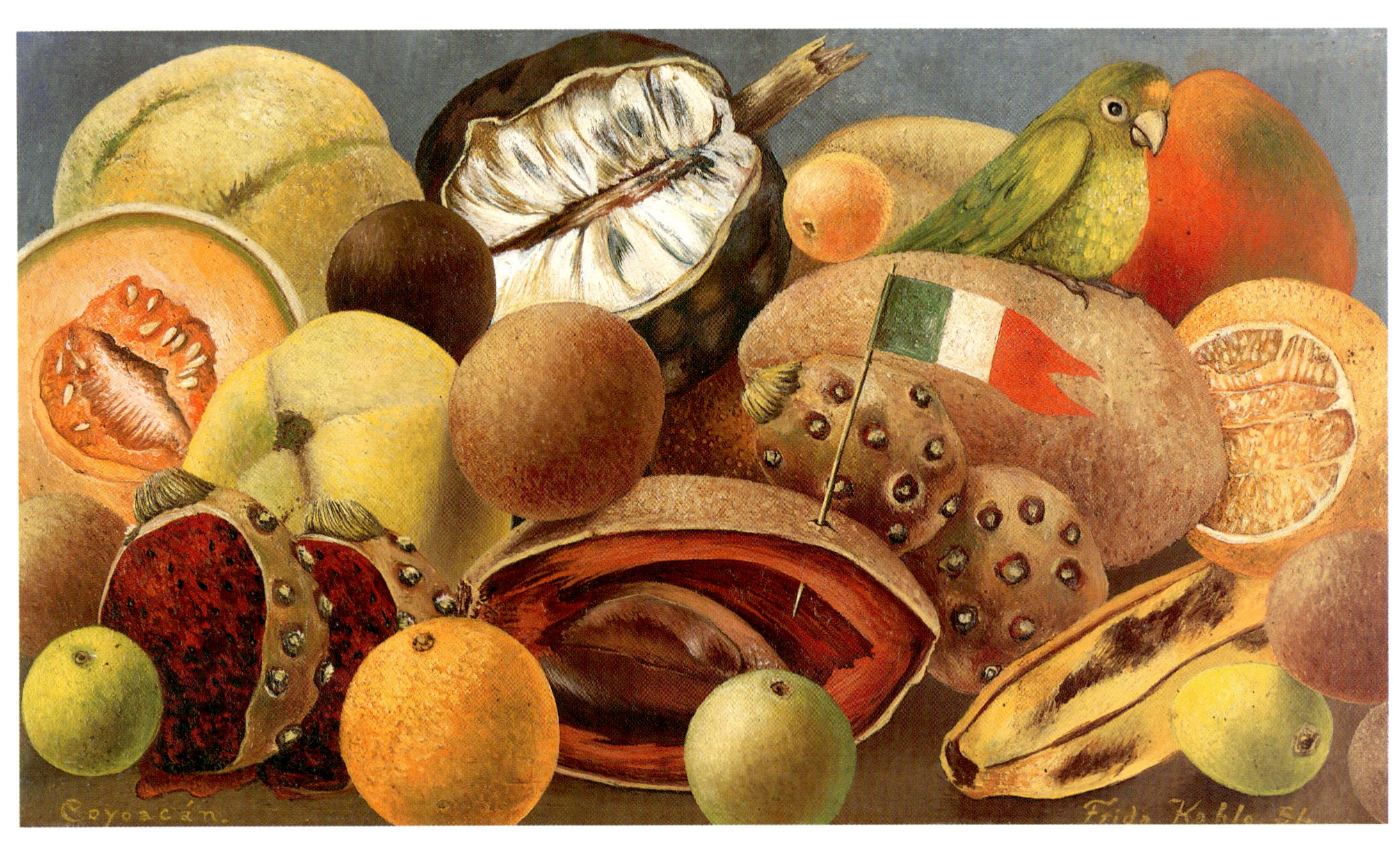

69 STILL LIFE WITH PARROT AND FLAG, 1951

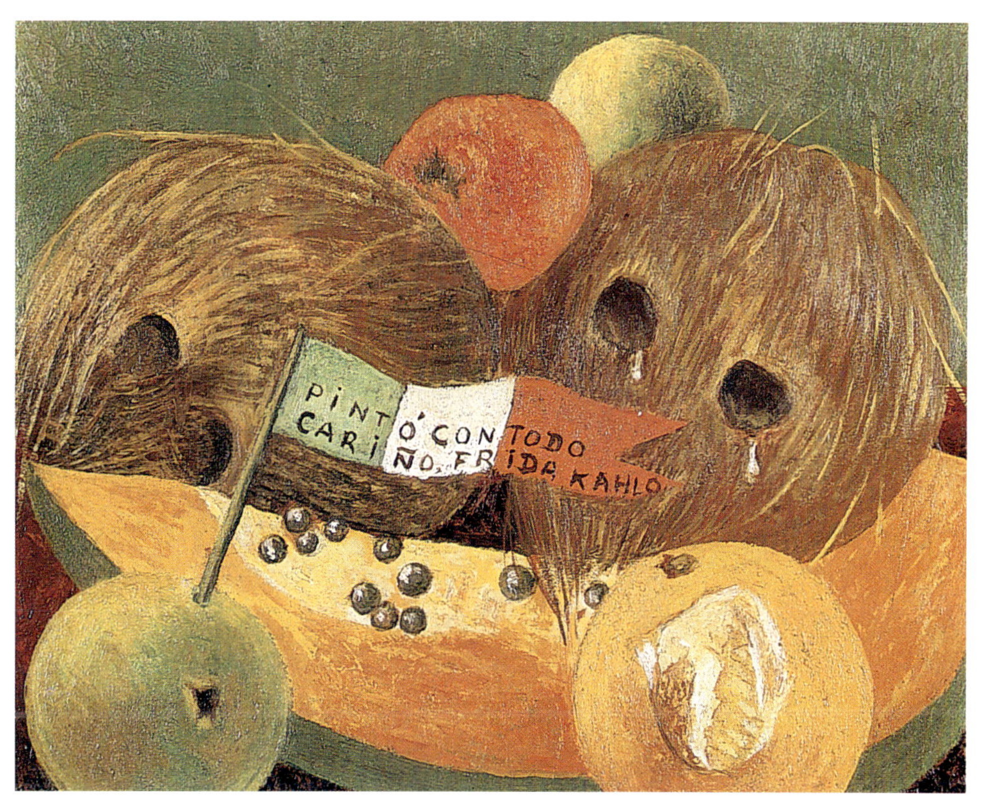

70 TEARS OF THE COCONUT (COCONUT TEARS), circa 1951

Alejandrito:

Me han dicho que estás muy triste y preocupado en un invento de radio telefonía inhalambrica porque padeces por las noches jaquecas y por eso te mando esta medicinita eh?

Mi ultimo retrato.

Estoy dando un concierto y tú lo estás oyendo en tu aparato

Ondas aereas.

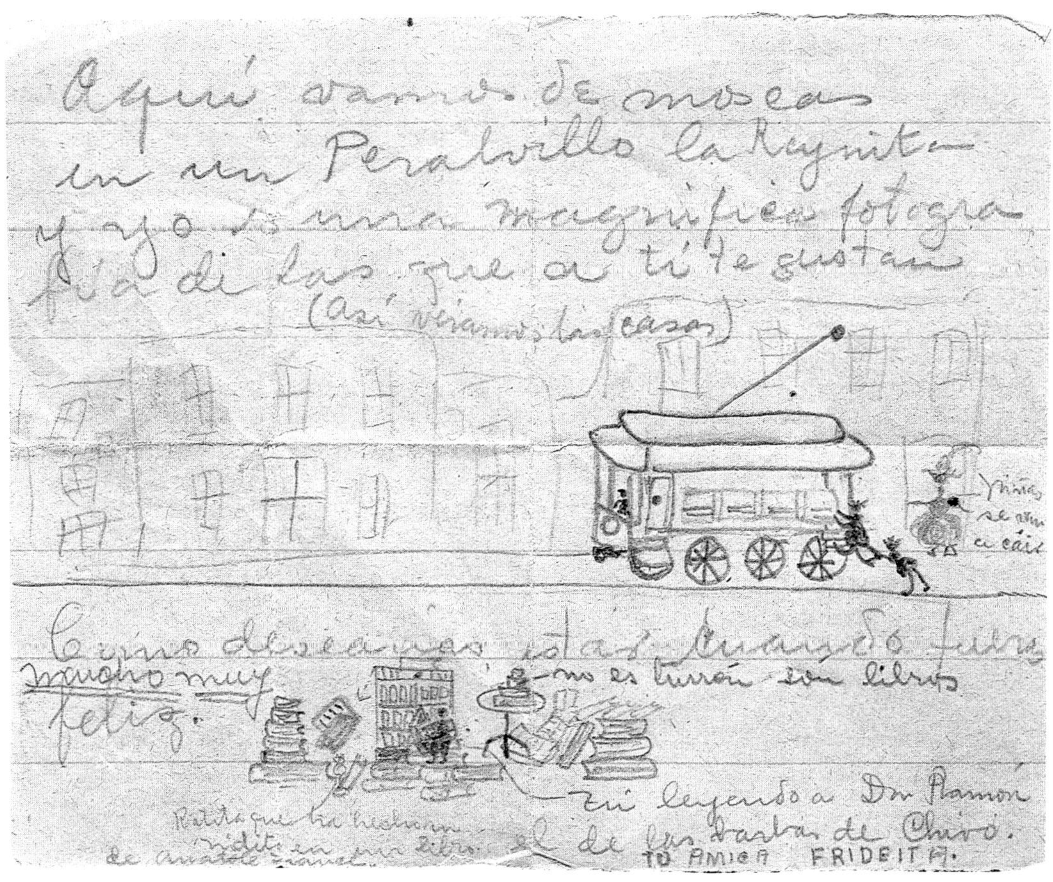

Aquí vamos de moscas en un Peralvillo la Reynita y yo es una magnifica fotografía de las que a ti te gustan

(Así veíamos las casas)

Niña se van a caer

Como descansas estás cuando fuiste mucho muy feliz.

no es turrón son libros

Tú leyendo a Dr Ramón el de las barbas de Chivo.

Retrato que te hicieron inédito en un libro de Anatole France.

TU AMIGA FRIDEITA.

76 LETTER, UNDATED

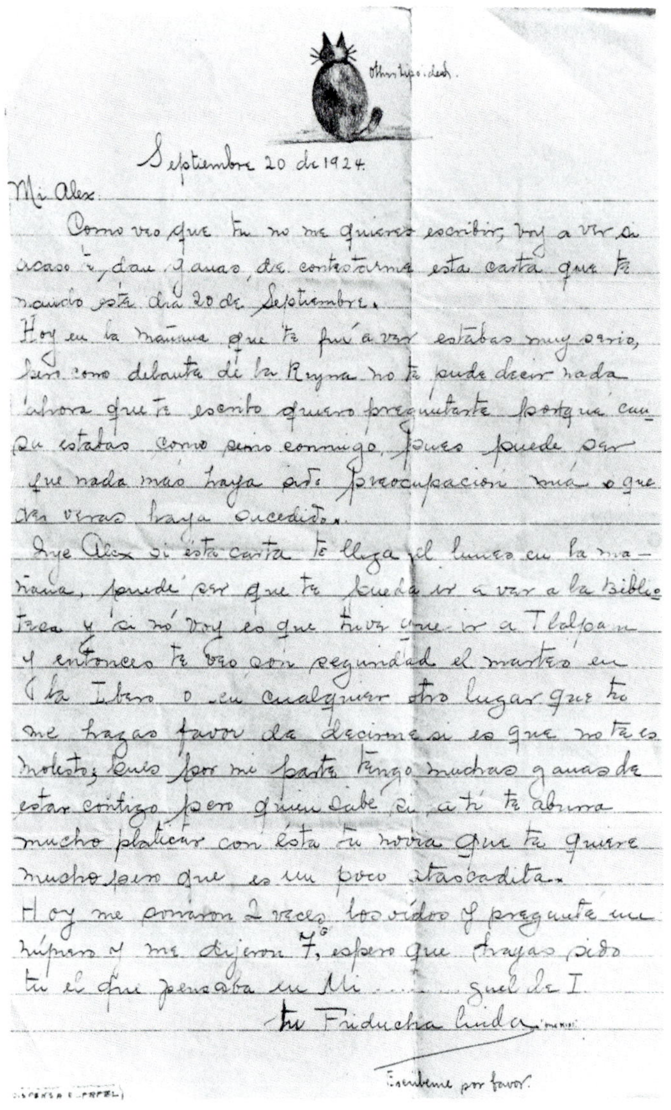

Septiembre 20 de 1924.

Mi Alex:

Como veo que tu no me quieres escribir, voy a ver si acaso te dan ganas de contestarme esta carta que te mando este día 20 de Septiembre.

Hoy en la mañana que te fuí a ver estabas muy serio, pero como delante de la Reyna no te pude decir nada ahora que te escribo quiero preguntarte porqué cuando estabas como serio conmigo, pues puede ser que nada más haya sido preocupación mía o que de veras haya sucedido.

Oye Alex si esta carta te llega el lunes en la mañana, puede ser que te pueda ir a ver a la biblioteca y si no voy es que tuve que ir a Tlalpam y entonces te veo con seguridad el martes en la Ibero o en cualquier otro lugar que tu me hagas favor de decirme si es que no te es molesto; pues por mi parte tengo muchas ganas de estar contigo pero quien sabe si a tí te aburra mucho platicar con ésta tu novia que te quiere mucho pero que es un poco atascadita.

Hoy me sonaron 2 veces los oídos y pregunté un número y me dijeron 7, espero que hayas sido tu el que pensaba en Mi ...... quel de I.

tu Friducha linda

Escríbeme por favor.

77 LETTER, 20 SEPTEMBER 1924

Contestame, contestame, contestame, contestame, contestame, contestame,

" " " " "

Salud la noticia → SE ACA... LAS PELONAS

1° de Enero de 1925.

Mi Alex: Hoy a las 11. recogí tu carta, pero no te contesté ahora mismo
porque como tu comprenderás, no se puede escribir, ni hacer
nada cuando está uno rodeado de manada, pero ahorita que
son las 10 de la noche, que me encuentro sola y mi alma. es
el momento más apropiado para contarte lo que pienso (aun
que no tengo en la mano izquierda linea de la cabeza) S. Mallén.
Acerca de lo que me dices de Anita Reyna, naturalmente ni
de chiste me enojaría, en primer lugar, porque no dices más
que la verdad, que es y será siempre muy guapa y muy chula
y en segundo lugar, que yo quiero a todas las gentes que
tú quieres o has querido(!) por la sencillísima razón de que
tú las quieres, sin embargo eso de las caricias no me gus
tó mucho porque a pesar de que comprendo que es muy
cierto que es chulísima, siento algo así... vaya, como te diré
como envidia sabes? pero eso es natural. El día que quieras
acariciarla aunque sea, como recuerdo, me acaricias a mí y te ha-
ces las ilusiones de que es ella eh? Mi Alex? Dirás que soy muy
pretenciosa, pero es que no hay otro remedio para consolarme,
de que aunque haya una Anita Reyna muy Chula, hay otra
Frida Kahlo no menos chula supuesto que le gusta a Alejandro
Gómez Arias según él y ella. Por lo demás Alex, me encantó
que fueras tan sincero conmigo y que me dijeras que la habías
visto muy linda y que, ella te había visto con su odio de
siempre, se conoce que eres un poquito llevado de por mal

———— CONTESTAME Y MANDAME UN BESITO

y recuerdas con cariño a los que te imaginas que no te han querido...
cosa que seguramente no me pasará a mí que te he querido como a
nadie, pero como tu eres muy bien cuatezón conmigo me vas a
querer aunque sepas que te quiero mucho verdad Alex? Oye herma
nito ahora en 1925 nos vamos a querer mucho eh?* No te parece que
[illegible]
vayamos arreglando muy bien la ida a los United States, quiero
que me digas que te parece que nos vayamos en Dic de este
año, hay mucho tiempo para arreglar todos los asuntos no crees?
Dime todo lo que le encuentres de malo y de bueno y si de veras
te puedes ir, porque mira Alex, es bueno que hagamos algo en la
vida no te parece, cómo nos vamos a estar nada más de mages toda
la vida en México, como para mí no hay cosa más linda que via
jar, es un verdadero sufrimiento el pensar que no tengo la
suficiente fuerza de voluntad para hacer lo que te digo, tú
dirás que no nada más se necesita fuerza de voluntad sino
antes que nada la fuerza de la moneda o (moscota) pero eso
trabajando un año se junta y ya lo demás pues es más fá
cil verdad? Pero como yo la mera verdad no sé muy bien de
estas cosas es bueno que tu me digas que tiene de ventajas
y qué de desventajas y si de veras son muy desgraciados
los gringos. Porque tienes que ver que de todo esto que te escri
bo, desde la crucesita* hasta this renglón, mucho hay de castillos
en el aire y es bueno que me desengañe de una vez para no ver
más allá del bien y del mal. (Porque todavía soy algo taruga
no creas)
Alas 12 de la noche pensé en ti mi Alex y tú? Yo creo que también porque me
zumbó el oído izquierdo. Bueno como ya sabes que "año nuevo vida nueva"
tu mujercita va a ser este año no peladilla de a 7 ps. Kilo sino lo más
dulce y bueno que hasta ahora se haya conocido para que te la comas enterita a puro beso
[illegible]

Enero 8 de 1925 - Jueves - -

Alex (propiedad asegurada) He estado buten de triste porque estás enfermo y yo quería haber estado todo el tiempo junto a tí, pero ya que no se puede me tengo que aguantar la parada hasta que te alivies que yo creo será muy pronto.
Estos días en las mañanas he venido al despacho del jefe y en las tardes estuve en la casa de tu cuate la Reynilla como habrás pensado en el momento que recibiste el bultito que te mandé con la gata o fámula, de la Reynis o no?
Ayer en la noche al único que ví fué a Salas que me dijo que lo habías felicitado de año nuevo, de una manera buten de alambicada y chistosa, y hasta creía que entre tú y yo lo habíamos hecho pero como yo no sabía nada, ~~pues~~ le dije que con toda seguridad habías sido tú porque era raro que a otro se le ocurriera hacer lo tan original y chispa. (Ya has de saber cual fué la felicitación por eso no te la explico) Antier sí no vi a nadie, mas que a la Reyna y anduvimos buscando decoraciones para el teatrito que se va a llamar TEATRO PELLO; y viendo la manera mas eficaz de conseguir chamba, le mandamos un telegrama a Chole de la siguiente alambicación,
Estimada Señorita.
Estudiantes ruegan respetuosamente se sirva concederles una entrevista.
Contestación a Pimentel 31. Srtas A. Reyna y F. K.
Yo creo que únicamente le regalamos al telégrafo nuestro tostón.

Contéstame luego luego en cartas de luto eh porque me gustan mucho.

pero todo es hacer la lucha. El lunes a las 8½ vamos a entrar a practicar taquigrafía y mecanog... a la Oliver para que no estemos tan atascadas en esa cuestión, pero sin embargo estoy mas triste que-qué bebés - porque de ninguna manera puedo conseguir chamba pronto y el tiempo se va como agua. La Güera Olaguíbel probablemente va a trabajar el El Globo de Palavicini y el otro día que me la encontré en un camión me dijo que le ofrecían una chamba en la Biblioteca de Educación pero que necesitaba una recomendación de algún poderoso de éstos y que si yo la podía conseguir me dejaba esa chamba porque ya tiene casi segura la del Globo y para eso quiero ver a Chole o a ver a quien demonios veo para que me haga la valedura. Pagan 4 o 4.50 y me parece que no está nada malo, pero antes que nada tengo que saber algo de máquina y de garabato. Así es que nada más figúrate qué atrasada está tu cuate! Pero ahorita lo único que quiero es que te alivies tú y ya lo demas viene en 5° y 6° lugar. porque del 1° al 4° lugar, són que te alivies y que me quieras. etc etc. Ya te habré fastidiado con tantas cosas, así es que ya me despido pero pronto doy la vuelta (Música del pájaro carpintero) Escríbele a Chong Lee que me mande saludar en tus cartas. Y tú escríbeme o si ya estás mejorcito dime cuando sales para poderte ver porque ya ves que yo soy muy chillona y si no te veo se me salen sin quererlas las de Sn Pedro. Que te alivies pronto pronto y que pienses un poquito en mí es lo que quiere tu hermana [illegible] Frieda

79 LETTER, 8 JANUARY 1925

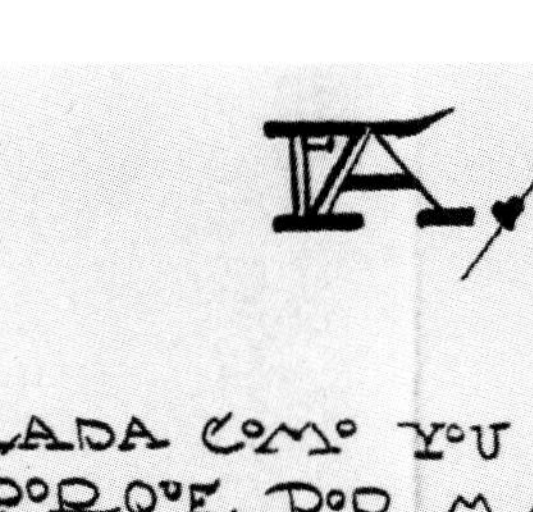

MY ALEX:

No soy one pelada como you pensó anoche, porque no me despedí of you, porque por más que hice, non pude ya salir al avise falaz. Pero espero que you me perdonará ¿no?

Si you want mañana viernes, mi lo verá in the night, in the little tree.............. pa' darnos al amor...

Mi telephoneará to las cuatro he! (non es "he" (el) you know.

Yo necesito que vareas veces you me diga.....

"Don't be lagrimilla" – it's very sweet for me.

"Yo am" to you very much. You lo cree?

Well, yo le suplico me perdone lo de ayer por haberse tratado of my mom.

Your forever.

Frieda.
Lagrimilla de Gómez Arias
or
I virgen lacri-morum.

"You no me escribe for the aicrón de anoche verdad?

One viento alicio buten de juerte.

— AGOSTO 21. 1926. =

PARA LA SONSA. V.gr. (COBRO $2.00 POR ILUSTRAR CARTAS)

80 LETTER, 21 AUGUST 1926

New. York. Junio 30/46

Alex darling,

No me dejan escribir mucho pero es solo para decirte que ya pasé the big trago operatorio. Hace tres weeks que procedieron al corte y corte de huesores. Y es tan maravilloso este medicamen, y tan lleno de vitalidad mi body, que hoy ya procedieron al paren en mis puper feet por dos minutillos, pero yo misma no lo belivo. Las dos first semanas fueron de gran sufrimienti y lágrima, pues los dolores no se los deseo a nobody. Son buten de estridentes y malignos, pero ya en esta semana se

aminoró el alarido y con ayuda de pastillamenes he sobrevivido más o menos bien. Tengo dos cicatrizotas en the espaldilla en this forma

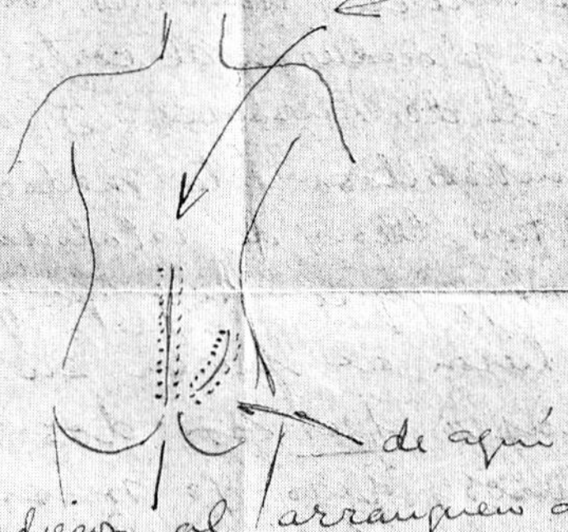

de aquí procedieron al arranquien del cacho de pelvis para injertarlo en la columnata, que es donde la cicatriz me quedó menos horripilante y mas derechita. Cinco vertebrillas eran las dañadas y ahora van a quedar cual riflamen. Nada más que

the latosidad es que tarda mucho el huesor para crecer y reajustarse y todavía me faltan seis semanas en cama hasta que me de den d'ialta y pueda huir de esta horripilante City a mi amado Coyoacán. ¿Como estás tú please escribeme y mandame one libraquito, please don't forget me. Como está tu mamasita? Alex, no me abandones solita solita en este maligno Hospital y escribeme. Cristi está rete aburridísima y ya nos cansamos de calor. Hace gran cuantiosidad de

calor y ya no sabemos que hacer.

¿Que hay en Mexico que pasa con la raza por allá?

Cuentame cosas de todos y sobre todo de ti.

tu
F.

Te mando buten de cariños y tantos besos – Recibí tu carta, que me animó tanto! No me olvides.

81 LETTER, 30 JUNE 1946

CARLOS MONSIVÁIS

FRIDA AND HER FRIENDS

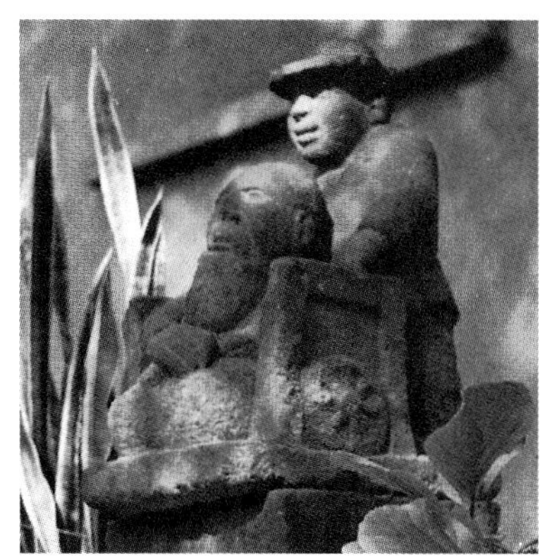

In the twenties, the middle classes of Mexico City were convinced, for various reasons, that the Mexican revolution was still in progress. Porfirio Diaz's dictatorship was over; what many considered the gravest danger, the peasant militia, had disappeared, but fighting between the factions continued. Clearly, there had been no radical transformation of the economic and social structures in Mexico. The government continued its incendiary harangues and, whether noticed or ignored, there has been a relentless change in mentality. Regardless of whether they supported, rejected, or felt alienated by it the Revolution compelled all artists and intellectuals to adopt emergency survival measures. There was no other alternative: governmental appreciation for culture was scant. Humanistic studies were limited to the study of law, there were hardly any museums or galleries, publishing houses languished, and an anti-intellectual climate prevailed in an environment dominated by a type of nationalism that meant too many things to too many people. Mexican artists and writers were thus compelled – like artists all over the world – to find in the friendship of their peers a chance for further growth. For all those who wanted to write, paint, or compose, the circle of friends became the university, discussions and debates the intensive courses. How else could the information gap – the lack of specialized publications, the hatred a mistrust of society and government for art and literature – have been mended?

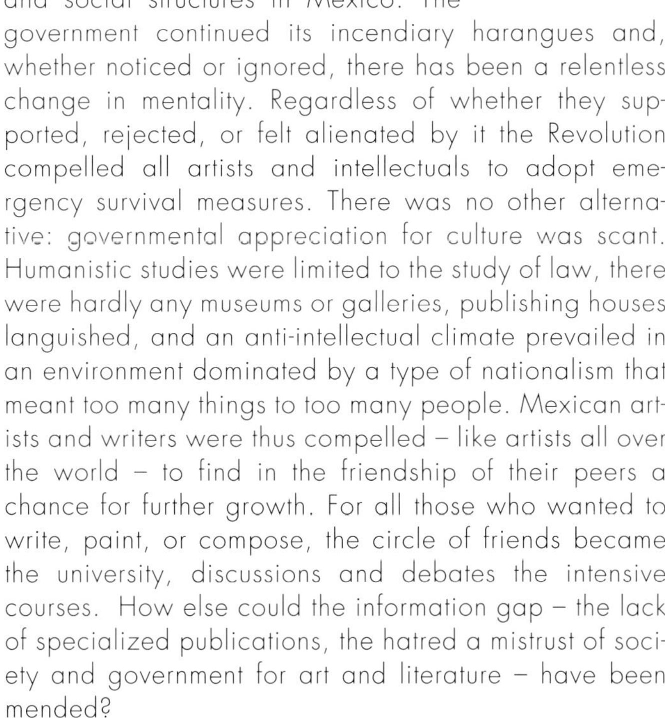

The difficulty of being a woman in a proudly male-oriented environment, an environment that throughout the nineteenth century ignored the existence of female painters and reserved for female poets a corner of barely tolerated sentimentalism, was an added obstacle. The support of their circle of friends was the only thing that nourished Frida Kahlo and María Izquierdo, another great contemporary artist. At the time, to consider a female artist seriously, without paternalistic condescension, was in itself a challenge to prejudice.

In the case of Frida Kahlo, her friends became a true "ecological niche" by offering her their knowledge, their humor, their trust, windows to a reality that confused and unnerved her. The group to which she belonged during her adolescence at the Escuela Nacional Preparatoría, called "Los Cachuchas" because of the distinctive caps they wore, was formed by young people who admired the power of the Revolution while rejecting the primitivism of the revolutionaries. Those young people would almost inevitably become politicians, writers, diplomats, and university professors. They would be instrumental in the psychological rescue of the shy young woman who suffers a tragic accident, the self-taught young woman who paints in order to fend off death. Among them, the brightest and the closest to Frida is Alejandro Gómez Arías, the leader of the student movement in 1929, an educated man, a tireless traveler, one of the first who embodied the humanism which, in spite of itself, the revolution engendered. Gómez Arías, Frida's first boyfriend, to whom she confided the process of separating from her dramatic childhood, was her spiritual shelter and her enduring friend.

When Frida met Diego Rivera, her circle of friends expanded. During the initial years of the muralist movement, Rivera was not only a well-known figure in the relatively small city but also a symbol of the endless possibilities of the Revolution at home and abroad. Rivera was outrageous, exhibitionistic, legendary because of the stories people told about him and those he told about himself, an indefatigable worker, he displayed his genius, his dogmatism and his fantasy. He became everything to Frida, her great translator of reality. He was her husband, her lover, her friend. He taught her fundamental lessons: to despise the criticism of conservative moralists, to appreciate vital liberties, to love work, to create a mystique – for Frida this was basically the calm serenity reincarnated in her own paintings.

Rivera's house, the center of the Mexican Renaissance, was an obligatory place to see and be seen. It was visited by travelers from Europe and the United States, painters, poets, writers, photographers, politicians, collectors of paintings and of "spine-tingling sensations," the first feminists, well-known eccentrics. Frida adopted this environment whose diversity spoke of the human and cultural wealth of a closed and fiercely homogeneous city. To her new friends Frida owed the broadening of

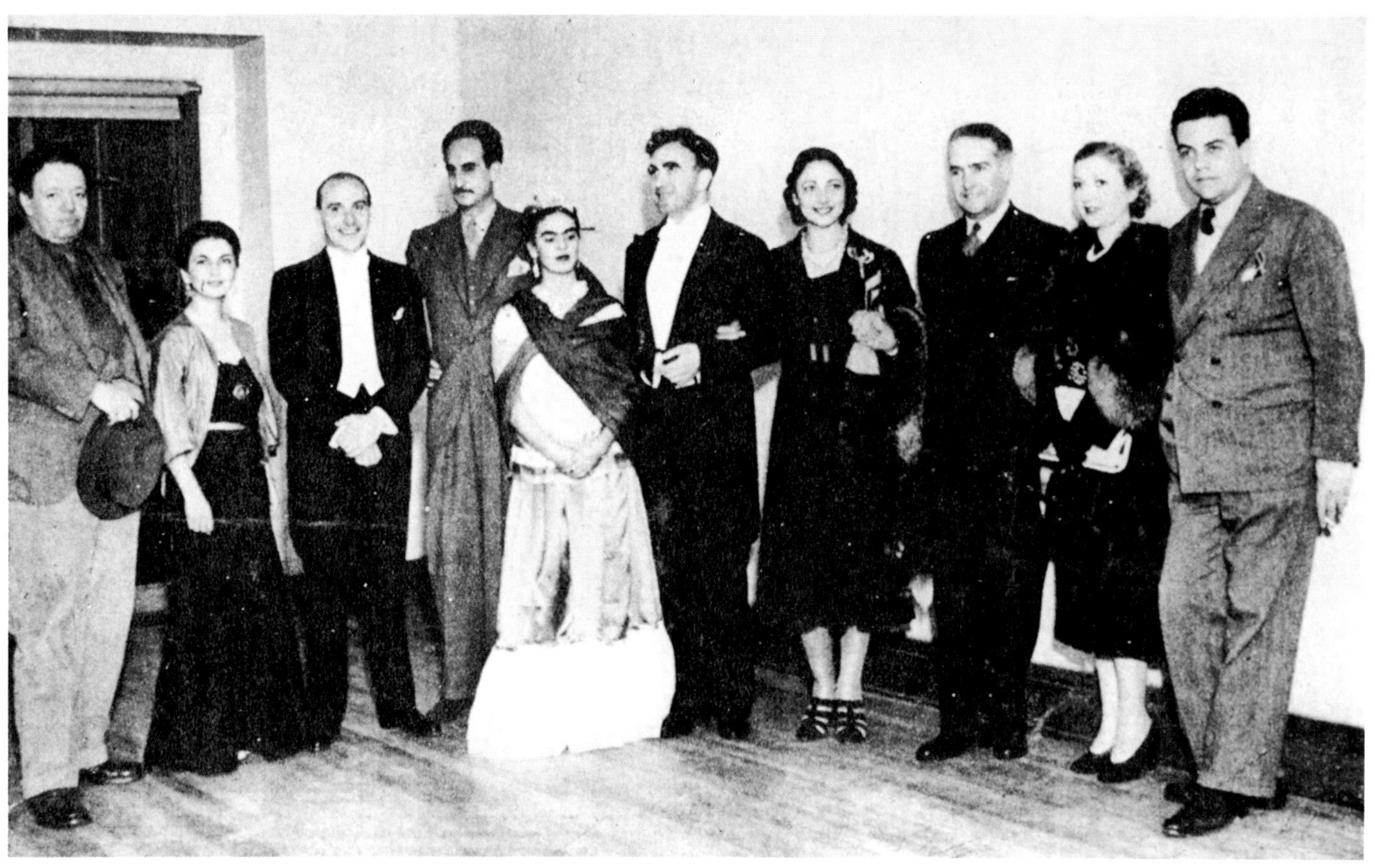

From left to right: Diego Rivera, Cristina Kahlo, Maestro Pittaluga, Fito Best, Frida Kahlo, Maestro Chávez, Rosita de Covarrubias, the architect Obregón Santacilia, Ana María de Pittaluga and Miguel Covarrubias.

her horizons, an escape from the spiritual limitations of her extremely conservative family.

Like so many others during that time of great militancy spanning the period between the twenties and the Cold War, Frida divided her friends into two, not easily reconcilable, groups. On the one hand, the Communists and nationalist revolutionaries, on the other, the bourgeois (who purchase paintings), the defenders of "pure art" (who believe in themselves and their paintings), the challengers of the dominant morality (who find in Frida a natural ally).

Only in later years would Frida consider herself personally committed to the revolutionary movement, rather than being associated with it through her loyalty to Rivera. Earlier, during three decades, her left-wing politics had a sentimental touch, closer to that of radical bohemians. As regards the political opposition, Frida did not befriend Marxist theoreticians or labor leaders but those who in the sixties would have become part of the counterculture. These constituted a motley assembly: intelligent, serious lesbians, composers of proletarian songs, promoters of a return to nature, art collectors. For instance, Concha Michel, a feminist when there were hardly any, who insisted on women's voting rights in meetings where she sang her own songs and claimed for members of her gender the double theological referent:

God is also Goddess, since only the patriarchal whim has so absolutely made him (her) male.

Frida was also, without condescension, a close friend of homosexuals, the worst-feared stigma at the time. Beginning in the twenties, largely due to the upheaval caused by the Revolution, homosexuals began to venture into a society in which most considered their very presence unthinkable, and only referred to them sarcastically as a non-existent species. Homosexuals were welcome only in the territory of romantic radicalism, and there Frida was a symbol; this was known and described by Salvador Novo, Xavier Villaurrutia, and Carlos Pellicer, three outstanding poets whose work was unknown outside Mexico because they came from a "Third World" country. Gay artists sought out Frida, dedicated poems to her, and were the first to recognize her uniqueness.

Novo, a personal and political enemy of Rivera and the one who most ostensibly exhibited his sexual preferences, saw Frida "as rocket, as grenade, as shattered glass, as tidings, as a telegraph in blood." Pellicer drew comparisons: "You, like a trampled garden on a skyless night. You, like a storm-beaten window; you, like a blood-soaked handkerchief; you, like a butterfly full of tears; like a prematurely broken day; like a tear on a sea of tears; singing and victorious araucaria: a beam of light for everybody."

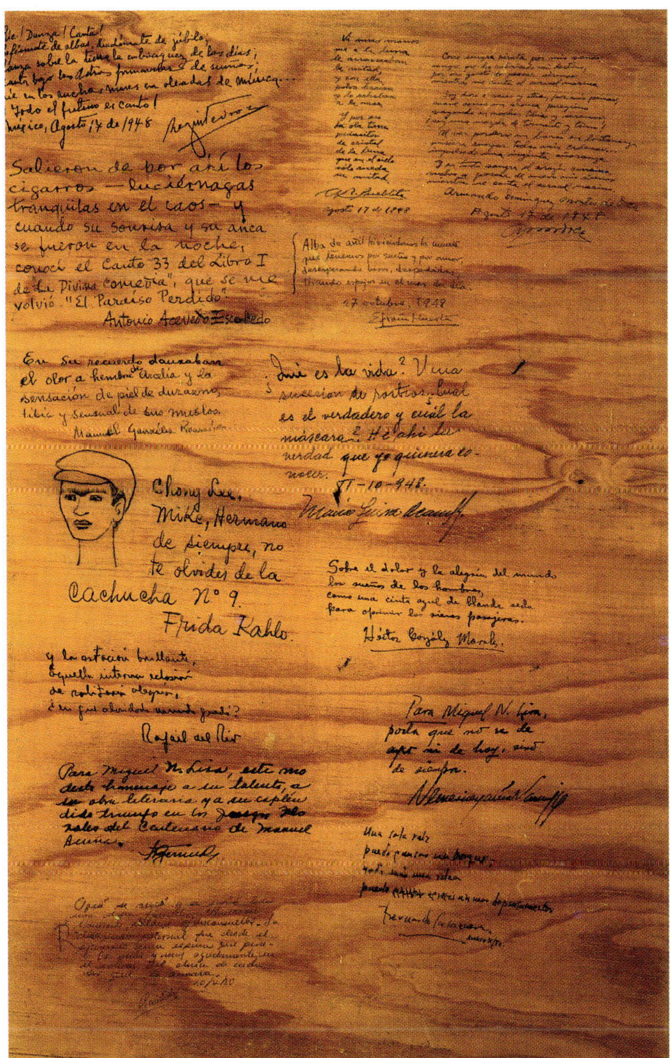

Plywood with various inscriptions, among them a drawing and text dedicated to Chong Lee (Miguel N. Lira) by Frida Kahlo.

"You, like a storm-beaten window..." This phrase by Pellicer admirably summarizes Frida's experience: one operation after another, torture upon torture, pulling herself up from her frailty and falling back into it, wrapped in her sickness, her other dramatic vision of the world. For Frida, the child of despair, friendship was also a strategy against pain. Although the obsessive theme of her paintings is the self-portrait – "narcissism" as invented health, a dialogue with herself in the mirror of permanence, the integration in one image (a votive painting) of the Virgin and the donor – in Frida's daily life her fellow human beings, as for all of us, more than for all of us, were irreplaceable. They offered their caring and strengthened her through contact, conversation, and love. In her house in Coyoacán, Frida was invariably surrounded by a circle of visitors, friends, and disciples, warm-hearted, she displayed concern for them and hid her suffering as best she could. Her friendships provided Frida with a means of distancing herself from her pain.

In her tumultuous and varied sexual relationships Frida's lovers, both male and female, represent not just physical attraction, but also her attempt to grow roots through friendship. Perpetually and almost maniacally in love with Rivera, she considered her other relationships – with Trotsky, with American artists, with unconditionally devoted women, with folk singers – as fleeting passions that stimulated her desire to live and to admire. Not surprisingly, two of her great romances were two of the great mythical figures of Mexican cinema, two unusual beauties: Dolores del Rio and María Felix. Frida was herself a beauty whose Mexican or Mexicanist presence Rivera cultivated; what enthralled her about Dolores and Maria was something that mattered to her above all else: not the embodiment of the excellence of the race but the perfect combination of features and decorum, of personality and attire, a seldom acknowledged strain of aesthetic nationalism, a tendency somewhat similar to the attitude of Black Americans in the sixties: "I'm Black and I'm beautiful."

In Dolores and María, Frida saw unusual beauties and, through an intuition that in time became ideology, she recognized the images favored by the country and rediscovered by movies, photography, and painting: the "intimate Mexico" of small towns, folk dress, vigorous Indian faces and landscapes, an idyllic world uncontaminated by civilization. In pursuit of these clues and signs of a

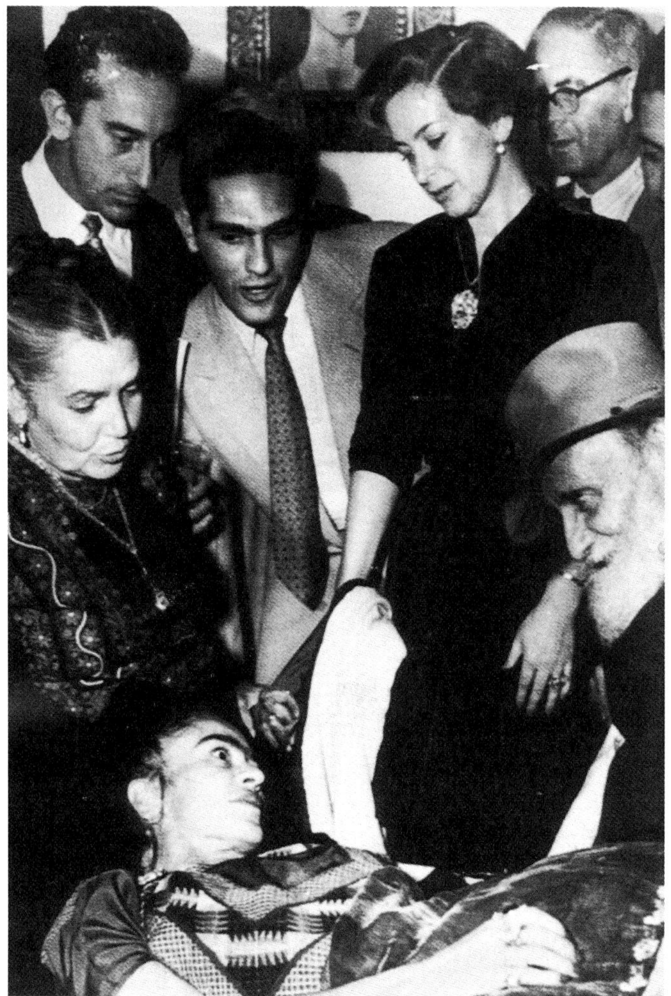

Dr. Atl greets Frida Kahlo at her exhibition at Lola Alvarez Bravo's gallery, 1953.

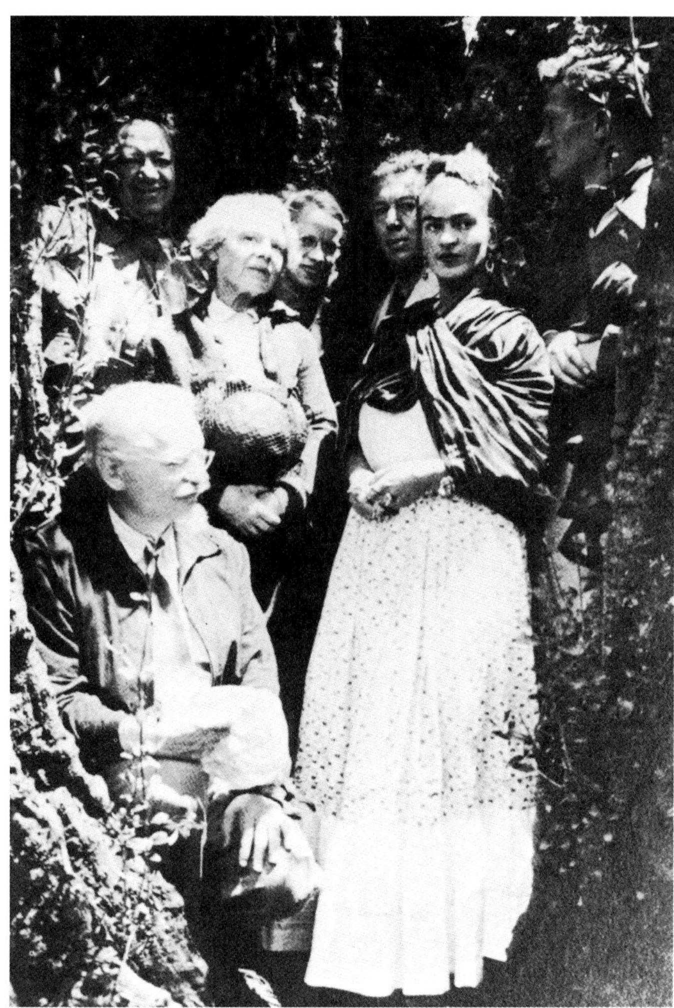

Frida Kahlo with Leo Trotzky, Natalia Trotzky, Reba Hansen, André Breton, and Jean Van Heijenoort (Trotsky's secretary), 1931.

Mexico where myth guides aesthetic perception ("Look for the myth and you will find visual achievements and events"), Frida encouraged her friends to wear typical Mexican attire and turned herself into an advertisement for thousand-year-old wonders; as hymns of joyous despair she adopted *canciones rancheras* (folk songs), the mournful songs of withdrawal into ideal rural solitude, which the *mariachi* had commercialized. This explains her close friendship with two notable interpreters of Mexican songs: Lucha Reyes and Chavela Vargas. In her home, in gatherings around the guitar, tequila and *mezcal* at hand, Frida conquered pain by conjuring it up. She even culled from "Cielito lindo," the well-known traditional song, the defiant motto of one of her paintings: "Arbol de la esperanza mantente firme" (Tree of hope keep firm). It could also have read: "Corazon apasionado disimula la tristeza" (Passionate heart hide your pain).

How did Frida understand, through her senses and feelings, rationally or irrationally, the extreme pain, the mourning over miscarriages, the despair over lost fetuses, the hypertrophied leg, the ulcers, the orthopedic prisons, the nails that mark her body, the endless operations, the surgical incisions, the dependency on alcohol, drugs, and painkillers, the resistance to madness that Demerol (drived from morphine) provided her? In her journeys through hospitals and between operating tables Frida gathered another most important group of friends, the physicians that advised her, took care of her, subjected her to destructive studies, prescribed medication and changed prescriptions, conjectured and proposed. Helpless, anguished, courageous, she painted herself with her doctor at her side or, as in her 1945 painting *Without Hope,* offered an account of her ordeal. Emaciated, she lies dejectedly in bed sucking nourishment from a huge funnel propped up on an easel, ironically evoking the horn of plenty. On the back of the painting is an inscription: "A mi no me queda ya ni la menor esperanza, todo se mueve al compas de lo que encierra la panza" (I don't have a shred of hope left, everything moves at the rhythm that the belly commands). For someone in a borderline situation like Frida Kahlo's, as enemies of a body she deeply loved, her physician friends provided the third formative or didactic space: the space of the daily difference between life and death. Every day, for hours, for seconds, amidst the worsening of her circulatory condition, amids surgeries on her right foot or her spine, amidst amputations and graftings, Frida experienced the most humiliating delirium, quite often unable to distinguish between reality and nightmare. The painting in which she painted herself next to the portrait of her friend Dr. Farill synthetizes the devastating experience: the palette that Frida uses is her own heart, and the brushes are blood-smeared scalpels, obvious symbols transformed by her sincerity. Protecting her from above in the painting is her physician, a friendly reality who does not ease the pain but to a certain extent makes it intelligible.

In friendship Frida Kahlo found and perfected her vision of the world.

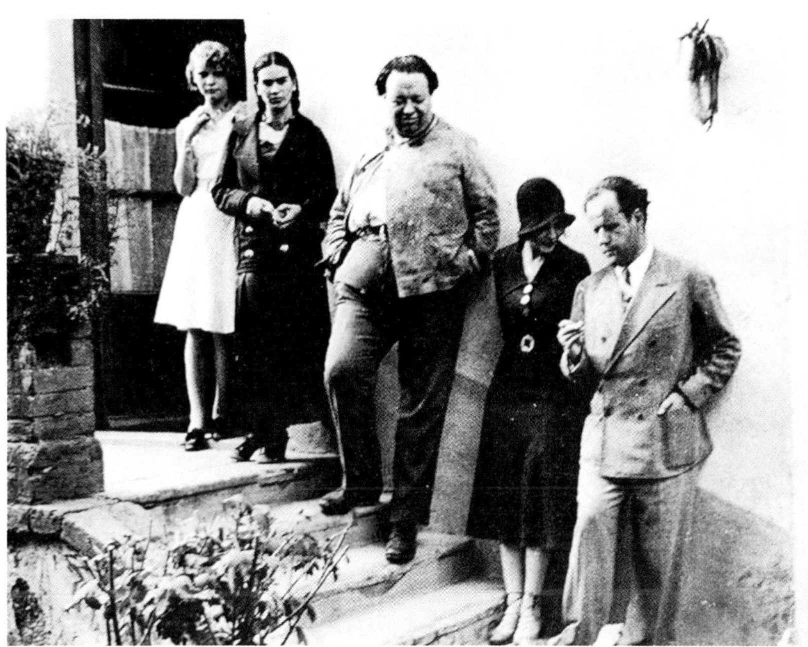

Frida Kahlo and Diego Rivera with Sergei Eisenstein in the Blue House, 1931.

ERIKA BILLETER

THE PAINTERS: FRIENDS AND CONTEMPORARIES

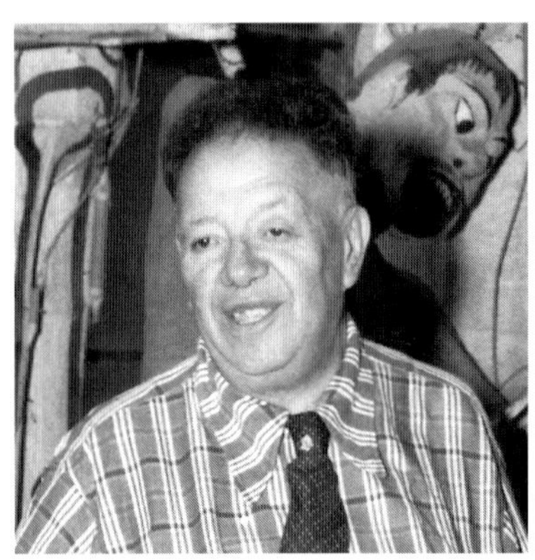

"Of all the Mexican painting of quality produced during the last twenty years Frida Kahlo's work shines like a diamond in the midst of many inferior jewels, clear and hard, with precisely defined facets." That is what Diego Rivera wrote in 1943 in his essay "Frida Kahlo and Mexican Art." The most famous wall painter of his time recognized the unique talent of his wife, Frida Kahlo, from the beginning. He saw her not only with the eyes of love but in his capacity as a profound authority on Mexican (and European) art of his time. He admired the unique value of her work. Indeed, among her contemporaries, Frida Kahlo's work occupies a special, sacrosanct place. She pursued her vocation for art during the seminal decades after the Revolution, which caused all the hidden powers that had been preserved within Mexican culture for centuries to awaken. As a painter Frida is part of those sweeping changes and, together with Rivera, the center of cultural and intellectual Mexico.

But she and Diego were not the only extraordinary personalities of those decades.

To let the cultural climate be experienced optically, we shall now present individually, the friends and contemporaries of Frida Kahlo and Diego Rivera. Uninfluenced by them, Frida evaded the different trends and tendencies current at the time, and practised her egocentric art apart from these others, and perhaps her work really does glitter like a diamond, as Rivera described it.

Frida had a friendly attachment to the Mexican muralists, who made their works accessible to the public and brought art to the people. The contrast between Frida's art and the monumental fresco paintings by Diego Rivera, José Clemente Orozco, and David Alfaro Siqueiros could not, however, be greater. The creators of a new, public art on the one hand, and Frida's small paintings, fixed entirely on her own life story – on the other – at the time of the Revolution in Mexico, everything was possible and conceivable. Wieland Schmid referred to her pictures as an "intimate biography." Her private mythology stands in contrast to the muralists' new picture of history, which ained to take possession of the myths of a people. "Those who paint murals always tell the story of mankind." Nevertheless, Frida, with her favorite students, "Los Fridos," once tried her hand at fresco: her mural at the pulquería "La Rosita" was produced in 1943 but was later destroyed.

In the thirties and forties the Surrealists caused a sensation in Mexico. Emigrés from Europe, they brought new impulses to a country in which myth was still alive and in which the fantasies of the predominantly Indian and *mestizo* population were Surrealistic in nature. In 1936 Antonin Artaud had come to Mexico yearning for an unspoiled, original culture. He saw it embodied in the paintings of María Izquierdo, a friend of Frida's who, like her, was inspired by the rituals and objects of Mexican folk art. Izquierdo did not transcend these elements, but used them as a direct pictorial theme. She did not adapt the style or composition of the retablo to her own pictorial theme, but rather painted the image of a *retablo*. But, like Frida, she demonstrated Mexicanidad and wore Indian dress. In the last years of her life she was lame on one side after suffering a stroke. She died in 1955, one year after Frida Kahlo. Rivera had promoted María Izquierdo's first exhibition in Mexico in 1929. At that time she was living with Rufino Tamayo. In the deepest sense, her entire work is dedicated to Mexico. In 1947 she herself wrote in her "cultural credo," "I try to make my work reflect the true Mexico, that I feel with and love. I avoid anecdotal, folkloric, and political themes because they have no expressive or poetic power. I believe that in the world of art a painting is an open window to human imagination."

In 1940 Frida Kahlo exhibited together with María Izquierdo in the famous exhibition of Surrealism in Mexico City. Together with Wolfgang Paalen, André Breton was the initiator of this exhibition, which took place in the gallery of Ines Amor. Two years before that Breton had visited Mexico and discovered in Frida the ideal of a female Surrealist. For him she was the quintessence of Surrealism, and her participation in the international exhibition of Surrealism was of great importance to him. Frida herself was less enthusiastic, because she did not think of herself as a Surrealist. But she exhibited *The Two Fridas* and *The Wounded Table* (a picture that is no longer in existence). Wolfgang Paalen and his wife, Alice Rahon, had emigrated to Mexico and they also took part in this exhibition. Although it caused a big sensation in Mexico, this show did not by any means establish a Surrealistic movement but rather stimulated the existing "surrealistic" element. Alice Rahon became an intimate friend of Frida's, although her art was entirely different in orientation. Remedios Varo came to Mexico with the poet Benjamin Péret in 1942, the same year in which Leonora Carrington made Mexico her chosen home. Both painters created their major works in Mexico. Neither is known to have been a friend of Frida Kahlo, but both painters further opened Mexico to Surrealism, which they interpreted in very personal ways. Gunther Gerszo, who made his first autodidactic attempts at art in 1940, also joined the Surrealist emigrants. In the fifties he painted Surrealistic compositions, until by degrees he turned to abstract art.

But Mexico's cultural scene is homogeneous and full of creativity. Dr. Atl (Gerardo Murillo), who had taken an active part in the Revolution and whose volcano pictures from the forties are very famous, was one of Frida Kahlo's oldest, closest friends. The Riveras, like many others, owed to him their awareness of Mexican folk art, which became just as important to them as the works of the Indian high cultures. There were other individuals who had a decisive influence in shaping Mexican art after the Revolution: Julio Castellano and Agustin Lazo, one of the founders of the "Contemporáneos," along with Frida's close friend Carlos Pellicer, who wrote a poem or two for her and who had the Blue House made into a museum after her death.

All these painters have something in common which gives Mexican art in the years after the First World War its special place within art history: an attempt to make the state of suspense between reality and unreality a concrete experience that is comprehensible, An architect and a painter, Juan O'Gorman was Rivera's closest friend. He built Rivera's studio house in San Angel as well as a house for Frida that is connected to Rivera's house by a bridge. While his architecture is related to European modernism, his paintings show Surrealistic elements in the surroundings that appear realistic. Manuel Rodriquez Lozano is one of those painters who combines idealism, realism, and fantasy. When he became director of the Escuela Nacional de Artes Plásticas, one of the first persons to whom he gave an assignment at the school was Diego Rivera.Those painters for whom the Indian element was an essential component in their art and are, therefore, instinctively close to Diego's and Frida's work are also worth mentioning: Chucho Reyes (Jesús Reyes Ferreira), advocate of Indian culture and a close friend of Luis Barragan, Miguel Covarrubias, and Roberto Montenegro. Montenegro had been friendly with Diego since his youth.

Carlos Merida was Rivera's assistant when he painted the mural in the Escuela Nacional de Preparatoría, the same school Frida attended as a young girl and in which she stole away to observe the famous painter at work. Since his move from Guatemala to Mexico in 1919, Carlos Merida had been one of Rivera's friends. Early in his career he, too, had become interested in the original inhabitants of his country. But he went a completely opposite direction from the Mexican painters and steered towards abstract art. Finally worth mentioning is Rufino Tamayo, who as a young man was María Izquierdo's lover. Coming after the pioneering decades of *muralismo,* Tamayo is the great integrative figure in Mexican art. He tries to connect the newly won "national identity to a universal tradition," in the words of Octavio Paz. He reduces his figures to basic geometrical patterns but the contents of his pictures remain Mexican just the same. The Tehuanas, the women from the isthmus of Tehuantepec, continue to be his favorite subjects. His watermelons – *sandías* – have left a strong impression as a Mexican theme. At the end of her life Frida painted them with ever-increasing enthusiasm – as an expression of life, an expression of *Mexikanidad.*

A glance at the painter friends and contemporaries of Frida makes it clear that she, as a painter, was amazingly lucky to have been surrounded by such important artists. We have presented only a few of them here. She did not work in a vacuum, although her art was the result of solitude. She was understood and loved by artists. She was admired as a painter. In that way she is different from quite a few female painters of her time. The open, artistic situation that prevailed in Mexico was the result of the Revolution, which made the forming of a versatile, engaged cultural scene in Mexico possible. Every single artist contributed with his or her own cultural vision to the picture of the new Mexico. In the background of that unique, overpowering situation the little diamond, Frida Kahlo, glitters.

[1] Wieland Schmid, "Der Elefant und die Taube," in the cataloguo *Diego Rivera* (Berlin, Neue Gesellschaft für Bildende Kunst, 1987), 191.

[2] *María Izquierdo,* ed. Miguel Cervantes (1986).

PAINTINGS BY FRIENDS AND CONTEMPORARIES

REALISM – SURREALISM – MAGIC REALISM

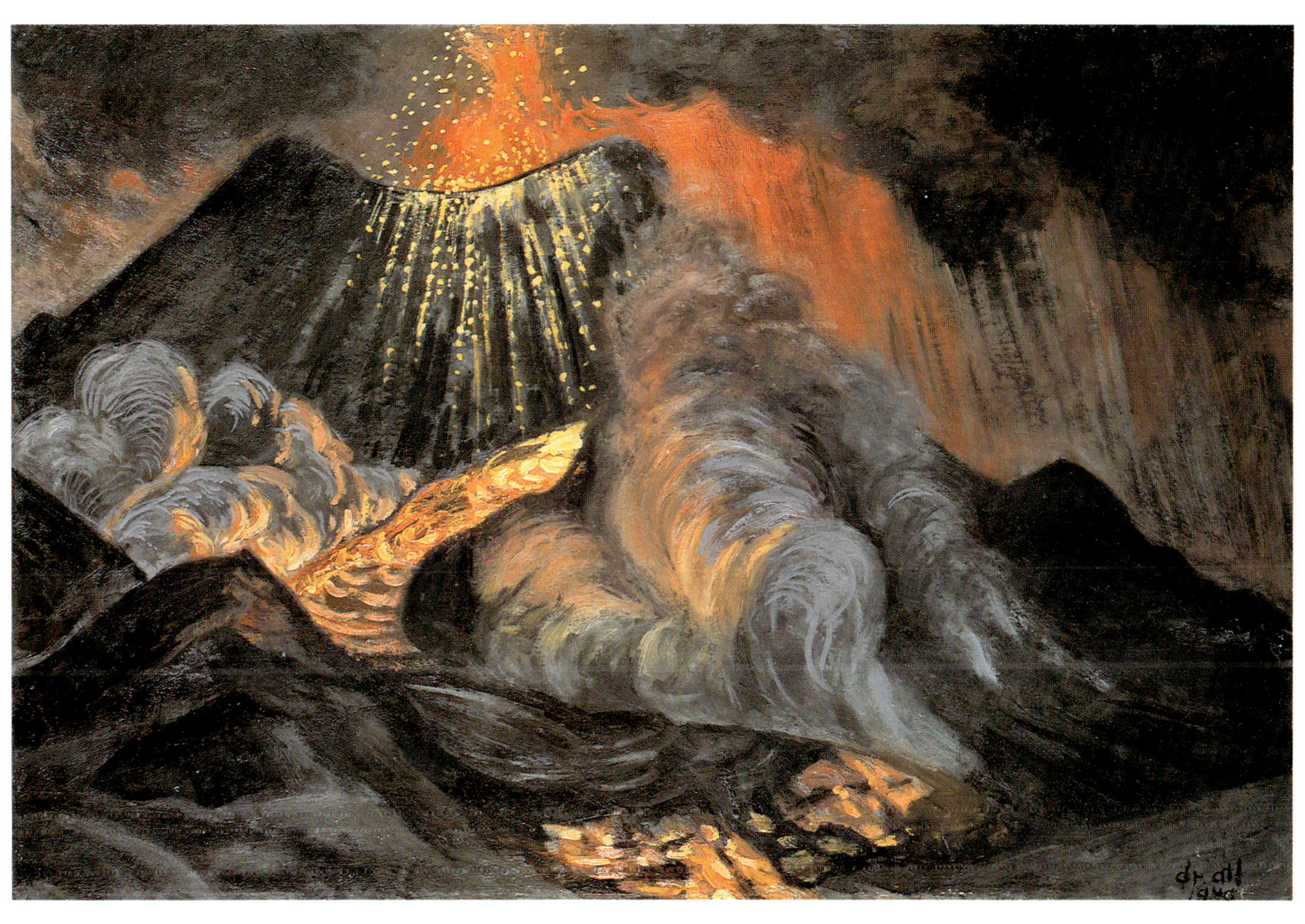

86 DR. ATL (GERARDO MURILLO), VOLCANO, 1945

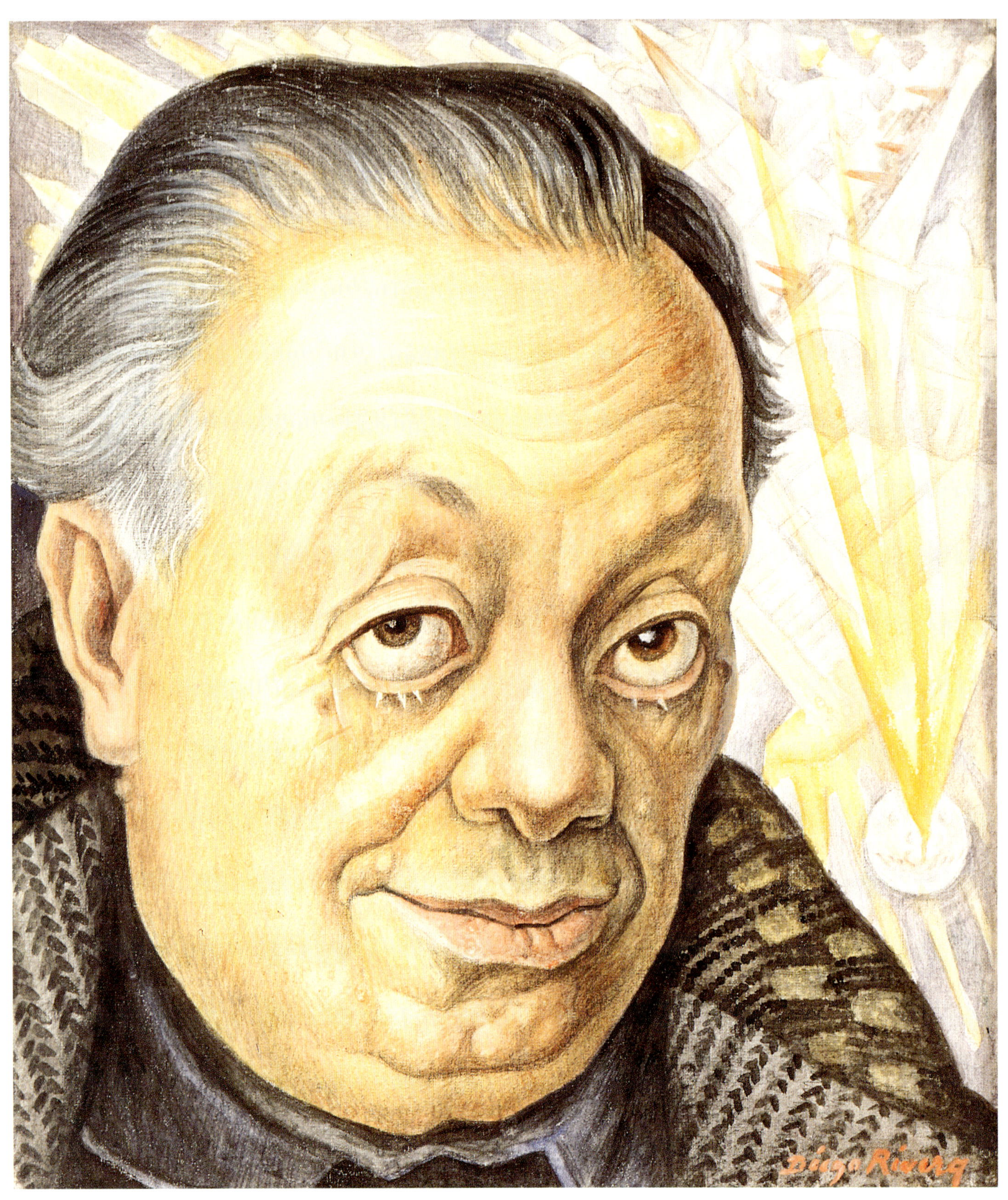

113 DIEGO RIVERA, SELF-PORTRAIT (THE RAVAGES OF TIME), undated

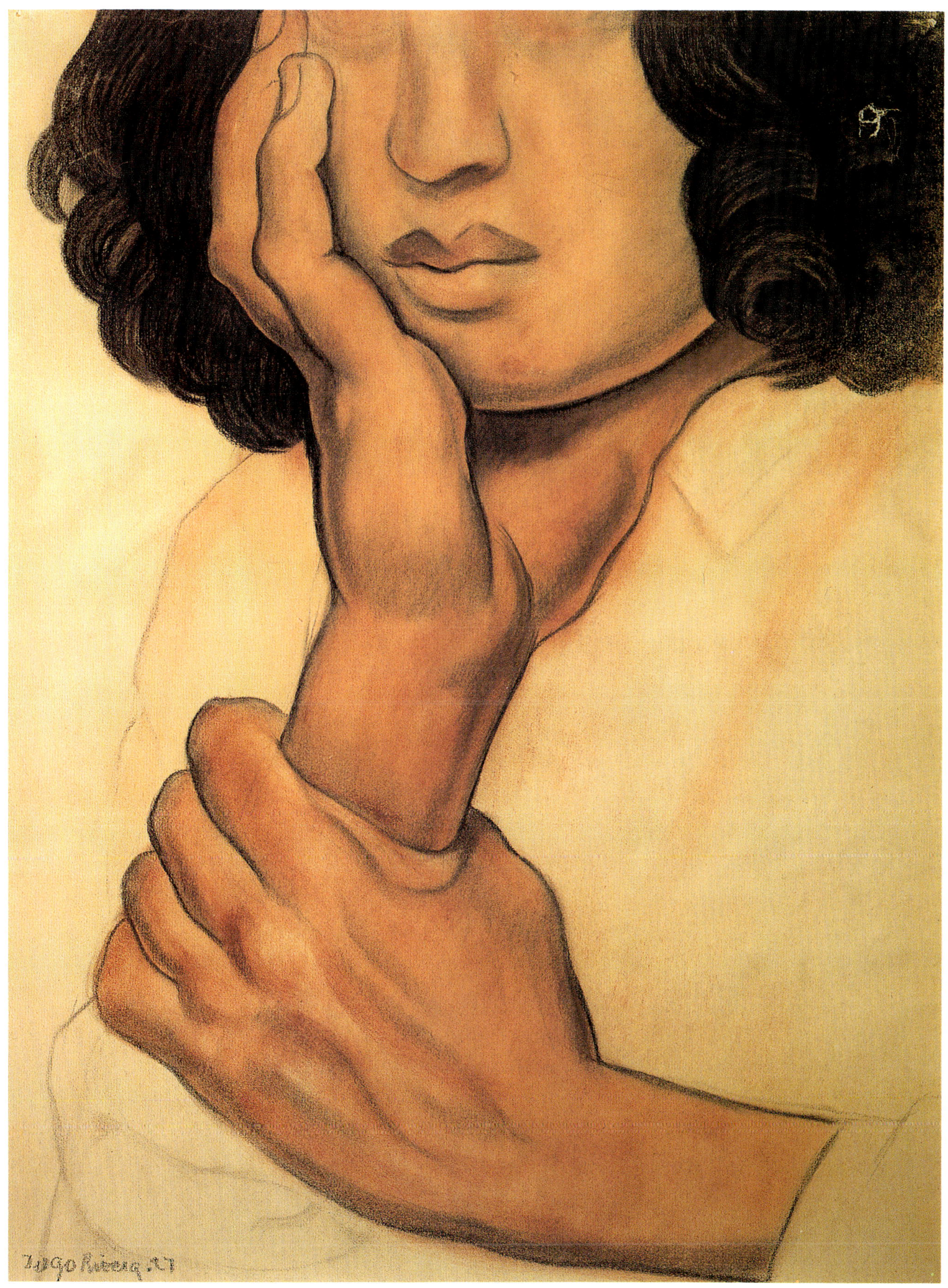

107 DIEGO RIVERA, PORTRAIT OF A WOMAN, 1927

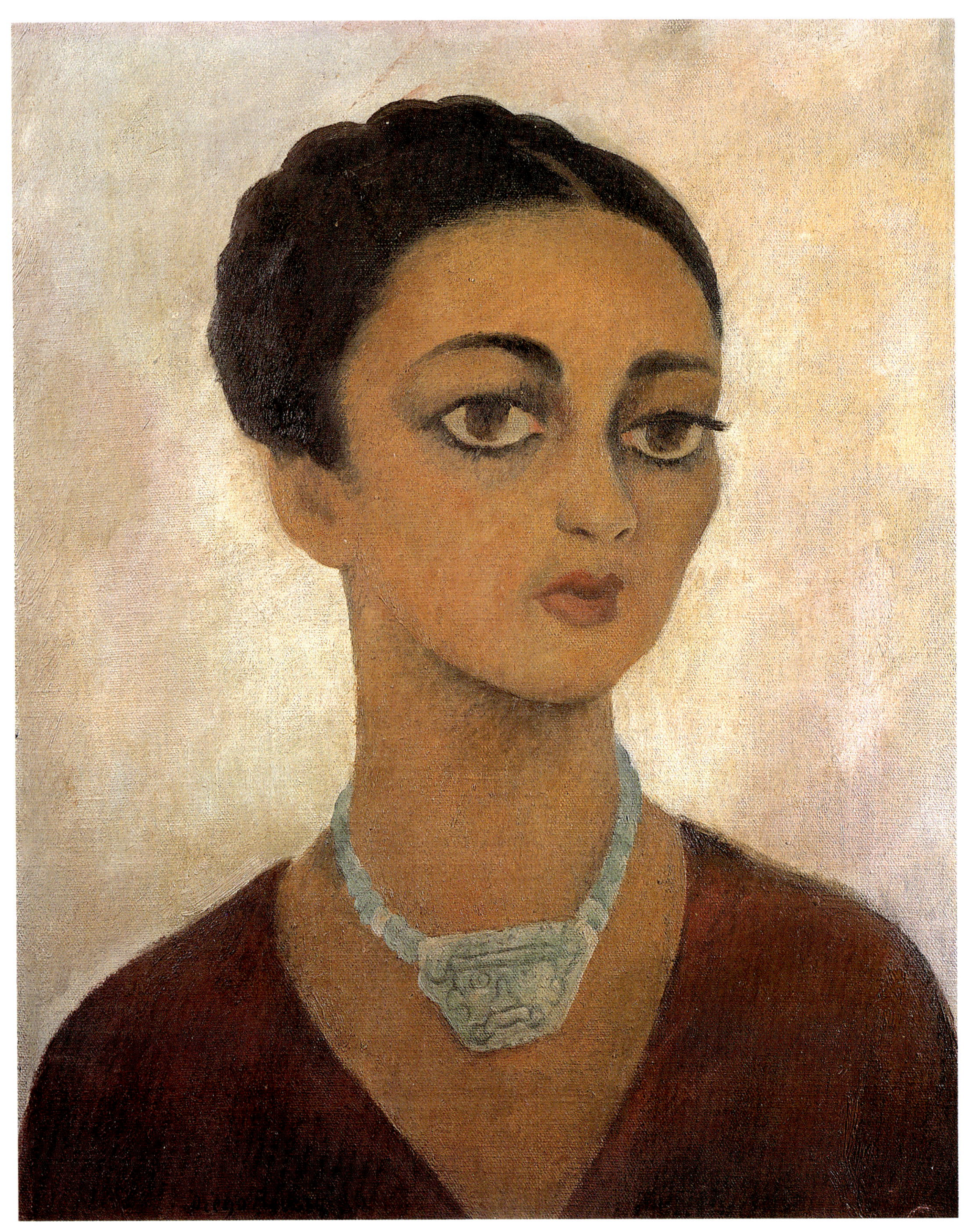

108 DIEGO RIVERA, PORTRAIT OF ROSA ROLANDO, 1930

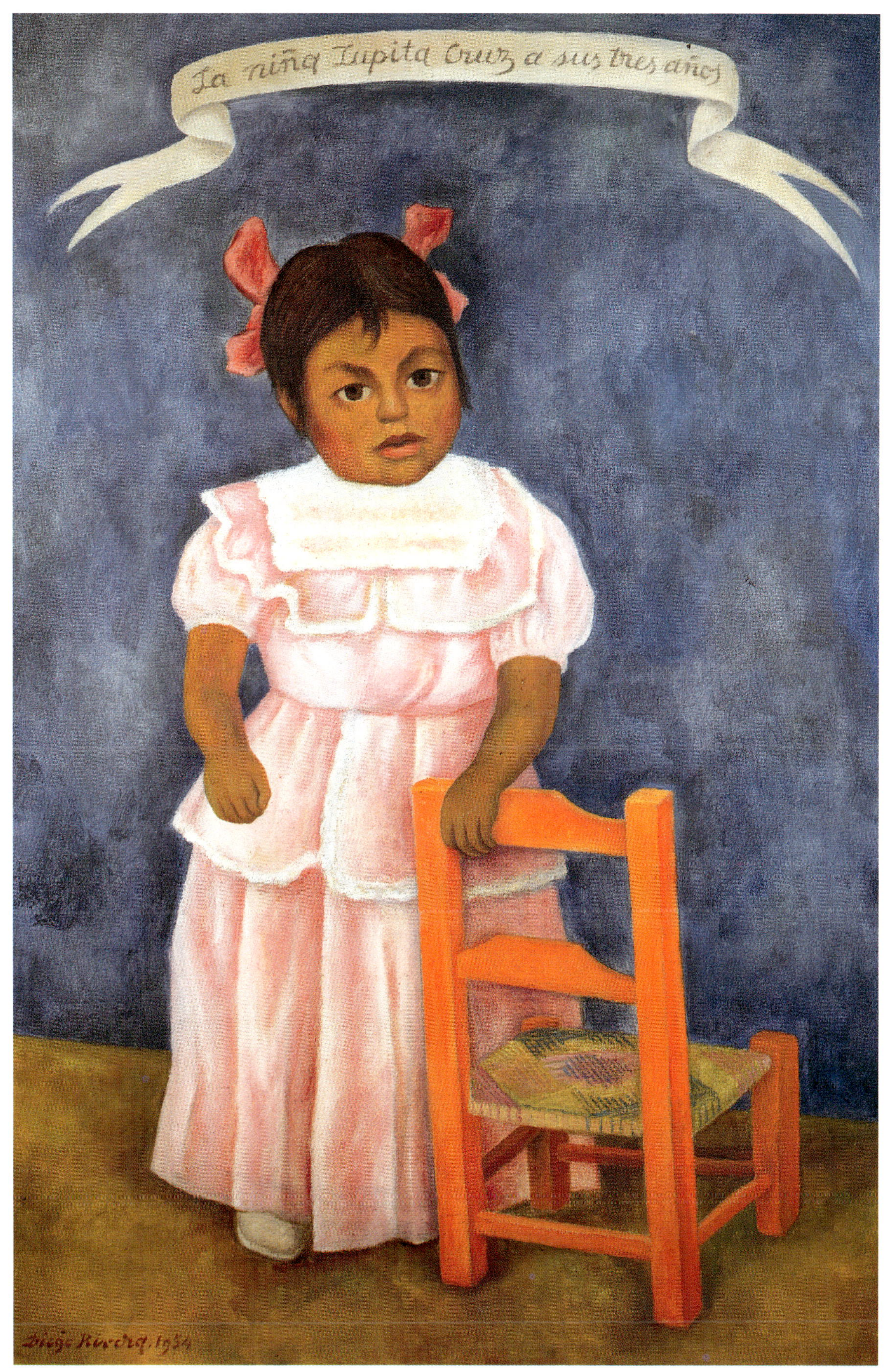

112 DIEGO RIVERA, LUPITA CRUZ AT AGE THREE, 1954

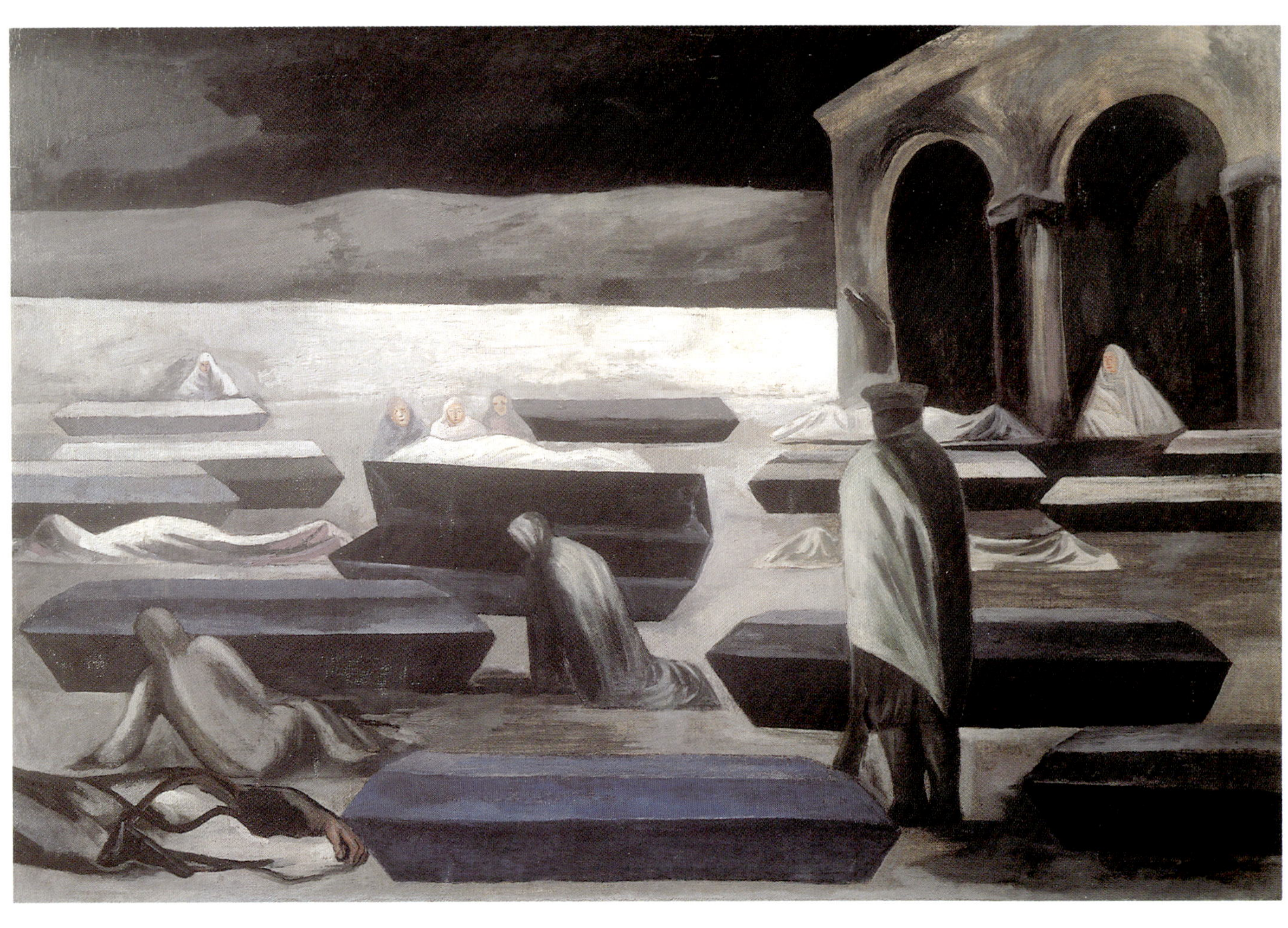

102 JOSÉ CLEMENTE OROZCO, THE CEMETERY, 1931

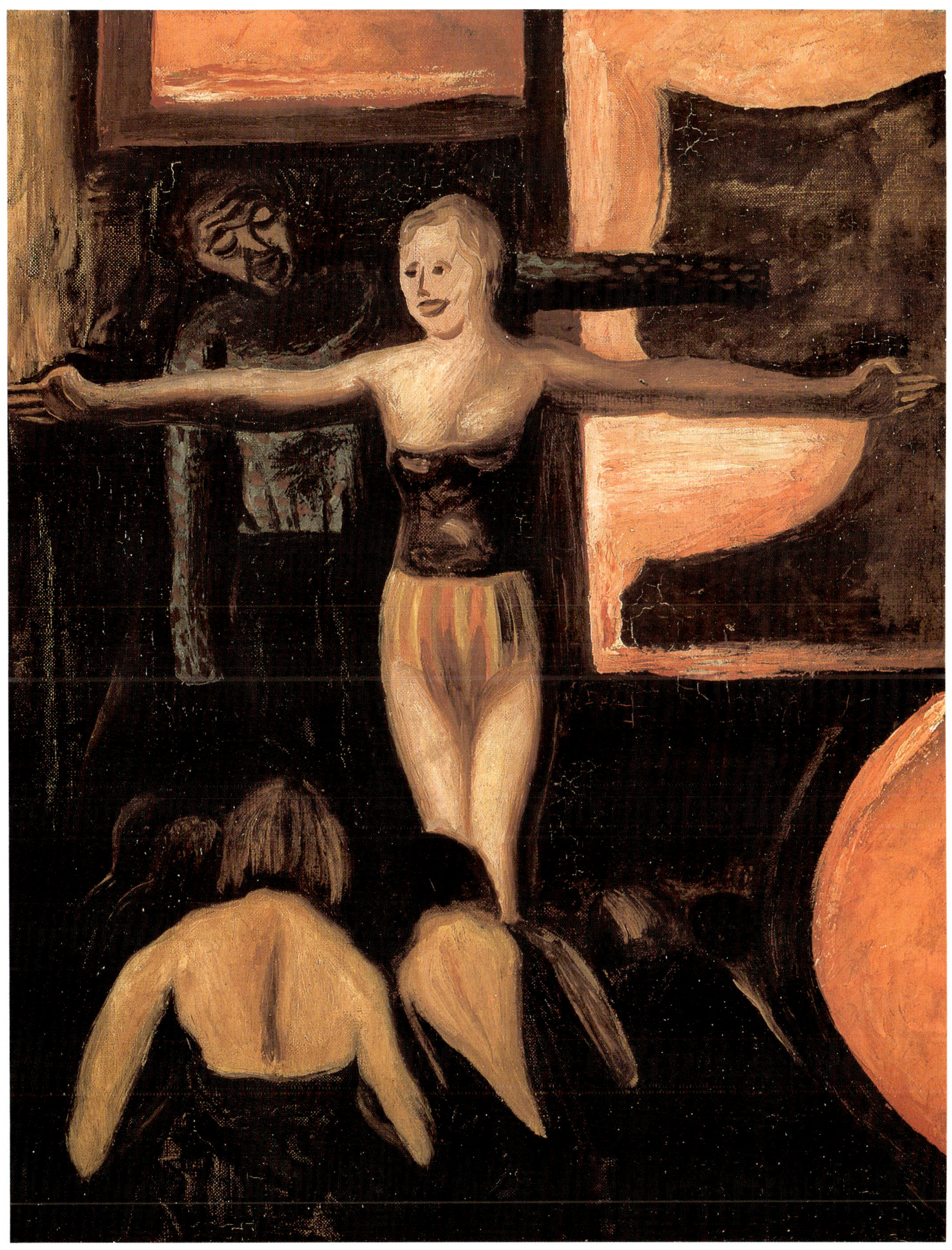

103 JOSÉ CLEMENTE OROZCO, CONEY ISLAND, circa 1930

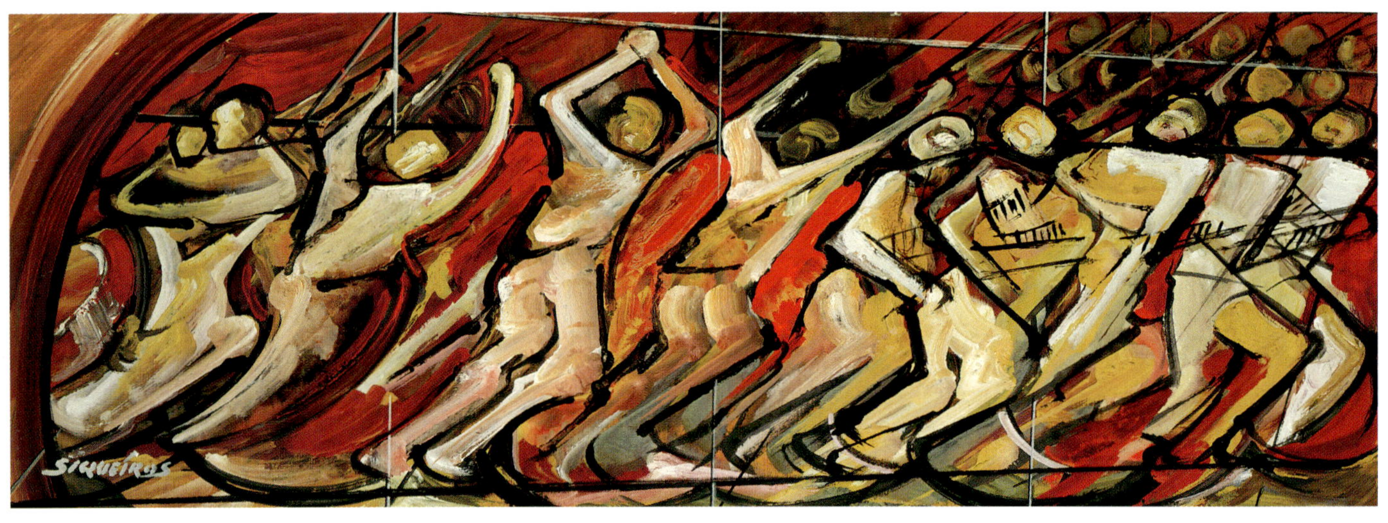

114 DAVID ALFARO SIQUEIROS, THE MARCH OF MAN TOWARD SOCIALISM, 1962

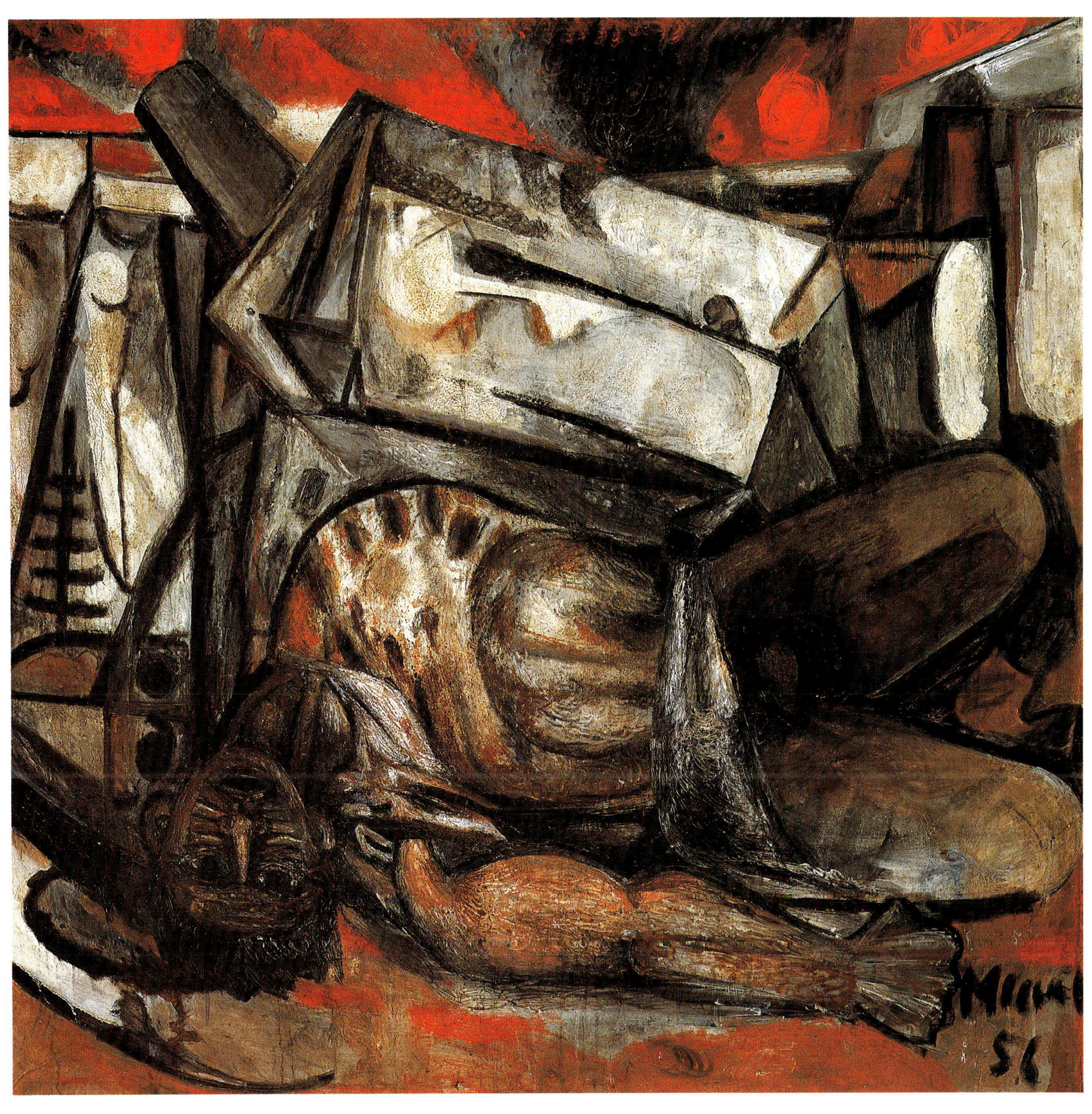

96 ALFONSO MICHEL, THE BARRICADE, 1956

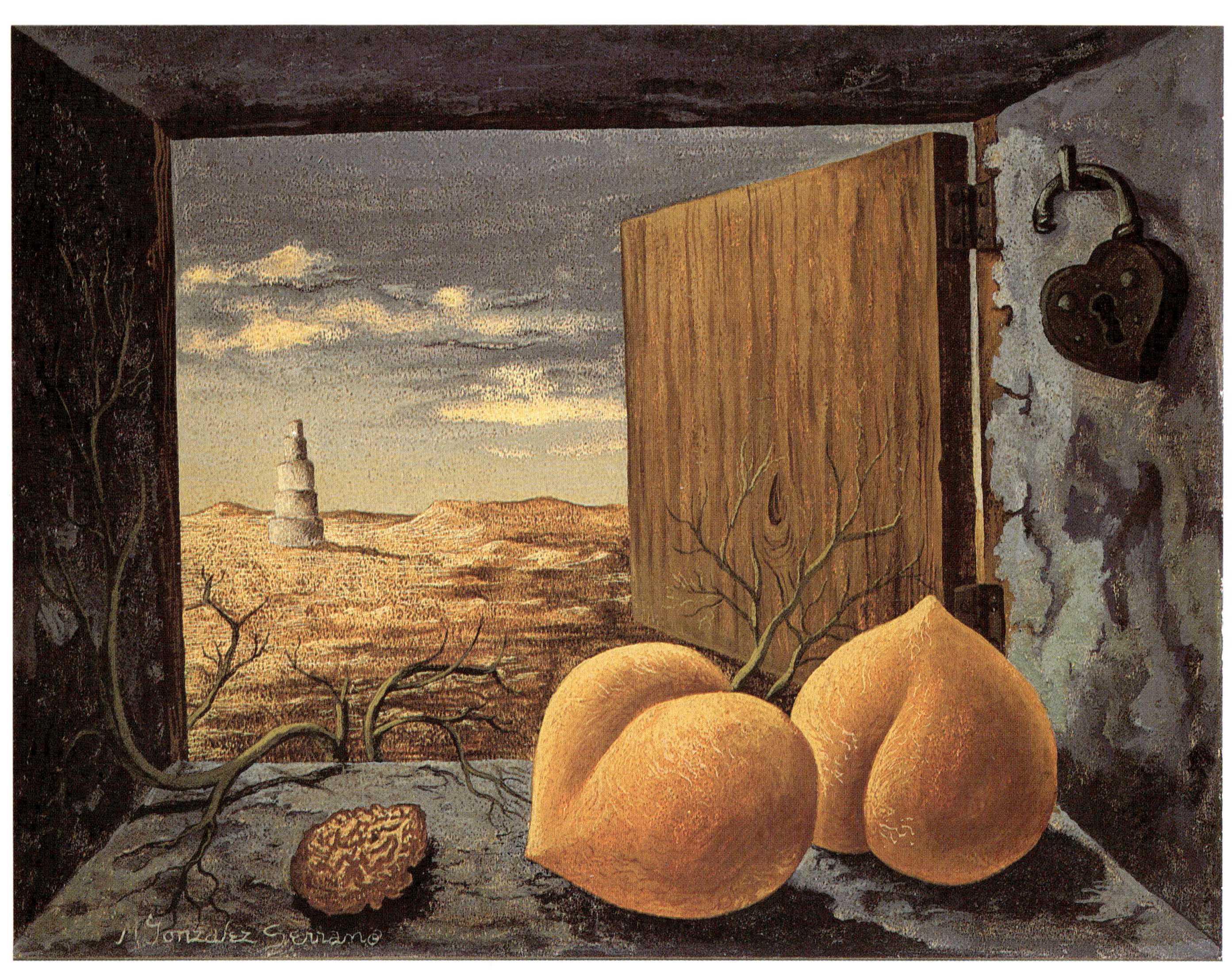

91 MANUEL GONZÁLEZ SERRANO, STILL LIFE WITH WINDOW AND LOCK, circa 1945

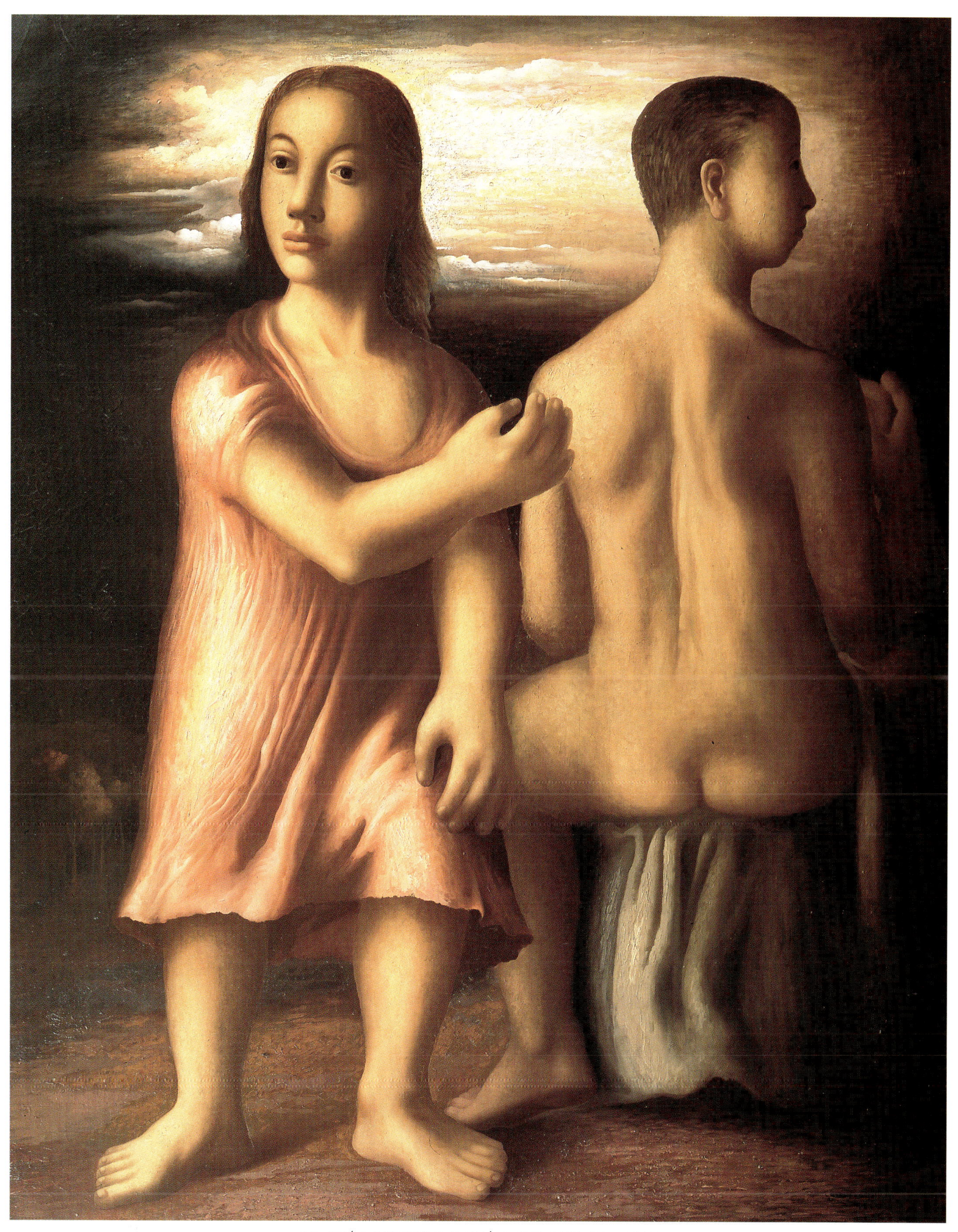

92 JESÚS GUERRERO GALVÁN, THE CHILDREN, 1939

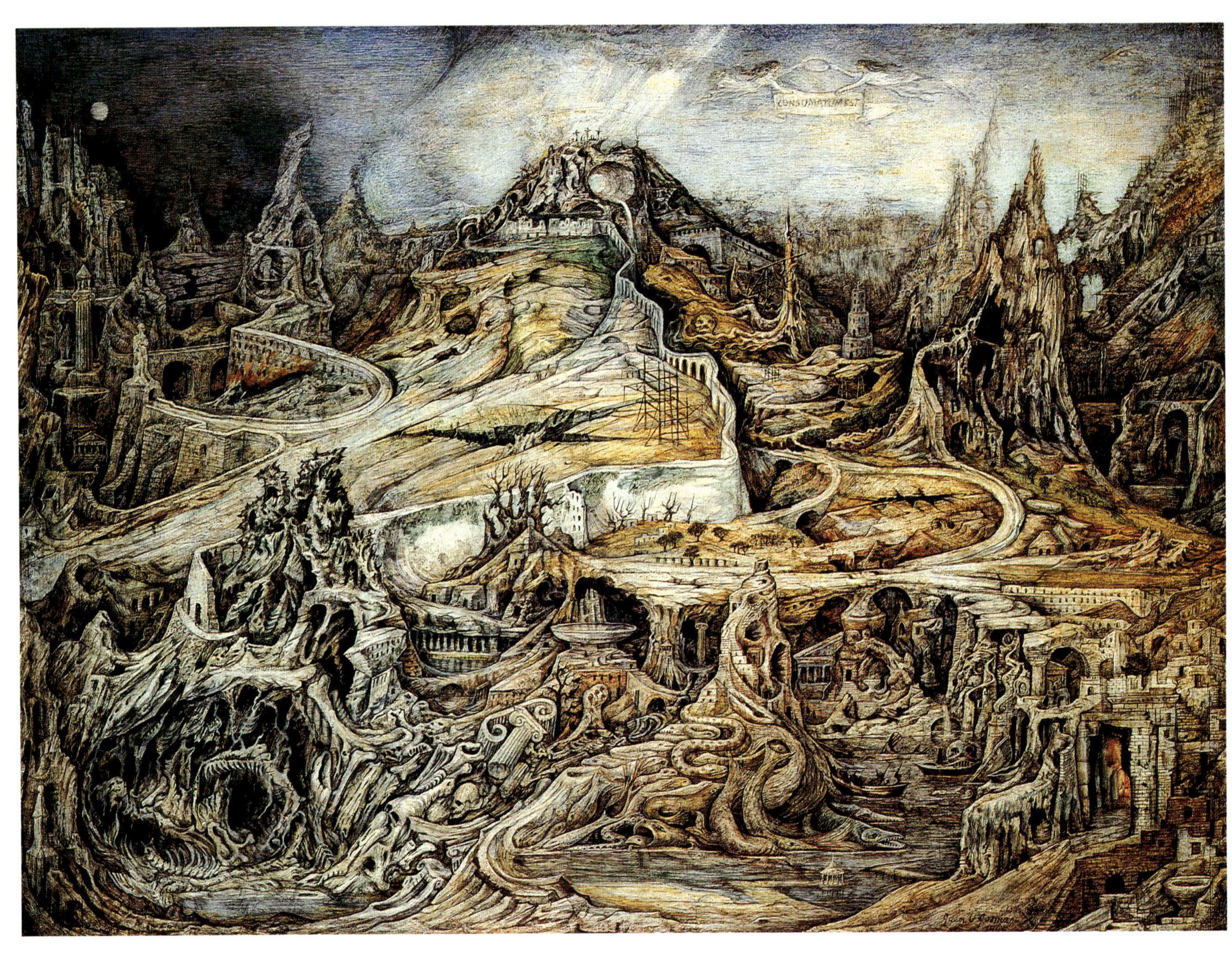

101 JUAN O'GORMAN, CONSUMATUM EST, 1942

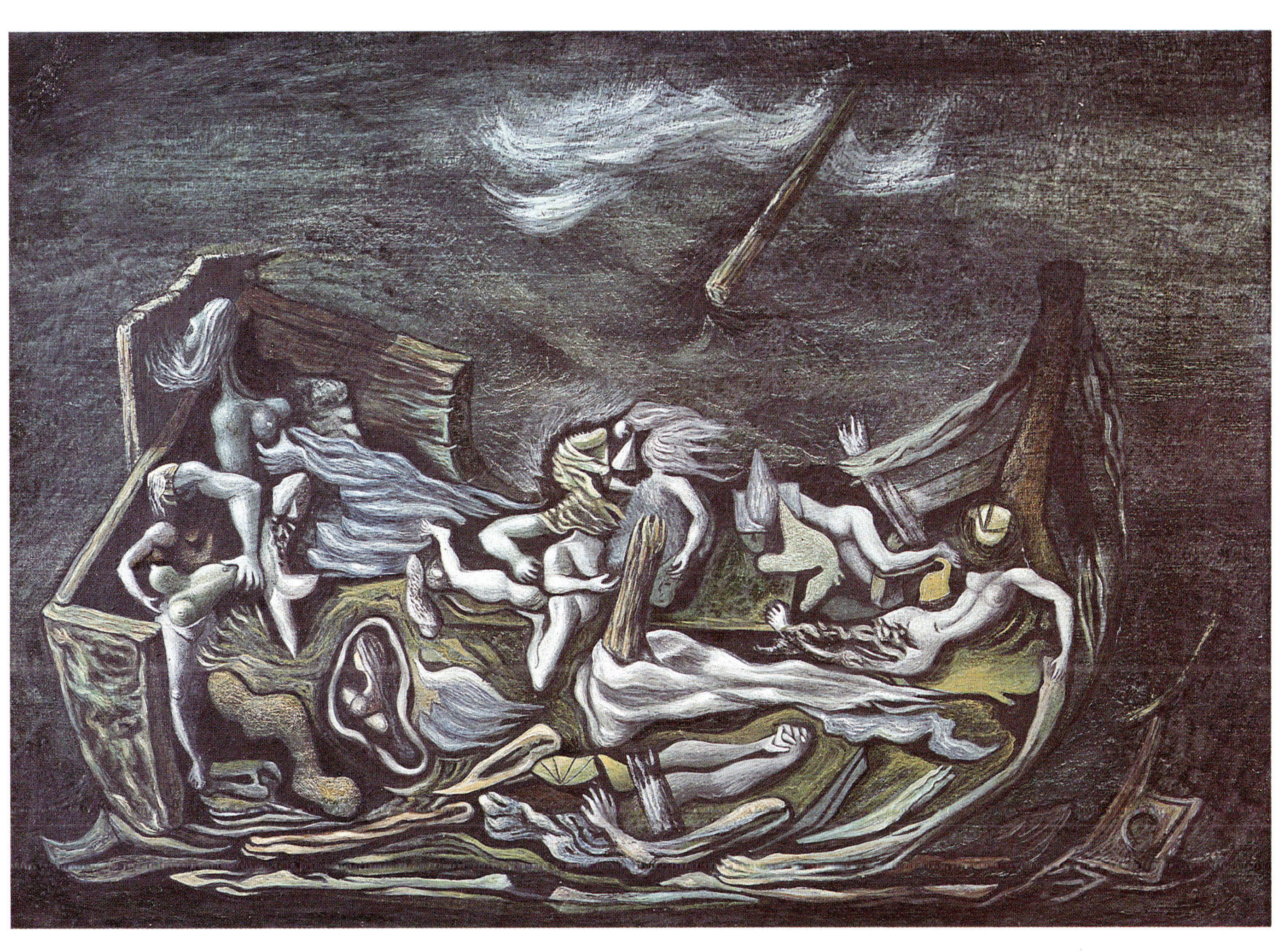

90 GUNTHER GERZSO, SHIPWRECK, 1945

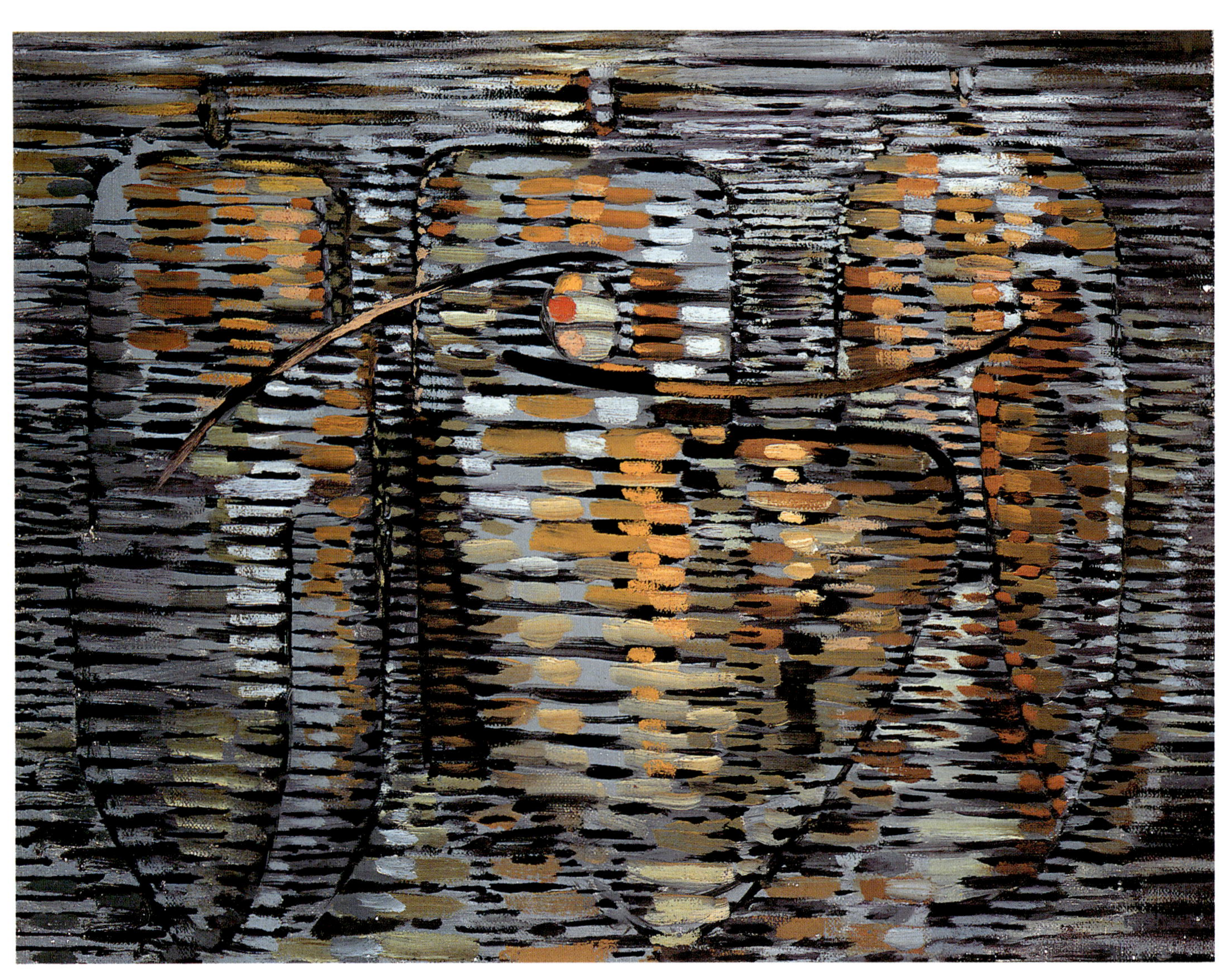

104 WOLFGANG PAALEN, FUTURE ANCESTORS, 1947

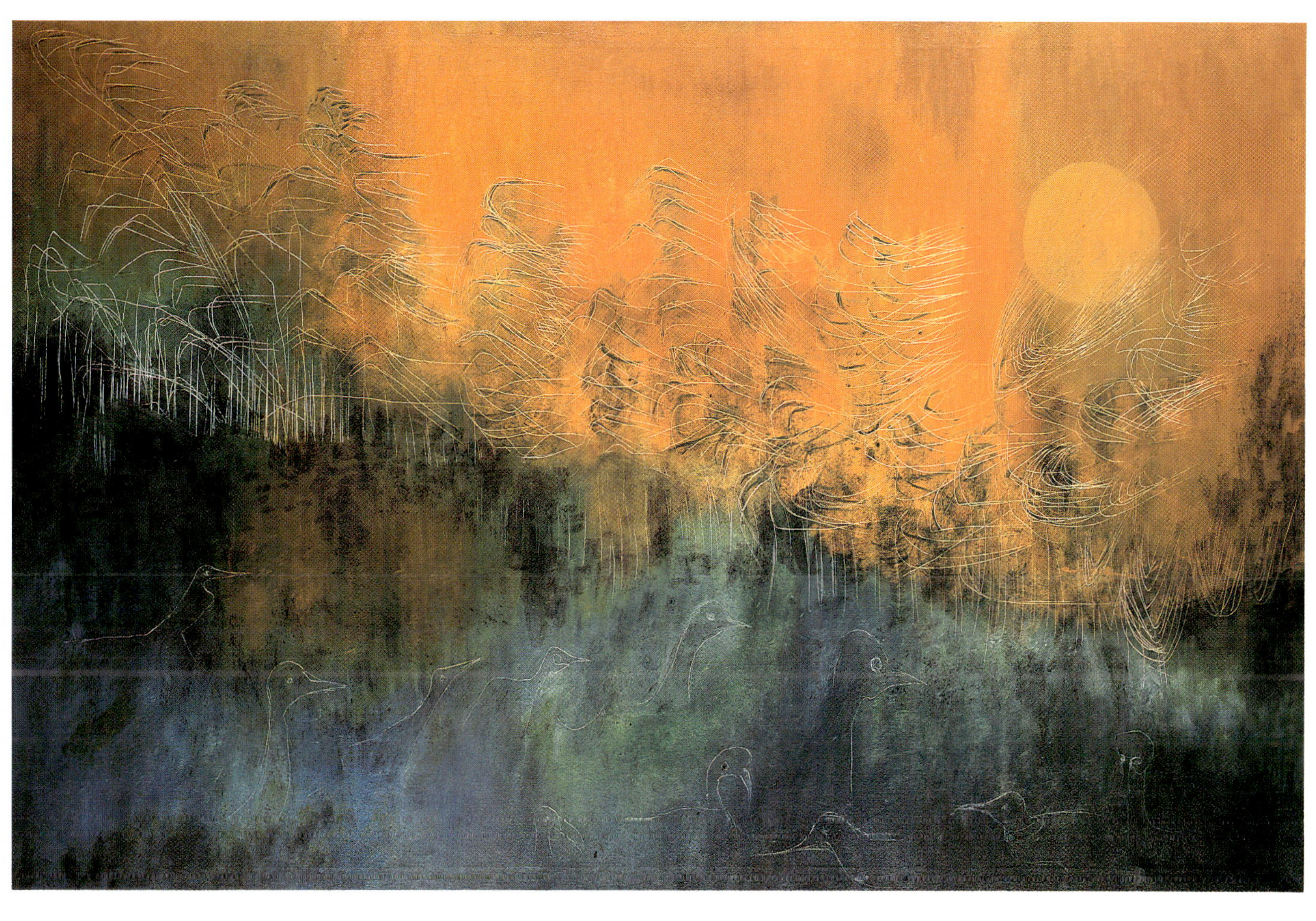

105 ALICE RAHON, THE WIND, 1954

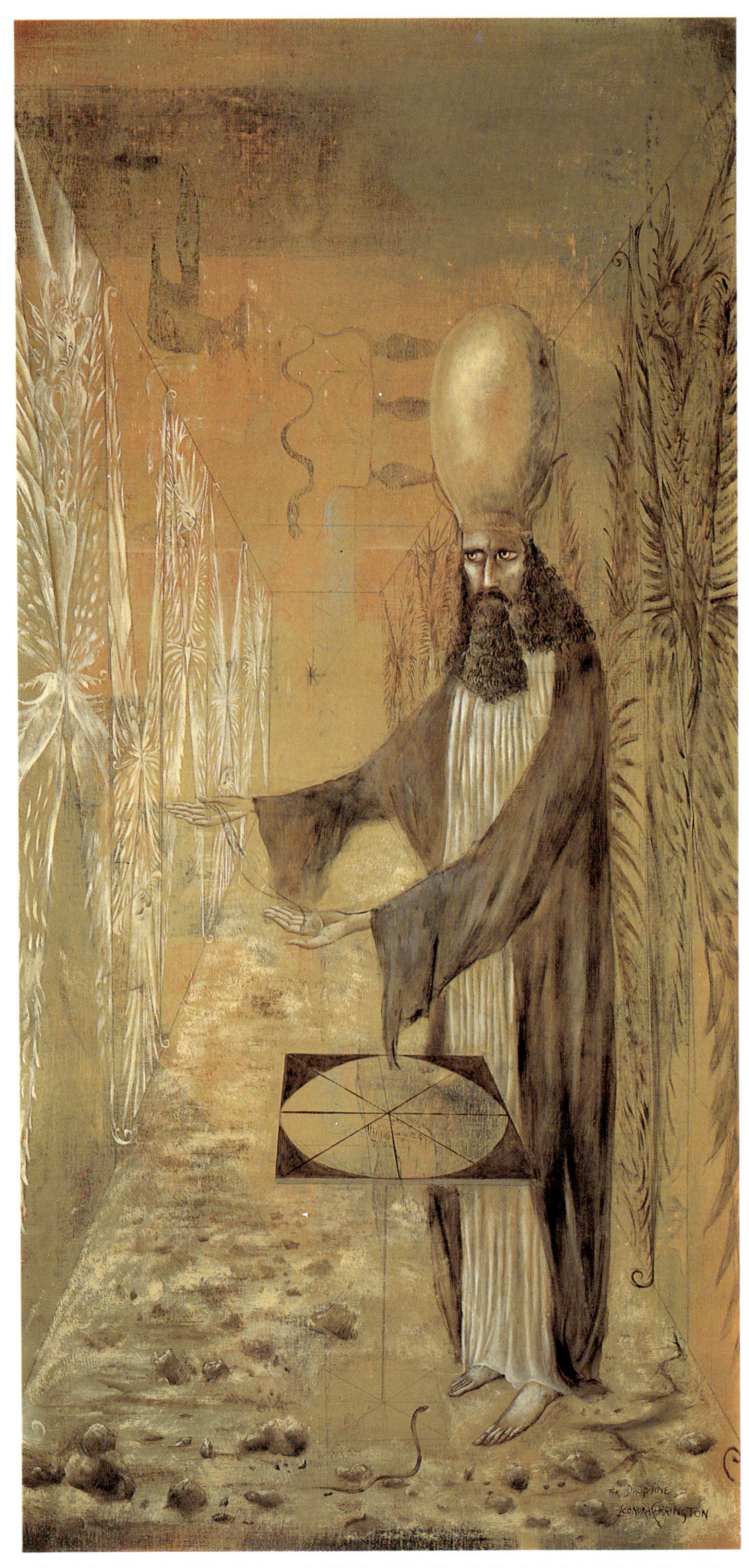

87 LEONORA CARRINGTON, UNTITLED (HIEROPHANTE, POUR DAUPHINE), 1958

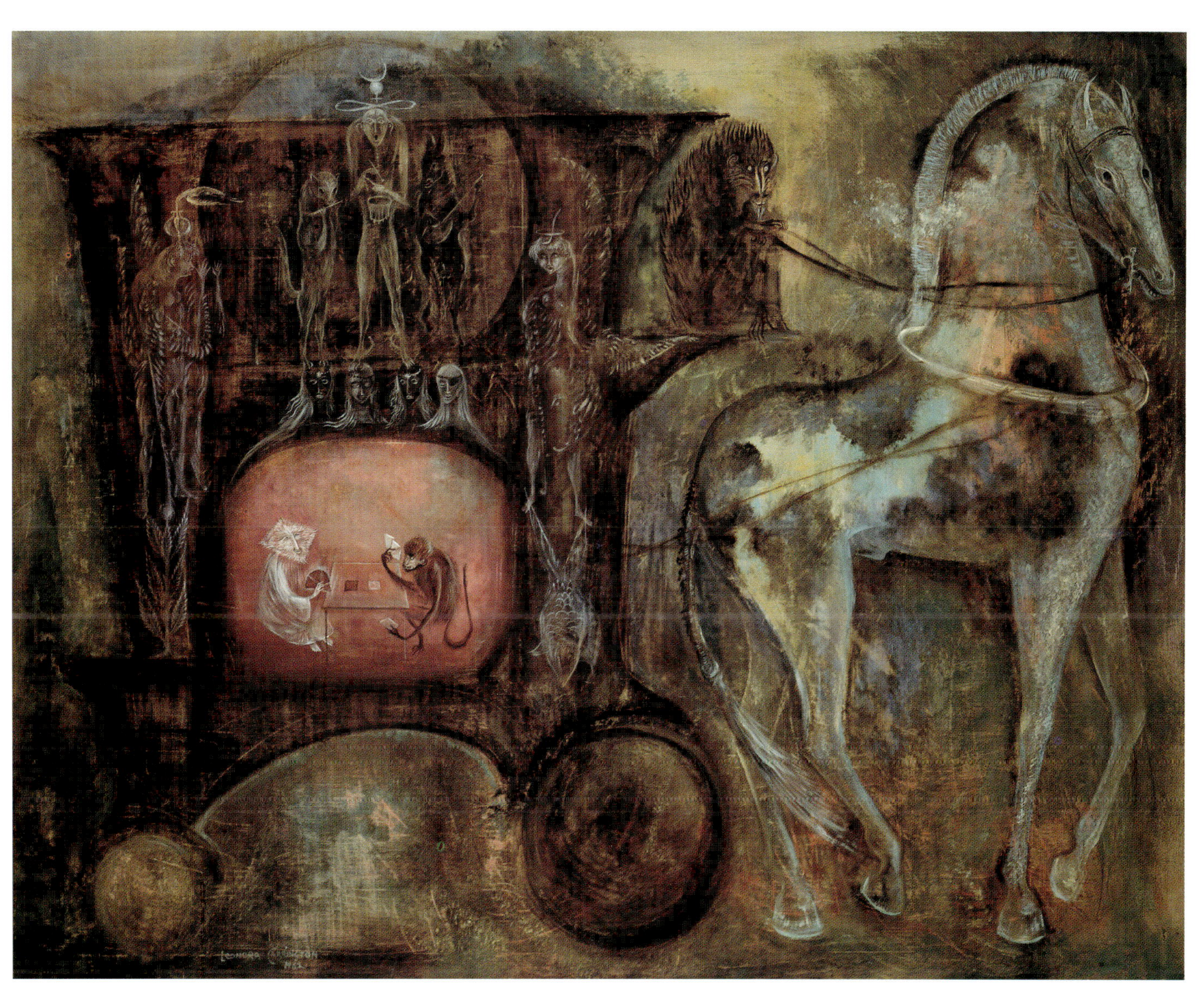

88 LEONORA CARRINGTON, TELUM PASSIONIS, 1962

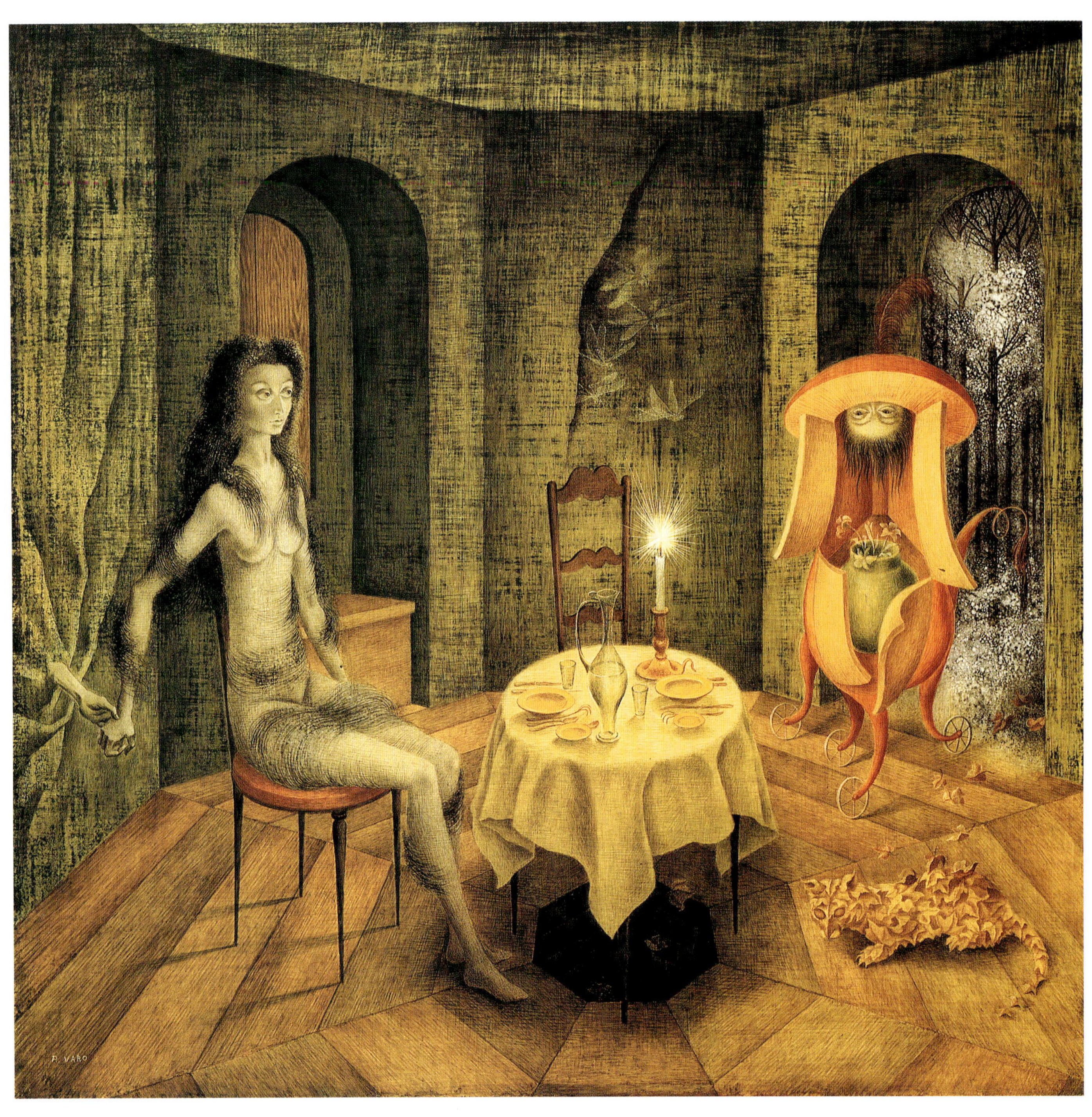

118 REMEDIOS VARO, UNEXPECTED VISITOR, 1958

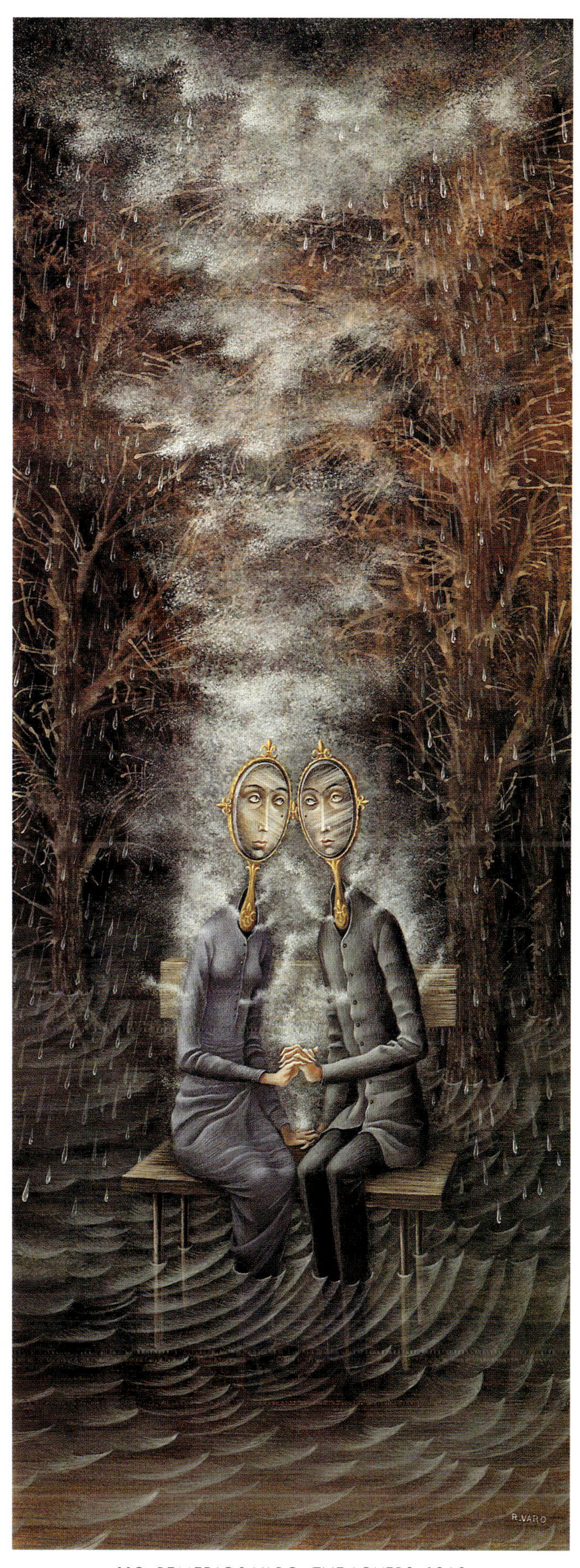

119 REMEDIOS VARO, THE LOVERS, 1963

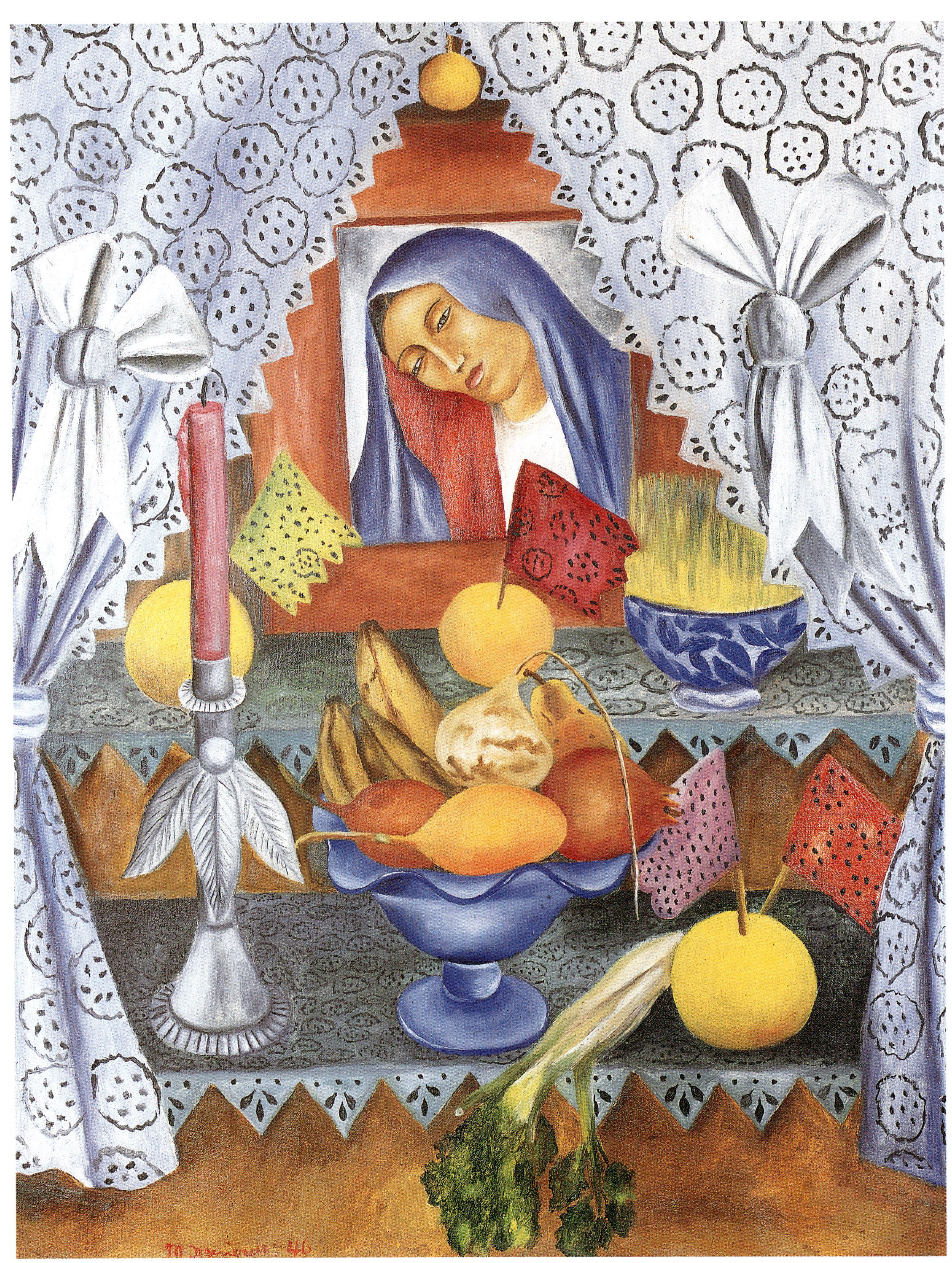

93 MARÍA IZQUIERDO, ALTAR TO THE VIRGIN OF SORROWS, 1946

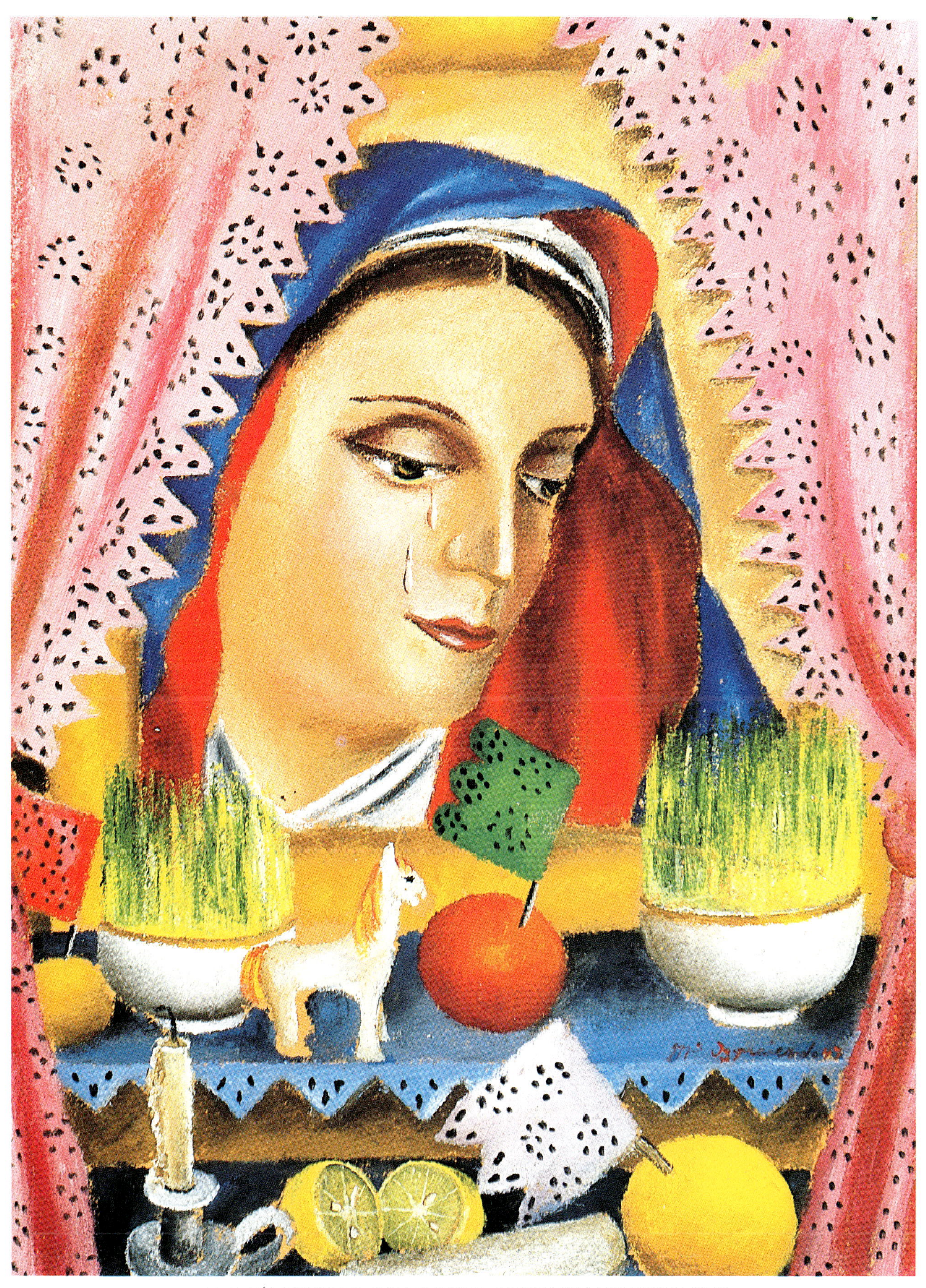

94 MARÍA IZQUIERDO, THE DOLOROSA OR THE VIRGIN DOLOROSA, 1947

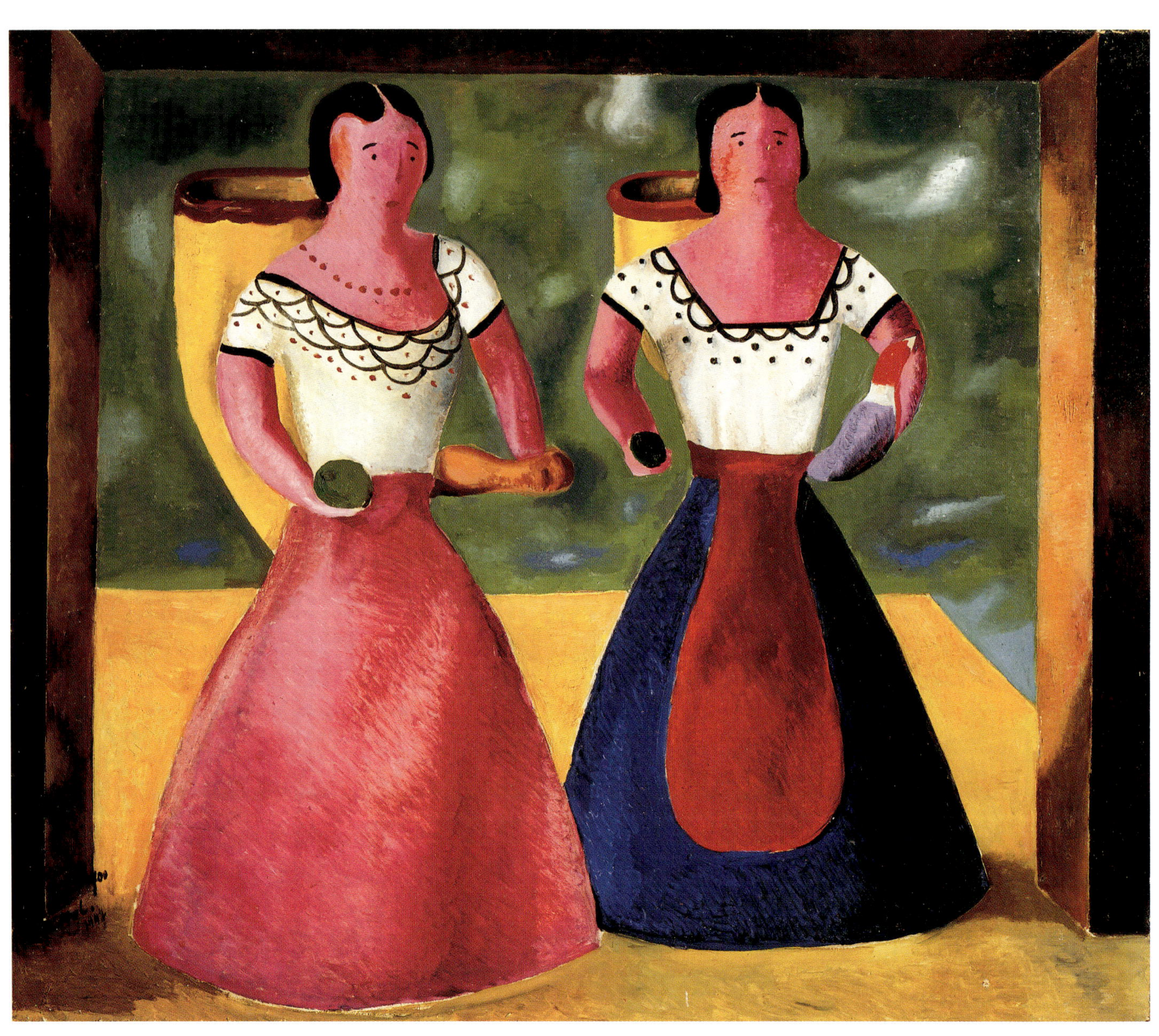

100 ROBERTO MONTENEGRO, TWO INDIAN GIRLS (CANDLESTICKS), 1947

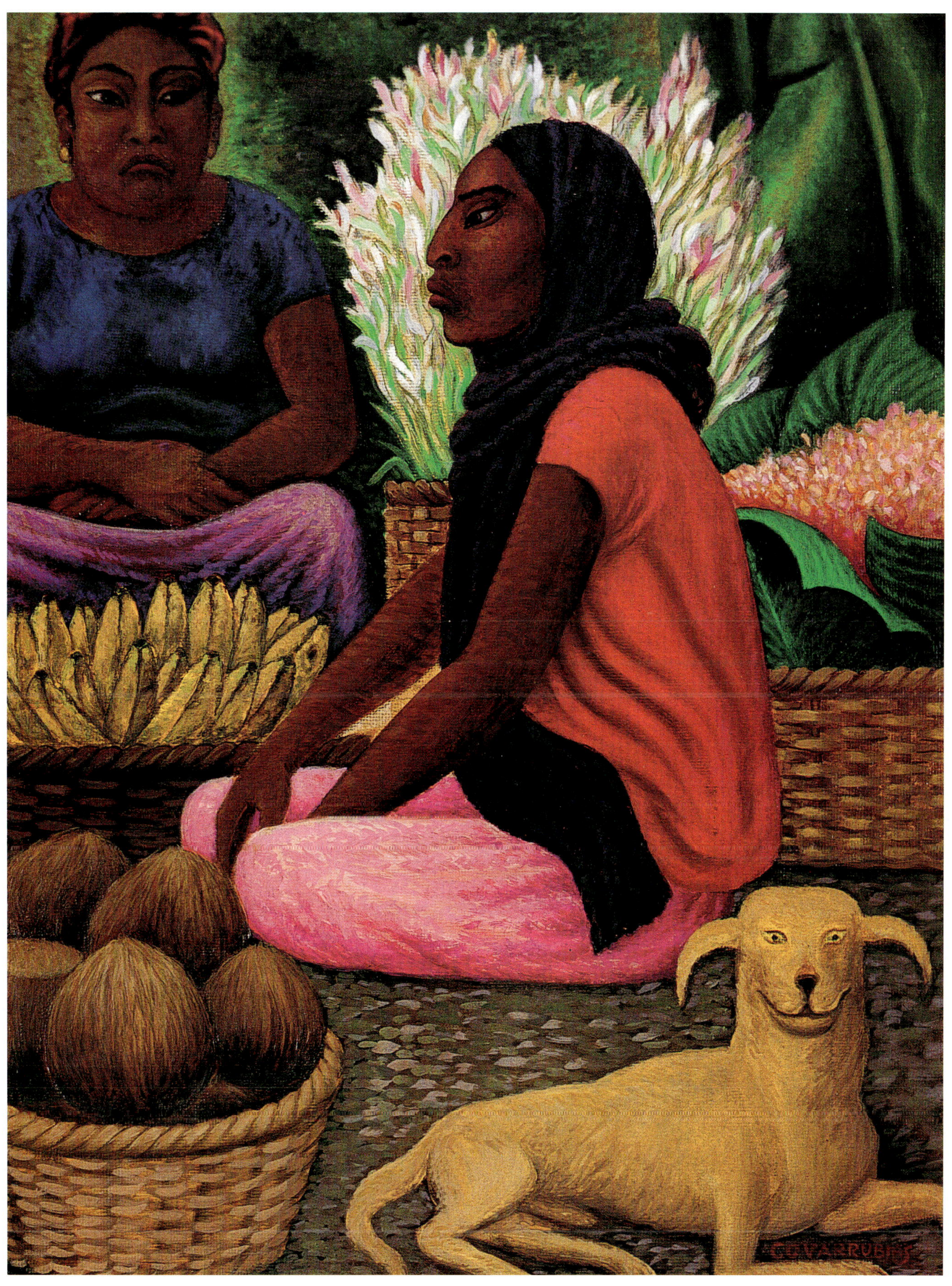

89 MIGUEL COVARRUBIAS, MARKET SCENE, undated

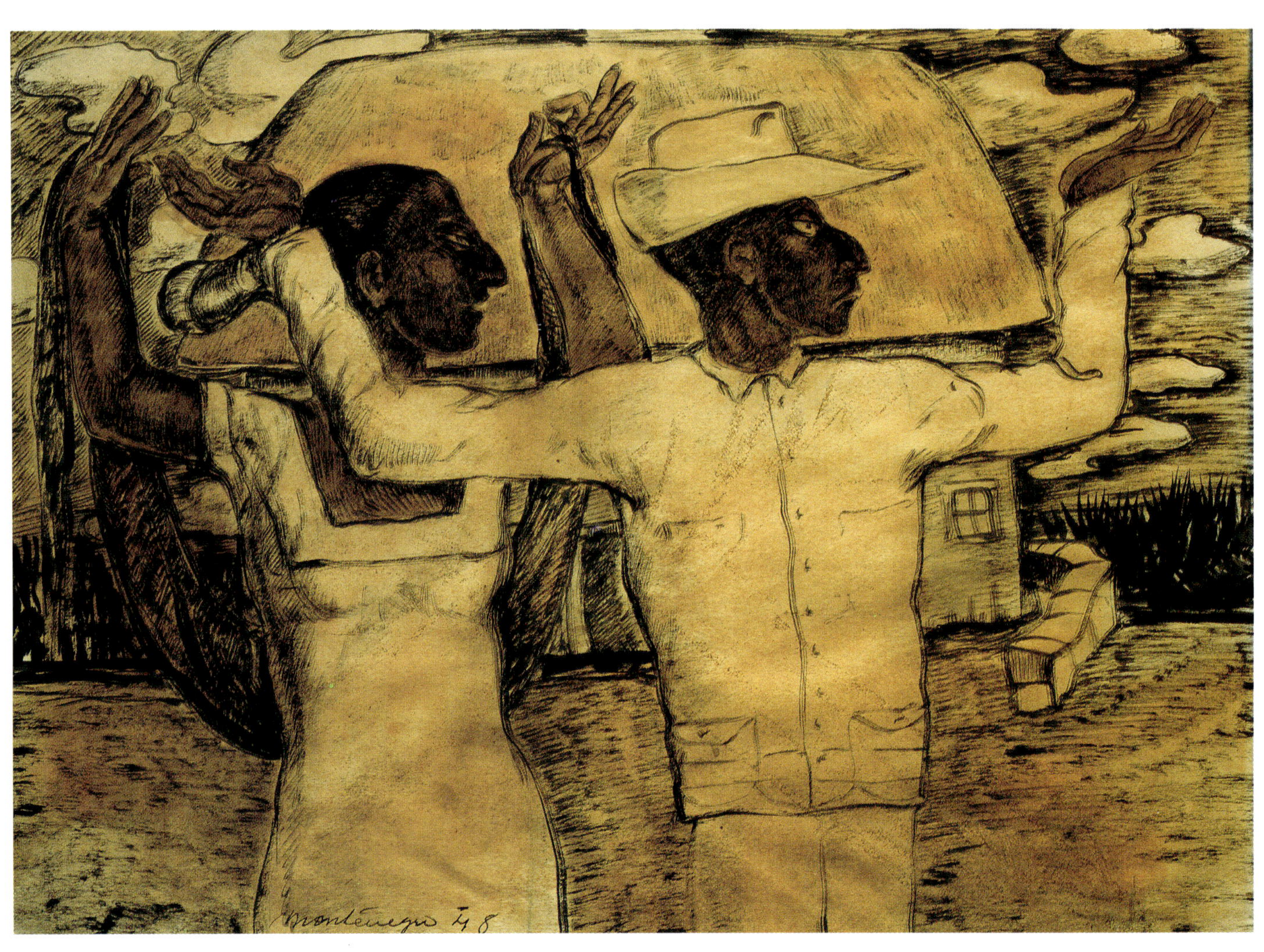

99 ROBERTO MONTENEGRO, BRIDAL COUPLE FROM VERACRUZ, 1948

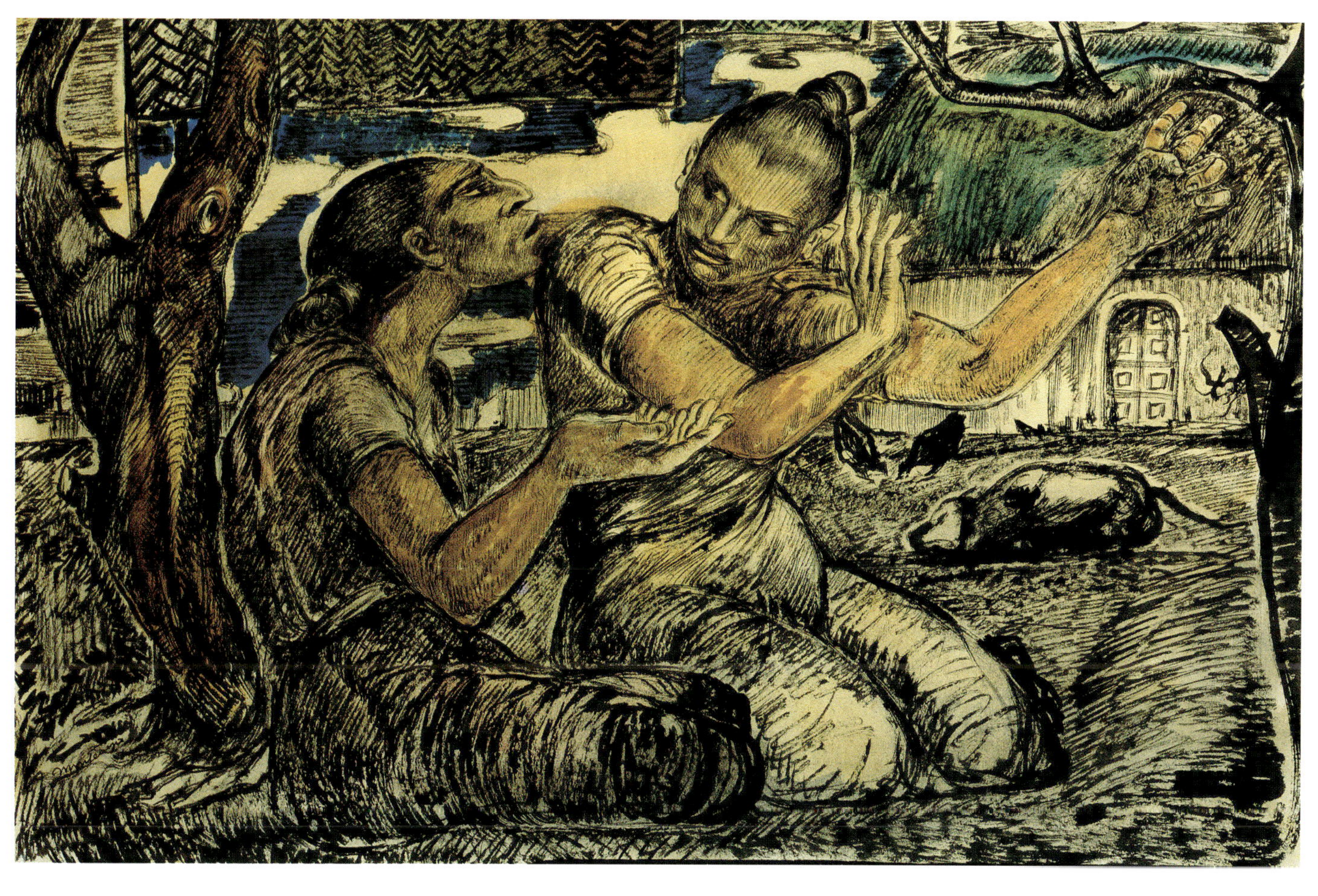

98 ROBERTO MONTENEGRO, TWO SEATED WOMEN, 1948

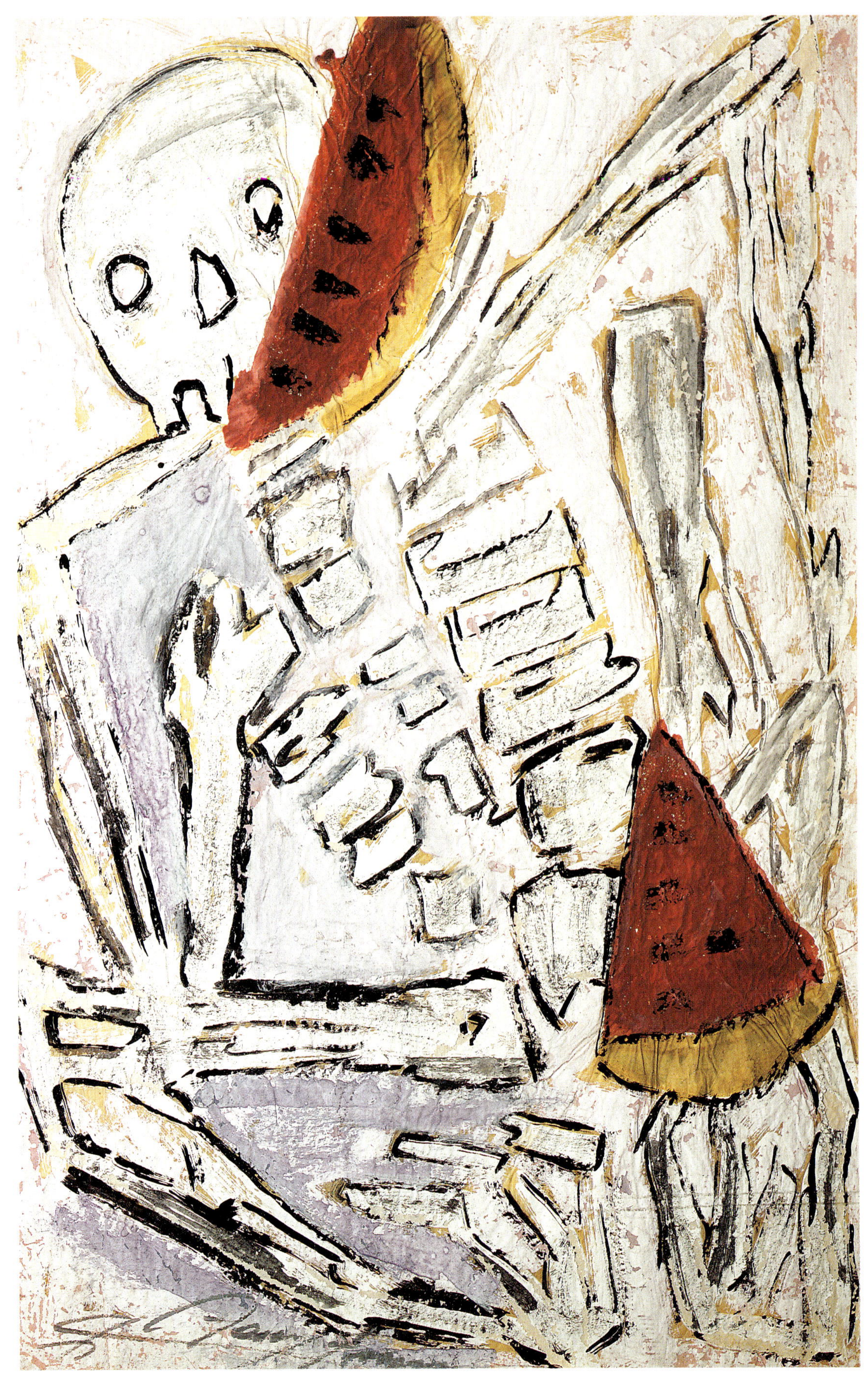

106 JESÚS REYES FERREIRA (CHUCHO REYES), SKULLS WITH WATERMELONS, undated

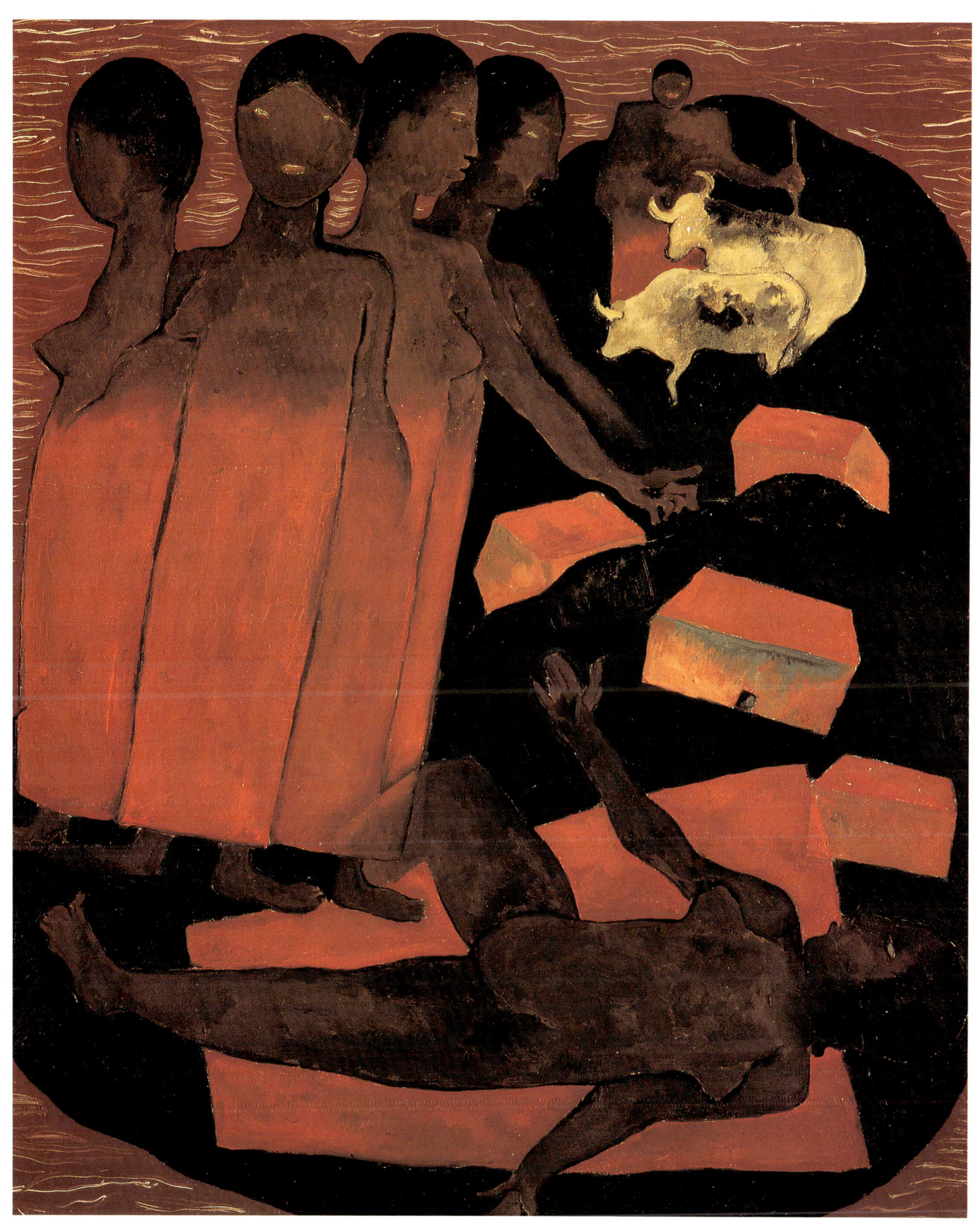

95 CARLOS MÉRIDA, VOODOO SCENE, 1929

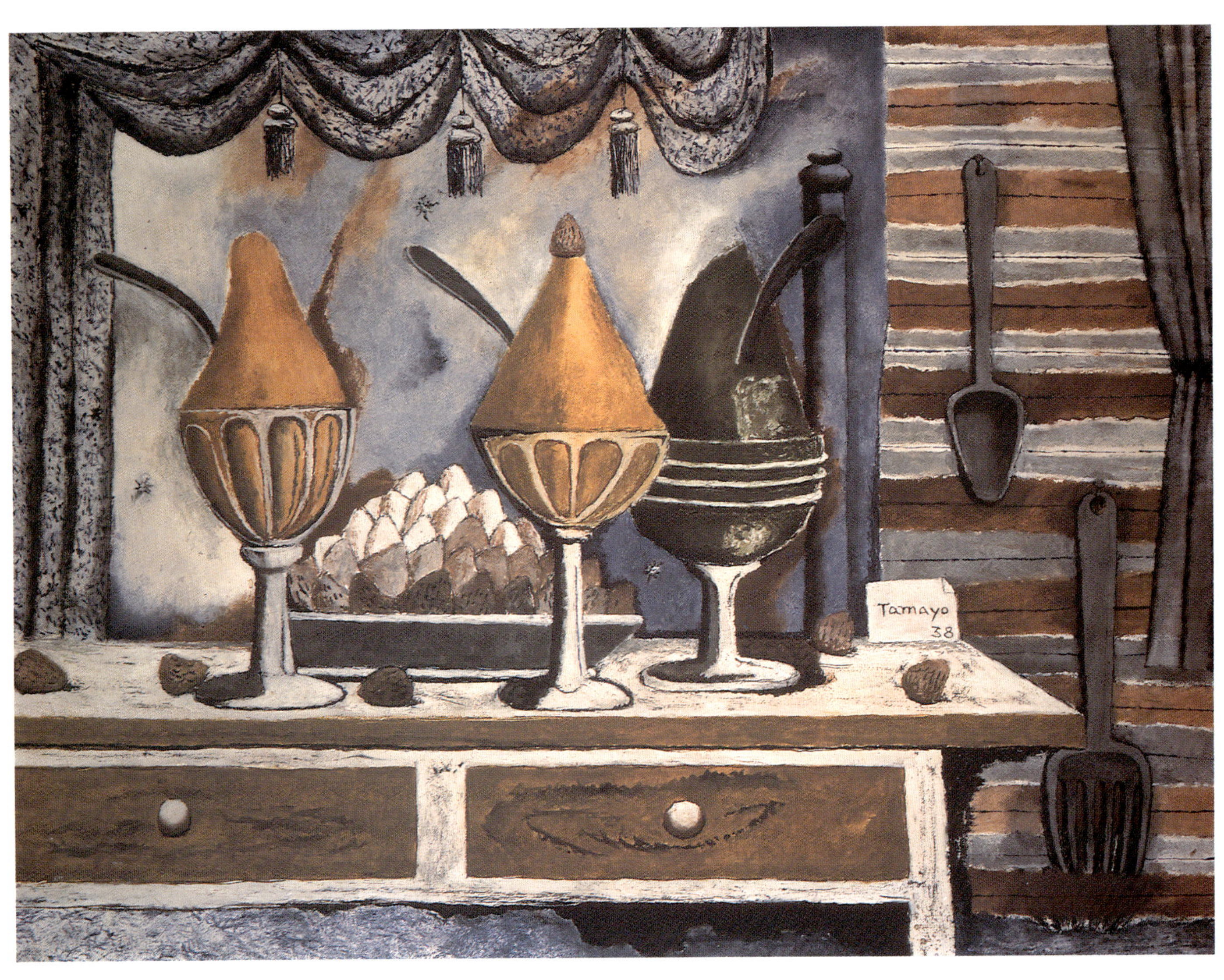

115 RUFINO TAMAYO, STILL LIFE WITH SHERBERTS, 1938

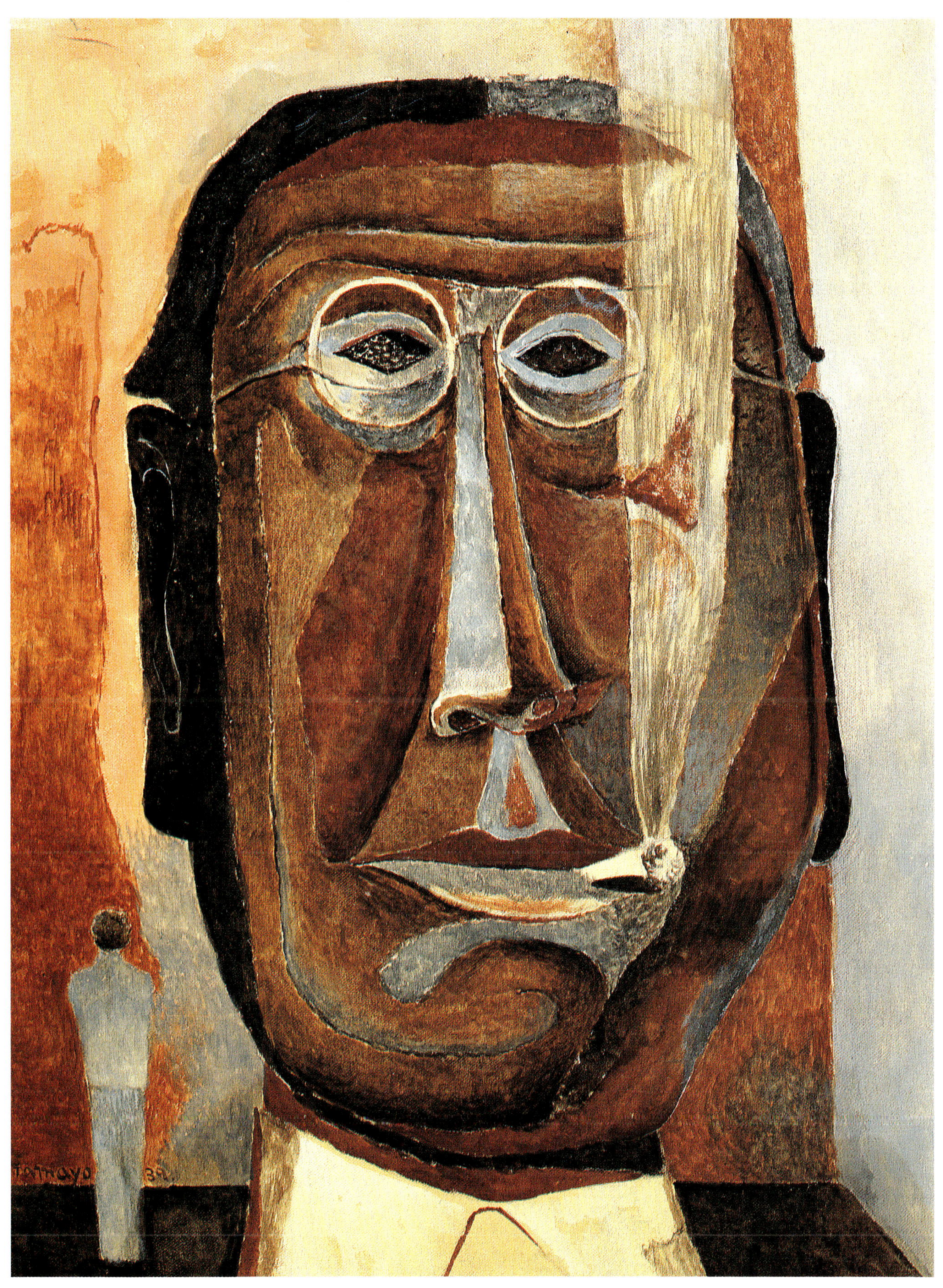

116 RUFINO TAMAYO, THE SMOKER, 1939

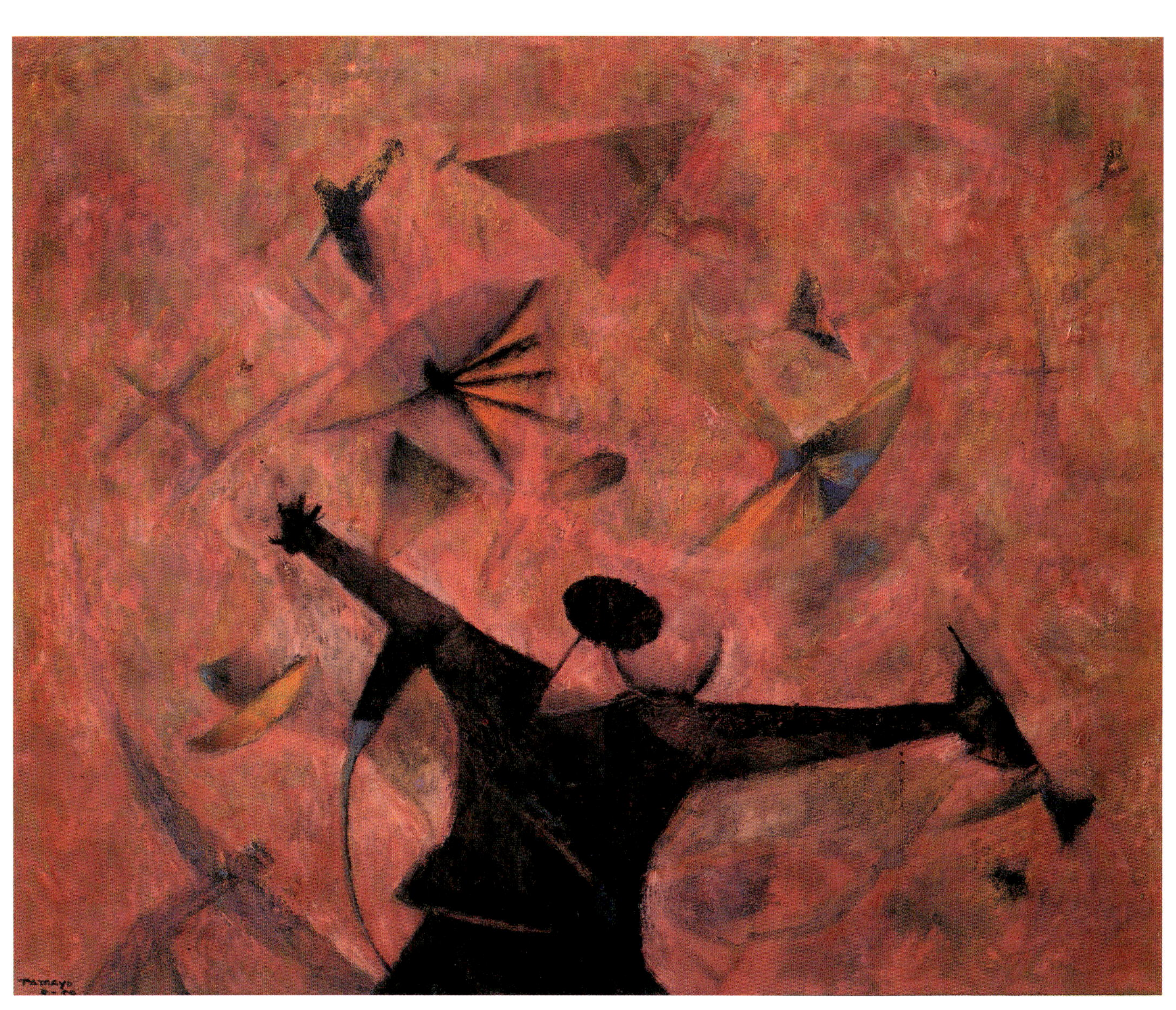

117 RUFINO TAMAYO, THE BIRDMAN, 1950

VICTOR FOSADO

THE INTUITION OF RETABLO PAINTERS AND THE PASSION OF FRIDA

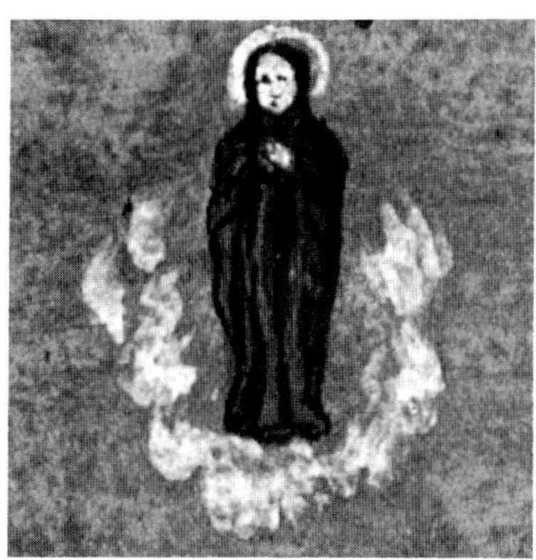

Intuition and a secret feeling for the sacred inspire the creators of votive paintings (or *retablos* as they are called in Mexico).[1] These impulses give them the strength to take on the responsibility of being imaginative intermediaries between inexplicable, even miraculous, events and their pictorial representation, which they achieve through the most direct means: the expressiveness of folk art.

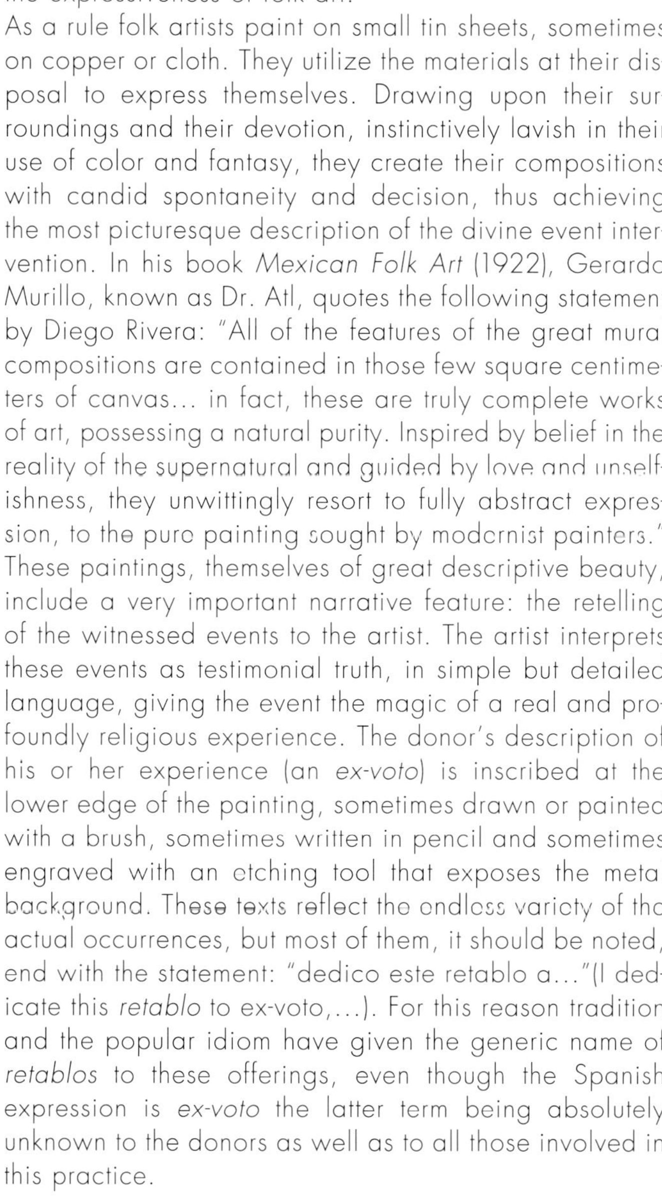

As a rule folk artists paint on small tin sheets, sometimes on copper or cloth. They utilize the materials at their disposal to express themselves. Drawing upon their surroundings and their devotion, instinctively lavish in their use of color and fantasy, they create their compositions with candid spontaneity and decision, thus achieving the most picturesque description of the divine event intervention. In his book *Mexican Folk Art* (1922), Gerardo Murillo, known as Dr. Atl, quotes the following statement by Diego Rivera: "All of the features of the great mural compositions are contained in those few square centimeters of canvas... in fact, these are truly complete works of art, possessing a natural purity. Inspired by belief in the reality of the supernatural and guided by love and unselfishness, they unwittingly resort to fully abstract expression, to the pure painting sought by modernist painters."

These paintings, themselves of great descriptive beauty, include a very important narrative feature: the retelling of the witnessed events to the artist. The artist interprets these events as testimonial truth, in simple but detailed language, giving the event the magic of a real and profoundly religious experience. The donor's description of his or her experience (an *ex-voto*) is inscribed at the lower edge of the painting, sometimes drawn or painted with a brush, sometimes written in pencil and sometimes engraved with an etching tool that exposes the metal background. These texts reflect the endless variety of the actual occurrences, but most of them, it should be noted, end with the statement: "dedico este retablo a..."(I dedicate this *retablo* to ex-voto,...). For this reason tradition and the popular idiom have given the generic name of *retablos* to these offerings, even though the Spanish expression is *ex-voto* the latter term being absolutely unknown to the donors as well as to all those involved in this practice.

The so-called style of these paintings has not changed much. Their format, size, and composition have remained fairly stable with only minor variations: the upper corners are dedicated to representation of the saint to whom the painting is dedicated, the space above the text shows scenes portraying the event, and to one side often appears a kneeling figure of the donor giving thanks for the miracle or the favor granted. These important details release the artist's creativity.

Votive paintings are an important source of information for ethnographers, who can, on the basis of their date and origin, identify different types of dress, utensils of daily use, decorations, architecture, means of transport, and even the different types of attire used to decorate images of the Virgin and the saints for special holidays, fairs, and pilgrimages held throught out the year.

Like other forms of folk art, retablos were considered vital by artists who foresaw, at the beginning of the century, the importance of the visual power that these expressions had for most people. During and after the Revolution of 1910, the nationalist feelings awakened by the intellectual movement (a kind of second independence or liberation) permeated the innovative ideas of Dr. Atl and his contemporaries, Xavier Guerrero, Orozco, Siqueiros, and Rivera among others, who express their ideals in murals as well as in easel paintings. Well into the "Mexicanist" era in the visual arts, the strange surrealism that characterizes the *retablos* had a powerful hold on Frida Kahlo's sensibility. Owing to the circumstances that entrapped her, she expressed her enormous artistic talent through painting herself, becoming a live *retablo* character. Frida is the constant protagonist who offers herself to herself, the honored saint as well as the donor who sometimes appears in the painting or who is present in delicately written narrations. Even when Frida paints or refers to others rather than herself, as in the painting *The Suicide of Dorothy Hale*, she nevertheless appears as the witness of the event by offering the *ex-voto:* "In her memory this *retablo* was exe-

[1] Votive paintings are intended as offerings of thanksgiving to holy personages, one of the saints or, most often the Virgin, for their intervention in the life of the donor, usually by saving him or her from some misfortune.

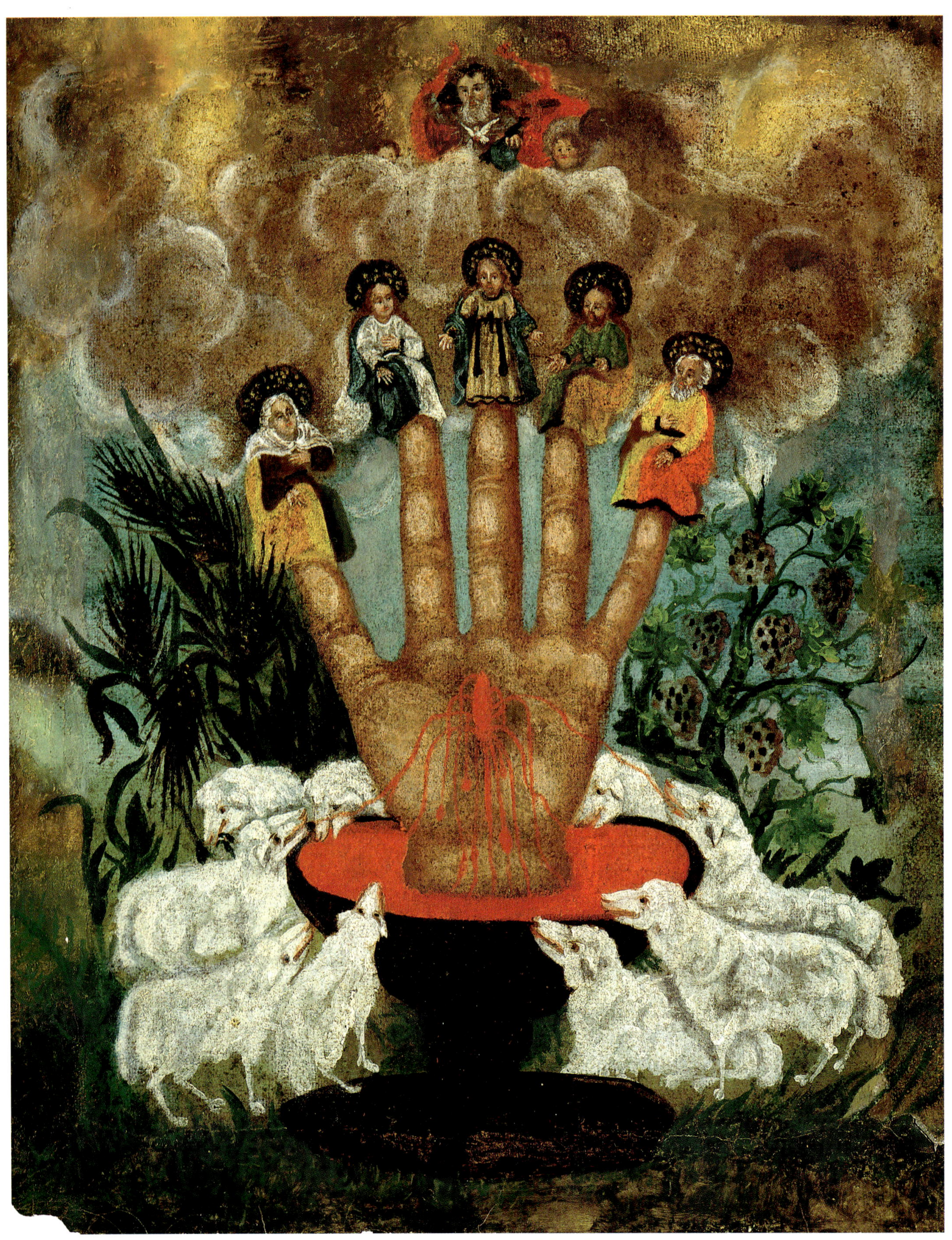

120 RETABLO, HAND OF WONDER, END OF THE 18TH CENTURY

cuted by Frida Kahlo." This text appears at the lower edge of the painting, following the type of composition traditionally used in votive paintings. In all of the paintings in which she is lying in bed, Frida is the patient (as in the *retablos*) who agonizes and languishes in a vast and mostly empty room. The place is arcane, cold, and solitary, reflecting the feeling of her own existence.

Is it not perhaps the transmutation of her pain and sadness to this imaginary otherworldly space that is achieved by transferring her suffering to the canvas? The donors of votive paintings also cross the threshold between the real world and the celestial miracle through their offerings.

Behind the facade of vanity, like a ceremonial figure who is always impeccable, festively decorated, and exotically attractive, Frida disguised her hidden, barely veiled humility.

The power of Frida's inexhaustible imagination was continually inspired by the enormous visual riches of Mexican *ex-votos*.

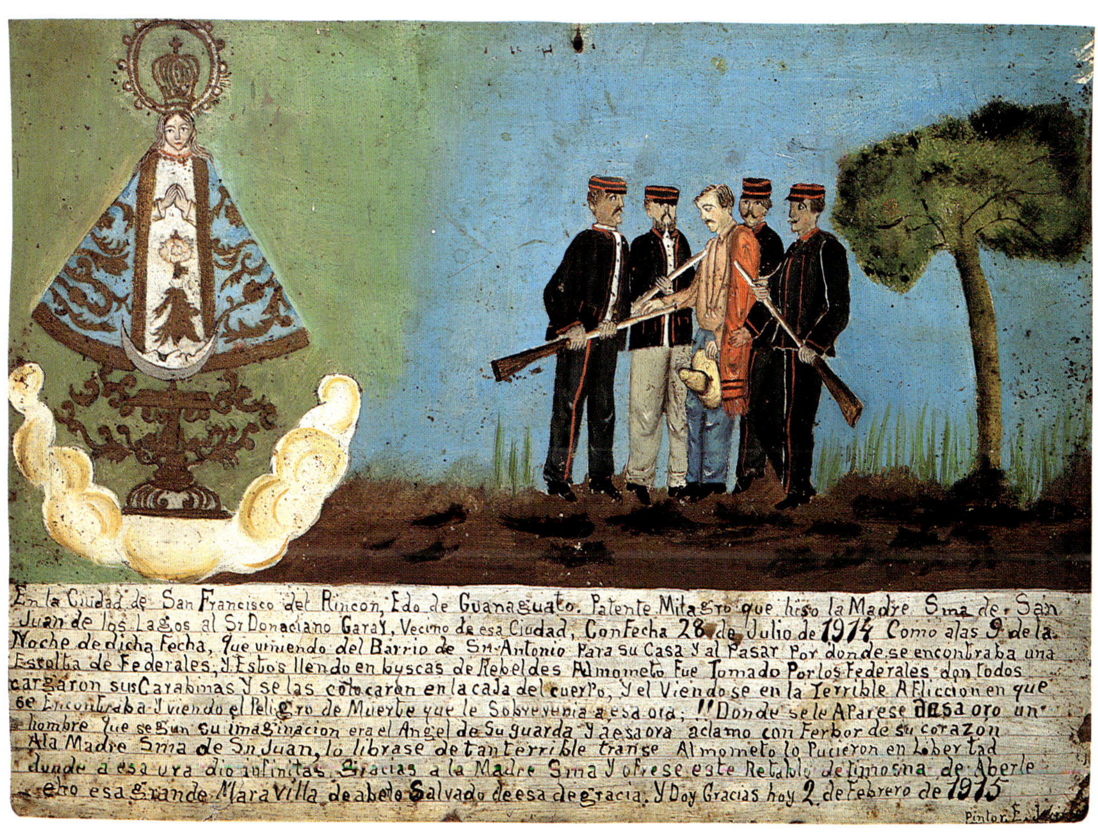

121 EX-VOTO, IN THE CITY OF SAN FRANCISCO, 1915

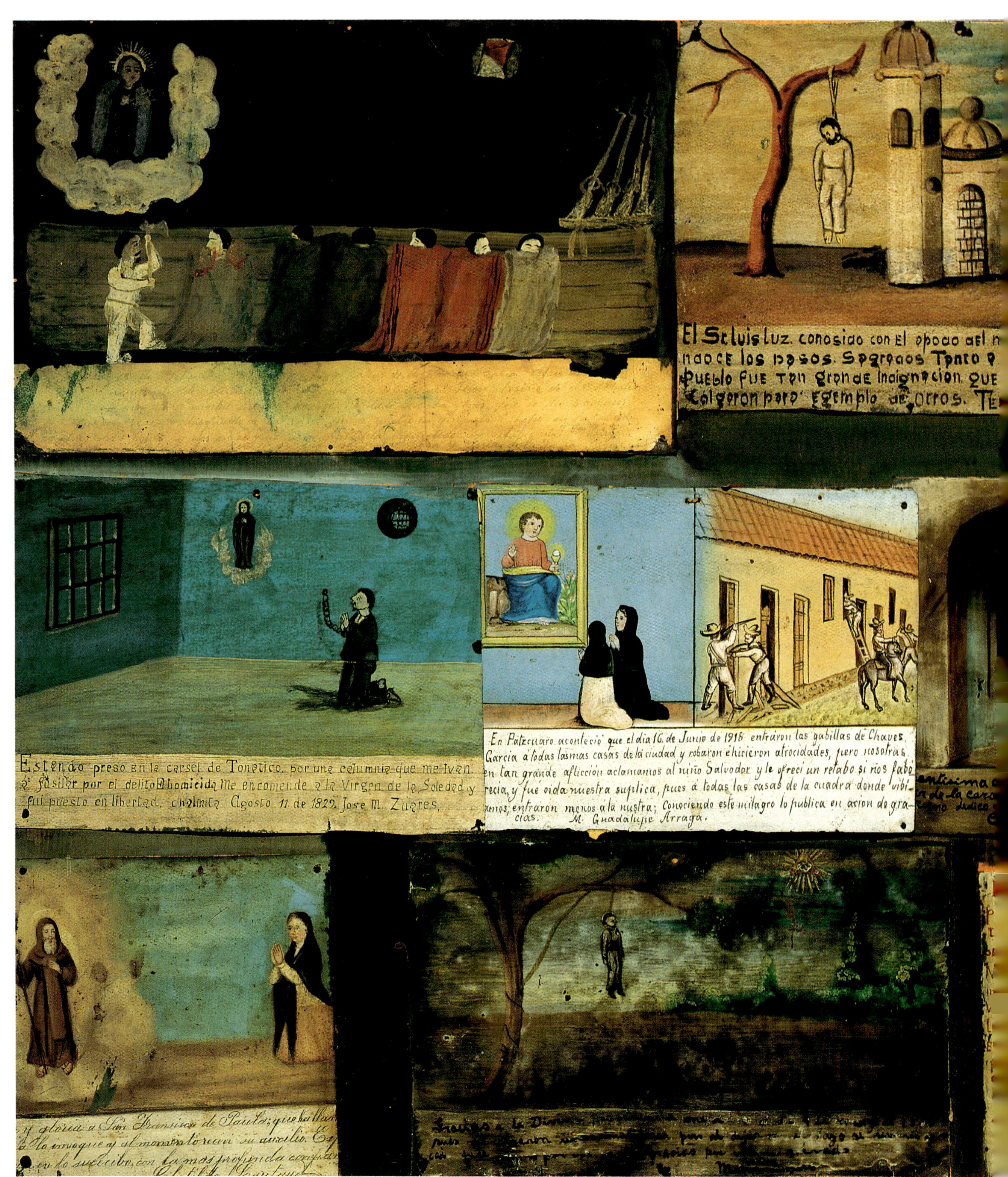

122 EX-VOTOS, 17TH–20TH CENTURY

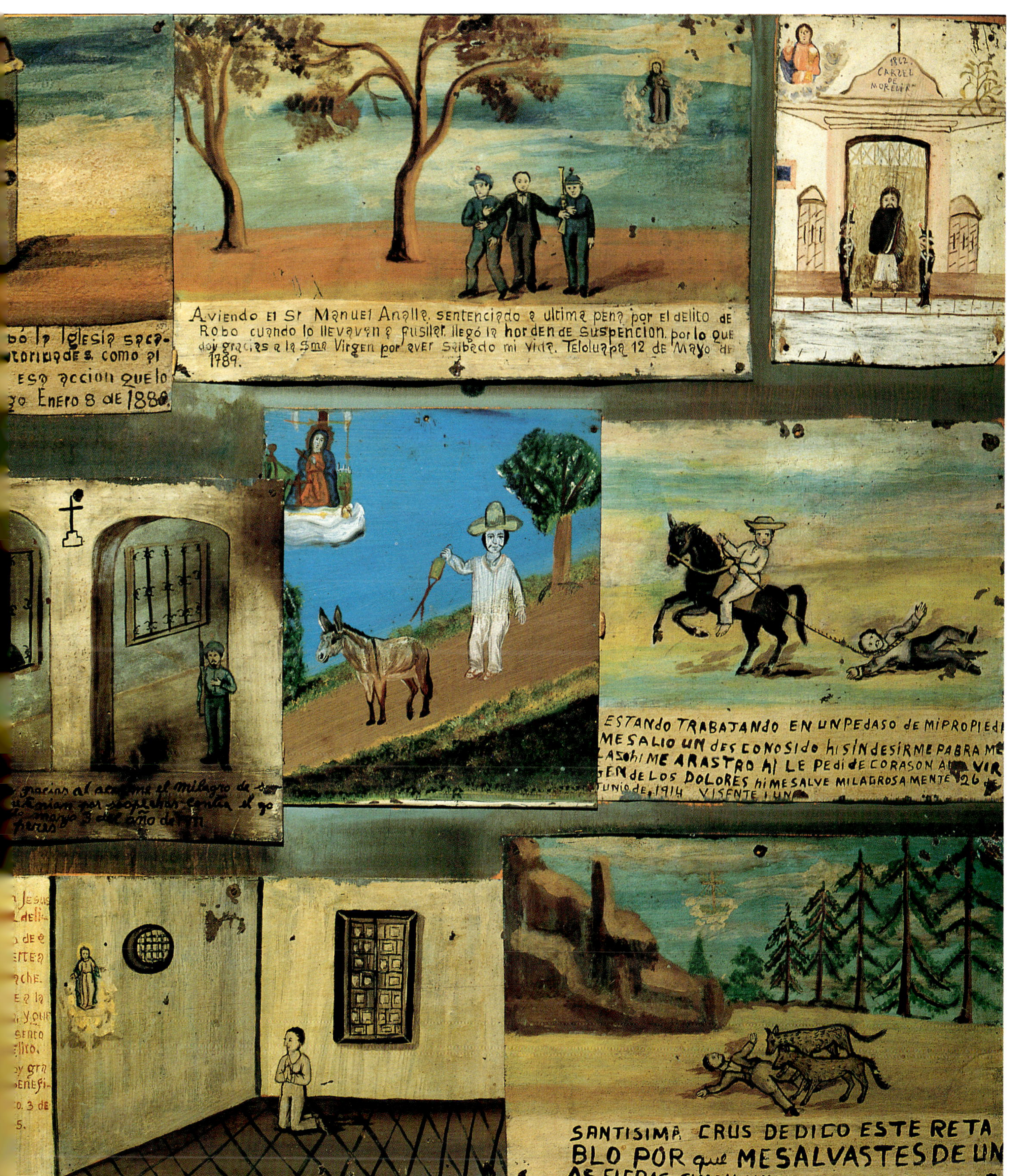
ó la Iglesia saca-
ESA accion que lo
Enero 8 de 1880
Aviendo el Sr Manuel Analla sentenciado a ultima pena por el delito de
Robo cuando lo llevavan a fusilar llegó la horden de suspencion. por lo que
doy gracias a la Sma Virgen por aver salbado mi vida. Teloluapa 12 de Mayo de
1789.
1842 CARCEL DE MORELIA
ESTANDO TRABAJANDO EN UN PEDASO DE MI PROPIED
ME SALIO UN DESCONOSIDO HI SIN DESIRME PARA ME
LASO HI ME ARASTRO AL LE PEDI DE CORASON A LA VIR
GEN DE LOS DOLORES HI ME SALVE MILAGROSAMENTE 26
JUNIO DE 1914
SANTISIMA CRUS DEDICO ESTE RETA
BLO POR que ME SALVASTES DE UN
AS FIERAS SIMON MATA

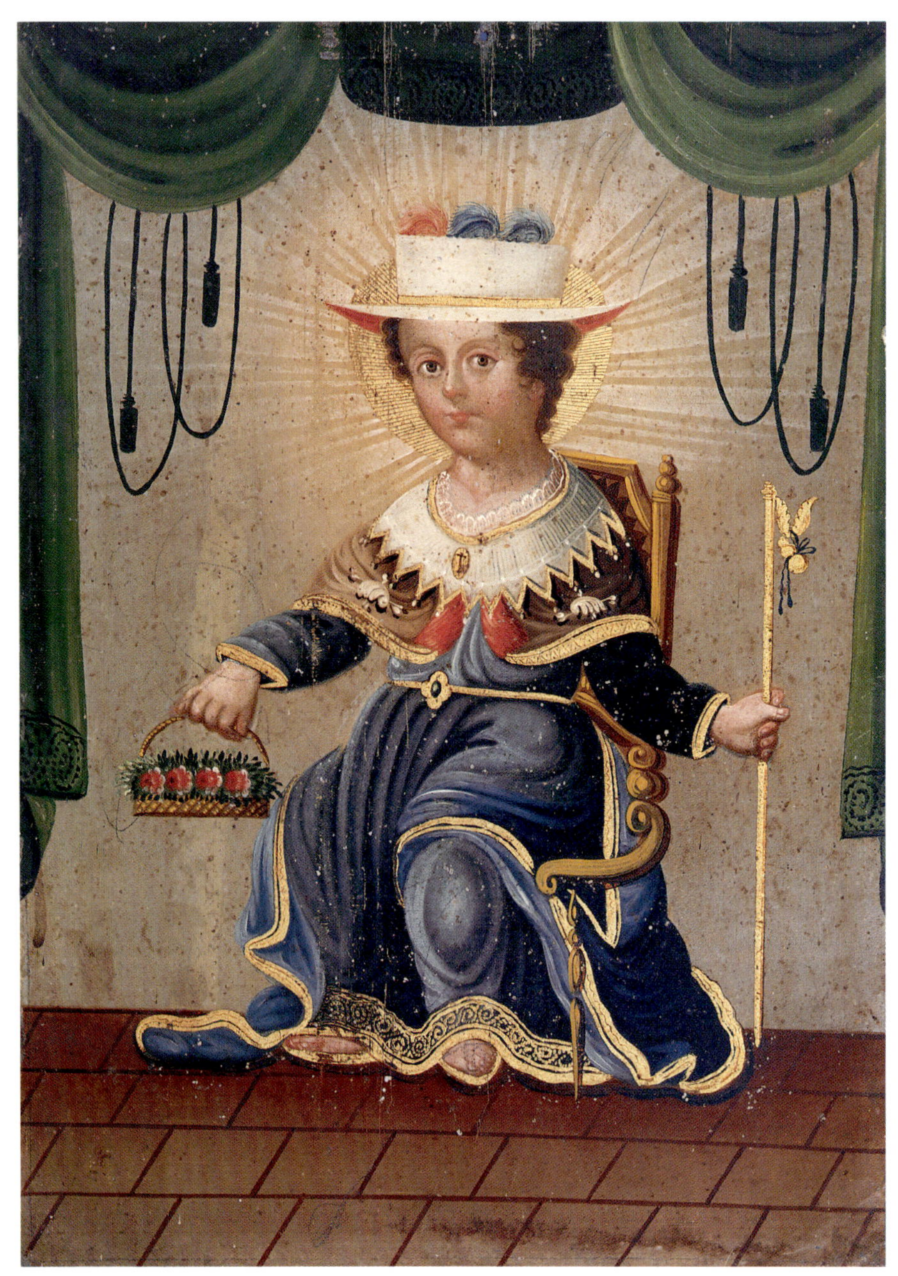

123 HERMENEGILDO BUSTOS, RETABLO OF THE CHILD OF ATOCHA

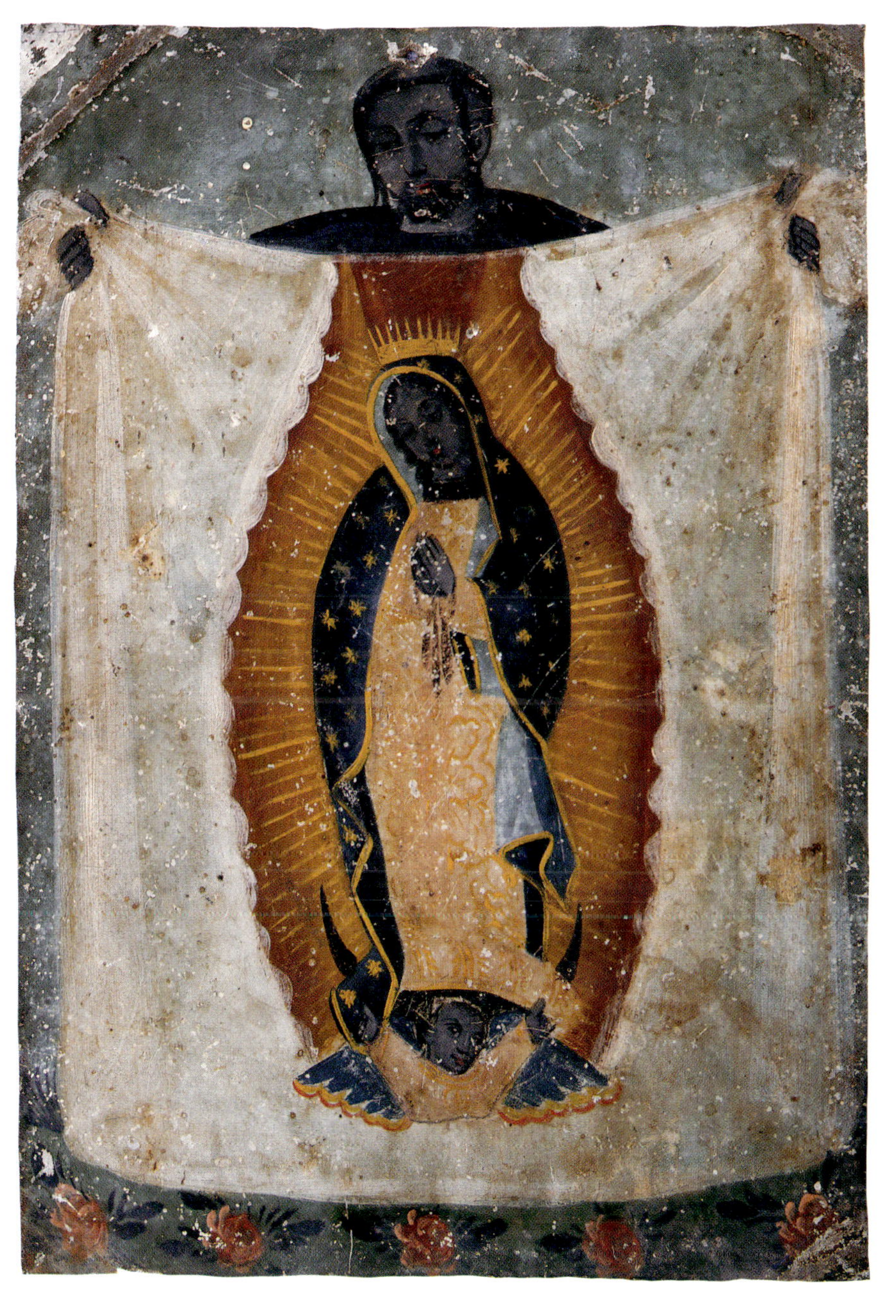

124 HERMENEGILDO BUSTOS, RETABLO OF THE VIRGIN OF GUADALUPE

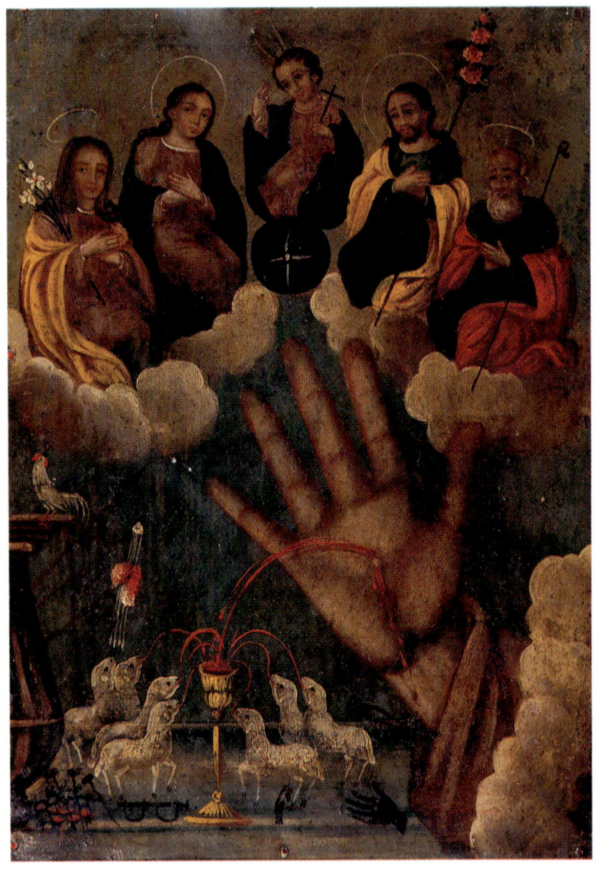

125 BUSTOS, RETABLO OF THE HAND OF GOD

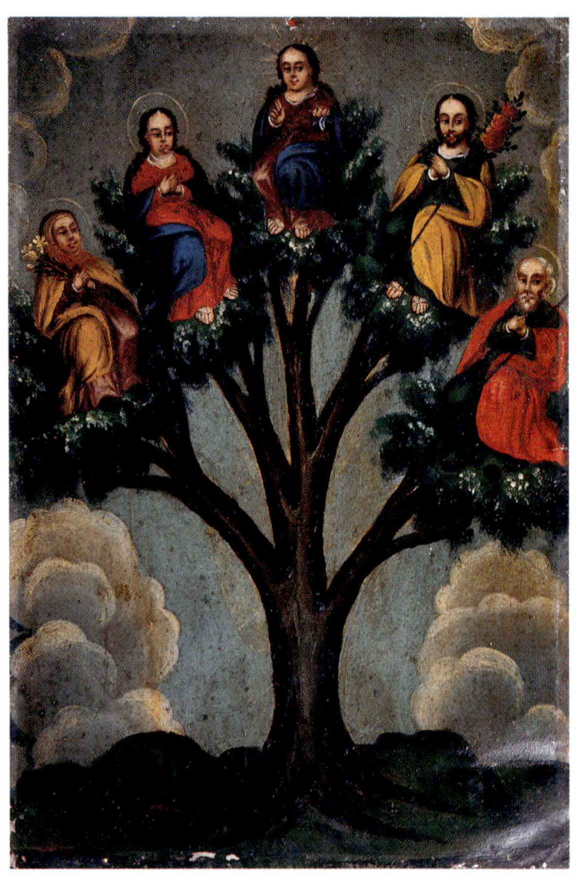

126 BUSTOS, RETABLO OF THE HOLY FAMILY

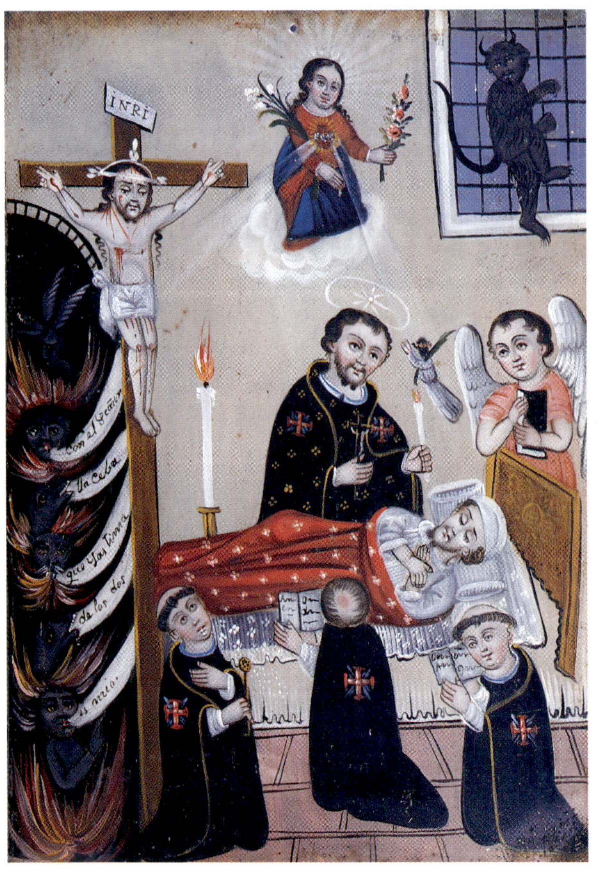

127 BUSTOS, EX-VOTO OF
THE DEATH OF SAINT CAMILO DE LELIS

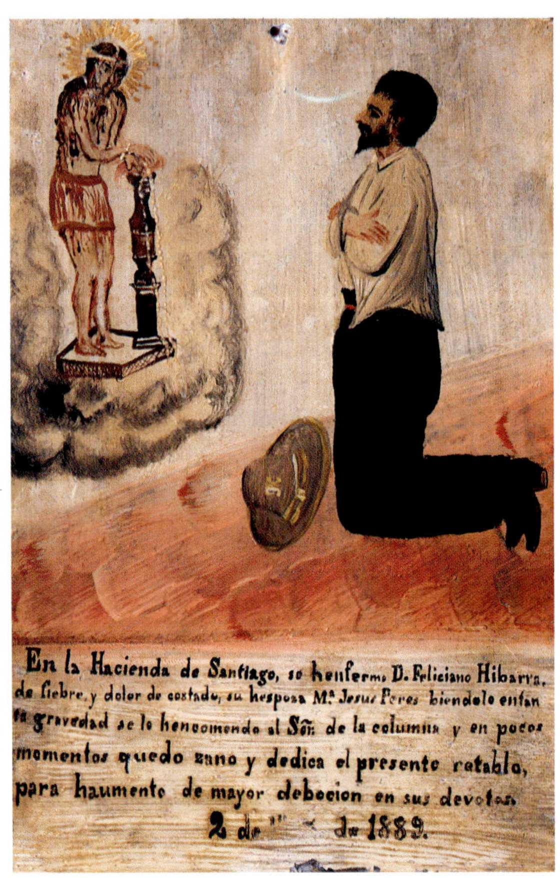

128 BUSTOS, EX-VOTO OF FELICIANO IBARRA

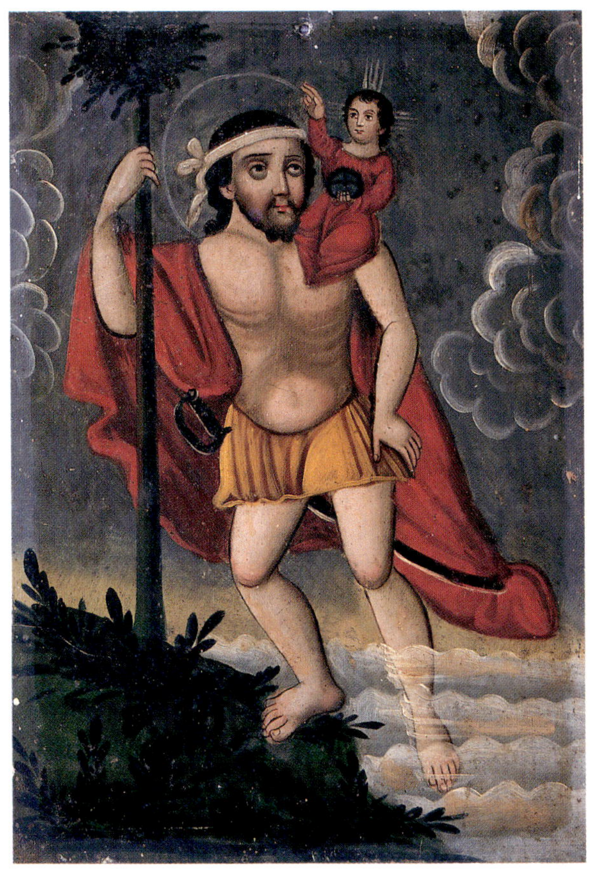

129 BUSTOS, RETABLO OF SAINT CHRISTOPHER

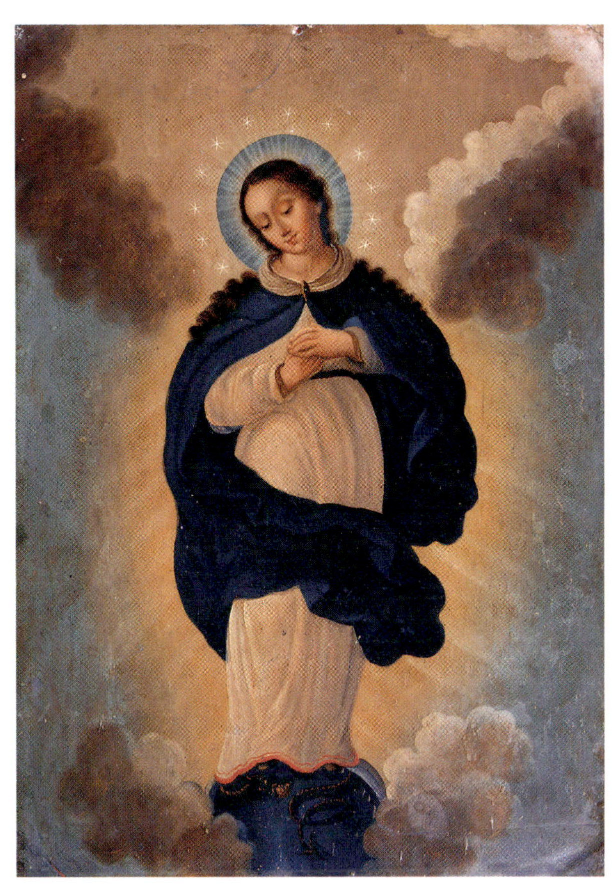

130 BUSTOS, RETABLO OF THE IMMACULATE VIRGIN

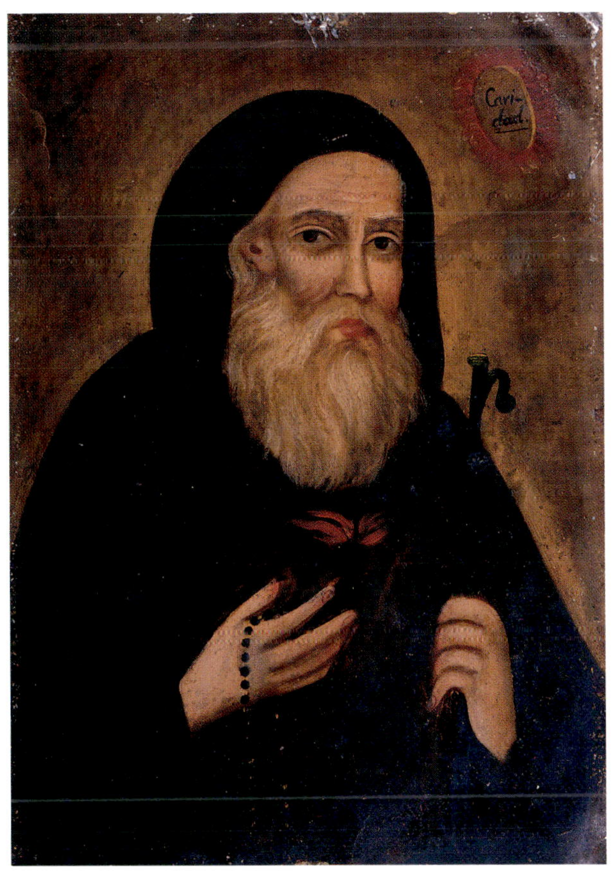

131 BUSTOS, RETABLO OF SAINT FRANCIS OF ASSISI

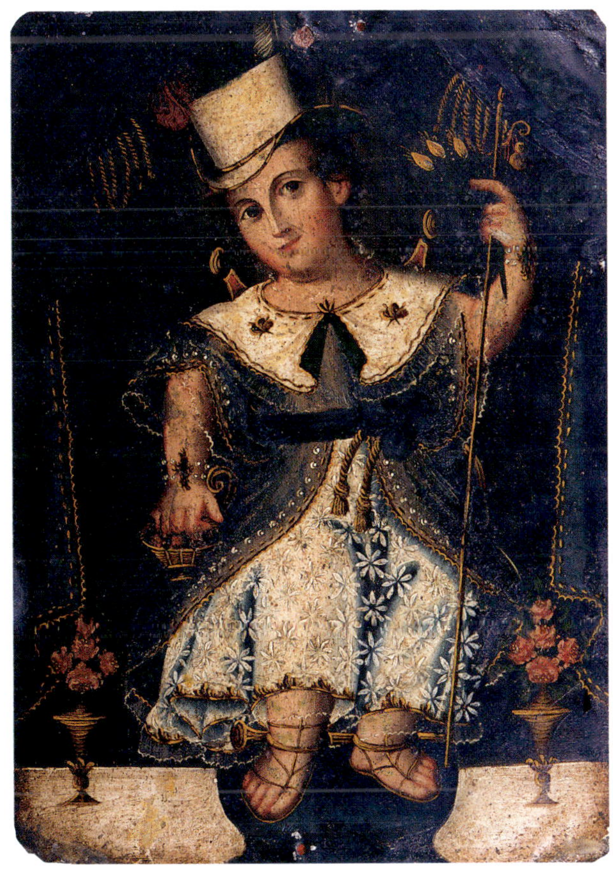

132 BUSTOS, RETABLO OF THE CHILD OF ATOCHA

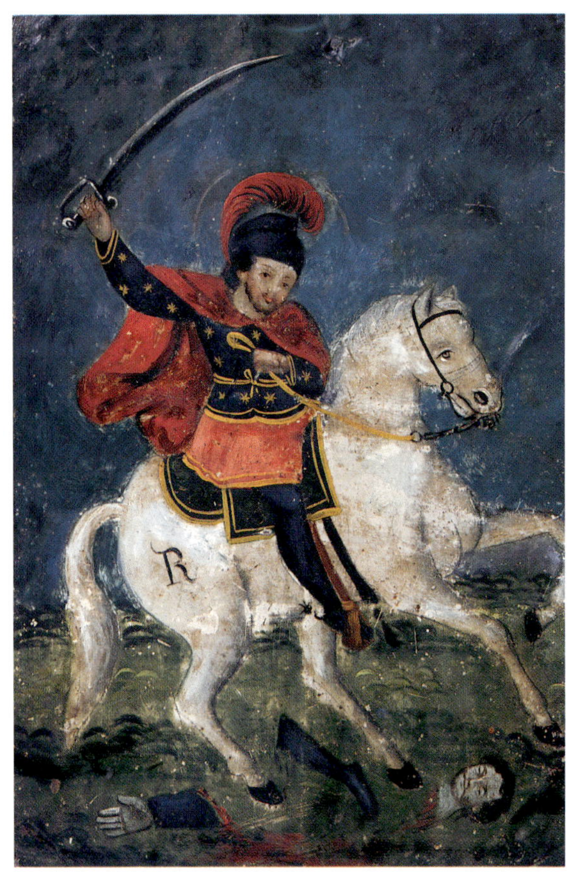

133 BUSTOS, RETABLO OF THE APOSTLE JACOB

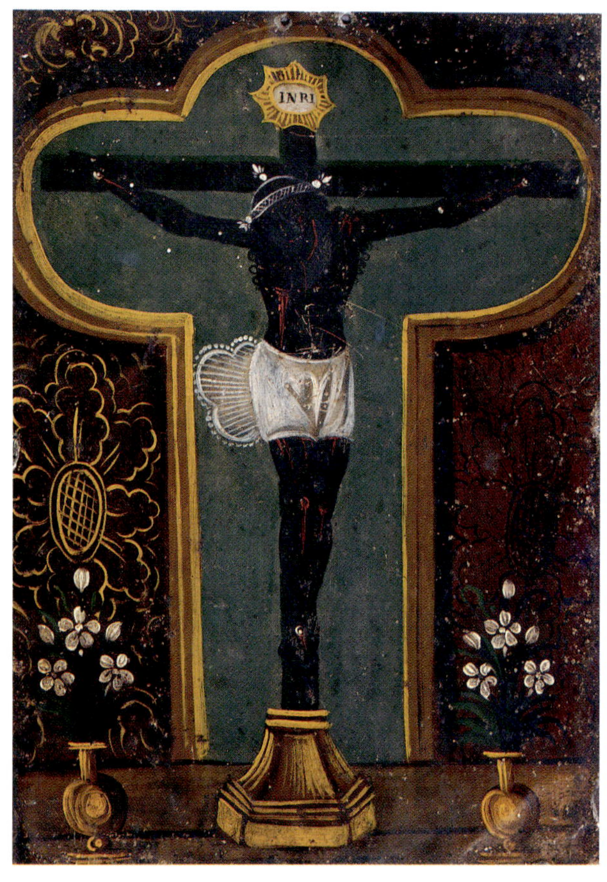

134 BUSTOS, RETABLO OF THE BLACK JESUS OF ESQUIPULA

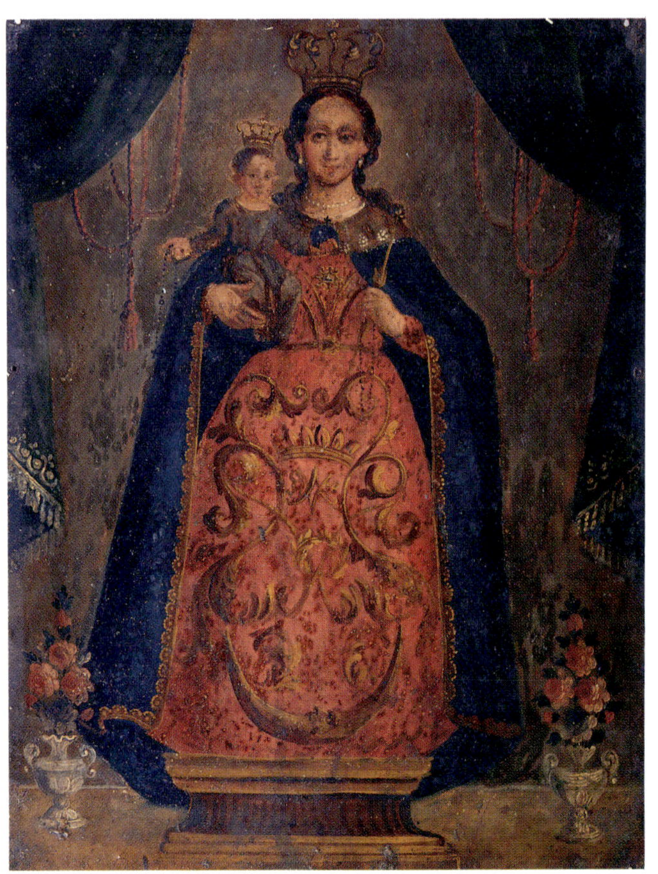

135 BUSTOS, RETABLO OF THE VIRGIN WITH THE HALF MOON

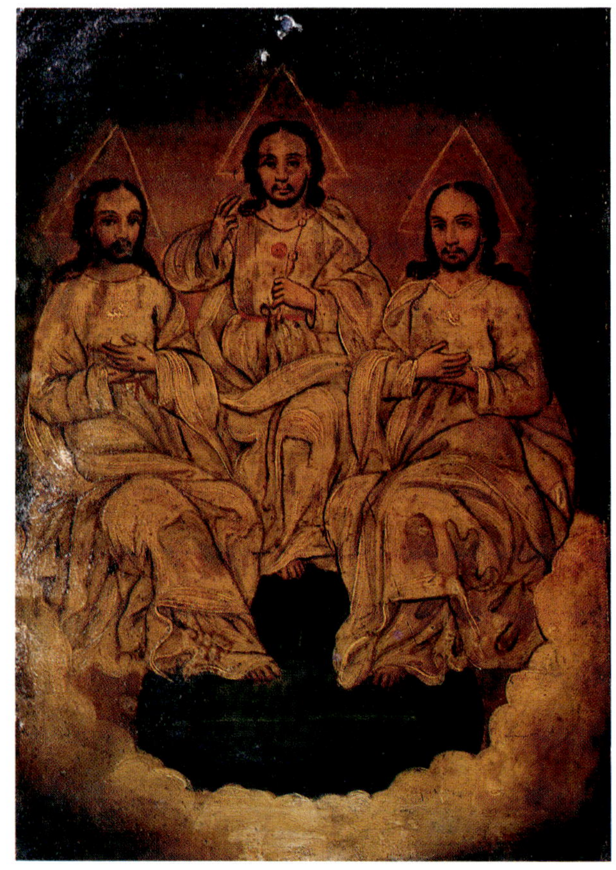

136 BUSTOS, RETABLO OF THE HOLY TRINITY

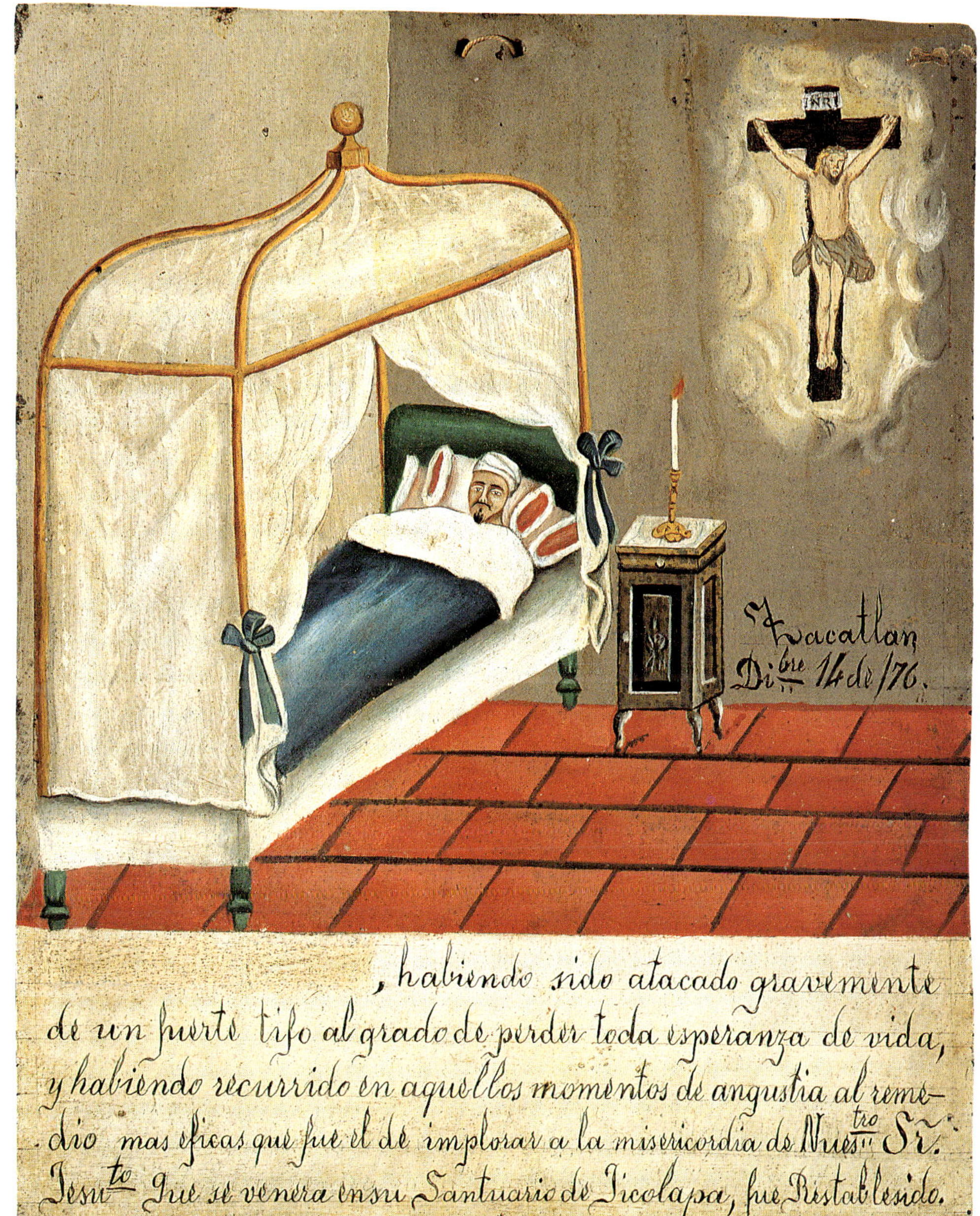

137 EX-VOTO "BEING SEVERELY ATTACKED BY A STRONG TYPHUS...," 1876

REMEMBRANCES OF MEXICO'S "BELLE ÉPOQUE" LOLA ALVAREZ BRAVO MAKES A MOVIE ABOUT FRIDA

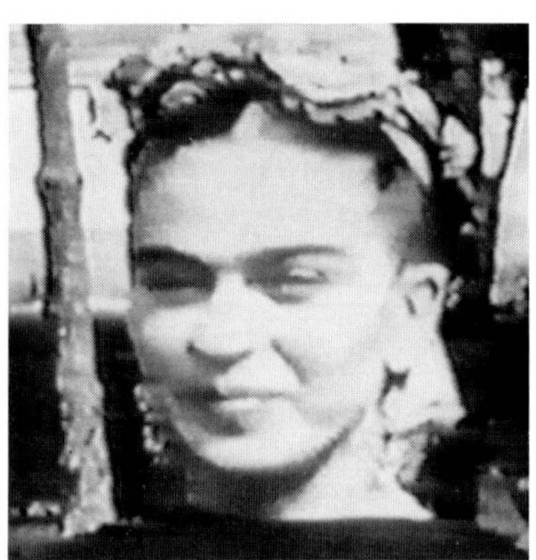

Between the end of spring and the beginning of summer 1951, Lola Alvarez Bravo, Raúl Abarca, the youngest Misrachi daughter (a striking young woman), and myself, decided to make an experimental movie with Frida Kahlo as the protagonist. Directing the photography workshop in San Carlos had awakened in Lola an interest in trying her luck at making movies. I believe the 16-millimeter camera, the only one we could afford, forever broke as we were, belonged to Abarca, who also financed a substantial share of the project. I contributed the script and an irresistible desire to be the director.

We entered Frida and Diego's house in Coyoacán as if it were a sanctuary. This was especially true for me since I had never seen the sacred monsters up close. The house looked almost the same as it does today, except then it was alive. Today I have come to realize, not without wonderment, that it was an artifice, an invention, a cultural artifact, the quintessence of a Mexican home: *equipales* (chairs with seats made out of woven palm leaves or strips of leather), armoires with mirrored doors, credenzas decorated with open woodwork, glazed casseroles, handcrafted tables, votive paintings on metal sheets that seemed to have alighted like butterflies on the walls, *petates* (rugs made out of woven palm leaves) on the floor, Itzcuintli breed pups, a couple of spider monkeys. And in the background a large inner patio: trees with hanging orchids, and a kind of Indian pyramid with ferns and ancient clay figures on the platforms. I became convinced that the house was an artifact, a nationalist thesis, a statement of belief in a Mexico no less profound for its colorful haphazardness – or vice versa; I understood all that when I stole into Frida's half-darkened room and saw the famous bed, covered with a white hand-crocheted lace cover, with the full-length mirror on the inside of its canopy.

On the whole, the house was not at all pretty. It was something more, it was beautiful; with a kind of steely, decadent, vaguely menacing beauty. However – perhaps because of its references to the revolution which would some day set the world on fire – it was austere, like certain colonial religious buildings dating from the time of the Viceroy, imbued with a sense of the end of time; in short, like any exceptional place, pregnant with history.

At the door of the receiving room Frida materialized (Frida never simply entered or arrived), dressed in a white *huipil* (a sleeveless blouse worn by indigenous women), a black *rebozo* (Mexican shawl), and colored ribbons braided into her hair. I was immediately smitten by her and even forgot the violent passion for the young Misrachi that had overcome me that very morning. I could not help it, I felt overpowered by a superior force. Frida was possessed by a consuming urge to be loved, by the air, by things, by insects, by people, by all of the people. Just as Saint Theresa prayed twenty-four hours a day, Frida consumed love. When she appeared that morning, she instantly realized that I had not yet submitted to her and on the spot engulfed me in flames that left me speechless, lost in the contemplation of her magical face. It was like standing in front of an open oven. What in fact opened up was a friendly conversation. Frida was prepared, in ten minutes we started to film: Lola was bent over a low tripod, her behind sticking up, one eye glued to the viewfinder and the other half-closed to ward off the smoke of the cigarette hanging from her lips. Abarca was holding up some tinfoil-lined cardboards serving as reflectors, and I was clumsily giving Frida instructions which she obediently followed.

This went on every morning, from Monday through Friday, for a week and a half; until paradise came to an end. Frida had to stay in bed. I felt guilty thinking I might have abused her patience and exhausted her. Although, to tell the truth, for several days we had been noticing a certain tension in Frida's smile, and a certain stiffness in her bearing as she waited for us seated on the *equipal* dressed in her white *huipil*.

About that time I obtained a contract to work in Rome for the FAO (Food and Agriculture Organization of the United Nations). The last time I saw Frida she was bedridden, the sheets revealing her bare arms and shoulders. Her hair was spread out on the pillow like rays of a black sun, the martyred face wore no makeup, her ring-decorated hands were resting on the blanket, her skin was as pale as wax.

I do not remember what we said to each other, I was

overcome with emotion. When I stood up she stretched out her arm searching her bedside table for a small round mirror with a red lacquer back on which she had etched her name. As she made this movement I saw the swelling of her breast and the fastening of her orthopedic corset. She placed the mirror in my hand, folding it close with hers. I bent down to kiss her knuckles, but she reached up and, holding my neck, pulled me down, and kissed me on the lips. We both had tears in our eyes. I left, holding the mirror tightly in my fist. Once outside, I joined Lola who was talking in the hallway to Diego; a massive bulk planted inside his large mountain-hiking shoes and wearing huge overalls that looked like a circus tent. I never saw Frida again. As regards the sections of film we had shot, in the sixties Lola, who was incapable of refusing any request, lent the rolls of film to somebody for a television program. He never returned them and they got lost.*

That is how, in the magical atmosphere created by Frida, one of the most cherished periods of my life, my friendship with Lola Alvarez Bravo, came to an end. That friendship had started for me about 1940, when she was thirty-three years old, in a hallway of the Palacio de Bellas Artes, in front of the office of Carlos Pellicer. I remember arriving, sitting down, and seeing in front of me a woman wearing a transparent dress of black voile over silk underwear, also black, which revealed her broad shoulders and well-shaped arms. She sat sideways in the armchair, her legs crossed; under her black silk stockings her knees, calves, and the insteps of her feet were visible. They were of the same unblemished matte white color, like porcelain or paper, as the skin of her decolleté up to the line of her steel-gray hair, which was combed up on top of her head. Her arched eyebrows, her long, pointed nose, her thin lips, all suggested cruelty, which was emphasized by some faint acne scars on her cheeks; the cruelty was countered, however, by the curve of her jaw and the shapely pillar of her neck, splendidly placed on those seventeenth-century shoulders. And what can I say about her breasts under the tight-fitting silk? I sat there, speechless, imbibing her with my eyes.

Pellicier told me her name: Lola Alvarez Bravo, a photographer, but warned me that she was having an affair with José Martínez, who was about twenty-two years old at the time. He was already well known for his *Tierra Nueva*, as well as for his elegance, good looks, and his teaching at the Prepa (the Escuela Nacional Preparatoria, an institution of higher education that prepared students for admission to the university, and one of the best in Mexico at the time). I understood that it was a waste of time to fix my longing glances on Lola.

* Fragments of the film have resurfaced and will be shown again during this exhibition for the first time.

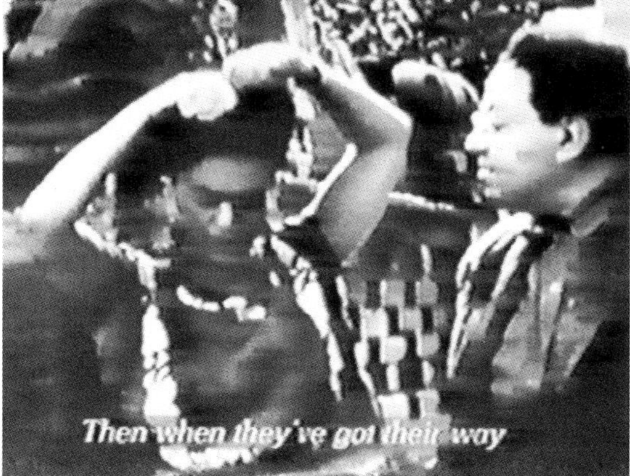

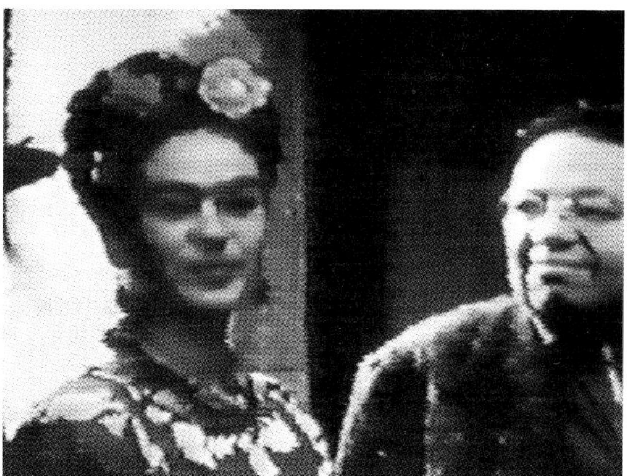

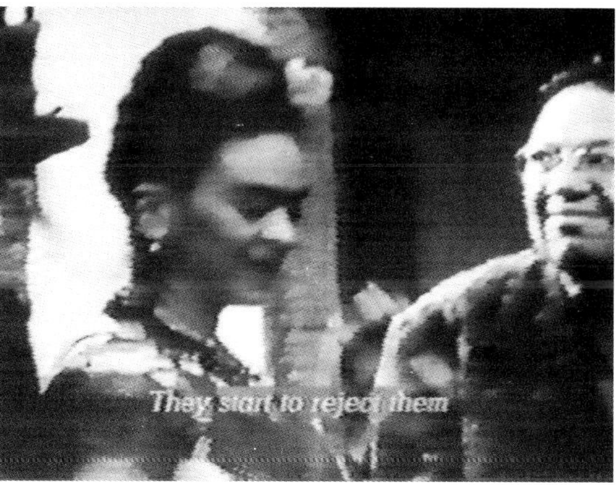

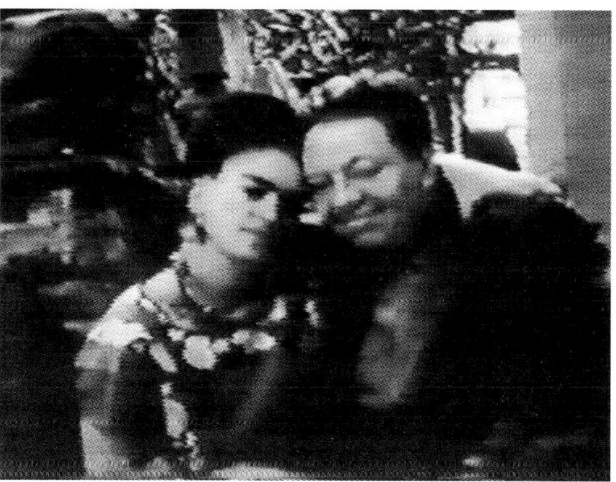

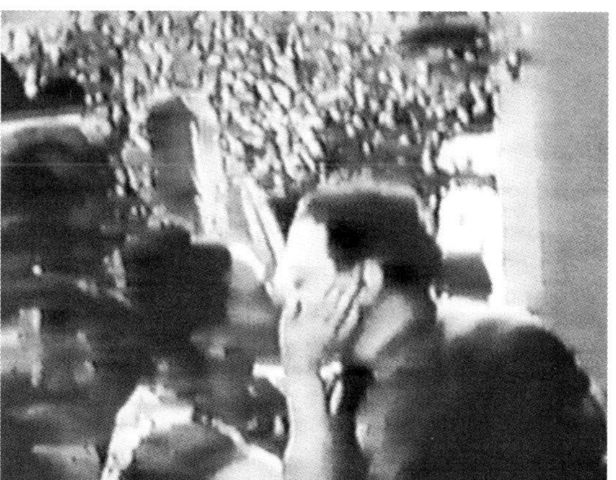

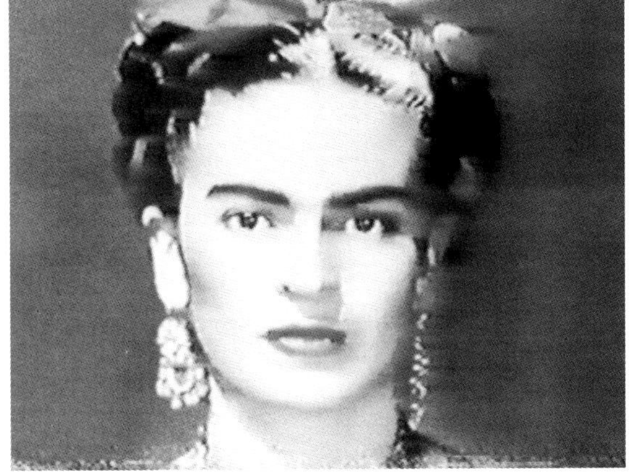

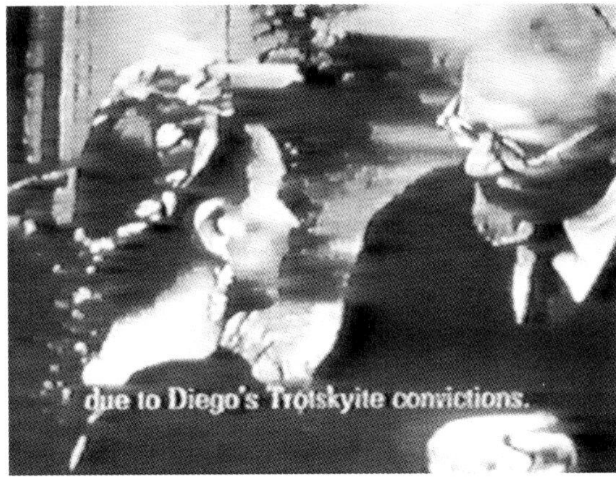

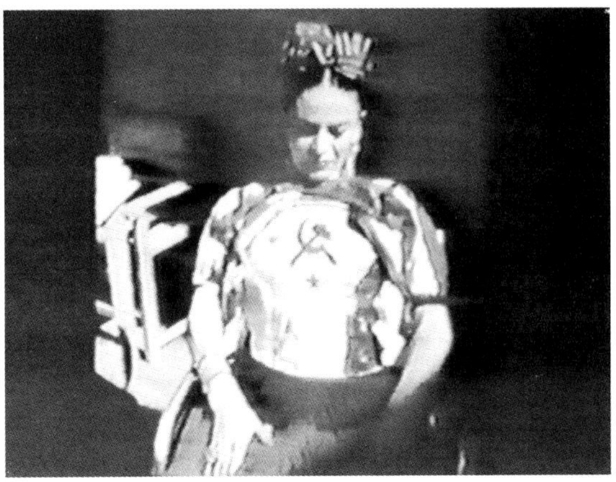

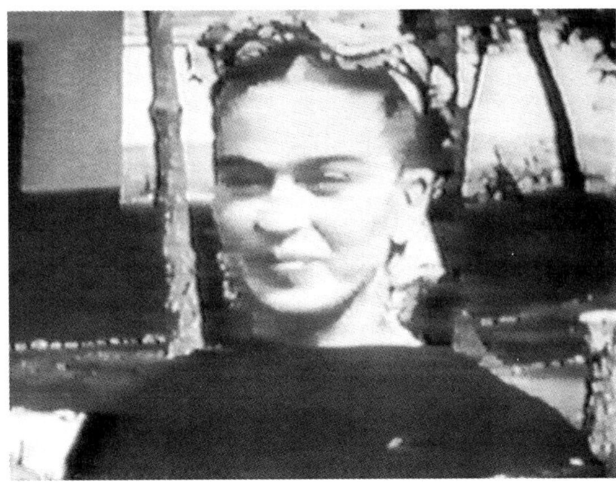

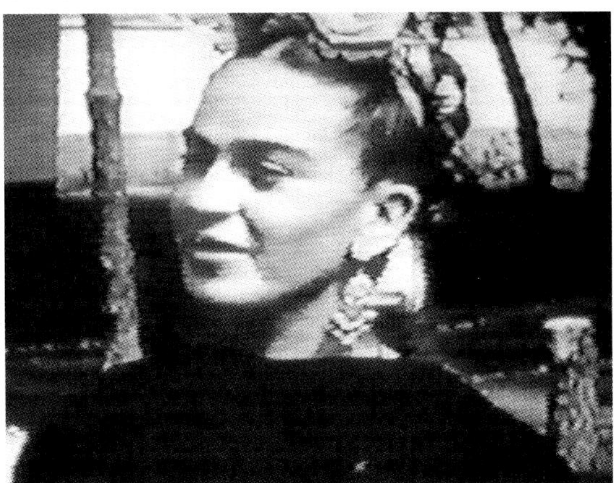

Nevertheless, I managed to run into her repeatedly, and after a few months, I do not recall how many, when Martinez had become a thing of the past, Lola accepted me as a member of her circle of friends. The core of the group were Lola, Juan Soriano, and Diego de Mesa, in addition to a varied ensemble of other characters who came and went; I joined them as a junior member. I seem to remember some of Lola's lovers: a future bull-fighter, for instance, who almost became famous. Then came the long years with Raúl Abarca, whom Lola adopted as her companion, her photography student, and her disciple in the art of living. I should add that in her love life, Lola was the embodiment of discretion and kindness. The ground rule for her life was to share her bed and her wisdom. She never hurt anybody; I cannot recall one argument, I never heard a complaint.

The group met almost every evening to eat at cheap restaurants or Chinese cafes, or to go to parties or to the movies. Those memories have become a rich broth that still feeds me, from which I take spoonfuls of recollection, beloved icons like Frida's kiss, or the night we went to the premiere of *Bicycle Thieves,* and later, around a bar table, cried over tacos we could not swallow because of the lump in our throats.

How did Lola live at that time? With modesty as moving as her talent, off small stipends and a few commissions. Today I have trouble reconstructing her apartment on Ejido street. I remember a confusing mixture of furniture and objects: handcrafted articles, boxes with photography supplies, shoes and other garments, lamps, tubes with chemicals. In her bedroom a perpetually unmade bed, not very wide, was surrounded by piles of books and portraits leaning against the walls.

Her tenderness is still alive, but I wonder about the end of her alliance with Eros. I left Mexico believing it would never end. Another icon, from the end of the forties: a dinner *cum* tequila at the home of María Izquierdo, who had decided to beat the stroke she had recently suffered. All of a sudden Abarca and Ricardo Garibay started fighting over one of Lola's shoes. Both holding onto the shoe, their ties pulled to one side, flushed faces and eyes bloodshot with anger, they started a lively dance that began in the dining room and ended in the patio, leaving a trail of overturned chairs in its wake. Meanwhile María Izquierdo, sitting in her armchair, laughed with half her mouth.

I tell about these memories which come to me from the full years that I spent among Lola Alvarez Bravo's friends, because they have stayed with me. Among them I particularly cherish my brief sojourn in the world of Frida Kahlo before the interrupted filming; I mention it because even today I remember that episode like a flash of light. I do not merely recall those times with a sense of nostalgia but for reasons that go beyond that meeting!

My meeting with Frida was the best gift that Lola gave me among all those she bestowed upon me by the simple fact of letting me be close to her for ten years. I have referred to her inclination to share with people she loved her knowledge, her experiences, and her search; for me she opened the doors of the culture of the forties. She was not the only one interested in a young man like myself, eager to enter the fabled circle (I could mention Carlos Pellicer, Octavio G. Barreda, Julio Castellanos, among others), but she was my most constant tutor. Still, that desire to share wisdom and friends, that inclination to shape human beings, was a feature of that culture. This spontaneous impulse, so intimately linked to the emotions inherent in human relationships was part and parcel of the emotional code which, at the time, marked the pursuit of any intellectual endeavor. It happened among friends, among lovers, among strangers. It was the foundation of any encounter. And, of course, it became apparent in the relationship that linked any work of art with its spectator, listener, or reader.

I believe this unique emotionality was the second achievement of the culture that José Vasconcelos clamored for with messianic fervor, when in 1921 he proclaimed: "Let us be the initiators of a crusade for public education, let us inspire our race with the same enthusiasm it has devoted in previous times to religion and conquest ... Let us be the initiators of an educational crusade, namely, the teaching of those who know to those who know nothing." For Vasconcelos the cultural process could not take place unless "there is a close relationship between proletarians and workers ... the workers of the mind ... Only close contact between laborers and intellectuals can lead to a spiritual renaissance that may lift our times above others."

Before Vasconcelos, the generation of 1915, the Seven Wise Men, then nineteen years old, had realized "whith stupefied optimism" – as Daniel Cosio Villegas says – that a new Mexico was emerging in front of their eyes and that "they could and had to participate in its construction." The result of this unbridled activism was, literally, the creation of a culture imbued with a hunger for education; in light of the Revolution and above the thinking heads appeared a new ethic and an aesthetic that was nevertheless rooted in a kind of universal humanism to which our historical heritage lent a uniquely beloved singularity.

Fired up by an urge toward discovery, we all became, in our own individual way, examples of how those ideals should be lived in daily life, including the realms of emotion and carnal knowledge. In coitus, even in the most primitive lust, Mexico revealed itself. Were we not redefining ourselves in our search for indigenous and *mestizo* beauty? To discover Mexico also meant for Mexicans to discover each other.

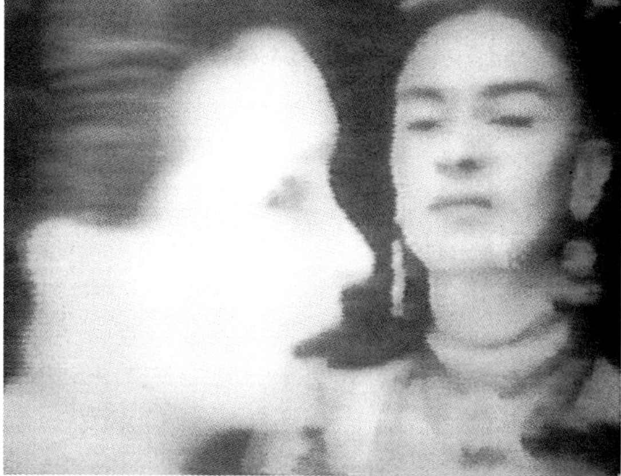

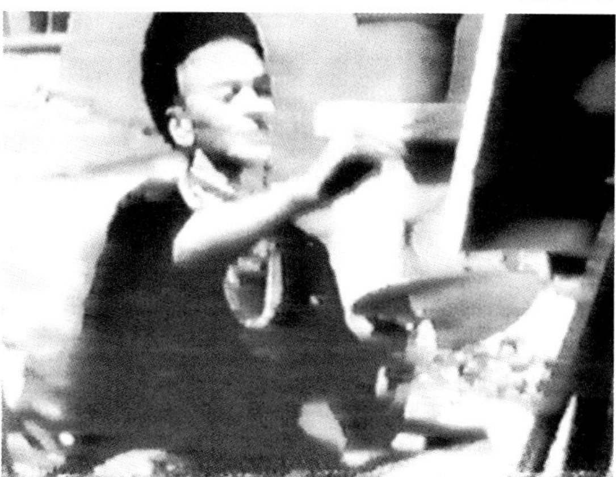

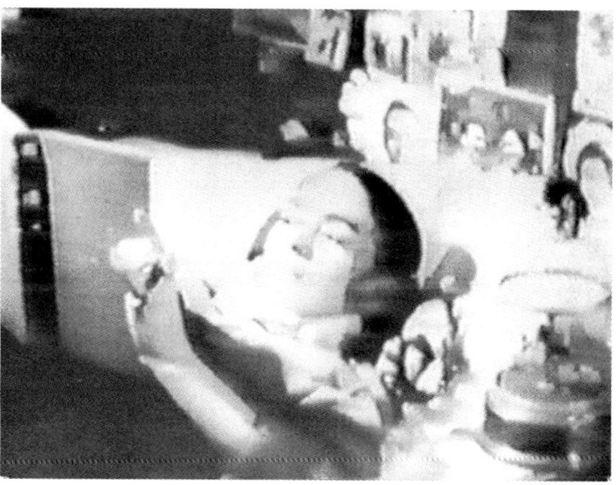

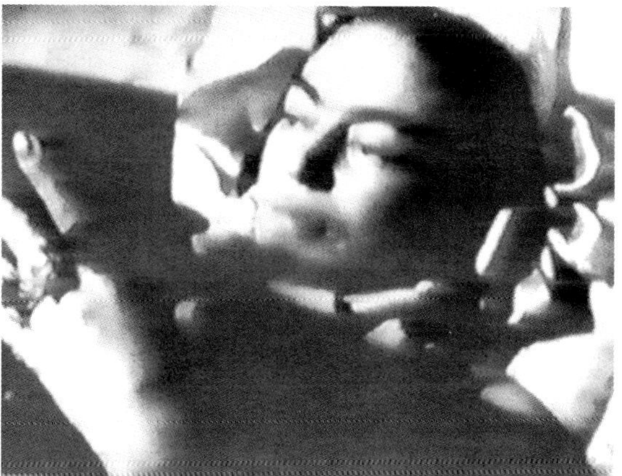

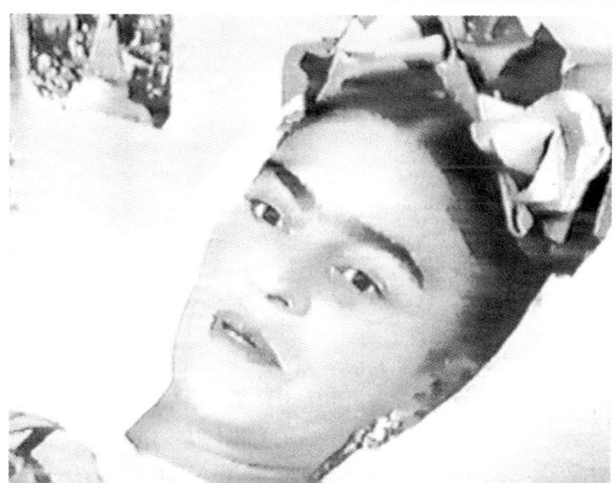

What I here recall I had forgotten. And I had forgotten it because I had stopped experiencing it; and I no longer experienced it because it had vanished. Because it *has* vanished. That emotionality, that way of relating to people, of feeling and shaping – crafting – a culture, namely by cultivating onself-among-others, has ceased to exist. And with it, because it was an integral part of it, that culture has vanished too. And along with it, the beloved city in which it reached its prime.

During the forties, Pellicer inaugurated a show in which we marveled at the discovery of works by José María Velasco. At that time the affinity between our habitat and the valley exalted in those paintings was still recognizable: we lived in the region with the most transparent air. We confirmed that, every time we looked out from any point of the city and could see the top of Iztaccíhuatl. Today Velasco's paintings are a testimony to immense riches lost forever. The landscape paintings by Velasco or by Atl can only be viewed with sadness. Are Lola Alvarez Bravo's paintings a reference to the past, like dried flowers? For me, they have enriched recent history. In order for the past, even the immediate past, to fill us with life, we need not only to interpret the events but also to recapture the emotional atmosphere, the range of emotions that served as the backdrop against which these events were shaped. We need to contrast them with the mettle of our current life, the affective codes of our present, so as to reconcile in the end the bitterness of our current life with the sweetness of what was, in fact, Mexico's true "belle époque." A belle époque first earned through a revolution, and next, through another revolution against that revolution.

That cultural climate had its political import, since it was a deliberate attempt to mold the country in accordance with values that contrasted drastically with the bloody code of violent passions that raged within the revolutionary caudillos. This is clearly illustrated in Martín Luis Guzmán's film *The Shadow of the Caudillo* . The former was the exact opposite of the latter. As stated by Antonio Caso, it was a matter of carrying out the mission of "defending the culture against the armed struggle between brothers." From 1920 on, in Cosio Villega's words, this cultural militancy – or countermilitancy? – turned into a search for our Mexican roots "not in order to set them against each other but to finally to reconcile them," thus ceasing to be, as Ramon Lopez Velarde wrote in 1921 "prodigal children of a motherland we cannot even define." I wonder whether we have achieved that reconciliation. But that is another story.

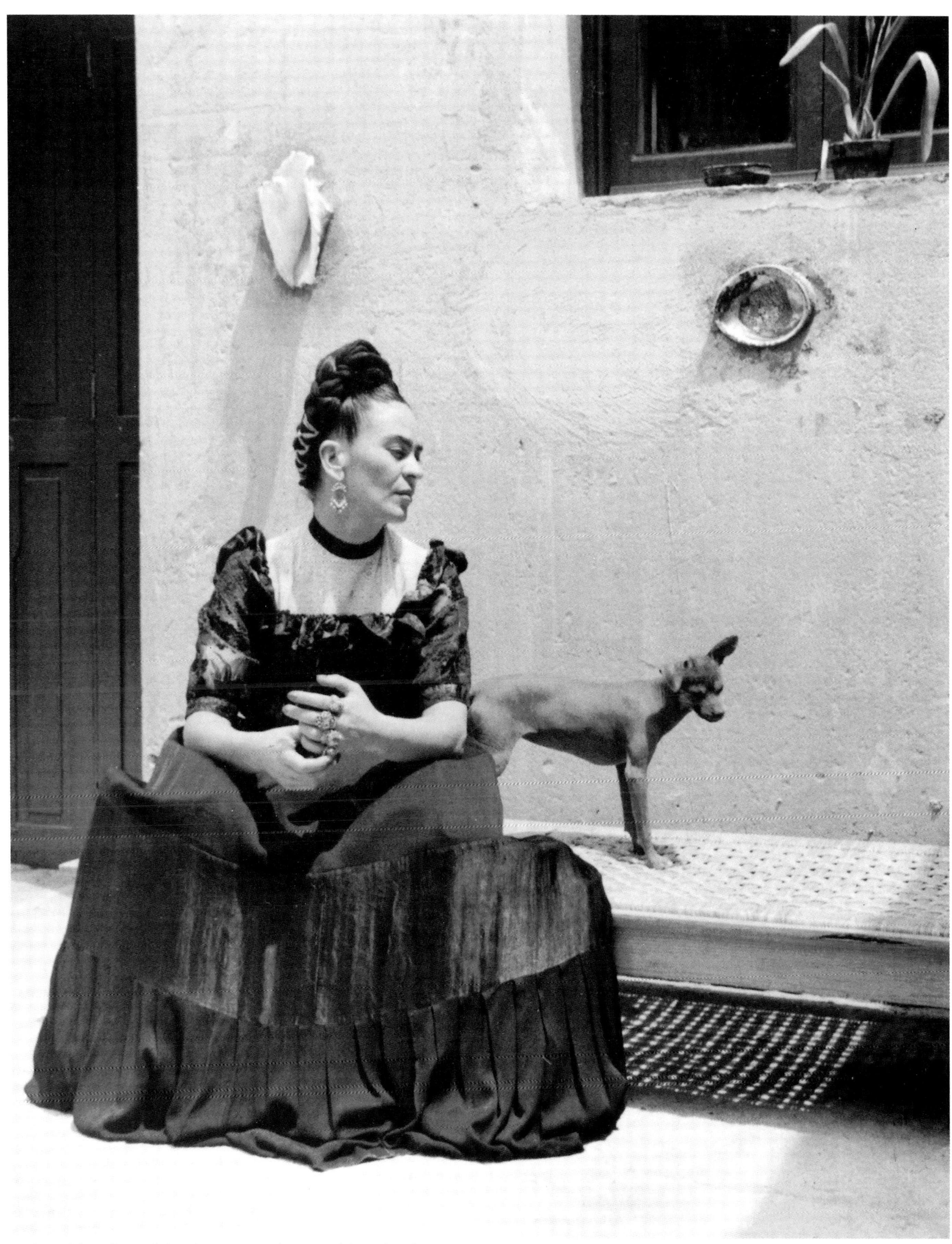

Frida Kahlo in front of the Blue House. Photograph by Lola Alvarez Bravo.

CHRONOLOGY

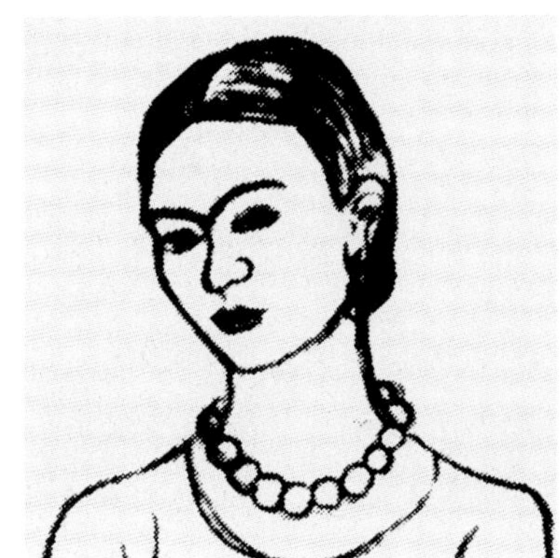

1907
Magdalena Carmen Frida Kahlo Calderón born on July 6 in the Coyoacán district of Mexico City. Her father, Guillermo Kahlo, a photographer of Jewish-Hungarian ancestry, was born in Germany, and her mother, Mathilde Calderón, in Mexico City. Married in 1898, they had four daughters: Matilde, Adriana, Frida and Cristina. Guillermo Kahlo also had two daughters, Luisa and Margarita, from a previous marriage in 1894 to María Cerdeña (died 1898).

1918
Frida suffers a contusion on her right foot that causes a slight atrophy. She is diagnosed with poliomyelitis and is bedridden for nine months. As a result of this illness, her right leg is permanently thinner than her left.

1922
She enters the Escuela Nacional Preparatoria, located in the old Colegio de San Ildefonso, with the intention of later studying medicine. She falls in love with Alejandro Gómez Arias, who is part of a group called "Las Cachuchas," which she also joins. Around this time, she decides to take three years off her age and to use 1910 as her birth date. This later causes confusion in the chronology of her life and work. Frida observes the famous and polemic artist Diego Rivera as he paints the mural *Creation* in the Anfiteatro Bolívar.

1923
Frida and Alejandro Gómez Arias begin their love affair.

1924
The relationship with Gómez Arias becomes intimate, and Frida makes plans to go with him to the United States. During the mornings she attends school and in the afternoons she helps her father in his photographic studio.

1925
Her first experience with art occurs when she becomes an apprentice engraver in the print shop of Fernando Fernández. There she copies three works by Anders Zorn. She studies shorthand and typing at the Academia Oliver. On September 17, while returning from school with Gómez Arias, she suffers a terrible accident when the bus in which they are traveling has a collision with a streetcar, and her life is forever changed.
Frida remembered that day: "I was a smart girl, but not very practical.... Perhaps, because of that, I did not correctly measure the situation and did not grasp the severity of my wounds.... The arms of the seat went through me like a sword into a bull."[1] At the news, the Kahlo family is plunged into grief: her father becomes ill, her mother cannot talk for a month. Only her sister Matilde remains at her side during her stay in the hospital.
Letter from Frida to Gómez Arias (October 13): "You, better than anybody else, know how sad I have been in this wretched hospital, as you can imagine it yourself, and also the boys must have told you. Everybody tells me not to be so desperate, but they don't know what it is like to be in bed for three months, even though that is where I need to be. Having roamed the streets all my life and loved it, this is difficult to cope with. But what can one do? At least Death didn't carry me away. Right?"[2]

1926
Her forced confinement causes Frida to think about dedicating herself to making scientific drawings for medical books. For that purpose she analyzes biological tissues under a microscope. Doctor Ortiz Tirado immobilizes her in a cast for nine months when he discovers that she has three vertebrae out of place. A device is placed on her foot, which Frida hides by wearing masculine clothes. She completes her "disguise" by having her hair cut short. Informed that she cannot conceive, she dedicates a few lines in a letter to an imaginary son, supposedly born when she suffered her accident. "Leonardo was born at the Red Cross in the year of our Lord 1925, in the month of September, and was baptized in the village of Coyoacán the following year. His mother was Frida Kahlo, his godparents Isabel Campos and Alejandro Gómez Arias."[3]

During her convalescence she starts to paint, after also attempting watercolor and engraving. Her mother fixes her bed with a special easel that makes it easier for her to draw or write and places a mirror in her room so that she can see her image. A year after her accident, Frida has matured, her bitter experience having forced her to face reality. She later considered 1926 to be a crucial year in her life because that is when she began to paint regularly.

Letter from Frida to Gómez Arias (September 29): "Why do you study so much? What secret are you looking for? Life will reveal it to you soon. I already know it all, without reading or writing. A little while ago, not much more than a few days ago, I was a child who went about in a world of colors, of hard and tangible forms. Everything was mysterious and something was hidden, guessing what it was was a game for me. If you knew how terrible it is to know suddenly, as if a bolt of lightning elucidated the earth. Now I live in a painful planet, transparent as ice; but it is as if I had learned everything at once in seconds. My friends, my companions became women slowly. I became old in instants and everything today is bland and lucid. I know that nothing lies behind, if there was something I would see it."[4]

Works: *Self-Portrait Wearing a Velvet Dress*[5]

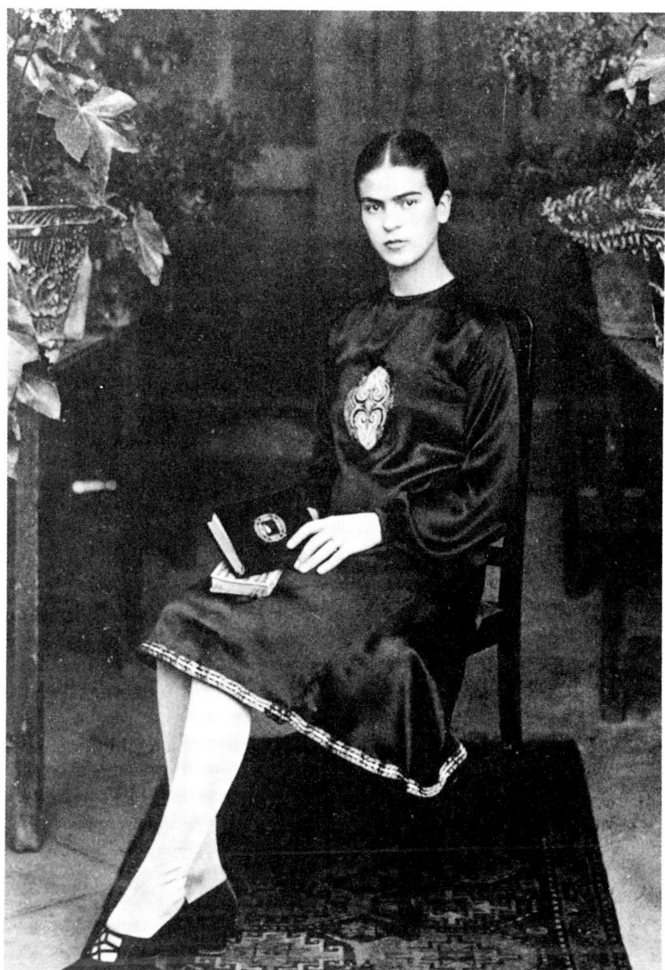

The eighteen-year-old Frida, 1926. Photograph by her father.

1927

In March, Gómez Arias goes to Germany to study. He and Frida communicate frequently by letter. On January 10 she writes: "I am as always, bad. You can see how boring this is. I don't know what to do because it has been over a year that I have been here. It is driving me to the wall to have so many ailments, like an old lady. I don't know how I will be at thirty years of age. You will have to carry me wrapped in cotton all day long. I am very very bored!!!"[6]

In another letter on April 22, she tells him about the corset they are going to put on her: "The only advantage this dirty thing has is that I am able to walk, but since walking hurts my leg so much, even this benefit is counterproductive." She adds that if this does not work an operation will be necessary to transfer a piece of bone from her leg to her spinal column.[7] A few days later (April 30), she writes again: "Last Friday a cast was put on and since then it has been real torture. It cannot be compared with anything. I feel suffocated. There is a dreadful pain in my lungs and all over my back. I cannot touch my leg, I cannot walk, and I sleep badly. Imagine, for two and a half hours, they had me hanging by my head only and after that resting on the tips of my toes for over one hour, while the cast was dried with heated air. But when I arrived at home, it was still completely damp. For three or four months I must bear this torture, and if I don't get relief I would sincerely like to die."[8]

On May 29 Frida writes to Gómez Arias that her father has promised to take her to Veracruz. She complains of her bad luck: "Some are born stars, others only see stars.... I am one of those who because of pain mostly just see stars dance before my eyes."[9] On May 31, she writes that she is about to finish the portrait of Chong Li (Miguel N. Lira). She says that the second corset did not work, the pain continues, and she is going to be operated on. "My sciatic nerve is damaged plus another one ... that branches off to the reproductive organs. Also damaged are two vertebrae. I don't know where and how and I weary of things that I cannot explain to you because I don't understand them."[10]

In a letter on June 4, Frida writes to Gómez Arias about the treatment she will be subjected to: "They are going to change the device for a third time. This time it will make me completely rigid so I will not be able to walk for two or three months, until the vertebrae join together perfectly.... After that... first a month in bed (the same way you left me), another month with different devices, then two more months in a cast, and finally six months once again in the small device so I will be able to walk. Then there will still be the wonderful prospect of being operated on."[11]

In a letter to Gómez Arias dated July 15 her attitude seems to have changed. She is content, with hopes of recuperation. Later in the letter she sounds sad and annoyed, but ready to endure everything in order to get better: "I hardly ever get desperate, and I seldom shed tears."[12] About this time, a mobile table is constructed that allows her to take sun baths. In a letter dated July 23 she says that she has finished the portrait of Lira but finds it horrible. "It has a very elaborate background, and he seems like a cardboard cutout."[13]

And another letter to Gómez Arias: "Today is September 17, the worst of all, because I am alone. If you came I could not offer you anything I would like to. Instead of being a flirt and brazen, I am merely brazen and useless, which is worse. All these things torment me constantly. All life is in you, but I will not be able to have it.... I am very simpleminded and I suffer a lot for things I should not. I am very young, and perhaps it is still possible to get well. Only I cannot believe it. Should I?"[14]

Works: *Pancho Villa and Adelita; Portrait of Miguel N. Lira; Portrait of Alicia Galant; If Adelita ("Las Cachuchas"); Portrait of Adriana Kahlo; Portrait of Ruth Quintanilla; Portrait of Angel Salas; Portrait of Jesús Ríos y Valle*

1928

Recently returned from the Soviet Union, Diego Rivera continues working on the murals at the Secretaría de Educación Pública. Frida decides to visit him to show him her works and get the opinion of a person who knows his trade, because, although she only knows him by sight, she admires him greatly.

Rivera later described in detail the strong impression of her beauty, her personality, and her works made on him. He considered this encounter one of the happiest moments of his life. "I felt deeply moved by admiration for this girl. I had to restrain myself from praising her as much as I wanted to. Yet I could not be completely insincere. I was puzzled by her attitude. Why, I asked her, didn't she trust my judgment? Hadn't she come herself to ask for it? 'The trouble is,' she replied, 'that some of your good friends have advised me not to put too much stock in what you say. They say that if it's a girl who asks your opinion and she's not an absolute horror, you are ready to gush all over her. Well, I want you to tell me only one thing. Do you actually believe that I should continue to paint, or should I turn to some other sort of work?' In my opinion, no matter how difficult it is for you, you must continue to paint, I answered at once."[15]

Frida serves as Rivera's model for the mural *In the Arsenal,* in the series known as the Ballad of the Proletarian Revolution, located on the third floor of the Secretaría de Educación Pública. Rivera helps her obtain a job as a teacher of drawing for children.

Works: *Portrait of Cristina, My Sister; Tiny Caballero; Portrait of Agustín M., Olmedo; Two Women; Seated Girl with Duck*

1929

On July 1 Frida receives a teaching appointment in the Section of Painting and Handicrafts in the Department of Fine Arts.[16]

On August 21 Frida becomes Rivera's third wife. He is forty-two years of age, she is twenty-two, but says she is nineteen. The ceremony takes place in the old Palacio Municipal in Coyoacán. The couple rents an elegant and spacious house at 104 Paseo de la Reforma. With this union, Frida's life changes completely. At Rivera's request she starts wearing traditional Mexican dresses.

On September 24 Frida requests a three-month leave of absence without pay, sometime later she asks for an extension, and is finally fired when she does not return to her job. Rivera is appointed director of the Academia de San Carlos but his revolutionary ideas about education provoke serious opposition, and he is dismissed within a year.

In December Frida and Rivera go to live in Cuernavaca in the house of Dwight W. Morrow, United States Ambassador to Mexico. They remain there for approximately a year, while Rivera paints the murals at the Palacio de Cortés.

Works: *The Bus; Portrait of a Girl Wearing a Necklace; Girl in Diapers; Portrait of a Girl; Portrait of Virginia Niña; Portrait of a Girl with a Ribbon around Her Waist;*

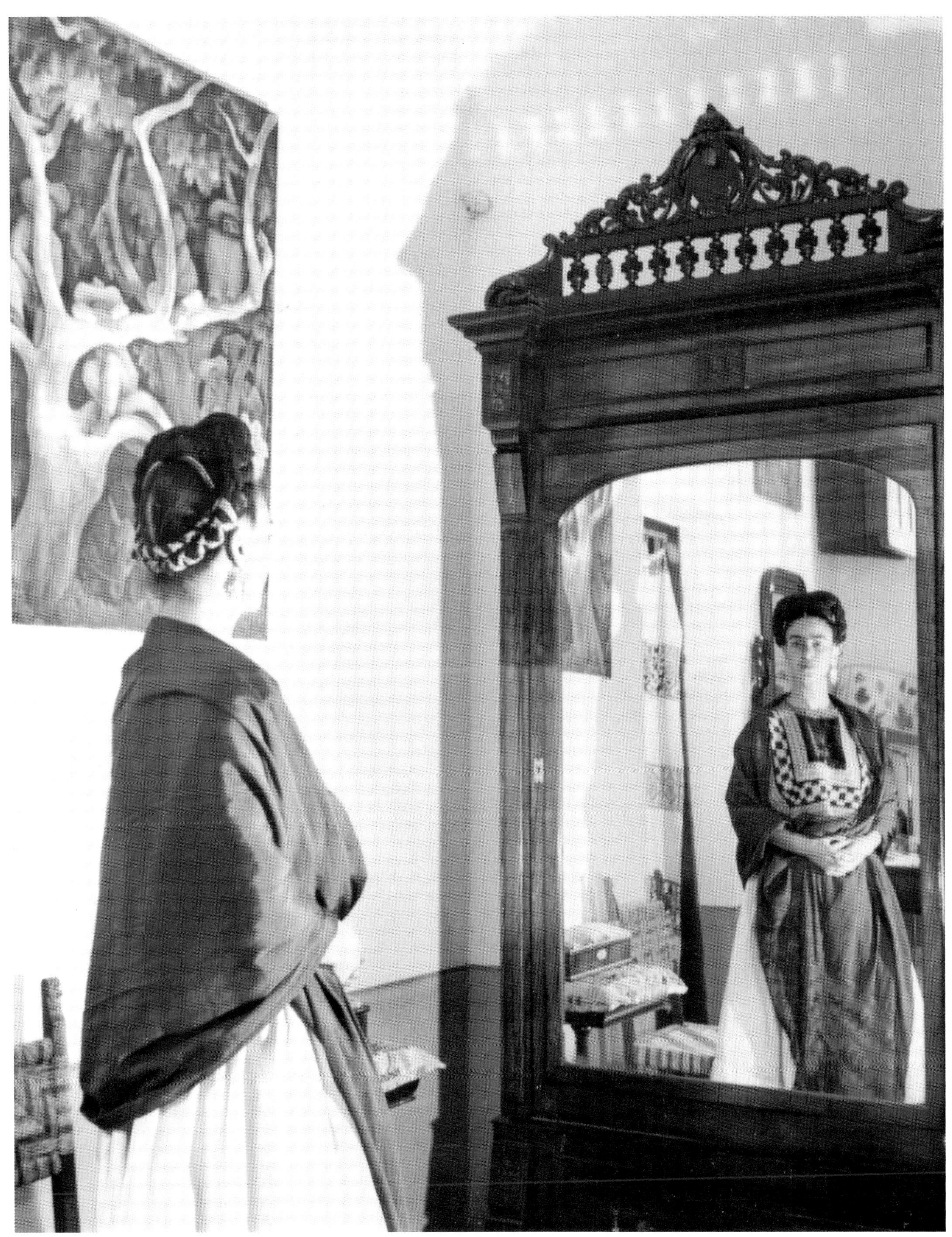

Frida Kahlo in the Blue House. Photograph by Lola Alvarez Bravo.

Self-Portrait "Time Flies"; Nude Indian Woman; Portait of Lupe Marín

1930
Frida's first pregnancy aborted at three months because of "pelvic malformation" by Dr. Jesús Marín, brother of Lupe Marín, Rivera's second wife.
In November Rivera and Frida travel to San Francisco, where he is to paint murals at the Luncheon Club of the Stock Exchange and at the San Francisco Art Institute. They reside in the studio of sculptor Ralph Stackpole. Frida explores San Francisco, visits Chinatown, and attends parties, lectures, and exhibitions. She meets photographer Edward Weston and Dr. Leo Eloesser.
Works: *Self-Portrait; Portrait of a Lady Wearing Earrings*

1931
On March 10 Rivera finishes the Stock Exchange mural, *Allegory of California,* and goes with Frida to rest in Atherton, California, at the country house of the Stern family. There Rivera paints a mural in the dining room, while Frida paints a portrait of horticulturist Luther Burbank. In April Rivera starts the mural at the Art Institute, while Frida dedicates herself to painting her wedding portrait. Dr. Eloesser examines Frida and orders several tests.
On May 3 Frida writes to Isabel Campos: "I have been very happy, only I miss my mother a lot. You have no idea how marvelous this city is.... The gringos are not completely to my liking. They are dull and all of them have faces like uncooked cakes *(bizcochos),* especially the old ladies. What is very good is Chinatown. ...I have never in my whole life seen more beautiful children than the Chinese.... I don't have any friends.... So I spend my life painting.... It has done me good to come here, because it opened my eyes and I have seen many new and beautiful things."[17]
Frida and Rivera return to Mexico in June. In November they visit New York to prepare an exhibition of Rivera's works; they stay at the Barbizon Plaza hotel. On November 23 Frida writes to Dr. Eloesser and tells him that the city is interesting, but, despite the many invitations she has received to go to the homes of rich and important people, she is bored. On December 22 she attends the inauguration of Rivera's retrospective exhibition at the Museum of Modern Art with her friends Lucienne Bloch and Anita Brenner.
Works: *Portrait of Mrs. Jean Wight; Frida Kahlo and Diego Rivera; Showcase in Detroit; Portrait of Luther Burbank; Portrait of Eva Frederick; Portrait of Dr. Leo Eloesser; Portrait of a Woman*

1932
In April Frida travels with Rivera to Detroit, where he paints murals about modern industry at the Detroit Institute of Arts. Rivera introduces her to the press under the name of Carmen. When they ask him if she is a painter, he answers: "Yes, she is the best one in the world." They stay at the Wardell Hotel and tour several factories.
Frida writes to Dr. Eloesser from Detroit (May 26) and comments that she does not like the city, only the industrial section. "The rest is, as in all of the United States, ugly and stupid."[18] She tells him she is going to have a baby and is two months pregnant, and that Dr. Pratt has advised her to have a Caesarean section. Frida has doubts but decides not to have an abortion. She has a miscarriage and goes to Henry Ford Hospital, where Dr. Pratt attends her. On July 17 she leaves the hospital.
In September Frida is told that her mother is very sick so she decides to go back to Mexico, accompanied by Lucienne Bloch. She arrives in Mexico on September 8 and on September 15 her mother dies. She remains five weeks in Mexico with her father. During this time architect Juan O'Gorman starts the construction of Rivera's and Frida's homes in the San Angel district of Mexico City. Frida departs for Detroit on October 16 and arrives on October 21. She attends a lithography workshop.
Works: *Frida and the Caesarean (The Hospital); Henry Ford Hospital (The Flying Bed); Self-Portrait on the Border between Mexico and the United States; My Birth (Birth)*

1933
In February Florence Davies interviews Frida for *The Detroit News.* The article, titled "Wife of the Master Mural Painter Gleefully Dabbles in Works of Art," shows that Frida had by now acquired personal assurance. "No," she explains, "I didn't study with Diego. I didn't study with anyone. I just started to paint." Then her eyes begin to twinkle. "Of course," she explains, "he does pretty well for a little boy, but it is I who am the big artist."[19]
In March the couple travels to New York with Ernst Halberstand and Andrés Sánchez Flores, Rivera's assistants for the commission he had received to paint the murals at the RCA Building in Rockefeller Center. Once again, they stay at the Barbizon Plaza. Rivera's inclusion of a figure of Lenin in the mural causes his dismissal and the destruction of the work. Rivera offers to reproduce the mural for free at the New Workers School, but the space is inadequate so he changes the theme to the history of the United States. Rivera and Frida move to an apartment near the New Workers School and later, in September, to the Brevoort Hotel. Rivera is attracted to his assistant Louise Nevelson.
On November 16 Frida writes to Isabel Campos: "Here in Gringoland, I spend life dreaming about returning to

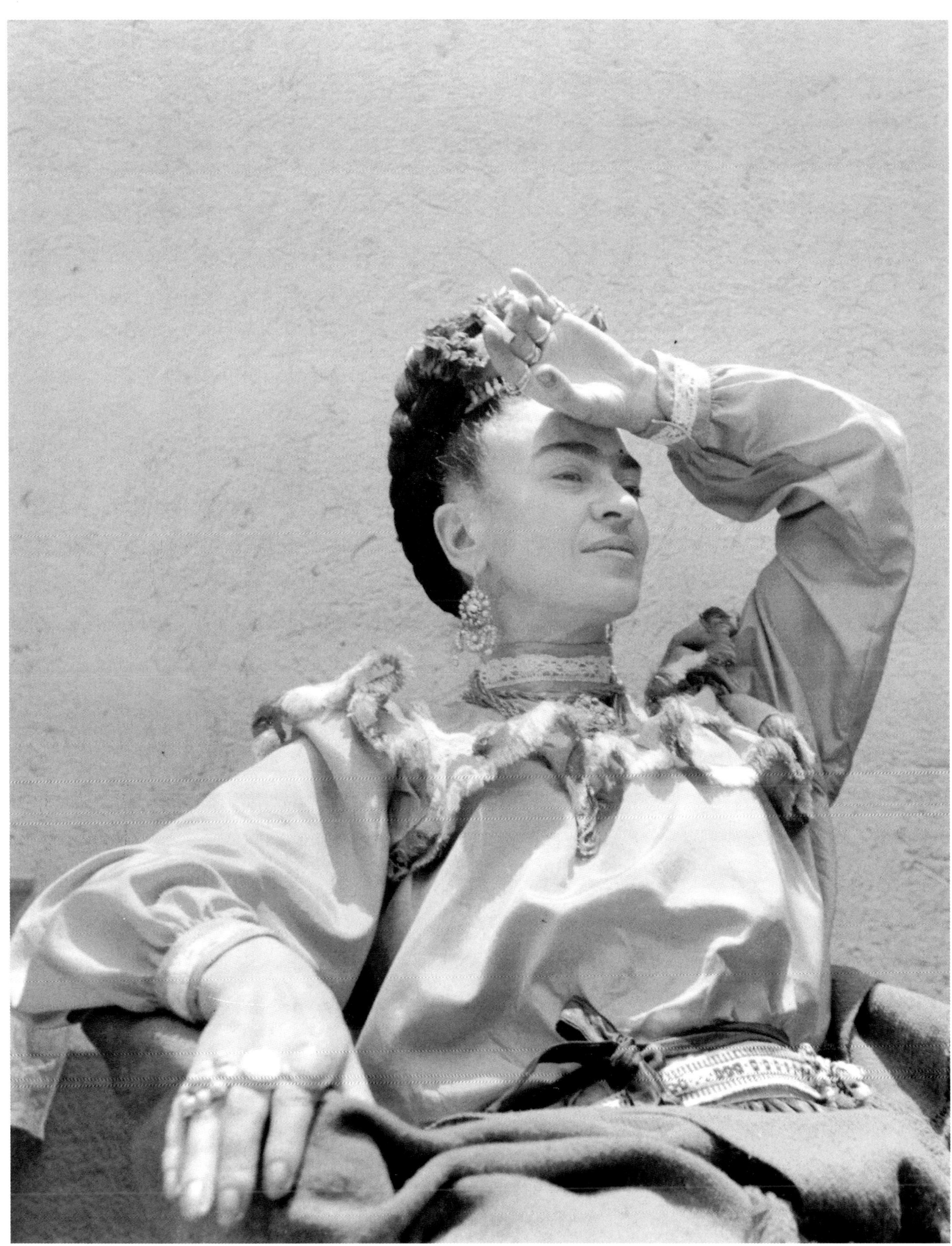

Frida Kahlo in front of the Blue House. Photograph by Lola Alvarez Bravo.

Mexico.... Yesterday it snowed for the first time.... It can't be helped, so we have to put on woolen britches and endure it. I like to believe that because I wear our famous long petticoats the cold will soak me less.... Some gringo ladies even imitate me and want to dress like "Mexicans," but the poor things look like turnips. The truth is they look ugly."[20]

Rivera enjoys living in the United States, but Frida prefers her own country. They have serious arguments about the details of returning to Mexico. Their economic situation has suffered because of the investment of their money in Rivera's recent murals, so their friends pay for their tickets home.

On December 20, Frida and Rivera travel on the ship *El Oriente* to Veracruz via Havana. Around this time Juan O'Gorman finishes their two homes at the corner of Palma (today Diego de Rivera) and Avenida Altavista in the San Angel district.

Works: *Self-Portrait "Very Ugly"; Self-Portrait with Necklace; My Dress Hangs There (New York); New York*

1934

Dr. Zollinger takes care of Frida when she has another miscarriage. Her right foot is operated on for the first time and some toes are removed. Rivera works on the murals at the Palacio de Bellas Artes to replace the ones destroyed at Rockefeller Center, and in November he starts the murals at the Palacio Nacional. Rivera has an affair with Cristina, Frida's younger sister.

Letter from Frida to Alejandro Gómez Arias (October 12): "Alex, the light ended and I am not painting little monkeys anymore. I keep thinking about the decoration of the wall separated by *another Wall* of wisdom. My head is full of microscopic spiders and hordes of vermin. I think we should build a microscopic wall also because in that way it would be difficult to do ugly and fallacious painting. Besides, do you believe that all silent wisdom could be contained in such a limited space? And what kind of trashy little books could contain *such* virtually *non*existent letters? *That is the big* problem, and it falls to you as an architect to solve it because, as you say, I can*not* put anything in order inside the *big reality* without getting into a quarrel, leaving everything undecided, or pulling what is distant into dangerous and fatal proximity. You will save everything with a ruler and compass."[21]

Letter from Frida to Dr. Eloesser (November 26): "The situation with Diego is worse each day. I know that much of the fault for what has happened has been mine because of not having understood what he wanted from the beginning and because of having opposed something that could no longer be helped. Now, after many months of real torment for me, I forgave my sister... It has left me in a state of such unhappiness and discouragement that I do not know what I am going to do. I know that Diego is for the moment more interested in her than in me, and I should understand that it is not his fault and that I am the one who should compromise if I want him to be happy."[22]

1935

Connubial problems separate Rivera and Frida. She moves from the house in San Angel to a small apartment on Avenida Insurgentes. She starts an affair with the sculptor Isamu Noguchi, and they plan to live together, but when Rivera learns of it the romance is thwarted.

Rivera provides houses for Frida and Cristina. He includes both sisters in the mural *Mexico Today and Tomorrow* at the Palacio Nacional. Frida decides to return to live in San Angel and forgives her sister Cristina who, together with her two sons, becomes an integral part of the family. Frida travels to New York with Anita Brenner and Mary Shapiro. She writes to Rivera (July 23): "[I know now that] all these letters, liaisons with petticoats, lady teachers of 'English,' gypsy models, assistants with 'good intentions,' 'plenipotentiary emissaries from distant places,' only represent *flirtations,* and that at bottom *you and I* love each other dearly, and thus go through adventures without number, beatings on doors, imprecations, insults, international claims – yet we will always love each other."[23]

Rivera hires Cristina Kahlo as his secretary. On August 26, during a lecture by Rivera at the Palacio de Bellas Artes about "The arts and their revolutionary role in the culture," Siqueiros attacks him verbally. Frida supports and defends him. Again she has a miscarriage and is cared for by Dr. Zollinger. In addition, her right foot ist operated on again, and it takes her six months to recuperate.

Works: *A Few Small Nips; Self-Portrait with Curly Hair*

1936

Frida undergoes a third operation on her right foot. She is very tired, nervous, anorexic, and suffers pains in her spinal column.

Works: *My Grandparents, My Parents, and I*

1937

In January Frida writes to Dr. Eloesser and tells him that Rivera is in the hospital with a liver infection and comments about his political activities helping the Spanish Republic. Accompanied by Max Shachtman, founder of the American Trotskyist movement, and George Novak, secretary of the American Committee for the Defense of Trotsky, Frida goes to Tampico to receive Trotsky and his wife Natalia. They travel to Mexico City on the train *El Hidalgo* sent by President Lazaro Cardenas. Rivera leaves the hospital to receive them and houses them in his Coyoacán home.

ARTIST IN NEW TROUBLE

Murals Removed From Hotel

"San Francisco Call-Bulletin" XI-24-36

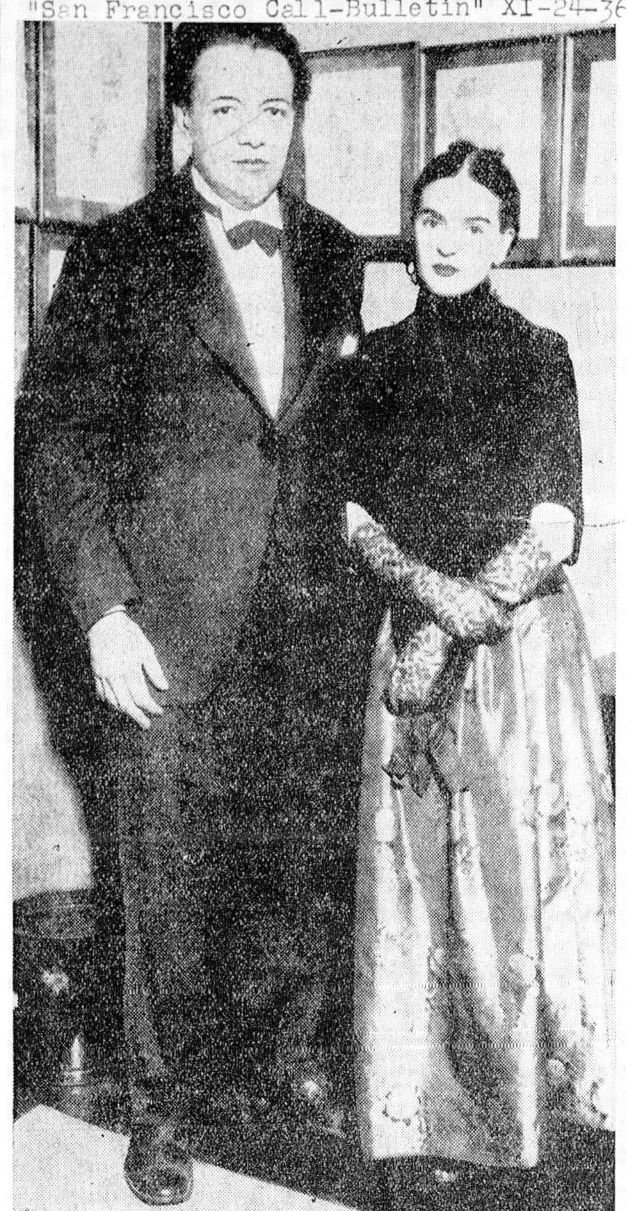

Troubles mounted today for Diego Rivera, fiery painter, shown above with his wife. Senora Rivera was to inform him before nightfall that his frescos have been removed from the walls of the new Hotel Reforma, in Mexico City. International News Photo by Call-Bulletin.

Diego Rivera Murals Spur Labor Revolt

Diego Rivera, with his satirical murals, today had landed in the midst of another battle, this time on home grounds.

It is a battle that has become a national issue in Mexico, and may well become an international one.

The fiery artist is well known to San Francisco because of his works and frequent visits. He has murals on display at the San Francisco Stock Exchange and the San Francisco Art Association. Among the city's artists and students are many of his dis-

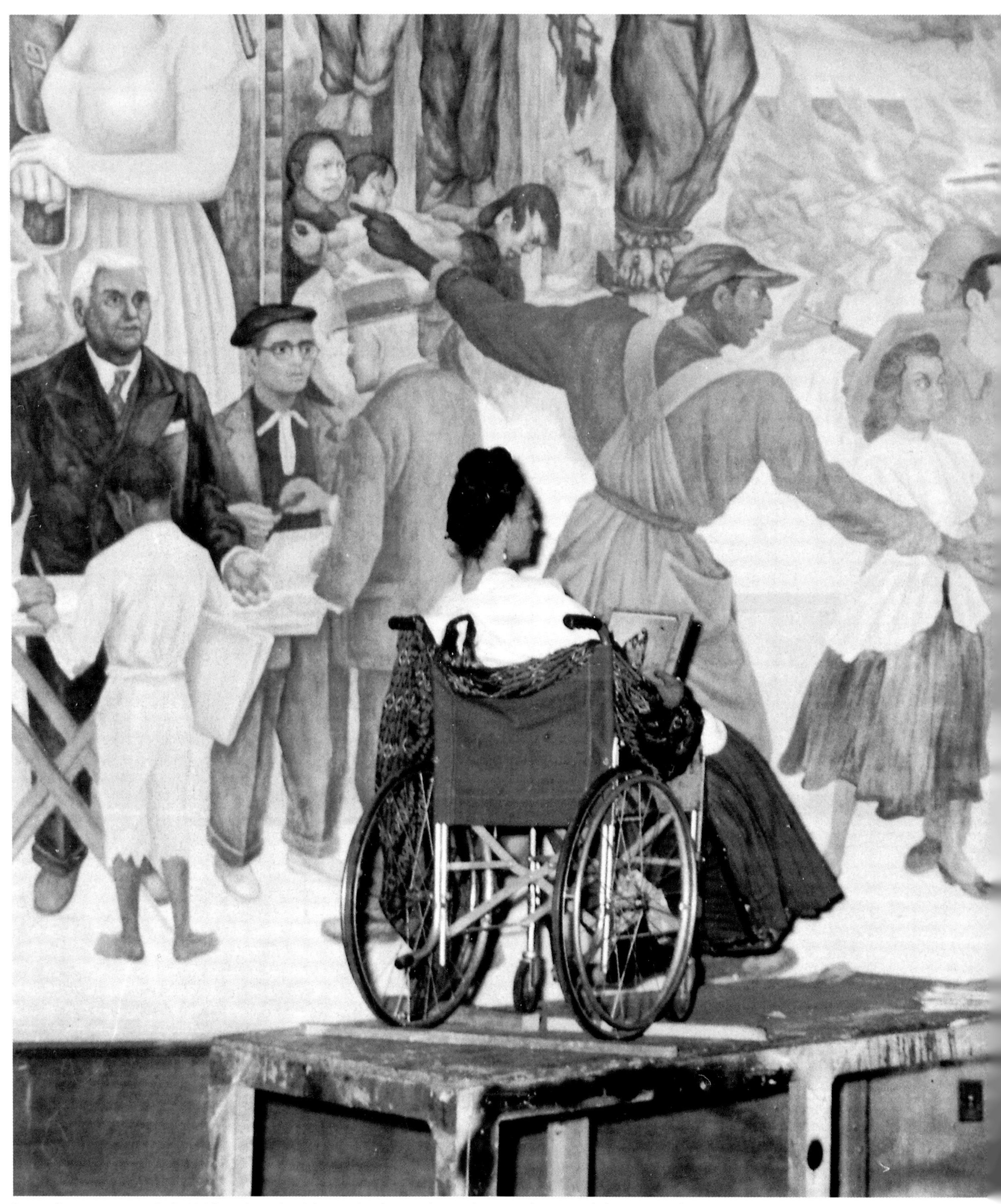

Diego Rivera portrays Frida Kahlo in her wheelchair in his fresco *The Nightmare of War and the Dream of Peace,* 1952, in the Palacio de Belles Artes in Mexico.

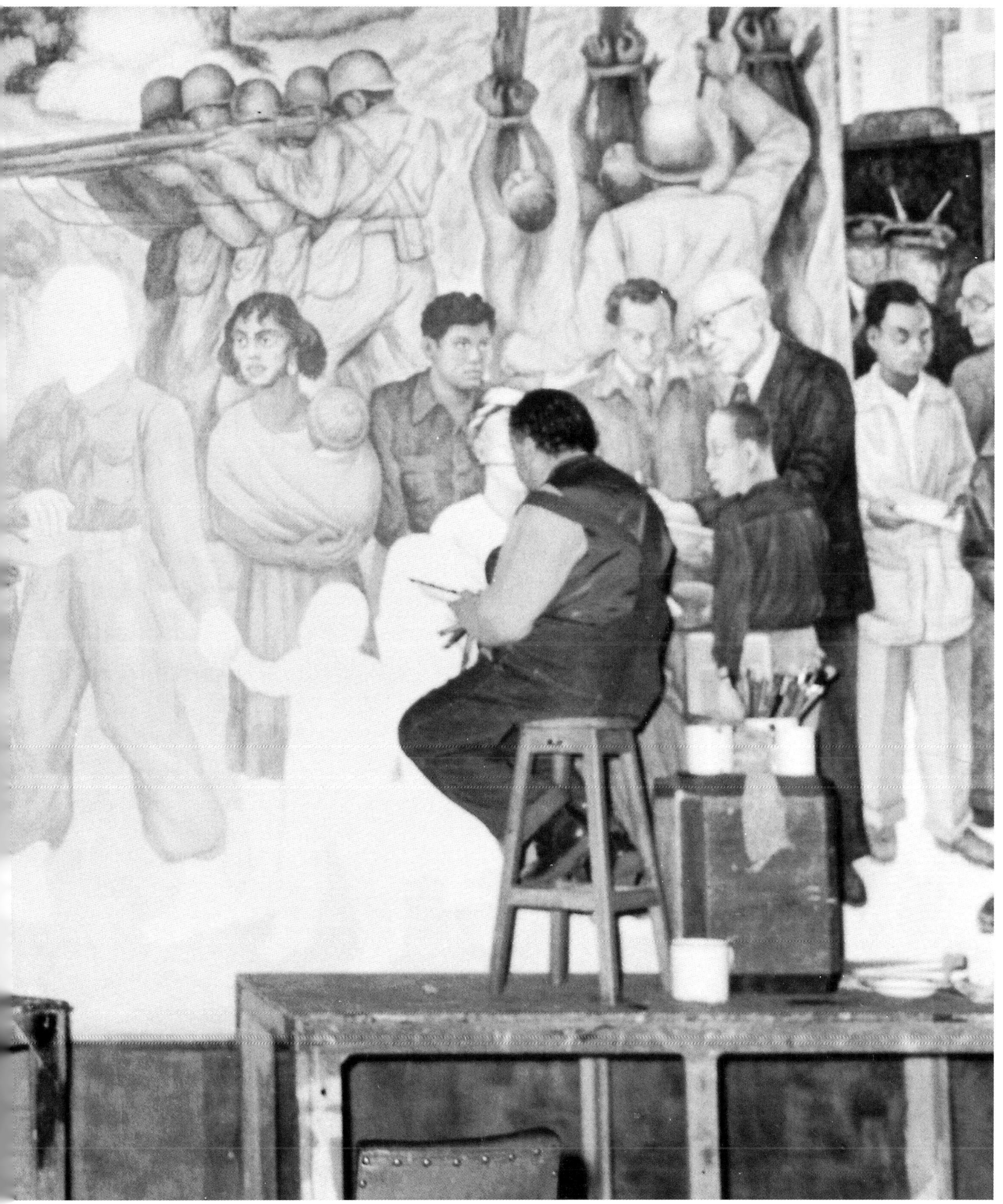

Photograph by Lola Alvarez Bravo.

On September 23 Frida's work *My Parents, My Grandparents, and I* is included in an exhibition at the Gallery of Art of the Social Action Department of UNAM (Universidad Nacional Autónoma de México). On November 7 she gives a self-portrait to Trotsky for his birthday.

She begins to dedicate more time to her profession and creates more paintings in this year than ever before.

Works: *Portrait of Alberto Misrachi; The Deceased Dimas; Portrait of Diego Rivera; Memory (The Heart); Self-Portrait on the Bed (Me and My Doll); My Nurse and I (Me Suckling); Fulang Chang and I; Self-Portrait Dedicated to Leon Trotsky (Between the Curtains); I Belong to My Owner*

1938

Poet André Breton visits Mexico with his wife Jacqueline, learns about Frida's work, and defines it as Surrealist. The Riveras, Bretons, and Trotskys travel to Michoacán. Frida sells several of her works to the North American actor Edward G. Robinson. Rivera writes to Sam A. Lewiston, an American movie critic, in words that reveal the respect he feels for Frida's work: "I recommend her to you, not as her husband, but as an admirer of her work: sour and tender, as hard as steel and as delicate and refined as the wing of a butterfly, adorable as a beautiful smile and deep and cruel like the bitterness of life."[24]

Frida has an affair with photographer Nickolas Muray. She travels to New York to prepare her first individual exhibition at the Levy Gallery, which takes place November 1–15. Twenty-five works are exhibited and half of them are sold. André Breton writes the catalogue's preface: "My surprise and joy were unbounded when I discovered, on my arrival in Mexico, that her work had blossomed forth, in her latest paintings, into pure surreality, despite the fact that it had been conceived without any prior knowledge whatsoever of the ideas motivating the activities of my friends and myself. Yet at this present point in the development of Mexican painting, which since the beginning of the nineteenth century has remained largely free from foreign influence and profoundly attached to its own resources, I was witnessing here, at the other end of the earth, a spontaneous outpouring of our own questioning spirit: what irrational laws do we obey, what subjective signals allow us to establish the right direction at any moment, which symbols and myths predominate in a particular conjunction of objects or web of happenings, what meaning can be ascribed to the eye's capacity to pass from visual power to visionary power?"

"The painting which Frida Kahlo de Rivera was just completing at that moment – *What the Water Yields Me* – illustrated, unbeknown to her, the phrase I had once heard from the lips of Nadja: 'I am the thought of bathing in the mirrorless room.'"

"This art even contains that drop of cruelty and humor uniquely capable of blending the rare effective powers that compound together to form the philtre which is Mexico's secret. The power of inspiration here is nourished by the strange ectasies of puberty and the mysteries of generation, and, far from considering these to be the mind's private preserves, as in some colder climates, she displays them proudly with a mixture of candor and insolence."

"While I was in Mexico, I felt bound to say that I could think of no art more perfectly situated in time and space than hers. I would like to add now that there is no art more exclusively feminine, in the sense that, in order to be as seductive as possible, it is only too willing to play alternately at being absolutely pure and absolutely pernicious. The art of Frida Kahlo is a ribbon around a bomb."[25]

Bertram Wolfe does not agree with this opinion and in a review in *Vogue* he clarifies: "Though André Breton, who will sponsor her show in Paris, told her she was a *surrealiste,* she did not attain her style by following the methods of that school.... Quite free, also, from the Freudian symbols and philosophy that obsess the official Surrealist painters, hers is a sort of 'naive' Surrealism, which she invented for herself.... While official Surrealism concern itself mostly with the stuff of dreams, nightmares, and neurotic symbols, in Madame Rivera's brand of it, wit and humor predominate."[26]

The opinions of art critics and historians make manifest the interest aroused by Frida's paintings: Parker Lesley calls them examples of "conscious, purposeful, and useful symbolic painting in opposition to the unconscious, totally obscure cabalistic productions of ingenious frauds such as Dali."[27]

After the exhibition she is seriously ill and is attended by Dr. Glusker, the husband of her friend Anita Brenner, who cures the ulcer on her foot. Frida is one of a group of artists who sign a document protesting the destruction of the murals by Juan O'Gorman in the Mexico City airport.

Works: *Tunas (Still Life with Prickly Pear Fruit); Fruits of the Earth; Xochitl, Flower of Life; Dear, How I Love You When I Have you; Self-Portrait "The Frame"; Me and Itzcuintli Dog; Girl with Death Mask; Self-Portrait with Monkey; The Suicide of Dorothy Hale; Girl with Death Mask II; Straw Wings (They Ask for Airplanes and Only Get Straw Wings); Remembrance of an Open Wound; Four Inhabitants of Mexico City; Air Crash (The Survivor)*

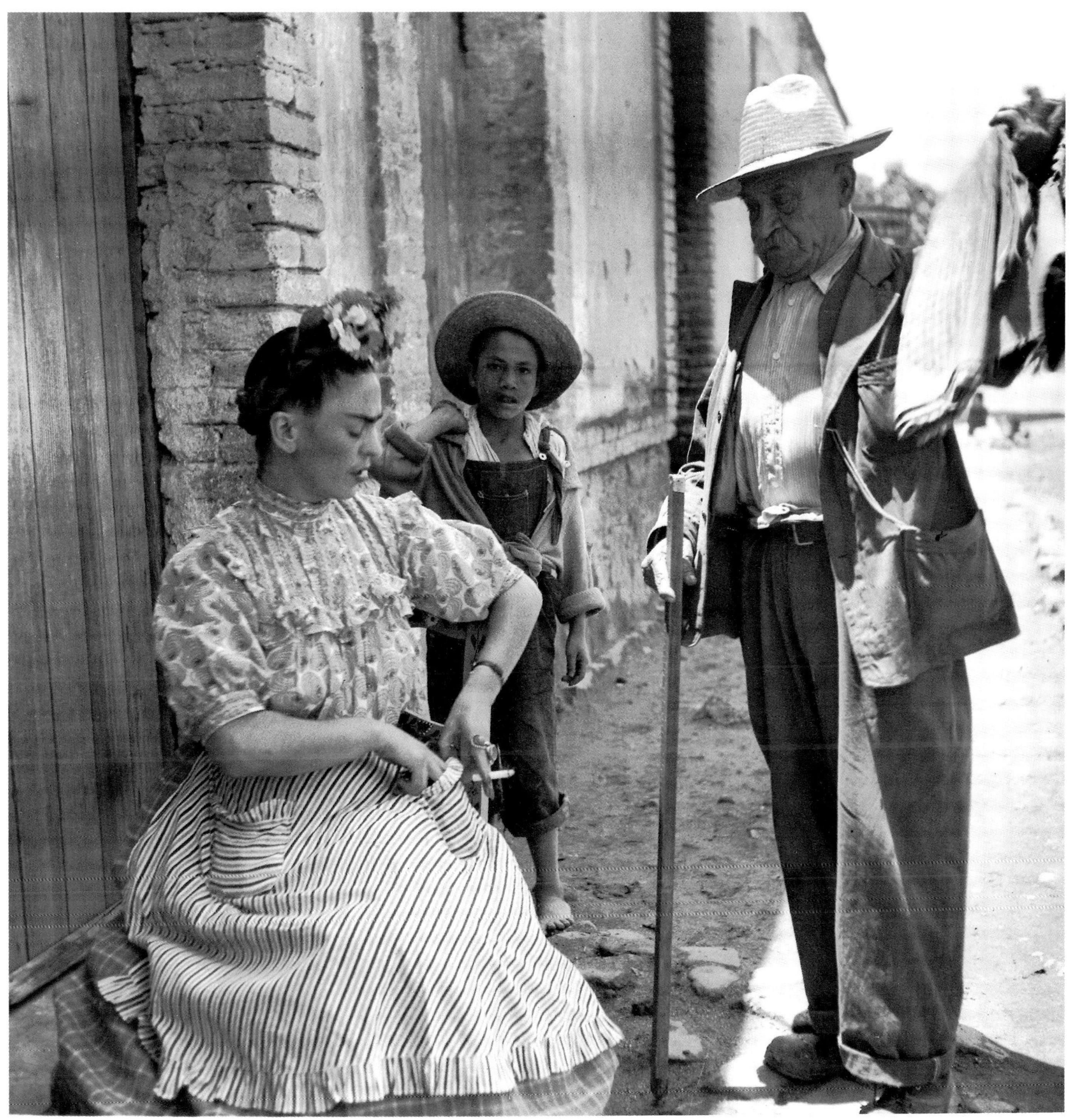

Frida Kahlo, 1946. Photograph by Leo Matiz.

1939

Frida goes to Paris to participate in the exhibition *Mexique* at the Pierre Colle Gallery. Also included are photographs by Manuel Alvarez Bravo and Mexican portraits of the nineteenth century. Rivera later commented on the effect Frida's work had on European artists, saying that Frida's painting moved Kandinsky so much that he embraced her and kissed her on her cheeks and forehead in the middle of the exhibition, while tears of emotion ran down his face, and that even Picasso sang praises to Frida's artistic and personal qualities, claiming that from their first meeting he was enchanted by her. Picasso later wrote to Rivera: "Neither Derain, nor you and I are capable of painting a head like Frida Kahlo."[23]
Not only Frida's work but also her beauty, her exotic appearance, her typical Mexican dresses, and her jewels make a great impression. Her ring-bedecked hand is reproduced in an issue of *Vogue* and her Tehuana dress inspires Schiaparelli to create a dress called "Madame Rivera."
In April Frida travels to New York, then returns to Mexico. She ends her relationship with Nickolas Muray. On November 6, Frida and Rivera are granted a divorce and Frida moves to the house in Coyoacán. Her economic situation is precarious, and she starts drinking to lessen her pain. During her separation from Rivera, Frida paints her two most important works, *What the Water Gave Me* and *The Two Fridas.*
Works: *What the Water Gave Me (What I Saw in the Water); Two Nudes in the Forest (Earth Herself* or *My Nurse and I); The Two Fridas*

1940

Two works by Frida, *The Wounded Table* and *The Two Fridas,* are included in the *International Surrealism Exihibition* at Ines Amor's Gallery of Mexican Art. In June Rivera travels to San Francisco, where he participates in the "Art in Action" section of the Golden Gate International Exposition held on Treasure Island. There the public observes him painting the mural *Pan-American Unity.*[29] Frida appears in one panel as the personification of the culture of the South (Mexico), dressed as a Tehuana, with a brush and a palette in her hand.
After Siqueiros assaults Trotsky, Frida's house is searched and she is taken into police custody for some hours. Frida suffers acute pains in her spinal column and travels to San Francisco for an operation by Dr. Leo Eloesser. She recovers her health and travels to New York.
After their divorce Rivera and Frida had continued to share a social life and in San Francisco they decide to remarry. She asks that they share the household expenses and cease sexual relations. Frida returns to Mexico two months before Rivera and again suffers acute back pains. She participates in the Golden Gate International Exposition and in an exhibition, *Twenty Centuries of Mexican Art,* in New York.
Works: *Self-Portrait with Cropped Hair; The Dream (The Bed); Self-Portrait Dedicated to Sigmund Firestone; Self-Portrait Dedicated to Dr. Eloesser; Self-Portrait with a Thorn Necklace and Hummingbird; Self-Portrait with Monkey; The Wounded Table*

1941

Her father dies and Frida decides to move again to the house in Coyoacán. Her economic situation is difficult and she tries to sell some works. She participates in the exhibition *Modern Mexican Painters* at the Institute of Contemporary Arts in Boston.
Works: *Self-Portrait with Bonito; Me and My Parrots; Self-Portrait with Braid; Self-Portrait; Flower Basket*

1942

Frida starts working twelve hours a week as a teacher of painting at the Escuela de Pintura y Escultura "La Esmeralda." After a few months due to her bad health she conducts her class in her home. Her students Arturo García Bustos, Guillermo Monroy, Arturo Estrada, and Fanny Rabel are known as "Los Fridos." Fanny describes her impressions when she met Frida: "I was fascinated when I met Frida because she has the talent of captivating people. She had enormous reserves of good humor and a passion for life."[30]
She is appointed founding member of the Seminario de Cultura Mexicana. *Self-Portrait with Braid* is included in the exhibition *Portraits of the Twentieth Century* at the Museum of Modern Art in New York.
Works: *Still Life; Portrait of Marucha Lavin; Self-Portrait with Monkey and Parrot; Lucha Maria, Girl from Tehuacán (Sun and Moon* or *Woman with Wrap)*

1943

Frida's students Lidia Huerta, María de los Angeles Ramos, Tomás Cabrera, Arturo Estrada, Ramón Victoria, and Erasmo V. Landechi paint a mural in the *pulquería* "La Rosita" under her direction.
Rivera writes "Frida Kahlo and Mexican Art," in which he underlines her importance: "In the midst of the panorama of all the Mexican painting of quality produced during the last twenty years the work of Frida Kahlo shines like a diamond in the midst of many inferior jewels, clear and hard, with precisely defined facets. Christ, the Virgin, and the saints disappeared from the *retablo.*"
"Instead of miracles, the theme of her painting is the permanent miracle–life. Life that is always in flux, always changing and always the same in its movement through the veins and through the universe. A single life that con-

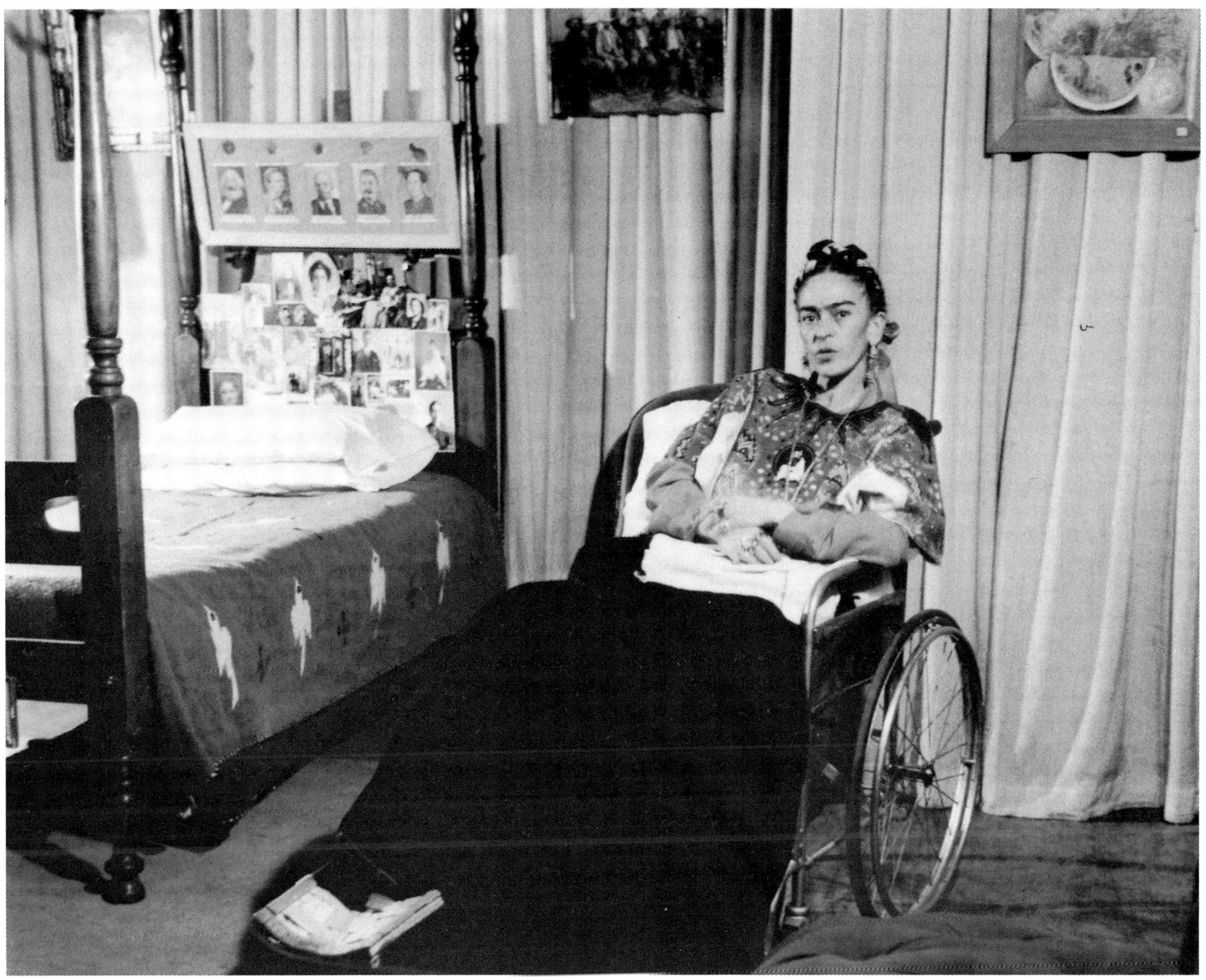

Frida Kahlo in her wheelchair. Photograph by Lola Alvarez Bravo.

tains the elements of all life. And if one tries to grasp its basis, one encounters abysmal depths, vertiginous heights, and an endlessly branching web that extends through the centuries, full of the light and shadows of life. The *retablos* of Frida are unique, unlike those of any other artist, unlike anything else. Frida's art is both collective and individual. Her realism is so monumental that everything has innumerable dimensions. Thus, at the same time she paints the exterior and interior of herself and the world and Frida is the only example in the history of art of an artist who tore open her chest an heart to reveal the biological truth of her feelings."[31]

She sends works to the following exhibitions, *One Hundred Years of the Mexican Portrait* at the Benjamin Franklin Library in Mexico City, where she exhibits *The Portrait of Marucha Lavin; First Salon of the Flower,* organized by the Secretaría de Agricultura y Fomento, where she exhibits *Xochitl* and *The Flower of Life; Mexican Art Today* at the Philadelphia Museum of Art; and *Women Artists* at the Art of This Century Gallery in New York. She helps coordinate the *Salón Libre 20 de Noviembre* at the Palacio de Bellas Artes, where she exhibits *The Wounded Table.*

Works: *Self-Portrait with Monkeys; Thinking about Death; Self-Portrait as a Tehuana (Diego on My Mind* or *Thinking of Diego); The Bride Who Becomes Frightened When She Sees Life Open; Flower of Life; Portrait of Natasha Gelman; Roots (Self-Portrait on Rocky Ground)*

1944

Frida begins her diary. Her health worsens and Dr. Velasco Zimbrón recommends rest and the use of an iron corset. She loses her appetite and considerable weight. She receives a commission for a mural for the Hotel Posada del Sol to be done by her students. However, the work does not please the owner, who has it destroyed. She participates in several collective exhibitions at the Gallery of Contemporary Painters in New York as well as two in Mexico City, *Second Salon of the Flower* and *The Child in Mexican Painting* at the Benjamin Franklin Library.

Works: *Portrait of Doña Rosita Morillo; Portrait of Eduardo Morillo Safa; Portrait of Alicia Morillo Safa and Her Son Eduardo; Portrait of Mariana Morillo Safa; Portrait of Lupita Morillo Safa; Portrait of Marta Porcel; Portrait of Marte R. Gómez; Corset (The Broken Column); The Broken Column; Diego and Frida 1929–1944 I; Diego and Frida 1929–1944 II*

1945

Frida continues having intense pains and must once again wear a cast. She wears a special shoe to compensate for the shortening of her leg. She obtains a commission for "Los Fridos" to create murals in the public baths, the so-called Casa de la Mujer Josefa Ortiz de Domínguez, in Coyoacán. Juan O'Gorman advises about fresco technique and Frida pays for the materials.

Works: *Moses (Nuclear Sun); Self-Portrait with Monkey; Self-Portrait with Small Monkey; The Mask; Without Hope; The Chick; Magnolias*

1946

Accompanied by her sister Cristina, Frida goes to New York to consult with Dr. Philip D. Wilson. She undergoes a complicated surgical operation in which a piece of pelvic bone is removed and inserted in her spinal column. On June 30 she writes to Alejandro Gómez Arias: "I came through the big calamitous operation. Three weeks ago they cut my bones. And this treatment is so marvelous and my body so full of vitality that today when they put me on my feet for two short minutes, I hardly dared believe it. The first two weeks were filled with great suffering and tears, I wish these pains on nobody. They are piercing and very mean, but already this week my crying has lessened and with the help of some pills I have survived more or less. I have two big scars on my little back.... They took a piece of my pelvic bone, where the scar looks horrible, to insert it in my spine. Five vertebrae were damaged and now they will always remain crushed together."[32] She must wear an iron corset for eight months, her health worsens, and she develops anemia.

She is elected to receive a government grant and in September receives a prize from the Secretaría de Educación Pública. Other artists receiving the honor are Dr. Atl, Julio Castellanos, and Francisco Goitia.

Works: *The Little Deer (The Wounded Deer* or *I am Just a Poor Deer); Tree of Hope, Keep Firm; Miniature Self-Portrait*

1947

Frida shows signs of depression and progressive weight loss. The Instituto Nacional de Bellas Artes organizes the exhibition *Forty-Five Self-Portraits by Mexican Painters,* in which only four women are included: María Izquierdo, Isabel Villaseñor, Olga Costa, and Frida, who sends her self-portrait *Diego on My Mind.* A catalogue is published in which Frida says about her work: "Really I don't know if my paintings are Surrealist or not, but I know for a fact that they are the most frank expression of myself, without ever taking into consideration either the opinions or the prejudices of anyone else."[33]

One of her works is selected for the opening of the Museo Nacional de Artes Plásticas at the Palacio de Bellas Artes. Rivera represents Frida in his mural, *Dream of a Sunday Afternoon in the Alameda.*

Works: *Self-Portrait with Loose Hair; Landscape; Sun and Life*

1948

La Sociedad para el Impulso de las Artes Plásticas organizes an exhibition in which she participates.
Works: *Self-Portraits*

1949

Her right foot worsens and she is attended by Dr. Gluker. Dr. Farill is of the opinion that the surgery performed in New York was not successful and he suggests another operation. At the inauguration of the Salón de la Plástica Mexicana she exhibits *The Love Embrace of the Universe, the Earth (Mexico), Diego, Me and Señor Xólotl*.

For the cataloque of the exhibition organized by the Instituto Nacional de Bellas Artes (INBA) to honor Rivera, Frida describes her husband's "shape" and "content": "Let me say that I am going to paint this portrait of Diego with unfamiliar colors–with words.... This is not going to be a biographical tale.... I am not going to talk about him as 'my husband,' that would be ridiculous. Diego has never been and never will be the 'husband' of anybody. Nor will I speak of him as a lover because he encompasses so much more that goes beyond sexual boundaries.... I will try to tell only the truth: my truth."

"His form: With his Asiatic head and his dark hair, so thin that it seems to float on air, Diego looks like a huge child, with a nice face and a sad look. His big eyes protrude almost out of their sockets... and are very far apart.... Seeing him naked you think immediately of a baby frog.... His childish shoulders, narrow and round, merge without angles into feminine arms that end in marvelous hands, small and finely made, sensible and subtle hands like antennas that can communicate with the whole universe... His abdomen, a huge, soft, and tender globe, rests on his strong legs which are like beautiful columns."

"His content: Diego is separated from any personal relationship, limited and precise. Conversely, like everything that supports life, he is, at the same time, a big caress and a discharge of violent and uniquely strong forces. He dwells inside like the seed treasured by earth and outside like a landscape. Some people will probably expect from me a very personal and 'feminine' picture of Diego, like an anecdote, funny, full of complaints, perhaps even a certain amount of gossip.... Maybe they expect to hear my lamentations of 'how much suffering' there is when you live with a man like Diego. But I don't think that the banks of a river suffer because you let it run, and the earth does not suffer because it rains, or the atom suffer when it discharges its energy.... for me everything has a natural compensation."

"There are three directions or principal lines that I consider basic in his portrait. The first one: he is a constant revolutionary, a dynamic fighter. He is extraordinarily sensitive and vital. He works without fatigue in his trade, which he knows like few painters in the world. He is enthusiastic, fanatic about life and at the same time discontented because he can't know more, build more, paint more. The second one: He is an eternally curious person, he is never tired of investigating everything. And the third one: He absolutely lacks prejudice... He fights at every moment to overcome mankind's fear and stupidity.... An acute observer, he has garnered experience that, together with his understanding–I could say his inside knowlegde of things–and his vast education, allows him to get to the bottom of things.... That is why Diego is not a defeatist or a sad person. He is fundamentally a researcher and among other things an architect. He is an architect in his paintings, in his thinking process, and in his passionate desire to build a functional, solid, and harmonious society.... The magnificent proofs of his genius are his murals which unite themselves to the buildings that shelter them, and live within their organized and material function."

"There are no words to describe the immense tenderness of Diego for things that have beauty, his love for those who have nothing to do with the present society of classes, or his respect for those oppressed by it."[34]

Works: *Diego and I; The Love Embrace of the Universe, the Earth (Mexico), Diego, Me, and Señor Xólotl*

1950

In the face of Frida's general decline in health, Dr. Farill recommends special care. During the time that she is at the English Hospital, Diego is often at her side. Her state of mind depends on the affection shown by her husband. On March 23 she undergoes another operation on her spinal column. This time the inserted bone becomes infected and she is operated on again on July 4.

Frida later described her situation: "I have been sick for a year, from 1950 to 1951. Seven operations on my spinal column. Dr. Farill saved me. He gave me back my joy in living. I am still in a wheelchair and I don't know if I will walk again soon. I have on this cast. It is a terrible nuisance, but it helps my spine feel better. I am not in pain. I feel only weariness...and, of course a lot of times, desperation. A desperation that no words can describe. Neverthcless I want to live. I have started to paint. I am uneasy about my painting. Above all, I want to transform it into something useful, because until now I have just painted honest expressions of myself, but these are completely unsuitable for serving the (Communist) Party. I must fight with all my strength so that the few positive things that my health allows me to will help the revolution–the only real reason to live."[35]

The Riveras celebrate the tenth anniversary of their second marriage. They dress formally for the occasion: the

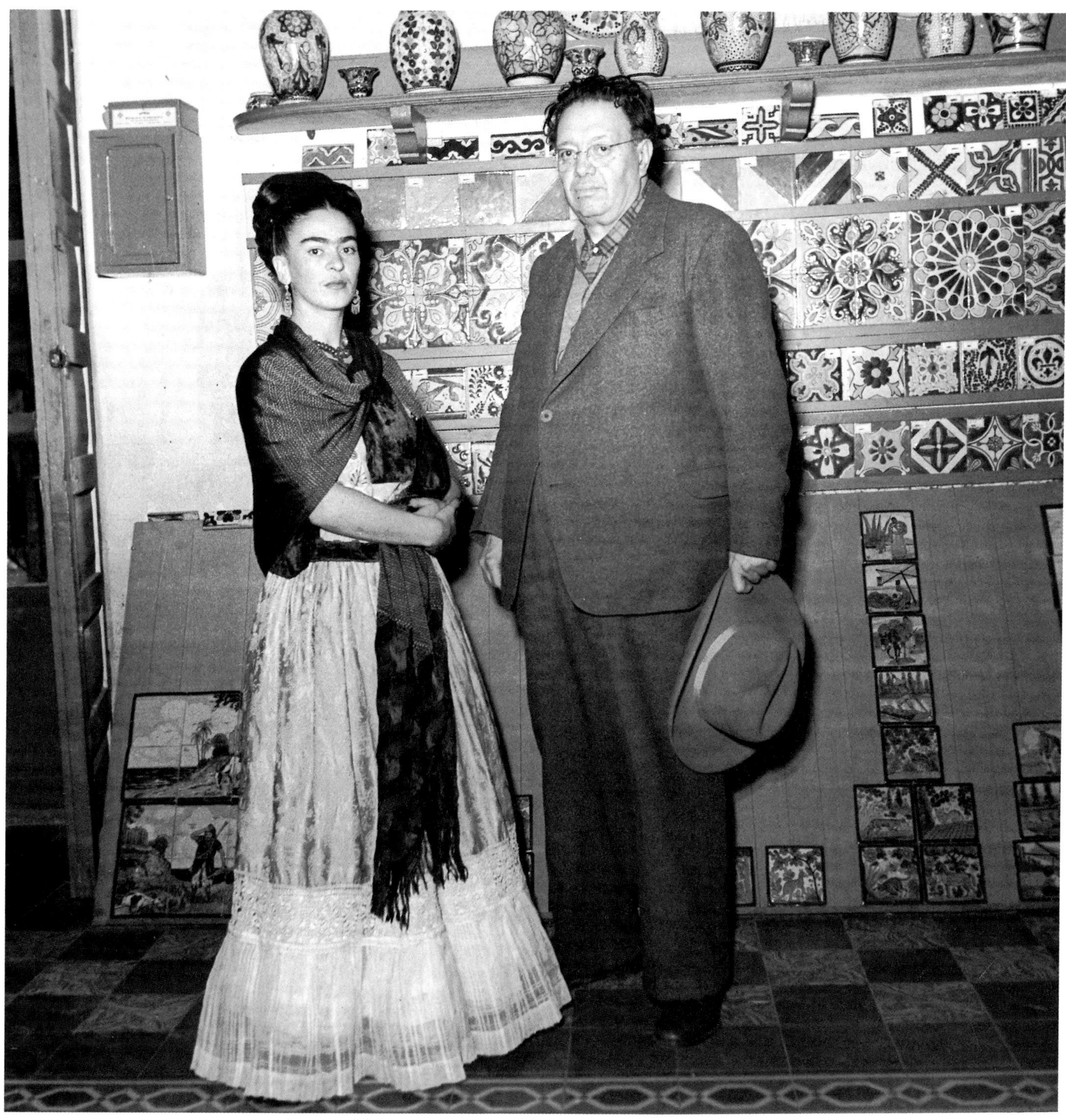

Frida Kahlo and Diego Rivera, 1946. Photograph by Leo Matiz.

bride wearing for the first time a veil and crown and Rivera in the traditional *capa* (cape) and *chambergo* (soft, broadrimmed hat). Frida writes and sketches in her diary.
Works: *Self-Portrait "The Circle"; Portrait of Frida's Family*

1951
On June 10 the newspaper *Novedades* devotes several articles to Frida in its supplement on Mexican culture. F. B. (Fernando Benítez) writes: "In this issue we want to offer a tribute to Frida Kahlo. She has deserved it for a long time. We thank her, a delicate flower attacked by misfortune, fot the lesson she teaches. The lesson of her hope, of her joy, of her heroic perseverance.... Here are her works made of dreams and transparent realities. There she is, lifting herself out of the pain like a tall and slender lily that creates its own atmosphere.... No exclamations and no fanfare.... Only the voices of her friends who don't want to disturb the enchanted intimacy, the silence of water and stone, in which she flourishes like a perfumed and marvelous lily."[36]
Works: *Portrait of My Father; Still Life "Long Live Life and Dr. Juan Farill"; Self-Portrait with Portrait of Dr. Farill (Self-Portrait with Dr. Juan Farill); Looks–Still Life–Coconuts; Still Life with Parrot and Flag; Tears of Coconut (Coconut Tears)*

1952
Rivera paints a portable mural on cloth, *Nightmare of War and Dream of Peace* at the Palacios de Bellas Artes. In it he represents Frida in her wheelchair. It was her habit to come visit him in her chair while collecting signatures for the Stockholm Peace Petition. Her health deteriorates and her right foot is worse. She is depressed.
Works: *People's Congress for Peace; Still Life; Living Life*

1953
Frida's illness worries Rivera, who prepares a retrospective exhibition of her work at Lola Alvarez Bravo's Gallería Arte Contemporaneo which opens in April. Frida attends her first individual exhibition (in Mexico) in an ambulance. Her bed is transferred to the gallery and becomes part of the show. Rivera comes to the realization that Frida's suffering is only a point of departure. "It is not tragedy that rules Frida's work. This has been misunderstood by many people. The darkness of her pain is just a velvet background for the marvelous light of her physical strength, her delicate sensibility, her bright intelligence, and her invincible strength as she struggles to live and show her fellow humans how to resist hostile forces and come out triumphant, how to reach superior happiness, against which nothing will prevail in the world of the future, while in this world the collective value of her life will lead to a truly historic and genuinely human epoch in our society."[37]
Looking retrospectively at her life and her work, Frida commented: "My painting carries within it the message of pain. I think that at least a few people were interested in it. It is not revolutionary. Why should I have any illusions that it is combative? I can't ... Painting completed my life. I lost three children that could have filled my horrible life. Painting took the place of all that."[38]
Dr. Guillermo de Velasco Polo and Dr. Farill decide to put her in the English Hospital because of a progressive infection in her right foot, which develops gangrene. In August they decide to amputate her leg below the knee. Frida commented on this in an interview given to her friend Bambi: "My leg was operated on and never in my life have I suffered like that. After that I had a nervous trauma, a general lack of equilibrium that changed everything even my blood circulation.... It's been seven months since the operation and here I am, I love Diego more than ever and I hope to serve him in something and keep on painting, full of joy. I hope nothing more happens to me. And I hope nothing happens to Diego either, because the day that Diego dies I will go with him, regardless of what anybody says. We should be buried together. I have already told them, 'Don't count on me after Diego.' I am not going to live without Diego. I can't. For me, he is my child, my son, my father, my lover, my husband, my all."[39]
Works: *Fruit of Life; Still Life with Watermelons*

1954
In February Frida writes in her diary: "They amputated my leg six months ago. It's been like centuries of torture and at moments I almost lost my mind. I keep wanting to commit suicide. Diego is the one that holds me back, for I am so vain that I believe he needs me. He has told me so and I believe it. But never in my life have I suffered more. I'll wait a while."[40]
In April she tries to commit suicide. She is admitted to the English Hospital from April 19 to April 27, where she is attended by Dr. David Glusker. She writes: "I came out well and I promise never to go back, a promise I will keep."[41] However, she is hospitalized again from May 6 to May 12. In July she celebrates her birthday and is visited by friends.
July 2 she goes with Rivera, Juan O'Gorman, and others to a rally protesting the intervention of the United States in Guatemala. Raquel Tibol praises Frida's brave attitude and describes her sad physical condition: "She is a bundle of pain, aware of her premature aging, yet she came out to express her disagreement with imperialism and its servants, instead of staying home to cry for her personal misfortunes. Like a victim of war she went

in her wheelchair with her amputated leg and her broken spine, her muscles weak after being forced to spend such a long time confined to her bed."[42]

This is her last public appearance. Her health, extremely delicate, worsens and she contracts pneumonia. On July 13 she dies at the age of forty-seven. A day later her body is cremated. Four years pass before the blue house where Frida lived and suffered is dedicated to her memory.

Works: *Still Life with Flag; Still Life, "Long Live Life"; Self-Portrait with Stalin; Marxism Will Give Health to the Sick; The Brick Ovens; Self-Portrait with the Image of Diego on My Breast and María on My Brow; Self-Portrait Inside a Sunflower*

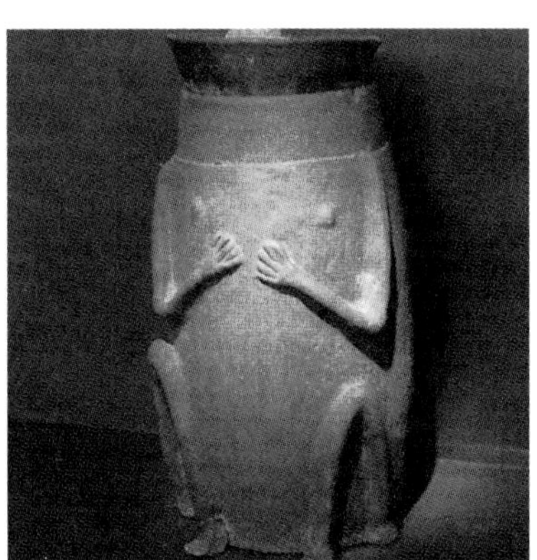

[1] Raquel Tibol. *Frida Kahlo: Una vida abierta* (Mexico: Editorial Oasis, 1983), 39–40.
[2] Ibid., 41.
[3] Ibid.
[4] Hayden Herrera, *Frida: A Biography of Frida Kahlo* (New York: Harper & Row, 1983), 75.
[5] The titles used here are based on those used by Hayden Herrera (see note 4 above) as well as those given in *Frida Kahlo: Das Gesamtwerk*, eds. Helga Prignitz-Poda, Andrea Kettenmann, and Salomon Grimberg (Frankfurt: Verlag Neue Kritik, 1988).
[6] Raquel Tibol, *Frida Kahlo*, 42–43.
[7] Ibid., 45.
[8] Ibid., 45–46.
[9] Ibid., 47.
[10] Ibid.
[11] Ibid., 47–48.
[12] Ibid., 48–49.
[13] Ibid., 49.
[14] Ibid., 51.
[15] Diego Rivera, *Mi arte, mi vida*, ed. Gladys March (Mexico: Editorial Herrero, 1963), 133. Translation from Hayden Herrera, *Frida*, 88.
[16] Archivo Historico de la Secretaría de Educación Pública. Fondo de personal sobresaliente, Frida Kahlo, box 19. These files contain information on Frida's various posts at the Secretaría de Educación and at the Instituto Nacional de Belles Artes.
[17] Raquel Tibol, *Frida Kahlo*, 52–53.
[18] Hayden Herrera, *Frida*, 136.
[19] Ibid., 159.
[20] Raquel Tibol, *Frida*, 51.
[21] Ibid., 56–57.
[22] Hayden Herrera, *Frida*, 184.
[23] Ibid., 186.
[24] Raquel Tibol, *Frida Kahlo*, 58.
[25] André Breton, *Surrealism and Painting*, trans. Simon Watson Taylor (New York: Harper & Row, 1972), 144.
[26] Bertram Wolfe, "Rise of Another Rivera," *Vogue* 10 (November 1938). Quoted in Hayden Herrera, *Frida*, 262.
[27] Letter from Parker Lesley to Frida. Quoted in Hayden Herrera, *Frida*, 262.
[28] Raquel Tibol, *Frida Kahlo*, 95.
[29] "Diego Rivera Tells of Attempt on Life." *New York Times*, June 6, 1940.
[30] Hayden Herrera, *Frida*, 329.
[31] Raquel Tibol, ed., *Diego Rivera, Arte y política* (Mexico: Editorial Grijalbo, 1979), 246–247.
[32] Raquel Tibol, *Frida Kahlo*, 62–63.
[33] Ibid., 98.
[34] "Retrato de Diego" in *Diego Rivera, 50 años de su labor artistica* (Mexico: INBA/ Secretaría de Educación Pública, 1950), 37–42.
[35] Raquel Tibol, *Frida Kahlo*, 63–64.
[36] "Homenaje a Frida Kahlo," *Novedades*, supplement, "México en la Cultura," June 10, 1951, 1–3.
[37] Raquel Tibol, *Frida Kahlo*, 13.
[38] Ibid., 50.
[39] Martha Zamora, *Frida el pincel de la angustia* (Mexico: Edición de la autora, 1987), 134.
[40] Raquel Tibol, *Frida Kahlo*, 64.
[41] Ibid.
[42] Ibid., 11.

This chronology is based on the documentation of Elizabeth Fuentes Rojas, published in Carlos Monsiváis and Rafael Vázquez Bayod, *Frida Kahlo: Una vida, una obra* (Mexico, 1992).

CHECKLIST OF THE EXHIBITION

PAINTINGS AND DRAWINGS BY FRIDA KAHLO

1
SELF-PORTRAIT
1923–1933
Fresco
24¾×19 inches (62.8×48.2 cm)
Private collection
Ill. p. 74

2
VILLAGE GIRL
before 1925
Watercolor and pencil on paper
9×5½ inches (23×14 cm)
Instituto Tlaxcalteca de Cultura, Tlaxcala, Mexico
Ill. p. 76

3
HAVE ANOTHER DRINK
before 1925
Watercolor and pencil on paper
7×9½ inches (18×24.5 cm)
Instituto Tlaxcalteca de Cultura, Tlaxcala Mexico
Ill. p. 78

4
THE ACCIDENT, 17 SEPTEMBER 1926
1926
Pencil on paper
7¾×10½ inches (20×27 cm)
Collection Juan Coronel Rivera, Milpa Alta, Mexico
Ill. p. 75

5
PANCHO VILLA AND ADELITA
before 1927
Oil on canvas
25½×17¾ inches (65×45 cm)
Instituto Tlaxcalteca de Cultura, Tlaxcala, Mexico
Ill. p. 79

6
PORTRAIT OF MIGUEL N. LIRA
1927
Oil on canvas
39×26½ inches (99.2×67.5 cm)
Instituto Tlaxcalteca de Cultura, Tlaxcala, Mexico
Ill. p. 83

7
PORTRAIT OF ALICIA GALANT
1927
Oil on canvas
42×36¾ inches (107×93.5 cm)
Museo Dolores Olmedo Patiño, Mexico City
Ill. p. 81

8
FRIDA IN COYOACÁN
circa 1927
Pencil on paper
4×5¾ inches (10.5×14.8 cm)
Instituto Tlaxcalteca de Cultura, Tlaxcala, Mexico
Ill. p. 77

9
FRIDA IN COYOACÁN
circa 1927
Watercolor on paper
6⅓×18⅛ inches (16×21 cm)
Instituto Tlaxcalteca de Cultura, Tlaxcala, Mexico
Ill. p. 77

10
UNTITLED – LITTLE LIFE (II)
circa 1928
Watercolor on paper
7×9¾ inches (18×25)
Private collection
Ill. p. 88

11
TINY CABALLERO
1928
Watercolor on paper
10½×13 inches (27×33 cm)
Private collection, United States
Courtesy Galería Arvil, Mexico
Ill. p. 89

12
PORTRAIT OF VIRGINIA (NIÑA)
1929
Oil on Masonite
30½×24 inches (78×61 cm)
Museo Dolores Olmedo Patiño, Mexico City
Ill. p. 85

13
THE BUS
1929
Oil on canvas
10×21 inches (25.8×55.5 cm)
Museo Dolores Olmedo Patiño, Mexico City
Ill. p. 87

14
FRIDA KAHLO AND DIEGO RIVERA
1930
Pencil and ink on paper
11½×8½ inches (29.5×21.6 cm)
Art Collection, Harry Ransom Humanities Research Center, The University of Texas at Austin
Ill. p. 86

15
NUDE STUDY OF MY COUSIN ADY WEBER
1930
Pencil on paper
24×19 inches (61×48 cm)
Museo Dolores Olmedo Patiño, Mexico City
Ill. p. 90

16
THE HAND
1930
Pencil on paper
8¾×6 inches (22.5×15 cm)
Museo Dolores Olmedo Patiño, Mexico City
Ill. p. 91

17
SELF-PORTRAIT
1930
Oil on canvas
25½×21½ inches (65×55 cm)
Courtesy Boston Museum of Fine Arts, Boston
Ill. p. 93

18
NUDE STUDY OF EVA FREDERICK
1931
Pencil on paper
24½×19 inches (62×48 cm)
Museo Dolores Olmedo Patiño, Mexico City
Ill. p. 94

19
PORTRAIT OF EVA FREDERICK
1931
Oil on canvas
24¾×19 inches (63×48 cm)
Museo Dolores Olmedo Patiño, Mexico City
Ill. p. 95

20
PORTRAIT OF LADY CRISTINA HASTINGS
1931
Pencil on paper
19⅓×11¾ inches (49×30 cm)
Museo Dolores Olmedo Patiño, Mexico City
Ill. p. 96

21
PORTRAIT OF MRS. JEAN WIGHT
1931
Oil on canvas
$24\frac{3}{4}$×18 inches (63.2×46 cm)
John Berggruen Gallery, San Francisco
Ill. p. 97

22
PORTRAIT OF LUTHER BURBANK
1931
Pencil on paper
12×$18\frac{1}{2}$ inches (30.3×21.5 cm)
Collection Juan Coronel Rivera, Milpa Alta, Mexico
Ill. p. 98

23
PORTRAIT OF LUTHER BURBANK
1931
Oil on Masonite
34×$24\frac{1}{4}$ inches (86.3 ×21.5 cm)
Museo Dolores Olmedo Patiño, Mexico City
Ill. p. 99

24
SELF-PORTRAIT DREAMING I
1932
Pencil on paper
$10\frac{1}{2}$×$7\frac{3}{4}$ inches (27×20 cm)
Collection Juan Coronel Rivera, Milpa Alta, Mexico
Ill. p. 108

25
SELF-PORTRAIT ON THE BORDER BETWEEN MEXICO AND THE UNITED STATES
1932
Oil on metal
$12\frac{1}{2}$×$13\frac{3}{4}$ inches (31.8×34.9 cm)
María Reyero Collection, New York
Ill. p. 101

26
STUDY FOR "HENRY FORD HOSPITAL"
1932
Pencil on paper
$5\frac{1}{2}$×$10\frac{1}{2}$ inches (13.9×26.7 cm)
Private collection, Courtesy of Mary-Anne Martin/ Fine Art, New York
Ill. p. 102

27
HENRY FORD HOSPITAL
1932
Oil on metal
12×15 inches (30.5×38 cm)
Museo Dolores Olmedo Patiño, Mexico City
Ill. p. 103

28
THE MISCARRIAGE
1932
Lithograph
$8\frac{3}{4}$×$5\frac{1}{2}$ inches (22.5×14.5 cm)
Museo Dolores Olmedo Patiño, Mexico City
Ill. p. 105

29
SELF-PORTRAIT, 9 JULY 1932
1932
Pencil on paper
8×$5\frac{1}{4}$ inches (20.5×13.2 cm)
Collection Juan Coronel Rivera, Milpa Alta, Mexico
Ill. p. 109

30
BEAUTY PARLOR
1932
Watercolor and pencil on paper
$10\frac{1}{4}$×$8\frac{2}{3}$ inches (26×22 cm)
Collection Agustin Cristóbal, Mexico
Ill. p. 110

31
HEAD
1932
Watercolor and pastel crayons on paper
$11\frac{7}{8}$×$8\frac{7}{8}$ inches (30×22.5 cm)
Museo Dolores Olmedo Patiño, Mexico City
Ill. p. 113

32
SELF-PORTRAIT "VERY ANGRY"
1932
Pencil on board
11×8 inches (28×20.3 cm)
Private collection
Courtesy Galería Arvil, Mexico
Not illustrated

33
MY DRESS HANGS THERE
1933
Oil and collage on Masonite
18×$19\frac{1}{2}$ inches (46×50 cm)
Private collection, Courtesy Christie, Manson & Woods, New York
Ill. p. 107

34
ALL-SEEING EYE
1934
Pencil on paper
$8\frac{1}{4}$×12 inches (21×30.5 cm)
Collection Juan Coronel Rivera, Milpa Alta, Mexico
Ill. p. 112

35
RECLINING SELF-PORTRAIT
1935
Pencil on paper
8×$11\frac{1}{2}$ inches (20.7×29.7 cm)
Collection Juan Coronel Rivera, Milpa Alta, Mexico
Ill. p. 112

36
A FEW SMALL NIPS
1935
Oil on metal
$11\frac{1}{2}$×$14\frac{1}{2}$ inches (29.5×39.5 cm)
Museo Dolores Olmedo Patiño, Mexico City
Ill. p. 115

37
SANTA CLAUS
circa 1932, dated 1937
Watercolor and pencil on paper
$8\frac{1}{2}$×$10\frac{1}{4}$ inches (22×26 cm)
Collection Juan Coronel Rivera, Milpa Alta, Mexico
Ill. p. 111

38
SELF-PORTRAIT
circa 1937
Pencil on paper
$11\frac{1}{2}$×$8\frac{1}{4}$ inches (29.7×21 cm)
Private collection, United States
Not illustrated

39
MY NURSE AND I
1937
Oil on metal
12×$13\frac{1}{2}$ inches (30.5×34.7 cm)
Museo Dolores Olmedo Patiño, Mexico City
Ill. p. 117

40
THE DECEASED DIMAS
1937
Oil on Masonite
$18\frac{3}{4}$×$12\frac{1}{2}$ inches (48×31.5 cm)
Museo Dolores Olmedo Patiño, Mexico City
Ill. p. 119

41
SELF-PORTRAIT DEDICATED TO LEON TROTSKY
1937
Oil on canvas
$11\frac{3}{4}$×$9\frac{1}{2}$ inches (30×24 cm)
The National Museum of Women in the Arts, Washington, D. C.,
Gift of Clare Booth Luce
Ill. p. 121

42
FRUITS OF THE EARTH
1938
Oil on Masonite
16×$23\frac{1}{2}$ inches (40.6×60 cm)
Collection Banco Nacional de México,S.A., Mexico City
Ill. p. 123

43
TUNAS (STILL LIFE WITH PRICKLY PEAR FRUIT)
1938
Oil on tin
$9\frac{1}{2}$×$7\frac{1}{4}$ inches (24×18.5 cm)
Private collection
Ill. p. 125

44
TWO NUDES IN THE FOREST
1939
Oil on sheet metal
$9^{7}/_{8}\times11^{7}/_{8}$ inches (25×30.2 cm)
Private collection, Courtesy
of Mary-Anne Martin/
Fine Art, New York
Ill. p. 127

45
THE TWO FRIDAS
1939
Oil on canvas
68×68 inches (173×173 cm)
Museo de Arte Moderno, Mexico City
Ill. p. 129

46
SELF-PORTRAIT WITH MONKEY
AND PARROT
1942
Oil on Masonite
21×17 inches (53.3×43.2 cm)
Collection IBM Corporation, Armonk,
New York
Ill. p. 131

47
ROOTS
1943
Oil on metal
$12\times19^{1}/_{2}$ inches (30.5×49.9 cm)
Pirvate collection
Ill. p. 133

48
FLOWER OF LIFE
1943, dated 1944
Oil on Masonite
$11\times7^{3}/_{4}$ inches (27.8×19.7 cm)
Museo Dolores Olmedo Patiño, Mexico City
Ill. p. 135

49
STUDY FOR "MY GRANDPARENTS, MY
PARENTS, AND I"
1943
$12\times13^{3}/_{4}$ inches (30.7×35 cm)
Michele and Howard Lazar,
Courtesy CDS Gallery, New York
Ill. p. 137

50
THINKING ABOUT DEATH
1943
Oil on canvas, mounted on Masonite
$17^{1}/_{2}\times14^{1}/_{4}$ inches (44.5×36.3 cm)
Private collection, Mexico
Ill. p. 139

51
DIEGO AND FRIDA 1929–1944 (II)
1944
Oil on Masonite (or oil on wood)
$5^{1}/_{3}\times3^{3}/_{4}$ inches (13.5×8.5 cm)
Private collection
Ill. p. 141

52
THE BROKEN COLUMN
1944
Oil on canvas, mounted on Masonite
$15^{3}/_{4}\times12$ inches (40×30.7 cm)
Museo Dolores Olmedo Patiño, Mexico City
Ill. p. 143

53
PORTRAIT OF DOÑA ROSITA MORILLO
1944
Oil on canvas, mounted on Masonite
$30\times23^{7}/_{8}$ inches (76×60.5 cm)
Museo Dolores Olmedo Patiño, Mexico City
Ill. p. 145

54
PORTRAIT OF LUPITA MORILLO SAFA
1944
Oil on Masonite
$22^{1}/_{2}\times19^{1}/_{2}$ inches (57×50 cm)
Private collection, Courtesy CDS Gallery,
New York,
Galería Arvil, Mexico
Ill. p. 147

55
PORTRAIT OF EDUARDO MORILLO SAFA
1944
Oil on Masonite
$15^{1}/_{2}\times11^{1}/_{2}$ inches (39.5×29.5 cm)
Museo Dolores Olmedo Patiño, Mexico City
Ill. p. 149

56
PORTRAIT OF MARTE R. GÓMEZ
1944
Oil on Masonite
$12^{1}/_{4}\times9^{3}/_{4}$ inches (31×25 cm)
Geraldo Contreras Gómez, Mexico
Ill. p. 151

57
FANTASY (I)
1944
Pencil on paper
$9^{1}/_{2}\times6^{1}/_{4}$ inches (24×16 cm)
Museo Dolores Olmedo Patiño, Mexico City
Ill. p. 153

58
MOSES
1945
Oil on Masonite
$24\times29^{3}/_{4}$ inches (61×75.6 cm)
Private collection
Ill. p. 157

59
SELF-PORTRAIT WITH SMALL MONKEY
1945
Oil on Masonite
$22^{1}/_{2}\times16^{1}/_{2}$ inches (57×42 cm)
Museo Dolores Olmedo Patiño, Mexico City
Ill. p. 159

60
THE MASK
1945
Oil on canvas
$15^{3}/_{4}\times12$ inches (40×30.5 cm)
Museo Dolores Olmedo Patiño, Mexico City
Ill. p. 161

61
WITHOUT HOPE
1945
Oil on canvas, mounted on Masonite
11×14 inches (28×36 cm)
Museo Dolores Olmedo Patiño, Mexico City
Ill. p. 163

62
THE CHICK
1945
Oil on Masonite
$10^{1}/_{2}\times8^{1}/_{2}$ inches (27×22 cm)
Museo Dolores Olmedo Patiño, Mexico City
Ill. p. 165

63
THE LITTLE DEER
1946
Oil on Masonite
$8^{3}/_{4}\times11^{3}/_{4}$ inches (22.4×30 cm)
Private collection
Ill. p. 167

64
SUN AND LIFE
1947
Oil on Masonite
$15^{3}/_{4}\times19^{1}/_{2}$ inches (40×50 cm)
Private collection
Courtesy Galería Arvil, Mexico
Ill. p. 169

65
SELF-PORTRAIT WITH LOOSE HAIR
1947
Oil on Masonite
$24\times17^{3}/_{4}$ inches (61×45 cm)
Private collection
Ill. p. 171 and cover

66
DIEGO AND I
1949
Oil on Masonite
$11\times8^{1}/_{2}$ inches (28×22 cm)
Private collection
Ill. p. 173

67
SELF-PORTRAIT "THE CIRCLE"
circa 1950
Oil on sheet metal
$12^{1}/_{2}\times12^{1}/_{4}\times6$ inches (32×31×15 cm)
Museo Dolores Olmedo Patiño, Mexico City
Ill. p. 175

68
STILL LIFE WITH PARROT
1951
Oil on canvas
10×11 inches (25.5×28 cm)
Art Collection, Harry Ransom Humanities Research Center, The University of Texas at Austin
Ill. p. 177

69
STILL LIFE WITH PARROT AND FLAG
1951
Oil on Masonite
11×15$\frac{3}{4}$ inches (28×40 cm)
Pivate collection
Courtesy Galería Arvil, Mexico
Ill. p. 178

70
TEARS OF THE COCONUT
OR COCONUT TEARS
circa 1951
Oil on Masonite
9×11$\frac{3}{4}$ inches (22.9×29.8 cm)
B. Lewin Galleries, Palm Springs, CA
Ill. p. 179

71
LANDSCAPE
1951
Watercolor on paper
4$\frac{3}{4}$×7 inches (12×18 cm)
Private collection, United States
Not illustrated

72
LANDSCAPE
1951
Watercolor on paper
4$\frac{3}{4}$×7 inches (12×18 cm)
Private collection, United States
Not illustrated

73
LANDSCAPE
1951
Watercolor on paper
4$\frac{3}{4}$×7 inches (12×18 cm)
Private collection, United States
Not illustrated

74
CHONG-LEE
circa 1948–1950
Ink and scorch-technique on wood
24$\frac{1}{2}$×16$\frac{1}{3}$ inches (62×41.5 cm)
Instituto Tlaxcalteca de Cultura, Tlaxcala
Ill. p. 189

RELATED WORKS

75
CORSET WITH HAMMER AND SICKLE
1950
Corset painted with oil
15$\frac{1}{2}$×12$\frac{1}{2}$×6$\frac{1}{4}$ inches (39.5×32×16 cm)
Collection Galería La Granja

76
LETTER, UNDATED
Pencil on paper
4×4$\frac{1}{2}$ inches (10.2×11.9 cm)
Private collection
Ill. p. 181

77
LETTER, 20 SEPTEMBER 1924
Ink on paper
10$\frac{1}{2}$×6$\frac{1}{2}$ inches (27×16.5 cm)
Private collection
Ill. p. 182

78
LETTER, 1 JANUARY 1925
Ink on paper
11×6$\frac{1}{2}$ inches (28×16.5 cm)
Private collection
Ill. p. 183

79
LETTER, 8 JANUARY 1925
Ink on paper (both sides)
10$\frac{3}{4}$×8$\frac{1}{4}$ inches (27.5×20.8 cm)
Private collection
Ill. p. 184

80
LETTER, 21 AUGUST 1926
Chinese ink on paper
9$\frac{1}{3}$×9$\frac{1}{2}$ inches (23.7×24 cm)
Private collection
Ill. p. 185

81
LETTER, 30 JUNE 1946
Ink on paper
9$\frac{1}{2}$×6 inches (24×15 cm)
Private collection
Ill. p. 186

81 A
RECEIPT FOR TWO PARROTS
July 25, 1941
Ink on paper
6$\frac{3}{4}$×8$\frac{1}{3}$ inches (17.2×21.3 cm)
Collection Sylvia Misrachi de Assael
Not illustrated

81 B
LETTER, 20 JUNE 1941
Ink on paper
10$\frac{3}{4}$×8 inches (27.5×20.5 cm)
Collection of Mr. Alberto Misrachi Samanon, from the Archive de Centro de Publicaciones "Librería Misrachi"
Not illustrated

82
LETTER, 12 JUNE 1937
Ink on paper
10$\frac{1}{2}$×8 inches (26.5×20.5 cm)
Collection of Mr. Alberto Misrachi Samanon, from the Archive de Centro de Publicaciones "Librería Misrachi"
Not illustrated

83
LETTER, 17 NOVEMBER 1941
Ink on paper
10$\frac{3}{4}$×8$\frac{1}{4}$ inches (27.5×21 cm)
Collection of Mr. Alberto Misrachi Samanon, from the Archive de Centro de Publicaciones "Librería Misrachi"
Not illustrated

84
LETTER, 17 JULY 1941
Ink on paper
Collection of Mr. Alberto Misrachi Samanon, from the Archive de Centro de Publicaciones "Librería Misrachi"
Not illustrated

85
«MURALS TAKEN FROM HOTEL»
November 24, 1936
Newspaper clipping
Not illustrated

Unless otherwise noted, catalogue numbers 86–119 are lent courtesy Galería Arvil, Mexico.

DR. ATL (MURILLO, GERARDO)

1875: born on October 3 in Guadalajara. Began painting in his home town in the atelier of Felipe Castro.
1896: began his studies at the Escuela Nacional de Bellas Artes in Mexico City.
1897: traveled to Europe. Studied philosophy and criminal law at University of Rome.
1901: painted his first mural in a Roman villa.
1903: returned to Mexico and the Escuela de Bellas Artes. Became involved with the revival of national art appreciation.
1910: organized an exhibition of work by independent Mexican artists. He planned an artistic center devoted to the painting of murals on public buildings, but the ideal was never realized owing to the outbreak of the Revolution.
1911: traveled to Paris. Organized various exhibitions in France and Germany.
1913: exihibited his own work in the Salon d'Automne and the Salon des Indépendents. Murillo became increasingly active in the field of politics and changed his name to Dr. Atl.
1914: returned to Mexico. Dr. Atl joined the revolutionary movement against Victoriano Huerta. Organized lectures and conferences in the service of the Revolution.
1916: left Mexico for political reasons and settled in Los Angeles, where he remained until 1920.
1921–1922: returned to his native land and painted murals on the walls of the Colegio Máximo de San Pedro y San Pablo in collaboration with Xavier Guerrero and Roberto Montenegro. Dr. Artl wrote a book entitled *Las Partes Populares en México* as the catalogue for the first exhibition dedicated to Mexican folk art. He also published a large-scale work on the churches of Mexico. Founded the "Comité Nacional de las Artes Populares."
1925: appointed president of the League of American Writers.
1932–1942: published numerous books, as well as a series of pro-Fascist articles.
1943: moved to the vicinity of the new volcano El Paricutín, which he observed with fascination and painted over and over again. He also wrote a book about the volcano.
1950: exhibition of his volcano paintings and drawings at the Palacio de Bellas Artes in Mexico City.
1958: exhibition in the Salón de la Plástica Mexicana of pictures which he called "Aeropaisajes" – landscapes seen from the air, from airplanes and helicopters, which in his opinion opened up new perspectives in landscape painting. Dr. Atl dreamed of founding a new cultural city in Mexico.
1964: Gerardo Murillo – Dr. Atl – died, in Mexico City at the age of 89.

86
DR. ATL (GERARDO MURILLO)
Volcano
Oil on Masonite
$24\frac{1}{2} \times 36\frac{1}{4}$ inches (62×92 cm)
Private collection, United States
Ill. p. 197

CARRINGTON, LEONORA

1917: born in Clayton Green, Great Britain. Her father is a rich and eccentric industrialist in the textile business. Her mother is from southern Ireland.
1920: the family lives in the castle of Crookney, in the vicinity of Lancaster. An Irish nurse, a French governess, and a private tutor, Father O'Connor, are in charge of the education of Leonora and her three brothers.
1926–1928: enrolled at two religious schools, one after another, but expelled from each since she showed only an interest in drawing.
1932–1934: attended private schools in Florence, where she starts to paint, and in Paris.
1936: convinces her family to let her study painting. Short period of study at the Amédée Ozenfant Academy in London.
1937: met Max Ernst in London. Lives with him for two years at Saint-Martin d'Ardèche. The horse becomes a frequent motif in her paintings.
1938: La Maison de la Peur, her first collection of Surrealistic poems; preface and illustrations by Max Ernst.
1939: "La Dame overale," a fantastic tale, illustrated by Max Ernst.
At the beginning of the war Max Ernst placed in an internnent camp as a German citizen. She suffered from a severe depression and was sent to a mental hospital in Santander, Spain, by her parents.
1940: "La débutante" and "Les soeurs," stories which have woman as bird-vampire as their theme.
1941: met the Mexican diplomat Renato Leduc in Madrid, married Leduc in Lisabon and with him emigrated to New York. Reunited with Ernst and other Surrealists. Her story "Waiting" published in the Surrealists magazine *View.*
1942: moved to Mexico City. Divorced Leduc.
1943: met Enrico Weisz, called Chiqui, a Hungarian photographer.
1944: the British multimillionaire Edward James became the most important collector of her works. "Down Below," a story about her stay in a psychiatric hospital in Spain, published in the Surrealist magazine *VVV* in New York.
1945–1946: wrote two plays "The Flannel Night Shirt" and "Penelope."
1946: married Chiqui, with whom she will have two sons.
1950: from the beginning of the 1950s her work was influenced by oriental metaphors and the reincarnation theories of G.I. Gurdiew and P.D. Ouspenskij.
1963: El Mundo magico de los Mayas, a large mural for the Museo Nacional de Antropología.
1974: publication of *Cornet accoustiqua,* an earlier, unpublished novel about woman as the rejuvenator of the world.
1976: publication of *La Porte de pierre,* an earlier, unpublished novel about the theme of love – passion.
Leonora Carrington lives today in Mexico and New York.

87
LEONOARA CARRINGTON
UNITLED (HIEROPHANTE, POUR DAUPHINE)
1985
Oil on canvas
$39\frac{3}{8} \times 19\frac{5}{8}$ inches (100×50 cm)
Private collection
Ill. p. 212

88
LEONOARA CARRINGTON
TELUM PASSIONIS
1962
Oil on canvas
$39\frac{3}{8} \times 31\frac{1}{2}$ inches (100×80 cm)
Private collection
Ill. p. 213

COVARRUBIAS, MIGUEL

1904: born in Mexico City. He cut short his studies at the Ecuela Nacional Preparatoria in order to devote his time to drawing caricatures. He found his themes during noctural observation in theaters and cafés. Published his drawings in newspapers and magazines.
1923: traveled to New York, where he became the official caricaturist at *Vanity Fair* (until 1936). Traveled to Java, Bali, India, Vietnam, Africa, and Europe on a Guggenheim scholarship.
1940: painted two large murals for the San Francisco International Fair. Covarrubias taught ethnography at the Escuela Nacional de Antropología. He was also appointed director of the Academia de Danza of the Instituto Nacional de Bellas Artes. He published numerous books of caricatures and drawings, and volumes on art and ethnography, for example, the book entitled *Indian Art of Mexico and Central America* (New York, 1957).
1957: Covarrubias died in Mexico City.

89
MIGUEL COVARRUBIAS
MARKET SCENE
undated
Oil on Masonite
22×11¾ inches (56×30 cm)
Private collection
Ill. p. 219

GERZSO, GUNTHER

1915: born on June 17 in Mexico City, the son of a Hungarian father and a German mother.
1922–1924: he spent these years in Europe with his mother, stepfather, brothers, and sisters.
1927–1931: lived with his uncle, the art historian and art dealer Hans Wendland, in Lugano (Switzerland). He made the acquaintance of many artists, including Paul Klee. Became friends with the Italian stage designer Nando Tamberlani.
1931–1933: lived with his mother in Mexico and attended the German school there.
1935–1940: Arch Lauterer, stage designer and professor at Bennington College in Vermont, recognized Gerzso's talent for drawing and recommended him to the Cleveland Playhouse, where Gerzso worked as a stage designer for four years. He continued his studies in New York.
1940: began to paint. Married the American musician Gene Rilla Cady.
1941: returned to Mexico. Began designing film sets. During the following twenty years he produced designs for nearly 250 films and worked with film directors like Luis Buñuel, John Ford, and Yves Allegret.
1944: made the acquaintance of a number of Surrealists who were in Mexico in exile: Benjamin Péret, Leonora Carrington, Remedios Varo, and Wolfgang Paalen. His own painting became more Surrealistic under the influence of Tanguy.
1959: traveled to Greece.
1962: introduced pre-Columbian motifs into his work.
1963: retrospective exhibition of his work at the Instituto Nacional de Bellas Artes in Mexico City.
1968: Gerzso designed a large glass window for the Hotel Aristos in Mexico City.
1974: first lithographs.
1976: one-man exhibition at the University of Texas in Austin.
1977: one-man exhibition at the Museo de Arte Moderno of the Instituto Nacional de Bellas Artes in Mexico City.
1981–1982: first designs for sculptures. Exhibitions in Europe and the USA.
Gunter Gerzso lives in Mexico.

90
GUNTHER GERZSO
SHIPWRECK
1945
Oil on canvas
13¾×19⅝ inches (35×50 cm)
Private collection
Ill. p. 209

GONZALES SERRANO, MANUEL

1917: born in Lagos der Moreno, Jalisco. Self-taught.
1937: for a few months attended "La Esmeralda" and the Academia de San Carlos, but discontinued his academic training because it did not suit him. During the *1940*s he developed a very personal Surrealism.
1944: his first exhibition at the Galería Arte y Decoration in Mexico. Followed by other exhibitions.
1950: retired and did not paint any more.
1960: Manuel Gonzales Serrano died in Mexico.

91
MANUEL GONZÁLEZ SERRANO
STILL LIFE WITH WINDOW AND LOCK
circa 1945
Oil on Masonite
14⅞×16 inches (37.7×40.6 cm)
Private collection
Ill. p. 206

GUERRERO GALVÁN, JESÚS

1910: born on June 10 in Tonlé (State of Jalisco).
1925: traveled to the USA with his mother. Studied at the Art School of San Antonio, Texas, for two years.
1928: attended the Escuela Libre de Pintura in Guadalajara.
1931: first mural for the telegraph office in Guadalajara.
1933: moved to Mexico City. Worked in the State of Michoacán on a commission from the Misiones Culturales.
1934: with Roberto Réyes Pérez, Máximo Pacheco, and Juán Manuel Anaya, co-founder of the Alianza de Trabajadores de las Artes Plásticas.
1936: became a teacher of painting at the Escuela de Arte para Trabajadores.
1938: worked as professor of painting and drawing at the Escuela Nacional de Artes Plásticas.
1942: invited by the University of New Mexico to give a course on contemporary Mexican art and to paint a mural at the university.
1952: takes an active part in the politics of his country as delegate of the Partido Popular.
1959: founding member of the "Unión de Pintores y Brabadores de México," with Raúl Anguiano, Juan O'Gorman, Carlos Orozco Romero, and others.
1960: spent a year in the Soviet Union at the invitation of a number of Russian artists.
1968: moved to Cuernavaca.
1973: Jesús Guerrero Galván died on May 11.

92
JESÚS GUERRERO GALVÁN
THE CHILDREN
1939
Oil on canvas
57⅝×39⅜ inches (146.5×100 cm)
Private collection
Ill. p. 207

IZQUIERDO, MARÍA

1960: born in San Juan de los Lagos (State of Jalisco).
1912: moved to Torréon (State of Coahuila). First art lessons.
1917: married Cándido Posados.
1923: moved to Mexico City.
1927: or *1928:* studied at the Escuela Nacional de Bellas Artes (Academia de San Carlos) for one year.
1929: first one-woman exhibition at the Galería de Arte Moderno. She established her own atelier, where she worked with Rufino Tamayo.
1930: one-woman exhibition at the New York Art Center.

1931: appointed teacher of painting at the Escuela de Pintura y Escultura of the Secretaría de Educación Pública.
1933: one-woman exhibition at the Galerie René Highe in Paris.
1934–1935: numerous exhibitions in Mexico, the USA, and Europe.
1940: participated in the International Surrealist Exhibition at the Galería de Arte Mexicano.
1945: planned a large mural at the Palacio de Gobierno in Mexico City. Diego Rivera and David Alfaro Siquieros prevented her from carrying out the project since they felt that she had no experience in wall painting.
1955: María Izquierdo died in Mexico City.

93
MARÍA IZQUIERDO
ALTAR TO THE VIRGIN OF SORROWS
1946
Oil on canvas
$29\frac{1}{8}\times22\frac{7}{8}$ inches (74×58 cm)
Galería de Arte Mexicano,
Señora Alejandra R. de Yturbe,
Señorita Mariana Pérez Amor
Ill. p. 216

94
MARÍA IZQUIERDO
THE DOLOROSA OR THE VIRGIN DOLOROSA
1947
Oil on Masonite
$15\times11\frac{7}{8}$ inches (38×30 cm)
Collection Francisco Osio Morales,
Ill. p. 217

MÉRIDA, CARLOS

1891: born in Guatemala City.
1896–1908: attended schools and took painting and music lessons in Guatemala City and Quetzaltenango.
1909: returned to Guatemala City and joined a group of young artists including Carlos Valenti and Jaime Sabartés.
1910: traveled to Europe for the first time with Carlos Valenti, who died prematurely in Paris. Mérida made the acquaintance of Kees van Dongen, Anglada Camarasa, Amadeo Modigliani, and Piet Mondrian. Became friends with Diego Rivera, Roberto Montenegro, Jorge Enciso, and Pablo Picasso.
1914: returned to Guatemala. Began working with local themes and Indian motifs in his paintings.
1917: first journey to the USA, where he settled in New York.
1919: married Dalila Gálvez and returned to Mexico for good.
1921: assisted Diego Rivera with his mural in the Anfiteatro Bolívar in the Escuela Nacional Preparatoria, together with Jean Charlot, Armando de la Cueva, and Xavier Guerrero.
1922: joined the Renascimento Mexicano muralist group.
1923: commissioned to paint the Biblioteca Infantil for the Secretaría de Educación Pública. Mérida was a co-founder of the Mexican Union of Painters, Sculptors, and Graphic Artists.
1927: back in Paris, he renewed his friendship with Paul Klee and Joan Miró.
1929: appointed director of the Galería del Teatro Nacional in Mexico City. Organized the school of dance for the Secretaría de Educación Pública in collaboration with Carlos Orozco and acted as director of the school for three years.
1934: first sketches for the ballet *La Virgen y las Fieras.*
1941–1942: teacher of art at North Texas State Teacher's College in Denton.
1944: in New York, became friends with Josef Albers, André Breton, Alexander Calder, Marcel Duchamp, Max Ernst, Albert Gleizes, David Hare, Fernand Léger, and Ossip Zadkine.
1950: third journey to Europe. Studied Venetian mosaic techniques in Italy.
1968: mosaic mural *La Confluencia de la Civilización* in San Antonio, Texas.
From 1914 on, he held numerous exhibitions in Guatemala, Mexico, the USA, and Paris.
1984: Carlos Mérida died.

95
CARLOS MÉRIDA
VOODOO SCENE
1929
Oil on canvas
24×20 inches (61×51 cm)
Private collection
Ill. p. 223

MICHEL, ALFONSO

1897: born on January 14 in Colima (State of Colima). His family moved to Guadalajara, where Alfonso attended school. Invited to California where he spent a short period at an art academy in San Francisco.
1918: traveled to New York and subsequently to Europe. Spent two years in Florence and some time in Paris.
1921: lived in Berlin between July and December. Worked as a fashion designer. His inclination towards the bohemian life resulted in frequent ill health.
1923: back in Paris, he worked in the daytime with the Russian painter Shokawaff and in the evenings he attended courses in the atelier of Lucien Simon. Spent the summer in Berlin and on the North Sea coast.
1926–1927: after a brief period in Mexico, he traveled to Nice and Italy.
1928: worked as an illustrator in Paris and dreamed of a career as a film director. Spent a short time in Spain.
1931: after his return to Mexico he settled in Colima where his family owned a country estate. Encouraged by Roberto Montenegro, he devoted himself whole-heartedly to painting.
1933: moved to Guadalajara. Shared a studio with José Guadalupe Zuno. Worked on murals for the Olimpo House with Jesús Guerrero Galván, Carlos Stahl, and Francisco Sánchez Flores.
1942: moved to Mexico City, where his work began to find recognition.
1945: first exhibition in Mexico and New York.
1949: traveled to Paris and subsequently to Greece and Egypt.
1950: one-man exhibition in the Galerie d'Art Pictorial in Paris.
1953–1957: various exhibitions in Mexico and in Lima (1954).
1957: Alfonso Michel died on February 18 in Mexico City.

96
ALFONSO MICHEL
THE BARRICADE
1956
Oil on Masonite
$47\frac{7}{8}\times46\frac{5}{8}$ inches (121.5×118.5 cm)
Patrimonio de la Pinacoteca de la Universidad de Colima, Mexico
Ill. p. 205

MONTENEGRO, ROBERTO

1887: born on February 19 in Guadalajara.
1903: began painting in Félix Bernardelli's studio.
1904: moved to Mexico City in order to study architecture. Enrolled at the Escuela Nacional de Arte, where he made the acquaintance of Saturnino Herrán, Diego Rivera, and others.
1905: traveled to France and Spain on a grant from the Secretaría de Educación Pública.
1906: moved in literary circles in Madrid. Was fascinated by the work of El Greco in Toledo. Traveled through Belgium and the Netherlands.
1907: traveled to Paris and attended the Ecole des Beaux Arts. Made the acquaintance of Jean Cocteau and Juan Gris.
1908–1909: traveled to Italy and lived for a short time in Venice.
1910: returned to Paris and then to Mexico.
1911: in contact with the artist's circle founded by Dr. Atl in Guadalajara.
1912: returned once again to Paris and exhibited in the Salon d'Automne.

1914: fled to Barcelona at the outbreak of World War I. He later settled in Pollenza on Mallorca, where he lived until 1918.
1918: first exhibition in Madrid. Published ten etchings.
1919: exhibitions in Madrid and on Mallorca. Returned to Mexico via Paris and New York.
1920: painted his first murals. He began to take an intense interest in Mexican folk art.
1920–1933: painted numerous murals in Mexico.
1928: painted scenery for the *Teatro de Ulises* with Manuel Rodriguez Lozano and Julio Castellanos.
1930: made the acquaintance of Sergei Eisenstein and accompanied him during the filming of *Que viva México*.
1934: Montenegro became director of the Museo de Artes Populares de Bellas Artes.
1935: helped Marc Chagall with the scenery for the ballet *Aleko*.
1935–1940: shared an atelier with Alfonso Michel.
1946: founded a museum of folk art in Toluca.
1965: big retrospective exhibition organized by INBA (Instituto Nacional de Bellas Artes).
1967: received the Mexican national art award.
1968: Roberto Montenegro died during a journey to Pátzcuaro.

97
ROBERTO MONTENEGRO
PORTRAIT OF FRIDA KAHLO
undated
Oil on canvas
31½×25⅝ inches (80×65 cm)
Private collection
Ill. p. 17

98
ROBERTO MONTENEGRO
TWO SEATED WOMEN
1948
Ink, watercolor, and gouache on paper
13×18⅛ inches (33×46 cm)
Agustín and Angel Cristóbal
Ill. p. 221

99
ROBERTO MONTENEGRO
BRIDAL COUPLE FROM VERACRUZ
1948
Ink watercolor, and gouache on paper
13⅜×18½ inches (34×47 cm)
Agustín and Angel Cristóbal
Ill. p. 220

100
ROBERTO MONTENEGRO
TWO INDIAN GIRLS (CANDLESTICKS)
1947
Oil on Masonite
23⅝×28 inches (60×71 cm)
Private collection
Ill. p. 218

O'GORMAN, JUAN

1905: born in Coyoacán.
1921–1925: studied architecture at the Escuela Nacional de Arquitectura.
1925–1928: worked as a trainee in the atelier of the architect Carlos Obregón S.
1928–1931: built the first functional houses in Mexico, including Diego Rivera's house in San Angel.
1932–1934: worked as the head of the Secretaría de Educación Pública's Departamento de Constructión de Escuelas. Developed the first year's program for school construction.
1932–1948: professor at the Escuela de Ingeniería y Arquitectura of the Instituto Politécnico Nacional.
1938–1939: built ten private houses in Mexico. Devoted more of his time to painting.
1948: first one-man exhibition in the Museo Nacional de Bellas Artes in Mexico City.
1949–1951: with the architects Martínez de Velasco and Gustavo Saavedra, he created a project for the University of Mexico City's Biblioteca Central, where he executed the mosaics.
1950–1951: one-man exhibitions in Mexico City, in the Palacio de Bellas Artes and in Morelia.
1961: one-man exhibition in the Instituto de Arte Mexicano.
1964: one-man exhibition in the Salón de la Plástica Mexicana in Mexico City and in the San Fernando Valley State College in California.
1968: exhibition of sketches for wall paintings in the Palacio de Bellas Artes in Mexico City.
1982: Juan O'Gorman died.

101
JUAN O'GORMAN
CONSUMATUM EST
1942
Tempera on Masonite
20⅞×23¼ inches (53×59 cm)
Private collection
Ill. p. 208

OROZCO, JOSÉ CLEMENTE

1883: born on November 23, in Zapotlán el grande, now known as Ciudad Guzmán (State of Jalisco).
1890: Orozco moved to Mexico City with his family, where he attended the maestro's preparatory school, an off-shoot of the Escuela Normal. Vanegas Arroyo's printing work was situated in the same street as the school. Arroyo printed illustrations by José Guadalupe Posada, Manilla etc., and Orozco later wrote in his autobiography that this provided the greatest possible stimulus for his imagination and inspired him to start scribbling his first figures. It was a revelation, his first introduction to the existence of drawing and painting.
1897–1904: studied agronomy at the Agricultural School of San Jacinto.
1908–1914: attended courses in drawing at the Academia de Bellas Artes. After his father died he started earning his living as a draughtsman in architectural offices and as a caricaturist.
1913: moved to Veracruz and painted a huge oil painting of the retreat of the Spanish troops in 1822 in what used to be the Museo de San Juan de Ulúa.
1916: first one-man exhibition in the Biblos bookshop in México D.F.
1917: unable to find a climate that suited him as an artist, he traveled to the USA where he lived for a year, at first in San Francisco, and then in New York.
1922: painted his first murals in the Escuela Nacional Preparatoria and became one of the first members of the Mexican muralist movement. Joined the Union of Painters, Sculptors, and Graphic Artists. Worked as a graphic artist for the movement's organ *El Machete*. The Minister of Education, Puig Cassauranc, forced him to discontinue work on the murals in the Escuela Nacional Preparatoria. Two years later, in 1926, he recommenced work on the murals.
1925: one-man exhibition in the Galerie Gernheim-Jeune in Paris.
1927: traveled to the USA. Made the acquaintance of Alma Reed and Mrs. Sikelianos in New York.
1929: one-man exhibition at the Galerie Fermé la Nuit in Paris and at the Art Students League in New York.
1930: the Delphic Studios, which were run by Alma Reed, were inaugurated by an exhibition of Orozco's work. Exhibitions at the Albertini Museum in Venice and the museum in Exposition Park in Los Angeles. Commissioned to paint murals for Pomona College.
1931: one-man exhibitions at the Downtown Gallery in New York, at the Grace Horn's Galleries in Boston and at the Wisconsin Union.
1932: he became acquainted with the leading museums of London and Paris during three months spent in Europe. He visited a big Picasso retrospective exhibition in Paris at the Galerie Georges Petit. He traveled through Italy and admired Leonardo's *Last Supper* in Milan, Giotto in Padua, Titian and Tintoretto in Venice. He visited Ravenna and Florence, Assisi and Arezzo, Rome and the Vatican, Naples, Pompei, Pisa, Genoa. Further stops on this journey were Marseilles, Barcelona, Zaragoza, Madrid, Toledo, and Avila.
1936–1939: painted frescos in the amphitheater of the University of Guadalajara, in the government palace and in the Hospicio Cabañas.

1940: once again in New York, he painted six panel pictures for the Museum of Modern Art. Exhibition of sketches and studies for his murales at the Galeria de Arte Mexicano.
1943: founding member of the "Colegio Nacional," an institution which united famous personalities from the worlds of art and science.
1945: traveled to the USA again.
1946: awarded the national art prize.
1947: comprehensive exhibition at the Palacio de Bellas Artes.
1949: José Clemente Orozco died on September 7 in Mexico City. His ashes were interred in the Rotonda of Famous Men in the Panteón Civil de Dolores.

102
JOSÉ CLEMENTE OROZCO
THE CEMETERY
1931
Oil on canvas
$27\frac{1}{2} \times 39\frac{3}{8}$ inches (70×100 cm)
Private collection
Ill. p. 202

103
JOSÉ CLEMENTE OROZCO
CONEY ISLAND
circa 1930
Oil on canvas
$19\frac{1}{4} \times 15\frac{3}{8}$ inches (49×39 cm)
Private collection
Ill. p. 203

PAALEN, WOLFGANG

1907: born in Vienna.
1918: starts to paint, encouraged by his father.
1927: art courses with Hans Hoffmann in Munich.
1928–1939: lives in Paris: He is interested in primitive art.
1931: marries Alice Rahon, poet and painter.
1933–1936: member of the group "Abstraction – Création".
1936: joins the Surrealists, but without becoming a member. Illustrates the works of Valentine Penrose.
1937: develops his own smoke technique by blackening the canvas with candle smoke. Creation of strange objects: "Nuage articulé" Cloud joined together), an umbrella made of natural sponges. Paints fantastic landscapes peopled by threatening ghosts.
1938: illustrates the "Ouvres complètes" by Lautréamont along with other Surrealists.
1939: trip to Alaska. Emigrates to Mexico. Collects Pre-Columbian objects.
1940: together with A. Breton and C. Moro the organizes the international exhibitions of Surrealists.
1942–1944: publishes "Dyn," a luxurious magazine with international dissemination. Founds the "Dynation" movement together with the painters Gorton Onslow-Ford and Lee Mullican.
1942: break with Surrealism.
1945: "Form and Sense," a collection of writings, published in New York.
1947: divorced from Alice Rahon, married Luz del Solar.
1949–1954: lived in New York, California, and Paris.
1951: organized the exhibition *Dynation* at the Museum of Modern Art in San Francisco.
1951–1953: repeated stays in Paris. Closer contact with Breton.
1954: returned to Mexico. Married Isabel Marin. Start of a long illness.
1959: Wolfgang Paalen committed suicide on a plateau near Mexico.

104
WOLFGANG PAALEN
FUTURE ANCESTORS
1947
Oil on Masonite
$14\frac{1}{8} \times 13\frac{3}{4}$ inches (36×35 cm)
Private collection
Ill. p. 210

RAHON, ALICE

1914: born in Trefley, France. Her father is an academic painter.
1928: encouraged by her father, she began to paint.
1931: married the painter Wolfgang Paalen.
1936: took part as a poet in the Surrealist movement. Collection of poems *Sablier couché*. Trip to India with Valentine Penrose.
1939: A même la terre, collection of poems, illustrated by Tanguy. Emigrated to Mexico with Paalen.
1940: took part in the exhibition of Surrealists organized by Wolfgang Paalen.
1941: Noir animal, collection of poems, illustrated by Paalen.
1942: worked on the publication of *Dyn,* founded by Paalen. For her paintings she used the dried left over paints on Paalen's palette. Painted visionary landscapes, fantastic architectural forms, but also worlds with archaic figures, animals, and hieroglyphics.
On the theme of the woman, she sought to find a connection between the modern feminine awareness and its historic and legendary sources. Of all the female Surrealist painters in Mexico, she was the one most influenced by the folk art of Mexico.
1947: divorced from Paalen.
1987: Alice Rahon dies in Mexico.

105
ALICE RAHON
THE WIND
1954
Oil on canvas
$42\frac{5}{8} \times 70\frac{7}{8}$ inches (108.4×180 cm)
Private collection
Ill. p. 211

REYES FERREIRA, JESÚS

1880: born in Guadalajara (State of Jalisco).
1894: worked as a trainee in an engraving and lithography shop and subsequently as a show window decorator in a shop for artist's materials.
1911: inherited antiques and objects of art after the death of his father. Began collecting.
1913–1915: opened a shop selling antiques and folk art.
1913–1937: began his own artistic activities.
1938: left Guadalajara and moved to Mexico City.
1942: made the acquaintance of Marc Chagall.
1950: first exhibition in Guadalajara. He frequently painted on India paper and cardboad, as well as sculpted, and made tapestries with Cynthia Sargen.
1962: the Instituto Nacional de Bellas Artes organized a large-scale retrospective exhibition on the occasion of his 80th birthday.
1972: traveled to Europe for the first time at the age of 90. Exhibition in Barcelona.
1974: started painting oil pictures after returning from his second trip to Europe.
1977: Jesús Reyes Ferreira died at the age of 97.

106
JESÚS REYES FERREIRA (CHUCHO REYES)
SKULLS WITH WATERMELONS
undated
Gouache on China paper
$29\frac{1}{2} \times 19\frac{5}{8}$ inches (75×50 cm)
Private collection
Ill. p. 222

RIVERA, DIEGO

1886: born on December 8 in Guanajuato.
1892: moved to Mexico City with his family.
1986: enrolled at the Academia de San Carlos at the age of 10. His teachers included Santiago Rebull, Andrés Rios, José Salomé Pina, Félix Parra, and José María Velasco.
1902: left the academy because he disagreed with the system of photographic realism introduced by the new director, Antonio Fabrés.

1907: first exhibition. Awarded a grant to study in Spain. Enrolled at the Academia de San Fernando in Madrid.
1908–1909: traveled through France, Belgium, Holland, and England. Exhibited his work with the Indépendants in Paris. Deeply impressed by the work of Cézanne.
1910: returned to Mexico and exhibited in the Academia de San Carlos. Experienced the beginning of the Mexican Revolution.
1911: returned to Paris. During this period his work was influenced by Pointillism and Cubism. Exhibited in the Salon d'Automne. Legalized his relationship with Angelina Beloff.
1914: traveled to Mallorca and Madrid shortly after the outbreak of World War I.
1915–1920: intensive work in Paris. 1919, discussions with Siqueiros on "the necessity of changing Mexican art in order to create a national people's movement."
1920–1921: traveled through Italy where he made sketches and studies of the paintings and frescos of the Old Masters. Returned to Mexico.
1922: first murals in the Anfiteatro Bolívar at the Escuela Nacional Preparatoria with 22 other artists, among them Orozco and Siqueiros. This group provided the impetus that triggered the muralist movement in Mexico. Rivera married Guadalupe Marín. Joined the Mexican Communist party. Co-founder of the Union of Revolutionary Painters, Sculptors and Graphic Artists. Began work on frescos for the Secretaría de Educación Pública.
1926–1927: murals for the Escuela Nacional de Agricultura in Chapingo.
1927: traveled to the Soviet Union at the invitation of the Committee for Public Education.
1928: divorced Guadelupe Marín and married Frida Kahlo the following year.
1929: Rivera became director of the Academia de San Carlos.
1930: moved to the USA, where he painted various murals in California.
1931: exhibition at the Museum of Modern Art in New York.
1932: designed the scenery and costumes for the ballet *H.P.* (*Horse Power*) by Carlos Chávez, which was performed in Philadelphia. Mural in the Detroit Institute of Arts.
1933: worked on a mural in the Rockefeller Center in New York. The painting was destroyed before completion because it contained a portrait of Lenin.
1934: returned to Mexico, where he painted the mural intended for the Rockefeller Center in the Palacio de Bellas Artes.
1936: Leo Trotsky was Rivera's guest at Frida Kahlo's house in Coyoacán.
1936–1940: devoted himself exclusively to easel painting: landscapes, portraits and a series of black dancers.
1940–1957: numerous murals in the USA and, above all, in Mexico.
1949: Diego Rivera honored with a national exhibition in the Museo Nacional de Artes Plásticas, Palacio de Bellas Artes in Mexico.
1954: Frida Kahlo died on July 13.
1955: Diego Rivera donated the house in Coyoacán, where Frida Kahlo was born, lived and died, to the Mexican people. The intention was to create a Frida Kahlo Museum. Rivera traveled to the Soviet Union for medical treatment.
1956: last exhibitions in the Galerie Diego Rivera.
1957: Diego Rivera died on November 24 in Mexico City. His ashes were interred in the Panteón Civil de Dolores.

107
DIEGO RIVERA
PORTRAIT OF A WOMAN
1927
Charcoal and red pencil on paper
$24\frac{1}{4}\times18\frac{3}{4}$ inches (61.5×47.5 cm)
Private collection
Ill. p. 199

108
DIEGO RIVERA
PORTRAIT OF ROSA ROLANDO
1930
Oil on canvas
$22\times17\frac{3}{4}$ inches (56×45 cm)
Private collection
Ill. p. 200

109
DIEGO RIVERA
SELF-PORTRAIT
1930
Lithograph (46/100)
$20\frac{3}{4}\times16$ inches (52.7×40.7 cm)
Not illustrated

110
DIEGO RIVERA
NUDE STUDY OF FRIDA KAHLO
1930
Lithograph (84/100)
$17\frac{3}{8}\times12\frac{5}{8}$ inches (44×32 cm)
Private collection
Ill. p. 18

111
DIEGO RIVERA
POSTHUMOUS PORTRAIT OF FRIDA KAHLO
1955
Colored print, overpainted in oil
$7\times9\frac{1}{2}$ inches (18×24 cm)
Private collection
Ill. p. 19

112
DIEGO RIVERA
LUPITA CRUZ AT AGE THREE
1954
Oil on canvas
$47\frac{1}{4}\times31\frac{1}{2}$ inches (120×80 cm)
Private collection
Ill. p. 201

113
DIEGO RIVERA
SELF-PORTRAIT (THE RAVAGES OF TIME)
undated
Oil on canvas
$12\frac{1}{4}\times11\frac{1}{2}$ inches (31×28.5 cm)
Private collection
Ill. p. 198

SIQUEIROS, DAVID ALFARO

1896: born on December 29, in Santa Rosalía de Camargo, Chihuahua.
1908: attended the Marist French-English School in Mexico City.
1911: in addition to preparatory school, he attended the Escuela Nacional de Bellas Artes (Academia de San Carlos) as a special pupil.
1913: enrolled at the Escuela al Aire Libre at Santa Anita, directed by Ramos Martínez. Took part in the students' and workers' conspiracy against the presidential usurper Victoriano Huerta and was subsequently persecuted.
1914: member of the revolutionary troops under Venustiano Carranza.
1915: appointed Second Captain in the regimental headquarters of General Manuel M. Diéguez.
1918: in Guadalajara he made contact with the artists of the collective avant-gardist workshop "Centro Bohemio" to which José Guadalupe Zuno, Amado de la Cueva, Xavier Guerrero, and others belonged.
1919: traveled to Europe. Became friends with Diego Rivera in Paris.
1922: after his return to Mexico, he joined the groups of artists who were painting at the Escuela Nacional Preparatoria.
1923: appointed to the executive committee of the Mexican Communist Party together with Rivera and Xavier Guerrero. Secretary General of the Union of Painters, Sculptors and Graphic Artists.
1924: Siqueiros, Guerrero, and Rivera formed the executive committee of *El Machete,* the official trade union organ – and later official organ of the Mexican Communist Party. Siqueiros settled in Guadalajara where he painted murals for the university with Amado de la Cueva.
1925–1930: he ceased his painting activities during these years in order to devote himself to his revolutionary trade union work.

1930: interned in a Mexican prison from May to December. Returned to painting with a series of pictures with social themes.
1932: first one-man exhibition in the Casino Español in Mexico City. Traveled to California as an outlaw, where he painted murals in the Chouinard School of Art and the Plaza Art Center. Threatened with deportation, he fled to South America.
1933: exhibitions in Uruguay and Argentina. Painted, wrote articles, and spoke about new aesthetics and a new social order.
1934: one-man exhibition in New York, at the Delphic Studios run by Alma Reed.
1935: discussions in Mexico with Diego Rivera: first collective self-criticism by the founders of the muralist movement. Back in New York, he founded the "Siqueiros Experimental Workshop, a Laboratory of Modern Techniques." One of his pupils was Jackson Pollock.
1937: with the militia, he fought at the front in the Spanish Civil War and finally became head of the 29th Division with the rank of Lieutenant-Colonel.
1938: lectured on Mexican art at the Maison de la Culture in Paris.
1939: returned to Mexico.
1943: traveled to Peru, Ecuador, Panama, and Cuba as part of a campaign for "American Art in the service of the victory of democracy."
1944: founded the "Centro Realista de Arte Moderno" in Mexico.
1950: took part in the XXV Biennale of Venice with Orozco, Rivera, and Tamayo.
1951: publication of his book *How to Paint Murals*. Traveled to Warsaw.
1955: traveled to Poland and the Soviet Union.
1958: took part in the 1st Inter-American Biennale of Painting and Graphic Art in Mexico with his own work and as a member of the jury.
1960: traveled to Cuba and Venezuela. Back in Mexico, he was arrested once more because of his public criticism of Mexican politics under President Lopéz Mateos. Sentenced to eight years imprisonment.
1964: released from prison after three years, eleven months and three days as a result of his plea for clemency. Produced numerous small paintings, sketches, and designs for prints during his imprisonment. Numerous commissions for murals.
1966: the Mexican government awarded him the national art prize.
1967: received the Lenin Peace Prize awarded by the Soviet Union.
1968: founding member and first chairman of the Mexican Art Academy.
1969: appointed honorary member of the Academy of Visual Arts in the Soviet Union.
1974: Siqueiros died in Mexico City.

114
DAVID ALFARO SIQUEIROS
THE MARCH OF MAN TOWARD SOCIALISM
1962
Oil on wood
$12\frac{3}{4} \times 36\frac{1}{4}$ inches (32.5×92 cm)
Collection Francisco Osio Morales
Ill. p. 204

TAMAYO, RUFINO

1899: born in Oaxaca.
1911: moved to Mexico City.
1917–1921: attended the Academia de Bellas Artes.
1921: appointed head of the ethnographic department of the Museo Nacional de Arqueología in Mexico City.
1926: first one-man exhibition in Mexico. Traveled to New York for the first time and exhibited in the Weyhe Gallery.
1928–1929: taught painting at the Escuela Nacional de Bellas Artes in Mexico City.
1932: became head of the Departamento de Artes Plásticas de la Secretaría de Educación in Mexico City.
1933: painted a mural for the National Music Conservatory in Mexico City.
1936: settled in New York for a long period. Became professor of painting at the Dalton School. Painted several murals in the USA and Mexico. Numerous exhibitions.
1946: appointed professor at Brooklyn Museum.
1948: retrospective exhibition of his work in the Palacio de Bellas Artes in Mexico City.
1949: traveled to Europe and settled in Paris.
1950: exhibited at the Biennale in Venice.
1953: received the grand prize for painting at the Biennale of São Paulo.
1958: mural for the UNESCO building in Paris.
1960: received a Guggenheim Foundation prize and the international prize at the Biennale of Mexico.
1963: wall paintings and an exhibition in Israel. Retrospective exhibition in Tokyo.
1964: awarded the national prize by the President of the Mexican Republic. Produced 26 lithographs for the Ford Foundation.
1967: painted a mural for the Mexican Pavillon at Expo 67 in Montreal.
1968: large retrospective exhibition at the Palacio de Bellas Artes in Mexico City.
1974: donated a museum of pre-Columbian art to his native town of Oaxaca. Large exhibition of his work from the 1960s and 1970s at the Musée d'Art Moderne de la Ville de Paris.
Since 1976: more large-scale exhibitions in Mexico, Tokyo, Caracas, San Salvador, Washington, New York, and London.
1991: Rufino Tamayo died in Mexico.

115
RUFINO TAMAYO
STILL LIFE WITH SHERBERTS
1938
Oil on canvas
$17\frac{3}{4} \times 23\frac{5}{8}$ inches (45×60 cm)
Private collection
Ill. p. 224

116
RUFINO TAMAYO
THE SMOKER
1939
Oil on canvas
17×13 inches (43×33 cm)
Private collection
Ill. p. 225

117
RUFINO TAMAYO
THE BIRDMAN
1950
Oil on canvas
$31\frac{1}{2} \times 39\frac{3}{8}$ inches (80×100 cm)
Private collection
Ill. p. 226

VARO, REMEDIOS

1908: born in Angles, Spain. Her father is Andalusian, her mother Basque. Moved frequently during childhood and teenage years, since her father works as an engineer in different towns in Spain and North Africa. Her father taught her to draw. Her mother, a fervent Catholic, enrolled her in parochial schools, where she showed an interest in mathematics and drawing

1924: left school. Attended the Academia de San Fernando in Madrid.
1930–1931: married the painter Gerardo Lizarraga.
1932: painting course at the art school of Barcelona.
1935: contact with Esteban Frances and his circle.
1936: met the poet Benjamin Péret, who is fighting in the Spanish Civil War. She left her husband.
1937: married Péret. Traveled to Paris and joined the activities of the Surrealists. Met Leonora Carrington, whom she is to meet again later in Mexico
1938: publication of her drawings, inspired by Oscar Dominguez, Max Ernst, and René Magritte, in the magazines *Minotaure* and *Trajectoire du rêve*.
1942: emigrated to Mexico, together with Péret. Wrote *Lady Milagra*, a short novel about the magic powers of women. Stoped painting the first years in Mexico. Close friend of Leonora Carrington and Natalia Trotsky. Joined pro-Trotsky groups.

1947: separation from Péret.
1949: stay in Caracas. Worked for several months in the Ministerio de Salud Publico.
1953: married Walter Gruen, an immigrant from Europe, who encourages her to paint again. She dedicated herself to painting strange worlds or lonely people, who fly on strange machines. Parodied the themes of Leonora Carrington sorceresses, witches, the world of children. Like Leonora she is influenced by the theories of G.J. Gurdiew and P.D. Ouspenskij.
1955: first successful exhibitions.
1961: suffered from severe depressions.
1963: Remedios Varos died in Mexico.

118
REMEDIOS VARO
UNEXPECTED VISITOR
1958
Oil on Masonite
$23\frac{5}{8} \times 24\frac{3}{8}$ inches (60×62 cm)
Private collection
Ill. p. 214

119
REMEDIOS VARO
THE LOVERS
1963
Mixed media on cardboard
$29\frac{1}{2} \times 11\frac{7}{8}$ inches (75×30 cm)
Private collection
Ill. p. 215

RETABLOS AND EX-VOTOS

120
RETABLO
HAND OF WONDER
End of the 18th century
Oil on canvas
$17 \times 13\frac{5}{8}$ inches (43×34.5 cm)
Collection Ruth D. Lechuga
Ill. p. 228

121
EX-VOTO
IN THE CITY OF SAN FRANCISCO
1915
Oil on metal
$9\frac{1}{2} \times 13\frac{1}{4}$ inches (24.1×33.7 cm)
Collection Victor Fosado
Ill. p. 229

122
13 EX-VOTOS
MOUNTED ON WOODEN BOARD
17th–20th century
Oil on metal
$24 \times 43\frac{3}{8}$ inches (61×110 cm)
Collection Ruth D. Lechuga
Ill. p. 230–31

BUSTOS, HERMENEGILDO

1832: born in Purisima del Rincon, Guanajuato, where he also died in 1907. Born to an Indian family, worked as ice-cream vendor and carpenter. In his youth he received six months of training in painting in Léon. For the most part self-taught. His largest paintings (*Birth of Christ, The Last Supper, Pilatus, Purgatory*), were painted for the church in his village. His oeuvre consists also of still lifes, portraits, and *retablos*.

123
HERMENEGILDO BUSTOS
RETABLO OF THE CHILD OF ATOCHA
Oil on metal
$14\frac{1}{8} \times 10\frac{1}{4}$ inches (36×26 cm)
Museo Regional de Guanajuato
Alhóndiga de Granaditas, Gto., INAH
Ill. p. 232

124
HERMENEGILDO BUSTOS
RETABLO OF THE VIRGIN OF GUADALUPE
Oil on metal
$10\frac{1}{4} \times 6\frac{7}{8}$ inches (26×17.5 cm)
Museo Regional de Guanajuato
Alhóndiga de Granaditas, Gto., INAH
Ill. p. 233

125
HERMENEGILDO BUSTOS
RETABLO OF THE HAND OF GOD
Oil on metal
$14\frac{1}{8} \times \frac{7}{8}$ inches (36×25 cm)
Museo Regional de Guanajuato
Alhóndiga de Granaditas, Gto., INAH
Ill. p. 234

126
HERMENEGILDO BUSTOS
RETABLO OF THE HOLY FAMILY
Oil on metal
$14 \times 9\frac{1}{2}$ inches (35.5×24 cm)
Museo Regional de Guanajuato
Alhóndiga de Granaditas, Gto., INAH
Ill. p. 234

127
HERMENEGILDO BUSTOS
EX-VOTO OF THE DEATH OF SAINT CAMILO DE LELIS
Oil on metal
$14\frac{3}{8} \times 10$ inches (36.5×25.5 cm)
Museo Regional de Guanajuato
Alhóndiga de Granaditas, Gto., INAH
Ill. p. 234

128
HERMENEGILDO BUSTOS
EX-VOTO OF FELICIANO IBARRA
Oil on metal
$6\frac{1}{4} \times 4\frac{1}{8}$ inches (16×10.5 cm)
Museo Regional de Guanajuato
Alhóndiga de Granaditas, Gto., INAH
Ill. p. 234

129
HERMENEGILDO BUSTOS
RETABLO OF SAINT CHRISTOPHER
Oil on metal
$10 \times 6\frac{7}{8}$ inches (25.5×17.5 cm)
Museo Regional de Guanajuato
Alhóndiga de Granaditas, Gto., INAH
Ill. p. 235

130
HERMENEGILDO BUSTOS
RETABLO OF THE IMMACULATE VIRGIN
Oil on metal
$13\frac{3}{4} \times 10$ inches (35×25.5 cm)
Museo Regional de Guanajuato
Alhóndiga de Granaditas, Gto., INAH
Ill. p. 235

131
HERMENEGILDO BUSTOS
RETABLO OF SAINT FRANCIS OF ASSISI
Oil on metal
$17\frac{7}{8}\times10\frac{1}{4}$ inches (45.5×26 cm)
Museo Regional de Guanajuato
Alhóndiga de Granaditas, Gto., INAH
Ill. p. 235

132
HERMENEGILDO BUSTOS
RETABLO OF THE CHILD OF ATOCHA
Oil on metal
$13\frac{3}{4}\times10$ inches (35×25.5 cm)
Museo Regional de Guanajuato
Alhóndiga de Granaditas, Gto., INAH
Ill. p. 235

133
HERMENEGILDO BUSTOS
RETABLO OF THE APOSTLE JACOB
Oil on metal
$10\times6\frac{3}{4}$ inches (25.5×17 cm)
Museo Regional de Guanajuato
Alhóndiga de Granaditas, Gto., INAH
Ill. p. 236

134
HERMENEGILDO BUSTOS
RETABLO OF THE BLACK JESUS
OF ESQUIPULA
Oil on metal
10×7 inches (25.5×18 cm)
Museo Regional de Guanajuato
Alhóndiga de Granaditas, Gto., INAH
Ill. p. 236

135
HERMENEGILDO BUSTOS
RETABLO OF THE VIRGIN WITH THE
HALF MOON
Oil on metal
13×10 inches (33×25.5 cm)
Museo Regional de Guanajuato
Alhóndiga de Granaditas, Gto., INAH
Ill. p. 236

136
HERMENGILDO BUSTOS
RETABLO OF THE HOLY TRINITY
Oil on metal
$9\frac{7}{8}\times6\frac{7}{8}$ inches (25×17.5 cm)
Museo Regional de Guanajuato
Alhóndiga de Granaditas, Gto., INAH
Ill. p. 236

137
EX-VOTO "BEING SEVERELY ATTACKED
BY A STRONG TYPHUS..."
1876
Oil on metal
$12\frac{3}{8}\times10$ inches (31.5×25.4 cm)
Collection Victor Fosado
Ill. p. 237

FOLK ART

138
CARMEN CABALLERO
JUDAS "LA PATERA"
Papier-mâché
$16\times22\frac{3}{8}\times35\frac{1}{2}$ inches ($193\times57\times90$ cm)
Museo Dolores Olmedo Patiño, Mexico City
Ill. p. 28

139
CARMEN CABALLERO
JUDAS "LA CALACA ROSA"
Papier-mâché
$115\frac{3}{8}\times24\frac{3}{4}\times16\frac{1}{8}$ inches ($293\times63\times41$ cm)
Museo Dolores Olmedo Patiño, Mexico City
Ill. p. 29

140
CARMEN CABALLERO
JUDAS "SKELETON"
Papier-mâché
$125\frac{1}{4}\times17\frac{3}{8}\times30\frac{3}{8}$ inches ($318\times44\times7$ cm)
Museo Dolores Olmedo Patiño, Mexico City
Ill. p. 30

141
PEDRO LINARES
JUDAS "ADELITA"
1974
Papier-mâché
$15\frac{3}{4}\times30\frac{3}{8}\times8\frac{5}{8}$ inches ($40\times77\times22$ cm)
Collection Ruth D. Lechuga
Ill. p. 27

142
TEHUANA COSTUME
circa 1940
Huipil and hooped skirt,
petticoat, large *huipil*
Collection Ruth D. Lechuga
Not illustrated

143
TEHUANA COSTUME
circa 1980
Huipil, hooped skirt and petticoat
Collection Ruth D. Lechuga
Not illustrated

144
TEHUANA COSTUME
circa 1930–1940
Hand-embroidered skirt and blouse
Museo Dolores Olmedo Patiño, Mexico City
Ill. p. 14

145
VARIOUS REBOZOS
(Shawls)
circa 1930–1940
Multi-colored hand-woven silk
Museo Dolores Olmedo Patiño, Mexico City
Ill. p. 14

146
NECKLACE
4 m long
18 karat gold
Museo Dolores Olmedo Patiño, Mexico City
Ill. p. 14

147
PENDANT
with three "Hidalgo" coins
18 karat gold and 20-peso "Hidalgo" coins
Museo Dolores Olmedo Patiño, Mexico City
Ill. p. 14

148
EARRINGS
Each with three 5-peso gold coins and one
2-peso gold coin, decorated with pearls
and gold balls
Museo Dolores Olmedo Patiño, Mexico City
Ill. p. 14

149
BOWL XICALPEXTLI
First half of 20th century
Lacquerwork on calabash
$5\frac{7}{8}\times17\frac{3}{8}$ inches diameter (15×44 cm
diameter)
Museo Dolores Olmedo Patiño, Mexico City
Ill. p. 13

PRE-COLUMBIAN CLAY SCULPTURE

150
DOG WITH SCORPION
Colima, western Mexico
Classic era, 200–600 A.D.
Clay vessel
10⅝×16⅛×9½ inches (27×41×24 cm)
Museo Dolores Olmedo Patiño, Mexico City
Ill. p. 31

151
DOG WITH MASK
Colima, western Mexico
Classic era, 200–600 A.D.
Clay vessel
13⅜×11×6¼ inches (34×28×16 cm)
Museo Dolores Olmedo Patiño, Mexico City
Ill. p. 32

152
DOG CRAWLING ON ALL FOURS
Colima, western Mexico
Classic era, 200–600 A.D.
Clay vessel
9⅝×12¼×7⅛ inches (24.5×31×18 cm)
Museo Dolores Olmedo Patiño, Mexico City
Ill. p. 32

153
SITTING DOG
Colima, western Mexico
Classic era, 200–600 A.D.
Clay vessel
10⅝×9½×6¾ inches (27×24×17 cm)
Museo Dolores Olmedo Patiño, Mexico City
Not illustrated

154
PAIR OF DOGS
Colima, western Mexico
Classic era, 200–600 A.D.
Clay vessel
Museo Dolores Olmedo Patiño, Mexico City
Ill. p. 32

155
BITCH WITH HER PUPS
Colima, western Mexico
Classic era, 200–600 A.D.
Clay vessel
9⅞×9×5⅞ inches (25×23×15 cm)
Museo Dolores Olmedo Patiño, Mexico City
Ill. p. 31

156
SITTING DOG
Colima, western Mexico
Classic era, 200–600 A.D.
Clay vessel
18⅞×18⅞×9½ inches (48×48×24 cm)
Museo Dolores Olmedo Patiño, Mexico City
Ill. p. 32

157
WOMAN GIVING BIRTH
Pre-Columbian
Clay vessel
18⅛×6¼×10¼ inches (46×16×26 cm)
Museo Dolores Olmedo Patiño, Mexico City
Ill. p. 70

158
WOMAN GIVING BIRTH
Pre-Columbian
Clay vessel
19⅝×7⅞×7⅞ inches (50×20×20 cm)
Museo Dolores Olmedo Patiño, Mexico City
Ill. p. 70

SELECTED BIBLIOGRAPHY

Billeter, Erika. *La Femme et le Surréalisme.* Lausanne: Musée Cantonal des Beaux-Arts, 1987.

Billeter, Erika, ed. *Images of Mexico: The Contribution of Mexico to 20th Century Art.* Exh. cat., Dallas: Dallas Museum of Art, and Bern: Benteli Verlag, 1987.

Billeter Erika, ed. *Einsame Begegnungen: Lola Alvarez Bravo fotografiert Frida Kahlo.* Bern: Benteli Verlag, 1992.

del Conde, Teresa. *Frida Kahlo, la pintora y el mito.* Mexico City: Instituto de Inverstigaciones Estéticas, Universidad Nacional Autónoma de México, 1992.

Frida Kahlo and Tina Modotti. Exh. cat., London: Whitechapel Gallery, 1982.

Frida Kahlo. Exh. cat., Madrid: Salas Pablo Ruiz Picasso, 1985.

Herrera, Hayden. *Frida: A Biography of Frida Kahlo.* New York: Harper and Row, 1983.

Herrera, Hayden. *Frida Kahlo: The Paintings.* New York: Harper Collins Publishers, 1991.

Monsiváis, Carlos, and Rafael Vázquez Bayod. *Frida Kahlo: Una vida – una obra.* Mexico City: Ediciones Era, 1992.

Poniatowska, Elena, and Carla Stellweg. *Frida Kahlo: The Camera Seduced.* San Francisco: Chronicle Books, 1992.

Prignitz-Poda, Helga, Andrea Kettenmann, and Salomon Grimberg, eds. *Frida Kahlo: Das Gesamtwerk.* Frankfurt: Verlag Neue Kritik, 1988.

Tibol, Raquel. *Frida Kahlo: Una vida abierta.* Oaxaca: Editorial Oasis, 1983.

Zamora, Martha. *Frida Kahlo: The Brush of Anguish.* San Francisco: Chronicle Books, 1990.